Armies in Retreat
Chaos, Cohesion, and Consequences

Edited by Timothy G. Heck
and Walker D. Mills

Army University Press
Fort Leavenorth, Kansas

Publisher's Note on the Use of Civil War Terms

The Army University Press supports the professional military education of Soldiers and leader development. Books are published by our press that describe the historical facts pertaining to the American Civil War and acknowledge that the legacy of that war is still at the forefront of our national conversation. We intend to describe the political and social situation of the Civil War in a neutral manner. For example, the traditional terms to describe the opposing sides, North and South, are only used for grammatical variety, as they ascribe generalities that certainly did not apply to the totality of the "North" or the "South." Many local citizens who resided in states that openly rebelled against the United States government were not in favor of secession, nor did they believe that preserving slavery warranted such a violent act.

Similarly, citizens in states who remained loyal to the United States did not all feel a strong commitment toward dissolving the institution of slavery, nor did they believe Lincoln's views represented their own. Thus, while the historiography has traditionally referred to the "Union" in the American Civil War as "the northern states loyal to the United States government," the fact is that the term "Union" always referred to all the states together, which clearly was not the situation at all. In light of this, the reader will discover that the word "Union" will be largely replaced by the more historically accurate "Federal Government" or "United States Government." "Union forces" or "Union army" will largely be replaced by the terms "United States. Army," "Federals," or "Federal Army."

The Reconstruction policy between the Federal Government and the former rebellious states saw an increased effort to control the narrative of how and why the war was fought, which led to an enduring perpetuation of Lost Cause rhetoric. The Lost Cause promotes an interpretation of the Civil War era that legitimates and excuses the secessionist agenda. This narrative has been wholly rejected by academic scholars who rely on rigorous research and an honest interpretation of primary source materials. To rely on bad faith interpretations of history like the Lost Cause in this day and age would be insufficient, inaccurate, and an acknowledgment that the Confederate States of America was a legitimate nation. The fact is that Abraham Lincoln and the United States Congress were very careful not to recognize the government of the states in rebellion as a legitimate government. Nonetheless, those states that formed a political and social alliance, even though not recognized by the Lincoln government, called themselves the "Confederacy" or the "Confederate States of America." In our works, the Army University Press acknowledges that political alliance, albeit an alliance in rebellion, by allowing the use of the terms "Confederate," "Confederacy," "Confederate Army," for ease of reference and flow of the narrative, in addition to the variations of the term "rebel."

Contents *page*

Publisher's Note on the Use of Civil War Terms iii

Chapter 1—Introduction
by Walker D. Mills and Timothy G. Heck 1

Chaos

Chapter 2—"Left Him Alone with His Glory": Sir John Moore and the Miracle of Corunna
by Andrew O. G. Young 9

Chapter 3—Clausewitzian Friction and the Retreat of 6 Indian Division to Kut-al-Amara, November–December 1915
by Nikolas E. Gardner 31

Chapter 4—Shattered: The XVth Brigade against Franco's 1938 Aragon Offensive
by Tyler D. Wentzell 55

Chapter 5—Polish Horsemen in the Chaotic Withdrawal of 1939
by Marcin Wilczek 77

Cohesion

Chapter 6—Fly by Night: Plataean Evacuation and Night-Fighting in the Peloponnesian War
by Jonathan H. Warner 99

Chapter 7—Hülsen's Retreat: The Campaign in Saxony, August–October 1760
by Alexander S. Burns 119

Chapter 8—Retreat to Victory: The Northern Army's Campaigns, 1775–1777
by Jonathan D. Bratten 137

Chapter 9—Airmen into Infantry: The Provisional Air Corps Regiment at Bataan, January–April 1942
by Frank A. Blazich Jr. 155

Chapter 10—Operation Ziethen: The Evacuation of the Demyansk Salient, February 1943
by Gregory P. Liedtke 179

page

Chapter 11—The German 7th Infantry Division and Retreat from the Rzhev Salient, February–March 1943
by Jeff Rutherford 195

Chapter 12—A Fighting Retreat: The Chosin Reservoir Campaign
by Charles P. Neimeyer 217

Chapter 13—The Railroad Saved Our Necks: United Nations Command Retreat in Korea, Winter 1950–51
by Eric Allan Sibul 241

Consequences

Chapter 14—Cornwallis in the 1781 Yorktown Campaign: When an Attack Becomes a Defense, a Siege, and a Surrender
by Patrick H. Hannum 277

Chapter 15—Disaster on the Scheldt, 1809: A British Defeat in Holland
by Jason D. Lancaster 303

Chapter 16—"We Did Retreat but Were Not Beat": The Irish-American Experience at Bull Run as Told through Civil War Songs
by Catherine V. Bateson 327

Chapter 17—The Flight into History: The XI Corps at Chancellorsville
by Anthony J. Cade 353

Chapter 18—Evacuating Gallipoli: Military Advice and the Politics of Decision-Making, 1915–16
by Aimée Fox 377

Chapter 19—The Retreat of Cyber Forces after Offensive Operations
by J. D. Work 401

Conclusion

Chapter 20—Conclusion
by Walker D. Mills 423

About the Authors 431

Figures   *page*

Figure 2.1. Map of Moore's retreat to Corunna 13
Figure 3.1. Map of Mesopotamia... 32
Figure 3.2. 120th Rajputana Infantry, 1915 35
Figure 3.3. Lower Mesopotamia. 1914... 37
Figure 3.4. Battle of Ctesiphon map 38
Figure 3.5. Battle of Ctesiphon map 39
Figure 3.6. Tigris River from Kut to Baghdad.. 40
Figure 3.7. British howitzer loading onto a raft, 1915........................... 43
Figure 3.8. Defense of Kut Al Amara 47
Figure 3.9. Wireless station receiving last message from Kut, 1916...... 48
Figure 3.10. Townshend Surrender 51
Figure 4.1. Nationalist axes of advance and XVth Brigade defensive positions, March 1938.. 59
Figure 5.1. Map of general situation, September 1939........................... 77
Figure 5.2. Cavalry Organizational Table 80
Figure 5.3. Cavalry Regiment antitank artillery platoon 80
Figure 5.4. Galloping horsemen on battlefield with rifle and sabres 81
Figure 5.5. Krojanty map 85
Figure 5.6. Mokra map.. 86
Figure 5.7. Milewo map.. 87
Figure 5.8. Brochów map.. 89
Figure 5.9. Cavalry Signal Troop radio station on two-wheel carriage... 92
Figure 5.10. Stream crossing by cavalry troop mounted unit 93
Figure 6.1. Plataea and its surroundings during Peloponnesian War..... 101
Figure 7.1. Prussian Order of Battle, 1760 123
Figure 7.2. Map of the Battle of Strehla, 20 August 1760 126
Figure 7.3. Prussian view from the Dürrenberg, August 2018 128
Figure 7.4. Hülsen's retreat, Saxony, August–October 1760................ 131

page

Figure 8.1. The Invasion of Canada, September 1775 to October 1776 .. 138

Figure 8.2. Northern New York Burgoynes Expedition, June to October 1777 145

Figure 9.1. Destroyed B-17 at Clark Field, December 1941 157

Figure 9.2. Map of the position of the Provisional Air Corps Regiment (PACR) in Sector B on Bataan, circa April 1942 160

Figure 9.3. Soldiers on Bataan used improvised antitank weaponry 161

Figure 9.4. Improvised tank traps on Bataan 165

Figure 9.5. Example of the dense jungle found on Bataan 170

Figure 10.1. Map of the Evacuation of the Demyansk Salient 184

Figure 11.1. The 7th Infantry Division and the Buffalo Movement 198

Figure 12.1. Battle of the Changjin Reservoir, 27–29 November 1950, and Withdrawal from the Reservoir, 6–11 December 1950 221

Figure 12.2. Crash landing of a Marine aircraft 223

Figure 12.3. "The Eternal Band of Brothers" 224

Figure 12.4. Combat Airlift Help Dates Back to Korea 225

Figure 12.5. Dead marines at Yudam-Ni waiting for burial 227

Figure 12.6. US marines march south from Hagaru-ri 228

Figure 12.7. Korean refugees during the Hungam evacuation 229

Figure 12.8. USS *Begor* (APD-127) stands offshore during the evacuation and demolition of Hungnam, Korea, 24 December 1950 ... 230

Figure 12.9. Chinese prisoners, 3–4 November 1950 232

Figure 13.1. The Korean railway network 242

Figure 13.2. Capt. Charles Mason, 3rd TMRS, gives final instructions to a Korean National Railroad conductor, 8 September 1950 244

Figure 13.3. Republic of Korea marines move from Inchon 245

Figure 13.4. Korean National Railroad employees begin repair work at Seoul Station 245

Figure 13.5. Supply train on the Wonsan-Hamhung railway line 247

page

Figure 13.6. First supply train arrives in Wonsan from Seoul, 15 November 1950 247

Figure 13.7. US Marine Corps troop train 248

Figure 13.8. Marines load a narrow-gauge supply train 249

Figure 13.9. X Corps Area of Operations, October–December 1950 ... 250

Figure 13.10. Hungnam destruction, 15 December 1950 252

Figure 13.11. Final destruction of station facilities in Wonsan 253

Figure 13.12. Hospital train rolling south at Pukchong, North Korea, 27 November 1950 254

Figure 13.13. Refugees flock aboard an evacuation train in Sariwon .. 255

Figure 13.14. As part of the Seoul Evacuation, evacuees prepare to board a southbound train at Seoul Station 257

Figure 13.15. Refugees climb aboard evacuation train at Yongdungpo .. 258

Figure 13.16. Refugees aboard an evacuation train south of Seoul 260

Figure 13.17. Supply train arrives at the 1st Marine Division Railhead .. 262

Figure 14.1. Surrender of Lord Cornwallis at Yorktown painting 277

Figure 14.2. Political cartoon "The American Rattlesnake" 278

Figure 14.3. 1781 Yorktown Campaign 281

Figure 14.4. Patriot Militia reenactors 282

Figure 14.5. British Dragoon reenactors 283

Figure 14.6. 1781 plan of the Town of York 287

Figure 14.7. Plan of the entrance to the Chesapeake Bay 290

Figure 14.8. French Infantry reenactors 292

Figure 14.9. 76th Highland reenactors 293

Figure 15.1. British Walcheren Expedition Command and Control 305

Figure 15.2. Map of the Scheldt Estuary 312

Figure 16.1. "The Battle at Bull's Run" illustration 331

Figure 16.2. Map of the Battles of Bull Run near Manassas 334

ix

page

Figure 16.3. Ruins of Mrs. Henry's House, March 1862 336
Figure 16.4. The Cost of the First Battle of Bull Run 340
Figure 17.1. Maj. Gen. Franz Sigel 357
Figure 17.2. General Oliver Otis Howard 359
Figure 17.3. "The Battle of Chancellorsville" sketch 360
Figure 17.4. Hooker at Chancellorsville, 3 May 1863 362
Figure 17.5. Map of Jackson's Flank Attack, 1700–1800 on 2 May 363
Figure 17.6. Men of Company C, 41st New York Infantry 366
Figure 17.7. General Carl Schurz 368
Figure 18.1. Gallipoli peninsula.. 379
Figure 18.2. Troops from the Australian 13th Battalion 381
Figure 18.3. Eastern Mediterranean map.. 382
Figure 18.4. Aftermath of heavy storms that swept the Gallipoli peninsula, November 1915 384
Figure 18.5. Australian soldiers stand in snow outside a dugout after inclement weather and storms battered the peninsula, November 1915..388

Chapter 1
Introduction
Walker D. Mills and Timothy G. Heck

Descriptions of retreats date back to ancient times. The earliest descriptions of a pitched battle are from the Battle of Megiddo, fought in the fifteenth century BCE, and include Canaanite forces fleeing the field to take refuge in the city from the Egyptian army of Thutmose III. Even the word Armageddon has its origin in the city's name.

In religious texts, warriors are often portrayed as those who do not flee or who stand tall in the face of the enemy due to faith in their chosen deity. In the Guru Granth Sahib, the sacred text of Sikhs, the warrior is admonished to "keep up and press on. He should not yield, and he should not retreat."[1] For Hindus, the Kshatriyas—the warrior caste—indicated that they "resolve[d] never to retreat from battle."[2]

The Quran recorded an admonition that those who retreat from the enemy in battle "will earn the displeasure of Allah, and their home will be Hell."[3] Only those who retreated with the intent of deception or regrouping to attack again would be spared this fate. Armies like the United Nations forces in Korea certainly retreated to regroup and attack again.

The warnings and descriptions against retreat present in the sacred texts' military history could as easily have been written about more recent retreats as well. In 605 BC, Jeremiah had a vision that prophesied the retreating Egyptian army after the Battle of Carchemish at the hands of the Babylonians:

> What do I see?
> They are terrified,
> they are retreating,
> their warriors are defeated.
> They flee in haste
> without looking back,
> and there is terror on every side.[4]

Certainly, the Egyptian retreat is not much different than that of 6 Indian Division in 1915. Both armies were paralyzed by fear, chaos, and terror permeating their forces.

From a practical perspective, how and why did these armies wind up retreating? Why do some make a conscious decision to retreat for a tactical, operational, or strategic advantage while others flee the battlefield in haste? Why does one army retreat in an orderly manner, capable of fighting another day, while another disintegrates and ceases to function? How do societies or even sub-elements of society view a retreating army? *Armies in Retreat* seeks to examine these questions in a rigorous and scholarly manner that can inform policymakers, practitioners, and scholars alike.

This volume emerged out of an idea that many recent publications focused on large-scale combat operations had a vaguely (or expressly) triumphant narrative. As the United States military shifts from two decades of counterterrorism and counterinsurgency operations to focus on great power competition and peer competitors, there has been a concurrent surge in publications that focus on these threats. The counterinsurgency and small war focus of French officer David Galula, war correspondent Bernard Fall, and Australian counterinsurgency expert David Kilcullen are being shelved in favor of narratives that focus on large armies fighting against peers. The Marine Corps *Small Wars Manual*, initially released in 1940, is being superseded by a volume of work that seeks to create a big wars manual.[5]

As authors, we are not immune from that trend. Our own chapters in the Army University Press *Large-Scale Combat Operations* series covered the Soviet Red Army's disemboweling of the Wehrmacht during the Vistula-Oder Campaign, its bloody capture of Berlin in 1945, and its rear-area operations after defeating the Japanese in Manchuria.[6] We focused on the victors, culminating in the raising of the red banner over the Reichstag and occupation of much of Manchuria.[7]

This shift of focus from small wars to big is not a bad one. But every battle has two sides. For every victor, there is a vanquished. Imagine the great retreats and defeats of the Western Allies in World War II. Much of the historiography of the 1940 Battle of France, for example, focuses on Rommel's Panzers slashing into the country, swiftly defeating the Allies. That narrative quickly gives way to a triumphant story about the evacuation of Dunkirk. In reality, numerically superior American and Filipino forces lost the fight at Bataan and Corregidor and spent four years in Japanese captivity.[8] General Jonathan M. Wainwright IV, who ordered the surrender of American forces at Corregidor, went into captivity thinking he had let the nation down. In reality, he was lauded in the United States, eventually awarded the Medal of Honor. And there is much to learn from these histories. It is the story and experience of retreating and defeated armies we want to analyze and tell.

Creating a thesis or central argument in an edited volume that was formed out of an open call for chapters is tricky. Each author adds a unique perspective to the volume through his or her chapter. As we read and analyzed these chapters, we recognized there was no singular theme when it came to retreats. Ultimately, we view retreating armies similar to Tolstoy's view of families in the opening line of *Anna Karenina*: "All happy families are alike; each unhappy family is unhappy in its own way."[9] Each retreating army has its own reason for its retreat; most have multiple reasons, some many reasons. Some failed on the battlefield while others retreated to prepare for counterattacks or to buy time. While retreating, some armies were unable to maintain cohesion and hold together while others succeeded. Some remained relatively stable, others did not. Similarly, research on desertion and surrender has revealed a wide variety of factors that influenced soldier decisions to desert or surrender.[10] Some retreats resulted in dire consequences for the armies or nations while others were relatively benign.

Thus, the broad themes of chaos, cohesion, and consequences coalesced in the framing of this book. We went back and forth about how best to organize and present the selected narratives before settling on these three themes. Much of the writing in these chapters focuses at the operational level and many are campaign histories like the chapters by Alexander Burns, Jonathan Bratten, and Jason Lancaster. Some like Aimée Fox's chapter examine strategic and political implications, while others like Catherine Bateson's examine how society outside the military converses with retreat in social memory. Rather than organizing our book chronologically or geographically, we framed the book thematically so readers can follow the underlying and common threads more clearly.

Our examination starts with armies retreating in the midst of chaos. As Patrick Hannum explores in his chapter, some retreats like Cornwallis to Yorktown have strategic consequences. Others like the English Brigade in the Spanish Civil War covered in Tyler Wentzel's chapter and the Polish cavalry in the Second World War recounted by Marcin Wilczek are tactical retreats in the midst of wars that are ultimately lost. For these commanders, their worlds devolved into chaos in Poland and Spain. These retreats, however, portend failure. Some armies retreating in the midst of chaos survive or thrive, as Andrew Young examines in his chapter on Sir John Moore at Corunna. Nikolas Gardner uses the Clausewitzian concept of friction to analyze the disastrous British retreat to Al-Kut during World War I.

This book's second section, by contrast, focuses on armies that maintained cohesion in the midst of retreat, regardless of the ultimate consequences. Jonathan Warner examines the oft-studied Peloponnesian War. Instead of looking at the famous Spartan stand at Thermopylae, however, Warner examines the successful escape and reconstitution of the Plataeans, showing that a retreat ultimately can lead to victory. At the operational level, both Alexander Burns and Jonathan Bratten examine eighteenth-century retreats that preserved their protagonists' combat power. Frank Blazich's chapter on the Provisional Air Corps Regiment in the Philippines reveals that strong leadership can hold units together longer and keep them more combat effective than expected. Switching to the Soviet-German war, both Jeff Rutherford and Greg Liedtke reveal some of the operational prowess of the German general staff as it retreats from superior Soviet strength and increased operational competency. Charles Niemeyer and Eric Sibul look at the role logistics played for United Nations forces during the Korean War (1950–53).

The final section looks at the consequences of retreat. Whether it is an Irish-American ballad that frames the narrative of a retreating army in Catherine Bateson's chapter or the ethnic bias and nativism shaping the way tactical action is passed into cultural memory in A. J. Cade's chapter on Chancellorsville, retreats matter in cultural memory. These chapters reveal that a retreat is not merely a battlefield event. Rather, retreat has a lasting cultural impact. As recent cyberattacks seem to indicate, perhaps the most applicable chapter for the near future will be J. D. Work's chapter on cyber operations.

Despite the seemingly obvious fact that someone wins in a war and someone loses, there is decidedly little meaningful and practical analysis on retreating armies. For example, much of the dominant Western historiography of the war between the Soviet Union and Nazi Germany was written many years after the events by defeated German generals—accounts that have been identified as problematic and inaccurate. These memoirs and reflections are largely self-serving and fail to credit the Soviets as competent opponents.[11] As a result, lessons at the operational level from one of the largest military defeats in history are significantly lacking in meaningful analysis or practical advice. Instead, the generals often blamed Hitler for their defeats, frequently using him as a scapegoat for their decisions and ultimate defeat.[12]

Beyond the Germans, existing memoirs and studies for retreating and defeated armies are often rife with political bias and self-serving content. In the United States, the survivors of the largest loser in our history, the

Confederate States of America, crafted a "Lost Cause" narrative that continues to impact and dominate the national security space today. Recent United States Department of Defense discussions about bases named after Confederate generals, memorials, and even the Confederate flag appearing on military installations all remind us that war does not exist in a vacuum. Legacies of retreat and defeat echo through the generations.[13]

In *Defeat and Memory: Cultural Histories of Military Defeat in the Modern Era*, John Horne identified five types of defeat:

1. Temporary defeat in battle or campaign that is later reversed by the outcome of the war.

2. Definitive defeat that shapes the subsequent peace.

3. Total defeat in which the vanquished is stripped of political sovereignty until it is rebuilt in the image of the victor.

4. Internal defeat in civil wars where total defeat of the rival is sought to rebuild unity in the image of the victor.

5. Partial defeat where a defeat shocks the military and diplomatic stability of the state but does not threaten its territorial or political integrity.[14]

The chapters in this book deal with retreats across all five types of defeats. Some are temporary setbacks, others have a marked impact on the subsequent peace, and others are swept aside to make way for something new. Regardless of the retreat's consequences, all can teach something about being on the losing end (even temporarily).

Centuries after the religious texts were authored, Cedric Delves, a British Special Air Service leader during the Falklands War/Guerra de las Malvinas, witnessed a defeated army in retreat. In his memoir, *Across an Angry Sea: The SAS in the Falklands War*, Delves described the retreating Argentinian forces:

> They moved slowly, drifting away from where our battle groups must be. A dark oozing mass flowed into Stanley, around Stanley, some even making their way out towards the airport. And over it all, silence. The guns had stopped. Nothing, just the sound of the wind. So, this was what a broken army looked like, for we knew what it meant, what we were gazing down upon. Even from that distance, we could see that they were done: a vast mass of spent men slowly departing.[15]

The chapter authors in this book provide that sense of personal observation through their research and writing. In the introduction to *Divided Armies:*

Inequality & Battlefield Performance in Modern War, author Jason Lyall remarks that "no consensus exists over what constitutes military effectiveness, a mark of both its importance and complexity."[16] Lyall divides existing analysis of effectiveness into two camps. The first is task-centered: the army that inflicts the most damage to the others at the least cost to itself is more effective. The second camp uses cohesion as its measure of effectiveness. "Cohesive forces are resilient, able to shoulder heavy losses without caving, and exhibit a 'will to fight' that stretches the breaking point of armies, prolonging the war."[17] When studying retreating armies, both analytical frameworks are valid. As such, both approaches find a home in this book as we seek to identify what it means to be that vast mass of men and women caught inside the conflict.

Ultimately, *Armies in Retreat* is about surviving defeat. It is designed to inform leaders about what to expect when the unexpected happens, to prevent the shock and mitigate some of the terror on every side. While triumphal narratives reign supreme, there is need for balance and preparation for the next war. While the United States wants to believe it will remain supreme in combat, the reality is that we face a possibility of defeat and must prepare for it. Retreat, while unpalatable, can ultimately lead to military or national survival, even victory. Though we hope that day will not come, we want to help leaders and forces be better prepared to respond with resilience and cohesion.

Notes

1. Guru Granth Sahib, 341, accessed 14 August 2022, https://www.srigranth.org/servlet/gurbani.gurbani?Action=Page&Param=341&english=t&id=15612#l15612.

2. Swami Mukundananda, Bhagavad Gita, Verse 43, accessed, 14 August 2022, https://www.holy-bhagavad-gita.org/chapter/18/verse/43.

3. "Quran 8," accessed 14 August 2022, https://quran.com/8.

4. Bible Gateway, Jeremiah 46:5, accessed 14 August 2022, https://www.biblegateway.com/passage/?search=Jeremiah%2046%3A5&version=NIV.

5. United States Marine Corps, *Small Wars Manual* (Washington, DC: US Government Printing Office, 1940). The big wars manual line comes from the title of Stanton S. Coerr's "The Big Wars Manual," *Marine Corps Gazette*, October 2013, 100.

6. See Timothy G. Heck, "From the Vistula to the Oder: Soviet Deep Maneuver in 1945," in *Deep Maneuver: Historical Case Studies of Maneuver in Large-Scale Combat Operations*, ed. Jack D. Kem (Fort Leavenworth, KS: Army University Press, 2018).

7. See Walker D. Mills, "To Take a City: Mobility and Countermobility in Berlin, 1945," in *Into the Breach: Historical Case Studies of Mobility Operations in Large-Scale Combat Operations*, ed. Florian L. Waitl (Fort Leavenworth, KS: Army University Press, 2018). See also, Timothy G. Heck and Walker D. Mills, "A Whirlwind of Violence: Soviet Consolidation of Gains in Manchuria, 1945-6," in *Enduring Success: Consolidation of Gains in Large-Scale Combat Operations*, ed. Eric M. Burke and Donald P. Wright (Fort Leavenworth, KS: Army University Press, 2022).

8. See Angry Staff Officer, "Training for Defeat," *The Angry Staff Officer,* 25 August 2018, https://angrystaffofficer.com/2018/08/25/training-for-defeat/.

9. Leo Tolstoy, *Anna Karenina* (London: J. M. Dent & Sons, 1878).

10. For desertion, see Theodore McLauchlin, *Desertion: Trust and Mistrust in Civil Wars* (Ithaca, NY: Cornell University Press, 2020). For surrender, see Todd C. Lehmann and Yuri M. Zhukov, "Until the Bitter End? The Diffusion of Surrender Across Battles," *International Organization* 73, no. 1 (2019): 133–69.

11. David Glantz, "The Failure of Historiography: Forgotten Battles of the German-Soviet War (1941–1945)," *Journal of Slavic Military Studies* 8, no. 4 (1995), https://www.tandfonline.com/doi/abs/10.1080/13518049508430217?-journalCode=fslv20.

12. For more on the shortcomings of the German memoirs, see David Glantz, "American Perspectives on Eastern Front Operations in World War II" (Fort Leavenworth, KS: Soviet Army Studies Office, 1987), 21–69, https://web.archive.org/web/20160610080127/http://fmso.leavenworth.army.mil/documents/e-front.htm. This paper was prepared for delivery at the first Soviet-American collegium on the problems of World War II history, held in Moscow on 23 October 1986. Thereafter the article was published in the August 1987 issue of the Soviet Academy of Sciences Journal *Voprosy Istorii* [Questions of History].

13. See Jenny Macleod, ed., *Defeat and Memory: Cultural Histories of Military Defeat in the Modern Era* (Basingstoke, UK: Palgrave Macmillan, 2008). Chapters in Macleod's edited volume address five broad themes related to defeat.

14. John Horne, "Defeat and Memory in Modern History," in *Defeat and Memory: Cultural Histories of Military Defeat in the Modern Era*, ed. Jenny Macleod (Basingstoke, UK: Palgrave Macmillan, 2008).

15. Cedric Delves, *Across an Angry Sea: The SAS in the Falklands War* (London: Hurst & Company, 2018), 316–17.

16. Jason Lyall, *Divided Armies: Inequality and Battlefield Performance in Modern War* (Princeton, NJ: Princeton University Press, 2020), 8.

17. Lyall, 9.

Chapter 2
"Left Him Alone with His Glory": Sir John Moore and the Miracle of Corunna

Andrew O. G. Young

According to Anglo-American strategist Colin S. Gray, an examination of British strategic history can remind strategists "of the hard cases when continental allies, as well as British expeditionary forces, failed in the field."[1] The power by which Britain was able to export her army also provided a place of refuge: British commanders and troops could expect, except in the rarest of cases, an avenue of escape so long as access to the sea was maintained.[2] Few cases are as rife with lessons as Lt. Gen. Sir John Moore's retreat across northern Spain in December 1808 to January 1809, and the army's eventual rescue from Corunna on 17 January. Its pertinence today is emphasized by the outcomes of the United Kingdom's 2021 "Integrated Review of Defence and Security" and "Defence Command Paper."

Fought under the most difficult circumstances imaginable, the British army faced not only a vastly superior foe, captained at one point by the most capable military commander of the time, but to deteriorating weather and in a place that was decidedly alien. The army had limited logistical capability as well as minimal intelligence of both ground and opposition movements, and was essentially isolated and alone. Despite acting as an auxiliary to the host nation, its allies were of mixed quality at best and wholly dependent on British supplies of stores and materiel. In fact, the only part of the entire campaign that could be called a resounding success was the amphibious aspect; the landing, sustainment, and extraction of the army was a feat unimaginable to even French emperor Napoleon Bonaparte. This combined expeditionary character is an enduring feature of the British way of warfare. The sea not only provides Britain with an avenue of maneuver and attack, but a place of refuge. Britain's army always acts in concert with its Navy (and, latterly, Air Force)—never alone. As was the case in 1808 to 1809, reaching a secure port or harbor is only part of the story; salvation and safety were only guaranteed if the force could be recovered to the home base.

Corunna was a campaign that had all the ingredients for a chaotic rout. It was an ad hoc campaign fought across unfamiliar territory in the worst possible circumstances. The army was largely untried and untested, reliant on a neutral-at-best population for local succour and support and a distant Navy for security and rescue. It bears no small similarity to Xenophon's

March of the Ten Thousand, a small army desperately seeking the sea and the promise of salvation. That the Corunna campaign, like Xenophon's, did not descend completely into chaos is remarkable. Amongst other perennial strategic insights, the enduring tactical lessons from Corunna are ones of leadership, discipline, and group cohesion.

This chapter is not intended as a detailed historical examination; there are numerous histories that explore the specifics. Rather, it is a deductive primer for military science students—an opportunity to discern general principles and considerations for modern planners, policymakers, and military practitioners. There are dangers in "raiding" historical case studies, yet few would argue against their use for informing, educating, and providing insight for practitioners who do not have relevant experience of their own.[3] Thus, rather than providing a detailed account of the retreat, this chapter will highlight patterns, parallels, and behaviors pertinent to current considerations.[4]

The Situation

Why was a British expedition in Spain? Despite Napoleon's ascendancy over Europe by the 1807 Treaty of Tilsit, 1808 was a year of promise for Robert Stewart, Lord Castlereagh.[5] The success of the 1807 Copenhagen expedition had proved Britain's ability to project power to the European periphery.[6] In early 1808, however, Britain stood alone against France; Prussia, Russia, and Austria had all been humbled by Napoleon in the preceding three years. Napoleon's march on Portugal and his 1808 usurpation of the Spanish throne offered an opportunity for Britain to find new allies. The imposition of Joseph Bonaparte on the Spanish throne resulted in a popular rising, followed by the capitulation of an 18,000-strong French army at Bailén (19 July 1808).[7] The spell of French invincibility, so recently forged at Jena-Auerstadt (14 October 1806) and Friedland (14 June 1807), was broken.[8] Now, Spain offered the kind of ally capable of "large-scale military campaigns that Britain needed from coalition partners" and a suitable theater in which to fight France on favorable terms.[9] Joseph Bonaparte fled Madrid and took up position north of the Ebro River awaiting his brother Napoleon's assistance.[10] In August, Lt. Gen. Sir Arthur Wellesley's army landed and then was victorious at Roliça and Vimeiro; French forces evacuated Portugal under the Convention of Cintra.[11] Subsequently, Wellesley, General Sir Hew Whitefoord Dalrymple, and General Sir Harry Burrard were recalled and Iberian command fell to the newly arrived Lt. Gen. Sir John Moore, whose expedition to Goteborg in support of Swedish efforts had been redirected to Portugal.[12]

Though he was considered one of the most competent officers of his generation and was known as "the Whig general par excellence," Moore faced private political attacks both from the incumbent Tory government and within his own command.[13] At that time, officers were promoted based on political allegiance as much if not more than competence and seniority. Moore, who was aligned to the parliamentary opposition, not only had to contend with the French in the field, but faced the political machinations of subordinates, to say nothing of being the ancillary, auxiliary force to the larger host nation. The campaign would necessitate close coordination with Spanish allies. Moreover, Moore's army was an amphibious force; he was utterly reliant on the Royal Navy retaining command of the sea to secure his supply lines. Moore's appointment was as much diplomatic as it was military, requiring him to cultivate good relations and communication with his Spanish and naval counterparts. With the latter he had experience; with the former, none.

The army he commanded was also a precious commodity. Foreign Secretary George Canning wrote: "It is, in fact, the British army. . . . Another army it has not to send."[14] Yet, Castlereagh instructed Moore and his army to concentrate on the border of Leon and Old Castile, and from there "cooperate with the Spanish armies in the expulsion of the French from that Kingdom."[15] Canning and Castlereagh, buoyed by propagandist reports extolling the Spanish Patriot cause and misperceptions of Spanish martial capabilities, envisioned a "dam against the floodtide of Napoleon's success. The nationalist reaction had begun; and if the spark caught flame and the flames were fanned and spread, all Europe might be caught up in the fire."[16] Such sparks were already evident in Prussia, Austria, and the German states.[17] Thus in September 1808, the British army was ordered to depart Portugal and cross northern Spain to support the Spanish armies now concentrating south of the Ebro and finish the liberation of the Peninsula. At no point had Moore's orders countenanced the possibility of Spanish defeat.

Moore's troubles began before he left Portugal, principally owing to the commissariat's inexperience and structure, which relied on indigenous logistical support.[18] There were never enough carts, and none capable of traversing mountainous roads in the depths of winter.[19] Moore's war chest was "desperately short of specie;" Portuguese and Spanish contractors insisted on silver; they "had a horror of Government bills and promissory notes."[20] Because the Portuguese were ignorant as to which roads could be traversed by artillery and heavy baggage, Moore was forced to split his command and order Sir David Baird's inbound convoy to disembark at Corunna; this decision led to costly delays.[21] Food stocks were "tenuous in the extreme," and establishing forward magazines on the route of march was impossible.[22] Further, the central Spanish *junta* lacked military experience and had no control over the regional commands; additionally, because the numerous generals were more intent to jealously guard their own power than cooperate with rivals, there was no agreed campaign plan.[23] To add insult to injury, the arriving British soldiers soon observed that the populace was at best resentful, at worst outright hostile toward them.[24] The British were not alone in overestimating Spain's capacity to support large numbers of troops; Napoleon, too, mistakenly believed that armies could live and move in Spain as easily as elsewhere in Europe.[25]

By the time Moore came close to the intended area of operations (Sahagun in Leon, bordering Old Castille), the Spanish armies had been scattered, Madrid had fallen, and Napoleon had gleefully turned his attention northward in an effort to trap the British army, commenting: "If only these 20,000 were 100,000, if only more English mothers could feel the horrors of war."[26] Such was Napoleon's optimism that on 27 December, he disingenuously ordered his brother in Madrid: "Put into the newspapers, and spread in every direction, that 36,000 English are surrounded."[27] What followed was a fifteen-day running fight as Moore raced to escape Imperial France's converging might.[28] It was an experience for which his army was singularly unprepared.

Doctrine, Training, and Experience

Amphibious powers and forces engaged in amphibious operations hold a nominal advantage over their continental, land-bound enemies: "a secure line of retreat if overwhelmed."[29] Yet despite the plethora of historical precedents, US and UK doctrine routinely overlooks "the difficult task of amphibious extraction—the recovery of embattled units under fire."[30] It is not a mistake made by the first proponent of amphibious doctrine; British Army officer Thomas More Molyneux devoted chapter 7 of *Conjunct Expeditions* to a force's "re-embarkment . . . with the bayonet pressing at their backs."[31] Molyneux seems alone in his detailed study of withdrawal; both French officer Maurice de Saxe and Prussia's Frederick the Great devoted less than a paragraph to discussing its tactical application.[32] Current US joint doctrine only contains two pages on amphibious withdrawals; capstone UK Maritime and Land doctrine, even less.[33] Given that both the US and UK are geographically expeditionary powers that will require the dispatch, employment, sustainment and extraction of amphibious forces

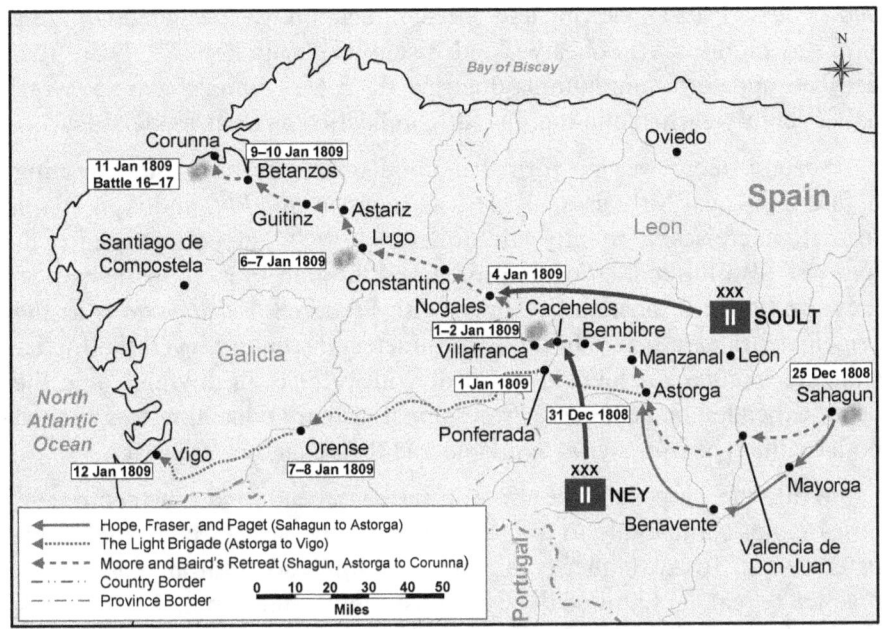

Figure 2.1. Map of Moore's retreat to Corunna. The British army marched nearly 300 miles across the mountains of Northern Spain to escape from Napoleon's forces. Created by Army University Press.

to engage with their competitors, one would expect doctrinal literature to be replete with studies of withdrawals. The absence of such information points to a failure to recognize that no plan survives first contact and that the enemy will always have a say. Indeed, across current publications, the assumption is that all withdrawals will be planned activities. This contradicts the musings of Britain's Lt. Col. James Wolfe: "In war, something must be allowed to chance and fortune, seeing it is in its nature hazardous, and an option of difficulties."[34] Evidently, it is an assumption not shared by our doctrinal forebears.

Unfortunately, these doctrinal defects are present in the Corunna campaign. First, treatises of the time were predominantly tactical—technical manuals for the employment and deployment of soldiers up to the battalion level; even recent historical studies of Napoleonic warfare refer to retreat in tactical terms.[35] British General Sir David Dundas's *Rules and Regulations for the Formations, Field-Exercise, and Movements of His Majesty's Forces* (1794) and Lieutenant General Moore's *Light Infantry Instructions of 1798–1799* (1798) both referenced "retiring" as a tactical evolution; there is no mention in the Duke of York's *General Regulations and Orders* (1798). Doctrine and officer education was designed with one aim: "to produce fit, cohesive, and disciplined battalions."[36] There had been no update to amphibious doctrine from Molyneux's seminal work half a century earlier, and there is little indication as to its readership.

Second, there was no formal method of British army staff training before the Royal Military College was founded in 1799, and regulations for field exercises were only laid down in 1795.[37] The college's curriculum was also limited; students progressed through French, mathematics, drawing, fortifications, and German with Frederick's *Instructions* as the principal strategic text.[38] In the early nineteenth century, even the higher strategic tracts available did not deal with retreats in anything like the detail expended on advances. Professional military education was limited both by the type of material available and the pedagogic approach.

While the purpose of doctrine in the eighteenth and nineteenth centuries is not comparable to modern writings, the lack of conceptual preparedness is. Today, higher commands and staffs do not train, educate, or practice retreat, and limited doctrine exists above the tactical level regarding its theoretical underpinnings. This is in direct contrast to Molyneux, who stated that "to make a safe retreat in the sight of a powerful enemy, has at all times been esteemed, one of the most shining qualities in a General."[39] Unfortunately, as he acknowledged, the defensive "is so far from exciting the genius that it turns some People's Heads, they become like Men in a Trance."[40] Indeed, criticism was leveled at Moore:

> [He] proved lamentably deficient in those qualities of decision and firmness which he had so often displayed on former occasions . . . [and] appeared to labour under a depression of spirits so different from his usual serene and cheerful disposition as to give a mournful expression to his countenance, indicative of the greatest anxiety of mind; and it seemed either that his judgement was completely clouded or that he was under the influence of a spell which forced him to commit the most glaring errors.[41]

Moore should not bear such criticism alone. In his General Orders, he commonly implored officers to do their duty and personally castigated as well as praised commanding officers during the final march from Burgo to Corunna.[42] One purpose of doctrine is to prevent cognitive dislocation by preparing individuals for unfavorable circumstances: neither Moore, his staff, nor the wider army were prepared for "precipitate retreat."[43] Are their professional descendants any better equipped today? In 2021, UK divisional-level wargames and rehearsal of concept (ROC) drills do not consider prolonged retreat, and modern doctrine refers to retreat only as a temporary tactical phase before transitioning to another action.[44] This failure to devote conceptual effort to understanding and preparing for retreat is similarly matched in the moral component, both then and now.

Morale and Resilience

Maintenance of morale is a central doctrinal tenet—second in the UK's Principles of War litany. What is less often described is the place of mental resilience, although this is being addressed in recent times. Group resilience was, and remains, a key component of section, company, battalion/regiment, or even army character.[45] Australian historian Rory Muir questions whether even Wellington's veterans would have been able to weather the morale shocks suffered by Prussian Gebhard Leberecht von Blucher's Prussians in the 1813–1815 campaigns.[46] The mark of a successful military is not the ability to win first time, every time, but to continue even after suffering a reversal of fortune. Blucher's army was defeated at Ligny on 16 June 1815, only to secure victory at Waterloo just two days later. Such recovery requires mental resilience, the willingness to accept failure as an occupational hazard, and learning from that experience.

Retreat is detrimental to both personal and group morale, and this is evidenced in the witness accounts. Advancing into Spain with the prospect of battle with Bonaparte, the army was in high spirits. Brig.-Gen. Robert Anstruther even proclaimed that if Napoleon beat them, "we shall be like the rest of the world. If we beat him, we shall be like ourselves alone."[47] As soon as the order to retreat was given, "all ranks called out to stop and not to run away . . . from the greatest pitch of exaltation and courage at once a solemn gloom prevailed."[48] Artist and diplomat Ker Porter, accompanying Sir John Moore, captured the "withering effect" of the order: "The army of England was no more. Its spirit was fled; and what appeared to me a host of heroes [became] men in arms without hope, wish, or energy."[49] The morale collapse was so intense that Moore castigated the army on 27 and 30 December, and then again on the 6 January—appealing to their honor, forbearance, and understanding of the situation. Moore's appeal was undermined by the behavior of the commissariat staff under his direction, who ordered troops to destroy, rather than distribute, stores of food and boots.[50]

Accounts of the retreat unanimously describe the horrendous conditions. Troops marched through freezing conditions over the mountainous terrain of northern Spain and suffered from malnutrition; uniforms quickly decayed while morale and discipline rapidly collapsed; and soldiers in the leading divisions looted and drank their way toward Corunna.[51] First at

Benevente on 28 December, then at Bembibre on 2 January, hundreds of troops became so inebriated that they were left to the elements or the enemy. British troops pillaged Astorga, stealing stores meant for Romana's Spanish division and later burned the town of Villafranca in an orgy of destruction. The army's pay chest was thrown into a gorge—£25,000 in silver dollars (equal to US $30,000). As snow fell and the weather deteriorated, pack animals and the wagon train collapsed. Wagons containing the sick and wounded were abandoned altogether at Monte Cebrero. Between Villafranca and Lugo, the road was marked with bloody footprints and littered with abandoned carts, equipment, and the bodies of men, women, and children who succumbed to the elements.[52]

As it was, Col. Digby Hamilton indicated that instances of "great irregularity and disorder" were prompted by three defects.[53] First, the commissariat (logistics corps) failed to create depots along the route of march. Second, because of the perennial lack of baggage transport and draft animals, much-needed equipment was lost or destroyed, and the wounded were abandoned. Third, military effectiveness was hampered by the number of non-combatants (primarily soldiers' wives and children) accompanying the retreating troops.[54] Detractors blamed Moore's enlightened approach to discipline, while his defenders looked to the ambivalence of regimental officers paying attention to their own comfort rather than their soldiers' needs.[55] Without discipline from above, unit cohesion collapsed as soldiers focused on their own and immediate comrades' survival, or simply gave up. A key failing was the lack of competent staff and commissariat to organize and supply the retreating brigades. Units were left to find their own billets, frequently leading to scuffles and confrontations between groups of soldiers, and supply depots often were destroyed so they could not be used by the enemy. Additionally, the stores that did exist were not distributed to the starving and ragged army and, as a result, the disciplined, ordered destruction rapidly turned into wanton, gleeful, and nihilistic devastation.

Yet the disorder and ill-discipline was not universal. Summerville highlighted that "the cavalry, artillery, [King's] German Legion [KGL], and Foot Guards maintained high levels of discipline, as did the 20th, 43rd, 52nd, and 95th regiments."[56] Among the rear-guard brigades (comprised of the cavalry, KGL, 20th, 43rd, 52nd and 95th regiments), the combination of proximity to the enemy, strict discipline (it was not uncommon for punishment parades to be held in sight of the French vanguard), and esprit de corps kept excesses against the civilian populace to the minimum. These units also suffered proportionately fewer casualties during the march and subsequent battle, despite successfully fighting several delaying actions.[57]

That these units had been chosen for the rear-guard duties was not coincidental. Moore trusted the Light Brigade as he trusted few other corps, having been instrumental in their raising and training. Moreover, the 20th, 43rd, 52nd, and 95th all had recent campaign experience, and the KGL was predominantly veterans recruited from former Hanoverian and German states now under Imperial French occupation.[58] This was unusual; it would be a mistake to assume that Moore's army was the same corps of veterans that Lord Wellington would lead into France in 1813. Of the thirty-five infantry battalions, only fifteen had fought with Wellesley at Vimeiro—for many their first campaign in over a decade. Of Moore's eleven infantry brigades, four had no operational experience.[59] Among the cavalry, only one unit had recent operational experience: the 20th Hussars. Yet because of the cavalry's esprit de corps, recent successes during the advance at Sahagun (21 December 1808), and the moral ascendancy they felt over their French counterparts, these units were able to blunt the pursuit. Most memorably, the cavalry captured General Lefebvre-Desnouettes (commanding a cavalry unit of Napoleon's Imperial Guard) in full view of the emperor.

Remarkably when the army turned to face its pursuers, group cohesion was sufficient to restore discipline. French witnesses were astonished that "when all order and discipline appeared to be lost in the British ranks, the slightest prospect of an engagement produced, as if by magic, the immediate restoration of both."[60] When the whole army turned and stood at Lugo, it checked Soult's advance guard—even though Moore declined battle and continued the retreat. The army's comradely fighting spirit was, seemingly, undaunted; the physical act of retreating—and the lax discipline combined with open criticism voiced by much of the officer corps—produced the most deleterious effects.[61] Moore acknowledged, however, that if the army was to stand in line of battle, they would need more than just fighting spirit. The ravages of the campaign would need to be undone.

Reconstitution

One assumption in modern doctrine is that the retreated force can, by dint of being embarked on its transports, be reconstituted and returned to the fight.[62] Moore firmly derided this premise in a letter to Castlereagh: "If I succeed in embarking the Army, I shall send it to England—it is quite unfit for further service until it has been refitted."[63] Oman estimated that total losses during the retreat and battle numbered some 5,998, including 3,809 "perished in battle, by the road, or in hospital."[64] Summerville quoted a higher figure of 7,035, but this did not include troops that made their way back to Portugal separate from their units.[65] In either case, of the 33,234 effectives in October 1808, 26,199 were returned to England, a 21-percent attrition rate. Although Moore's main army of some 22,000 troops entered Corunna on 11 January, the shipping did not arrive from Vigo until the 14th; in the meantime, Moore was able to rest, recuperate, and refit much of the infantry.[66] When transports did arrive, more than fifty of the army's guns were immediately embarked, along with the remaining cavalry and sick.[67] Remarkably, the cavalry suffered just 222 casualties (less than 10 percent), yet that too was still a spent force; weather and ground were ruinous to horses' health.[68]

The vast quantities of stores abandoned or destroyed is another matter. Because of the industrial and fiscal revolution, Britain could accommodate the wanton and deliberate destruction of such commodities—able to supply and pay for the re-equipping of its own armies and those of its allies.[69] Prior to Wellesley's dispatch to Portugal, the Spanish *juntas* received "£1.5m in silver [£60 million/US $73 million in modern reckoning] . . . 120,000 muskets, millions of cartridges, 155 artillery pieces, 100,000 uniforms, and an assorted glut of other military supplies."[70] In more recent times, the gifting of artillery systems and missiles to Ukraine underscores the continued utility of military aid, albeit with some caveats.[71] In this post-industrial world, one must wonder about the UK's capacity to absorb such materiel losses and expenditure.

What could not be made good were cavalry mounts. A total of 2,000 horses were deemed unfit and butchered on the quayside, much to the army's distress; only approximately 10 percent of the cavalry mounts shipped from England were saved, with priority given to officers' horses.[72] As with the 1940 evacuation of the British Expeditionary Force from Dunkirk, the army sacrificed its mobility in order to survive. A 1796 board of enquiry noted the difficulty of securing suitable mounts and, as a result, reformed the procurement system.[73] Even so, the training and climatization of horses to the cavalry role was a time-consuming process. A cavalry unit returned from Corunna was unlikely to see field service for "four to five years," leaving the army chronically short of reconnaissance and shock-action capabilities; for example, the 10th, 15th, and 18th Hussars did not return to the Peninsular War until 1813.[74]

The manpower problem proved the most acute. Reconstituting Britain's expeditionary army was never an easy task: despite numbering more than 200,000 by 1809, two thirds of the army was scattered in garrison duties across the empire.[75] Moreover, the casualty rate among those returning to the UK was as high as initial campaign losses. Howard estimated

5,000 to 6,000 sick and injured were received from the transports, with an average mortality rate of 17 percent; many more were discharged as invalids.[76] Unfortunately, the Inspector of Army Hospitals had closed facilities at Gosport, Plymouth, and Deal in an effort to save money; this resulted in the mass mobilization of medical students and general practitioners, and conversion of barracks and prison hulks into "wholly unsatisfactory" hospitals.[77] In total, approximately a third of Moore's army was incapacitated or killed; Castlereagh called for 28,000 volunteers from the militia to replace the losses; within the year, the majority of the infantry battalions were back on campaign in northern Europe.[78]

The same could not be said today. The British military has closed all its hospitals, moving treatment and medical personnel into the National Health Service where the focus is no longer to return personnel effectively and quickly to operations.[79] Defence Medical Services is also suffering a severe personnel retention crisis, placing yet more strain on an already fragile system. Further, with the decrease in regular personnel, units are now required to "back-fill" from the Army Reserve; large elements are already committed, either to discrete specialist missions such as cyber command or providing additional maneuver sub-units to undermanned regular formations. Additionally, the British army struggled to sustain a casualty rate of just 4.7 percent at the peak of its Helmand campaign (2007–2014).[80] The recent experience of forces engaged in high-intensity warfighting should be salutary; battle casualties, even in limited wars, are in the thousands rather than hundreds.[81]

Amphibious Sustainment

Moore well recognized that success hinged on access to and support from secure sea lines of communication; British expeditionary capability was only possible thanks to total dominance of the ocean.[82] After Trafalgar, French attempts to build fleets were unrealistic, lacking both men and materiel; squadrons that did evade blockade were snapped up by the ubiquitous Royal Navy.[83] Napoleon's attempts to purloin fleets from neutrals or allies were foiled, as at Copenhagen. Indeed, one reason for British intervention in Portugal was both the presence of the Portuguese fleet and Admiral Dmitry Siniavin's Russian squadron at Lisbon in November 1807 (Russia was then allied to France). Rear Admiral Sir Sidney Smith first blockaded the Tagus, denying Siniavin freedom of movement, then removed the greater part of the Portuguese fleet and the Royal family to Brazil.[84] Admiral Sir Charles Cotton then escorted Siniavin's squadron to Portsmouth in September 1808.[85] Thus, sea control assured Moore's lines of communication and retreat—something he knew from personal experience would be vital.[86]

Vice Admiral Cuthbert Collingwood's command was typical of the numerous squadrons blockading Napoleon's coastlines; such "familiar occurrences" included his "gallant young men" assaulting forts, landing raiding parties, strangling coastal trade, and cutting out fighting ships.[87] By constantly harassing and denying French maritime freedom, Britain dominated the sea-lanes, both commercially and militarily. Consequently, British forces enjoyed uninterrupted passage to almost any chosen landing place. Yet, maintaining this command of the sea came at an enormous cost. Britain maintained 140,000 seamen and more than 800 ships, including 100 that were line-of-battle, and devoted nearly a quarter of its total government spending to the cause (£11 to 14 million/US $13.3 to 17 million per annum).[88]

Battle at sea may be an operational function of a fleet but is not its strategic purpose—a lesson the Royal Navy has had to relearn on numerous occasions.[89] Castlereagh's amassing of civilian shipping under the Transport Board ensured the initial dispatch and successful extraction of Moore's army.[90] At a minimum ratio of 1¼ tons per man, the Peninsular army required in excess of 40,000 tons of shipping for the infantry alone. A single regiment of horse (600 troopers) required a further 20,000 tons; artillery and commissariat needed yet more.[91] Parliament requested overall figures for maritime transport during the Corunna campaign: 803 vessels, totalling 196,670 tons, were taken up from trade at an exorbitant £1,292,781 (equal to US $1.57 million).[92] The transport fleet that saved Moore's army was only loitering on the Spanish Atlantic and Biscay coasts fortuitously; of the 150 vessels available in January, many had only recently finished unloading troops and stores destined for Baird's Division or their now-scattered Spanish allies.[93] Today, no western navy has such a mass of transports; the UK possesses just four strategic roll-on/roll-off ferries and a similar number of amphibious landing platforms. Many of those assets are aging, due out of service or permanently employed in other roles. If Britain mounts another amphibious expedition of consequence in the future, it will once again have to resort to Ships Taken Up from Trade (STUFT) as it did in the 1982 Falklands Conflict.[94] Today, however, Britain's merchant marine is even smaller than it was in 1982, and a fraction of the comparative capacity that Castlereagh could call upon.

Shipping alone is not enough to guarantee salvation; the location and organization of embarkation points is also crucial. During the evacuation from Flanders in 1799, General Guillaume-Mathieu Dumas observed that "those who have executed or followed the details of the embarkation of an army with its artillery, hospitals, baggage, and ammunition may be astounded at the speed of British preparations."[95] Baird, in conjunction with Admiral Michael de Courcy, had initially suggested Vigo, which was a better anchorage and had greater capacity for holding troops prior to embarkation.[96] In the end, only 3,500 men of the elite Light Brigade and the KGL embarked at Vigo.[97] The vast majority of Moore's troops made for the smaller, but nearer, Corunna port, but not without loss and a brief brush with chaos; the order to head for Corunna rather than taking the road to Vigo was lost when the dragoon carrying the dispatch to Fraser's 3rd Division succumbed to drunkenness. In retracing its steps, the Division lost some 400 stragglers, and much-needed time.

The 100 transports arrived at Corunna on 14 January, three days after Moore's army. They had been delayed by bad weather and the failure to deliver Moore's initial message ordering the shift in base of operations—a further example of the friction of war and possibility of the retreat descending into chaos. While forced marches had cost Moore approximately 10 percent of his strength, the time it bought him was invaluable. The delay between the army's arrival and that of the transports was fortuitous. In the days preceding the events, with the bridge at Burgo blown and Paget's Reserve Division holding Soult's advance guard at bay, the army was able to recuperate and rearm itself from the vast quantities of arms and materiel within the port.[98] Discipline was restored, and the troops were brought back under control. With hot meals and secure lodgings, the disorganized rabble quickly became an army again. When they did engage on the 16th of January, Soult's army suffered from the immediate deprivations of forced marches in poor country.[99] Surpluses were destroyed, although much was missed in the confusion and eventually fell into the hands of the French.[100] Once the British ships arrived, the priority was to embark the sick, the army's guns, and the cavalry; thirty-four so-laden vessels departed from Corunna on the 16th.[101] Lack of horse transports—twenty-seven had returned to England on 31 December—at least in part contributed to the dispatch of so many cavalry mounts, but the need to convert transports for hospital ships and embark bulky limbers, caissons, and other artillery impedimenta must have also factored.[102]

From the moment of their arrival on the 14th, the pace was frenetic; the British commissaries and transport officers had no rest for three days and two nights. The Royal Navy established two evacuation points: the quay under the Citadel for the sick, cumbersome baggage, and horses and the open beach at nearby St Lucia for the majority of the troops. Having fought Soult to a standstill at the Battle of Corunna on the 16th, embarkation continued through the evening, day of the 17th, and finally into the small hours of the 18th. Even when the French brought up a battery overlooking St Lucia on the 17th, there was little interruption to embarkation; four vessels were lost when their masters panicked and cut their moorings, yet crews and cargo were rescued with only nine lives lost.[103] Descriptions of the evacuation over the beaches are reminiscent of Dunkirk; troops waded out neck-deep into the Atlantic swell awaiting pick-up by ships' boats. Unlike the boat crews from the Naval vessels who could work in shifts, the minimally crewed merchantmen had no rest; the civilian sailors were exhausted by the constant effort of rowing against wind and tide.[104] Although Howard described the embarkation as "disorderly," with some transports over-crowded and units hopelessly intermixed, Corunna was probably one of the "Transport Board's finest moments."[105] The recent prior service of agents and transport officers during the 1807 Baltic expeditions and 1808 landings undoubtedly provided much-needed experience and precedent at the tactical and operational levels. That the embarkation was carried out in winter, across an open bay, on a lee shore, and without serious loss is testament to their professionalism, but also the good conduct of the troops. The trying situation could easily have descended into a chaotic free-for-all. One of the key lessons from the Corunna evacuation was to have strategic shipping on standby in the locale. Subsequently, a transport fleet was kept in the Tagus below Lisbon throughout the Peninsula campaign of 1809–1813, though this required a huge commitment and expense.

Conclusion

There are many lessons to be learned from Corunna. At the strategic level, expeditionary powers such as the US and UK must realize that it is not a cheap option and requires excessively large outlays of resources and capability; the cost of shipping, a support function, was ruinous. Moreover, the need for properly constituted, mobilized, and capable continental allies is paramount; expeditionary forces are only ever auxiliaries. Those allies must be paid for and supplied, as was the case throughout the French Wars; seven coalitions were subsidized by the British, and even Napoleon's army quite literally marched in British boots. Without allies, the expeditionary force would be dangerously exposed and vulnerable. Further, expeditionary forces can only operate against the continental hegemon's extremities, and only then after securing total command of the sea. Without this vital element, all other considerations are moot.

Operationally, commanders and their subordinates must be prepared for defeat and/or withdrawal. This is not the same as being defeatist; rather it is an acceptance of friction and willingness to plan for the worst-case scenario. In the case of Corunna, there was no preparation until the campaign was too far advanced; politically, militarily, and doctrinally, retreat had not been considered until after Moore's forces had been committed. The lack of preparation across all three components of fighting power (physical, conceptual, and moral) led to the collapse in morale and subsequent chaotic scenes marked by looting and destruction of stores and towns along the route of march. By contrast to both contemporary and modern doctrine, Molyneux and the German Army's *Truppenführung* both devote entire chapters to withdrawal. Further, failure to prepare for the campaign with forward establishment of depots, lack of knowledge about the terrain and local conditions, and the failure to win populace support all contributed to the army's breakdown during the retreat. Effective leadership, esprit de corps, group discipline and coherence were much in evidence in those units that maintained their unity.

The retreat showcased unfounded assumptions at all levels, such as that forces can be withdrawn by ship, "reconstituted," and sent back to the area of operations. The fact that the Royal Navy and army were able to concentrate in the same location, albeit with some delay, emphasizes the difficulty of coordinating across multiple domains, locations, and force components. Joint or combined operations are hazardous because they occur at the seams. For expeditionary powers, joint thinking and awareness is vital and must be worked at. This was not a lesson solely learned at Corunna. Gallipoli, Dunkirk, Crete, and numerous others all demonstrate the fallacies of such lazy assumptions. Moreover, even if successfully evacuated to the home-base, reconstitution is not assured. Failing to maintain military health systems and hospital capability in peacetime, relying on civilian surge, is also dangerous; civil health services are not orientated to military requirements and have limited spare capacity. The serious materiel losses—particularly by the army's reconnaissance and maneuver arm as well as logistical capabilities—hampered operations for several years. That these losses were eventually made good was owing to huge inter-generational investment in military industrial capability by both the public purse and the private sector.

Much has been made of Moore's battlefield victory at Corunna, with commentators viewing it as a vindication of the British soldier and an invaluable morale boost. Yet the campaign was a defeat. "Wars," as British Prime Minister Winston Churchill said, "are not won by evacuations."[106] Molyneux noted some fifty years earlier that retreats are the most difficult operations for any commander and force. Neither Moore, his army, or his political masters were psychologically or physically prepared for retreat. For British and US personnel, it is a lesson that should be remembered and prepared for.

Notes

1. Colin S. Gray, *Strategy and History* (Abingdon, UK: Routledge, 2006), 55.

2. Donald D. Horward, "British Seapower and Its Influence upon the Peninsular War (1808–1814), *Naval War College Review* 31, no.2, Fall 1978: 54–71.

3. Gray, *Strategy and History*, 57; and Sir Michael Howard, "The Use and Abuse of Military History," in *The Causes of Wars, and Other Essays* (London: Unwin, 1983), 208–17.

4. Andrew Young, "History: A Neglected Discipline," *The Naval Review* 104, no. 1, February 2014: 39–43.

5. Hereafter simply Castlereagh. He served as Secretary State for War and the Colonies twice between 1804 and 1809, resigning briefly in 1806 during the tumultuous "Ministry of all the Talents." As Secretary for War, Castlereagh set the military strategic targets and mobilized resources to meet Foreign Secretary George Canning's policy ends.

6. Ranking alongside the destruction of the French fleet at Mers-el-Kebir, Algiers, in 1940, the expedition to secure the Danish fleet is a lesson in British self-interest. In June 1807, Napoleon issued both Denmark and Portugal an ultimatum to close their ports to British shipping or face the consequences. (Napoleon famously quipped to the Portuguese ambassador: "The English declare they will no longer respect neutrals on the sea; I will no longer recognize them on land.") The risk of the Danish fleet falling into Napoleon's hands was deemed too great in London, and when the Danish court refused to accept British offers of alliance, a force of 25,000 troops was conveyed to Copenhagen. After a three-day bombardment, the Danes surrendered their fleet. The example stiffened Portuguese resolve. Gunther Rothenberg, *The Napoleonic Wars* (London: Cassell 2004), 113; David Gates, "Transformation of the Army, 1783–1815," in *Oxford History of the British Army*, ed. David Chandler (Oxford: Oxford University Press, 1996), 132–60; and Robert K. Sutcliffe, *British Expeditionary Warfare and the Defeat of Napoleon, 1793–1815* (London: Boydell & Brewer 2016), 182.

7. The *dos de Mayo,* which later precipitated the guerrilla, or "Little War," that characterized what Napoleon later referred to as his "Spanish Ulcer." Christopher Hibbert, *Corunna* (London: Pan Books, 1967), 18–19.

8. Charles Esdaile, *The Peninsular War* (London: Allen Lane, 2002), 62–86.

9. Esdaile, *The Peninsular War*, 3.

10. Charles Esdaile, *The French Wars* (London: Routledge, 2001), 51; and Rothenburg, *The Napoleonic Wars,* 114.

11. Sutcliffe, *British Expeditionary Warfare and the Defeat of Napoleon,* 187 and 189; Godfrey Davies, "English Foreign Policy," *Huntington Library Quarterly* 5, no.4 (July 1942): 419–78; Rothenberg, *The Napoleonic Wars,* 115; Hibbert, *Corunna,* 21–24; and Esdaile, *The Peninsular War,* 101–3. Lieutenant General Wellesley's army landed in stages, and only reached its full strength of 37,000 late in the campaign. By the time Wellesley defeated Major-General Jean-Andoche Junot at Vimeiro, he had officially been superseded by Lieutenant

General Burrard, who in turn gave over command to Lieutenant General Dalrymple. The Convention of Cintra returned Junot's 24,735-strong army—complete with standards, cannon, stores, and "personal effects" (including a significant quantity of looted goods)—to France in British merchant ships. This controversial movement caused consternation at home and fury in Lisbon. Its architects, Generals Dalrymple and Burrard, attempted to shift blame onto Sir Arthur Wellesley; all three were recalled, but only Wellesley emerged unscathed.

12. Philip Haythornwaite, *Corunna 1809: Sir John Moore's Fighting Retreat* (Oxford: Osprey 2001), loc. 33, Kindle; and Esdaile, *The French Wars*, 51.

13. J. H. Anderson quoted in Haythornwaite, loc. 50; and Hibbert, *Corunna*, 39.

14. George Canning to Hookham Frere, quoted in Hibbert, 30.

15. Esdaile, *The Peninsular War*, 105; and Hibbert, 29.

16. Hibbert, 19–20.

17. Esdaile, *The Peninsular War*, 85–86.

18. Hibbert, *Corunna*, 35; and Haythornwaite, *Corunna 1809*, loc. 441.

19. Hibbert, 34.

20. Esdaile, *The Peninsular War*, 142; and Hibbert, 37.

21. Moore marched north through Portugal toward Salamanca with some 15,000 on 18 October, while his cavalry, artillery, and a strong escort totaling 5,000 crossed via a southerly route. Lieutenant General Baird's force of 12,000 finally landed at Corunna between 26 October and 4 November, with his delayed cavalry landing on 13 November. Between 31 October and 23 November, Napoleon's commanders launched a series of overwhelming assaults on the separated Spanish armies. Haythornwaite, *Corunna 1809*, loc. 528–49.

22. Esdaile, *The Peninsular War*, 143; and Hibbert, *Corunna*, 35.

23. Haythornwaite, *Corunna 1809*, loc. 114; Charles Esdaile, "War and Politics in Spain, 1808–1814," *The Historical Journal* 32, no.2, June 1988: 295–317; Esdaile, *The French Wars*, 51–52; and Esdaile, *The Peninsular War*, 143.

24. Hibbert, *Corunna*, 49–52.

25. Rothenberg, *The Napoleonic Wars*, 116.

26. Napoleon quoted in Hibbert, *Corunna*, 90.

27. Napoleon to Joseph Bonaparte, quoted in Haythornwaite, *Corunna 1809*, loc. 779.

28. Horward, "British Seapower and Its Influence upon the Peninsular War," 57.

29. Col. C. E. Callwell, *Military Operations and Maritime Preponderance* (1906; repr., Annapolis, MD: Naval Institute Press, 1996), 274.

30. Col. (USMC) Joseph H. Alexander, "Amphibious Warfare: What Sort of Future?," in *Assault from the Sea: Essays on the History of Amphibious Warfare*, ed. Lt. Col. (USMC-Ret.) Merrill L. Bartlett (Annapolis, MD: Naval Institute Press, 1983), 419–25.

31. Thomas M. Molyneux, *Conjunct Expeditions* (London: R&J Dodsley, 1759), 149–77.

32. Maurice de Saxe, *Reveries, or Memoirs Concerning the Art of War* (Edinburgh: Sands, Donaldson, Murray, and Cochran, 1759), 100–62.

33. Development, Concepts, and Doctrine Centre, Joint Doctrine Publication 0-10, *UK Maritime Power* (Wiltshire, UK: 2017); Land Warfare Development Centre, *Land Operations* (Wiltshire, UK: 2017); Frederick the Great, "Military Instructions for the Generals," in *Roots of Strategy*, ed. Maj Thomas Phillips (London: John Lane, 1943), 167–218; and Joint Forces Command, Joint Publication 3-02, *Amphibious Operations* (Washington, DC: 2014).

34. Lt. Col. James Wolfe, letter to Maj. William Rickson, in Robert Wright, *The Life of Major General James Wolfe* (London: Chapman and Hall, 1864), 396–97.

35. Gates, "Transformation of the Army," 141; and Rory Muir, *Tactics and the Experience of Battle in the Age of Napoleon* (Yale: London 1998), 240–47.

36. B. Collins, "Effectiveness and the British Officer Corps, 1793–1815," in *Britain's Soldiers: Rethinking War and Society, 1715–1815* ed. K. Linch and M. McCormack (Liverpool: Liverpool University Press), 57–76.

37. Mark Urban, *Generals (*London: Faber and Faber, 2005), 104–5.

38. Anthony Morton, "From Flanders to Waterloo: The Origins of the Royal Military College," *Sandhurst Occasional Papers* 28, Royal Military Academy (2019): 15 and 34–35.

39. Molyneux, *Conjunct Expeditions,* 163 and 153.

40. Molyneux, 163 and 153.

41. Hibbert, *Corunna,* 196.

42. Christopher Summerville, *March of Death: Sir John Moore's Retreat to Corunna* (Barnsley UK: Frontline Books, 2004) loc. 2237, Kindle.

43. Harold Høiback, *Understanding Military Doctrine* (Abingdon: Routledge 2013); Howard, "The Use and Abuse of Military History," 208–17; and Hibbert, *Corunna,* 196.

44. Army Doctrine Publication C71940, *Land Operations,* 8–22.

45. Edward J, Goss, *All for the King's Shilling* (Norman, OK: University of Oklahoma Press, 2010), 191–210.

46. Rory Muir: 244.

47. Haythornwaite, *Corunna 1809,* loc. 549; and Hibbert, *Corunna,* 38.

48. Haythornwaite, loc. 756; and Hibbert, 92.

49. Haythornwaite, loc. 756.

50. Summerville, *March of Death,* loc. 1139.

51. Goss, *All for the King's Shilling,* 105; and Esdaile, *The Peninsular War,* 150–54.

52. Hibbert, *Corunna,* 99–136.

53. Janet Macdonald, *Sir John Moore: The Making of a Controversial Hero* (Barnsley, UK: Pen and Sword, 2016), 249.

54. Macdonald, 249.

55. Haythornwaite, *Corunna 1809,* loc. 898–910.

56. Summerville, *March of Death,* loc. 1169.

57. Sir Charles Oman, *A History of the Peninsular War,* vol. 1 (Kingston, TN: Pickle Partners, 2014), 734–36, Kindle.

58. Alistair Nichols, "It's not just about desertion: foreign soldiers and the British army during the Napoleonic Wars," in *The Sword and the Spirit: Proceedings of the first 'War & Peace in the Age of Napoleon' Conference,* ed. Zach White (Helion, Warwick: 2021): 116–33.

59. Haythornwaite, *Corunna 1809,* loc. 344.

60. Haythornwaite, loc. 1045.

61. Goss, *All for the King's Shilling*, 153 and 191–210; Oman, *A History of the Peninsular War,* 746; and Summerville, *March of Death,* loc. 1169.

62. Army Doctrine Publication C71940, *Land Operations*: loc. 7–12.

63. Moore to Castlereagh, 13 January 1809, in Macdonald, *Sir John Moore,* 260–74.

64. Oman, *A History of the Peninsular War,* 869–74.

65. Summerville, *March of Death,* loc. 3108–61.

66. Oman, *A History of the Peninsular War,* 869–74.

67. Oman, 754.

68. Oman, 754 and 869.

69. Davies, "English Foreign Policy," 420–21; and Piers Mackesy, "Problems of an Amphibious Power: Britain against France, 1793–1815," *Naval War College Review* 30, no. 4 (Spring 1978): 17.

70. Summerville, *March of Death,* loc. 196–205.

71. Samuel Cranny-Evans, "What Do UK Weapons Deliveries Add to Ukraine's Armed Forces?", *RUSI Commentary,* 21 January 2022, https://rusi.org/explore-our-research/publications/commentary/what-do-uk-weapons-deliveries-add-ukraines-armed-forces. A full evaluation of the limits of military aid to partner nations is made by Dr. Jack Watling and Nick Reynolds in *War by Others' Means: Delivering Effective Partner Force Capacity Building* (London: Routledge, 2021).

72. Sutcliffe, *British Expeditionary Warfare and the Defeat of Napoleon,* 192–93; Oman, *A History of the Peninsular War,* 754; Haythornwaite, *Corunna 1809,* loc. 1194; Sutcliffe, *British Expeditionary Warfare and the Defeat of Napoleon,* 193; and Mark T. Gerges, "Command and Control in the Peninsula: The Role of the British Cavalry 1808–1814" (PhD Thesis: 2005), 51, https://diginole.lib.fsu.edu/islandora/object/fsu:182486/datastream/PDF/view.

73. Richard Holmes, *Redcoat* (London: Harper Collins, 2002), 227; and Gerges, 22.

74. Gerges, 342.

75. Robert K. Sutcliffe, *British Expeditionary Warfare and the Defeat of Napoleon, 1793–1815* (London: Boydell & Brewer 2016), 241; and Gates, "Transformation of the Army," 138.

76. M. R. Howard, "Medical Aspects of Sir John Moore's Corunna Campaign, 1808–1809," *Journal of the Royal Society of Medicine* 84 (May 1991): 300; and Saul David, *All the King's Men* (London: Viking, 2012): 394–95.

77. Howard, "Medical Aspects of Sir John Moore's Corunna Campaign," 300.

78. Corelli Barnett, *Britain and Her Army* (London: Allen Lane, 1970), 258. Throughout the French and Napoleonic Wars, the army lost 16–24,000 troops per annum; the 1793–1796 expeditions to the French Sugar Islands cost 80,000 men dead or invalided (Gates, 138; and Barnett, 234).

79. Since 1990, all thirty-two British Military Hospitals have closed. The last to close were Cambridge Hospital in Aldershot (1996); Haslar Hospital in Gosport (2009); and The Princess Mary Hospital in Cyprus (2012).

80. Jason W. Davidson. "The Costs of War to United States Allies Since 9/11," Watson Institute for International and Public Affairs, Brown University, May 2021.

81. Ministry of Defence of the Republic of Azerbaijan, "List of Servicemen who Died as Shehids in the Patriotic War," 14 June 2021, https://mod.gov.az/en/news/list-of-servicemen-who-died-as-shehids-in-the-patriotic-war-36332.html.

82. David Syrett, "The Role of the Royal Navy in the Napoleonic Wars after Trafalgar, 1805–1814,0, *Naval War College Review* 32 no. 5 (September–October 1979): 71–84; and Sutcliffe, *British Expeditionary Warfare and the Defeat of Napoleon*, 123.

83. Andrew Lambert, *War at Sea in the Age of Sail, 1650–1850* (London: Cassell, 2005), 185–86.

84. N. A. M. Rodger, *The Command of the Ocean* (London: Penguin 2005), 551.

85. Donald D. Horward, "Portugal and the Anglo-Russian Naval Crisis (1808), *Naval War College Review* 34, no. 3 (May–June 1981): 48–74.

86. Macdonald, *Sir John Moore*, 6–7. Moore, a captain-lieutenant and regimental paymaster, distinguished himself during the 1779 Penobscot expedition. There, two British regiments found themselves besieged by the New England militia and navy. The arrival of a squadron from Halifax dispersed the American fleet and relieved the garrison.

87. Rodger, *The Command of the Ocean*, 555.

88. Lambert, *War at Sea in the Age of Sail*, 187; Holmes, *Redcoat*, 86; and Rodger, *The Command of the Ocean*, 474.

89. Sir Julian S. Corbett, *England in the Seven Years War*, vol 1. (London: Longman Greens & Co, 1907), 1–7.

90. Sutcliffe, *British Expeditionary Warfare and the Defeat of Napoleon*, 189.

91. Mackesy, "Problems of an Amphibious Power," 20.

92. Sutcliffe, *British Expeditionary Warfare and the Defeat of Napoleon*, 204.

93. Sutcliffe, 199–200.

94. Andrew Young, "Littoral Response Groups: It's About Mass," *RUSI Defence Systems*, 12 July 2021, https://rusi.org/explore-our-research/publications/rusi-defence-systems/littoral-response-groups-its-about-mass.

95. Mackesy, "Problems of an Amphibious Power," 21.

96. Sutcliffe, *British Expeditionary Warfare and the Defeat of Napoleon*, 199.

97. Hibbert, *Corunna,* 146–52.

98. Summerville, *March of* Death, 2237–70; and Oman, *A History of the Peninsular War,* 755.

99. Haythornwaite, *Corunna 1809,* 1456–63.

100. Summerville, *March of Death,* 2299–310; and Hibbert, *Corunna,* 162–63.

101. Sutcliffe, *British Expeditionary Warfare and the Defeat of Napoleon,* 202.

102. Sutcliffe, 199 and 202.

103. W. Napier, "Chapter V," in W. Napier, *History of the War in the Peninsula and in the South of France: From the Year 1807 to the Year 1814* (New York: D. & J. Sadlier, 1828), 473–501, Cambridge Library Collection-Naval and Military History, Cambridge University Press; and Summerville, *March of Death,* 2794.

104. Sutcliffe, *British Expeditionary Warfare and the Defeat of Napoleon,* 202.

105. Howard, "Medical Aspects of Sir John Moore's Corunna Campaign," 229–302; and Sutcliffe, 201–3.

106. Winston Churchill, speech to House of Commons, 4 June 1940.

Chapter 3
Clausewitzian Friction and the Retreat of 6 Indian Division to Kut-al-Amara, November–December 1915[1]
Nikolas E. Gardner

Theorists of maneuver warfare have often viewed chaos as an opportunity to be exploited. American military strategist John Boyd, for example, advocated using speed, unpredictability, and deliberate deception to create "an amorphous, menacing, and unpredictable world of uncertainty, doubt, mistrust, confusion, [and] chaos," with the aim of rendering the enemy incapable of organized resistance.[2] In practice, however, it can be difficult to insulate one's own force from the disorder afflicting one's adversary. Any interaction between hostile forces lacking perfect situational awareness will invariably result in human errors and unintended consequences for both sides. This in turn will produce friction, which Prussian theorist Carl von Clausewitz described as "the force that makes the apparently easy so difficult."[3] Boyd maintained that experience and cohesion based on mutual trust could help members of an armed force cope with friction. But as casualties, fatigue, and uncertainty accumulate, even the most capable personnel can succumb to its debilitating effects. This chapter examines the impact of friction on British imperial forces operating in Mesopotamia in late November 1915. After an unsuccessful attempt to outmaneuver a larger Ottoman army holding positions south of Baghdad, the 6th Indian Division embarked on an extended retreat during which doubt, mistrust, confusion, and chaos profoundly affected personnel performance and the decisions of its commander.

The retreat ended at the Iraqi town of Kut-al-Amara, where the division was surrounded by Ottoman forces. The subsequent siege of Kut-al-Amara remains the most controversial episode of the British campaign in Mesopotamia during the First World War. This campaign began immediately after Britain declared war on the Ottoman Empire on 5 November 1914. The following day, Indian Expeditionary Force D (IEFD) landed near the port of Basra, aiming to secure the nearby oil fields of the Anglo-Persian oil company from Ottoman forces in the vicinity. Composed of British and Indian personnel, IEFD captured the port by the end of November. By mid-1915, it had established control over most of the Basra *vilayet*, the Ottoman province encompassing what is today southern Iraq. As the summer of 1915 progressed, however, British ambitions expanded. Facing setbacks on the Western Front and at the Dardanelles, political and military leaders increasingly focused on capturing the historic city of Baghdad, which appeared to be an attainable prize that would burnish British prestige throughout the Muslim world.[4]

Thus, in September 1915, Major-General Charles Townshend's 6 Indian Division, the vanguard of IEFD, began advancing up the Tigris River with the intent of reaching Baghdad. From 22 to 25 November, however, the division engaged superior Ottoman forces at Ctesiphon, less than thirty miles from its objective. After sustaining heavy casualties, Townshend's force withdrew from the battlefield on the evening of 25 November. Eight days later, after retreating more than ninety miles downriver with the enemy in pursuit, 6 Indian Division reached the town of Kut-al-Amara, where Townshend halted. Ottoman forces subsequently surrounded the town and established defensive positions farther down the Tigris. Despite multiple

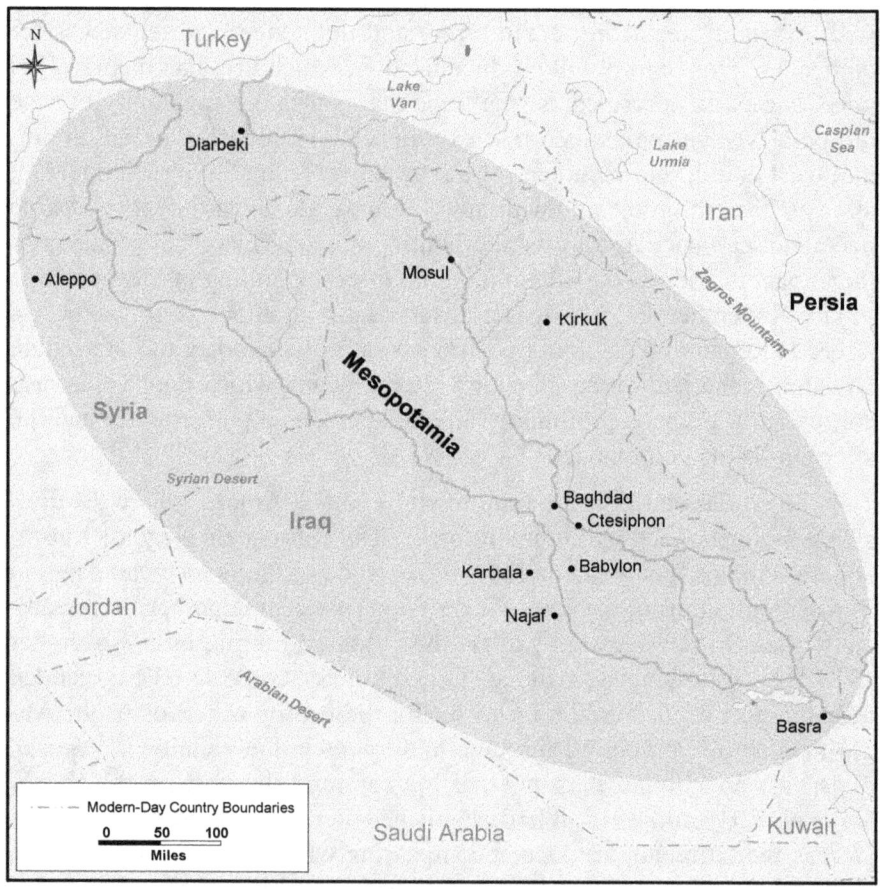

Figure 3.1. Map of Mesopotamia. Created by the Army University Press.

unsuccessful attempts by British forces to break through these positions, disease and starvation forced the division to surrender in late April 1916. The origins of the siege remain poorly understood. Influenced by Townshend's memoir of the campaign, scholars have assumed that the British commander resolved to seek refuge at Kut-al-Amara during the engagement at Ctesiphon or shortly afterward.[5] If this was the case, then the siege appears to have been a foregone conclusion. Yet a careful assessment of 6 Indian Division's retreat from Ctesiphon demonstrates that Townshend's decision to halt at Kut was not preordained. In fact, it was a result of mounting fatigue, ongoing uncertainty about the location of enemy forces, and increasing concern about the morale of Townshend's own subordinates.

All of these factors are elements of general friction, which Clausewitz described as "the only concept that more or less corresponds to the factors that distinguish real war from war on paper."[6] The factors that cause general friction include danger, physical exertion, imperfect intelligence, and unexpected interaction between the components of an armed force as well as the interaction between that force and the external environment. Strategic analyst Barry Watts has refined Clausewitz's broad conceptualization, incorporating insights from economics, evolutionary biology, and complexity theory to develop a taxonomy of general friction comprising three categories. The first consists of "constraints imposed by human physical and cognitive limitations," such as fatigue, emotion, and the brain's finite ability to process information. The second category results from uncertainty due to the inaccessibility of relevant information, because it is obscured by our own preconceptions, hidden by other actors, or dependent on future events. Watts's final category is friction caused by the nonlinearity of combat, specifically its tendency to produce unpredictable results, with minor events producing disproportionately large consequences and vice versa.[7] Drawing on theories that did not exist in the nineteenth century, Watts's taxonomy is not an exact reproduction of Clausewitz's ideas. But his identification of reasonably distinct categories of friction enables us to see more easily its impact on the conduct of war. Therefore, the following discussion will employ Watts's taxonomy to explain Townshend's retreat to Kut-al-Amara.

Townshend's Army

To understand Charles Townshend's decisions during the retreat, it is helpful to become acquainted with the 6 Indian Division commander and the force he led. Fifty-four years old in 1915, Townshend had built his career in British colonial campaigns in India and Africa. He first gained renown as a captain when he led the successful British defense of the Chitral fort in India's North West Frontier region against a siege by local forces in 1895. Three years later, he commanded an African regiment during the successful British campaign in Sudan.[8] Townshend's career progressed steadily during the first decade of the twentieth century. By 1911, he had attained the rank of major-general. Townshend proved restless, however, continually lobbying for new opportunities in Britain and India in an effort to gain promotion and acclaim.[9] The outbreak of the First World War appeared to be just such an opportunity. But as commander of the Rawal Pindi Brigade in August 1914, Townshend watched with frustration as other Indian formations embarked on operations to Europe, Africa, and the Middle East while he remained on garrison duty. Thus, when Lieutenant-General Sir John Nixon, the IEFD commander in Mesopotamia, offered him command of 6 Indian Division in the spring of 1915, Townshend seized the opportunity.

Despite Townshend's extensive imperial service, however, he had little experience commanding the Indian personnel who composed the majority of the division. Each of 6 Indian Division's three infantry brigades included three battalions of Indian *sepoys* alongside a single British battalion.[10] Attached to the division was an additional infantry brigade of similar composition, as well as a cavalry brigade comprising three regiments of Indian mounted troops (referred to as *sowars*), three companies of Indian sappers and miners, six British artillery batteries, and an additional battery of "mixed race" Eurasian personnel. Accompanying the division were an additional 3,500 Indian followers, who performed support functions such as food preparation and animal care. Altogether, Indian personnel comprised more than 80 percent of Townshend's force.[11] These Indians were members of what colonial authorities termed "martial classes," ethnic and religious groups that purportedly possessed innate qualities conducive to military service. While British authors attributed different virtues to specific ethnic and religious groups, all the groups shared a willingness to accept colonial rule. Inhabiting rural areas with authoritarian social structures and low rates of literacy, they had little exposure to notions of self-government circulating in India during this period.[12] To reduce the likelihood that these Indian personnel would unite in rebellion, as had been the case in 1857, the British encouraged distinctive dietary and religious practices among the groups they recruited.[13] They also reinforced the identities of individual units by recruiting from specific communities. Thus, at the outset of the First World War, the Indian Army was a patchwork of distinct units, with entire companies or even battalions consisting of *sepoys* or *sowars* as well as non-commissioned officers (NCOs) and Indian Viceroy's Commissioned Officers (VCOs), all of the same ethnic and religious background. At full strength, each Indian battalion also included thirteen British King's Commissioned Officers (KCOs), who served as a vital link between the command structure of the army and the Indian personnel, who were largely illiterate.[14] The unique makeup of Indian units made it difficult for senior British officers to assess the morale of their members. While many had experience commanding Indians, few were familiar with all the languages and cultural practices of the different ethnic and religious groups that comprised the army as a whole. This was particularly true of Charles Townshend. Despite his extensive service in the Indian Army as a staff officer and a senior commander, he had never served as a regimental officer in an Indian unit.

The harsh conditions IEFD experienced in Mesopotamia increased the uncertainty of British commanders for several reasons. The British logistical system was inadequate, which left British and Indian personnel without tents, clothing, and even boots. Indians, in particular, also suffered due to inadequate food supplies.[15] Traditionally expected to supplement their rations by purchasing food locally, they were unable to do so in Mesopotamia; the food shortages led to outbreaks of deficiency diseases such

Figure 3.2. 120th Rajputana Infantry, 1915. Courtesy of Wikimedia Commons.

as beriberi and scurvy.[16] Soldiers also suffered from dysentery and malaria—further complicated because the aforementioned logistical shortcomings left them, as well as those wounded in battle, without adequate medical care. To make matters worse, soldiers who became casualties in Mesopotamia were not immediately discharged back to India, which had long been an expectation of Indians who became sick or wounded on campaign.[17] Those soldiers who escaped death or injury felt keenly the loss of comrades and leaders with whom they had served for years or even decades. The small communities that traditionally provided recruits for specific companies and battalions ran out of able volunteers as the war progressed. As a result, it became increasingly difficult to maintain the cohesion of Indian units. As historian Edwin Latter has explained: "Recruiting was too localized, and specialized, to permit the replacement of wastage without changing the social, and even ethnic makeup of company-level units."[18] The British also had trouble finding officers with Indian language skills and experience leading Indian personnel. By the fall of 1915, it had become increasingly difficult to find any replacements for officer casualties in Mesopotamia; an average of only seven British officers remained in each Indian battalion.[19] Sir Walter Lawrence, commissioner of Indian military hospitals in France and England, described the overall impact of these losses in a letter to the Secretary of State for War, Lord Kitchener. Indian personnel, he explained, "have become accustomed to look upon their regiment as a family: they have lost the officers whom they knew, and the regiment, which formerly was made up of well-defined and exclusive castes and tribes, is now composed of miscellaneous and dissimilar elements. . . . This is no longer a regiment. It has no cohesion."[20] The conditions in which soldiers served in Mesopotamia, along with the impact of sustained casualties, corroded Indian morale as 1915 progressed.

In this context, some soldiers expressed religious objections to the campaign. Muslims comprised approximately 40 percent of the Indian Army at the beginning of the war.[21] Many Sunnis had reservations about fighting against the Ottoman sultan, who they recognized as the spiritual leader of the Muslim world. Shias were reluctant to fight near holy sites like Karbala and Najaf. Reassured by the British that the Ottomans had initiated hostilities, and that they would not attack religious sites, most Muslim soldiers participated in the campaign. But trans-frontier Pathans, whose homes lay in independent tribal territory between India and Afghanistan, were more likely to resist. Religious objections to service may also have been motivated by Pathans' concerns for the safety of their property and families, which were outside the control of British authorities.[22]

Lieutenant-General Arthur Barrett, Townshend's predecessor in command of 6 Indian Division, unsuccessfully requested to replace four companies of Pathans twice in early 1915.[23] The fact that the Pathans remained in Mesopotamia increased British concerns about the morale of the entire force. Thus, like any commander assuming a new role in an unfamiliar environment, Charles Townshend experienced real uncertainty as he arrived in Mesopotamia in the spring of 1915. But his lack of experience leading Indian personnel, combined with suspicions about their loyalty, compounded this uncertainty. It would become an acute source of friction under the stress of active operations.

The Battle of Ctesiphon and the Beginning of the Retreat

Townshend took command of 6 Indian Division as British forces were advancing north and west in an effort to establish control over the Basra *vilayet*. He distinguished himself almost immediately, capturing the town of Amara in early June with fewer than 100 troops and compelling the surrender of an enemy force ten times larger. Sickness forced his return to India shortly afterward, but he "lied to the doctors" about his health

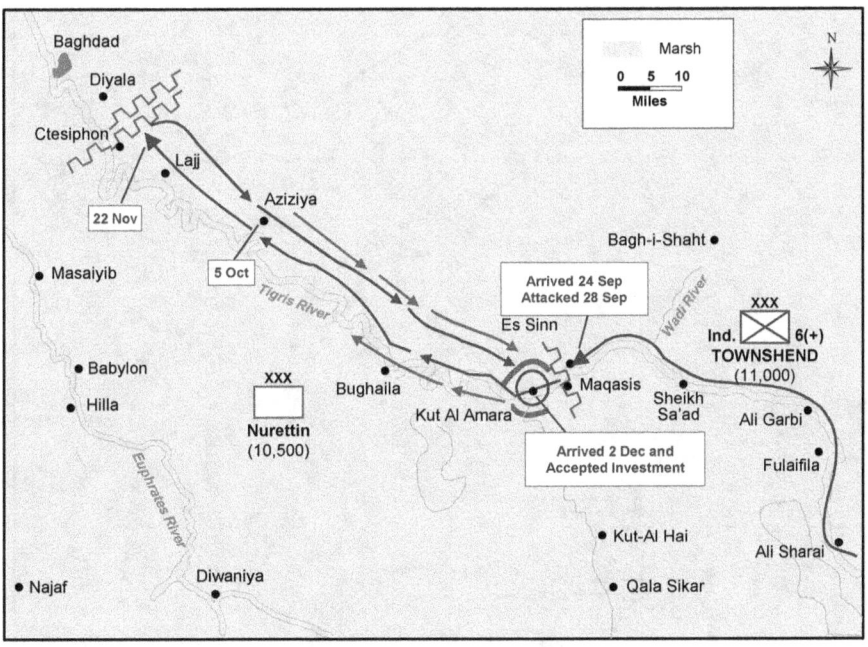

Figure 3.3. Lower Mesopotamia. 1914. First Advance on Baghdad, Situation 30 November 1915, and Operations since July 1915. Courtesy US Military Academy, recreated by Army University Press.

and was back in Mesopotamia in late August.[24] A month later, Townshend achieved further success on the battlefield, dislodging Ottoman forces from defensive positions at Es Sinn, several miles down the Tigris from Kut-al-Amara.

Townshend became increasingly concerned about the vulnerability of his force as it advanced farther up the Tigris in October, leaving the British base of operations at Basra hundreds of miles behind. He also expressed doubts about the reliability of his Indian subordinates, some of whom had retired in disorder during the engagement at Es Sinn. Nonetheless, Townshend continued his offensive, advancing against Ottoman forces at Ctesiphon on 22 November. Townshend's force had a fighting strength of approximately 14,000 troops supported by a relatively meager complement of 35 artillery pieces.[25] Against an adversary of equal or greater strength, he recognized that success would depend on speed. Therefore Townshend eschewed a preparatory artillery bombardment and developed a plan involving sequential frontal and flank attacks to disorient the enemy army and compel its retirement toward Baghdad.

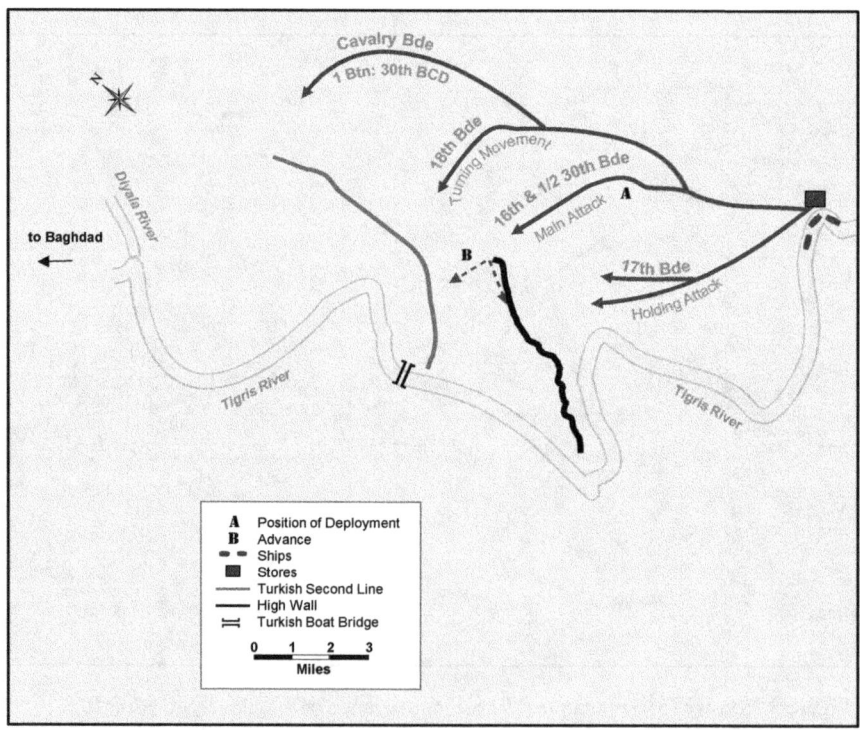

Figure 3.4. Battle of Ctesiphon map. Created by Army University Press.

But Townshend underestimated the strength of the Ottoman force, which comprised four divisions, commanded by Nurettin Pasha. Two of these, 35 and 38 divisions, consisted of Arab conscripts with a limited commitment to the Ottoman cause. The other two, 45 and 51 divisions, were composed of Anatolian soldiers with better training and morale than their Arab counterparts. Altogether the force totaled more than 30,000 troops, including 18,000 infantry.[26] Moreover, Nurettin had spent nearly two months preparing elaborate defensive positions at Ctesiphon. He also

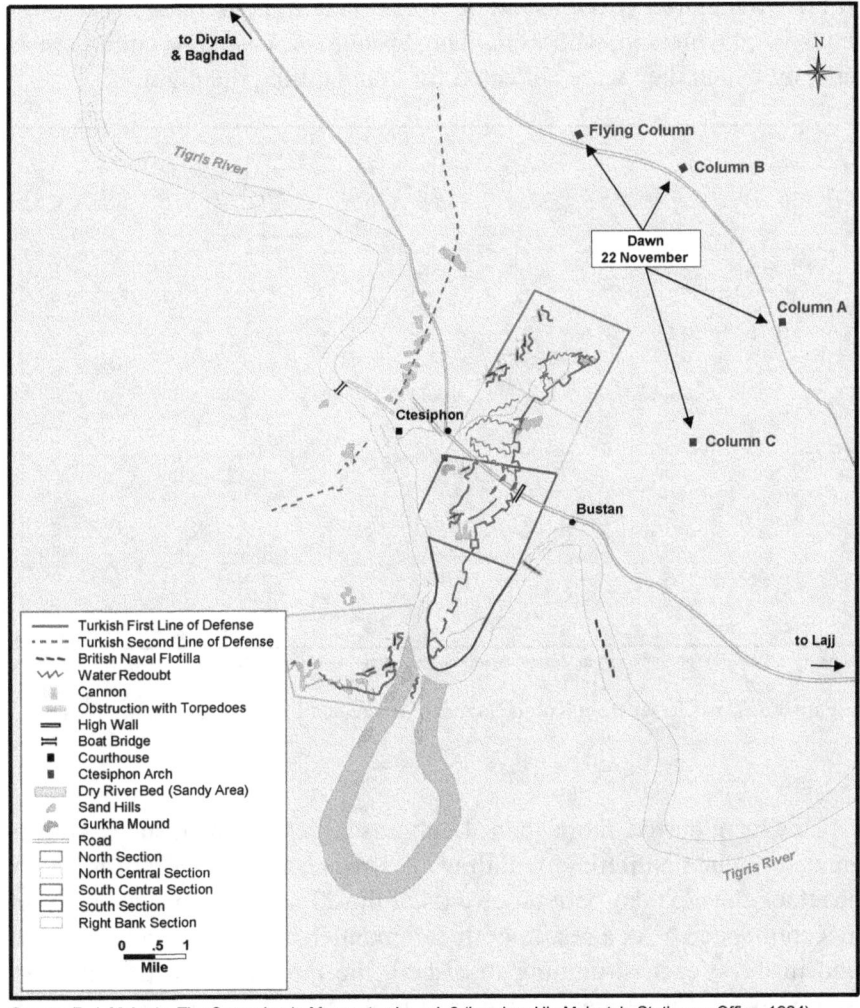

Source: F. J. Moberly, The Campaign in Mesopotamia, vol. 2 (London: His Majesty's Stationery Office, 1924).

Figure 3.5. Battle of Ctesiphon map. Recreated by Army University Press.

held 51 Division, the strongest of his formations, in reserve to counter an attack on his flank.²⁷ Thus, while Townshend's force inflicted significant casualties on the Ottomans on the morning of the 22nd, it was unable to induce them to retire. By early afternoon, Ottoman counterattacks increased. Commanding near the front, Townshend witnessed able Indian soldiers retiring voluntarily, a worrying development that he attributed to the fact that "there were not enough white officers to keep them steady and in hand."²⁸ That night he remained at the front as wounded personnel were collected at a makeshift field hospital. Townshend recalled in his memoir: "If I live a hundred years, I shall not forget that night bivouac . . . amongst hundreds of wounded, who were being brought in, loaded on commissariat carts, by which they were collected for hours during the night."²⁹

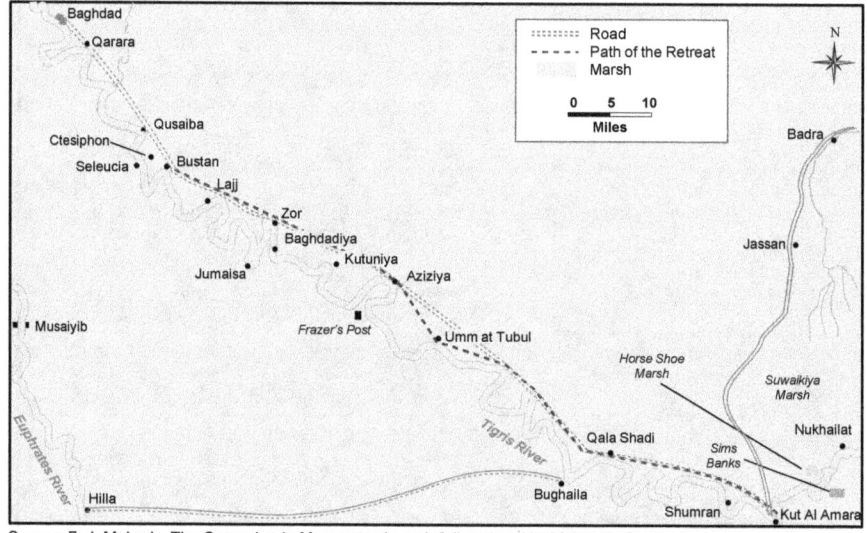

Source: F. J. Moberly, The Campaign in Mesopotamia, vol. 2 (London: His Majesty's Stationery Office, 1924).

Figure 3.6. Tigris River from Kut to Baghdad. Recreated by Army University Press.

Having incurred more than 4,000 casualties in an unsuccessful attempt to induce Nurettin's withdrawal, Townshend elected not to renew the attack the next day. But the events of the 22nd had also shaken Nurettin's confidence.³⁰ As a result, both commanders acted cautiously on subsequent days, each struggling to discern the intentions of his adversary using imperfect intelligence-gathering tools. While Nurettin relied solely on reports from observers on the ground, Townshend had several reconnaissance aircraft. Neither method, however, provided accurate or timely information. The flat terrain and prevalence of mirage conditions hampered visibility and made it difficult to judge distances. Moreover, in the absence of portable real-time communication devices, intelligence reports could take hours to reach commanders. As a result, Nurettin did not realize until early afternoon on 23 November that Townshend was no longer attacking. By the time the Ottoman commander initiated a counterattack, darkness had fallen and his force struggled even to find its enemy. Ottoman units that did locate Townshend's force suffered heavy casualties.[31]

Nevertheless, given the losses sustained by 6 Indian Division and continued Ottoman pressure, Townshend concluded on 24 November that his position was untenable. Therefore, he ordered a limited retirement six miles down the Tigris to Lajj, beginning on the morning of the 26th.[32] Nurettin was also apprehensive. Upon receiving false reports that Townshend was advancing late on the evening of the 24th, he ordered his force to retire the next morning. When daylight revealed no advance by 6 Indian Division, however, Nurettin ordered the reoccupation of his positions at Ctesiphon.[33] Believing that this activity indicated the arrival of Ottoman reinforcements, Townshend expedited his own retirement, directing his force to move out on the evening of the 25th. This decision resulted directly from human limitations and informational uncertainty, two of Watts's categories of friction. A tired commander, concerned about the morale of his depleted force after several days of combat, misinterpreted vague intelligence reports of an enemy advance and accelerated his withdrawal. Townshend's decision also exemplifies Watts's third category of friction: the non-linearity of combat processes. Initiating a limited withdrawal on relatively short notice transformed a standoff between two exhausted and anxious armies into a retreat that placed additional physical and psychological demands on 6 Indian Division while reducing the information available to its commander regarding the whereabouts of his adversary.

The Retreat, 26 November to 3 December

Townshend did not foresee an extended retreat. His goal was simply to retire to a position where he could safely await reinforcements. Accompanied by ships carrying supplies and wounded personnel, 6 Indian Division could not venture away from the Tigris. But Townshend showed little concern for the vulnerability of his force. Notwithstanding the tenacity of the Ottoman defense at Ctesiphon, Townshend doubted that Nurettin would pursue him vigorously. Thus, on the evening of 25 November, his force halted at Lajj, where it spent the next day preparing defenses in anticipation of an extended stay. Townshend informed Nixon that he intended to remain at Lajj for a week, until available rations had been consumed. On the morning of 27 November, however, reconnaissance revealed the approach of a large force of more than 10,000 Ottoman troops. This news disabused Townshend of his assumption that 6 Indian Division would be able to reorganize in the vicinity of its enemy. He immediately issued orders for a further withdrawal to Aziziyah, the closest point downriver where there were sufficient rations to sustain his force while he awaited the arrival of reinforcements from Basra.[34]

The rapid retirement to Azizyah put additional pressure on 6 Indian Division and its commander. The force departed Lajj in a hurry, abandoning supplies in the process. After a march of more than twenty miles, it arrived at Aziziyah between 0400 and 1000 on 28 November. Tired and hungry after the forced march, British and Indian personnel began looting stockpiles of food and supplies in the town.[35] The lack of careful planning preceding the retirement had additional consequences, as Townshend discovered to his annoyance that the town held enough rations for only six days; he had anticipated twenty days' rations for his British personnel and seven days' rations for his Indian personnel.[36] Despite mounting fatigue and fraying discipline within his force, the 6 Indian Division commander recognized that he could not stay at Aziziyah for long. On the afternoon of the 29th, he received an aerial reconnaissance report indicating that Nurettin was still moving down the Tigris.

Townshend was not yet convinced, however, that he faced an urgent threat. Rather than ordering an immediate withdrawal, he directed his force to remain at Aziziyah until 0900 on 30 November, and then march to Umm at Tubul, less than eight miles downriver.[37] Moreover, when Nixon sent a message asking if he could spare troops to help protect IEFD headquarters from Ottoman and Arab forces downriver from Kut, Townshend dispatched an entire infantry brigade along with a cavalry regiment and artillery. By this point, Townshend intended to retire to Qala Shadi, approximately thirty miles farther downriver. There he planned to entrench positions to cover the concentration of reinforcements at Kut, twenty miles farther down the Tigris.[38] But the fact that he halted at Umm at Tubul on 30 November after only a three-hour march, with a weakened force of approximately 6,000 infantry, 1,250 cavalry, and 36 guns, indicates that Townshend still did not believe his force was in imminent danger, despite Nurettin's continued pursuit.[39] Townshend's deliberate conduct of the retreat in its initial stages is understandable. Given his concerns regarding the morale of his subordinates, particularly after the battle at Ctesiphon, he did not want to increase trepidation in the ranks by ordering a hasty withdrawal or unnecessarily conceding territory to the enemy. Nor did he wish to drive his force to the point of exhaustion. But Nurettin's pursuit eventually gained momentum. On the afternoon of 30 November, Ottoman forces reached Azizyah, where they discovered discarded supplies, documents, and other evidence of a hurried departure. While this discovery slowed Ottoman progress temporarily, it also emboldened Nurettin, who ordered the resumption of the advance after a halt of only two hours.[40]

Figure 3.7. British howitzer loading onto a raft, 1915. Courtesy of the National Army Museum.

By expediting his pursuit late in the day, the Ottoman commander was taking a significant risk. Aircraft had joined his force on 27 November, but they could not conduct reconnaissance after dark. For information regarding enemy whereabouts, Nurettin relied primarily on his cavalry, which he believed to be advancing in front of his force. As a result, when Nurettin and his staff spotted campfires around 1900 on 30 November, they assumed that they were approaching their own advance guard. Unbeknownst to the Ottoman commander, however, the cavalry had fallen behind the rest of the army. The Ottomans soon discovered that they had actually stumbled upon elements of 6 Indian Division. Nurettin directed his artillery to fire on the enemy personnel, who quickly extinguished their fires and lights in response. Further efforts to locate the British were met with sporadic small-arms fire, but in light of reports from local Arabs that Townshend's force had withdrawn from the vicinity, Nurettin assumed that he had encountered a British rearguard that had subsequently departed.[41] He ordered his force to halt until the next morning.[42]

In fact, the two armies spent the night camped only two miles apart. While Townshend was just as surprised as Nurettin by the unexpected encounter on the evening of the 30th, he was quicker to grasp the gravity of the situation. The sudden burst of enemy artillery fire, the sound of cart wheels moving in the darkness, and the subsequent appearance of enemy campfires convinced Townshend that the Ottoman force was nearby.[43] He recognized that his ships could not navigate the Tigris in the dark but also realized that once dawn broke around 0645, his army could not possibly escape enemy notice. Townshend, therefore, resolved to attack at dawn so his ships and land transport could escape.[44] By 0630 on 1 December, the three 6 Indian Division infantry brigades had formed a line facing the enemy, with Townshend's remaining cavalry on their right flank. At the same time, the land transport began withdrawing. The Ottomans had detected the movement of the British force in the dark, and Nurettin had ordered his 51 Division to advance with 45 Division in support. When the two armies became visible to one another as the sun rose, both were advancing. It was Townshend's artillery, however, that struck first, halting the advance of 51 Division and forcing 45 Division to retire. The barrage also had a devastating effect on the Ottoman command structure, killing or wounding a corps commander and several other senior officers.[45] In the ensuing chaos, some Ottoman soldiers retired toward Aziziyah.[46]

Townshend's subordinates commented on their commander's composure at Umm at Tubul. According to G. W. R. Bishop, a dispatch rider: "I was struck by his immaculate appearance and utter calm and detachment, although standing periodically in the gunfire, and with the Turks 1000 yards or so away."[47] But Townshend's calm demeanor belied his growing fears for the safety of his force. Having dispatched one of his brigades to assist Nixon two days previously, he was now engaged with an Ottoman force of unknown strength and disposition. In addition, after the initial shock of Townshend's artillery barrage, enemy resistance stiffened; the Ottomans destroyed or captured several British boats on the Tigris.[48] Therefore, after throwing Nurettin's army into temporary disarray, Townshend quickly moved to extricate his force from Umm at Tubul. By 0830, the retreat had resumed "under heavy enemy gunfire," with Ottoman artillery and cavalry badgering the retiring units for the rest of the morning.[49]

While Ottoman pressure lessened on the afternoon of 1 December, Townshend's narrow escape at Umm at Tubul had a disproportionate impact on his subsequent decisions, leading him to accelerate the pace of his retreat. Fatigue undoubtedly affected his judgment, as did uncertainty about the intentions of his adversary, who had surprised him the previous night. It was not only the pursuing enemy, but also the prospect of his own force's eroding discipline that impelled him forward. When asked for a short rest around dusk to allow soldiers to drink from the Tigris, the 6 Indian Division commander refused: "Once these men get down to the river bank, we shall not collect them for hours. They will lie by the water, drink, and fall asleep like logs. I do not know that the Turks are not a few miles behind."[50] Instead, Townshend continued the retreat into the night. He finally allowed his force to halt briefly at Qala Shadi, more than thirty-five miles from Umm at Tubul. The last 6 Indian Division units arrived at Qala Shadi well after midnight, and the retirement resumed at dawn on the 2nd. During the day, the force marched another eighteen miles to Shamran, where they ate for the first time in forty-eight hours and spent the night.

Just six miles west of Shamran, Kut-al-Amara was a tempting sanctuary for Townshend's beleaguered force. The town held enough rations to sustain Townshend's force for at least a month, as well as stockpiles of ammunition. The British had also begun preparing defensive positions around Kut. Moreover, its position at the junction of the Tigris and the Shatt-al-Hai theoretically allowed 6 Indian Division to prevent the Ottomans from moving farther down either river. Nonetheless, as historian Patrick Crowley has explained: "Kut was vulnerable, surrounded on three sides by water leaving little space for the defenders to manoeuvre, prone to flooding, and an easy target for artillery."[51] It was also relatively easy to trap the town's occupants—soldiers and civilians alike—by establishing positions along the base of the peninsula on which it was located. Since 29 November, Townshend had been in contact with the commander of the British garrison at Kut, Brigadier-General J. C. Rimington, who had explained the position's shortcomings. Rimington also maintained that he could evacuate all of the supplies inside the town within forty-eight hours. He recommended that 6 Indian Division withdraw six miles farther down the Tigris to Es Sinn, where Townshend had defeated Nurettin in late September. There, he maintained, the force would be less vulnerable to encirclement.[52]

Rimington's recommendation was feasible. After the engagement at Umm at Tubul, Nurettin had halted, losing track of Townshend's force for forty-eight hours. The Ottoman force arrived at Shamran on 4 December, two days after 6 Indian Division, but did not close off the base of the Kut peninsula until late on the 6th.[53] Townshend's force could likely have withdrawn to Es Sinn with a significant proportion of the ammunition and supplies stored in the town. But the possibility of continuing the retreat was not evident to its commander, who was increasingly doubtful about the reliability of his subordinates. By the time he reached Shamran, Townshend had decided to take refuge inside Kut. After informing Rimington of his decision on the afternoon of 2 December, Townshend sent a message to Nixon the next morning explaining the benefits of holding the town. The 6 Indian Division commander also explained that the force was "too exhausted to move a yard farther at the moment," much less evacuate supplies from Kut.[54] Townshend was particularly concerned about the Indian personnel under his command. As he recalled in his memoir: "Never have I seen anything like the exhaustion of the troops after we reached Kut. The great bulk of the Indian troops would not march at all, although I got the British to work on 4th December, just as the Turkish advanced guard came into sight!"[55]

Some of Townshend's subordinates disagreed with his assessment. One of his brigade commanders, Brigadier-General W. S. Delamain, maintained that both British and Indians under his command were ready to continue retreating after a single day's rest. R. V. Martin, a medical officer, contended that with the exception of Gurkhas, who "were no good marching," Indian personnel were "in very good shape" upon arriving in Kut.[56] Townshend's lack of familiarity with Indian soldiers undoubtedly influenced his assessment of their condition, as did his own fatigue. The fifty-four-year-old commander had been engaged in active operations since returning prematurely from his convalescence in India in August. After arriving at Umm at Tubul on 30 November, he had planned and executed an attack to extricate his force from contact with the enemy, and then retreated more than fifty miles with no more than a few hours' sleep. With Nurettin's whereabouts unknown, Kut appeared to be a refuge where the exhausted commander and his force could await reinforcements. Townshend's assessment would soon change. After recuperating for two days, he learned on 5 December that a relief force might not arrive for two months. Therefore, on 6 December, he proposed withdrawing from Kut. With the Ottomans now closing in, however, it is doubtful that Townshend's force could have escaped without abandoning significant quantities of supplies and suffering heavy casualties. Moreover, Nixon accepted Townshend's explanation of the strategic benefits of holding Kut and, therefore, ordered him to remain there.[57] By 7 December, the Ottomans had encircled the town, and the siege of Kut-al-Amara began.

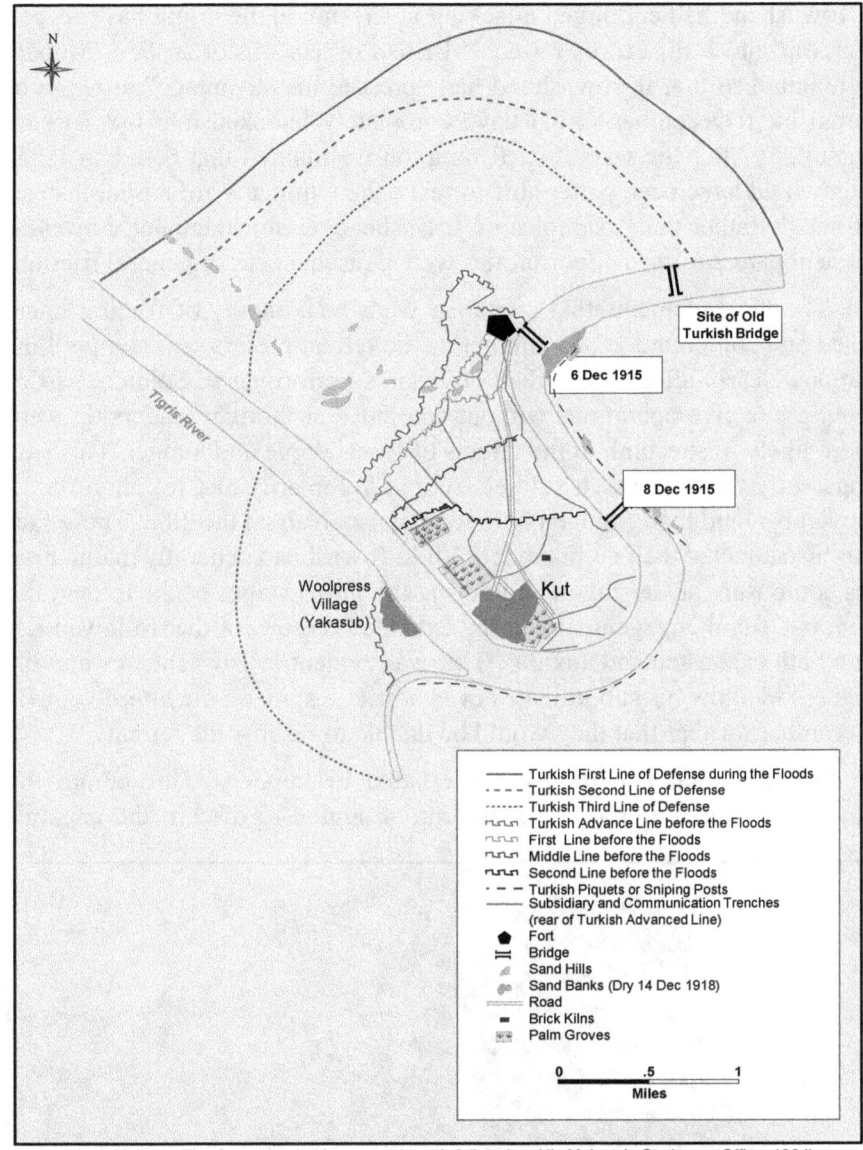

Source: F. J. Moberly, The Campaign in Mesopotamia, vol. 2 (London: His Majesty's Stationery Office, 1924).

Figure 3.8. Defense of Kut Al Amara. Recreated by Army University Press.

Conclusion

A variety of writers have criticized Charles Townshend's conduct of operations in November and December 1915. A staff officer involved in the Ottoman pursuit of 6 Indian Division, Muhammed Amin, suggested that if Townshend had continued attacking at Ctesiphon, he might have forced Nurettin into a disastrous retreat.[58] British official historian F. J. Moberly maintained that if Townshend had "pressed his advantage" at Umm at Tubul on 1 December, "he'd have completely knocked into the Turkish pursuit."[59] After the war, J. C. Rimington maintained that 6 Indian Division would have been better able to resist the Ottomans at Es Sinn instead of Kut.[60] Rather than examples of Townshend's poor judgment, however, these apparent missed opportunities were consequences of general friction.

The three elements that comprise Watts's taxonomy of friction interacted and compounded one another as the retreat progressed. Human limitations clearly affected 6 Indian Division's performance. Soldiers participating in active operations without comrades or familiar leadership were more likely to succumb to the effects of fear, fatigue and hunger. This was apparently the case when soldiers retired voluntarily at Ctesiphon on 22 November, and then engaged in looting at Aziziyah on the 28th. These factors also affected their commander. While Townshend generally maintained his composure at Ctesiphon and during the initial stages of the retreat, the Umm at Tubul engagement and the extended retirement that followed left him both exhausted and anxious. This was evident in Townshend's unwillingness to allow his subordinates even a brief respite on the afternoon of 1 December for fear that they would be unable to resume the retreat.

Informational uncertainty exacerbated his anxiety. Throughout the period under examination, Townshend struggled to discern the capabil-

Figure 3.9. Wireless station receiving last message from Kut, 1916. Courtesy of the National Army Museum.

ities and intentions of the Ottomans. The intelligence-gathering tools at his disposal provided only fragmentary information about his adversary's location, and even less about their plans. At Ctesiphon, he interpreted the Ottoman reoccupation of previously held positions as the arrival of reinforcements and accelerated his withdrawal as a result. During the retreat itself, Townshend remained largely unaware of the enemy's location until he was surprised by Nurettin's force at Umm at Tubul. Townshend also experienced increasing uncertainty about his own force as the retreat progressed. Skeptical of the motivation and morale of some of his Muslim subordinates from the outset of the offensive, Townshend became more apprehensive as he witnessed scenes of indiscipline at Ctesiphon and during the retreat. Significantly, this indiscipline never spread. Even during the siege that followed, only a small minority of Indian soldiers deserted or committed acts of insubordination. Townshend can be criticized for failing to distinguish between the Indians under his command, but he was not alone. While officers serving in Indian units were expected to possess specific linguistic skills and cultural knowledge, few if any senior commanders were familiar with the numerous languages and cultural traits of the diverse groups that made up the Indian Army. Like many British officers, Townshend relied on generalizations and stereotypes that did little to enhance his understanding of his subordinates. As a result, he grew increasingly uncertain about their morale as the retreat progressed.

Mounting fatigue and uncertainty led Townshend to take actions that had nonlinear effects. His decision to conduct a limited withdrawal from Ctesiphon conceded the initiative to his adversary, and subjected himself and his force to increasing fatigue and uncertainty as the withdrawal became an extended retreat. Similarly, at Umm at Tubul, human limitations and informational uncertainty led Townshend to take actions that had disproportionate consequences for his force. Although he succeeded in breaking contact with the Ottomans, the unexpected battle and persistent enemy pursuit afterward led Townshend to accelerate his retreat, leaving his force exhausted. Fatigued himself, and fearful of a morale collapse among his Indian subordinates, Townshend decided to seek refuge at Kut. This decision did not seal the fate of 6 Indian Division, but it certainly increased the likelihood of its eventual defeat.

In the past century, the advent of motorized transportation and computers, as well as electronic communications and surveillance capabilities, have significantly reduced many of the friction sources encountered by Townshend and his division. Armies today can move faster, and with greater awareness of their adversaries, while their commanders make decisions based on unprecedented amounts of data. But these new technologies have not eliminated the impact of human limitations and uncertainty on the conduct of war. In operations against adversaries with similar capabilities, commanders will have to evaluate larger quantities of information and more quickly. As the volume of information and the speed of operations increase, so will the likelihood of unanticipated events with disproportionate consequences. Moreover, Western armed forces often operate alongside allies and partners whose capabilities and morale, even if exemplary, are obscured by linguistic or cultural differences. They will thus encounter barriers similar to those that contributed to Charles Townshend's uncertainty about his subordinates in 1915. While it may appear in different forms, general friction will continue to bedevil Western armed forces in the twenty-first century.

In closing, it is worth recalling that the 6 Indian Division's prolonged retreat began after Townshend's failed attempt to defeat a larger Ottoman force holding defensive positions at Ctesiphon. Authors and military strategists like J. F. C. Fuller, Sir Basil Liddell Hart, and John Boyd have advocated using speed, deception, and ambiguity to disorient a stronger adversary and induce collapse. While this is possible, commanders must recognize the risks inherent in any attempt to impose chaos on the enemy. Any force employing such measures will experience its own uncertainty, errors, and unexpected outcomes while interacting with its opponent and the surrounding environment. Well-trained, cohesive forces may be better able to cope with unforeseen developments. Their ability to do so, however, will deteriorate over time due to cultural barriers, loss of experienced personnel, and the physical and psychological stress of prolonged engagements. Townshend's force suffered from low morale and a lack of cohesion from the operation's outset. These limitations and their consequences became more pronounced as the retreat progressed. Ultimately, 6 Indian Division and its commander succumbed to the chaos that they sought to create.

Figure 3.10. Townshend Surrender. Courtesy of Wikimedia Commons.

Notes

1. This chapter is based on research published in Nikolas Gardner, *The Siege of Kut-al-Amara: At War in Mesopotamia, 1915–1916* (Bloomington, IN: Indiana University Press, 2014), particularly chapter 3.

2. John R. Boyd, *A Discourse on Winning and Losing*, ed. Grant T. Hammond (Maxwell AFB, AL: Air University Press, 2018), 155.

3. Carl von Clausewitz, *On War*, ed. and trans. Michael Howard and Peter Paret (Princeton, NJ: Princeton University Press, 1976), 121.

4. David French, "The Dardanelles, Mecca, and Kut: Prestige as a Factor in British Eastern Strategy, 1914–1916," *War & Society* 5, no. 1 (May 1987): 45–61.

5. For examples, see A. J. Barker, *The Bastard War: The Mesopotamia Campaign of 1914–1918* (New York: Dial, 1967), 115; Russell Braddon, *The Siege* (London: Jonathan Cape, 1969), 105; Charles Townshend, *When God Made Hell: The British Invasion of Mesopotamia and the Creation of Iraq, 1914–1921* (London: Faber and Faber, 2010), 167.

6. Clausewitz, *On War*, 119–20.

7. Barry Watts, *Clausewitzian Friction and Future War*, McNair Paper 68 (Washington, DC: National Defense University, 2004), 76–77.

8. Justin Fantauzzo, "Townshend, Charles Vere Ferrers, Sir," in *1914–1918-online International Encyclopedia of the First World War*, ed. Ute Daniel et al. (Berlin: Freie Universität Berlin, 2018).

9. Erroll Sherston, *Townshend of Chitral and Kut* (London: Heinemann, 1928), 184–236.

10. A *sepoy* was an Indian infantry soldier serving under British or other European orders.

11. Patrick Crowley, *Kut 1916: Courage and Failure in Iraq* (Stroud, UK: Spellmount, 2009), 46.

12. David Omissi, *The Sepoy and the Raj: The Indian Army, 1860–1940* (London: Macmillan, 1994), 26–29.

13. Kaushik Roy, "The Construction of Regiments in the Indian Army: 1859–1913," *War in History* 8, no. 2 (April 2001): 127–48.

14. Jeffrey Greenhut, "Sahib and Sepoy: An Inquiry into the Relationship between British Officers and Native Soldiers of the British Indian Army," *Military Affairs* 48, no. 1 (January 1984): 16.

15. On the shortcomings of the logistical system in Mesopotamia, see Kaushik Roy, "From Defeat to Victory: Logistics of the Campaign in Mesopotamia, 1914–1918," *First World War Studies* 1, no. 1 (March 2010): 35–55.

16. Mark Harrison, "The Fight against Disease in the Mesopotamia Campaign," in *Facing Armageddon: The First World War Experienced*, ed. Peter Liddle and Hugh Cecil (London: Leo Cooper, 1996), 475–85.

17. "Sir Walter Lawrence to Lord Kitchener, 27 December 1915," Lawrence Papers, MSS Eur F143/65, India Office Records (IOR), British Library, London, hereafter cited as IOR.

18. Edwin Latter, "The Indian Army in Mesopotamia, 1914–1918, Part II," *Journal of the Society for Army Historical Research* 72, no. 291 (Autumn 1994): 168.

19. Charles V. F. Townshend, *My Campaign in Mesopotamia* (London: Butterworth, 1920), 230.

20. "Sir Walter Lawrence to Lord Kitchener, 15 June 1915," Lawrence Papers, MSS Eur F143/65, IOR.

21. Claude Markovits, "Indian Soldiers' Experiences in France during World War I: Seeing Europe from the Rear of the Front," in *The World in World Wars: Experiences, Perceptions, and Perspectives from Africa and Asia*, ed. Heike Liebau et al. (Leiden, NL: Brill, 2010), 34.

22. Latter, "The Indian Army in Mesopotamia," 167.

23. "Telegram from Viceroy, dated 11 March 1915" and "Telegram from Viceroy, dated 3 March 1915," Edmund Barrow Papers, MSS Eur E420/10, IOR.

24. "Townshend to Curzon, 7 November 1915," Curzon Papers, MSS Eur F112/163, IOR.

25. Crowley, *Kut 1916*, 33.

26. Edward J. Erickson, *Ottoman Army Effectiveness in World War I: A Comparative Study* (Abingdon, UK: Routledge, 2007), 69–74.

27. Mesut Uyar, *The Ottoman Army and the First World War* (London: Routledge, 2021), 141; and Edward Erickson, *Gallipoli and the Middle East: From the Dardanelles to Mesopotamia*, The History of World War I (London: Amber, 2011), 132–33.

28. Townshend, *My Campaign in Mesopotamia*, 176.

29. Townshend., 179.

30. Staff Bimbashi Muhammed Amin, "Battle of Ctesiphon (Suliman Pak) 1915 Nov.–Dec.," 69, CAB 44/33, The National Archives (TNA), London, hereafter cited as TNA.

31. Amin, 92–93.

32. B .T. Reynolds, "The Battle of Ctesiphon and the Retreat to Kut, Part 2," *Military Engineer* 30, no. 170 (March–April 1938), 127.

33. Amin, "Battle of Ctesiphon," 111.

34. F. J. Moberly, *The Campaign in Mesopotamia*, vol. 2 (London: His Majesty's Stationery Office, 1924), 110–11.

35. "Chalmers Diary, 28 November 1915," T.A. Chalmers Papers, Imperial War Museum, London.

36. Townshend, *My Campaign in Mesopotamia*, 190.

37. Townshend, 189–90.

38. Moberly, *The Campaign in Mesopotamia*, 112–13; and "From Nixon, 29 November 1915," Curzon Papers, MSS Eur F112/163, IOR.

39. W. D. A. Bird, *A Chapter of Misfortunes: The Battles of Ctesiphon and of the Dujailah in Mesopotamia, with a Summary of the Events that Preceded Them* (London: Forster Groom, 1923), 91.

40. Uyar, *The Ottoman Army and the First World War*, 144; and Amin, "Battle of Ctesiphon," 153–54.

41. Uyar, 156–65.
42. Uyar, 156–65.
43. Townshend, *My Campaign in Mesopotamia*, 192.
44. Moberly, *The Campaign in Mesopotamia*, 118.
45. Uyar, *The Ottoman Army and the First World War*, 144.
46. Amin, "Battle of Ctesiphon", 180–83.
47. "G. W. R. Bishop to A. J. Barker, 1 June 1965," Charles Townshend Papers, Liddell Hart Centre for Military Archives (LHCMA), King's College, London.
48. Uyar, *The Ottoman Army and the First World War*, 144.
49. Amin, "Battle of Ctesiphon," 168 and 174; and Moberly, *The Campaign in Mesopotamia*, 121.
50. Townshend, *My Campaign in Mesopotamia*, 196–97.
51. Crowley, *Kut 1916*, 42.
52. "Narrative from Memory Written by Lt. Col. S. De V. Julis of Events at the End of November 1915 at Kut in Mesopotamia," CAB 45/91, TNA; and J. C. Rimington, "Kut-al-Amarah," *Army Quarterly* 6, no. 1 (April 1923): 21–26.
53. F. E. G. Talbot, "The Siege of Kut al Amarah from the Turkish Point of View," 2, CAB 44/34, TNA; and Erickson, *Gallipoli and the Middle East*, 136.
54. Townshend, *My Campaign in Mesopotamia*, 198 and 212.
55. Townshend, 198 and 212.
56. Moberly, *The Campaign in Mesopotamia*, 160; R.V. Martin to H. H. Rich, 13 June 1971, General H. H. Rich Papers, Liddle Collection, University of Leeds, Leeds UK.
57. Moberly, 135–38.
58. Amin, "Battle of Ctesiphon," 105.
59. "F. J. Moberly to W. D. Bird, 29 August 1921," CAB 45/90, TNA.
60. Rimington, "Kut-al-Amarah," 26.

Chapter 4
Shattered: The XVth Brigade against Franco's 1938 Aragon Offensive

Tyler D. Wentzell

The Spanish Civil War erupted in July 1936, the result of many layers of conflict within the Second Spanish Republic. Led and widely supported by the Spanish Army, this Nationalist coup initially achieved only modest results. After the German Luftwaffe intervened later that summer, however, the Nationalists moved their Army of Africa from Morocco to Spain and made quick advances. The Republic retained Madrid and Valencia, and reasserted itself in Barcelona during the summer of 1937, but achieved few offensive military victories. Spanish Republican troops successfully seized the city of Teruel in Aragon in late 1937 in a bid to spoil a Nationalist offensive against Madrid; while this initially seemed to signal a change in the trajectory of the war, the Nationalists retook Teruel in February. By late winter 1938, the Spanish Republic was diplomatically and economically isolated, receiving only limited support from the Soviet Union and Mexico, and its armed forces were depleted, exhausted, and precariously positioned.[1] While they retained most of southeastern Spain, the Nationalists held a salient in the Aragon, pointing toward the Mediterranean.

In the spring of 1938, Generalissimo Francisco Franco launched the Aragon Offensive, a bold attack driving a wedge between the Madrid-Valencia corridor and the Spanish Republican industrial base in Catalonia. It would signal to Franco's German and Italian supporters that his victory was inevitable, and they would further augment his already significant military aid—including modern German and Italian tanks and artillery, Ju-87 Stuka dive bombers and other modern aircraft, as well as trainers, advisors, staff officers, and fighting army and air force units.[2] Franco's Nationalists attacked with marked local superiority, a decided advantage in tanks, trucks, aircraft, and materiel, and the element of surprise. The XVth International Brigade, composed largely of English-speaking foreign volunteers, unknowingly stood in the path of General Fidel Dávila Arrondo's five Nationalist army corps, the Italian *Corpo Truppe Volontarie* (CTV), and German Condor Legion land and air forces.[3] Although Franco insisted that the German tanks not be massed and instead be distributed to support the attacking infantry, the attack was otherwise very similar to the *blitzkrieg* that soon overtook Europe.[4]

This chapter examines the Nationalist Aragon Offensive as experienced by the XVth International Brigade. After the necessary background, it looks at the battle in two distinct phases: first, from the opening of the Nationalist offensive on 9 March through the brigade's 17 March defense of Caspe, and second, the brigade's engagements around Gandesa after the Nationalist offensive resumed on 30 March. The Nationalists held almost every conceivable advantage in their attack, and employed maneuver in ways not yet experienced by the defenders. The scale and speed of the attack came as a shock to the XVth Brigade, and at no point was it able to bring its whole force to bear; its constituent battalions mostly fought separate engagements. Lacking mutual support from units with which they had communications, attacked from the air, and perpetually threatened by encirclement, cohesion within the brigade predictably broke down. The XVth Brigade lost most of its combat power not to death or injury at the hands of the Nationalists, but to a chaotic mix of fear and exhaustion, breakdowns in communication, and the physical separation of soldiers and units. The chaos of the experience was such that many survivors referred to the period simply as "the retreats."

Background

Raised in February 1937, the XVth Brigade was the fifth of the Spanish Republic's International Brigades.[5] It was a *brigada mixta,* a "mixed brigade," meant to contain all of the combat, combat support, and logistics elements needed to conduct independent operations. In reality, the brigade was dependent on the corps-level *Regimiento de Tren* for motorized troop transport and had almost no integral combat support elements.[6] Apart from a few ambulances and trucks for transporting items like field kitchens, it possessed almost no vehicles of its own. Troops moved long distances by rail or *Regimiento de Tren* trucks, and then marched. The brigade's integral combat support was limited to a scout platoon, a brigade machine gun company, a company of engineers, and an anti-tank gun battery.

The XVth Brigade was principally a light infantry organization with approximately 3,500 soldiers organized into four battalions: the British Battalion, the Abraham Lincoln Battalion, the Mackenzie-Papineau Battalion (the Mac-Paps), and the Spanish Battalion.[7] These battalions rarely fielded their authorized strength of 600, and had to overcome language barriers. The foreign volunteers largely spoke English, but there were large numbers of volunteers whose first language was Finnish, Ukrainian, or various Slavic languages, and each of the nominally English battalions had a Spanish company and Spanish soldiers scattered throughout their organization. As the war ground on, the proportion of Spanish soldiers to foreign volunteers increased; as early as August 1937, Britons made up less than half of the soldiers in the British Battalion.[8] Foreign soldiers were encouraged to learn Spanish and vice versa—and many did—but the different languages created an additional challenge for the organization.

While the first volunteers received had almost no training at all, by the winter of 1937–38, most had benefited from some kind of formal training.[9] Training deficiencies were most notable among commanders and staff officers. While some were graduates of an Officer Training School, many had been thrust into leadership positions upon arriving in Spain based on their often-limited previous military experience.

The brigade commander, Yugoslav Vladimir Copic, for instance, had some experience in the Austro-Hungarian army during the First World War but spent most of the conflict in Russian prisoner-of-war camps. He served as a brigade commissar at Jarama, then as the brigade commander until the summer of 1938.[10] The brigade chief of staff, the energetic and respected American Robert Merriman, had been part of the Reserve Officers' Training Corps in California, where he received some training in platoon-level operations. He became a battalion commander shortly after arriving in Spain. Wounded in his first battle, Merriman worked in the International Brigade training system as a commander and instructor while he convalesced, and then served as brigade chief of staff until he disappeared in April 1938.[11] Given the scale of their responsibilities, this was much less training and experience than one might expect. Merriman and Copic had knowledge of the Russian language; both had spent time in Moscow, which facilitated their interactions with the brigade's two Russian military advisers.[12]

The situation was much the same at the battalion level, exacerbated by the quick turnover in leadership. The British and Lincoln battalions retained commanders only briefly. The commanders departed because of promotion, illness, or injury, and sometimes due to intervention by their home Communist parties.[13] Edward Cecil-Smith, commander of the Mac-Paps from November 1937 until the end of the war, was the brigade's longest-serving battalion commander. Prior to this appointment, he was a regimental sergeant major in the Canadian militia and had received some training in company command in Spain, but none in battalion command. Cecil-Smith felt very unprepared for the challenges of battalion command.[14]

Much of the brigade had significant combat experience by the spring of 1938. Some soldiers had fought for more than a year, first in the defense of Madrid and then the failed Brunete Offensive during the summer of 1937. Most of the brigade had been especially active in a series of offensive actions in the Aragon region during the summer and fall of 1937; Cecil-Smith and the Mac-Paps joined the brigade for the battalion's first battle in October 1937. In January and February 1938, the XVth Brigade doggedly retained Teruel against determined Nationalist attacks and conducted successful raids against hill forts around Segura de los Baños. Though significant, these feats of arms were also limited in terms of preparing the soldiers for the challenges that lie ahead. The brigade had only twice maneuvered as a single entity—at Brunete and Fuentes de Ebro in October 1937—and there were few veterans of both actions remaining. The brigade had not yet been forced to maneuver in retrograde, nor had they defended against tanks or fast-moving truck-mounted infantry. Notwithstanding the courage shown by so many members of the XVth Brigade, they were ill-prepared to face the Nationalist's Aragon Offensive.

Part 1: Belchite to Caspe

By March 1938, the Nationalists had seized the north and west of Spain, while the Republicans retained Madrid and the routes to Valencia, much of the Mediterranean coast, and industrial Catalonia. While the Soviet Union had initially been a helpful ally to Republican Spain, Japan's rising threat in the Far East increasingly diverted Soviet resources that might have otherwise been used in Spain.[15] Franco's repeated efforts to seize Madrid had failed, and by 1938 he needed a significant victory to convince his patrons to send further aid. After the resource-intensive effort of retaking the city of Teruel from Republican forces (December 1937 to February 1938), the Nationalists were ready for a deep offensive through the Aragon region by early April. On 9 March, 150,000 Nationalist soldiers, supported by 700 artillery pieces, 200 tanks, and 1,000 aircraft, cut through the Republican lines.

The XVth Brigade laid in the path of the Nationalist attack centered on the Fuentetodos Road. By the time it reached the XVth Brigade, the Nationalist attack advanced along four axes. In the north, two Nationalist divisions (the 5th Navarre and the 150th Mixed) would converge on Belchite, with the 5th Navarre Division proceeding to the rail hub at Caspe. Meanwhile, a smaller force would advance between Fuentetodos and Azuara, on to Hijar and Alcaniz. Lastly, the tank and truck-heavy Italian CTV would move cross country in a pincer to the south to link up with the forces in Alcaniz.[16] The XVth Brigade had never faced an offensive of this size, speed, or complexity. They were consistently surprised by the Nationalists' rate of advance and ability to harry their flanks.

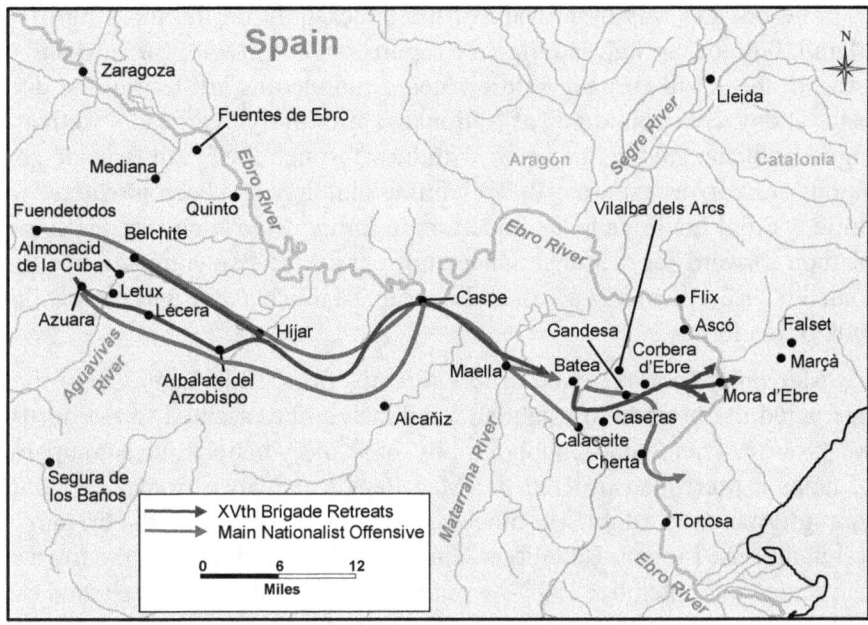

Figure 4.1. Nationalist axes of advance and XVth Brigade defensive positions, March 1938. Created by the author and Army University Press.

As the Nationalists prepared for the offensive, the XVth Brigade rested in reserve positions twenty kilometers (12.5 miles) behind the front lines. Although the brigade was nearly up to full-strength—having taken on 800 replacements following Teruel and Segura de los Baños—key leaders went on leave, including the brigade commander, Copic; brigade commissar, American David Doran; and brigade chief of operations, Briton Malcolm Dunbar.[17] The XVth Brigade's report states that Red Army adviser Nicolay Monselinzef (known as Maxim) was appointed as brigade commander from 9–17 March, but it is also clear from other records that brigade chief of staff Merriman exercised many command functions.[18] Both the Lincoln Battalion's commander and commissar went on leave, as well, leaving David Reiss in command. Reiss had previously served as a company commander, but this was his first time commanding a battalion.[19]

Merriman learned on 6 March that a Nationalist offensive was expected, but he had no details as to the attack's strength, location, or objectives.[20] Leadership did not cancel leave, fighting positions were not prepared, and no one but the brigade scouts conducted reconnaissance of routes, forward positions, or retrograde positions. Historian Cecil D. Eby wrote: "They did nothing but lounge under olive branches."[21] The XVth Brigade's leadership clearly did not anticipate the scale of the attack to come.

59

The brigade was first aware of the attack only on the morning of 9 March, but not through intelligence reports or liaison with forward units. Instead, the XVth Brigade soldiers heard thunderous artillery in the distance and watched hundreds of Nationalist aircraft fly overhead.[22] Retreating Republican soldiers began to withdraw through the XVth Brigade positions at Letux as early as 1000, claiming that they had been instructed to retire.[23] From his brigade headquarters in Letux, Merriman sent his scout platoon forward for reconnaissance and sent a Mac-Pap company two kilometers (1.2 miles) northwest of Letux to establish a guard to protect the bulk of his forces.[24]

Merriman soon received orders directly from 12th Army Corps that instructed the brigade to establish a defensive line oriented to the northwest toward Fuentetodos, supported by an artillery battery and a company of tanks.[25] Merriman ordered the Mac-Paps to advance from Letux and through Azuara to establish a blocking position, establishing the brigade's left flank. The Lincoln Battalion—already billeted in Belchite, the town it had seized in September 1937—would advance west immediately and establish a position to the south of the Fuentetodos road. The British Battalion, in Lecera, would establish the unit's right flank north of the Lincolns. The Spanish Battalion (sent at first to Azuara with the Mac-Paps, and then recalled) would establish the center of the line along with the brigade machine gun company northwest of Almonacid de la Cuba.[26] Unfortunately, Merriman's message to the Lincolns sent by runner at 2200 did not reach Reiss until Merriman himself arrived in Belchite at about 0200 the next day. The runner must have gotten lost. The Lincolns departed in an administrative fashion—ranks of four on the road—as they did not expect to encounter the Nationalists before reaching their positions. They left just as the British Battalion arrived at about 0300.[27]

The brigade was unable to form an integrated defensive position west of Belchite. On the left, the Spanish Battalion and the XVth Brigade Machine Gun Company—finding their assigned positions already occupied by the Nationalists—defended from the abandoned village of Almonacid de la Cuba. Lacking communications with the Lincoln Battalion to their right, or brigade headquarters, they withdrew under heavy attack. In the center, the Lincoln Battalion came under Nationalist machine gun fire shortly after dawn and scrambled to create a defensive position in the hills near an abandoned hermitage.[28] Soon, they were under heavy artillery fire and air attack. Reiss and nine others in the battalion command post were killed by an artillery strike.[29] On the right, the British Battalion fought a separate action from the Lincolns. At about 1400, British Battalion commander Sam Wild intervened when he saw the Lincolns withdrawing from their positions; he told the troops to stand fast, only to learn that "Comrade Maxim" had ordered a withdrawal. Wild's battalion had received no such order. The British Battalion withdrew into the town at 1600 and then withdrew again later that day as the Nationalists moved to encircle them.[30]

By the end of the day, the Lincoln and British battalions took heavy casualties; the Spanish Battalion, machine gun company, and engineer company disintegrated entirely; and the British anti-tank battery lost all its guns.[31] The XVth Brigade had lost much of its infantry and all of its supporting arms during the first day of the offensive, largely because they did not know the Nationalists' location or rate of advance. Without this information from troops in contact or reconnaissance elements, the XVth Brigade advanced blindly toward its main defensive area under the incorrect assumption that they had the time to do so. In fact, they were advancing to contact in the dark. The brigade would likely have been better served by a more deliberative advance, especially outside Belchite once the delay in the Lincolns' departure was known. Had the British and Lincoln battalions, along with supporting anti-tank guns, advanced west of Belchite under the command of the brigade headquarters, they likely would not have advanced as far, but they would have had considerably greater options upon making contact and might have retained greater cohesion in their withdrawal.

Farther to the south, Cecil-Smith and the Mac-Paps held their positions northwest of Azuara for most of 10 March despite artillery and air attack, and having no contact with flanking units or communications with brigade headquarters.[32] After dark, with Nationalist forces firing on the Mac-Paps from the flanks and behind, Cecil-Smith withdrew the battalion into the town of Azuara and emplaced machine guns in the cliffs above. Although Cecil-Smith did not have any news from brigade, a runner found the division commander and relayed a message through the civilian telephone lines. Cecil-Smith was to receive orders from division in the rear at 0400 the next morning. He returned to the Mac-Paps at dawn on 11 March with orders to retire to Lecera.[33] Although several machine gunners were unable to withdraw from their positions in the cliffs, the battalion otherwise withdrew in good order while under contact.[34] The soldiers linked up with the rest of the brigade outside Lecera at 1600 but were not able to rest because Lecera was already under attack. As the largest remaining battalion, still with between 200 and 300 soldiers, the Mac-Paps provided the rear guard for the brigade's march east.[35]

Orders were issued and quickly countermanded; Cecil-Smith recorded that he received three conflicting sets of orders within fifteen minutes at Lecera, and ultimately acted on the last set of orders—adopting a defensive position south of the town. There, he provided a reserve to a Mexican officer who was attempting to retake the town, before "Comrade Nicholai" (also known as Maxim) gave him orders for the march east.[36] Conflicting orders were presumably the product of the dynamic situation, but some likely resulted from a lack of unity of command. The XVth Brigade report states that Maxim was formally in command, oral accounts mostly describe Merriman's leadership role in the battle, and contemporaneous accounts written by Sam Wild and Cecil-Smith indicate that they received and accepted orders issued by Merriman and either of the brigade's two Red Army advisers.[37] Similarly, the Mexican staff officer referenced by Cecil-Smith was likely not Mexican at all; the descriptor was often applied to obscure the origin of Russian equipment and advisers. Though we can only speculate as to how well Merriman worked with the Red Army advisers—his diary for this period has not been found—this presumably collaborative command arrangement surely created space for further confusion and chaos.[38]

The XVth Brigade was to fall back sixty kilometers (thirty-seven miles) from Lecera to Alcaniz. Fatigue, panic, and confusion were beginning to take a toll. The XVth Brigade recorded that 12 March was "the day when the tragic part of the retreat had begun."[39] Units mixed together and commanders lost control of their formations. Soldiers dispersed when attacked from the air or by tanks or cavalry on their flanks. Over time, they were disinclined to come back together. Cecil-Smith recorded: "A panic developed on the highway," with different units mixed together and widespread confusion.[40] Commissar Sandor Voros described the state of the XVth Brigade:

> The Brigade as a unified fighting force no longer exists. There is no chain of command, no liaison, no battalions, no companies, only isolated groups of men putting up last-ditch resistance, holding until surrounded, retreating to other posts, holding with diminished numbers, dispersed, falling back in isolated groups to rally again. The planes attack constantly; the greatest damage they do is to morale. Our poorly trained men panic at the appearance of the Fascist planes, they bolt and run leaving their equipment behind.[41]

This state of affairs was worsened when the brigade was ordered to pivot from Alcaniz (already threatened by the Italian CTV) to mount a defense of Caspe. The message was not received by everyone in the brigade; many continued toward Alcaniz.[42]

By 13 March, David Doran, the brigade commissar returned from leave in Valencia and took command of the XVth Brigade's defense at Caspe. At that point, Merriman was missing. Doran assembled a force of 700 or so soldiers to repel the 5th Navarre Division approaching from the west.[43] Sam Wild led the British Battalion in blocking the rail line through the hills and into the town, the route by which the Nationalists tried to infiltrate on 15 March. A mixed force led by Finnish-Canadian volunteer Niilo Makela fought to hold Reservoir Hill, the terrain feature dominating the routes into the town.[44] Makela's force withdrew around dusk; a Nationalist tank shell wounded him as they pulled off the position and he later died of his wounds.[45]

Cecil-Smith arrived in Caspe at roughly the same time as Makela's force withdrew. The Mac-Pap commander had been among those who had not received word of the direction change. He had continued to Alcaniz and ran into a CTV roadblock. Fleeing cross-country to Maella, he found pockets of isolated and exhausted soldiers who had no practical means of quickly advancing twenty kilometers (12.5 miles) forward to Caspe. Cecil-Smith was only able to make it forward by hitchhiking. The XVth Brigade had lost a considerable portion of its force to the breakdown in communications. Many soldiers were killed or wounded by the CTV, and many more were simply in the wrong place to assist in the defense of Caspe.

Doran immediately gave Cecil-Smith the task of retaking Reservoir Hill.[46] Attacking with 100 soldiers in the early hours of 16 March, they successfully seized the hill, along with 30 prisoners of war, three Fiat heavy machine guns, 50 to 60 rifles, and 10 mules. The brigade report called the attack "something worthy of glory."[47] By dawn, however, Cecil-Smith's force was low on ammunition, and the Nationalists who infiltrated the town were firing on his force from behind. Cecil-Smith's troops withdrew—he confessed: "I had lost control of the men"—and the door to Caspe was open.[48] The Nationalists took Caspe on 17 March.[49]

Part 2: Caspe to the Ebro River

The Nationalists achieved their immediate objectives, smashing the Republican frontlines and pushing their mobile forces forward rapidly along multiple axes. The offensive surpassed Franco's expectations; on 15 March, he issued orders to drive on to the Mediterranean.[50] Republican units rushed from the south were able to check the Nationalist advance so that units like the XVth Brigade could withdraw and reorganize. The brigade converged on the town of Batea, forty kilometers (twenty-five miles) southeast of Caspe, where they had a welcome respite. They took stock of their losses, evacuated the wounded, took on reinforcements, and conducted both military and political training in preparation for the next phase of the operations.[51] Copic returned to take command of the brigade, and the Russian advisers apparently departed or at least began playing a diminished role.[52]

In the first eight days of the retreats, the Nationalists inflicted heavy casualties on the XVth Brigade. The Lincoln Battalion began the fight with 230 soldiers; more than half were killed, injured, or captured.[53] The Mac-Paps began with 500 soldiers and ended with 250, but only half were still armed.[54] The British Battalion only mustered twenty soldiers.[55] Replacements arrived from leave, hospitals, and training facilities. Some were veterans, either with earlier experience in battle or valuable time in the training system, but many were largely untrained Spanish conscripts. The influx of untrained troops required that even the most junior among the foreign soldiers were propelled into leadership positions.[56] Sandor Voros recalled, "We're an International Brigade in name only by now."[57] The reinforcements brought the brigade up to an overall strength of 2,329.[58]

On the evening of 30–31 March, just after receiving a welcome influx of Russian and Czechoslovakian weapons, the brigade received orders from both division and corps.[59] The 35th Division ordered the Lincolns to advance 9.5 kilometers (six miles) northwest of Gandesa and support the XIth Brigade's left flank along the road to Caspe. A few hours later, the 12th Army Corps ordered the British Battalion to advance northwest of Calaceite to reinforce General Enrique Lister's determined defense of Alcaniz. Without guides from Lister's forward units, George Fletcher, now the British Battalion commander, advanced along the main road carefully with scouts and a vanguard company. At about dawn, the vanguard walked past what they thought were Republican tanks. Battalion Commissar Wally Tapsell approached one, thinking it was part of Lister's force, only to be killed by its Italian crew. The Italian CTV inflicted terrible casualties on the British Battalion in the ensuing mêlée; tanks even ran over wounded soldiers, and the battalion sustained 350 casualties.[60] The British action at Calaceite was much like the Lincolns' advance from Belchite; they did not have the information they needed from troops in contact or reconnaissance elements. The British Battalion thought they were advancing to reinforce an existing friendly line and, despite taking precautions in their advance, still found themselves in a meeting engagement against an armored force.

Meanwhile, the Lincolns reached their positions in good order and defended against the 1st Navarre Division on 31 March and 1 April, unaware that the Navarese were advancing unimpeded along the highway east toward Vilalba dels Arcs and south toward Gandesa, where they would link up with the Italian CTV. With the destruction of the British Battalion in the south, the Lincolns were unwittingly inside a pincer closing in both directions.[61]

In the early hours of 1 April, Copic received orders from Corps to secure eleven different hills northeast of Caseras, presumably an attempt to block the CTV as it made good time from the west along the Alcaniz road but also cross-country and along parallel secondary roads.[62] Copic sent the Mac-Paps (less a company held in reserve) and the Spanish Battalion to secure these objectives. At least two of the hills were already in Nationalist hands by the time the battalions arrived. The Nationalists captured company and battalion leaders during their reconnaissance efforts, and the mobile Italians consistently threatened the flanks of any positions the two battalions attempted to hold. By 1100 on 1 April, soldiers from the Mac-Paps and Spanish Battalion began to withdraw through the brigade command post outside Gandesa.[63]

With the brigade's left and center collapsed, both Copic and Merriman conducted separate reconnaissance of the right flank, examining the road to the Lincolns position and the parallel route from Gandesa to Vilalba dels Arcs. Upon discovering that the Lincoln Battalion was being outflanked, Copic departed for Mora d'Ebre on the far bank of the Ebro River, claiming he had departed to acquire reinforcements from division.[64] He did not return. Merriman went forward to inform the Lincoln Battalion of the closing trap and lead them out of it.[65]

The Lincolns hastily departed their positions, moving cross country toward Mora d'Ebre, where they could cross the river to safety.[66] They left so quickly that orders from twenty-two-year-old Battalion Commander Milton Wolff did not reach the company on the left flank. The Lincoln Battalion left without them.[67] The remaining Lincolns managed to avoid contact with the enemy, though the force became separated and disorganized in the dark.[68] By the morning of 2 April, 200 Lincolns reached Gandesa—but not in time to escape the encirclement. The CTV had advanced from the west and encircled the town. The 1st Navarre Division, having easily taken and passed through Vilalba dels Arcs, now attacked Gandesa from the north. Merriman led an attack with the intention of breaking out, but the bulk of this force was killed during the attack or captured and then executed by the Nationalists.[69] Wolff waited until after dark and led a group of thirty as far as the Gandesa-Corbera d'Ebre Road. A few made it to the river and on to safety of the far bank.[70]

The vast majority of the XVth Brigade had been caught in the pincer between the 1st Navarre and the CTV. Brigade Chief of Operations Malcolm Dunbar, himself wounded at Calaceite and now returned to the front from medical treatment, rallied everyone he could find two kilometers (1.2 miles) west of Gandesa on 1 April. He sent a patrol to make contact with the Lincoln Battalion, but the patrol evidently arrived after Merriman.[71] Dunbar withdrew his force from Gandesa on 2 April, mustering his force at another blocking position south of the town toward Cherta. They put up a laudable defense against tanks, infantry, and cavalry, only withdrawing at dusk. Dunbar's stand was the XVth Brigade's last organized resistance.[72]

The XVth Brigade was now well and truly shattered. Parts of the brigade reached the Mora d'Ebre crossing before its demolition on 3 April and joined the chaotic scene of fleeing civilian families and soldiers filing across the only bridge in the area.[73] Most did not. Those trapped on the far bank scavenged for food and hid from the Nationalists as they searched for sites to ford the fast-flowing river, 200 meters wide in places. Some commandeered boats while others swam. Many more were captured by the Nationalists.[74] On 5 April, the brigade mustered only 160 of all ranks on the far side of the Ebro. The next day, after more soldiers had crossed the river on their own and been collected, the XVth Brigade numbered 798. The Nationalists had killed, wounded, or captured 1,531 members of the brigade in just seven days.[75]

Analysis and Conclusion

The Nationalist offensive achieved its objectives, pushing the Republican Army (including the XVth Brigade) east of the Ebro River and securing a pathway from their territory in the north all the way to the Mediterranean by 15 April. The Republic was divided; Nationalist-held territory now separated Madrid-Valencia in the west from Catalonia and the French border in the east. The Republican Army suffered tremendous casualties and, despite the initial success of its July offensive across the Ebro River, would never regain the initiative. The Spanish Republic demobilized the foreign volunteers in the International Brigades in September 1938 in a bid to secure better terms in their negotiations with the Nationalists. Some of the foreigners languished in Franco's prisoner-of-war camps for years, but most foreign survivors of the Aragon Offensive returned to their home countries by February 1939. The Spanish Republicans fought until the final defeat on 1 April 1939.

The outcome of the Aragon Offensive was likely inescapable given the Nationalists' clear local overmatch in numbers, modern weapons, and logistics. Policies of neutrality left the Spanish Republic on a starvation diet of necessary materiel, while Germany and Italy provided the Nationalists with plentiful supplies. At the tactical level, it is a mostly useless exercise to imagine how the XVth Brigade would have fared if they had more anti-tank guns or if the Nationalists had fewer modern aircraft. However, there may be some utility in considering how the XVth Brigade might have better preserved its forces and retained its cohesion in the face of almost-impossible odds. Three related lessons seem especially transferable to other situations: the interdependence of concentration of force, timely communications, and maintenance of morale.

First, accepting the dynamic nature of the situation, the XVth Brigade too often faced the Nationalists as separate battalions, not as a coordinated and mutually supporting brigade. In large part, they consistently underestimated the Nationalist rate of advance. Security was sacrificed for speed in the Republican race to reinforce or reestablish defensive lines. Consequently, despite efforts during the brigade's opening moves at Belchite and Gandesa, at no point did two full and mutually supporting battalions enter combat together. Each fought a separate fight and paid dearly for it.

Second, the brigade did not have sufficient communications for maintaining command and control in a dynamic situation. This is related to the first point: concentration of force was difficult without adequate communications. Lacking reliable information about the Nationalist location from forward and flanking units, as well as its higher headquarters, the XVth Brigade headquarters made ill-informed choices. Certainly, language barriers within the brigade caused difficulties, as did the brigade's dependence on runners and landlines. However, the issue was not merely linguistics or technology. Communications within the brigade appear to have been an afterthought. During the initial battle in and around Belchite, for instance, the brigade had no plan for communicating with the Spanish Battalion or the Mac-Paps. The Spanish Battalion did not establish communications, and the Mac-Paps achieved only moderate success by sending runners on reconnaissance missions and cutting into the civilian telephone system.[76] During the first phase of the battle, these shortcomings were likely exacerbated by the unclear command roles played by Merriman and the Red Army "advisers." Likely there were moments of contradiction and confusion. From 30 March to 1 April, the brigade's battalions departed Gandesa on separate axes without adequate plans for communicating across the brigade. Additionally, there were not enough trained signallers or soldiers dedicated to serving as runners.[77] Lacking a robust plan with contingencies at the outset, the situation descended into chaos once combat began. Despite their extraordinary efforts, the International Brigade's soldiers and signallers could not overcome the lack of planning.

Third, while leaders at the battalion and brigade levels struggled to gather information and coordinate across their organizations, junior leaders proved unable to maintain or reestablish cohesion at the squad and platoon levels. Individual soldiers routinely found themselves on their own, rather than fighting as part of an isolated squad or platoon.[78] Also noteworthy was the tendency to discard weapons. Canadian machine gunner Jim Higgins recalled that after days of fighting without sleep, having run out of food and water, and not knowing where any other soldier in his brigade was: "I dismantled my light machine gun and threw away parts as I moved, to prevent the enemy finding it in one piece. I could carry it no more. At some point, I got rid of my pistol."[79] He hid the two hand grenades he still had, understanding that if he was captured "with weapons, you were shot on the spot."[80] Higgins was not unique in this action or understanding, as shown by the fact that half of the Mac-Paps arrived in Batea unarmed.[81] Because the XVth Brigade soldiers understood that Nationalists murdered and mistreated their prisoners of war, many left accounts of discarding weapons, equipment, identifying insignia, and membership cards in efforts to shed weight to move faster and also disguise their identity.[82] Individual fatigue, fear of mistreatment if captured, and breakdowns in team cohesion (exacerbated by poor communications and an inability to concentrate forces) degraded the XVth Brigade to the point that the individual components could not function as a whole.

These lessons, taken together, serve as a reminder that much of the damage done in battle occurs at the psychological level. In addition to the brigade's devastating losses—those killed, wounded, and captured—many soldiers were neutralized by fear and disorganization. Chaos was their constant companion. Not knowing what to do or where to go, they went to the rear. With their flanks constantly threatened, the soldiers rightly feared encirclement and withdrew again and again. Afraid they would be executed if captured with weapons, they threw their weapons away. While some of these soldiers lived to fight another day, at that moment they were as much out of the fight as if the Nationalists had killed or wounded them. Conversely, where leaders organized and regrouped—bringing temporary order to the chaos—the XVth Brigade was able to slow the Nationalist advance, however briefly, and even conduct limited counterattacks. These observations are not a criticism of soldiers who reacted in a very human way, but rather a caution to future commanders who face seemingly insurmountable odds on the battlefield. Fighting the chaos of panic and confusion within the force—surviving an unexpected onslaught and quickly adapting to changing circumstances—can prove decisive in snatching victory from the jaws of defeat.

Notes

1. For example, between August 1937 and June 1938, the Republic received only twenty-five tanks and thirty-one fighter aircraft from the Soviet Union. Gerald Howson, *Arms for Spain: The Untold Story of the Spanish Civil War* (London: J. Murray, 1998), 298–300.

2. Hugh Thomas, *The Spanish Civil War*, 2nd ed. (London: Penguin Books, 1965), 394–95, 467–72, 594.

3. Paul Preston, *Franco: A Biography* (London: HarperCollins, 1993), 301–2; and Thomas, 797–98.

4. Thomas, 798.

5. The first five International Brigades were numbered XI to XV in order of creation. Thomas, 968–69.

6. For more on the *Regimiento de Tren,* see David Goutor, *A Chance to Fight Hitler: A Canadian Volunteer in the Spanish Civil War* (Toronto: Between the Lines, 2018), 74–82; and Cary Nelson and Jefferson Hendricks, *Madrid 1937: Letters of the Abraham Lincoln Brigade from the Spanish Civil War* (New York: Routledge, 1996), 333–58.

7. The structure of the XVth Brigade changed over time. In spring 1937, two Spanish battalions were transferred to the brigade, the 21st and 24th. The 21st was broken up to increase the strength of the other battalions. A second "American" battalion was subsequently created (the George Washington Battalion), but because of severe casualties in the Lincoln and Washington battalions during the Brunete Offensive, the brigade merged the two units to form the Lincoln-Washington Battalion, often referred to as the Lincoln Battalion. The decimated 6th of February Battalion was transferred out of the XV Brigade after Brunete. The Dimitrov Battalion transferred out of the XVth Brigade after Belchite in September 1937. The Mackenzie-Papineau Battalion (named after William Lyon Mackenzie and Louis-Joseph Papineau, leaders of the 1837 Upper and Lower Canada Rebellions) formed during the summer of 1937 and joined the XVth Brigade for the Battle of Fuentes de Ebro in October 1937. In fall 1937, the International Brigades were formally incorporated into the Spanish Popular Army and the battalions were renumbered. The British became the 57th; the Lincoln-Washington, the 58th; and the Mackenzie-Papineau, the 60th. The Spanish 24th Battalion was renumbered 59th. For simplicity, the 24th/59th Battalion is referred to here as the Spanish Battalion. Charles J. Esdaile, *The Spanish Civil War: A Military History* (London and New York: Routledge, 2019), 100–2, 355–57; Michael Petrou, *Renegades: Canadians in the Spanish Civil War* (Vancouver: UBC Press, 2008), 22–23; and Arthur H. Landis, *The Abraham Lincoln Brigade* (New York: Citadel Press, 1967), 317. Landis was an American volunteer in the Mackenzie-Papineau Battalion.

8. Esdaile, *The Spanish Civil War*, 259–60; and Richard Baxell, *British Volunteers in the Spanish Civil War: The British Battalion in the International Brigades, 1936–1939* (London: Routledge, 2004), 89. For more on the flow of North American recruits, see Tyler Wentzell, "Canada's Foreign Enlistment Act and the Spanish Civil War," *Labour/Le Travail* 80 (Fall 2017): 232–45.

9. Petrou, *Renegades*, 21.

10. See the newsletter of the XVth Brigade, *Volunteer for Liberty,* 17 November 1937 and 30 June 1938.

11. See *Volunteer for Liberty,* 13 December 1937; Adam Hochschild, *Spain in Our Hearts: Americans in the Spanish Civil War, 1936–1939* (Boston: Houghton Mifflin Harcourt, 2016), 289–90; and Marion Merriman and Warren Lerude, *American Commander in Spain: Robert Hale Merriman and the Abraham Lincoln Brigade* (Reno, NV: University of Reno Press, 1986).

12. For specifics of the brigade's training system, and the role played by Red Army trainers, see Robert Merriman's diary entries from the summer of 1937. A copy of his diary, as transcribed and annotated by Raymond Hoff, is held at the Tamiment Library and Robert F. Wagner Labor Archives at New York University, http://digitaltamiment.hosting.nyu.edu/s/digtam/item/5848. Regarding the role played by Red Army advisers during the battle, see RGASPI, Fond 545, Opis 3, Delo 475, "The Withdrawal of Aragon" (April 1938) [XVth Brigade Phase I Report], Library and Archives Canada (LAC), MG30 E173, Makenzie-Papineau Battalion Collection, Cecil-Smith Papers, report by Edward Cecil-Smith, n.d., c. April 1938 [Cecil-Smith Report]. Also reproduced in William Beeching, *Canadian Volunteers: Spain, 1936–1939* (Regina, SK: Canadian Plains Research Centre, 1989), 96; RGASPI, Fond 545, Opis 3, Delo 497, report by Sam Wild, 28 April 1938 [Sam Wild Report]; and Landis, *The Abraham Lincoln Brigade*, 406.

13. Because of space limitations, this chapter does not include a proper treatment of the role of communism, the Soviet Union, and national Communist Parties in the structure, training, and organizational culture on the XVth Brigade. Interested readers can learn more on this matter in Baxell, *British Volunteers in the Spanish Civil War*; Richard Baxell, "Myths of the International Brigades," *Bulletin of Spanish Studies* 91, no. 1–2 (February 2014): 11–24; Petrou, *Renegades*; Ronald Liversedge, *Mac-Pap: Memoir of a Canadian in the Spanish Civil War* (Vancouver: New Star Books, 2017); and Tyler Wentzell, *Not for King or Country: Edward Cecil-Smith, the Communist Party of Canada, and the Spanish Civil War* (Toronto: University of Toronto Press, 2020). Regarding the role of the British Communist Party in recalling officers, see Baxell, *British Volunteers in the Spanish Civil War*, 88–89, 150.

14. Wentzell, *Not for King or Country*, 117, 186–88.

15. Daniel Kowalsky, "Operation X: Soviet Russia and the Spanish Civil War," *Bulletin of Spanish Studies* 91, no. 1–2 (February 2014): 172–73.

16. Cecil D. Eby, *Comrades and Commissars: The Lincoln Battalion in the Spanish Civil War* (University Park, PA: Pennsylvania State University Press, 2007), 288–89.

17. Eby, 287; and Landis, *The Abraham Lincoln Brigade*, 405; Carl Geiser, *Prisoners of the Good Fight: The Spanish Civil War, 1936–39* (Westport, CT.: L. Hill, 1986), 42. See Russian State Archive of Socio-Political History (RGASPI) Records of the International Brigades, Comintern Archives, Moscow [RGASPI], Fond 545, Opis 6, Delo 40 for various incomplete lists of reinforcements in late February and early March.

18. Arthur Landis, a survivor of the battle and author of *The Abraham Lincoln Brigade,* cautiously declared Merriman to be the brigade commander: "A Russian colonel named Nicholaivitch was acting as 'advisor' to the Brigade. Whether this means he was nominally in command during Copic's absence is not certain. In the ensuing campaign both Colonel Nikolaievitch and his mentor, 'Maxim,' seemed lacking in decision and command capacities; they contributed little to the battle maneuvers of the Brigade. Major Robert Merriman, the highest-ranking American officer in Spain, seems to have offered the only real leadership through the long days and nights of retreat, encirclement, and battle." Landis cites "consensus" among the volunteers he knew and interviewed. He would not have had access to the XVth Brigade's report, although he was certainly aware of controversy on this point. For instance, in Landis's recorded interview with John Gerlach, an American commissar in the brigade headquarters, Gerlach stated that the Red Army advisers were actually in command during the battle and that Merriman "just had the stripes." XVth Brigade Phase I Report; Tamiment Library and Wagner Labor Archives, Oral History Collection, Arthur Landis interview with John Gerlach (1965); and Landis, *The Abraham Lincoln Brigade,* 406. See also Sandor Voros, *American Commissar* (Philadelphia: Chilton Co., Book Division, 1961), 387–88.

19. Eby, *Comrades and Commissars,* 287.

20. See RGASPI, XVth Brigade Phase I Report; Sandor Voros, *American Commissar* (Philadelphia: Chilton Co. Book Division, 1961), 387–88; and Eby, 288.

21. Eby, 289.

22. The timeline of these opening events has been confused in the early scholarship on the Spanish Civil War volunteers. For instance, Victor Hoar's account states that Republican soldiers began withdrawing through the Mac-Pap lines at 1000 on 8 March, whereas Cecil-Smith and the XVth Brigade's contemporaneous accounts clearly state that this occurred on 9 March. Similarly, Beeching's account indicates Maurice Constant and the brigade scouts were sent forward on the afternoon of 8 March, whereas the Cecil-Smith and brigade's report state that this occurred on 9 March. Cecil-Smith Report, 1; XVth Brigade Phase I Report, 6–7; Victor Hoar, *The Mackenzie-Papineau Battalion: Canadian Participation in the Spanish Civil War* (Toronto: Copp, Clark Pub. Co., 1969), 175–76; and Beeching, *Canadian Volunteers: Spain, 1936–1939,* 95–96. Note that Beeching was himself a Canadian volunteer in the Lincoln Battalion during this battle.

23. CBC Radio Archives, Mac Reynolds interview with Lawrence Cane (1964). See also Cecil-Smith Report and XVth Brigade Phase I Report, 6–7.

24. Cecil-Smith Report, 1.

25. Merriman's initial direction was to send the Mac-Paps, Spanish Battalion, his engineer company, and an anti-tank gun west from Letux to reinforce the Spanish line. The remainder of his forces would advance from Belchite to the same effect. Given that these forces would have been advancing to contact, in the dark, toward an advancing enemy and against the flow of retreating Republican units, it is likely just as well that these orders were soon countermanded. The

Mac-Paps, Spanish Battalion, engineers, and anti-tank gun established a position outside Letux, although Merriman recalled the entire force (less the Mac-Paps) to go to Belchite instead. XVth Brigade Phase I Report, 6–7; and Cecil-Smith Report, 1. The brigade report stated that the artillery battery "did not perform a remarkable job," and that the company of tanks "did little work, refusing to defend the north side of the village." XVth Brigade Phase I Report, 10.

26. XVth Brigade Phase I Report, 6–7.

27. Report by Milton Wolff and George Watt regarding the Lincoln Battalion's actions, dated 22 April 1938. RGASPI, Fond 545, Opis 3, Delo 503, ll. 105–11. See also Eby, *Comrades and Commissars*, 289–90; Robert A. Rosenstone, *Crusade of the Left: The Lincoln Battalion in the Spanish Civil War* (New York: Routledge, 2009), 276–79; and Landis, *The Abraham Lincoln Brigade*, 415.

28. Landis, 410, 415; and Eby, 290.

29. XVth Brigade Phase I Report, 10; Battalion 58 casualty lists at RGASPI, Fond 545, Opis 6, Delo 51; Landis, *The Abraham Lincoln Brigade*, 415; and Eby, 293.

30. Sam Wild Report.

31. XVth Brigade Phase I Report, 9, 10, 13–14, 30; Landis, *The Abraham Lincoln Brigade*, 416, 422; Baxell, *British Volunteers in the Spanish Civil War*, 94–95; Eby, *Comrades and Commissars*, 496–97; and Beeching, *Canadian Volunteers*, 109. Note that while the XVth Brigade report states that the Spanish Battalion made their retreat "in perfect order . . . [to an assigned position] at 1800," it also later states that the battalion had disintegrated following the withdrawal.

32. XVth Brigade Phase I Report, 14.

33. Cecil-Smith Report, 2–3; and XVth Brigade Phase I Report, 14–15.

34. XVth Brigade Phase I Report, 18; and Wentzell, *Not for King or Country*, 159–62. See also Jim Higgins, *Fighting for Democracy: The True Story of Jim Higgins (1907–1982)* (Toronto: Friesen Press, 2020), 51.

35. XVth Brigade Phase I Report, 17; Landis, *The Abraham Lincoln Brigade*, 424; and Voros, *American Commissar*, 387.

36. Cecil-Smith Report, 3–4.

37. Cecil-Smith Report, 3–4; and Sam Wild Report, 1–2.

38. Cecil-Smith stated the Mexican officer was from the XIIIth "Dabrowski" Brigade. Given that the Dabrowski Brigade was principally composed of Eastern European volunteers, it seems more likely that the commander in question was Russian rather than Mexican.

39. XVth Brigade Phase I Report, 20.

40. Cecil-Smith Report, 4–5.

41. Voros, *American Commissar*, 406.

42. Cecil-Smith Report, 4–5; XVth Brigade Phase I Report, 15–27; Voros, 402–5; and Wentzell, *Not for King or Country*, 162–65.

43. Estimates of numbers at Caspe vary widely. Landis estimates 700 soldiers at Caspe, which likely includes the soldiers cobbled together from other Spanish units and international brigades, including three companies of

soldiers from the XIVth Brigade that later refused to participate in counter-attacks. Eby estimates 300 soldiers from the XVth Brigade specifically. The XVth Brigade's own report indicates that they were not sure how many soldiers they had at their disposal at this point, but it was no more than 700 effective soldiers. They held "a large part" of the British Battalion with rifles and "some machine guns," "a group of" Lincolns armed only with rifles, "only some men" from the Spanish Battalion, and "part of" the Mac-Paps with rifles and machine guns. At this point, the report notes, the brigade had lost its machine gun company, its engineer company, its anti-tank battery, and most of the Spanish Battalion. XVth Brigade Phase I Report, 30, 35; Landis, *The Abraham Lincoln Brigade*, 430; and Eby, *Comrades and Commissars*, 306.

44. There is some confusion about the name of the hill where Makela died and Cecil-Smith subsequently attacked; some sources call it Cemetery Hill and others refer to it as Reservoir Hill. A 7 November 1938 *Volunteer for Liberty* article eulogizing Makela stated that he was wounded on Cemetery Hill; in Beeching's book, Paddy McElligott recalled that Makela was killed on a hill with an "earth-covered water reservoir;" and based on interviews with veterans, Victor Hoar referred to Makela's death and Cecil-Smith's attack as both occurring on "the cemetery hill." Cecil-Smith himself described the hill as "the cemetery hill" in his own report, but later corrected himself and called it Reservoir Hill in a subsequent newspaper article. The XVth Brigade report also refers to Reservoir Hill. Consequently, it is referred to here as Reservoir Hill. Ed Cecil-Smith, "Canadian Volunteers, Home from Spanish War, Lauded by Leader for Valour and Endurance," *Globe & Mail,* 4 February 1939; Sam Suto, "Captain Niila Makela [sic]," *Volunteer for Liberty*, 13 August 1938; Beeching, *Canadian Volunteers*, 113; and Hoar, *The Mackenzie-Papineau Battalion*, 183–84.

45. Landis, *The Abraham Lincoln Brigade*, 431; Baxell, *British Volunteers in the Spanish Civil War*, 95–96; and Eby, *Comrades and Commissars*, 308–9.

46. Cecil-Smith Report, 5–6; and Wentzell, *Not for King or Country*, 163–65.

47. XVth Brigade Phase I Report, 32.

48. Cecil-Smith Report, 6; XVth Brigade Phase I Report, 32–34, Sam Wild Report, 2–3; Eby, *Comrades and Commissars*, 310; and Wentzell, *Not for King or Country*, 165–67.

49. Thomas, *The Spanish Civil War*, 800.

50. Preston, *Franco: A Biography*, 303.

51. XVth Brigade Phase I Report, 36–38. See also Robert Merriman's last letter to his wife, dated 28 March, stating, "Needless to say the general situation is serious enough and requires rigid control and intense political work." Merriman and Lerude, *American Commander in Spain*, 207–8.

52. The XVth Brigade reports did not mention the Russian advisers during the second phase of the battle. RGASPI, Fond 545, Opis 3, Delo 475, The Operations in the Sector Batea-Cuadret-Calaceite-Mudefes-Gandesa March 30 to April 3, 1938 (April 1938) [XVth Brigade Phase II Report],

53. Eby, *Comrades and Commissars*, 311, 315.

54. Cecil-Smith Report, 6.

55. Baxell, *British Volunteers in the Spanish Civil War*, 312.

56. CBC Radio Archives, Mac Reynolds interview with Jules Paivio (1965); CBC Radio Archives, Mac Reynolds interview with Lionel Edwards (1965); Geiser, *Prisoners of the Good Fight*, 53; and Dan Bessie, ed., *Alvah Bessie's Spanish Civil War Notebooks* (Lexington, KY: University Press of Kentucky, 2002), 12–15. See also RGASPI, Fond 545, Opis 3 Delo 453, ll. 83–97 and RGASPI, Fond 545, Opis 6, Delo 40, which include various records from the training establishments on or about 13 March 1938 detailing students and instructors to be sent to the front as reinforcements.

57. Voros, *American Commissar*, 410. See also Eby, *Comrades and Commissars*, 313–14; D. P. (Pat) Stephens, *A Memoir of the Spanish Civil War: An Armenian-Canadian in the Lincoln Battalion* (St. John's, NL: Canadian Committee on Labour History, 2000), 75–76.

58. XVth Brigade Phase II Report, 56.

59. XVth Brigade Phase II Report, 45, 46; and Landis, *The Abraham Lincoln Brigade*, 446.

60. XVth Brigade Phase II Report, 48; RGASPI, Fond 545, Opis 3, Delo 497, Report by George Fletcher, 5 May 1938; and Baxell, *British Volunteers in the Spanish Civil War*, 98–99.

61. See Alvah Bessie, *Men in Battle: A Story of Americans in Spain* (New York: Veterans of the Abraham Lincoln Brigade, 1954), 94–106.

62. XVth Brigade Phase II Report, 49.

63. XVth Brigade Phase II Report, 49–50, 57; RGASPI, Fond 545, Opis 3, Delo 497, Report by Bob Cooney, n.d., c. April 1938 [Bob Cooney Report]; CBC Radio Archives, Mac Reynolds interview with Lawrence Cane and Carl Geiser (1964); Geiser, *Prisoners of the Good Fight*, 65–72; Voros, *American Commissar*, 415–18; and Beeching, *Canadian Volunteers*, 116–18.

64. XVth Brigade Phase II Report, 52; and Voros, *American Commissar*, 423–24.

65. Landis, *The Abraham Lincoln Brigade*, 459–60.

66. Bessie, *Men in Battle*, 109–13.

67. Eby, *Comrades and Commissars*, 328.

68. Bessie, *Men in Battle*, 113–16.

69. Merriman's fate has been a longstanding matter of controversy. It appears most likely that he was executed on capture. See Edwin Rolfe, *The Lincoln Battalion: The Story of the Americans Who Fought in Spain in the International Brigades* (New York: Veterans of the Abraham Lincoln Brigade, 1939), 210–14; Merriman and Lerude, *American Commander in Spain*, 219–33; and Chris Brooks, "The Death of Robert Hale Merriman," *The Volunteer*, 13 March 2016, https://albavolunteer.org/2016/03/the-death-of-major-robert-hale-merriman/.

70. Eby, *Comrades and Commissars*, 332–36; and Landis, *The Abraham Lincoln Brigade*, 462–64.

71. XVth Brigade Phase II Report, 53.

72. Bob Cooney Report; Baxell, *British Volunteers in the Spanish Civil War*, 99–100; and Landis, *The Abraham Lincoln Brigade*, 468–69.

73. Bessie, *Men in Battle*, 123–26; and Bessie, *Alvah Bessie's Spanish Civil War Notebooks*, 24–26.

74. Petrou, *Renegades*, 91–92; Higgins, *Fighting for Democracy*, 76–77; Hochschild, *Spain in Our Hearts*, 302–5; Eby, *Comrades and Commissars*, 340; and Landis, *The Abraham Lincoln Brigade*, 467–68. See also CBC Radio Archives, Mac Reynolds interview with Bill Beeching (1965).

75. XVth Brigade Phase II Report, 45. See RGASPI, Fond 545, Opis 3, Delo 453 II, 98–104, for detailed casualty lists of battalion and company leadership.

76. Cecil-Smith Report; and Baxell, *British Volunteers in the Spanish Civil War*, 96. See also signaller Harry Fisher's letters home describing the difficulties in laying, maintaining, and recovering wire at Batea and Gandesa in Nelson and Hendricks, *Madrid 1937*, 373–75, 376–77.

77. For example, Signaller Tom Bailey recalled being employed as infantry during these actions. On 1 April, almost immediately after the Mac-Paps deployed from Gandesa, the battalion communicated with brigade headquarters by sending its commissar, Carl Geiser, as a runner to brigade headquarters. Geiser found Robert Merriman, who informed him that he no longer had any runners of his own to communicate with the battalions. LAC, MG30-E-173, vol. 1, file 16, letter from Tom Bailey to Maurice Constant, c. June 1939; and Geiser, *Prisoners of the Good Fight*, 66.

78. For example, see CBC Radio Archives, Mac Reynolds interview with Lawrence Cane (1964); CBC Radio Archives, Mac Reynolds interview with Bill Beeching (1965); Cecil-Smith Report; and Higgins, *Fighting for Democracy*, 75.

79. Higgins, 75. See also Higgins, 63–65.

80. Higgins, 75. For more on the contentious issue of discipline and the discarding of weapons, see XVth Brigade Phase I Report, 32–35; Voros, *American Commissar*, 339–40, 411–12; Hochschild, *Spain in Our Hearts*, 298–99; Petrou, *Renegades*, 108–24; Baxell, "Myths of the International Brigades," 21–22; Bessie, *Men in Battle*, 84; and Rosenstone, *Crusade of the Left*, 309–11, 373–75.

81. Cecil-Smith Report, 6; and XVth Brigade Phase I Report, 42–43.

82. See also Voros's recollection that it was understood Communist party members like himself were to be executed. Carl Geiser understood that the Nationalists would execute all captured officers, such as himself. Although the Nationalists did not execute prisoners with consistency, the Nationalists routinely committed war crimes against their prisoners. Geiser's research, for instance, identified forty-one Americans killed following their capture between 10 and 17 March, and ninety-nine Americans killed following their capture between 30 March and 14 April. Voros, *American Commissar*, 391–92; Geiser, *Prisoners of the Good Fight*, 67, 263–66; Bessie, *Men in Battle*, 118; and Mark Zuehlke, *The Gallant Cause: Canadians in the Spanish Civil War, 1936–1939* (Vancouver and Toronto: Whitecap Books, 1996), 210–11.

Chapter 5
Polish Horsemen in the Chaotic Withdrawal of 1939
Marcin Wilczek

The German Invasion of Poland is frequently regarded as the actual beginning of the Second World War. The Polish effort to repel advancing German troops was the first organized military attempt to stop German expansion. Although Polish military intelligence anticipated the German offensive of September 1939, the tempo and coordinated use of armor and military aviation surprised the *Wojsko Polskie* (Polish Army).

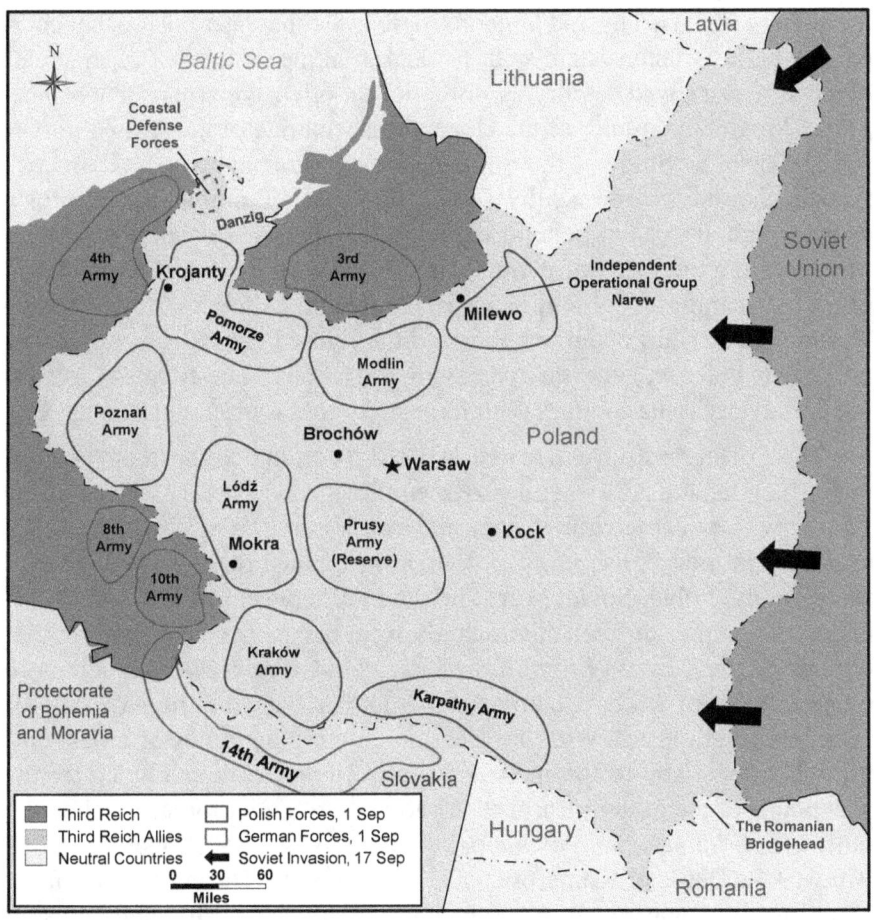

Figure 5.1. Map of general situation, September 1939. Created by the author and Army University Press.

The Polish forces were quickly forced to retreat. Withdrawals are always the toughest challenge for any army—often leading to deteriorating morale and discipline among the retreating troops. The worst possibility was an unplanned withdrawal, ordered ad-hoc, as a reaction to the overall defeat on the front. Such circumstances often made it impossible to plan and coordinate an effective combat operation. The September 1939 campaign was full of examples of defensive actions that devolved into a chaotic and disorderly retreat.

Stark disparities existed between the Polish defenders and the German aggressors, and popular memory has made the Polish cavalry a symbol of the lost campaign. The myth of saber and lance charges against German armor persists despite being debunked many times.[1] Regardless of the myths, the cavalry was used by and large in a defensive character during that campaign; this was inconsistent with tactical thinking of many Polish senior officers, who viewed cavalry as primarily an offensive arm. For instance, Stefan Mossor, an officer of the General Inspectorate of the Armed Forces and author of a "Study of the Strategic Plan of Poland against Germany," thought that the Polish cavalry should be kept as a mobile reserve for a decisive fight instead of being used in the initial phase of war.[2] Polish field manuals from the interwar period also prioritized the use of the cavalry in offensive operations.[3] Witold Sawicki, the scientific director of the Cavalry Training Center in Poland, emphasized the limited capabilities of cavalry not only in defense, but even in delaying operations.[4] The effects of assigning the cavalry tasks contrary with its primary role warrant closer analysis.[5]

The Polish Army was created in 1918. With the collapse of the German, Russian, and Austro-Hungarian empires—and after 123 years of the *Partitions*—Polish territorial integrity was restored.[6] Only two years later, newly formed Polish units took up arms against the Soviet Bolshevik forces in the Polish-Soviet War. The conflict between the nascent Polish and Soviet armies differed significantly from the static trench warfare that dominated the Western Front of the First World War. It was a much more dynamic form of warfare, similar to the combat waged during World War I on the Eastern Front. With the frontline moving hundreds of miles, mobility became a key factor and cavalry proved an excellent choice for the vast plains of the eastern Europe.[7] Although the Soviet forces reached the outskirts of Warsaw, the Poles repelled them. A key Polish victory in this war was the Battle of Komarów on 31 August 1920. During this old-fashioned cavalry engagement, 1,500 men of the Polish 1st Mounted Division defeated the Soviet 1st Horse Army, which was four-times larger. As a result, the Bolsheviks lost the initiative on the southern front. Eventually, the

Polish Army pushed the Soviets back and secured the eastern border of the newly formed country. The cavalry had a significant role in this outcome.

Following the war's conclusion, Polish military planners and politicians saw a need to maintain a strong cavalry. The Soviet threat remained at the forefront of Polish strategic thought, a threat magnified by its significant manpower advantage. To the Polish Army, mobility was a central factor to offset Soviet numerical superiority.[8]

Doctrinally, Polish field manuals in the 1930s treated the cavalry as a mounted infantry unit that travelled on horseback and fought dismounted.[9] Between 1920 and 1939, it was organized into forty regiments—differing in name, traditions, and colors but similarly equipped, organized, and tactically trained.[10] Sabers and lances remained in the inventory, but rifle and grenades were the primary weapons for each trooper. A cavalry regiment had four company-sized line troops (*szwadrony liniowe*), and each of these troops divided into three platoons.[11] Therefore, the actual combat power of the cavalry regiment was similar to an infantry battalion. Its total combat power was diluted while dismounted, as a number of men constantly had to the guard the horses.[12] Unlike the infantry, cavalry regiments had no organic field artillery or mortars; fire support was provided by a heavy machine gun troop (*szwadron CKM*).[13] The motorized anti-aircraft artillery battery (*bateria motorowa artylerii przeciwlotniczej*) at the cavalry brigade level had only two 40-mm Bofors AA guns that provided little more than symbolic air defense. The regiments had to rely on their heavy machine guns for air defense.[14] Furthermore, the majority of the brigade's armored squadron vehicles were armed with machine guns (only a few were equipped with an effective 20-mm autocannon), reducing the cavalry's value as an offensive asset.[15] Anti-armor capabilities partially compensated for these gaps. Each cavalry regiment had an anti-tank platoon with four modern guns, and all the line platoons were issued anti-tank rifles.[16] Additionally, the brigade horse artillery squadron (*dywizjon artylerii konnej*) could use its 75-mm wz.02/26 light field gun as a heavy anti-tank weapon.[17] The cavalry brigades, with their mobility and anti-tank firepower, made a potent operational reserve capable of thwarting enemy armor; however, their armament and equipment were not adequate for more varied tasks.

Communications, especially important for independent and highly mobile forces, were a noteworthy weakness for the Polish cavalry. The Polish Army based its communications plans on civilian ground telephone lines, supplemented with field-expedient military lines.[18] There

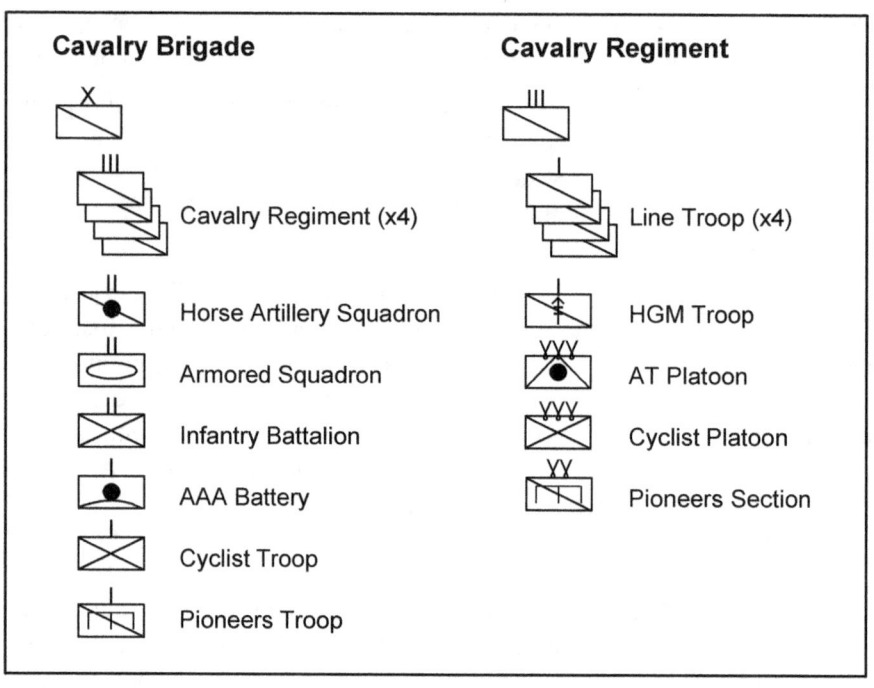

Figure 5.2. Cavalry Organizational Table. Created by the author and Army University Press.

Figure 5.3. Cavalry Regiment antitank artillery platoon with 37-mm Bofors cannon. Courtesy of the Polish National Digital Archive.

were only two radio sets per cavalry regiment and an additional three at each brigade headquarters.[19] This was an especially inconvenient solution for a mobile unit. The supply system, based on wagon trains, additionally limited the mobility.[20] The long logistics column that followed the units slowed the rate of march and increased the chance of enemy detection. Additionally, Poland's weaker economy precluded the scale of modernization of neighboring Germany and the Soviet Union. As a result, the horse remained the primary mode of transportation for the entire Polish Army. By 1939, only one motorized brigade gained combat-ready status.[21] The vast majority of the Polish cavalry—eleven brigades—went to war as horse-mounted units.[22]

In addition to cavalry brigades, Polish infantry divisions also formed divisional cavalry troops (*kawaleria dywizyjna*) to serve as their reconnaissance and mobile reserve.[23] It is worth mentioning that in the peacetime army, Poles did not have independent, specialized reconnaissance units. In 1936, infantry regiments received mixed (horse- and bicycle-mounted) reconnaissance companies that could only be used at the lowest tactical level. To gain some additional capabilities at the operational level during the 1939 alarm-mobilization, peacetime armored battalions formed independent reconnaissance tank companies (*samodzielne kompanie czołgów rozpoznawczych*). The same battalions were simultaneously detaching their forces for cavalry brigade armored squadrons. As a result, the re-

Figure 5.4. Galloping horsemen on battlefield with rifle and sabres. Courtesy of the Polish National Digital Archive.

source-constrained army was not equipped with a sufficient number of reconnaissance tank companies. The Poles formed only fifteen of them, which meant that less than half of existing infantry divisions could have one attached.[24] In most cases, the divisional cavalry troop remained the unit best-suited for operational reconnaissance tasks.

The cavalry was an elite branch within the Polish Army. Its training centers accepted only the brightest officer candidates who had to complete the demanding course before being commissioned.[25] For enlisted men, serving in the cavalry was a privilege, so the army had few problems finding troopers—despite terms of service that were often much stricter than in other units. Compulsory military service for mounted branches was longer than for other ground branches.[26] The extended service allowed the cavalry regiments to maintain a combat-ready status for the entire training cycle. An effective training system, together with the romantic belief that cavalrymen were direct heirs of the noble knights, created strong bonds between soldiers and shaped high unit morale.[27]

Cavalry also played a role in national-level mobilization plans. Polish mobilization relied on cavalry units to provide cover and protection when the rest of the armed forces were assembling troops and equipment for war.[28] During the first days of combat when the infantry units would be still concentrating, the cavalry was to conduct reconnaissance and, when possible, harass the enemy in hit-and-run raids.[29]

In 1939, with tensions running high between Germany and Poland, cavalry units located close to the border were ordered to conduct regular patrols of the frontier to prevent German infiltration.[30] These patrols also allowed some Polish troops to become familiar with the terrain as well as their own strengths and weaknesses.[31] Overall, however, these preparations were inadequate. Defensive strategy—based on the operational plan "West"—envisaged that after fighting the initial battle in western borderlands, the Polish Army would move in an orderly withdrawal to the main defense positions. The final line at which German forces were to be withheld was established along the rivers (mainly Wisła, Narew, and San) and other central Poland terrain obstacles. This plan emphasized ensuring a signaling effect to the Germans and Poland's allies, France and Great Britain, rather than providing mass or flexibility to commanders. At the war's outbreak, most Polish forces were stretched along the borders, often disregarding terrain features and unit capabilities. For example, pre-war field manuals indicated infantry divisions were supposed to cover no more than eight kilometers of frontage; in practice, some infantry units protected sectors of up to thirty kilometers.[32]

When the Germans invaded on 1 September 1939, the Polish cavalry was as ready as possible. The fully manned regiments and brigades were already in their areas of responsibility. Garrisons, left by the frontline units, were converted into reserve centers, forming marching troops with the rapidly mobilizing Polish population.[33] Period memoirs mention the cavalry's high morale; troopers believed they would be able to defend their country. As events revealed, this belief proved false.

The Polish strategic plan of defending forward turned out to be a tragic miscalculation. Despite having declared war on Germany, French and British actions were limited to a symbolic effort. The Polish Army was left alone, attempting to defend disadvantageous positions. By contrast, German tactics were highly effective. After quickly breaking through the Polish lines, *Wehrmacht* motorized and armor units brought chaos to the defenders' rear as the *Luftwaffe* ranged overhead almost unchallenged.

Overall, Polish forces collapsed. Entire armies started to retreat though some local commanders attempted counterattacks, most of which were unsuccessful. The Polish retreat grew more disorganized as the war continued. Roads were filled with refugees, hampering military movement. Furthermore, many of the vital static civilian communication lines were knocked out, which limited command-and-control abilities. Polish units, including cavalry brigades, became separated, forcing elements down to the platoon level to retreat alone in some cases. Despite heroic efforts by individual soldiers and commanders, attempts to establish a solid second line of defense were futile.

On 5 September, the central government offices in Warsaw were evacuated. Two days later, the Polish forces commander-in-chief, Marshal Edward Śmigły-Rydz, ordered the army to prepare a new defensive line on the Romanian bridgehead, clearly implying that most of the Polish territory had already been lost. Despite suffering heavy losses, some divisions were still able to establish defenses. However, Poland's fate was all but sealed on 17 September when Soviet troops invaded the eastern part of the country as a result of the Molotov-von Ribbentrop Pact. Regardless, Polish soldiers continued to fight. Though Warsaw fell on 28 September, regular combat operations did not cease until 5 October when the last fighting units expended their remaining ammunition.

According to the Polish military doctrine, defending mobile forces should have remained in reserve, allowing commanders flexibility to use them against enemy actions.[34] In 1939, however, as part of the forward defense strategy, most Polish cavalry brigades formed a cordon on the borders, tied into the infantry divisions. This tactic stripped the cavalry units of opportunities to use their mobility and gain initiative in battle. Rather than being able to maneuver to meet the Germans, the cavalry fought in fixed positions. As a result, some cavalry units were immediately engaged on 1 September while others had a chance to organize prior to facing the advancing *Wehrmacht*.

Two particular battles fought on 1 September demonstrated the Polish cavalry's fate, becoming symbols of loss and victory in the process. The first took place near the village of Krojanty in Pomerania, a region of strategic importance to the Germans. Pomerania was an interwar German objective, as the Germans planned to establish a land communication line between East Prussia and the rest of the Third Reich.[35] As in other areas of the campaign, the Germans enjoyed a qualitative and quantitative advantage over the defenders. Nevertheless, the German 4th Army's advance was rather cautious, as commanders were unfamiliar with the scope and disposition of Polish troops. The 18th Uhlan Regiment, under the command of Col. Kazimierz Mastalerz, counterattacked elements of the German 20th Motorized Infantry Division to prevent encirclement of the main body of Polish forces in the area. Two troops of his regiment (each lacking a platoon), dismounted and supported by the cavalry brigade's organic artillery and tankettes, effectively stopped the advancing enemy columns; meanwhile, the commander with a reinforced two-troop squadron rode behind enemy lines, intending to attack the German rear.[36] In the vicinity of the village Krojanty, the squadron engaged a battalion of German infantry that was resting and unprepared for the Polish onslaught. The Poles attacked mounted, an on-the-spot decision by Mastalerz, which precluded the German's ability to organize a defense. The cavalry's charge with sabers drawn completely surprised the Germans, and the battalion dispersed. Unfortunately for the Polish horsemen, German armored cars joined the battle shortly thereafter. The effect was devastating. The Uhlans suffered numerous casualties, including their commander. By day's end, the regiment had lost more than half of its men and horses— proving how fragile the Polish cavalry was when confronted with modern forces, even while performing basic tasks such as screening and covering. The action, however, gave the Polish infantry time to withdraw. After the campaign, German propaganda used pictures of the Krojanty battlefield showing fallen Polish horsemen and unscratched German armor as a cornerstone for building the myth of inferior Polish soldiers who were incapable of opposing superior invaders.[37]

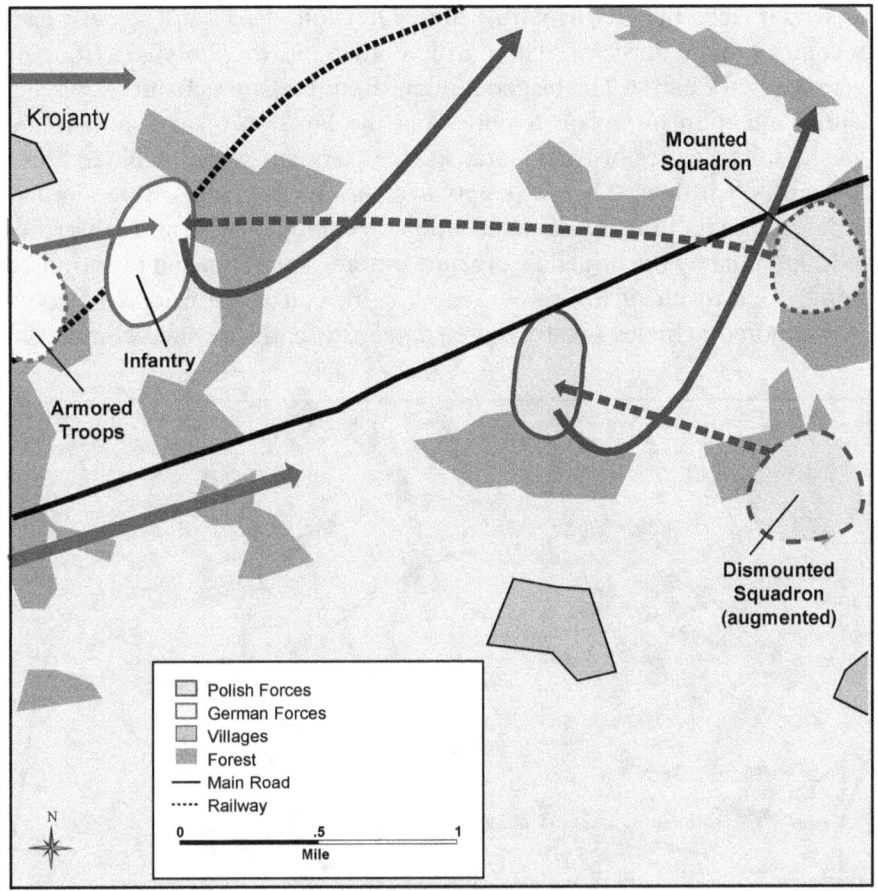

Figure 5.5. Krojanty map. Created by the author and Army University Press.

As the Polish Army retreated farther in the following days, the Pomorska Cavalry Brigade sustained severe losses, eventually shrinking to the size of a single regiment. In contrast to the ad-hoc counterattack and subsequent losses at Krojanty, the Wołyńska Cavalry Brigade commanded by Col. Julian Filipowicz faced a significantly different fight at the village of Mokra, more than 300 kilometers south-southeast from Krojanty. In the days preceding the outbreak of the war, the Brigade was reinforced with the 12th Uhlan Regiment from the Podolska Cavalry Brigade, an infantry battalion, and an armored train. The Polish General Staff believed the now-four-regiment brigade sat astride one of the main German directions of attack, a belief that turned out to be correct. On 1 September, the Polish horsemen faced the German 4th Panzer Division, the assault's spearhead. In contrast to the improvised actions in Pomerania, the Wołyńska troopers were ready for battle. The brigade fought from prepared positions, paying careful attention to terrain features and the location of anti-tank weapons. Despite a series of frontal attacks, the Germans were unable to break through Polish lines. Their attempts to flank the defenders were similarly defeated, this time by mounted troopers equipped with anti-tank rifles and supported by the brigade's organic armored squadron and the armored train.[38] As a result of Polish actions, the 4th Panzer Division lost about fifty armored vehicles (destroyed or damaged) and remained combat-in-

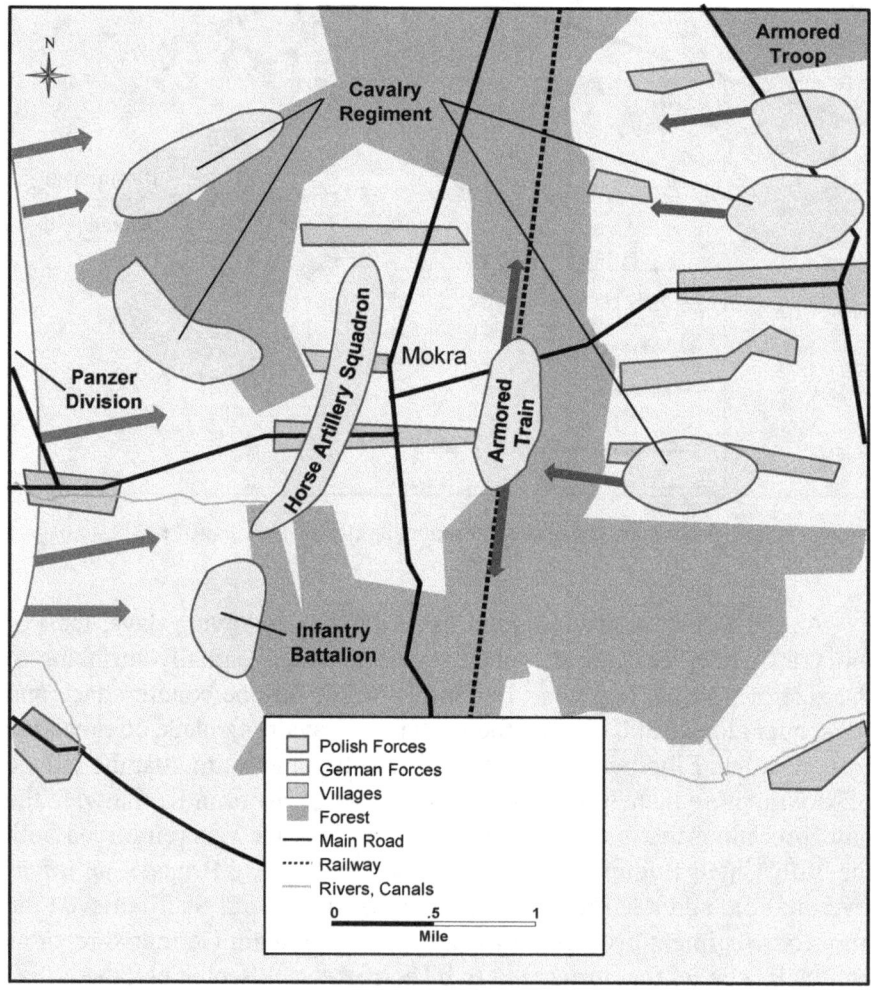

Figure 5.6. Mokra map. Created by the author and Army University Press.

effective for several days following the battle.[39] That evening, despite still holding their lines, the Poles were ordered to retreat. Abandoning the positions, the cavalry fell back, having taken significant losses. More than 500 troopers had been killed or injured, the horse artillery squadron had lost almost half of its guns, and several anti-tank guns were destroyed. The unit sustained further casualties during the subsequent retreat. Due to the weakening situation across the army, lost men, horses, and equipment could not be replaced and the brigade never regained its initial potential.

Cavalry brigades defending quieter sectors of the frontier were in a slightly better position. Their commanding officers had a chance to choose

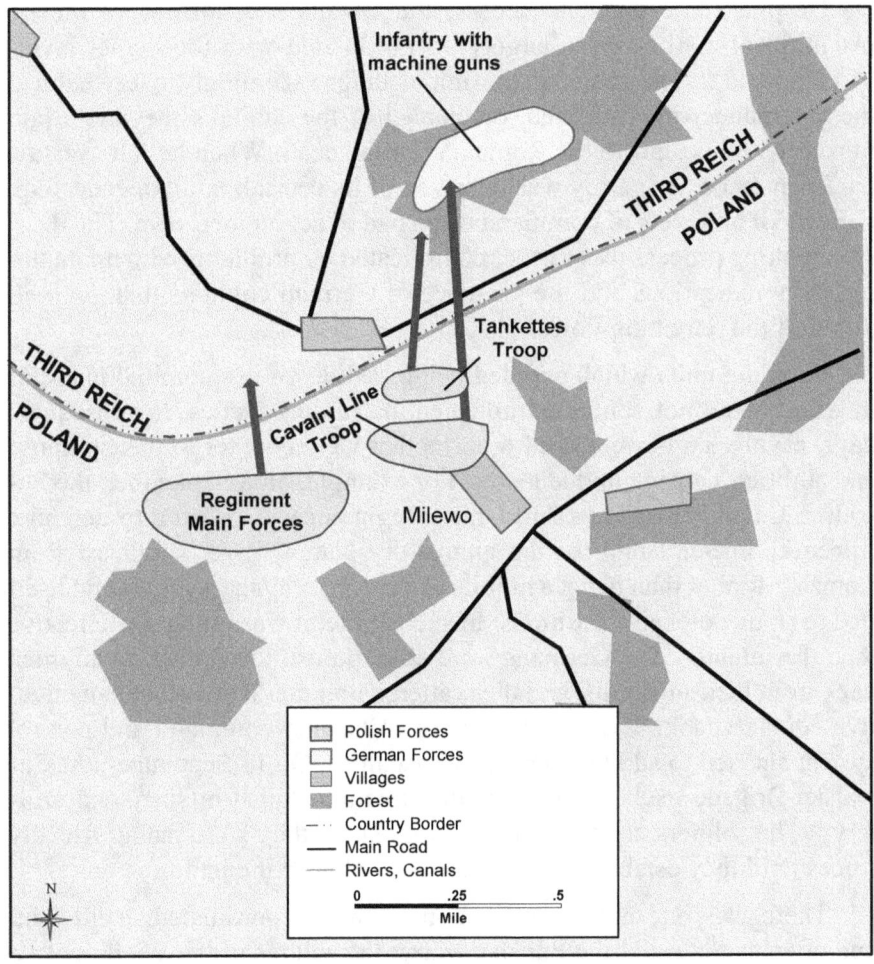

Figure 5.7. Milewo map. Created by the author and Army University Press.

the place and time of the first engagement. The Suwalska and Podlaska cavalry brigades guarding the border between Poland and Eastern Prussia conducted raids inside German territory, attacking enemy units in rear areas. On 4 September, 9th Mounted Rifles Regiment dismounted horsemen, supported by the Podlaska Brigade armored squadron, approached a dug-in German infantry unit sheltering in the forest near Milewo. Cavalry troopers followed the tankettes and later were covered by their fire. When the troopers reached German lines, they attacked with fixed bayonets, prompting the Germans to flee in panic. Polish officers later remarked that even during the peacetime exercises, they had not seen such an effective combination of maneuver, fire, and use of terrain.[40]

Despite some tactical success, the cavalry's actions were mostly insignificant as they were largely uncoordinated with the higher levels of command.[41] The scale of the initial defeat seemingly overwhelmed the commander-in-chief who, convinced of the capital's inevitable fall, moved with his staff to the Romanian bridgehead. When he left Warsaw on 7 September, the army was deprived of its central, unified leadership. Officers of all levels of command often had to act on their own. The decision-making process was further complicated by problems with maintaining communications and the presence of German columns that got well ahead of the retreating Poles.

Even the units which avoided being tied down in the initial phase of invasion could not continue implementing raiding tactics. In subsequent days, cavalry units were used in tasks that were counter to their purpose and abilities, causing undue losses. For example, on 8 September, the Suwalska Cavalry Brigade's 2nd Uhlan Regiment was ordered to defend a fifteen-kilometer length of the almost-dry Narew River southeast from Łomża.[42] Rather than being a mobile reserve, the cavalry again found itself tied to static defensive positions. In such a role, it was much less effective than the infantry. The Germans were able to push the Polish cavalrymen back from their positions, and the scattered unit could not mount an effective counterattack. The Polish Army's collapsing command and control system also led to additional cavalry casualties. On 11 September, the Suwalska Brigade exchanged fire with retreating Polish infantry and artillery.[43] The soldiers and troopers did not realize they were facing friendly forces until they established close contact between the units.

There was one notable exception to the uncoordinated, inefficient, and often static use of the Polish cavalry: the actions of the Wielkopolska Cavalry Brigade commanded by General Roman Abraham. The brigade, after engaging some minor German forces in the area of Poznan, had to withdraw with the rest of the army in the direction of central Poland. The retreat was one of the better-planned and executed operations of the entire campaign. Although neighboring Polish armies were defeated and virtually destroyed, General Tadeusz Kutrzeba, commander of the Poznan Army, kept his units largely intact as they retreated. Kutrzeba also recognized and

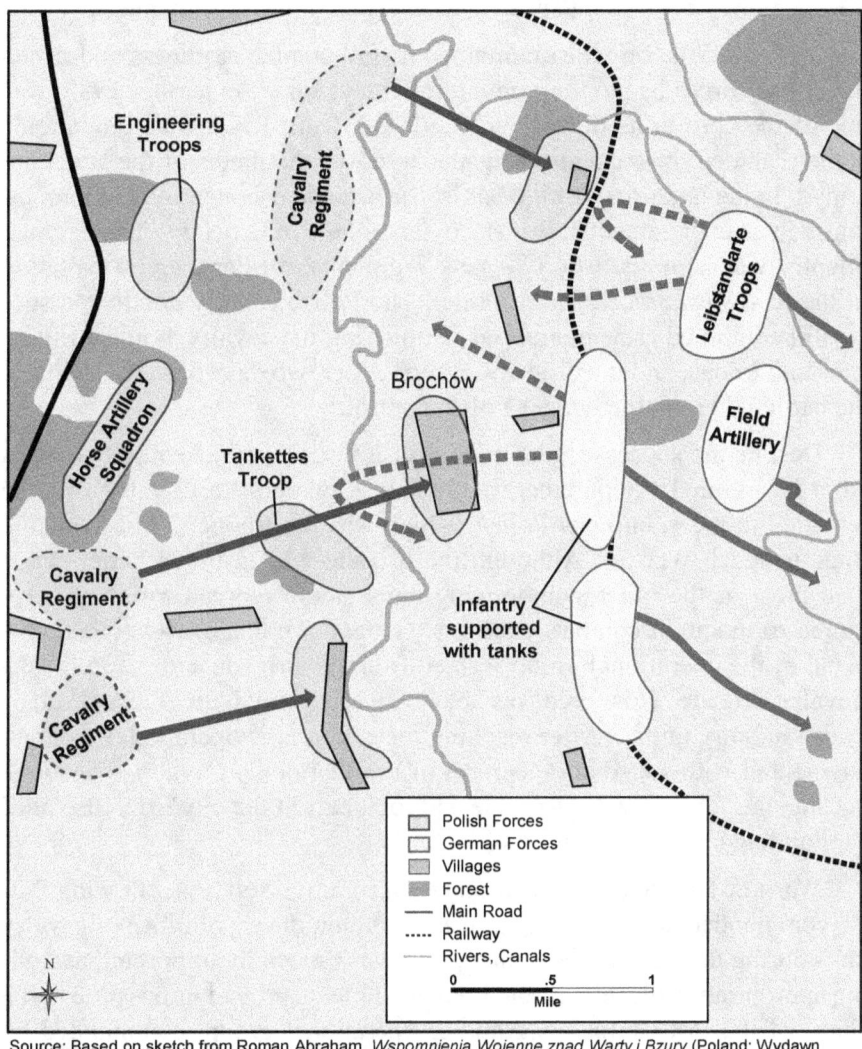

Source: Based on sketch from Roman Abraham, *Wspomnienia Wojenne znad Warty i Bzury* (Poland: Wydawn Ministerstwa Obrony Narodowe, 1969; repr., Poland: Wydawn Ministerstwa Obrony Narodowe, 1990).

Figure 5.8. Brochów map. Created by the author and Army University Press.

appreciated the potential of the cavalry.[44] During the retreat, he treated the Wielkopolska Brigade as his mobile asset, employing it as a reconnaissance element, rearguard, tactical reserve, and a force to seize significant terrain such as river crossings. The cavalry actions (always coordinated with the rest of his units) were crucial for the efficiency of the main force's movement. As a result of its constant employment, the troopers spent most of their time on the march, with limited opportunities to rest. Despite this, they kept their movement speed at rates listed in pre-war manuals.[45]

Moreover, the brigade maintained its full combat readiness and, when the Polish forces began their counteroffensive on 9 September 1939, was one of the core units during the Battle of Bzura River. The operation's battle plan deployed cavalry brigades to cover the flanks of the attacking army.[46] In the latter days of the battle, the brigade encountered German infantry in an engagement at the Mazovian village of Brochów. The German infantry was supported by two tank regiments, artillery, and a battalion of the SS-*Leibstandarte* Adolf Hitler. The Polish cavalry conducted successful combined arms operations, employing the cavalry, horse artillery, anti-tank troops, and the brigade's armor. After two days of fierce fighting, the battlefield remained under Polish control.[47]

Despite the successes, the main Polish forces were eventually defeated at Bzura on 19 September 1939. The Wielkopolska Cavalry Brigade retreated to the Kampinos Forest, which was the troopers' last available route to reach Warsaw. Although the brigade was in much better shape than most of the other withdrawing units, some reorganization was required to maintain combat readiness. General Abraham was given command of the operational group formed from his brigade and the Podolska Cavalry Brigade. This force was able to sweep through the forest ahead of Polish infantry units.[48] After reaching the capital, the operational group—augmented with surviving elements of the Pomorska Cavalry Brigade—became the Joint Cavalry Brigade and took part in the city's defense until capitulating on 28 September.

Wartime ad-hoc reorganization was a common solution, allowing Polish commanders to increase or at least maintain the capabilities of cavalry units during the September campaign. It was especially important, as finding appropriate replacements and replenishments proved impossible in the chaos of the lost campaign. Another operational group, commanded by General Władysław Anders, was created from the Nowogródzka, Wołyńska, and Kresowa cavalry brigades, while elements of Suwalska and Podlaska cavalry brigades were integrated into General Zygmunt Podhorski's

Cavalry Division "Zaza."⁴⁹ This unit made its final stand during the Battle of Kock, ending the entire campaign.⁵⁰

The Polish cavalry also provided intangible benefits to retreating forces. Their morale remained high despite heavy combat, losses, and constant employment. In contrast to the infantry, which could not evade German units, the troopers were able to move, allowing them to retain some sense of initiative and efficiency.⁵¹ As a result, during later stages of the campaign, intact cavalry units often marched upstream against the flow of retreating soldiers and civilian refugees.⁵² In some cases, just the presence of a cavalry unit among the withdrawing forces raised morale, and separated outfits often joined the horsemen. On 28 September, a 5th Infantry Regiment heavy machine gun platoon joined the 2nd Uhlan Regiment near Ostrów Lubelski. Rather than simply accompanying the Uhlans, the infantrymen attempted to obtain horses, spurs, and sabers to become cavalry themselves.⁵³

While morale and mobility were certainly factors in the September campaign, cavalry deficiencies could not be fully overcome. The use of horses was more of an asset than a weakness. In fact, horses were easier to support than motorcars due to the lack of infrastructure in the Polish countryside of the 1930s. It was often much easier to obtain forage for horses than fuel for vehicles.⁵⁴ Structural issues, however, were harder to overcome. For example, the insufficient quantity of specialist equipment and arms at the regimental and brigade level was detrimental to Polish capabilities. A two-gun anti-aircraft battery was incapable of providing effective protection for the brigade headquarters. A moving cavalry force required significantly larger numbers of anti-aircraft weapons once squadrons and troops were split into their tactical formations. Using machine guns as anti-aircraft weapons also turned out to be ineffective. Modern German aircraft bombed and strafed Polish forces with near-impunity.⁵⁵ As a result, during the latter phase of the campaign, Polish forces were only able to move relatively unhampered at night when German aerial reconnaissance was grounded.⁵⁶

Further challenging the Polish cavalry was a lack of accurate intelligence and command-and-control assets. Without substantial aerial assets or the ability to send the fixed-in-place cavalry out as scouts, commanders could only acquire limited information on the enemy. Polish situational awareness, so essential for effective decision-making, was additionally reduced by communications system inefficiency.⁵⁷ Using the civilian networks or setting military ground lines during a rushed retreat was techni-

Figure 5.9. Cavalry Signal Troop radio station on two-wheel carriage. Courtesy of the Polish National Digital Archive.

cally impracticable. With a small number of radios, often treated by the signal troops as secondary equipment, establishing communications was a great challenge.[58] Commanders frequently found themselves disconnected from both subordinates and superiors, unaware of what was happening around them.[59] General Podhorski, for example, commanded his improvised cavalry division based on rumors, aware there were Germans to the west and north of his position and Soviets to the east but with no details about their locations or strength.[60]

Due to the lack of radios and telephones, mounted messengers and couriers became vital for cavalry brigades and regiments.[61] The use of couriers, however, increased transmission time which, in turn, slowed the Polish decision-making tempo. Further complicating the situation, a messenger could only be sent to a known place, and the exact location of the moving troops was often unknown. For instance, the separated elements of the 14th Horse Artillery Squadron were trying to find each other simply by checking for gun carriage tracks at passed crossroads.[62]

In September and October 1939, Polish horsemen shared the fate of the rest of Polish Army. High command mistakes and miscalculations during the planning phase took an especially heavy toll on cavalry. However, on several occasions Uhlans, Mounted Rifles, and Light Horses proved their combat value during the withdrawal and their cavalrymen high spirit was a crucial factor.[63] Polish horsemen were slower to succumb to low morale than soldiers from other military branches. Because of their superior mobility, cavalry troopers were hopeful they would retake the initiative and additionally were less tired than infantrymen who covered the same distance on foot. Equipping cavalry forces with assets allowing them to conserve their strength turned out to be essential in the environment of withdrawal. Nevertheless, resources saved this way could have been easily lost.

The mass retreat had devastating effects on more than just soldier morale. Chaos ensuing from each lost battle, and revelations about surrendered cities heavily affected the command-and-control system. Communication efficiency and intelligence data quality were gradually

Figure 5.10. Stream crossing by cavalry troop mounted unit—more efficient when water levels were high. Courtesy of the Polish National Digital Archive.

worsening. As a result, numerous decisions and orders were based on erroneous information. One of the most important conclusions drawn from the actions of the Polish Cavalry in the September campaign thus regards the command-and-control system. Connection with higher echelons of command and with subordinate units—as well as up-to-date intelligence on friendly and enemy forces—were and still are vital to give commanders operational awareness in any kind of military operation. Communication and intelligence are even more important during a withdrawal or retreat, because they allow the troops to act in the most effective manner and to clearly understand the objective and purpose of their actions when the world around them is collapsing.[64]

Notes

1. Matthew S. Palmer, "The Grand Delusion: The Creation and Perseverance of the September Campaign Mythos," *The Journal of Slavic Military Studies* 30, no. 1 (2017): 61–81.

2. The General Inspectorate of the Armed Forces (*Generalny Inspektorat Sił Zbrojnych, GISZ*), established in 1926 was responsible for defense planning. Commanding officer of the Inspectorate was designated to become a commander-in-chief in wartime. Stefan Mossor, "Kawalerja strategiczna w obliczu przyszłej wojny," *Przegląd Kawaleryjski* 4, no. 138 (1937): 391–425.

3. *Regulamin Kawalerji* (Warsaw: Główna Księgarnia Wojskowa, Cavalry Department, 1922).

4. Witold Sawicki, "Walki opóźniające mniejszych oddziałów kwalerji," *Przegląd Kawaleryjski* 8, no. 130 (1936): 137–56.

5. Because the fights ended with a total defeat of the Polish Army, very few Polish documents from the campaign (including orders and reports) were preserved. Fortunately for researchers, the Polish Government in Exile was particularly interested in obtaining all available sources on the reasons for that disaster. Polish Armed Forces, formed in the West, ordered officers who avoided capture and reached Allied countries to prepare post-action reports. These reports—Relacje z kampanii wrześniwoej, 1939 (Relations of the September campaign, 1939)—are part of the Polish Institute and Sikorski Museum archival collection and were used as a primary source for this chapter. Additionally, the author referred to pre-Second World War Polish cavalry field manuals, military journals from the period, and veteran memoirs published both in Poland and in exile after the war. Mentioned memoirs include works of senior officers like Roman Abraham and Klemens Rudnicki as well as company grade officers like Grzegorz Cydzik or Stanisław Koszutski. Of the academic monographs, which were used as secondary sources, a book by Juliusz S. Tym on the use and training of the cavalry proved especially valuable. Together, these scholarly works and archival documents help reconstruct the Polish cavalry's organization and role with the 1939 campaign, and provide an analysis of its efficiency in the chaotic circumstances of a mass retreat.

6. At the end of eighteenth century, the political situation of the Polish-Lithuanian Commonwealth deteriorated significantly. Neighboring Prussia, Russia, and Austria undertook diplomatic and military actions to seize the land of the weakened dualist monarchy. As a result, independent Poland and Lithuania were erased from the map of Europe for 123 years.

7. Fights of the Soviet 1st Horse Army were an extraordinary example of the mass use of the cavalry in this conflict.

8. Juliusz S. Tym, *Kawaleria w operacji i w walce: Koncepcje użycia i wyszkolenia kawalerii samodzielnej wojska polskiego w latach 1921–1939* (Warsaw: Historyczna, 2014), 40–43. The Soviet Union also maintained a sizeable cavalry component through the end of World War II. See John S. Harrel, *Soviet*

Cavalry Operations during the Second World War: The Genesis of the Operational Manoeuvre Group (Barnsley, UK: Pen & Sword Military, 2019).

9. *Regulamin Kawalerii* (Warsaw: Ministry of Military Affairs, Cavalry Department, 1938).

10. These included twenty-seven Uhlan regiments (*pułki ułanów*), three Light Horse regiments (*pułki szwoleżerów*), and ten Mounted Rifle regiments (*pułki strzelców konnych*). The Light Horses and Uhlans were the most prestigious units, tracing their roots back to the pre-partition cavalry troops or to the Napoleonic era's Polish regiments of the French Guards. The Mounted Rifle units were less esteemed than the other two.

11. A line troop consisted of 112 officers and enlisted men.

12. Klemens Rudnicki, *Na polskim szlaku: wspomnienia z lat 1939–1947* (Wroclaw, PL: Ossolineum, 1990), 20.

13. The HMG troop was equipped with twelve heavy machine guns.

14. Relacje z kampanii wrześniowej: Suwalska Brygada Kawalerii, B.I.18/A, 21, Instytut Polski i Muzeum im. Gen. Sikorskiego (The Polish Institute and Sikorski Museum), hereafter cited as IPMS.

15. The Armored troop had eight armored cars and thirteen light tanks.

16. Relacje z kampanii wrześniowej: Suwalska Brygada Kawalerii, B.I.18/A, 63–65, IPMS. By 1939, a four-regiment cavalry brigade had sixteen 37-mm Bofors anti-tank guns and forty-eight *Wz. 35 Ur* anti-tank rifles.

17. Relacje z kampanii wrześniowej: Suwalska Brygada Kawalerii, B.I.18/A, 21, IPMS. A horse artillery squadron was composed of three or four horse artillery batteries, each with four 75-mm *wz.02/26* guns.

18. Relacje z kampanii wrześniowej: 4 Dywizjon Artylerii Konnej, B.I.18/G, 47, IPMS.

19. Relacje z kampanii wrześniowej: Sztab Suwalskiej Brygady Kawalerii, B.I.18/B, 134, IPMS.

20. There were wagons attached to particular platoons and troops. Each line troop, for example, had seven wagons while the heavy machine guns troops had fourteen. The logistic troop (*szwadron gospodarczy*) of the cavalry regiment was equipped with more than fifty wagons. In total, a regimental wagon train consisted of about 100 wagons. Only part of those were military issue; the rest, in case of war, were mobilized together with horses from the local farms and estates. The quality of wagons drafted into military service differed significantly. The worst situation was usually in the eastern garrisons, which received mostly simple, low-capacity, and fragile ones.

21. Piotr Potomski, *Generał broni Stanisław Władysław Maczek (1892–1994)* (Warsaw: WUW, 2008), 112–15.

22. Only three regiments (1st and 10th Mounted Rifles and 24th Uhlan) were motorized. The thirty-seven remaining horse regiments, together with supporting elements and combat support service units, were assigned to cavalry brigades.

23. Relacje z kampanii wrześniowej: 33 Dywizja Piechoty, Kawaleria Dywizyjna, B.I.15/D, 1–6, IPMS.

24. These tanks were, in fact, lightly armored tankettes that lacked essential reconnaissance equipment like radios.

25. Grzegorz Cydzik, *Ułani, ułani* (Warsaw: MON, 1983), 5–6.

26. Cydzik, 65–71.

27. Rudnicki, *Na polskim szlaku*, 7–8, 10.

28. Rudnicki, 12.

29. Relacje z kampanii wrześniowej: 10 Pułk Ułanów, B.I.17/D, 42–43, IPMS.

30. Relacje z kampanii wrześniowej: 2 Pułk Ułanów, B.I.18/D, 6, IPMS.

31. Relacje z kampanii wrześniowej: Dowódca i dowództwo Podlaskiej BK, B.I.17/A, 4, IPMS.

32. Rudnicki, *Na polskim szlaku*, 54.

33. Marching troop (*szwadron marszowy*) was a cavalry unit formed from the supernumerary called-up reservists, after filling the regiment's wartime headcount. It may have been used to replace casualties or form an entirely new squadron, or assigned independently for some specific tasks. Similarly, there were infantry marching companies or battalions in infantry and marching batteries in artillery.

34. Tym, *Kawaleria w operacji i w walce*, 425.

35. A claim for an exterritorial corridor through the Polish territory was one of the German pretexts to start a war.

36. Leszek Moczulski, *Wojna polska 1939* (Warsaw: Bellona, 2009), 620.

37. Andrzej Lorbiecki and Marcin Wałdoch, *Chojnice 1939* (Warsaw: Bellona, 2014), 244–47.

38. Moczulski, *Wojna polska 1939*, 623–24.

39. Stanisław Koszutski, *Wspomnienia z Różnych Pobojowisk* (London: Wydawnictwo Przeglądu Kawalerii i Broni Pancernej, 1972), 74.

40. Relacje z kampanii wrześniowej: Łączność Podlaskiej Brygady Kawalerii, B.I.17/H, 31, IPMS.

41. Tym, *Kawaleria w operacji i w walce*, 424.

42. Relacje z kampanii wrześniowej: 2 Pułk Ułanów, B.I.18/D, 6, IPMS.

43. Relacje z kampanii wrześniowej: 4 Dywizjon Artylerii Konnej, B.I.18/G, 28–29, IPMS.

44. Rudnicki, *Na polskim szlaku*, 12.

45. Tym, *Kawaleria w operacji i w walce*, 428–32.

46. Rudnicki, *Na polskim szlaku*, 17.

47. Roman Abraham, *Wspomnienia wojenne znad Warty i Bzury* (Warsaw: MON, 1990) 137–54.

48. Rudnicki, *Na polskim szlaku*, 23.

49. Tym, *Kawaleria w operacji i w walce*, 426–27.

50. Relacje z kampanii wrześniowej: 2 Pułk Ułanów, B.I.18/D, 16–17, IPMS.

51. Rudnicki, *Na polskim szlaku*, 17–22.

52. Relacje z kampanii wrześniowej: 4 Dywizjon Artylerii Konnej, B.I.18/G, 46; and 33 Dywizja Piechoty, Kawaleria Dywizyjna, B.I.15/D, 10, IPMS.

53. Relacje z kampanii wrześniowej: 2Pułk Ułanów, B.I.18/D, 13, IPMS.
54. Tym, *Kawaleria w operacji i w walce,* 551.
55. Relacje z kampanii wrześniowej: Suwalska Brygada Kawalerii, B.I.18/A, 46, IPMS.
56. Relacje z kampanii wrześniowej: 14 Dywizjon Artylerii Konnej, B.I.17/F, 56–57; 33 Dywizja Piechoty, Kawaleria Dywizyjna, B.I.15/D, 12; and Łączność Podlaskiej Brygady Kawalerii, B.I.17/H, 56, IPMS.
57. Relacje z kampanii wrześniowej: Łączność Podlaskiej Brygady Kawalerii, B.I.17/H,68-69, IPMS.
58. Relacje z kampanii wrześniowej: Szwadron Pionierów, Szwadron Kolarzy Podlaskiej BK, B.I.17/G, 7, IPMS.
59. Relacje z kampanii wrześniowej: Dowódca i dowództwo Podlaskiej Brygady Kawalerii, B.I.17/A, 28–29; and 9 Pułk Strzelców Konnych, B.I.17/E, 125, IPMS.
60. Relacje z kampanii wrześniowej: Suwalska brygada Kawalerii, B.I.18/A, 47-48, IPMS.
61. Relacje z kampanii wrześniowej: Szwadron Pionierów, Szwadron Kolarzy Podlaskiej BK, B.I.17/G, 4, IPMS.
62. Relacje z kampanii wrześniowej: 14 Dywizjon Artylerii Konnej, B.I.17/F, 60, IPMS.
63. Rudnicki, *Na polskim szlaku*, 53–55.
64. The author dedicates this chapter to the memory of his grandfather, Karol, who as a young boy witnessed the tragic events of 1939.

Chapter 6
Fly by Night: Plataean Evacuation and
Night-Fighting in the Peloponnesian War
Jonathan H. Warner

Although the Spartans' fight to the death at Thermopylae may be among the most famous and sentimentalized military defeats from Classical Greece, an episode from the beginning of the Peloponnesian war may offer a more useful example for contemporary leaders considering defeat and withdrawal rather than a valiant final stand. The small city of Plataea, an ally of Athens, found itself surrounded and outmatched by a Spartan army. In the winter of 428–427 BC, a few hundred Plataeans fled their besieged city under cover of darkness. By carefully planning and executing a retreat, the Plataeans recovered from utter defeat and reconstituted as an important member of a military coalition.

This chapter contributes to the understanding of retreat and combat specialization in antiquity by offering a comprehensive analysis of the success of the Plataeans. It includes hitherto-overlooked connections between the participants in this night retreat and other episodes in the war, arguing that the Plataeans were able to use withdrawal to develop skills in night operations that helped their allies later in the war. Withdrawal under exigent circumstances, although perilous, allows a force not only to survive to fight another day but to improve cohesion and master capabilities in reconnaissance, planning, and coordination that are indispensable to an allied coalition.

The first part of the chapter narrates the escape from the besieged city of Plataea in 428–427 BC. Due to their intelligence-gathering, timing, coordination, and allied support, the Plataeans were able to penetrate the enemy circumvallation, escape the destruction of their city, and find safe haven in Athens, where they could safely plot to avenge their fallen comrades.

The second part of the chapter addresses the connection between the night withdrawal of 428–427 BC and two other events in the war. Just four years earlier, the Plataeans had repulsed a poorly executed night raid from their city, and it is likely that the Plataeans learned the virtues of preparation and initiative from this negative example. Later in the war, in 424, some of them were selected by an Athenian commander for an important nocturnal operation at Nisaea, likely because of their demonstrated proficiency in urban night-fighting. The example of the Plataeans shows how irregular tactics and specializations can emerge from contingent circumstances and experiences, even defeat and withdrawal.

This chapter uses the terms "retreat," "withdrawal," and "evacuation" somewhat interchangeably. The central distinction between the former terms and evacuation depends on whether a force is disengaging from contact with the enemy (retreat or withdrawal) or merely clearing an area of military personnel, materiel, or civilians (evacuation).[1] In the central episode of this chapter, the Plataeans escaped from a lengthy siege; this preplanned movement out of static, prolonged contact with the enemy satisfies the definitions of both retreat/withdrawal and evacuation. On the other hand, the Theban and Athenian retreats discussed toward the end of the chapter constitute "routs;" unlike the withdrawal of the Plataeans, these forces disengaged without planning or cohesion.

The Escape from Plataea

The siege and riveting flight from Plataea are narrated in the third book of Thucydides's *History of the Peloponnesian War*.[2] With only later, derivative accounts, such as those of Diodorus Siculus and Apollodorus of Acharnae to supplement Thucydides's narrative, we might be cautious to accept the historian's presentation of the Plataeans at face value.[3] Still, the historian's access to sources and topographical information lends credence to Thucydides's otherwise-plausible narrative.[4] Regardless, his framing of events and presentation of incidental details conveys important lessons to military leaders and historians interested in retreats.

Plataea, the site of the decisive battle of the Persian Wars, was the stage on which the first phase of the Peloponnesian War, the so-called Archidamian War, began. Thebes and Plataea, Boeotian cities and traditional enemies, were allies of Sparta and Athens, respectively. Peace between the Peloponnesian League, led by Sparta, and the Delian League, under the hegemony of Athens, broke down; in the spring of 431, the Thebans launched a surprise night raid on Plataea, which failed.[5] Although the attack did not "begin the war in any important causal sense," Thucydides marks this as the moment when "the treaty had quite obviously been broken" and both sides prepared for war.[6] After invading Attica during the first two summers of the war and forcing the Athenians to retreat behind their "Long Walls," the Spartan king Archidamus instead marched on Plataea in 429.[7] He offered neutrality if the Plataeans would abandon their alliance, but the Plataeans, after consulting the Athenians, refused.

The Peloponnesians promptly surrounded the city and began a siege.[8] The Plataeans had already evacuated their women, children, and men of

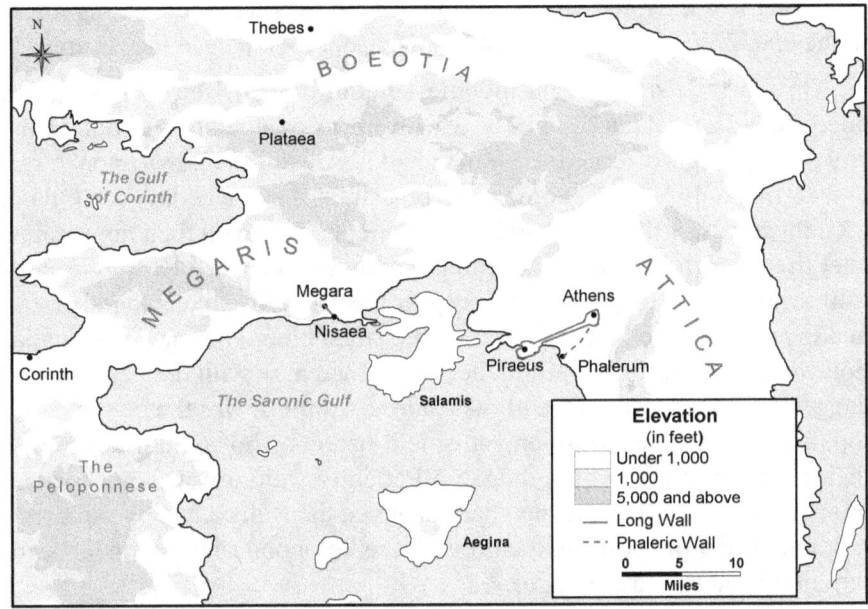

Figure 6.1. Plataea and its surroundings during the Peloponnesian War. Created by Army University Press.

non-military age to Athens, both ensuring the safety of their civilians and prolonging their rations. The only people left were 400 Plataean men, 80 Athenians sent to help, and 110 women, perhaps slaves, to bake bread.[9] The Spartans built ramps against the Plataean walls and surrounded them with circumvallations, but the Plataeans countered with reinforced walls and countermines of their own.[10] With no progress being made, Archidamus left a small Peloponnesian garrison to keep the defenders hemmed into the city.[11]

Relief never came for the defenders. In 428, the Peloponnesians invaded Attica and trapped the Athenians by land. Although a fleet could have navigated up the Gulf of Corinth, the Athenians could hardly afford a campaign of their own to save such a minor city so close to their Boeotian enemies. As the siege wore on, the outnumbered Plataeans saw their supplies dwindle and began to consider their options. An all-out sally stood little chance of success. Barring outside help, surrender or death seemed likely, but a few daring Plataeans—the soothsayer Theaenetus, who perhaps had a family connection to Athens, and the general Eupompides—proposed that they risk escape rather than face death or dishonor at the hands of the Peloponnesians.[12] Many backed out of the plan out of fear, or,

101

according to a later and probably embellished version, after casting lots.[13] In the end, 220 men, roughly half the garrison, took part in the escape.

On a windy, stormy, and moonless night, the garrison formed up on opposite sides of Plataea. Those who were to escape slipped out of the city quietly. Lightly armed, each man had his own task and weapon.[14] The first carried only ladders. Some wore breastplates and had daggers. Others brought spears. Still others carried only shields. Based on their appearance later in the narrative, archers apparently held up the rear.[15] Everyone carefully walked far enough apart to keep from striking weapons together and making noise.[16] The Plataeans approached the Peloponnesian circumvallation with their carefully built ladders. First, the men with breastplates and daggers scaled the wall. One of the leaders, Ammias, was the first over the top, followed by the spearmen and shield-bearers who could give them to their counterparts if fighting began.[17] Patiently waiting for the opportune moment, nearly half of the men had ascended the walls when one soldier's foot knocked a tile down to the ground; the Peloponnesian sentinels heard the sound and raised the alarm.[18]

Just then and surely as part of a previously conceived plan, "the Plataeans who were left behind in the city made a sortie and attacked the wall at a point opposite to the place where their comrades were climbing up."[19] Fearing an all-out attack, the Peloponnesians did not dare abandon any part of the wall. Instead, they dispatched an emergency reserve of 300 men to respond to the disturbance.[20] Meanwhile, the first men up the ladders slew the guards and took up posts from which they could hurl missiles and shoot arrows at approaching men. With the towers secure, the Plataeans smoothly moved and coordinated missile fire at the remaining enemy, and they used their ladders, perhaps as bridges, to make their way across to the outer wall and down to the outer ditch.[21]

At that moment, the 300 Peloponnesians of the emergency reserve arrived bearing torches which made it simultaneously harder to see and easier to be seen by the Plataeans, a result of the human eye's adaptation to low light.[22] The Plataeans dispersed them with the help of arrows and javelins and waded through the icy water to the other side.[23] By the time they were clear of the walls, only 8 of the original 220 Plataeans had failed to escape.[24]

The Plataeans had escaped the city and made it over the besieger's walls, but they still needed to avoid being intercepted on their way to Attica. Foremost among their concerns was that the Peloponnesians would signal Thebes to send reinforcements to intercept them. Their enemies had lit fire-signals to try to alert the Thebans, but the Plataeans inside the city were ready with fires of their own.[25] The confused array of fires interfered with the message and prevented the Thebans from knowing what was happening.[26] To reduce their chance of interception, the Plataeans took the road north to Thebes before turning east and then south-east toward Athens instead of choosing the direct route across Mount Cithaeron, because "they imagined that this road, leading into their enemies' country, would be the very last one that they would be suspected of having taken."[27] They evaded the Peloponnesians sent to pursue them and reached Athens the next day, surely exhausted by their harrowing escape and elated to be reunited with their families in Attica.

Keys to Success

Because of their thorough knowledge of their home terrain and the static nature of the ongoing siege, the Plataeans had the ability to time, prepare, and execute their escape.[28] They carefully observed the disposition of the enemy and planned to attack the most vulnerable point in their circumvallation. Thucydides does not give the exact length of time from the conception of the plot to its execution, but it likely took weeks of planning to account for the necessary deliberation, explanation of the plan and individual roles to all members of the garrison, construction of equipment and preparation of fire signals, practice (such as they could without betraying their intentions), and waiting for the right coincidence of lunar and meteorological conditions.

This last point was perhaps the most important factor in allowing the Plataeans to keep the initiative throughout their operation. Thucydides explicitly states that the Plataeans waited for a night with the right lunar and meteorological conditions, adding later that there was also a substantial amount of snow that night.[29] These weather conditions helped the Plataeans in three critical ways. They had observed beforehand that the Peloponnesians did not man the battlements on rainy nights, but only posted a few sentries in the roofed towers.[30] Fewer guards meant an easier escape. At the same time, the blustery wind drowned out the sound of their footsteps.[31] Finally, cloud-cover must have reduced the light of the stars, and this darkness, which "substitutes for cover and concealment," proved vital when the Plataeans encountered the Peloponnesian reserves.[32] Thucydides says that it was mostly due to the weather that they escaped, but it would have also taken intelligence and patience to identify the most opportune time to attack.[33] It may have helped that one of the Plataean leaders, Theaenetus, was a soothsayer (*mantis*) and may have had rudimentary meteorological and astronomical expertise.[34]

The Plataeans' equipment was also specially chosen for the operation, and the troops were arrayed to traverse obstacles quickly and silently. The Plataeans had all counted the bricks on an unplastered section of wall and, after averaging their results to minimize the possibility of human error, estimated the height of a brick and calculated the height needed for the ladders.[35] The first men up these ladders lacked armor besides the cuirass (*thōrax*), surely meant to maximize their mobility. Likewise, their daggers (*xiphidia*) were ideal for combat on ladders or in the narrow confines of an enemy fortification. These men were followed by soldiers with spears (*doratia*) and then an equal number carrying shields (*aspides*), a careful division of the hoplite panoply between different soldiers. Thucydides even uses the diminutive of "spear" (*doratia* vs. *doru*), perhaps suggesting smaller arms that would not clang together and alert the defenders.[36] The Plataeans carefully stuck to preassigned roles, carrying the minimum amount of equipment to maximize mobility and minimize noise.

The rearguard of archers was critical. Thucydides recounts how the Plataeans, when they encountered the 300 Peloponnesians with torches, not only shot in their direction, but targeted specific parts of their bodies.[37] Classicist Wallace McLeod marshaled a number of historical examples, from Homer down to the eighteenth century, to show "a recurrent connection between the dark of night, the bow, and aiming at lights."[38] In fact, several early-modern archery manuals recommend night target practice to improve accuracy.[39] Perhaps the Plataeans had trained at night in preparation for their mission, practicing "off-centered vision" of targets or closing one eye to preserve "visual purple" (*rhodopsin*, the protein that allows sight in low-light conditions before exposure to bright light).[40]

One of the most peculiar aspects of the Plataean preparation was their choice of footwear. Thucydides reports that the men "only wore shoes on the left foot, to stop them slipping in the mud."[41] Many scholars are skeptical that this "monosandalism" would have worked as Thucydides thought; given the presence of a religious expert in the operation, some have offered ritual explanations, suggesting that the practice reminded the Plataeans of their training in their youth when they may have similarly donned only one shoe in imitation of Greek heroes.[42] As yet another explanation, the Plataeans, who had already shown their capacity for compromise when estimating wall height, were seeking a middle course between shod and unshod. The difficult terrain they had to negotiate could have inspired their asymmetric footwear. Taking time to undo a stuck sandal is time-consuming, so a soldier could instead rely on his bare foot if he encountered a particularly thick patch of mud. At the same time, he could favor his protected foot when traversing splintery ladders, jagged walls, and rocky terrain.[43] Modern fencers, with differential impact to the left and right feet, often prefer extra support on their front foot.[44] By analogy, the Plataeans might have benefited from similar footwear variation, with the left foot being the lead foot in most ancient sword-techniques and thus benefiting from the firmer cushioning of a shoe.[45] Moreover, if there were any metal fittings on their shoes, having one foot unshod could prevent any clanging of metal, an especially important consideration when prioritizing stealth.[46] The Plataeans had carefully planned every detail of the operation, down to their footwear.

The final ingredient of the Plataeans' success was the support and encouragement of their Athenian allies. They only decided to resist the Spartan onslaught after Athens pledged to honor their alliance and defend the city. An Athenian contingent assisted the garrison, and Plataean civilians evacuated to Attica. Athens' support, however, was not entirely high-minded. Both the Plataean civilians in Athens and the Athenian soldiers in Plataea served as collateral to prevent the Plataeans from surrendering their city to the Spartans. And the Athenians in Plataea may have played a decisive role in the choice to retreat from the besieged city. Although Thucydides does not fractionate precisely who stayed behind and who fled the city; an analysis of his numbers reveals that a higher proportion of Athenians than Plataeans joined the endeavor.[47]

Preparation and allied support were indispensable to the Plataeans' successful retreat, but in the course of the war, their retreat may not have had huge strategic significance. The Plataeans who remained succumbed to starvation and surrendered in the following summer (427). In a rare moment of pathos, Thucydides describes how the city was razed with a temple to Hera built in its place.[48] But from another vantage point, the daring night retreat sheds light on the importance of safeguarding experience and specialization within a coalition. The Plataeans who chose to undertake the risky escape self-selected into a cohesive team with strong mutual commitment and resolve to execute a prearranged plan.

The Escape in Context: The Theban Night Raid and Retreat

The failed Theban raid on Plataea in the spring of 431 imparted tactical and strategic lessons from which the Plataeans could draw during their own retreat almost four years later. Before general hostilities had broken out, a small band of Thebans, little more than 300 in number, launched a surprise night attack on Plataea under a waning moon and during a religious festival.[49] The gates were opened by Plataean accomplices who led the Thebans to the agora, where they issued a proclamation and invited the Plataeans to join them and legitimize their coup.[50]

The Plataeans, unable to judge the size of the Theban force due to the darkness, agreed to come to terms; but after realizing that the Thebans were not as numerous as they had first thought, the Plataeans secretly sent word throughout the city.[51] Armed with whatever was at hand, the inhabitants advanced in small groups toward the agora, moving through buildings and alleys to avoid open sight-lines.[52] Just before dawn, the Plataeans sallied forth from their hiding places and fell upon the unsuspecting Thebans. Men rushed into the melee from all sides, and women, slaves, and children hurled stones and tiles from the rooftops.[53] The Plataeans attacked sporadically, and the Theban soldiers held off several waves. The darkness had helped them infiltrate Plataea, but now it prevented them from seeing any means of escape.

Outnumbered and exhausted, most of the Thebans broke and ran through the unfamiliar city. Those who made for the gate were dismayed to find it shut.[54] Some tried in vain to scale the walls; others fled through muddy alleys or large houses, looking for an escape route.[55] Most met their deaths. One group found an unguarded gate, procured an axe, and broke through the crossbar, but the Plataeans caught most of them before they could escape.

The Thebans' botched plan is instructive of the challenges and opportunities of night operations. Rather than using the element of surprise to their advantage, they "grounded arms"—taking up defensive positions in the agora—and announced their presence through a herald.[56] In seizing a central and politically significant space, they privileged optics over good tactics. Knowing their location and strength, the Plataeans surrounded the Thebans and exploited their insufficient topographic knowledge. Had the Thebans eliminated the leaders of the pro-Athenian party, as Nauclides and his men suggested, or in some other active way taken the initiative, they might have prevented the Plataeans from rallying at the edges of the city center. By adopting a passive defensive posture and inviting the Plataeans to join them in the agora instead, the Thebans let a symbolic proclamation derail their chances of keeping the Plataeans in the dark as to the exact tactical situation.

The Thebans' second failure was coalitional. Their Plataean guides largely disappear from Thucydides' narrative after the opening of the gate. These insurgents offered poor advice and shared insufficient topographical and political information. As a result, the Thebans underestimated the popular support for the pro-Athenian party in Plataea. Once the attack had failed, the allied guides did not provide any support to the Thebans, who initiated a chaotic and disastrous retreat.

Finally, poor communication and understanding of the physical landscape exacerbated their situation. The Thebans failed to reconnoiter and secure an escape route in advance. When they scattered down the unfamiliar streets of Plataea, they gave up all ability to communicate and put themselves at the mercy of the city's inhabitants who had built wagon barricades to block off some escape routes.[57] The Plataeans took advantage of their superior knowledge of the terrain:

> Their idea was that if they attacked in daylight, their enemies would be more sure of themselves and would be able to meet them on equal terms, whereas in the night they would not be so confident and would also be at a disadvantage through not knowing the city so well as the Plataeans did.[58]

The Thebans, under the very conditions which demand the most disciplined organization and detailed planning failed to prepare for the contingency of escape.

This botched night raid and disastrous retreat must have left an impression on the citizens and soldiers of Plataeans. Within four short years, the garrison of Plataeans, having learned from their previous experience and their enemies' missteps, executed their own night retreat. Unlike the Thebans of 431, these Plataeans knew the topography and disposition of the enemy, took full advantage of the element of surprise, and maintained unit cohesion even when the enemy were alerted to their presence. A study of night fighting commissioned by the US Army after the Second World War and contributed to by German generals with experience from the Eastern Front concluded that night operations "are inexpedient when a certain minimum amount of orientation is impossible because terrain conditions and the enemy situation are too uncertain."[59] The Plataeans had learned firsthand about this principle that the Thebans failed to understand.

The Escape in Context: The Attack on Nisaea

No accounts remain about what the Plataeans did between 428–427 and 424. If they stayed in Attica, they could have helped guard Athens against the invasions of 427 or 425.[60] The exiles finally arrived on the scene again during Athens' campaign to take Megara.[61] The popular party within Megara had secretly communicated its willingness to betray the city to the Athenian generals, so Athens dispatched a small contingent of hoplites and light troops to Minoa, an island near Megara.[62] From there, they moved to the mainland and prepared to launch their night-attack against Nisaea and the "long walls" leading to Megara.

One of the Athenian generals, Hippocrates, posted his 600 hoplites in some quarry pits. Meanwhile, Demosthenes, another commander, personally led some light-armed Plataeans and *peripoloi* (Athenian recruits between the ages of eighteen and twenty) closer to the city near an otherwise-unknown shrine to Enyalius, the war god.[63] Seeing that their Megarian contacts had blocked the gate with a cart, they "came out of their ambush, running as fast as they could, so as to get there before the gates were shut again and while the cart was still in the entrance to stop them being shut."[64] Meanwhile, the Megarian accomplices slew the guards at the gate, but more Peloponnesians, alerted by the alarm, came rushing to defend the compromised walls. At just that moment, the Plataeans and *peripoloi* broke through the gate and defeated the Peloponnesians, allowing Hippocrates' infantry to enter. The rest of the garrison soon fled into Nisaea.

The larger attack on neighboring Megara did not go as well for Athens. Their Megarian allies failed to open the gates before the arrival of the Athenian army, and a Peloponnesian army arrived and cut short their hopes of taking Megara itself.[65] Even so, the Athenians besieged and quickly took Nisaea, and then commemorated their victory at the long walls, spearheaded by the Plataeans, with a trophy.[66] In a fitting exchange at the peace negotiations of 421—because the Peloponnesians insisted on keeping Plataea—the Athenians held onto Nisaea, itself captured with the aid of Plataean exiles.[67]

Nisaea was not the strategic boon that the Athenians had hoped for; much like the escape from Plataea, its capture sheds light on the importance of tactical and coalitional expertise. At a tactical level, the attack had the hallmarks of a successful night operation: careful timing, the element of surprise, and preparation for the exigencies of nocturnal conditions. The details of the attack were closely held secrets.[68] The vanguard of Plataeans was lightly armed to rush in more easily.[69] Megarian insurrectionists had coordinated with Demosthenes ahead of time to block the gate, and, in a peculiar detail, had covered their bodies in oil to be identified more easily by night.[70]

But aside from these tactical insights, the presence of the Plataeans suggests a conscious choice of experts in night operations. Given Plataea's small population and the even smaller remnant in exile, a substantial proportion of the able-bodied Plataeans available in 424 would have been the very men who orchestrated the daring night retreat of 428–427 BC.[71] Many of those same troops had also repulsed the ill-fated Theban night raid of

431. In both of those engagements, the Plataeans had already demonstrated an ability to react to unforeseen circumstances while maintaining unit cohesion. Until now scholars have not made the corollary argument that their presence at Nisaea may have been the result of deliberate selection. Against the backdrop of "the Greeks' entrenched military amateurism," the Plataeans at Megara stand out as a suggestive instance of the ad hoc use of tactical expertise.[72]

The personal participation of Demosthenes in the night attack, obliquely referenced by Thucydides, suggests a high degree of involvement in its planning and execution.[73] It is plausible that Demosthenes, the recent victor at Sphacteria, would have had the clout to select troops for his raid, and a deliberate choice of forces with nocturnal experience would be consistent with his innovative tactics and troop selection—"the first Greek general to begin regularly to use tricks to overcome numerical, strategic, or armament inferiority."[74] The supplement of *peripoloi*, added "in addition" to the Plataeans, is another suggestive detail.[75] Demosthenes may have added them to the operation to supplement the veteran Plataeans with youth and agility. The Plataeans' shared national identity and combat experience could have bolstered bonding, commitment, and resolve, and their experience in previous nocturnal engagements offered a foundation on which the vanguard force could build confidence and cohesion.[76]

If Demosthenes deliberately chose a Plataean contingent to draw on the night-fighting experience of some veterans, it would fit with a pattern of commanders hand-picking men for such attacks. Epic and biblical accounts depict dramatic night raids in which soldiers were selected for night operations based on age and competence.[77] More reliable sources attest the practice in Classical Greece. Diodorus called the Thebans who infiltrated Plataea "picked men" (*epilektous*).[78] Prior to the Peloponnesian War, there are eight reported instances of night operations in Greece, and many of these involved conscious selection.[79] In one noteworthy episode recorded by Polyaenus, a late source, king Elnes of Arcadia (early sixth century BC) "sent his choicest troops to a peak above the enemy and ordered them to attack in the middle of the night" while old men and young boys lit fires as a diversion.[80] The Greek for "choicest troops" (*hosoi men en akmēi*) connotes youthfulness, perhaps reminiscent of Demosthenes's experienced Plataeans and young *peripoloi*.

A decade later, Demosthenes hastily prepared for a night assault on the Epipolae, the heights overlooking Syracuse. Perhaps overconfident, he took with him masons, carpenters, and equipment to fortify his position should he prove successful.⁸¹ The attack, "the only full-scale night-battle (*nyktomachia*) between large armies in this war," was a complete failure, and the Athenians were soon routed, unable to communicate or identify friend from foe.⁸² The retreat was a disaster:

> The way down again from Epipolae was only a narrow one, and in the pursuit many men lost their lives by throwing themselves down from the cliffs. As for those who got down safely from the heights to the plain, most of them . . . escaped to the camp, but there were a number of those who had recently arrived who lost their way and wandered about the country. When day came, these were rounded up and killed by the Syracusan cavalry.⁸³

The experienced Plataeans, present in the Sicilian expedition but nowhere to be found in the *nyktomachia*, were sorely missed.⁸⁴

Contemporary Lessons

In the 431 Theban raid and their own 428–427 BC retreat, the Plataeans cultivated unit cohesion and developed abilities in intelligence gathering, operational planning, and coordination of different responsibilities. They also honed expertise peculiar to night fighting and exhibited equipment and tactics suited to nocturnal conditions. These Plataeans appear to have drawn on this experience in the night assault on Nisaea in 424. Given how little training and specialization there was in Classical Greek armies, the Plataeans show how retreat could be an important factor in developing and preserving tactical expertise and unit cohesion.

History rarely offers simple morals or straightforward lessons, but ancient tactics and strategy can prove instructive, especially as greater distance severs past events from contemporary passions and prejudices. Just as this remnant of Plataea reconstituted as a valuable ally of Athens, modern leaders should not forget their own vulnerable partners, whose valiant efforts in defeat may yield opportunities for future success. One might think of parallel situations today. In Northern Iraq and Syria, the Kurds have often been abandoned by their American allies.⁸⁵ An American diplomat recently noted that the acquiescence of Turkish incursions caused the United States to "[lose] significant leverage and [inherit] a shrunken, less stable platform to support both our [counterterrorism] efforts and the mission of finding a comprehensive political solution for Syria."⁸⁶ Whatever the strategic calculations when the United States chooses to intervene, there is a potential strategic benefit in welcoming partners who possess special skills and bonds of commitment forged by a perilous escape from conflict. Even a modest, largely symbolic show of support for a minor ally, such as Athens offered to Plataea, can safeguard tactical expertise and coalitional capital for future campaigns. The Athenians could not save the Plataeans for strategic reasons, but the Athenians sent a token relief force and welcomed Plataean evacuees, even in the wake of a deadly plague. They did not foresee the Plataean contribution at Nisaea but anticipated there would be long-term strategic benefits to such a relationship. Similarly, the United States might offer special immigrant visas to dedicated and skilled partners, such as Afghan translators and guides.

To an ancient Greek, few things could be worse than losing one's homeland. Those who suffer disasters abroad can at least rest assured that their homes, temples, and families are safe, but if they should fail in defense of their city, "no hope of salvation would be left."[87] From this perspective, the Plataeans' is a sad story interrupted by a daring but largely inconsequential retreat. Even in exile, though, they could maintain hope of rebuilding elsewhere, as other Greek communities had.[88] They returned home for only a short interlude (386–73) before finally reestablishing their *polis* in 338, more than ninety years after they had first fled.[89] In the interim, the Athenians gave the Plataeans legal protections and a safe haven, first offering Scione as a new home in 421 and then granting citizenship rights in 373, perhaps earlier.[90] All that time, Athenian orators trumpeted the generosity of their city to the Plataeans, who could be seen frequenting the cheese market and participating in civic life.[91]

This Plataean example suggests that strategic considerations can also buttress the moral and humanitarian case for supporting vulnerable allies. It sends a message of solidarity, a reminder that retreat can offer a safe harbor from which partners may thrive and avenge their losses. Even if geopolitical realities prevent direct intervention, as was the case for the Athenians at Plataea, a generous refugee policy offers a refuge to which allies may flee if their enemies prevail. Just as the Athenians broadcasted their support for the Plataeans in the fourth century, the welcoming of allies in retreat is a testament to a military power's reliability in the worst of circumstances.[92]

Notes

1. Compare NATO's distinction between a "withdrawal operation" ("A planned operation in which a force in contact disengages from an enemy force," from *NATOTerm: The Official NATO Terminology Database*, 2021, https://nso.nato.int/natoterm/content/nato/pages/home.html?lg=en, hereafter *NATOTerm*, AAP-06, AAP-39) and an "evacuation" ("The clearance of personnel, animals, or materiel from a given locality," from *NATOTerm*, AP-39). Although the escape also bears some similarities to a breakout, this term is not used as the Plataeans' chief strategic objective was withdrawal to Athens rather than continued engagement in the area. Compare NATO's definition of a breakout as "an operation conducted by an encircled force to regain freedom of movement or contact with friendly units. It differs from other attacks only in that a simultaneous defence in other areas of the perimeter must be maintained" (from *NATOTerm*, AAP-39).

2. H. Stuart Jones and J. E. Powell, ed., *Thucydidis Historiae*, emended ed., 2 vols. (Oxford: Clarendon Press, 1942), hereafter cited as Th., 2.71–79, 3.20–24, and 3.52–68. All citations of ancient sources follow the abbreviations in the *Liddell, Scott, and Jones Greek-English Lexicon* (*LSJ*). All quotations of Thucydides come from Rex Warner, trans., *History of the Peloponnesian War* (Baltimore: Penguin Books, 1954) unless otherwise noted.

3. Diodorus Siculus 12.56, in *Library of History,* vol. IV, ed. and trans. C. H. Oldfather (Cambridge, MA: Harvard University Press, 1946), hereafter cited as D.S.; and Pseudo-Demosthenes, 59.101–3, in *Orations*, vol. VII, ed. and trans. A. T. Murray (Cambridge, MA: Harvard University Press, 1939), hereafter cited as D.

4. Given Thucydides's presence in Athens prior to his exile, his detailed Plataean narrative, and his own statements about his historical method (Th., 1.22.2), he likely spoke with Plataeans who had escaped by night or survived the sack. See Michael F. Quinn, "Beyond the Phalanx: Hoplites at War in Thucydides' History of the Peloponnesian War, 432–404 BC" (PhD diss., University of Washington, Seattle, 2010), 159; N. K. Rutter, *Thucydides: Books III-V* (London: Bristol Classical Press 1996), 5; and Andreas Konecny, Vassilis Aravantinos, and Ron Marchese, *Plataiai: Archäologie und Geschichte einer boiotischen Polis* (Vienna: Österreichisches Archäologisches Institut, 2013), 61. Interestingly, the patronym of one of the Plataean leaders—Eupompides, son of Daimachus—matches that of a fourth-century writer of a lost treatise on siegecraft as observed by Simon Hornblower, *A Commentary on Thucydides*, 3 vols. (Oxford: Clarendon Press, 1991–2008), 1:405–6; see Felix Jacoby, *Fragmente der griechischen Historiker* (Berlin: Weidmann, 1923), nos. 65, 66, and 716. It is possible that these men belonged to the same clan and carried on a family history of the escape from Plataea, oral or written. Thucydides and even Diodorus could have had access to this narrative tradition. Although archaeologists have not found material remains of the siege-works, the topography of Plataea's southern fortifications is a plausible site for a siege ramp described by Thucydides, and the

surrounding environs are accurately described in Konecny et al., *Plataiai,* and Th., 2.75-7 3.24, 3.68. This does not entirely discount a rhetorical and philosophical reading; see Bernard J. Dobski, "Escape from Plataea: Political and Intellectual Liberation in Thucydides's *History*," *Philosophy and Literature* 42, no. 1 (2018): 201–16.

5. Th., 2.2–5.

6. Jeffrey S. Rusten, *The Peloponnesian War,* Thucydides Book II (Cambridge: Cambridge University Press, 1989), 97; and Th., 2.7.1.

7. Th., 2.71.

8. Th., 2.71–74.

9. Th., 2.78.3–4 with Robert B. Strassler, ed., *The Landmark Thucydides: A Comprehensive Guide to the Peloponnesian War*, trans. Richard Crawley (New York: Simon & Schuster, 1996).

10. Th., 2.75–78; and Yvon Garlan, 1974. *Recherches de poliorcétique grecque* (Athens: Bibliothèques de l'Ecole française d'Athènes et de Rome, 1974), 111–2. A circumvallation is a double rampart erected around 100 meters from walls.

11. Th., 2.78.1–2.

12. Th., 3.20.1–2; Pausanias, Description of Greece, vol. I, ed. and trans. W. H. S. Jones (Cambridge, MA: Harvard University Press, 1918), 1.27.5; and Gabriel Herman, "Nikias, Epimenides and the Question of Omissions in Thucydides," *The Classical Quarterly*, New Series 39, no. 1 (1989): 91.

13. D., 59.103.

14. Th., 3.22.3.

15. Th., 3.23.2, 3.23.4, and 3.24.2.

16. Th., 3.22.2.

17. Th., 3.22.3.

18. Th., 3.22.4–5; and Raymond Weil and Jacqueline de Romilly, *Thucydide: La Guerre du Péloponnèse, Livre III* (Paris: Les Belles Lettres, 1969, 3:14.

19. Th., 3.22.5.

20. Th., 3.22.6–7.

21. Th., 3.23.1; E. L. Harrison, "The Escape from Plataea: Thucydides III, *Classical Quarterly* 9 (1959): 30–33; and Paul Bentley Kern, *Ancient Siege Warfare* (Bloomington, IN: Indiana University Press, 1999), 110.

22. Th., 3.23.4; and Andrew N. Morris, *Night Combat Operations* (Fort Leavenworth, KS: Combat Studies Institute, 1985, 33–34.

23. Th., 3.23.4–5.

24. Th., 3.24.2. None are mentioned who died; Thucydides only says that some turned around and one archer was captured at the trench.

25. Th., 3.22.7–8.

26. For discussion, see Daniel Walker Moore, "Proof through the Night: Representations of Fire-Signaling in Greek Historiography," *Histos: The On-Line Journal of Ancient Historiography* 11 (2017): 115. Polyaenus, adds that the types of fire-signals were different and that this was the cause of the difficulty;

see *Stratagems of War*, ed. J. Melber, trans. P. Krentz and E. L. Wheeler (Chicago: Ares Publishers, 1994), 6.19.2, hereafter cited as Polyaen.

27. Th., 3.24.1.

28. For a literary analysis of this aspect of Thucydides's siege of Plataea, see Jacqueline de Romilly, *The Mind of Thucydides*, trans. Elizabeth Trapnell Rawlings, ed. Hunter R. Rawlings III and Jeffrey S. Rusten (Ithaca, NY: Cornell University Press, 2012), 98.

29. Th., 3.22.1, 3.23.5.

30. Th., 3.21.4.

31. Th., 3.22.1.

32. Morris, *Night Combat Operations*, 4; and Th., 3.23.4.

33. Th., 3.23.5.

34. Th., 3.20.1; see Herodotus, *The Persian Wars*, vol. IV, ed. and trans. A. D. Godley (Cambridge, MA: Harvard University Press, 1925), hereafter cited as Hdt., 8.27.3, for another *mantis* devising a night raid.

35. Th., 3.20.3–4. The height needed to exceed that of the wall (Weil and de Romilly, *Thucydide*, 3:87). It is uncertain whether they used the arithmetic mean, median, or mode. See Aristotle, *Politics*, ed. and trans. H. Rackham (Cambridge, MA: Harvard University Press, 1932), 3.11 for an ancient discussion of the wisdom of crowds in problem-solving.

36. Thucydides elsewhere uses δοράτιον once of missile weapons (4.34.3) and once generically of spears (7.84.3). Other examples of δοράτιον from the fifth century cannot prove a clear distinction between δοράτιον and δόρυ. Herodotus used the word generically (1.34.3) as did Aristophanes as described in *Peace*, ed. and trans. Jeffrey Henderson (Cambridge, MA: Harvard University Press, 1998), 553. Xenophon employed the term in a sense almost like "pole," as noted in Xenophon, *Anabasis,* ed. Carleton L. Brownson (New York: G. P. Putnam's Sons, 1932), 224–25). Aeneas Tacticus used the word to describe the smuggling of arms into a city (29.6). Much later, Onasander used the word for a method of signaling (26.1). In most of these examples, δοράτιον refers to a spear as an object to be carried and moved rather than as a deadly weapon.

37. Th., 3.23.4.

38. Wallace McLeod, "The Bow at Night: An Inappropriate Weapon?" *Phoenix* 42, no. 2 (1988): 123.

39. McLeod 1988, 121–22; and Center of Military History (CMH) Publication 104-3, *Night Combat* (Washington, DC: US Army Center of Military History, 1986), 43–45.

40. Department of the Army, Field Manual (FM) 21-75, *Combat Training of the Individual Soldier and* Patrolling (Washington, DC: 1962), 44-8; and Morris, *Night Combat Operations*, 33–34. For an ancient awareness of *nyctalopia* (inability to see in low-light), see the remedies in Hippocrates, *Coan Prenotions, Anatomical and Minor Clinical Writings*, ed. and trans. Paul Potter (Cambridge, MA: Harvard University Press, 2010), hereafter cited as Hp.

41. Th., 3.22.2.

42. Pierre Lévêque and Pierre Vidal-Naquet, "Épaminondas pythagoricien ou le problème tactique de la droite et de la gauche," *Historia: Zeitschrift Für Alte Geschichte* 9 (1960): 298; Pierre Vidal-Naquet, *The Black Hunter: Forms of Thought and Forms of Society in the Greek World* (Baltimore: Johns Hopkins University Press, 1986), 64, 69–70, 75–76; Edmunds 1984, 71–75; and Sue Blundell, "One Shoe off and One Shoe on: The Motif of Monosandalism in Classical Greece," in *Shoes, Slippers, and Sandals: Feet and Footwear in Classical Antiquity*, ed. Sadie Pickup and Sally Waite (Boca Raton, FL: Routledge, 2018), 218–21.

43. Blundell, 219.

44. Craig Harkins, "The Comprehensive Guide to Fencing Shoes," Fencing.net, 2 November 2016, https://www.fencing.net/4197/the-comprehensive-guide-to-fencing-shoes/.

45. Brian F. Cook, "Footwork in Ancient Greek Swordsmanship," *Metropolitan Museum Journal* 24 (1989), 58–60; and Simon James, *Rome and the Sword: How Warriors and Weapons Shaped Roman History* (New York: Thames & Hudson, 2011), 78. In contrast, see Vegetius, *Epitoma rei militaris*, ed. M. Reeve (Oxford: Oxford University Press, 2004), 1.20.23, which identifies the right foot as the lead foot. The Hippocratic *On Joints* (Hp. *Art.* 62) specifically mentions the greater support of "mud shoes" (*pēlopatides*), as noted in Hippocrates, *On Wounds in the Head in the Surgery, On Fractures. On Joints. Mochlicon*, ed. and trans. E. T. Withington (Cambridge, MA: Harvard University Press, 1928).

46. Elizabeth M. Greene, "Metal Fittings on the Vindolanda Shoes: Footwear and Evidence for Podiatric Knowledge in the Roman World," in *Shoes, Slippers, and Sandals: Feet and Footwear in Classical Antiquity*, ed. Sadie Pickup and Sally Waite (Boca Raton, FL: Routledge, 2018). See Department of the Army, FM 21-75, 22–24, 206 for advice to secure all loose metal.

47. Two hundred or more Plataeans and 25 Athenians were left when the city surrendered (Th., 3.68.2). When the retreat happened, 212 escaped, 1 was captured, and 267 remained. If Thucydides's starting numbers are accurate (400 Plataean men and 80 Athenians), at most 42 died over the course of the siege. Taking this number of deaths and assuming casualties were evenly distributed following the retreat between the remaining Athenians and Plataeans, 30 Athenians were left behind in the city after the retreat. This would mean 50 Athenians were part of the escape-group, a much higher proportion of the total number of Athenians (63 percent) than the proportion of the Plataeans that chose to join the escape (41 percent).

48. Th., 3.68.4, with Hornblower, *A Commentary on Thucydides*, 1:465. D.S., 12.56.6, closes with a similarly emotional statement.

49. Th., 2.4.2, 3.56, 65. In contrast, Hdt. 7.233 gives the number 400.

50. Th., 2.2.4, 2.4.8. An agora is a public open space used for assemblies and markets.

51. Th., 2.3.2. Aeneas Tacticus, 2.3–4, probably without an independent source, reasons that the Plataeans intentionally decided to entertain negotiations

to give time to prepare an attack, as noted in Illinois Greek Club, ed. and trans., *Aeneas Tacticus, Asclepiodotus, and Onasander* (Cambridge, MA: Harvard University Press, 1923), hereafter cited as Aen.Tact..

52. Th., 2.3.4. Aen.Tact., 2.4, adds the detail, absent from Thucydides, that the Plataeans moved in twos and threes to avoid drawing attention to themselves. On the agora in urban fighting, see John W. I. Lee, "Urban Warfare in the Classical Greek World," in *Makers of Ancient Strategy: From the Persian Wars to the Fall of Rome*, ed. Victor Davis Hanson (Princeton, NJ: Princeton University Press, 2010), 145.

53. Th., 2.4.2 lists only women and slaves while D.S., 12.41.6 mentions slaves and children. On tiles in urban combat, see William D. Barry, "Roof Tiles and Urban Violence in the Ancient World," *Greek, Roman, and Byzantine Studies* 37, no. 1 (1996), 55–74.

54. Th., 2.4.3.

55. Th., 2.4.4–7.

56. Th., 2.2.4. On this idiom, see *LSJ*, s.v. τίθημι, A.10.a.

57. Th., 2.3.3. Unlike Thucydides, Aeneas Tacticus (2.6) directly attributes the Thebans' confusion while navigating the city to the presence of the barricades.

58. Th., 2.3.4.

59. CMH Publication 104-3, *Night Combat*, 1.

60. Th., 3.26, 4.2. The invasion of 426 was called off due to an earthquake.

61. For an overview of the diplomatic and strategic situation, see Donald Kagan, *The Archidamian War* (Ithaca, NY: Cornell University Press, 1990), 260–78.

62. Th., 4.66-67.

63. Th., 4.67.2; Strassler, *The Landmark Thucydides*, 259; and Hornblower, *A Commentary on Thucydides*, 2:234–35.

64. Th., 4.67.4.

65. Th., 4.68, 4.70–74.

66. Th., 4.69, 4.67.5.

67. Th., 5.17.2.

68. Th., 4.67.2.

69. Th., 4.67.2.

70. Th., 4.67.3–4, 4.68.5. Contrasting information is provided in Hdt., 8.27.3.

71. Iain A. F. Bruce, "Plataea and the Fifth-Century Boeotian Confederacy," *Phoenix* 22 (1968): 198; and Andreas Konecny, Michael J. Boyd, Ronald T. Marchese, and Vassilis Aravantinos. "The Urban Scheme of Plataiai in Boiotia: Report on the Geophysical Survey, 2005–2009," *Hesperia: The Journal of the American School of Classical Studies at Athens* 81, no. 1 (2012): 135. Identification inferred by David Cartwright, *A Historical Commentary on Thucydides* (Ann Arbor, MI: University of Michigan Press, 1997), 183. In contrast, the more equivocal remarks in Quinn, "Beyond the Phalanx," 159, give a nod to their experience in urban fighting.

72. Roel Konijnendijk, *Classical Greek Tactics: A Cultural History* (Leiden, NL: Brill, 2018), 70.

73. Th., 4.67.2 ("οἱ δὲ μετὰ τοῦ Δημοσθένους τοῦ ἑτέρου στρατηγοῦ Πλαταιῆς τε ψιλοὶ καὶ ἕτεροι περίπολοι ἐνήδρευσαν") and 4.67.5 ("καὶ πρῶτον μὲν οἱ περὶ τὸν Δημοσθένη Πλαταιῆς τε καὶ περίπολοι ἐσέδραμον").

74. A. W, Gomme, Antony Andrewes, and Kenneth Dover, *A Historical Commentary on Thucydides,* 5 vols. (Oxford, UK: Clarendon Press 1945–81), 3:530; and Graham Wrightson, *Combined Arms Warfare in Ancient Greece: From Homer to Alexander the Great and His Successors* (London: Routledge, 2019), 108. For more on Demosthenes's inventiveness, see Joseph Roisman, "The General Demosthenes and His Use of Military Surprise," in *Historia* (Stuttgart: F. Steiner, 1993); and Quinn, "Beyond the Phalanx," 260.

75. Th., 4.67.2, "Πλαταιῆς τε ψιλοί και ἕτεροι περίπολοι" (author's translation). For this meaning of ἕτερος, see Johannes Classen and Julius Steup, *Thukydides* (Berlin: Weidmann, 1885), 4:134.

76. Department of the Army, Army Techniques Publication (ATP) 6-22.6, *Army Team Building* (Washington, DC: 2015), 3-33: "Every new mission gives the team leader a chance to strengthen internal bonds and challenge the team to reach new levels of performance, accomplishment, and confidence."

77. Hom. *Il.*, 10.131–348, as noted in *Iliad:* vol. I, ed. and trans. A. T. Murray, rev. William F. Wyat (Cambridge, MA: Harvard University Press, 1924); Gen. 14:14–15; and Judg. 7. In contrast, see Smith-Christopher 2008 for a skeptical reading of biblical battle narratives.

78. Th., 2.2; and D.S., 12.41.4.

79. Drawn from the list of deceptive actions found in Peter Krentz, "Deception in Archaic and Classical Greek Warfare," in *War and Violence in Ancient Greece*, ed. Hans van Wees (Swansea, UK: Classical Press of Wales, 2000), 167–200. London: Duckworth and the Classical Press of Wales 2000, 183–99. Polyaen, 1.8 (580–560 BC, the Arcadians attack Lacedaemonians at night); Polyaen, 1.11 (Lacedaemonians attempt to take Tegea by night); Plutarch, *Moralia:* vol. III, ed. and trans. Frank Cole Babbitt (Cambridge, MA: Harvard University Press, 1931), 223ab (Cleomenes attacks Argives at night); Hdt. 8.27 (490–480, Phocians covered in gypsum attack Thessalians by night); Frontinus, *Stratagems, Aqueducts of Rome*, ed. Mary B. McElwain, trans. Charles E. Bennett (Cambridge, MA: Harvard University Press, 1925); *Strat.* 3.2.5 (470, Cimon captures a city by luring the Carians out by lighting a fire); Th., 1.115.4 (440, Samian exiles and mercenaries cross over to Samos by night and take control of the island); and Polyaen., 6.53 (437, Hagnon makes a truce and secretly works by night to fortify his position). Krentz leaves out the Spartan night attack at Thermopylae on Xerxes's tent, as noted in D.S., *Library of History*, vol. IV, ed. and trans. C. H. Oldfather (Cambridge, MA: Harvard University Press, 1946), 11.10), presumably because he considers it ahistorical.

80. Polyaen., 1.8: "Ἕλνης, βασιλεὺς Ἀρκάδων, Τεγέαν πορθούντων Λακεδαιμονίων, ὅσοι μὲν ἐν ἀκμῇ, κατὰ κορυφῆς ἔπεμψε τῶν πολεμίων νυκτὶ

μέση κελεύσας ἐπιθέσθαι· ὅσοι δὲ γέροντες καὶ παῖδες, τούτους ἐκέλευσε πρὸ τῆς πόλεως τὴν ἴσην ὥραν φυλάξαντας πῦρ ἀνακαῦσαι μέγιστον" (author's translation). For the date, see Krentz, 184 and 199 with Hdt. 1.65–66, as noted in *The Persian Wars*, vol. I, ed. and trans. A. D. Godley (Cambridge, MA: Harvard University Press, 1920).

81. Th., 7.44.2.

82. Th., 7.44.1 (author's translation).

83. Th., 7.44.8.

84. See the expeditionary catalog, Th. 7.57.5: "Only the Plataeans, though Boeotians themselves, fought against the other Boeotians for the good reason that they were their enemies." Had they fought at the Epipolae, a battle in which the enemy Boeotians are explicitly mentioned (7.43.7), Thucydides likely would have mentioned them.

85. Steven A. Cook, "There's Always a Next Time to Betray the Kurds," *Foreign Policy*, 11 October 2019. https://foreignpolicy.com/2019/10/11/kurds-betrayal-syria-erdogan-turkey-trump/.

86. William V. Roebuck, "Present at the Catastrophe: Standing By as Turks Cleanse Kurds in Northern Syria and De-Stabilize our D-ISIS Platform in the Northeast," *New York Times*, 7 November 2019, https://www.nytimes.com/2019/11/07/us/politics/memo-syria-trump-turkey.html.

87. Aen.Tact., praef.2 (author's translation). Isoc., vol. III, ed. and trans. La Rue Van Hook (Cambridge, MA: Harvard University Press, 1945), 14.55, offers a similar sentiment regarding the Plataeans.

88. As an example, Hdt. 1.169–71.

89. Samuel David Gartland, "New Boiotia? Exiles, Landscapes, and Kings," in *Boiotia in the Fourth Century B.C*, ed. Samuel David Gartland (Philadelphia: University of Pennsylvania Press, 2016), 149.

90. Th., 3.55.3, 5.32.1; Xenophon, *Hellenica, Volume II*, ed. and trans. Carleton L. Brownson (Cambridge, MA: Harvard University Press, 1921), 6.3.1; and D.S. 15.46.4-6. A perhaps earlier date is argued for by Konstantinos A. Kapparis, "The Athenian Decree for the Naturalisation of the Plataeans," *Greek, Roman and Byzantine Studies* 36, no. 4 (1995): 359–78.

91. Isoc. vol. I, ed. and trans. George Norlin (Cambridge, MA: Harvard University Press, 1928), 4.109, 14; D., 59.94–107; Lysias, *Orations,* ed. and trans. W. R. M. Lamb (Cambridge, MA: Harvard University Press, 1930), 23.6; and Stephen D. Lambert, Voula N. Bardani, and Stephen V. Tracy, ed*., Inscriptiones Graecae II et III: Inscriptiones Atticae Euclidis anno posteriors*, 3rd ed. (Berlin: Berlin-Brandenburg Academy, 2012), 1 345, 1 352, 1 480.

92. The author would like to thank the peer reviewer for offering helpful comments and suggesting improvements as well as Barry Strauss, Peter Osorio, Kathleen Garland, Mary Danisi, and Evan Allen for their valuable feedback on early versions of this chapter.

Chapter 7
Hülsen's Retreat: The Campaign in Saxony, August–October 1760
Alexander S. Burns

During the European portion of the Seven Years War, the Prussian Army of Lt. Gen. Johann Dietrich von Hülsen conducted a defensive retreat across the electorate of Saxony between August and October 1760. Despite having his forces outnumbered by more than three to one, Hülsen managed to preserve his own army. Hülsen's retreat demonstrates the possibilities that a small, veteran, and motivated army can realize when led against (or perhaps, away from) a larger, less-experienced force. During the retreat, Hülsen skillfully led his troops in the Battle of Strehla, inflicting a sharp tactical defeat on his Austrian opponents before retreating to yet another strong defensive position. Although expelled from the province of Saxony by the end of the campaign, Hülsen bought time for the main Prussian Army commanded by King Frederick II "the Great" to arrive and reclaim this vital province. Hülsen repeatedly utilized excellent terrain analysis to protect his small army throughout this retreat in the face of overwhelming odds. In doing so, Hülsen demonstrated the pinnacle of military art in his time: conducting a skillful retreat in the face of a superior enemy while seizing excellent defensive positions to play for time and inflict greater losses on the larger enemy forces.[1]

This campaign offers historians the opportunity to study the retreat of a small but veteran army which tried to play for time against a larger, but less-experienced opponent. Despite occurring at the very dawn of the modern period, the autumn 1760 campaign in Saxony offers military lessons for commanders moving into the middle decades of the twenty-first century. Additionally, although the intricacies of European power politics may seem disconnected from US Army history, there is a connection between the 1760 campaign and the United States: Friedrich Wilhelm—Freiherr de Steuben—was the famous "Baron von Steuben" who served in George Washington's Continental Army, likely also served as an officer on Hülsen's staff during this campaign.[2]

The Seven Years War, even just in Europe, was fought in diverse natural environments. Ranging from the Hessen area of what is today Germany and was then the Holy Roman Empire, the fighting spread across German Central Europe with battlegrounds in modern Germany, the Czech Republic, Poland, and the Kaliningrad Oblast of the Russian Federation.

Broadly, the forces of Frederick II of Prussia—allied with Hessen-Kassel, Hanover, Great Britain, and smaller western German principalities—fought against the Austrians, French, Russians, Swedes, and forces of the Holy Roman Empire, the *Reichsarmee*. This chapter discusses the 1760 campaign fought between the Prussians, Austrians, and *Reichsarmee* in the Saxony electorate.

Frederick II targeted the Saxon electorate as part of a 1756 pre-emptive strike against a large enemy coalition; indeed, this action started the European Seven Years War. The forces of both coalitions subsequently fought over Saxony, which, while occupied, provided the Prussians a great deal of materiel and personnel resources. Saxony was bisected by the River Elbe, which formed an important communications backbone and a barrier to movement through the province. Because of its good soil, the western side of the Elbe was fertile country before the Seven Years War. This flat land marked by wheat, barley, and corn; forests and hills broke up the landscape, particularly near the river itself.[3] By August 1760, Friedrich Michael, Count Palatine of Zweibrücken-Birkenfeld (Zweibrücken), commanded the *Reichsarmee* and Austrian forces attempting to liberate Saxony. Through training and leadership, Zweibrücken had done much to restore the *Reichsarmee*'s reputation after its embarrassing defeat at Rossbach by Frederick's Prussians in 1757. Zweibrücken, having already liberated many large Saxony towns such as Leipzig, prepared to drive the Prussians from the electorate entirely. Starting from their entrenched camp at Plauen in the extreme south of Saxony, Zweibrücken's 30,000 men advanced on Hülsen's Prussians, who were defending Meissen.

In August 1760, Frederick II had taken the main royal army into the neighboring province of Silesia, leaving General Hülsen to defend Meissen with an outnumbered army of 12,000 men. Hülsen, aged sixty-seven, had been a regimental officer during the last major war in the 1740s, and only attained army command as a result of good performance in the current war. At the Battle of Kolin in 1757, Hülsen's advanced guard fought obstinately in a losing battle, earning Frederick's praise. Hülsen had likewise fought with personal courage at the Prussian defeats of Kay and Kunersdorf, and his victorious days still lay ahead. By 9 August 1760, two armies, representative of the middle years of the Seven Years War, moved toward a clash in Saxony.

The Contending Forces

For much of the mid-twentieth century, both German and Anglophone historians contended that the Prussian Army—and eighteenth-century armies generally—were composed of unwilling recruits who feared their cane-wielding officers and were only kept together by rigid attention to the minutiae of military drill. Our new understanding of the Prussian Army, gleaned from the work of scholars such as Christopher Duffy, Ilya Berkovich, and Sascha Möbius, is wholly different. We now understand that the Prussian Army was a highly motivated force of conscripted native sons leavened with mostly willing volunteers. Both Prussian natives and foreigners were volunteers. Prussian recruiters undoubtedly snatched a small number of unwilling men, but the myth of a dictatorial army dragooned by force is not tenable. Once in the army, the Prussian recruits were trained through a developed and humane system of mentorship with noncommissioned officers and only subjected to corporal punishment after they had perfected the basics of military life.[4]

The Prussian Army under Hülsen reflected this composition: five battalions of grenadiers, six battalions of musketeers from senior regiments, four battalions of fusiliers, two battalions of lower-quality *Frei-Infanterie* and dragooned Saxons, and two companies of *Jäger* riflemen. Most of his officers were men with years of combat experience. His cavalry consisted of ten squadrons of excellent regular dragoons, ten squadrons of Hussars from the Kleist Frei-Korps, and four squadrons of dragoons from the same. Hülsen possessed thirty-five pieces of field artillery, mostly an assortment of twelve-pound guns and a few howitzers. Altogether, his force numbered about 12,000 men.[5]

Historians have also revised our understanding of the Austrian and *Reichsarmee* forces. Arthur Brabant's three-volume study of the *Reichsarmee*, now more than one hundred years old, is still the starting place for the serious researcher.[6] Increasingly, however, historians such as Christopher Duffy have begun to stress the importance of taking the army of the empire seriously.[7] British scholar Peter Wilson has dismissed the myth of a hopelessly ineffective *Reichsarmee*; he contends that while their combat record was inferior to many contemporaries, the troops were capable of putting up a fight.[8] The Austrian Army, by contrast, was one of the finest fighting forces in Europe by the middle of the Seven Years War—capable of inflicting heavy defeats on the Prussian Army in battles such as Kolin, Hochkirch, and Kunersdorf (while supporting the Russians). As a result of fresh research in the twenty-first century, historians such as Christopher Duffy and Michael Hochedlinger have shown that the Austrian military of the Seven Years War was a first-rate organization capable of matching the Prussians in battle.[9]

At the beginning of the campaign, the Austro-*Reichsarmee* force under Zweibrücken possessed thirty-six battalions of infantry, twenty-six companies of grenadiers, and forty-three cavalry squadrons in addition to a number of heavy guns.[10] Some of the *Reichsarmee* troops were extremely well-trained and proficient, such as the *Kreisinfanterieregiment* Hessen-Darmstadt, while others were not. Of the Austrian troops, the two battalions of Nikolaus Esterházy's Hungarian infantry were some of the most veteran troops. This force would eventually be reinforced to a strength of approximately 35,000 men.[11] In addition, halfway through the campaign, this force was joined by a Württemberg contingent of approximately 10,000 men commanded by Carl Eugen, Duke of Württemberg. This force consisted of twenty-one companies of grenadiers, six regiments of the line, a heavy and light cavalry brigade, and twenty guns.[12]

Despite recent scholarly revisions regarding both of these military forces, from a tactical perspective, the Prussians retained an edge of their opponents in the Austrian, *Reichsarmee*, and Württemberg contingents. An Austrian government report comparing the military qualities of the Prussian and Austrian armies from the early Seven Years War noted the Prussians possessed a greater speed of firing.[13] Likewise, a May 1758 military report indicated the Prussians figured more accurately, and also made better provision for target practice than the allied forces.[14] These observations were confirmed by a Prussian junior officer writing in 1760, who noted that their troops loaded more quickly and also that their own musket fire was more dangerous at a greater range.[15] Combined with the Prussian cavalry's maneuverability and initiative, the Prussian Army was a dangerous and experienced force on the battlefield.[16]

The Withdrawal from Meissen

At the beginning of August 1760, King Frederick II took his main army out of Saxony, leaving Hülsen and his small corps defending the town of Meissen on the Elbe River. From an operational perspective, he faced serious challenges. His mission was to play for time to allow King Frederick to gain success in other theaters. Hülsen was faced with an enemy force that was larger than his own but slightly inferior in quality. The Saxony terrain provided Hülsen with the opportunity to slow his enemy down if he could effectively use pre-existing defensive positions combined with the significant obstacle of the Elbe River. His troops could act offensively or defensively and, importantly, were skilled at quick operational movement. Hülsen had plenty of time available; indeed, his goal was to generate time and delay the enemy. Finally, although operating in

Prussian Army in Saxony
Lt. General Johann Dietrick von Hülsen

Grenadier Battalion 7/30 Lubath	Infantry Regiment IR7 Braunschweig-Bevern (2 Bns)	Frei-Infanterie F-7 Wunsch (1 Bn) + (2 Jäger Coys)
Grenadier Battalion 38/43 Burgsdorff	Infantry Regiment IR19 Markgraf Carl (2 Bns)	Dragoon Regiment DR 6 Schorlemmer (10 Squadrons)
Grenadier Battalion 11/14 Beyer	Infantry Regiment IR22 Schenckendorff (2 Bns)	Hussar Regiment H1 Kleist (5 Squadrons)
Grenadier Battalion G-I/G-XI Lossow	Infantry Regiment IR44 Grant (2 Bns)	Frei-Korps FC 12 von Kleist (5 Squadrons Hussars) (4 Squadrons Dragoons)
Grenadier Battalion 2/G-II Nesse	Infantry Regiment IR48 Salmuth (2 Bns)	Artillery 35 pieces (30 12pdrs, 5 howitzers)
	Infantry Regiment S-55 Hauss (1 Bn)	

Prussian Forces: ~ 12,000

Figure 7.1. Prussian Order of Battle, 1760. Created by the author and Army University Press.

occupied territory, Hülsen's disciplined troops spoke the same language as the civilian population, so he had minimal civilian concerns.

The campaign opened with the 9 August movement of the Austrian and *Reichsarmee* troops under Zweibrücken from the entrenched camp at Plauen. From Plauen, their initial movement took them to Kesselsdorf and Wilsdruf. Reaching Wilsdruf on 13 August, the allied force began to move closer to Hülsen's position at Meissen.[17] On the 14th, Austrian troops began to drive in the outposts of the Prussian Army. The rising hills around Meissen, a small porcelain manufacturing hub, provided the Prussian Army with a serious defensive position. This area had been fought over twice in the preceding year of 1759. The Meissen position on the high ground around the town provided good observation and clear fields of fire. The enemy forces had limited avenues of approach, the key terrain of the town was protected by hills, and the Prussians—having occupied this position previously—had constructed small earthworks to provide cover and concealment. To effectively use this terrain, however, Hülsen would have had to divide his already small army, deploying it on both sides of the valley in which the Triebisch stream flowed. To allow Frederick the time to gain successes in other theaters, Hülsen prepared to withdraw to other defense positions in Saxony.

On 16 August, the Prussians received reports that a portion of the enemy army had marched around to the left of the Prussian position at Meissen and was encamped at Ziegenhain, about five miles west of Meissen.[18] A Prussian officer described the scene:

> In the afternoon the left wing of the enemy made their way to Zeigenhain. It was worried that this Corps would march further in the night, and get around to stand behind us. Since we had the defiles of the Ketzerbach [stream] behind us, we would be cut off. This prompted GL [*Generalleutnant*] von Hülsen to leave the camp of Meissen, and make his base of supply Torgau. The retreat march began at eight in the evening, the supply train was sent ahead, and we passed the Ketzerbach in three columns, and came to Riesa before noon on the 17th.[19]

Hülsen—knowing that his objective of delaying the enemy's progress would not be achieved by being cut-off, surrounded, and captured—began his long retreat across the province of Saxony.

On the 17th, both armies continued their movements. The Prussians retreated with a rearguard under the command of Colonel Kleist, staying approximately eight miles ahead of the Austrians and *Reichsarmee* forces under Zweibrücken as they advanced to Lommatsch.[20] After taking stock of the ground around Riesa, Hülsen continued his withdrawal, deciding that the ground was not appropriate for the current needs of the Prussian Army.[21] On the 18th, Hülsen continued the retreat northward toward Strehla, marching in two columns.[22] Reaching Strehla on the evening of August 18, the troops took up an excellent defensive position previously utilized by the Prussian Army in 1759.

The Combat at Strehla

The Prussians camped with their left wing secured by the river and the town of Strehla itself. The Strehla position was commanded by a wooded hill (the Dürrenberg) approximately two miles from the town. To the south and west of town, gentle hills sloped down from the Dürrenberg. Hülsen's Strehla position provided good observation and clear fields of fire. The river ensured that the enemy had limited avenues of approach, and the Prussians viewed their fortified camp by the town and the Dürrenberg as key terrain. Earthworks, which had been strengthened during the Prussian occupation in 1759, provided cover and concealment for portions of the Prussian Army. The Prussian infantry stood in two camps: one near the town and the other on the Dürrenberg. Maj. Gen. August Wilhelm von Braun commanded the detached camp on the Dürrenberg. The two infantry camps were separated by approximately 1,600 yards.[23] The Prussian cavalry encamped between these two positions.

The next day, 19 August, was a busy day for the Prussian Army, full of news from different quarters. Hülsen received a worrying report that the enemy forces would be reinforced in the near future by a corps of 10,000 Württembergers.[24] The general immediately informed Frederick of this development, writing to request reinforcements for Saxony; Frederick informed Hülsen that this was a long shot and he was likely on his own.[25] The Prussians remained in place and in the afternoon received news that Frederick had won a defensive battle at Liegnitz in neighboring Silesia province, and Hülsen considered launching a surprise attack on the enemy's forward encampments within a few miles of Strehla.[26] Leaving camp just after midnight, however, Hülsen realized the enemy was already in motion to attack his force and immediately ordered his troops back to their defensive positions.

Zweibrücken had maneuvered his vastly larger army within striking distance of Strehla and was beginning preparations for an attack. The troops moved forward in several different bodies. The attack began with ten squadrons of hussars commanded by Maj. Gen. Stephan de Vécsey, driving in the Prussian outposts. Swinging far to the left, the reserve corps under Christian Carl Prince zu Stolberg (eight battalions and five squadrons) and the infantry of Maj. Gen. Wenzel Matthais von Kleefeld (four battalions, four companies of grenadiers, and ten squadrons) marched together. Approaching directly from the south, Graf Franz Guasco led the army's massed grenadiers (four battalions, twenty-four companies of grenadiers, and five squadrons). All these units were to mass for a combined assault on the Prussian camp on the Dürrenberg, while the main army under Zweibrücken and Hadik (twenty-two battalions and eighteen squadrons) approached the Prussian entrenchments outside Strehla and fixed them with an artillery barrage.[27] This type of attack had overcome Frederick's Prussian Army at Hochkirch in 1758, as well as the corps of General Finck at Maxen in 1759; considering their numerical superiority, the allies anticipated success. Altogether, the allies had approximately forty-five battalions and forty-three squadrons to mass against Hülsen's eighteen battalions and twenty-six squadrons. Although regimental returns are not available, it is likely the allies had more than twice as many troops as Hülsen.[28]

Vécsey's hussars began attacking the Prussian outposts at approximately 0330 on 20 August 1760. Although heavily outnumbered by the enemy light troops, the Prussian grenadiers and *Jägers* managed to hang onto the village of Rüglen southeast of Strehla. Artillery fire from Prussian positions on the Dürrenberg helped cover the withdrawal of most of these advanced guards.[29] Prussian forces began to note the appearance of enemy infantry columns to their south and west. As the Prince of Stolberg and Major General Kleefeld reached the village of Liebschütz, the allies began firing at the Dürrenberg from a small hill southeast of the village.

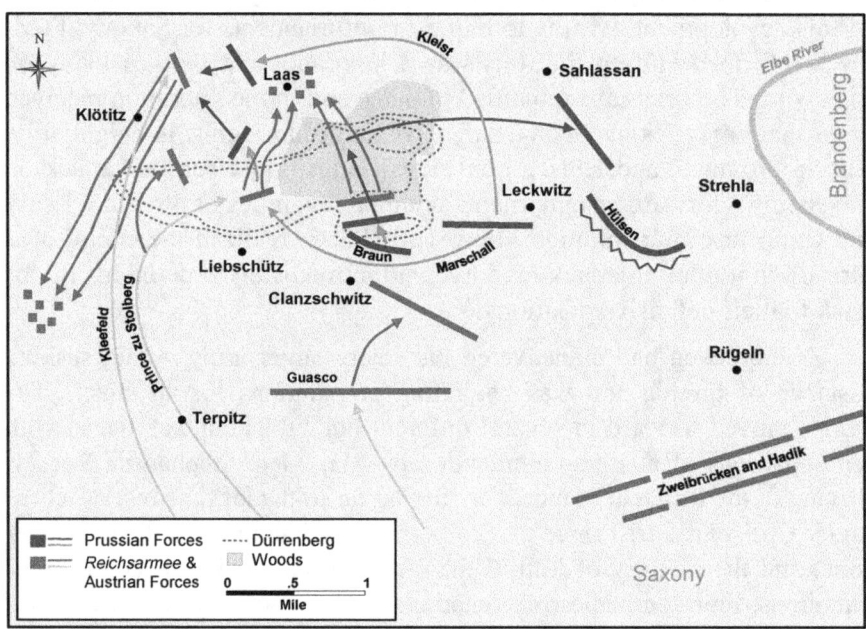

Figure 7.2. Map of the Battle of Strehla, 20 August 1760. Created by the author and Nicholas Burns.

Both of their columns continued in a wide arc to the west of the Dürrenberg, eventually approaching the river from the northeast while covered by woods. Forces on the Dürrenberg were further distracted by the appearance of Guasco's massed grenadiers directly to their south past the village of Clanzschwitz. Slowed by heavy Prussian artillery fire, Guasco stopped short of launching a full attack and was drawn into an artillery duel with Prussian guns on the Dürrenberg.[30]

Hülsen—aware of the danger to his right-wing position on the Dürrenberg—personally moved additional forces there, bringing the excellent Regiment of Bevern and three companies of Hauss Fusiliers composed of native Saxons that the Prussian Army forcibly recruited in 1756. Major-General Braun detached the Lubath Grenadier battalion and two heavy cannons from the Dürrenberg to seize high ground farther to the west and delay the enemy. These troops, however, were repulsed in the direction of the village of Laas when seven enemy infantry battalions advanced on their position; they returned to Braun. Realizing that the threat was appearing more and more from the west and not from the south as originally expected, Braun left the Burgsdorff Grenadier Battalion and two heavy cannons to continue checking Guasco's advance, and moved with his remaining battalions to face west. At this juncture, just before 0600, General Kleefeld's fusiliers, grenadiers, and Croats made an unexpected appearance—coming out of the woods north of the Prussian position. The Dürrenberg position was surrounded on three sides, bombarded by artillery from the south and west, and facing an infantry assault from the north.

Wheeling to meet this new threat with the battalions of Lubath, Beyer, and Lossow along with three companies of Hauss fusiliers, Braun found himself in a serious situation. After the battle, Hülsen sent this report to the Prussian state ministry: "The enemy attacked . . . the advanced force now from all sides at six in the morning . . . the affair had apparently become a crisis."[31] Indeed, the standard German General Staff history of the war asserts that this was the crisis of the battle.[32] Braun, fifty-nine years old and a thirty-eight-year Prussian Army veteran, had begun a quick ascension through the ranks due to his courage under fire and combat losses in higher ranks. Recently given a Fusilier Regiment (Nr. 37) as a colonel-proprietor, Braun introduced "good order and discipline" into the unit.[33] As his grenadiers wheeled into the correct north-facing position, his men began to open fire on the enemy.[34] A heavy firefight erupted at close range, likely under 150 yards.[35]

As Braun dealt with the enemy emerging from the woods, Hülsen arrived at the Dürrenberg, bringing both Bevern Infantry Regiment bat-

Figure 7.3. The Prussian view from the Dürrenberg toward the emerging allies, August 2018. Courtesy of the author.

talions to stabilize the position. Hülsen took stock of the situation and observed another column of enemy infantry, the Hungarian soldiers of Nikolaus Esterházy's regiment, approaching the Prussian flank from the northwest. Realizing his position was in serious danger from these excellent troops, Hülsen sent word for the Schorlemmer Dragoon battalion commanded by Maj. Anton Rudolph Marschall von Bieberstein to charge the deploying enemy forces.[36] These cavalrymen, the best at Hülsen's disposal, swept across the Dürrenberg to the south of the infantry firefight and smashed into the right flank of the Hungarians and their supporting troops. This use of a mobile reserve saved the Dürrenberg position, and saved the Prussian Army from disaster at Strehla.

Realizing the momentum of battle had begun to shift in the Prussian's favor, General Braun launched his grenadiers forward in a bayonet attack; they chased the *Reichsarmee* and Austrians in the woods then back through the village of Laas. Col. Friedrich Wilhelm von Kleist, commanding the remaining Prussian cavalry reserve, moved his forces around to the north of the Dürrenberg and the village of Laas and won a brief cavalry engagement against enemy horsemen in that section of the field. The Schlorlemmer Dragoons, having broken through the enemy, supported Kleist in this final engagement. It was now 0700; all firing had ceased and the battle drew to a close.[37] Approximately 1,000 Prussians had been killed and wounded, while the allies had lost 1,200 men as prisoners, and 1,800 killed and wounded.[38] Although the *Reichsarmee* and Austrian forces under Zweibrücken had suffered a sharp tactical defeat in the northern sector of the battlefield, they remained threateningly close to Hülsen's front.

The military values of the period dictated that whoever held the battlefield at the close of the engagement was victorious. Hülsen's troops had inflicted a proportionally higher loss on the enemy and repulsed the allied effort to drive them from the Dürrenberg, but they were still in a dangerous position with a much-larger enemy army in close proximity. If Hülsen retreated now, the allies could claim that the combat at Strehla had been a defeat for the Prussians.[39] From 0700 to 1000, the Prussian force maneuvered, shifting troops around in its defensive position. Then at 1300, Hülsen began to detect that the enemy was again trying to bypass him on the road to the city of Torgau. Choosing his army's safety over the traditional measure of victory, Hülsen immediately ordered his troops to retreat toward Torgau.[40] Noticing the retreat, Zweibrücken stopped his own advance and instead ordered his army to take up the position that the Prussians had abandoned. The *Reichsarmee* and Austrian soldiers camped there the night of the 20th.

Upon reaching Torgau on the evening of 21 August, Hülsen took up a strong defensive position; as at Strehla, this was a classic post that had been used by previous Prussian commanders. Hülsen reported his success to Frederick in a 21 August letter and received two letters in return. In the 24 August message—before he heard about Strehla—the king commented: "I do not have a word to say against your conduct up to the present, but see that you cannot have acted other, than what you have done, very, very sensibly."[41] Frederick was more effusive in his next letter written after he learned about the action at Strehla:

> You may judge yourself with what great joy I received from your letter of the 21st . . .that tells me of the action on the . . . Dürrenberg and the good disposition against the Austrians and the Reichsarmee made there. I therefore congratulate you and give assurance of my real appreciation . . . give my most gracious compliments to your senior officers and staff, who have distinguished

themselves on this occasion and who have shown themselves as persons of distinction.[42]

Frederick also awarded General Braun the Order of Merit, the highest Prussian military distinction, for his performance at Strehla.[43]

The Withdrawal from Torgau and Wittenberg

After the battle, the allies followed to Torgau on 25 August, camping in the same general area but taking care to maintain some distance between their army and the Prussians. Over the next month, the Prussians and the allies kept each other busy in the *petit guerre* or war of posts as small parties of hussars, *Jägers*, and frei-infanterie skirmished to gain positional advantages. By 12 September, the Württemberger auxiliary corps had arrived in Saxony, and by the 21st, the Württembergers had unified with elements of the allied army above Torgau on the Elbe at Pretzsch. By 26 September, the allies had constructed bridges across the Elbe at multiple points, potentially leading to a situation where Hülsen's force could be completely surrounded. At 1300 on the 26th, the Prussian force retreated once again, this time crossing the Elbe at the Torgau bridge by two columns across two separate bridges. It was here that the Prussians ran into trouble; their baggage train slowed their retreat, giving the enemy time to detect what was happening.

The allies immediately swung into action, advancing hussars against the tail of the Prussian column and firing artillery against both the bridges and the withdrawing Prussian troops. A Prussian officer with Hülsen described the scene:

> The enemy artillery of General Kleefeld moved closer, but General Hülsen from across the Elbe deployed his heavy guns, and answered the enemy fire. [The enemy] artillery took the Torgau bridge in their sights, and tried to stop the second column by lighting the bridge on fire, which they nearly succeeded in doing, but the fire was put out, and our column crossed the bridge. By 4 p.m., our Corps, under constant fire from the enemy, had completely cleared the Elbe. Hülsen sent word for the commander of the garrison at Torgau to resist the enemy vigorously.[44]

The 1,800 garrison troops left at Torgau covered Hülsen's escape, but surrendered the following day. Having escaped from a dangerous position, Hüslen then followed the course of the river to the friendly garrison at Wittenberg, where the army encamped on 30 September. The final drama

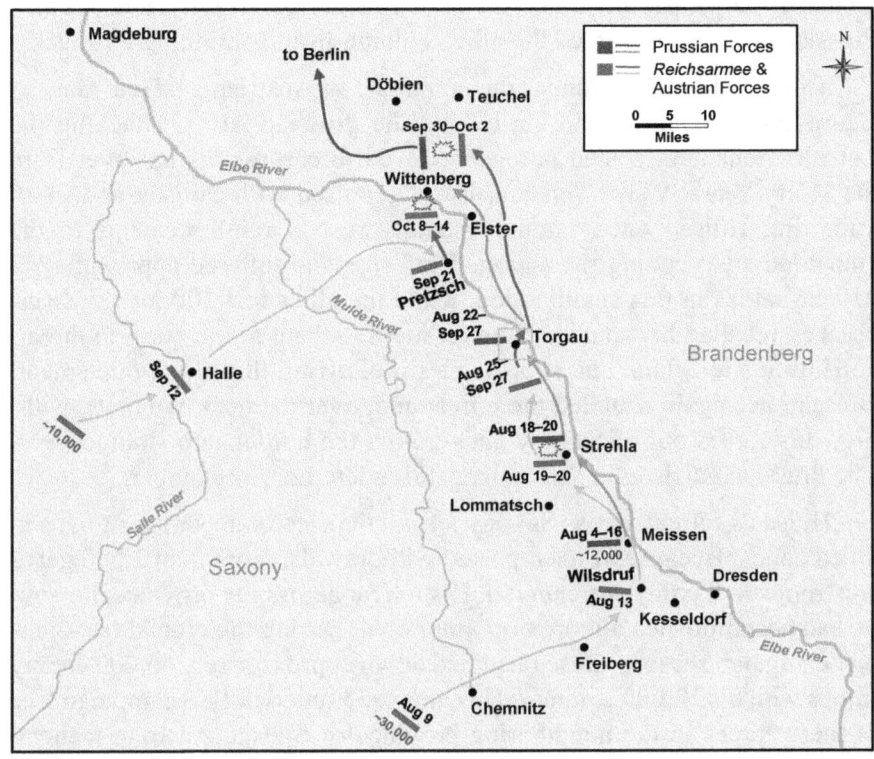

Figure 7.4. Hülsen's retreat, Saxony, August–October 1760. Created by the author and Nicholas Burns.

of Hülsen's retreat across the Saxon electorate unfolded at the town of Wittenberg, the birthplace of the Protestant Reformation.

Establishing a defensive position just north of the town, Hülsen used the Elbe to secure his right flank and rising ground near the villages of Teuchel and Döbien to secure his left. On 2 October, the two allied forces arrived in the area; the Austrians and *Reichsarmee* approached Hülsen from the east on the same side of the river, while the Württemberger Corps watched from the opposite bank to the south. Zweibrücken tried to bag Hülsen one more time, turning his left flank and trapping the Prussian troops against the river. In two columns, the allies approached Hülsen's position from the east from their camp at Elster.[45] Both columns reached the heights near the village of Targun opposite the Prussian left. From this position, the allied army's massed artillery began bombarding the Prussian-held positions. The first allied column containing the Austrian

131

grenadier corps assaulted the village of Teuche, but heavily concentrated Prussian artillery prevented the allied column from continuing its attack.

The second column under the command of Austrian Lt. Gen. Gabriel Georg Luzinsky moved to get behind the Prussian Army, attacking the Lubath Grenadiers posted in ancient Swedish earthworks left over from the Thirty Years' War.[46] This attack was repulsed with canister and small arms fire; Hülsen once again personally rushed reinforcements to the embattled area, ending the action. The Prussians suffered approximately 230 casualties in this small action, while the allies lost 300 men.[47] Zweibrücken recalled his attacking forces, moving them to the north to threaten Hülsen's left flank and supply lines. Following this allied movement, Hülsen once again sounded the retreat and, over the next two days, withdrew his forces out of Saxony back across the border into Brandenberg. The Prussian garrison in Wittenberg surrendered on 14 October.

Hülsen's retreat across Saxony left all the electorate's major towns in allied hands. Because of his repeated withdrawals, more than 3,000 garrison troops in Saxony surrendered. His retreat across the province, however, had accomplished a more important goal. During the crucial late-summer campaign season, Hülsen had tied down approximately 45,000 enemy troops with his 12,000 soldiers. This allowed Frederick II to campaign free of these forces in the neighboring province of Silesia. Austrian General Andreas Hadik, who accompanied Zweibrücken throughout the campaign, assessed Hülsen's performance:

> We must give due justice to the enemy general Hülsen and his corps. He acted as a far-sighted and experienced commander, as shown by the great skill with which he maintained his positions until night, and exploiting the features of the ground to the full.[48]

Hülsen returned to Saxony less than a month later on 3 November to serve together with Frederick's army at the famous Battle of Torgau. Frederick, believing the battle was lost, had given up hope. The Prussians were saved when Hülsen, wounded in the foot, ordered his men to drag him forward on the carriage of a twelve-pound cannon for one final attack. Such was the determination of Frederick the Great's officers. This attack, combined with the forces of the Hussar commander Ziethen, won the battle and drove the Austrians from most of Saxony. Hülsen, retreating with sound tactical and operational principles, had saved his army to fight and be victorious another day.

Conclusion

In their retreat across Saxony, the Prussians benefitted from *both* their own efficiency and their opponents' failure to coordinate effectively. At Meissen, Strehla, Torgau, and Wittenberg, the *Reichsarmee* and their Austrian allies were unable to effectively fix Hülsen's force in place and destroy it against the river despite outnumbering that force by almost four to one. Hülsen made errors as well: his failure to properly coordinate the retreat from Torgau caused delays as the Prussians crossed the Elbe. On balance, however, Hülsen anticipated and planned for his opponent's likely move at each stage of the campaign, allowing his smaller, more disciplined, and mobile force to stay one step ahead of an enemy which could have defeated and destroyed them in open battle.

When confronted tactically with enemy forces, Hülsen and his subordinate commanders such as Braun, Marschall von Bieberstein, and Kleist all acted aggressively to place their numerically superior opponents in a reactive position. The results at Strehla were clear: Braun's infantry used firepower to recover from the surprising emergence of enemy troops in their rear, and then launched a counterattack. Likewise, Marschall von Bieberstein and Kleist both used the maneuverability of their cavalry reserve to deal crushing blows to incoming enemy forces. These successes indicate that tactically, Prussian troops still were superior to their opponents.

Hülsen's retreat demonstrates the importance of sound operational decision-making, tactical flexibility and initiative, and thorough terrain analysis. His forces could not rely on superior technology to solve operational and tactical problems. Instead, they employed superior training, instincts, and leadership to survive a series of incredibly dangerous encounters across the Saxon electorate in 1760. Hülsen, a long-serving commander who benefited from a veteran army, reminds us that a properly managed withdrawal can provide tactical and operational advantages to the retreating force.

Notes

1. Christopher Duffy, *Military Experience in the Age of Reason,* (Atheneum, New York, 1987), 194; and De Jeney, *Le partisan ou l'art de faire la petite-guerre* (La Haye, NL: Constapel, 1759), 137.

2. John Palmer, *General von Steuben* (New Haven, CT: Yale University Press, 1937), 38.

3. Joseph Marshall, *Travels through Holland, Flanders, Germany, Denmark, Sweden, Lapland, Russia, the Ukraine, and Poland in the Years 1768, 1769, 1770,* vol. 3 (London: Almon, 1772), 289–94.

4. Glenn A. Steppler, "The Common Soldier in the Reign of George III, 1760–1793" (PhD diss., Oxford, 1984); Peter H. Wilson, "Prusso-German Social MIlitarization Reconsidered," in Jörg Muth, *Flucht Aus Dem Militärischen Alltag: Ursachen Und Individuelle Ausprägung Der Desertion in Der Armee Friedrichs Des Grossen: Mit Besonderer Berücksichtigung Der Infanterie-Regimenter Der Potsdamer Garnison,* Preussen, Deutschland, Und Europa 1701–2001, (Freiburg im Breisgau, DE: Rombach Verl., 2003); Alan L. Forrest, *Napoleon's Men: The Soldiers of the Revolution and Empire* (London: Hambledon Continuum, 2006); Marcus Von Salisch, *Treue Deserteure: Das Kursächsische Militär Und Der Siebenjährige Krieg* (München: R. Oldenbourg, 2009), 10; Sascha Möbius, *Mehr Angst Vor Dem Offizier Als Vor Dem Feind?: Eine Mentalitätsgeschichtliche Studie Zur Preußischen Taktik Im Siebenjährigen Krieg* (Saarbrücken: AV: Akademikerverl, 2012); Don N. Hagist, *British Soldiers, American War: Voices of the American Revolution* (Yardley, PA: Westholme, 2014); Yuval Harari, *Ultimate Experience: Battlefield Revelations and the Making of Modern War Culture, 1450–2000* (London: Palgrave Macmillan, 2014); and Ilya Berkovich, *Motivation in War: The Experience of Common Soldiers in Old-Regime Europe* (Cambridge: Cambridge University Press, 2017).

5. Großen Generalstabe, *Die Krieges Friedrichs des Großen,* vol. 13 (Berlin: E. Mittler und Sohn, 1914), 161.

6. Artur Brabant, *Das Heilige Römische Reich Teutscher Nation in Kampfe mit Friedrich dem Großen,* 3 vols. (Berlin and Dresden, DE: G. Paetel, 1904–1931).

7. Christopher Duffy, *Prussia's Glory: Rossbach and Leuthen 1757* (Chicago: Emperor's Press, 2003), 23–29.

8. Wilson provided a significant reevaluation in his study of a longer period: Peter H. Wilson, *German Armies: War and German Politics, 1648–1806* (London: University College London Press, 1998).

9. The leading study of the Austrian Army in this period is undoubtedly Christopher Duffy, *The Austrian Army in the Seven Years War,* 2 vols. (Chicago: Emperor's Press, 2000, 2008). See also Michael Hochehlinger, *Austria's Wars of Emergence, 1683–1797* (London: Longman, 2003).

10. Großen Generalstabe, *Die Krieges Friedrichs des Großen,* 160.

11. Großen Generalstabe, 162.

12. Peter H. Wilson, "The Württemberg Army in the Seven Years War," in Alexander S. Burns, *The Changing Face of Old Regime Warfare: Essays in Honour of Christopher Duffy* (Warwick, UK: Helion & Co., 2022).

13. Haus-, Hof-, und Staatsarchiv, (HHStA) Kriegsakten 333-1, quoted in Christopher Duffy, *Army of Frederick the Great* (Chicago: Emperor's Press, 1994), 129.

14. Kriegsarchiv, Feldakten, Alte Feldakten, 1758 Hauptarmee III, 1, and Lieutenant-Colonel Rebain, 10 May 1758, quoted in Duffy, *Army of Frederick the Great,* 129.

15. Ernst von Barsewisch, *Meine Kriegs-Erlebnisse Während Des Siebenjährigen Krieges 1757–1763; and Wortgetreuer Abdruck Aus Dem Tagebuche Des Kgl. Preuß. General-Quartiermeister-Lieutenants C. F. R. Von Barsewisch* (Berlin: Warnsdorff, 1863), 113.

16. Duffy, *Army of Frederick the Great*, 263.

17. Geheimes Staatsarchiv Preußischer Kulturbesitz (GStA PK) I. HA GR. Rep 63, Nr. 1132 fol. 1.

18. Anonymous, *Sammlung ungedruckter Nachrichten, so die Geschichte der Feldzüge der Preußen von 1740 bis 1779,* vol. 2 (Dresden, DE: Walther, 1782) 7.

19. GStA PK I. HA GR. Rep 63, Nr. 1132 fol. 1.

20. Riesa to Lommatsch.

21. Großen Generalstabe, *Die Krieges Friedrichs des Großen,* 167.

22. Anonymous, *Sammlung ungedruckter Nachrichten,* 8.

23. This is the equivalent of 2,000 German paces or *Schritte*. Anonymous.

24. GStA PK I. HA GR. Rep 63, Nr. 1132 fol. 2.

25. Gustav Volz et al., *Politische Correspondenz Friedrich's des Grossen*, vol. 19 (Berlin: Duncker, 1892), 550–51.

26. Anonymous, *Sammlung ungedruckter Nachrichten,* 10.

27. Großen Generalstabe, *Die Krieges Friedrichs des Großen,* 170.

28. Großen Generalstabe, Anlage 8–9.

29. Anonymous, *Sammlung ungedruckter Nachrichten,* 10.

30. GStA PK I. HA GR. Rep 63, Nr. 1132 fol. 2.

31. GStA PK I. HA GR. Rep 63, Nr. 1129 fol. 6.

32. Großen Generalstabe, *Die Krieges Friedrichs des Großen,* 174.

33. Kurt von Priesdorff, *Soldatisches Führertum,* vol. 1 (Hamburg, DE: Hanseatische Verlagsanstalt, 1937), 483.

34. Anonymous, *Sammlung ungedruckter Nachrichten,* 14.

35. This estimate is based on the author's walk along the Dürrenberg in 2019, taken together with the description of textual sources.

36. Anonymous, *Sammlung ungedruckter Nachrichten,* 14–15.

37. GStA PK I. HA GR. Rep 63, Nr. 1132 fol. 2.

38. Großen Generalstabe, *Die Krieges Friedrichs des Großen,* 178.

39. Hülsen was right to worry, because the Reichsarmee and Austrians did claim they won the battle. See the report of the French observer comte de Mara-

inville, in Antoine-Henri Jomini, *Precis de l'art de la guerre* (Brussels: J.-B. Petit, 1841), 474–75.

40. Anonymous, *Sammlung ungedruckter Nachrichten,* 14–15.

41. Volz et al, *Politische Correspondenz,* 559.

42. Volz et al., 561.

43. Anton Balthasar König, *Biographisches Lexikon aller Helden und Militarpersonen,* vol. 1 (Berlin: Wever, 1788), 216.

44. Anonymous, *Sammlung ungedruckter Nachrichten,* 31.

45. Großen Generalstabe, *Die Krieges Friedrichs des Großen,* 196.

46. Anonymous, *Sammlung ungedruckter Nachrichten,* 41.

47. Großen Generalstabe, *Die Krieges Friedrichs des Großen,* 197.

48. Hadik Levéltár, Hadtörténeti Intézet és Múzeum, Hadik's Journal, 2 October 1760, quoted in Christopher Duffy, *By Force of Arms* (Chicago: Emperor's Press, 2008), 279.

Chapter 8
Retreat to Victory: The Northern Army's Campaigns, 1775–1777

Jonathan D. Bratten

A year after its birth, the US Army took its first halting steps—backward. The birth of the US Army lies in retreat. In 1775, the fledgling Continental Army launched an audacious two-pronged attack campaign into Canada. The at-first-promising offensive lost momentum, stalled, was overpowered, and then collapsed into a long and terrible retreat. Retreat followed retreat, losing key terrain as well as territory. That horrible 350-mile-long retreat from Canada ultimately led to victory in 1777 at Saratoga. This dramatic reversal is not only part of the great American mythos, but also carries valuable lessons for students of military history and theory. Victory at Saratoga following the horrible retreats was not guaranteed. Rather, that victory came from the actions of forward-thinking leaders who refused to accept defeat, realized that people were more important than positions, were willing to take risks, and knew how to use the terrain in their favor.

Actions at Lexington and Concord were scarcely news when the unlikely duo of Benedict Arnold and Ethan Allen swiftly seized Fort Ticonderoga and Crown Point on Lake Champlain in May 1775. Both were aggressive, larger-than-life men with egos to match. Arnold and Allen recognized what all military planners waging war in North America had: control of the Lake Champlain-Hudson Valley corridor was critical to victory. That control was key in every colonial conflict that pitted New France against New England over the previous century and a half, and Native nations used it to raid each other before the Europeans arrived.

Entering at the mouth of the Saint Lawrence River in Quebec, an eighteenth-century ship could sail up the river past Quebec City's towering bluffs and Trois-Rivieres, and then arrive at Montreal. From there, shallow-draft vessels would head south up the Richelieu River to its source in Lake Champlain. The next route was overland—west into the heart of New York or east into the Hampshire Grants (present-day Vermont). Heading farther south, a traveler—or invading army—could take a one-mile portage past the walls of Fort Ticonderoga to Lake George. Although not a major waterway, Lake George has one excellent feature: its southernmost reaches are but a few miles from the Hudson River, with access to Albany and New York City. During an era when over-the-road logistics was impractical, expensive, and slow, a nearly unimpeded waterway was a godsend for any army.

This corridor had another benefit: it divided the New England colonies from those of the mid-Atlantic. An enemy that controlled the Lake Champlain corridor could strike the New York capitol in Albany, move on New York City, or cut off New England from the rest of the colonies. And if the corridor were held by friendly troops, it offered an enticing route to strike into Canada.

This was the situation in 1775 when the new overall Continental Army commander, General George Washington, authorized two military expedi-

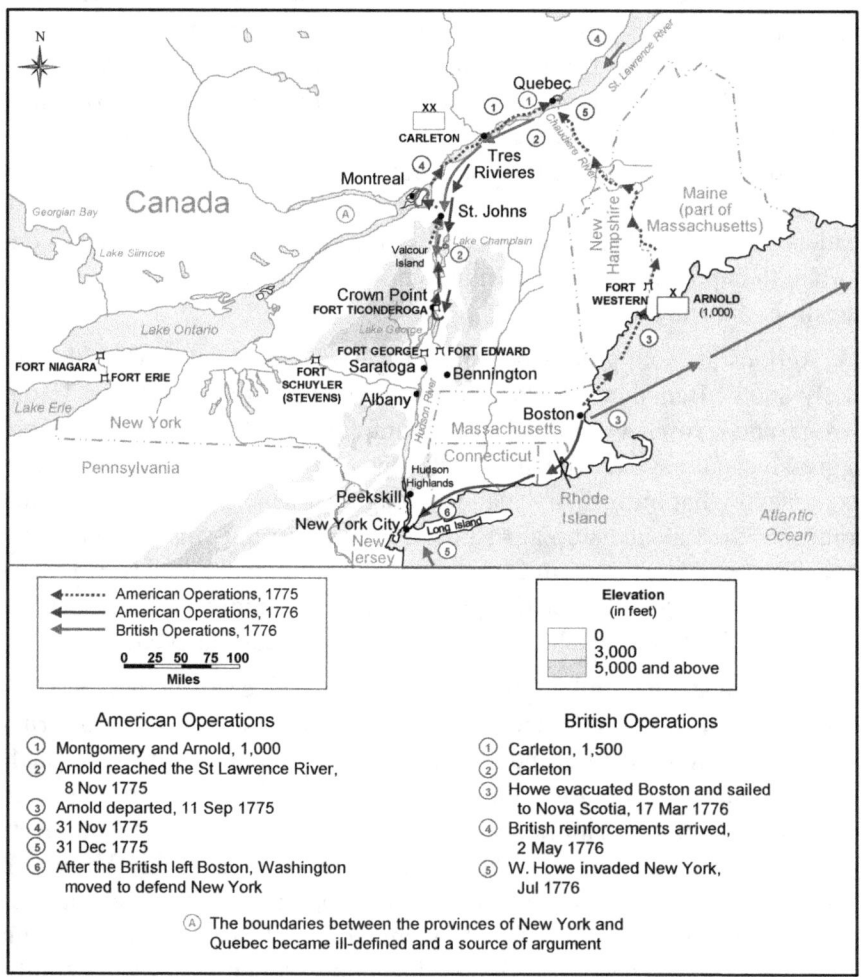

Figure 8.1. The Invasion of Canada, September 1775 to October 1776. Courtesy of the US Military Academy History Department.

tions to strike at British Canada. The first under General Richard Montgomery used the Lake Champlain corridor to seize Montreal. The second under the ubiquitous Benedict Arnold traversed Maine's rugged wilderness via the Kennebec and Chaudière Rivers to arrive outside Quebec City.

From there, however, the expedition began to unravel. Montgomery and Arnold united their tattered forces at Quebec City in December 1775. Even united, their forces were too few—only slightly more than 800 effectives—and too ill-supplied to conduct a siege.[1] In a daring three-pronged assault during a 31 December snowstorm, the revolutionary forces made a lodgment in the lower city but were unable to break through to the city's interior. Montgomery was killed and Arnold wounded during the fighting, and the assault lost all momentum. The remainder of the force pulled back, waiting to continue their largely ineffective siege after more reinforcements arrived.[2]

And reinforcements did arrive during the winter and spring of 1776, reaching more than 2,000 by April.[3] Even as his Main Army was occupying New York City and building strength against the expected British attack, General George Washington siphoned off much-needed regiments to reinforce what was fast becoming a failing venture in Canada. Nominal command of the Northern Army fell to Maj. Gen. Philip Schuyler, who remained in New York due to poor health but continued to send supplies and men to his army in Canada while he recovered. Schuyler's true genius was organization and logistics. Field command of the Northern Army laying siege to Quebec City had passed from Montgomery to Arnold, and then from Arnold to Brig. Gen. David Wooster. Wooster, in turn, was relieved of command on 2 May by Maj. Gen. John Thomas.[4] Thomas was in command for one month before promptly dying of smallpox, one of hundreds of American soldiers who died during this 1776 epidemic in Canada.[5]

On 6 May 1776, British General Guy Carleton slowly pushed his reinforced British army out from Quebec City toward the tired, sick, and dispirited Northern Army troops besieging the city—barely 1,000 effectives plus 1,200 sick. Confronted by 900 healthy British Regulars, Marines, and militia, the Northern Army cracked like an egg.[6] In a letter to Schuyler, Arnold described it as a rout rather than a retreat:

> Of course a most precipitate and confused retreat ensued with the loss of all our cannon, ammunition, &etc, &etc. . . . store of provisions, and about 200 of the sick fell into the enemy's hands.[7]

The hard work of the preceding fall and winter campaigns had come to naught.

Still, all was not lost. More reinforcements arrived by 1 June, including sixteen new units, bringing the numbers of Continental soldiers in Canada to 8,048.[8] With them came a new commander: Maj. Gen. John Sullivan. Sullivan and Brig. Gen. William Thompson pushed for a renewed effort to oppose the British, even though neither had reviewed the ground or spent much time with the army. Both believed they could restore a victorious spirit in an army in which hundreds died from smallpox—a problem that neither leader seemed to fully understand. Thompson, a Pennsylvanian, mocked the New Englanders who "are so much infected with or afraid of the small pox as almost to prevent their doing duty."[9]

The Americans tried one last time to turn and fight the pursuing British at Trois-Rivieres, about seventy-five miles above Montreal on the St. Lawrence. On 8 June, Thompson led an attack on the suspected British position without having conducted a reconnaissance. The approximately 2,000 Americans outnumbered the British two to one but squandered their advantage through uncoordinated assaults in five separate columns over poor ground. The force attacked piecemeal and gave the British defenders time to focus on defeating each one in turn. Swamps and marshes broke up the orderly lines, and the American units lost the cohesion so vital to eighteenth-century tactics. Regimental and battalion commanders like Arthur St. Clair and Anthony Wayne endeavored to create order from chaos, but British artillery and naval gunfire was too much for them. Around 700 to 800 men left the field in reasonable order. The last gasp of the offensive floundered in the swamps and marshes around Trois-Rivieres, including Thompson, who surrendered to the British.[10]

As stragglers made their way back to Montreal, 236 were snapped up as prisoners. The bulk of the best American fighting force in Canada had been wasted in a poorly planned, poorly executed attack. Lacking supplies, weighed down by the sick and wounded, and without a strong enough force to hold the St. Lawrence against a joint British Army and Navy attack, Sullivan had no option but to retreat. Arnold, who had done everything in his power to sustain the American forces in Quebec, agreed as early as 10 June:

> Shall we sacrifice the few men we have yet, endeavoring to keep possession of a small part of the country which can be of little or no service to us? The junction of the Canadians and the colonies—an object that had brought us into this country—is now at an end. Let us quit them and secure our own country before it is too late.[11]

On 15 June, the Continental troops began their long retreat to Fort Ticonderoga.

The Northern Army made its way south to Fort Saint-Jean, torching fortifications and leaving behind valuable artillery and supply depots. The rear guard, still in good order, destroyed bridges behind them as they moved south. At Saint-Jean, Sullivan held an 18 June council of war where it was agreed that to attempt to hold out in Canada "would be to Expose the whole Army to inevitable Ruins."[12] Anywhere that the Royal Navy could use its greater mobility and firepower was a liability. Once again, the army turned south and sailed toward the small island of Ile-aux-Noix. Arnold remained nearly to the last moment at Saint-Jean, having set the fort alight; he pushed off in the very last bateaux, as if taking ownership for the campaign that had begun more than a year prior.[13]

The retreat did not bring any relief to the already exhausted and broken army. Capt. John Lacy recalled: "Our bateaux loaded were moved up the rapids six miles: one hundred of them were towed by our wearied men up to their armpits in water. This was performed in one day."[14] From the now-burning Fort Saint-Jean, the ragged remnant proceeded to the tiny Isle-aux-Noix, a swampy island in the Richelieu River just ten miles from Lake Champlain. Several thousand smallpox patients had already been brought there from Montreal; the island was littered with the sick, dying, and dead. Nearly half the little army was infected with smallpox or dysentery, and all were suffering from exposure.[15] "The confusion the army was in is beyond description," recalled Capt. Charles Cushing of the 24th Connecticut.[16] The British were never far behind, entering Saint-Jean mere hours after Arnold's departure; this spurred Sullivan and Arnold to get the army out of Canada for good. By 20 June, the first boatloads of sick and wounded were headed to Crown Point. Evacuation of the remainder began on 25 June. The army's final elements reached Crown Point on 1 July 1776.[17]

The disaster might have been greater but for the energetic efforts of leaders like Arnold and Wayne to keep their units together, and for those of General Philip Schuyler. Nominally the commander of the northern theater, Schuyler had not advanced into Canada but instead used his important political and family connections to provide logistical support to the army in Canada. As early as 12 June, Schuyler had begun planning for the army's evacuation based on dispatches from Arnold.[18] He moved bateaux north from Lake George and Lake Champlain to help transport the Northern Army back to Crown Point and Fort Ticonderoga. At the same time, with an eye for the future, Schuyler arranged to rush shipwrights, sailors, and shipbuilding equipment to Fort Ticonderoga.[19]

Schuyler and Arnold realized that their relief would be temporary. British strength lay not merely in numbers, but in the Royal Navy. Unable to move their ships over the rapids of the Richelieu River, the British would have to build a new fleet. In addition to constructing ships at Saint-Jean, Carleton ordered existing British ships to be disassembled then transported to Lake Champlain for reassembly. This painstaking and laborious process would take months—but the end result would be assured mobility and dominance of Lake Champlain.[20]

At the same time, Northern Army leaders took stock of what forces they had remaining and how best to halt the anticipated British onslaught. Schuyler, Maj. Gen. Horatio Gates, Arnold, and other officers met to formulate their best course of action. They decided to abandon the advanced post at Crown Point and consolidate at Mount Independence across the Lake from Fort Ticonderoga. The second motion they agreed to was the immediate construction of "Naval Armament of Gundolas, Row Gallies, Armed Batteaus."[21]

Arnold threw himself into the construction efforts with his whole self, as he did with everything. He chose Skenesborough, New York, as the site for his shipyard, and work began almost immediately to build a force of vessels to confront Carleton. As the fleet took shape, Gates—now the acting field commander after Schuyler returned to Albany to manage logistics and recruiting—provided Arnold with strict instructions on what to do with the fleet. He also provided a clear commander's intent for the coming operations: "Preventing the Enemy's invasion of our Country, is the ultimate End of the important Command, with which you are now intrusted. It is a defensive War we are carrying on."[22]

On 11 October, Arnold's scratch fleet of fifteen vessels of dubious make and seaworthiness confronted the British fleet of thirty, sparking six hours of naval combat near Valcour Island on Lake Champlain.[23] Although Arnold and his men fought bravely, the little American force could not overcome the larger Royal Navy ships and superior British naval gunnery. Running low on ammunition and with many vessels lost, Arnold slipped his remaining forces through the British blockade that evening; only four of the fifteen vessels made it to Ticonderoga.[24] Once again, the Americans were in retreat. But once again, the British had not scooped up the entire rebel force.

But what awaited Carleton up Lake Champlain was not the disease-ridden remnants of the Northern Army—although disease remained a problem for the Northern Army. As the result of a burst of activity on Mount Independence during late summer and fall, Northern Army batteries now loomed over the lake and new battalions of Continentals and militia paraded across the works. A force of more than 9,000 officers and men held this strong bulwark. Lacking sufficient transports, Carleton had brought only a few thousand troops with him. After a reconnaissance of American positions, Carleton concluded that any attack, especially this late in the year, would be foolhardy; he did not want to make the same mistakes as Montgomery and Arnold the previous year.[25] Instead, Carleton withdrew down the Lake and ended his campaign for the year.[26]

This was only a respite. With Carleton's withdrawal, Gates reduced the number of troops assigned to the Northern Army; he sent much-needed reinforcements, including Arnold, to Washington to help with his winter campaigns at Trenton and Princeton. Gates would soon follow as well, leaving command of the cold outposts to Col. Wayne.[27] But over the winter, the British were making strategic decisions of their own. The war was dragging on too long. They needed to take territory. Lieut. Gen. John Burgoyne—who had been Carleton's second-in-command in Canada—identified what he considered a weak point with the Champlain corridor. He believed that advancing and seizing Ticonderoga and its supporting defenses would open options for further advances either into New England or west to Albany. The overall goal *might be* the junction of his Army and General Howe's New York City-based Army somewhere along the Hudson.[28] *Might be* because Burgoyne left the objectives to be defined by King George III.[29] The king reviewed the plans and approved them, ordering Burgoyne to seize Albany and then await orders from General Howe—even though the king had just recently approved Howe's own plan to advance against Philadelphia. Burgoyne was made aware of this but remained convinced that he could seize Albany and—after opening the lines of communication to New York—would "remain upon the Hudson's-River, and thereby enable that general [Howe] to act with his whole force to the southward."[30]

Burgoyne returned to Canada in May 1777 and immediately implemented his invasion plans, moving his forces piecemeal to the theater of operations. By 30 June, Burgoyne had assembled a force of about 8,200 British and German regulars at the ruins of Crown Point in New York. Additional Canadian provincial forces and Native American allies bolstered his forces to more than 9,000 troops as he began the campaign and advanced into New York.[31]

The formerly strong Northern Army at Ticonderoga and Mount Independence had dwindled to just around 4,000 Continentals and militia units now all under the command of Maj. Gen. Arthur St. Clair. Sickness had plagued the camps through the winter and spring, killing many. Even now there were more than 500 on the sick list. The harsh winter had also slowed or even halted work on improving the defenses of both works.[32]

On 13 June, one day after St. Clair took over, he sent his assessment of the troops and their position to Schuyler: "very ill prepared."[33] The situation wasn't much better in terms of arms, equipment, gunpowder, uniforms, and shoes: "the greater part of them are barefoot."[34] Although holding a strong position, the Northern Army was in no condition to repel a determined attack and had provisions on hand for only seven weeks—hardly enough for a siege.[35]

Schuyler, St. Clair, and Brigadier Generals Enoch Poor, John Paterson, and Alexis de Fermoy met in council of war on 20 June. None were suffering under the illusion that they were in a good position. Militia enlistment contracts would be running out over the next month.[36] Rumors of Burgoyne's intentions had already drifted south, as well as reliable intelligence as to his strength. If the Northern Army abandoned Ticonderoga—seen as the linchpin for the north—Congress and the nascent nation would be aghast. The blow to national morale would be devastating. Yet if they remained, the army's vital manpower might be entirely captured by surrounding British forces, leaving the roads to Albany and New York City wide open. These officers did not have to imagine such an event; they had the example of their commander-in-chief just the year prior.

In the summer of 1776, as the Northern Army was collecting itself after the disaster in Canada, George Washington faced a similar dilemma about holding posts or abandoning them. With just over 20,000 men at hand, Washington was confident he could defeat the British and retain New York City and its environs.[37] He was outmaneuvered during this campaign, however, and forced to abandon position after position despite hard fighting by his troops. Worse, the British took more than 4,000 of his men as prisoners, many who had been garrisoning forts that Washington elected to try to hold. For example, the British captured more than 2,800 Main Army officers and men at Forts Washington and Lee, along with huge quantities of stores, small arms, and artillery.[38] "This was a most unfortunate affair," wrote Washington after the 16 November loss of the forts, "and has given me great mortification."[39] Howe's army systematically drove him from Long Island in August, then Manhattan in September, and finally into New Jersey by November.

Despite these defeats, Washington managed to keep his army intact in the field through battles, defeats, and frequent escapes. Though no more than about 5,000 men of Washington's Main Army marched into New Jersey in November and then slipped into Pennsylvania in December, it was still an army.[40] This army gave the cause of independence a severely needed morale boost with Washington's twin victories at Trenton and Princeton

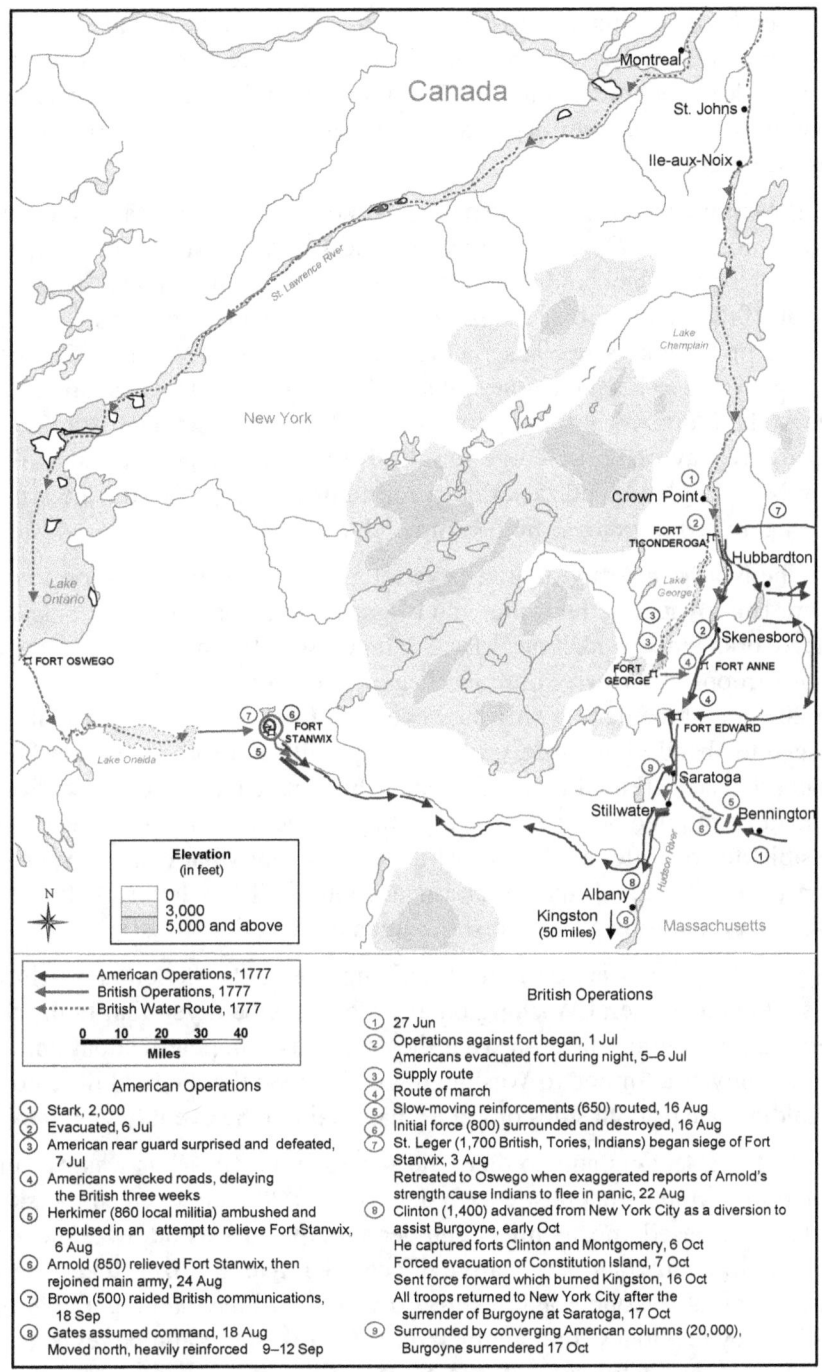

Figure 8.2. Northern New York Burgoynes Expedition, June to October 1777. Courtesy of the US Military Academy History Department.

in December and January. Washington had learned in the brutal campaign of 1776 that escaping with his army intact was more important than risking a battle. This knowledge would stay with him throughout the war and made him much cannier about assuming risks. Keeping his army intact was his greatest goal.[41]

Preserving the army was also the intent of Washington's far-flung lieutenants in June 1777. They agreed to hold the fort and Mount Independence as long as they could, focused on retaining the mount and its line of retreat. If they were forced from the mount, they would retreat southward in boats up the lake as well as via the road to Castleton, Vermont. The primary goal was to keep the army intact. They also agreed to send an urgent plea to the Main Army for reinforcements. With that, Schuyler set off for Albany by way of Fort George to rally New York troops, request militia from New England, and raise funds for additional supplies for the army; once again he turned over field command to St. Clair.[42]

The Northern Army did not have long to wait for the situation to develop. Burgoyne's native scouts and light infantry had been probing the outer works since mid-June.[43] By 25 June, St. Clair had intelligence of British troops at Crown Point and began to change his mind concerning the 20 June agreement: "This, however, is clear to me, that we shall be obliged to abandon this side, and then they will soon force the other from us; nor do I see a retreat will in any shape be practicable." He rallied, however, and reminded Schuyler: "Every thing, however, shall be done, that is possible, to frustrate the designs of the enemy; but what can be expected from troops ill armed, naked, and unaccoutred."[44] His letter of the 28th noted that the troops "began to show signs of dejection already."[45]

Both St. Clair's increasingly frantic updates to Schuyler, and Schuyler's letters to General Washington and Congress betrayed that both men were putting a brave face on what they felt was a hopeless situation. Indeed, Schuyler admitted to Washington on 25 June that he held little hope of holding one or both sides of Lake Champlain in the event of an attack.[46]

And yet, leaders and soldiers did not give up. St. Clair was rushing to improve Mount Independence's defenses on 28 June even as the skirmishing increased; meanwhile, Schuyler anticipated a withdrawal and was working to counteract its negative effects. Schuyler realized that even if Burgoyne took Ticonderoga, his troops would still have a long and arduous journey to Albany. In that much time, the disaster could be reversed.[47] To that end, he instructed half the New York militia to march to join St. Clair, with a reserve to be ready to march at a moment's notice.[48] He also ordered up the four regiments of Massachusetts troops from Peekskill that Washington had arranged as a department reserve and instructed the Connecticut militia to rendezvous at Albany.[49] A master logistician, Schuyler also arranged to move supplies and ammunition to supporting positions where he could sustain his troops, as well as giving orders to remove cattle and other goods from the enemy's path.[50]

On 5 July, as Burgoyne's forces closed in on Ticonderoga on the west side and Mount Independence on the east side of the lake, St. Clair held a council of war with his brigadiers. All were unanimous that Ticonderoga could not be held and that they should immediately withdraw. Further, they gauged that although Mount Independence might have provisions for some weeks, its water supply was vulnerable to attack; additionally, the entire garrison would be cut off if the enemy took control of the road to Castleton. They resolved on a general withdrawal to save the army.[51]

That same day Schuyler wrote the commander-in-chief, emphasizing the same conclusion as St. Clair and his commanders:

> Inclose your Excellency a return of the army at Ticonderoga. Should any accident befal us in that quarter, and the troops be lost, we shall be in a disagreeable situation, with little else besides militia, with not a single piece of heavy or light artillery, and not one artillery-man.[52]

If the army were lost, nothing would stand in Burgoyne's way. Thus, the army had to be saved.

Even so, abandoning the forts was gut-wrenching, and the evacuation was done hastily. Tadeusz Kościuszko, a department engineer, later said: "The troops pushed out of Mount Independence without order or regularity, in a great deal of confusion."[53] Attempts to move men and supplies in batteau up the lake were slowed by heavy winds and poor troop morale.[54] Many of the militia simply disappeared as the main body of the force retreated down the road toward Castleton, but some order was regained when the main body reached Hubbardton and halted for a rest. St. Clair initially stayed at Hubbardton to await the rear guard but then departed for Castleton, fearing the loss of the main force if he delayed further. Col. Seth Warner's Vermonters were left at Hubbardton with instructions to follow the main body when the rear guard arrived.[55]

Due to fatigue, however, the rear guard under Colonel Francis decided to remain at Hubbardton overnight. Warner agreed, and the approximately 800 troops went into camp for the night. The next morning as the troops were cooking breakfast and beginning the march back to Castleton, they were confronted by about the same number of British troops under Brig. Gen. Simon Fraser. An intense skirmish began at Hubbardton and raged for approximately two hours. German reinforcements arrived, forcing the Continentals to withdraw in haste. Casualties were nearly the same on both sides, but the smart fight had blunted Fraser's enthusiasm for further engagements until he received more troops.[56] For the moment, the Northern Army was secure from immediate destruction.

Still, there were setbacks for the patriot cause. Boats loaded with baggage, artillery pieces, and powder made it safely onto Lake Champlain but then were intercepted by the British at Skenesborough. Most of the men ferrying the boats escaped, setting fire to as much as they could. But the British still managed to seize additional artillery, supplies, and the entire shipwright site at Skenesborough.[57] The powder and artillery were a major loss to the Northern Department.[58]

The loss of Ticonderoga, the "Gibraltar of the North'" came as a shock even to those who anticipated its eventual fall. Schuyler commented: "An event so alarming has not yet happened since the contest began . . . and yet, by strenuous exertions, we may still prevent the enemy from penetrating, but not unless every man of the militia turns out."[59] As Schuyler moved available Continentals and militia into New York, he was aware that Burgoyne might see Vermont and then New Hampshire as a temptation, so he detailed Seth Warner's Regiment and newly arriving New Hampshire militia to hold Vermont and annoy Burgoyne's flank.[60] Burgoyne would later complain that this force "hangs like a gathering storm on my left."[61] Schuyler arrived at Fort Edward—about twenty-four miles south of Skenesborough—on 8 July. That evening, the Fort Anne garrison as well as remnants from the Skenesborough disaster reached Fort Edward.[62] On 12 July, St. Clair's army arrived at Fort Edward after leaving a small detachment at Saratoga, having completed a circuitous march to avoid British troops at Skenesborough.[63]

Schuyler began to take stock of his now-united forces at Fort Edward, which included some of the militia he had requested, four regiments of Massachusetts Continentals, and Nixon's Brigade of Continentals from the Highlands Department that had been ordered north by Washington.[64] Schuyler sent Nixon's Brigade north to Fort Anne to gather intelligence on the British, evacuate all livestock, and make good on the promise he had made to Washington: "I will throw every obstacle in their route I possibly can, and retard their progress as much as possible."[65] Nixon's troops felled trees on the road and knocked planking out of bridges. Burgoyne scarcely needed these delays, as logistics were already keeping him pinned to his supply base even as the Northern Army reconsolidated.

The situation had stabilized for St. Clair and Schuyler but was still precarious. On 14 July, Schuyler lamented to Washington: "Desertion prevails and disease gains ground. . . . We are besides in great want of every kind of necessary, provision excepted."[66] As July dragged on and Burgoyne did not arrive, much of the militia from New York and the Berkshires began to head home. One welcome addition was the return of Benedict Arnold, sent north at Washington's request. Schuyler was able to pass off much of the field work to the enthusiastic Arnold. Maj. Gen. Benjamin Lincoln also arrived, with orders to take "Command of the Eastern Militia . . . who place confidence in you."[67] Lincoln took over responsibility for the eastern sector of the theater in Vermont—more help for Schuyler.

Unable to hold Fort Edward much longer, Schuyler and St. Clair abandoned Fort Edward and retreated to Saratoga on 30–31 July. After the advance guard was mauled in severe fighting with British light infantry, Canadians, and Native allies on 3 August, the Northern Army retreated once again, this time to Stillwater, fourteen miles south.[68] Further withdrawals came until 17 August when the army was ten miles from Albany and Schuyler deployed the brigades in an arc covering the river crossings to the city.[69] This marked the final point of the Northern Army's retreat—more than 350 miles from Quebec City where it had begun the year prior.

Schuyler had managed to keep the Northern Army together and supplied the entire time. Thanks to his exhaustive work, food, ammunition, tents, uniforms, and other supplies reached camp daily. The Northern Army also received news that John Stark's New Hampshire militia and Warner's Vermonters had utterly routed a German foray against Bennington, depriving Burgoyne of yet more troops and, even more importantly, cutting off critical supplies he needed to carry on his campaign.[70] The "gathering storm" that Burgoyne complained of had finally struck. Ironically as Schuyler was seeing the fruits of his labors, he received word that he had been relieved of command by the Continental Congress. They blamed St. Clair and Schuyler for the loss of the northern forts. Congress sent Major General Horatio Gates to take command, which he did on 19 August.[71] Schuyler returned to Albany, where he continued to work to improve the situation of the Northern Department. He held meetings with Native nations to gain additional support and strip them away from the British, coordinated resupply efforts, and continued efforts to push more New York militia to the Northern Army.[72]

Over the next ten days, additional Continental regiments arrived, including Col. Daniel Morgan and his elite corps of riflemen, detached from the Main Army by Washington.[73] It is remarkable that Washington released Morgan and his men to the Northern Department while he was trying to protect the nascent nation's capitol at Philadelphia from William Howe. Washington assessed the risk and realized that while the Continental Army—and the cause of independence—could survive the loss of Philadelphia, it could not handle losing the vital Champlain-Hudson corridor. These actions also demonstrated that Washington trusted Schuyler, who kept him well-informed throughout the disaster-riddled summer of 1777.

The coming months would see Washington's assessment vindicated. Although the British took and held Philadelphia in September, they could do little with it. Meanwhile, the reinforcements Washington sent to the Northern Army played a critical role in the battles of Freeman's Farm (19 September) and Saratoga (7 October), which resulted in the first surrender of a British field army on 17 October. This surrender would have strategic consequences, the chief of which was to bring France and its fleet into the conflict, which changed the nature of the war entirely. In comparison, Howe found Philadelphia a paltry prize, and he resigned that winter. His successor, Gen. Sir Henry Clinton, decided to pull the army back to New York City. Washington—reinforced by troops from the Northern Department—harried Clinton the entire way back, including a battle at Monmouth. Clinton's army would remain penned up in New York City for the remainder of the war.

The Northern Army had found victory at long last—a total victory. And while the technology and tactics were different than those used today, the lessons learned from this retreat are timeless. First, the Northern Army owed much to the dogged determination of leaders like Schuyler and Arnold, who did not accept defeat even when events seemed hopeless. Neither man contemplated surrendering or disbanding the Northern Army. Indeed, Arnold used his force of will—and spent his own considerable fortune on supplies—to keep his soldiers together through the dismal 1775 trek through Maine and then back up the lake in 1776. Leaders shared the hardships of their soldiers and led by personal example. Arnold and St. Clair did not leave their force during the retreat from Saint-Jean, a la Douglas MacArthur when he left the Philippines for Australia in 1942. Instead, they remained and helped pull their men through to safety, exhorting their soldiers to greater efforts and trying to bolster their morale. Leaders who are willing to retreat and have plans for it—and do not give up—will set conditions for an eventual counterattack.

Second, this campaign demonstrates that people are more important than places or things. By preserving the nucleus of the Northern Army, Schuyler and St. Clair preserved the will to fight. While reinforcements would be needed to gain victory, these leaders and their soldiers bought the time to concentrate more forces. This was very much in keeping with Washington's strategy during the war: to avoid decisive battle if there was no hope for a victory and then trade space for time. Schuyler bought more than a month of time with his slow retreat from Ticonderoga to Fort Edward to Stillwater. Each retreat came from not wanting to risk the loss of personnel even though the retreat meant giving up fortified positions and equipment. In this case, Schuyler and St. Clair did not allow their pride, ego, or contemporary beliefs about the superiority of positional warfare to get in the way of saving their people. The Continental Army—Northern, Main, and Southern—made up the center of gravity for the rebellion. As long as the army survived, so did the war effort.

Third, the Continental Army benefitted from a strong commander-in-chief. Washington was willing to take operational risks but did not gamble. He assessed risk and probability and then made his decision. Washington's style contrasted with a wide spectrum of risk takers in this campaign. For example, Benedict Arnold took risks whenever he saw a mere spark of an opportunity for victory. On the opposite side of the spectrum was Horatio Gates, who preferred to let opportunity come to him. In the middle, Schuyler weighed pros and cons evenly. Washington's ability to assume prudent risk created the opportunity for future victory.

Fourth, the terrain favored the Continental cause—dividing the enemy in a largely hostile country with poor lines of supply. By retreating into interior lines, the Northern Army was able to rapidly resupply and refit for a further offensive. Leaders should consider not just the geographical terrain of their area of operations, but also the human terrain. If both are reinforcing, a leader can gain unexpected advantages.

Last, and possibly most important, leaders at all levels did not lose their fighting spirit or desire to seize the momentum again. Warner at Hubbardton (despite his tactical defeat), Stark at Bennington, and Arnold at Saratoga are all examples of leaders who seized the opportunity to regain the tactical and operational initiative from the enemy. That spirited resolve brought final victory at Saratoga in 1777 and continues to inspire the US Army to this day.

Notes

1. Mark Anderson, *The Battle for the Fourteenth Colony: America's War of Liberation in Canada, 1774–1776* (Hanover, NH: University Press of New England, 2013), 191.

2. Rick Atkinson, *The British Are Coming: The War for America, Lexington to Princeton, 1775–1777* (New York: Henry Holt and Company, 2019), 211.

3. Atkinson, 276.

4. Anderson, *Battle for the Fourteenth Colony*, 310.

5. Anderson, 323.

6. Atkinson, *The British Are Coming*, 282.

7. Peter Force, *American Archives Consisting of a Collection of Authentic Records,* vol. IV, no. 6 (Washington, DC: self-pub., 1844), 451.

8. Harry Schenawolf, "Canada Lost: The American Retreat from Quebec January—June 1776," *The Revolutionary War Journal*, 20 September 2018, http://www.revolutionarywarjournal.com/american-tragedy-retreat-from-quebec-january-june-1776-the-battle-of-three-rivers-resulting-in-the-loss-of-canada/.

9. Force, *American Archives*, 684.

10. Anderson, *Battle for the Fourteenth Colony*, 328–29.

11. Schenawolf, "Canada Lost."

12. Anderson, *Battle for the Fourteenth Colony*, 330.

13. Anderson, 330. A bateaux is a flat-bottomed boat common to the Great Lakes and northern US regions.

14. Douglas R. Cubbison, *The American Northern Theater Army in 1776: The Ruin and Reconstruction of the Continental Force* (Jefferson, NC: McFarland Publishing, 2010), 122.

15. Atkinson, *The British Are Coming*, 292.

16. Cubbison, *The American Northern Theater Army in 1776,* 123.

17. Anderson, *Battle for the Fourteenth Colony*, 331.

18. Force, *American Archives*, 926.

19. Force, 926.

20. Eric Schnitzer and Don Troiani, *Don Troiani's Campaign to Saratoga—1777: The Turning Point of the Revolutionary War in Paintings, Artifacts, and Historical Narrative* (Guilford, CT: Stackpole Books, 2019), 4.

21. Schnitzer and Troiani, 4.

22. Horatio Gates to Benedict Arnold, 7 August 1776, in *Naval Documents of the American Revolution*, vol. 6, ed. William James Morgan (Washington, DC: Government Printing Office, 1972), 95–96.

23. Atkinson, *The British Are Coming*, 417.

24. Schnitzer and Troiani, *Don Troiani's Campaign to Saratoga*, 11.

25. Schnitzer and Troiani, 12.

26. Atkinson, *The British Are Coming,* 425.

27. Atkinson, 428.

28. Schnitzer and Troiani, *Don Troiani's Campaign to Saratoga*, 16.

29. John Luzader, "The Coming Revolutionary War Battles at Saratoga," in *The Saratoga Campaign: Uncovering an Embattled Landscape*, ed. William Griswold and Donald Linebaugh (Lebanon, NH: University Press of New England, 2016), 9.

30. Schnitzer and Troiani, *Don Troiani's Campaign to Saratoga*, 16–18.

31. Luzader, "The Coming Revolutionary War Battles at Saratoga," 12.

32. Philip Schuyler to Congress, 23 June 1777, *Proceedings of a General Court Martial, held at Major General Lincoln's quarters, near Quaker-Hill, in the state of New-York, by order of His Excellency General Washington, commander in chief of the army of the United States of America, for the trial of Major General Schuyler*, accessed 10 February 2021, https://quod.lib.umich.edu/e/evans/N12773.0001.001/1:3?rgn=div1;view=fulltext, hereafter cited as *Schuyler Court Martial*, 34.

33. Luzader, "The Coming Revolutionary War Battles at Saratoga," 13.

34. Schnitzer and Troiani, *Don Troiani's Campaign to Saratoga*, 40,

35. *Schuyler Court Martial*, 4–5.

36. Schnitzer and Troiani, *Don Troiani's Campaign to Saratoga*, 39.

37. Atkinson, *The British Are Coming*, 357.

38. Atkinson, 459.

39. Atkinson, 459.

40. Atkinson, 485.

41. Atkinson, 553.

42. Luzader, "The Coming Revolutionary War Battles at Saratoga," 14.

43. Arthur St. Clair to Philip Schuyler, 18 June 1777, *Schuyler Court Martial*, 5.

44. Arthur St. Clair to Philip Schuyler, 25 June 1777, *Schuyler Court Martial*, 6.

45. Arthur St. Clair to Philip Schuyler, 28 June 1777, *Schuyler Court Martial*, 7.

46. Philip Schuyler to George Washington, 25 June 1777, *Schuyler Court Martial*, 34–35.

47. Extract of Orders from Philip Schuyler to Jacob Cuyler, 12 July 1777, *Schuyler Court Martial*, 46.

48. Philip Schuyler to the Committee of Safety of the State of New-York, 28 June 1777, *Schuyler Court Martial*, 36.

49. Philip Schuyler to General Putnam, 28 June 1777, *Schuyler Court Martial*, 36.

50. Schuyler, 43.

51. Arthur St. Clair, *Proceedings of a General Court Martial, held at White Plains, in the state of New-York, by order of His Excellency General Washington, commander in chief of the army of the United States of America, for the trial of Major General St. Clair, August 25, 1778, Major General Lincoln, president* (Philadelphia: Hall and Sellers, 1778), hereafter cited as *St. Clair Court Martial*, 26.

52. Philip Schuyler to George Washington, 5 July 1777, *Schuyler Court Martial,* 41.

53. Testimony of Tadeusz Kosciusko, *St. Clair Court Martial*, 22.

54. Testimony of Jeduthan Baldwin, *St. Clair Court Martial*, 29.

55. Schnitzer and Troiani, *Don Troiani's Campaign to Saratoga*, 49.

56. Schnitzer and Troiani, 50–60.

57. Schnitzer and Troiani, 63.

58. Testimony of Lt. Col. Stevens, *St. Clair Court Martial*, 30.

59. Philip Schuyler to the Committee of Berkshire, 7 July 1777, *Schuyler Court Martial*, 47.

60. Philip Schuyler to Arthur St. Clair, 8 July 1777, *Schuyler Court Martial*, 47.

61. Snow, Dean, *1777: Tipping Point at Saratoga* (New York, NY: Oxford University Press, 2016), 15.

62. Schnitzer and Troiani, *Don Troiani's Campaign to Saratoga,* 74.

63. Schnitzer and Troiani, 74.

64. Schnitzer and Troiani, 74–75.

65. Philip Schuyler to George Washington, 10 July 1777, *Schuyler Court Martial*, 48

66. Philip Schuyler to George Washington, 14 July 1777, *Schuyler Court Martial*, 49

67. Schnitzer and Troiani, *Don Troiani's Campaign to Saratoga*, 148

68. Schnitzer and Troiani, 89.

69. Schnitzer and Troiani, 149.

70. Snow, *1777*, 14.

71. *Schuyler Court Martial*, 55.

72. Extract of a letter to Congress, dated Albany, 27 September 1777, *Schuyler Court Martial*, 56.

73. Schnitzer and Troiani, *Don Troiani's Campaign to Saratoga*, 149.

Chapter 9
Airmen into Infantry: The Provisional Air Corps Regiment at Bataan, January–April 1942
Frank A. Blazich Jr.

On 7 February 1945, General of the Army Douglas MacArthur visited recently liberated prisoners at Santo Tomas University and Old Bilibid Prison in Manila, the Philippines. As MacArthur walked through Bilibid's prison wards, emaciated men clad in filthy rags with gaunt faces silently came to attention. Among them was Lt. Col. David L. Hardee. "Hardee," said the general, "the last time I saw you I was sending you to make infantry of the Air Corps."[1] MacArthur referenced a January 1942 meeting when the fighting on Luzon had reached a critical juncture. At month's end, the United States Army Forces in the Far East (USAFFE) ordered career infantry officers Hardee and Col. Irvin E. Doane to turn a group of aviators, ground crew, and mechanics into a competent infantry regiment capable of holding the main defensive line on the Bataan peninsula.

Following attacks by Imperial Japanese forces in December 1941, America's initial entry into World War II was marked by a series of defeats and losses of territory, personnel, and materiel in the Pacific. The Japanese struck Allied military forces broadly in the opening weeks of the war at Hawaii, Guam, Wake Island, Malaya, Singapore, the Dutch East Indies, and the Philippines. For the latter, American and Filipino forces facing the Japanese included career army officers and enlisted personnel, some World War I veterans, recently arrived US military forces, and green, hastily mobilized Filipino units with only rudimentary training. As the struggle for the Philippines unfolded and hope of resupply of equipment—much less personnel—proved fleeting, MacArthur and USAFFE attempted to hold back the Japanese with every available resource. The loss of the Far East Air Force (FEAF) and the urgent need to check the Japanese advance gave birth to one of the most unusual units in the history of the US Air Force: the Provisional Air Corps Regiment (PACR).

Within the literature of the fighting on Bataan, the most noteworthy example of the use of improvised infantry was during the Battle of the Points. From 23 January to 13 February 1942, a force of Philippine Constabulary, grounded American airmen, and a naval battalion composed of sailors and marines, fought two Japanese 20th Infantry Regiment battalions which had landed at Anyasan, Longoskawayan, Quinauan, and Silaiim Points on the southwest coast of Bataan. Aside from the marines, these forces were essentially untrained and completely inexperienced in infantry tactics or weapons. The improvised infantry stationed in the service command area of the southern tip of the peninsula, however, effectively contained the isolated Japanese forces but not dislodge or destroy them. When the enemy threat was finally annihilated, the infantry required reinforcements of armor, artillery, naval surface units, Filipino infantry and scouts, and support from the last remaining FEAF aircraft.[2]

The PACR's operational history, by comparison, remains obscure but provides a valuable case study into how a retreating force can be reconstituted and repurposed as a viable asset for defensive purposes. Unlike the units which fought in the Battle of the Points, the PACR was a formally established provisional regiment tasked with occupying a sector of what became the main line of resistance (MLR) on Bataan from late January to April 1942. Though these airmen lacked infantry training and small arms familiarity, they were aided by experienced senior infantry officers; with this expert advice, the PACR established potent defensive positions and conducted both scouting patrols and small raids. Through the twin pillars of experienced senior leadership and preservation of existing unit organization, the PACR maintained strong unit cohesion and became a stalwart element of the Bataan defense. The only American regiment on the MLR, the PACR airmen remain a singular example in American military aviation history of airmen converting into a line infantry regiment, an act born of necessity by a beleaguered retreating army.

Destroyed and Grounded

The PACR originated during the fall 1941 situation in the Philippines. After being recalled to active duty that July and placed in command of the newly established USAFFE, MacArthur attempted to mobilize, train, and equip ten Philippine Army reserve divisions to supplement the existing Philippine Department.[3] By 30 November, MacArthur had added American armor, artillery, a contingent of officers and enlisted personnel as trainers, and 107 P-40 fighters and 35 B-17 heavy bombers on Luzon; the additions bolstered his forces to approximately 31,000 American and 100,000 Filipino uniformed personnel. In the minds of MacArthur, Army Chief of Staff George C. Marshall, and Secretary of War Henry L. Stimson, this infusion of airpower for FEAF provided a formidable deterrent to aggressive Japanese expansion.[4]

One day of air attacks, however, transformed vaunted airpower into smoldering ruins. On 8 December, Imperial Japanese Army and Navy air units decimated the FEAF, destroying half of the B-17s and a third of

P-40s on the ground or in the air with considerable loss of personnel. By 10 December, Maj. Gen. Lewis H. Brereton, FEAF commander, ordered his remaining twenty-two P-40s and eight obsolete P-35s fighters to cease interdiction operations and instead fly aerial reconnaissance to spot enemy ground movements. Shortly thereafter on 22 December, the main Japanese ground force under command of Lt. Gen. Masaharu Homma landed at Lingayen Gulf and began moving toward Manila. Meanwhile, a second force landed at Lamon Bay on 24 December to move north. With Homma's pincers closing, MacArthur ordered a withdrawal into defensive positions on the Bataan peninsula. In the rush to move into Bataan, vast stores of food, medicine, and other war materiel were abandoned or ruined. On 24 December, Brereton and a skeleton staff evacuated to Australia and FEAF command passed to Col. Harold H. George of the Fifth Interceptor Command. George lacked aircraft but commanded approximately 5,000 personnel.[5]

With several squadrons permanently grounded on Bataan, the troops contributed any way they could in the withdrawal into Bataan. Some airmen drove supply trucks while others guarded hastily constructed airfields at the barangays of Mariveles, Cabcaben, and Lucanin (called Bataan Airfield) to shelter the few remaining aircraft in southern Bataan.[6] Early in

Figure 9.1. Destroyed B-17 at Clark Field, December 1941. Source: Record Group 127, Bill Bartsch Collection, MacArthur Memorial, Norfolk, VA.

1942, George initiated efforts to arm, equip, and train the airmen to serve as infantry. Within that first week of January, Col. Harrison H. C. Richards, MacArthur's senior air corps officer, assumed command of air corps personnel and thereafter decided to supplement USAFFE forces on the frontlines with the grounded airmen, albeit organized as a reserve force.[7]

Richards graduated from the US Military Academy in 1911 and served in the cavalry before earning his military aviator rating in 1918. Stationed stateside during World War I, he held a variety of posts in the 1920s and also graduated from the Air Corps Tactical School and the Command and General Staff School. He joined the Philippine Department in 1939.[8] Chaplain (Maj.) Leslie F. Zimmerman, based at Nichols Field in Luzon, recalled in his diary in early 1942: "It was the opinion of many of us that Col. Richards was mentally not quite capable of exercising good judgement, and that he had in mind making a wonderful name for himself by commanding a regiment of Air Corps men that were going to become heros [sic] like the 'Light Brigade' of poetic fame."[9] MacArthur's predecessor commanding the Philippine Department, Maj. Gen. George Grunert, requested a replacement for Richards in March 1941, deeming him "a hard worker [but] entirely too verbose, capable in a measure but apparently unable to get necessary cooperation.... Youngsters in the Air Corps ... have no confidence" in Richards with his antiquated ideas or in other senior air corps commanders.[10] Effective 19 November 1941, Richards was relieved as air officer of the Philippine Department and reassigned to FEAF as a senior air staff officer on MacArthur's staff.[11]

Starting in early January 1942, FEAF ordered the commencement of improvised training for the airmen. Pilots, mechanics, and ground personnel who had never handled a rifle received World War I-vintage M1903 Springfield or M1917 Enfield rifles, practiced extended order rifle drill, and learned how to clean and maintain the weapons. A squadron went south to the beach at Cabcaben for daily target practice, with each man issued five rounds. Other training consisted of bayonet drill, basic scouting, and patrol work. Compounding the strain of hurried training, on 5 January, USAFFE ordered everyone on half rations. On the evening of 8 January 1942, Lt. Col. William H. Maverick, who commanded the 20th Air Base Group (Reinforced) near Kilometer Post 165 by Limay, received orders to form the airmen into a provisional regiment and prepare for immediate movement into a reserve battle position near Bilolo. USAFFE Chief of Staff Maj. Gen. Richard K. Sutherland had assured George that the air corps men would man the reserve line with individuals on loan to infantry commanders until replacement aircraft and reinforcements arrived to reactivate the FEAF.[12]

From Wings to Rifles

What became the PACR stood up near Barrio Bilolo, two kilometers (1.2 miles) west of Orion. Numbering approximately 1,500 grounded officers and men, the regiment was organized into two battalions of five squadrons each, with the component air corps squadrons serving as infantry company equivalents. Retention of the Air Corps unit organization preserved the existing elements of identity and cohesion. Without then disrupting previous personnel arrangements, this ensured that previous bonds of mutual trust, cooperation, and confidence among airmen would exist on the field of battle.[13] The 1st Battalion, commanded by Col. Newman R. Laughinghouse with Maverick as his executive officer, consisted of the 20th Air Base Group Headquarters and Headquarters Squadron; 19th Air Base Squadron; and 7th, 27th, and 28th Materiel squadrons. The 2nd Battalion, commanded by Maj. (later Lt. Col.) John W. Sewell, consisted of the 27th Bombardment Group Headquarters and Headquarters Squadron, 48th Materiel Squadron, 2nd Observation Squadron, and the 17th and 91st Bomb squadrons.[14]

Thanks to the regimental cohesion tied to the Air Corps structure, PACR began with strong teamwork at the company and battalion level. Richards's poor leadership and reputation with the airmen, however, represented a risk. Held in low regard by junior Air Corps officers serving as infantry commanders of impromptu platoons and companies, Richards needed to regain the confidence of his subordinates during a period of marked uncertainty as to the regiment's organization and combat effectiveness. "By thinking objectively himself and by causing his men to perform tasks involving thought and movement," a leader could "instill in the men a sense of confidence and security," noted the Infantry School's influential publication, *Infantry in Battle*.[15]

In the rear battle position reserve line, stretching from Orion to Bagac (hereafter the Orion-Bagac Line), the PACR was assigned to the II Philippine Corps on the eastern half of Bataan and commanded by Maj. Gen. George M. Parker Jr.[16] Located eight miles behind the MLR, Parker assigned the airmen to Sector B, responsible for 2,200 yards of the line. The 31st Infantry Philippine Army (PA) was on the regiment's right in Sector A, and the 32nd Infantry (PA) on its left in Sector C. The 1st Battalion held the right flank, with 2nd Battalion on the left.[17] "The men with me were not professional infantrymen," recalled Capt. Mark M. Wohlfeld,

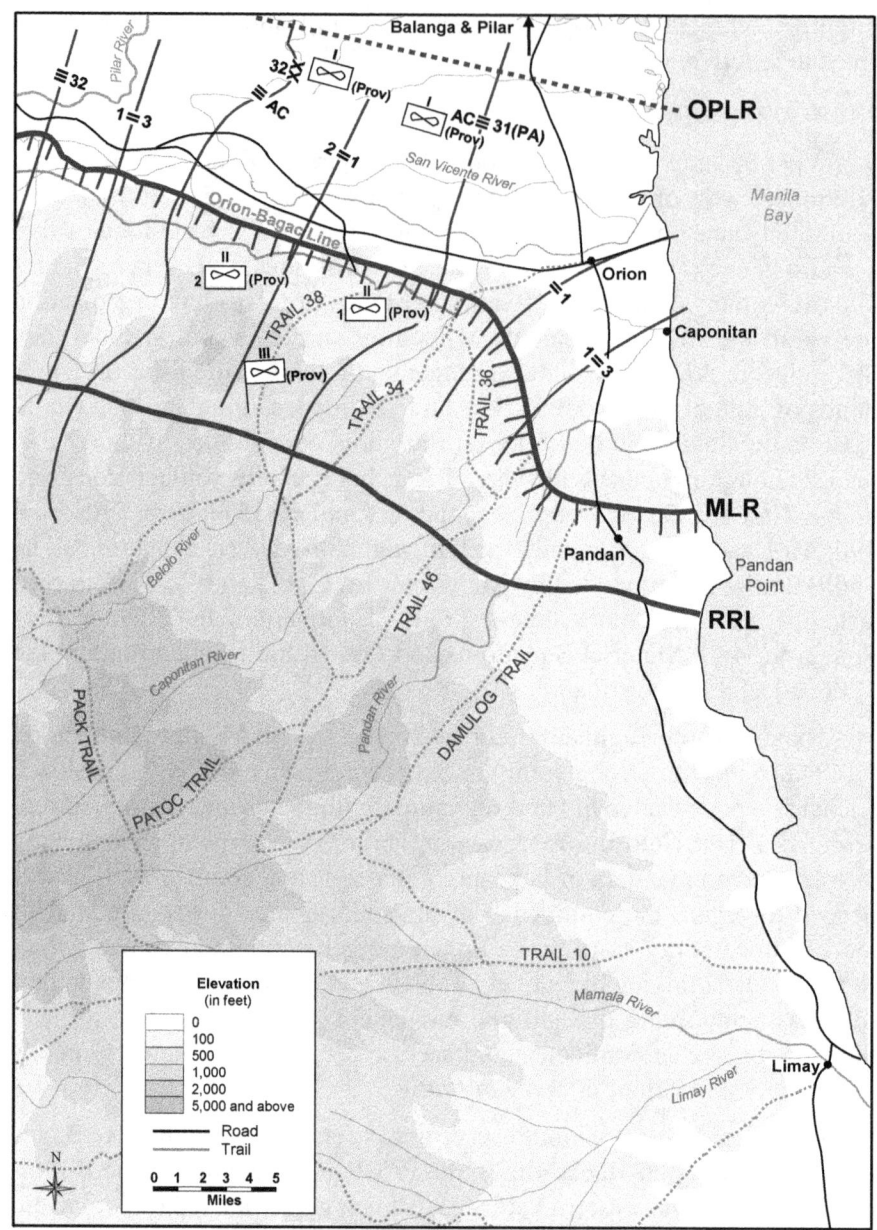

Figure 9.2. Map of the position of the Provisional Air Corps Regiment (PACR) in Sector B on Bataan, circa April 1942. Created by Army University Press.

27th Bombardment Group executive officer. "They were Air Force mechanics, technicians, or communications men. Some of the officers were pilots. They didn't know what to expect. They were just remotely acquainted with the rifles they carried."[18] Inexperience did not deter the airmen; morale appeared high.[19]

The airmen assembled a patchwork arsenal to defend their sector, including Marlin M1917 and water-cooled Browning machine guns, Browning automatic rifles, and masses of .30- and .50-caliber air-cooled machine guns salvaged from destroyed aircraft.[20] M1917 Lewis guns mounted in triplicate or M2 machine guns in improvised dual mounts served as anti-aircraft weapons. Most men carried bolt-action rifles, but some airmen managed to acquire the new semi-automatic M1 Garand. Fire support for Sectors A and B came from forty 75-mm guns of the 24th Field Artillery and 1st Battalion, 88th Field Artillery as well as 1st Battalion, 21st Field Artillery, which also had four 2.95-inch guns. Both subsectors also received support from the 192nd Tank Battalion. The regiment had no anti-personnel mines or anti-tank guns or mines, and only Molotov

Figure 9.3. Soldiers on Bataan resorted to improvised antitank weaponry, in this instance a Molotov cocktail. Courtesy of the National Archives and Records Administration.

cocktails to confront Japanese armor. In addition to lacking mortars, they experienced significant shortages of grenades, bayonets, and armor-piercing .50-caliber ammunition. For communication, the regiment used wired field telephones and some radio equipment; runners filled in for limited electronic means of communications.[21]

Sector B's terrain aided the ill-prepared regiment. The San Vincente River paralleled the front 400 to 800 yards from the MLR. Its steep sides and deep channel created a viable anti-tank barrier. Bilolo Creek branched from the river in the right flank of the sector, and the road from Orion crossed the creek. Engineers demolished the road crossing and dammed the creek, flooding the wide-open rice paddies between the river and the regiment's right flank with six inches of water to thwart direct tank or infantry assault. Richards, unfamiliar with defensive preparations, turned for advice to the regiment's few personnel with prior infantry experience. Lt. Col. Jasper E. Brady Jr., who commanded 3rd Battalion, 31st Infantry (US), and other regimental personnel gave advanced training to the airmen, based on their recent combat experiences. With few entrenching tools, the novice infantrymen dug foxholes and trench lines, prepared and sighted machine gun emplacements, strung barbed wire, manned observation posts, and commenced combat patrols. Mango trees provided concealment. First Lt. Sheldon H. Mendelson recalled the fields of fire were "generally good," and "the right flank of the regiment was able to give enfilade fire across a portion of subsector A."[22] Persistent attacks by enemy dive bombers harassed the men but produced few casualties. Some regiment members found diversions in Filipino-supplied alcohol, and junior officers complained about Richards's lack of competence in leadership and infantry knowledge.[23]

The Japanese launched the Battle of Bataan on 9 January against the II Philippine Corps line extending from Mabatang to the northeast slopes of Mount Natib in northern Bataan. On 15 January, the PACR's 1st Battalion received orders to move north to Abucay, just south of the Abucay-Mauban MLR. While the American-advised Filipino regiments held fast through the initial attacks, the relentless Japanese forces weakened the center of the MLR and threatened to turn the II Corps left flank near Mount Natib. In the darkness of the fifteenth, the 1st Battalion moved up on the Guitol Ridge to a plateau between the Abo-Abo and Tidwir rivers. Here the men made contact with soldiers of the Filipino 31st Division (PA) as Richards had managed to march the battalion right into the division command post of Brig. Gen. Clifford Bluemel. The airmen then relocated several miles rearward and engaged in anti-sniper activity. Over the following days, the airmen engaged in light scouting patrols and anti-sniper work. Inexperienced and jittery, the airmen mistook Filipino forces for Japanese infantry and bird songs for Japanese communications, and inadvertently killed monkeys thought to be enemy infiltrators. By 22 January, Japanese forces had destroyed the 51st Division (PA) and drove in the II Corps left flank as American and Filipino counterattacks failed to dislodge the enemy. The 1st Battalion and all other Filipino and American forces received orders to withdraw back to the Orion-Bagac Line, now the MLR on Bataan. The assembled PACR reoccupied Sector B of the line from 22 to 24 January.[24]

Operating as a frontline unit, the PACR's importance and combat effectiveness became paramount. The regiment's personnel, however, had completely lost confidence in Richards's leadership, and this threatened the regiment's cohesion. The regimental chaplain, Zimmerman, recalled "after we came back to our original position, it was soon evident that we could never get any sort of esprit de corps as long as Col. Richards was commanding us. The officers hated him, and the men had no respect for him."[25] On 26 January 1942, USAFFE issued General Order No. 13, establishing the PACR from the 27th Bombardment and 20th Air Base Groups. Concurrently, MacArthur's headquarters also issued Special Orders No. 24, again relieving Richards of command, replacing him with newly promoted Colonel Doane, executive officer of the 31st Infantry (US); Hardee, then on temporary duty at USAFFE headquarters, joined Doane to serve as his executive officer.[26]

Both officers provided a wealth of career infantry experience. A Maine native, Doane enlisted in the Maine National Guard in 1910 and received his commission in June 1916. After service with General John J. Pershing's Punitive Expedition of 1916, Doane headed to France in 1917 with the 103rd Infantry Regiment, 26th Division. In June 1918, he organized and led volunteers who braved artillery fire to capture a group of Germans, an act which helped him earn the nickname "Devil Doane." He remained in the postwar Army, graduating from the Infantry School Company Officers Course and staying on as an instructor. He held several instructor posts in the 1930s before reporting in 1939 to the Philippine Department. In October 1941, the Army retained Doane in the Philippines, where he served as the 31st Infantry (US) intelligence officer and executive officer prior to taking command of the PACR.[27]

A North Carolina native, Hardee enlisted in the Army in January 1918 and shipped out to France as a member of the 28th Infantry Regiment, 1st Infantry Division. He received a commission in September 1918 and entered combat in October in the Meuse-Argonne and Maison-Sedan offensives, being thrice cited for valor. In the 1920s, Hardee graduated from the Infantry School Basic Course and became the first infantry officer and non-aviator to graduate from the Air Corps Tactical School. As a member of the 31st Infantry in 1932, Hardee deployed to Shanghai to guard a section of the International Settlement against Japanese hostilities. While training infantry recruits at Camp Wheeler, Georgia, in September 1941, Hardee received orders to report to the Philippines to help train new Filipino infantry divisions. After arriving in November, Hardee spent the first weeks of the war on temporary duty with USAFFE, organizing the command post for the Bataan Echelon of the North Luzon Force, among other tasks.[28]

Doane and Hardee began honing the PACR's position and training men in the finer points of offensive and defensive infantry combat. Hardee considered the regiment "a particularly difficult assignment," noting problems such as the PACR's lack of "headquarters and service companies so necessary to proper infantry operations."[29] Recalling the work in 1945, he explained: "We had to improvise these as best we could from personnel and materials available. The men and officers, however, were up against hard propositions and we found them ready, able, and willing."[30] Doane—familiar with the terrain and the unit's position on the front line from his time with the 31st Infantry (US)—visited squadrons on the line, surveyed defenses, and implemented improvements. Fortunately, Japanese attacks on the Orion-Bagac failed to make inroads and on 8 February, Homma issued orders for a general withdrawal to regroup. During the initial fighting along the line, Sector B experienced small, albeit violent, engagements between Japanese and American patrols but no main assault. These trials by fire cost the regiment its first combat deaths, with six men killed on patrol duty.[31]

The change in leadership proved a boon for the regiment. "Our organization changed almost overnight. Under their guidance, our position was strengthened," reflected Zimmerman on Doane and Hardee's role.[32] Through their clear direction and authoritative experience in infantry warfare, Doane and Hardee instilled confidence in the men, and overall unit cohesion and teamwork improved. Existing foxholes were consolidated into continuous trenches along the line, a communication trench was built, and new positions were dug on the outpost line of resistance (OPLR) on an open plain about 1,000 yards north of the San Vicente River.[33] All the while, "machine guns had to be sighted, dead spaces covered with rifle fire and grenade pits, and a thousand and one little details attended to which make up an infantryman's work," noted Hardee.[34] With an overwhelming mass of former aircraft machine guns, excellent fields of fire, and tank and infantry defenses, Sector B stood poised to thwart any frontal assault.[35]

Figure 9.4. Improvised tank traps on Bataan akin to defensive measures taken by the PACR in Sector B. Courtesy of the National Archives and Records Administration.

Brig. Gen. Hugh J. Casey, USAFFE chief engineer, reported PACR positions were "outstanding" following his inspection of the line in March 1942.[36] Doane kept up the men's spirits and inspired them through his leadership. In contrast to Richards, he was "loved by everyone for his courageous and optimistic outlook when the going was toughest," reported Capt. Damon "Rocky" Gause of the 27th Bombardment Group. Gause emphasized how Doane "was especially appreciated by the airmen who served under him on Bataan because of his sincere respect for the Air Corps even though he was an infantry officer."[37]

Proficiency through Patrols

Having reinforced the main line defenses, PACR personnel improved their infantry skills. Throughout February and into March, "Our Air Corps men soon learned the tricks of the infantry trade and became as much at home in the slit trench or foxhole as a professional infantryman," wrote Gause. "Morale was good."[38] The regiment's improvised anti-aircraft mounts even downed two enemy dive bombers, further boosting morale. Doane restructured the regimental patrol system more efficiently, rotating platoons from the main to the OPLR approximately 2,000 yards in front of the MLR, then to a regimental reserve line (RRL) approximately 1,500 yards to the rear of the MLR to keep men rested and alert.[39] Together with Hardee, leadership made sure all personnel remained active and busy. Periodic intelligence patrols penetrated Japanese lines to monitor enemy forces. These intelligence patrols often worked with Filipino 31st Infantry (PA) scouts, who on one occasion alerted leaders about a Japanese ammo dump in Balanga. Capt. Mark M. Wohlfeld of the 27th Bombardment Group led a volunteer force armed with grenades and Molotov cocktails which, under the cover of darkness, located and destroyed the dump.[40]

During such patrols, airmen observed that the Japanese in Pilar and Balanga were using church steeples as observation posts. On 25 February, 2nd Lt. Arthur B. Amron of the 48th Materiel Squadron led a patrol to scout the area around the church in Balanga. Amron guided his twenty men six kilometers (nearly four miles) forward of the outpost line of resistance to reach the church. After killing guards outside, Amron and a sergeant entered the church and used rifle fire and grenades to kill several Japanese soldiers using it as an observation post. While exiting the church, Amron was critically wounded by enemy machine gun fire from a hidden enemy soldier but managed to exit the church before collapsing. When members of the patrol ran to help him, Amron yelled: "Damn it! Get the men the hell out of here. I can't make it." He died shortly after; his body was left behind and never recovered. Amron posthumously received the Silver Star for his heroic efforts. Following the Balanga incident, MacArthur withdrew restrictions on using artillery to destroy the houses of worship.[41]

Unfortunately, the regiment's lack of manpower left a glaring hole in the sector's defenses. With the MRL secure and OPLR operating smoothly, Hardee began work to establish the RRL. Unlike a standard infantry regiment, the PACR lacked a third battalion for the reserve line; as a result, Hardee could only order the men to clear out a line in the jungle and then thin vegetation to create open fire lanes. So the position would not be obvious to aircraft, lateral footpaths were created to mark the reserve line linking Trail 38, in the middle of the sector, with Sectors C and A on the regiment's flanks. Foxholes dotted areas where the paths and trails intersected in the event the regiment had to fall back to the line. Doane's rotational patrol system provided Hardee the labor to build the regimental reserve line and become familiar with it, but it largely remained unoccupied.[42]

Critical shortages of food and medicine further hampered reserve line construction and weakened the peninsula's defenders. In the jungles of Bataan, mosquitos and malaria proved devastating due to insufficient stocks of mosquito bars (nets) and prophylactic quinine. Practically everyone in the PACR suffered from malaria, including Doane, who was bedridden with the disease in February and March. Hardee attempted to maintain daily inspection and training tours but had to curtail them as hunger and malaria sapped his strength. By March, men barely received 1,000 calories daily. Rather than hunting the Japanese, the airmen began scrounging for food when on patrol, either capturing supplies from the Japanese or eating horses, mules, carabao, monkeys, and anything else they could find in the jungles.[43] To make the carabao palatable, Capt. William E. Dyess recalled the preferred formula: "you put a stone in the pot with it and when the stone melted the carabao was cooked."[44]

By mid-March, the multiple shortages, compounded by poor morale, worsened the situation for the PACR and the entire Bataan force. Daily bombing attacks and occasional artillery fire frayed the men's already jangled nerves. Uniforms and footwear rotted in the jungle conditions, and less than half the frontline men rated as combat-effective. On 11 March, MacArthur, his family, and select staff—including Maj. Charles H. Morehouse, the PACR surgeon—left Corregidor for Australia. Doane and Hardee withheld the news from the regiment until official word reached the troops. Weeks prior during a 23 February fireside chat, President Franklin D. Roosevelt had publicly acknowledged that relief for the Philippines would not come.[45]

Trial by Fire

On Good Friday, 3 April 1942, Japan commenced its new offensive. Approximately 150 Japanese artillery pieces began shelling the Orion-Bagac Line from 1000 to 1500. Bombers joined the barrage, dropping more than sixty tons of ordnance on American and Filipino positions. Hardee compared the barrage to his first war experience: "It far exceeded any preparation fire I had seen in the Meuse-Argonne in 1918."[46] The bulk of the fire was targeted on the narrow II Corps front on Sector D that was thinly held by the 21st and 41st divisions (PA). The Japanese placed their 65th Brigade and 4th Division, both heavily reinforced, in front. The barrage effectively destroyed the 41st Division (PA) even before Japanese armor and infantry crossed the line of departure. Following the bombardment, the Japanese force advanced forward and swiftly pushed through the routed 41st Division (PA) before moving on Mount Samat. By 5 April, the Japanese had seized the summit and held the entire MLR for II Corps' Sector D.[47]

Two sectors to the east, PACR braced for a 6 February frontal assault which never came. Maj. Gen. Edward P. King Jr., now in command of all

Bataan forces, positioned troops along the left flank of Sector B to launch a counterattack to protect the II Corps' left flank. On PACR's left, the 31st Division (PA), commanded by Bluemel, together with remnants of the 32nd and 51st Infantry regiments (PA) formed a line on the east bank of the San Vincente River; Doane and Hardee believed the line would hold. Hardee noted: "I went to bed reasonably satisfied, but fully expecting the artillery to come down on us early next morning. When daylight came, we went to breakfast as usual. No artillery."[48] On the morning of 7 April, however, a detachment of 4,000 men under Maj. Gen. Kameichiro Nagano attacked the 32nd Infantry (PA). Led by armor supported by infantry, the Japanese swiftly cut through the Philippine battalions and turned east to strike the PACR.

Previously on the sixth, Doane had pulled back his OPLR platoons and positioned them behind the MLR, facing west towards the 32nd Philippine Army Regiment on the PACR's left flank. Early on the morning of the seventh, he ordered 1st Battalion, now commanded by Maverick, to move its plethora of .50-caliber heavy machine guns, ammunition, and mounts rearward.[49] Around dawn, Nagano's force penetrated the left flank of the PACR in the rear of the MLR in the vicinity of the unoccupied RRL. By 0700, the PACR command post (CP) ordered the 1st Battalion units to relocate and position themselves along the junction of Trail 38 and the RRL, roughly diagonal across Sector B. Japanese small arms fire intensified as their force struck the 48th Materiel Squadron, 27th Bombardment Group, and 2nd Battalion's 2nd Observation Squadron on the PACR's left flank. Fire from the 48th Materiel Squadron delayed the Japanese advance, allowing remaining 2nd Battalion troops to fall back to the position at Trail 38 under Doane's orders by 1000.[50]

Doane now sought to withdraw the regiment and form new defensive lines. With permission from Parker, he ordered a withdrawal to the RRL. Doane and Hardee wanted to establish a new CP. But by 1100, deteriorating conditions necessitated moving the post farther south near a more a more defensible line along the Damulog Trail. Hardee recalled that "neither the high command nor anyone else could conceive of the battle lasting after our Orion-Bagac line had been overrun, so no plans beyond this line had been made."[51] Every regimental commander had to make their own decision to retreat while preserving the cohesion and combat effectiveness of their unit.[52]

Just after noon when the San Vincente River line collapsed, Hardee located the new CP on the trail near the Pandan River, several miles south of the RRL. Maverick and Sewell—commanding the PACR at the front while Doane and Hardee shifted the CP—waited two hours for information on the new CP location but received no reply. With Japanese fire intensifying, both battalion commanders walked until they finally located the CP several miles behind the RRL; there they found Doane, Hardee, and the staff having lunch, seemingly oblivious to the communications failure. Doane ordered both commanders to relocate along the Potoc Trail, with the junction of Trail 38 dividing the 2nd and 1st battalions.[53]

Returning to the regiment by staff car, Maverick issued orders to 1st Battalion for the withdrawal. Sewell, however, apparently failed to transmit withdrawal orders to 2nd Battalion and instead chose to withdraw to the rear on his own. These increasing communication failures and the leadership's apparent lack of situational awareness damaged the confidence between Doane and Hardee and the battalion commanders Maverick and Sewell. The unease expanded into broader fragmentation of regimental cohesion during the withdrawal south.

Maverick ordered Capt. John S. Coleman of the 27th Materiel Squadron to proceed with the 48th Materiel Squadron to cover the battalion's withdrawal. While 1st Battalion withdrew to the reserve line in an orderly fashion, 2nd Battalion's unit integrity began disintegrating as men became separated due to a combination of muddled orders and limited visibility on the jungle trails.[54] Recalled Pfc. Elbert Hampton of the 48th Materiel Squadron: "When the front lines gave way, the Japs were pushing hard, and we were scrambling to get out of there. We thought we would wind up on Corregidor, but that never happened."[55]

At 1400, the regiment formed a new line paralleling the Pandan Trail. When Maverick went to the CP, he found that Doane and Hardee had abandoned it. They left after receiving reports that Japanese armor and infantry had broken the lines of Col. Jack Irwin's 31st Infantry (PA) and were advancing south along the main East Road, forcing the PACR to relocate to the Damulog Trail. Throughout the withdrawal, Japanese aircraft dive-bombed, strafed, and harassed exhausted American airmen and Filipino soldiers. Once at the Damulog Trail, Doane ordered Maverick and Sewell to hold the regiment on the trail while he and Hardee attempted to reach II Corps. Doane met up with Irwin, then in contact with II Corps. Parker's headquarters ordered PACR to position itself near Limay, on the south bank of the Mamala River.

Maverick, hearing nothing back from Doane or Hardee for two hours, moved the regiment to the East Road junction with the Damulog Trail. He then received verbal orders by a runner from Doane to move to Limay and

Figure 9.5. Example of the dense jungle found on Bataan. The conditions complicated the repeated withdrawal and relocation of the PACR in the retreat of 7–8 April 1942. Courtesy of the National Archives and Records Administration.

await further instructions. Meanwhile, Japanese observation planes flew overhead dropping flares. Capt. Theodore C. Bigger remembered: "No anti-aircraft shells were bursting around them. We wondered why, for these planes were sitting ducks."[56] The PACR reached Limay around 0300 on 8 April and deployed along the East Road to rest. While marching south during the night, Bluemel decided that since high bluffs on the north bank of the Mamala River "completely commanded" the line on the south shore, the position was untenable. He ordered a withdrawal to the Alangan River three kilometers (nearly two miles) south of Limay. The weary columns of ragged airmen reached the far left of the new Alangan Line at dawn and then stopped for a breakfast of one cup of milk, one of rice gruel or lugao, and a can of tomatoes and one of corned beef for every five men.[57]

Continuous air attacks caught the regiment exposed on open ground. Japanese dive bombers dropped incendiaries and inflicted numerous casualties.[58] The PACR's heavy machine guns, ordered rearward by Doane on the morning of the seventh, were nowhere to be found. Wohlfeld remembered the dive bombers plastered his men, who lacked shovels to dig foxholes: and "blew some of our men into fragments. Some of the trees were blown down. The grass was on fire. The officers kept hollering, 'Get moving! Get across! Go! Go!' The smoke was everywhere."[59] Lt. Bert Schwarz recalled the dive bombers "blasted the hell out of us and killed quite a few guys."[60] By the afternoon of the eighth, Japanese infantrymen could be seen just 400 to 500 yards away, and small arms fire intensity increased.

Around 1800, the Japanese breached the Alangan line on the PACR's right flank. Doane ordered another withdrawal and reassembly at Cabcaben six kilometers (nearly four miles) farther south, the last defendable position before the Bataan hospital areas. Here the exhausted regiment splintered; Hardee and Doane accidentally separated in the confusion of American and Filipino forces retreating in disarray along dark, unmarked jungle footpaths and truck trails. Some men moved south to Cabcaben, while others ended up in Mariveles. Bluemel assumed overall field command of the remaining forces and positioned what remained of the PACR, 31st Infantry (US), 57th Infantry (PA), 26th Cavalry (PS), and 14th Engineer Battalion (PS) near Trail 20 on the south side of the Lamao River north of Cabcaben. This last defensive line numbered roughly 1,300 men. Late on 8 April, Wohlfeld could muster only 75 2nd Battalion officers and men out of the original 770. Maverick and 1st Battalion did marginally better, mustering approximately 325 men. During the midnight hours between 8 and 9 April, Major General King decided to surrender to avoid a possible slaughter. By noon on 9 April, the largest surrender in American history was official.[61]

Retrospective

Evaluating the PACR's combat performance from fragmentary records is difficult. From 28 January to 6 April 1942, the PACR was the only American infantry unit of II Philippine Corps stationed on the MLR.[62] From 7 to 8 April, the regiment managed to execute six retrograde movements despite its disintegrating cohesion and overall unit integrity. The experienced infantry leadership of Doane and Hardee, so essential to transforming airmen into infantry in the preceding months, had prepared the regiment for battle. But in the critical hours of 7 April, Doane's leadership—or nerves—faltered badly. The break among the regiment's senior leaders caused a loss of confidence with the two battalion commanders, themselves hampered by poor communication and situational disorientation.[63]

Combat performance is shaped by logistical constraints. Having been defeated as an air force, MacArthur's retreat necessitated reestablishing airmen into line infantry. As career infantrymen, Doane and Hardee provided effective leadership that strengthened the regiment's defensive position.

Retaining the air corps' organizational structure together with the combination of small unit training, patrol operations, and establishment of lines of resistance helped sustain a regimental esprit de corps and cohesion under constantly deteriorating conditions. Minimal Japanese contact during February and March proved advantageous as the regiment reoriented itself.

By April 1942, PACR personnel were at the end of their endurance and combat effectiveness. Communication failures and diminishing confidence in regimental leadership contributed to a collapse of unit cohesion during the chaotic day of 7 April. Factors beyond the control of the regimental command further contributed to the unit's defeat and surrender in conjunction with the wider surrender of the Bataan Force. Without a third battalion, the regiment lacked the personnel to maintain a reserve line to guard its left flank. The initial retreat into Bataan left the American-Filipino force without anti-tank weaponry, proper rations, and medicines. These shortages impacted every unit on the Orion-Bagac Line, including the PACR.

Had PACR possessed the logistical resources for a prolonged defense on Bataan, the regiment likely could have endured until a relief force arrived. Even in its weakened state, PACR would have inflicted heavy losses on the Japanese if Homma launched a frontal assault against Sector B. Airmen fell back under orders only after being flanked and under pressure from the weight of enemy armor and air cover; at that point they joined with other surviving Filipino and American forces moving south on Bataan to surrender, resulting in three horrific years of imprisonment and survival.

The PACR experience emphasizes the importance of infantry training and leadership skills. Just as the 29th Commandant of the Marine Corps, General Alfred M. Gray, promulgated the adage "every Marine is a rifleman," essentially every combat soldier regardless of occupation may find themselves fighting as an infantry soldier.[64] With experienced leadership and strong unit organization, overall unit cohesion and combat effectiveness can be achieved—and a retreat transformed into a defensive stand against almost-impossible odds.[65]

Notes

1. David L. Hardee, *Bataan Survivor: A POW's Account of Japanese Captivity in World War II*, ed. Frank A. Blazich Jr. (Columbia, MO: University of Missouri Press, 2016), 197; Douglas MacArthur, *Reminiscences* (New York: McGraw-Hill Book Co., 1964), 247–48; and David L. Hardee, *The Eastern North Carolina Hardy–Hardee Family in the South and Southwest* (Raleigh, NC: self-pub., 1966), 86–89.

2. Louis Morton, *The Fall of the Philippines* (1953; reprint, Washington, DC: Center of Military History, 1989), 296–324; John W. Whitman, *Bataan: Our Last Ditch, The Bataan Campaign, 1942* (New York: Hippocrene Books, 1990), 249–323; Samuel Eliot Morison, *The Rising Sun in the Pacific, 1931–April 1942*, History of United States Naval Operations in World War II, vol. 3 (Boston: Little, Brown and Co., 1948), 200–2; John Gordon, *Fighting for MacArthur: The Navy and Marine Corps' Desperate Defense of the Philippines* (Annapolis, MD: Naval Institute Press, 2011), 127–59; Donald J. Young, The *Battle of Bataan: A Complete History*, 2nd ed. (Jefferson, NC: McFarland and Co., 2009), 75–129; J. Michael Miller, "From Shanghai to Corregidor: Marines in the Defense of the Philippines" (Washington, DC: Marine Corps Historical Center, 1997), 20–23; William F. Prickett, "The Naval Battalion on Bataan," *US Naval Institute Proceedings* 86, no. 11 (November 1960): 72–81; William H. Bartsch, "'I Wonder at Times How We Keep Going Here': The 1941–42 Philippines Diary of Lt. John P. Burns, 21st Pursuit Squadron," *Air Power History* 53, no. 4 (Winter 2006): 28–47.

3. The Philippine Division included the main American contingent organized in the Philippine Division, composed of three regiments: the American 31st Infantry (US), and the famed Philippine Scouts of the 45th and 57th Infantry (PS).

4. Morton, *Philippines*, 15–50, 71; William H. Bartsch, *December 8, 1941: MacArthur's Pearl Harbor* (College Station, TX: Texas A&M University Press, 2003), 93–105; Wesley Frank Craven and James Lea Cate, *Plans and Early Operations, January 1939 to August 1942*, The Army Air Forces in World War II, vol. 1 (1949; reprint, Washington, DC: Office of Air Force History, Government Printing Office, 1983), 177–79; and John Burton, *Fortnight of Infamy: The Collapse of Allied Airpower West of Pearl Harbor* (Annapolis, MD: Naval Institute Press, 2006), 40–53.

5. Morton, *Philippines*, 79–96, 123–44, 161–65; Craven and Cate, *Plans*, 201–19; Burton, *Fortnight*, 118–48, 188–204, 279; Bartsch, *December 8, 1941*, 267–409; Adrian R. Martin and Larry W. Stephenson, *Operation Plum: The Ill-Fated 27th Bombardment Group and the Fight for the Western Pacific* (College Station, TX: Texas A&M University Press, 2008), 51–65; E. Kathleen Williams, *Army Air Forces in the War Against Japan, 1941–1942*, Army Air Forces Historical Studies, no. 34 (Washington, DC: Historical Division, Assistant Chief of the Air Staff, Intelligence, 1945), 20–36; and Walter D. Edmonds, *They Fought with What They Had: The Story of the Army Air Forces in the*

Southwest Pacific, 1941–1942 (Boston: Little, Brown, and Co., 1951), 74–109, 167–68, 188–97.

    6. Also referred to as a barrio, this is Filipino term for a district, village, or ward. A barangay is the smallest administrative division in the Republic of the Philippines.

    7. Allison Ind, *Bataan: The Judgement Seat* (New York: Macmillan Co., 1944), 168, 178–82, 188–202, 214–15, 221; Leslie F. Zimmerman, "Diary of Lieutenant Colonel Leslie F. Zimmerman, POW in Philippines, World War II" (Unpublished memoir, transcribed by US Air Force Historical Research Agency, December 1989), 49–52; and James B. McAfee, ed., "The 27th Reports, or How to Get Scrogged, Bugger All" (unofficial unit history, 1942), 47.

    8. George W. Cullum, *Biographical Register of the Officers and Graduates of the U.S. Military Academy at West Point, New York, Supplement, Vol. VI-B, 1910–1920*, ed. Wirt Robinson (Saginaw, MI: Seemann and Peters, 1920), 1539–40.

    9. Zimmerman, "Diary," 52.

    10. Bartsch, *MacArthur's Pearl Harbor*, 67.

    11. Edmonds, *They Fought with What They Had*, 196; and Bartsch, 205.

    12. John S. Coleman Jr., *Bataan and Beyond: Memories of an American POW* (College Station, TX: Texas A&M University Press, 1978), 19–20; Martin and Stephenson, *Plum*, 72; Sheldon H. Mendelson, "Operations of the Provisional Air Corps Regiment in the Defense of Bataan Peninsula, P.I., 8 January–10 April 1942" (Fort Benning, GA: US Army Infantry School, 1946–1947), 4, 8–9; Zimmerman, "Diary," 52–59; Ind, *Judgement*, 221. Both Laughinghouse and Maverick received temporary promotions to colonel and lieutenant colonel, respectively, on 5 January 1942. Laughinghouse left the regiment around 4 to 5 April to become Lt. Gen. Jonathan Wainwright's air officer on Corregidor, at which point Maverick became battalion commander. Calvin F. Chunn, "Provisional Air Corps Regiment," 1942, Folder "Historical Data–Provisional Air Corps Regiment," Box 1480, Entry 1113, Record Group (RG) 407, Records of the Adjutant General's Office, Philippine Archives Collection, National Archives and Record Administration, College Park, MD (NARA), hereafter NARA; Adjutant General's Office, *Official Army Register, January 1, 1943* (Washington, DC: Government Printing Office, 1943), 516, 576; "Col. Laughinghouse Safe and Well on Corregidor," *Albuquerque Journal*, 30 April 1942, 3; "Altadena Air Corps Officer Safe in Mukden," *Pasadena Star-News and Pasadena Post*, 29 August 1945, 15; and email to author from Jim Burnett, 30 November 2020.

    13. Department of the Army, Field Manual 6-22, *Leader Development* (Washington, DC: 2015), 1–6.

    14. General Orders No. 13, 26 January 1942, Headquarters, USAFFE, Box 53, Entry 541, Record Group 496, Records of General Headquarters, Southwest Pacific Area and United States Army Forces, Pacific, USAFFE (RG496), NARA.

    15. C. T. Lanham and Edwin F. Harding, eds., *Infantry in Battle*, 2nd ed. (Richmond, VA: Garrett and Massie, 1939), 355.

    16. Under Richards in early January 1942, the PACR began organizing the portion of the rear battle position astride the East Road north of Putting

Buhangin. The overall rear battle position paralleled the Pilar-Bagac road, and which in prewar plans represented the main battle line on Bataan. Morton, *Philippines*, 247–48; and George M. Parker Jr., Report of Operations of South Luzon Force, Bataan Defense Force, & II Philippine Corps in the Defense of South Luzon and Bataan from 8 December 1941 to 9 April 1942, 22, Annex V of Report of Operations of USAAFE and USFIP in the Philippines Islands, 1941–1942, Box 1157, RG407, NARA.

17. Morton, *Philippines*, 247, 327; Frank E. McGlothlin, *Barksdale to Bataan: History of the 48th Materiel Squadron, October 1940–April 1942* (Covington, LA: self-pub., 1984), 75–75a; and Mendelson, "Operations," 9. Sewell wrote his wife that he received his promotion to lieutenant colonel on 12 February 1942. "Days on Bataan," *Corvallis* (OR) *Gazette-Times*, 10 September 1942, 2. The figure of 2,200 yards is taken from a map overlay at the MacArthur Memorial, Norfolk, VA, hereafter MM.

18. Martin and Stephenson, *Plum*, 96.

19. Mendelson, "Operations," 8.

20. Lt. Bert Schwarz of the 27th Bomb Group, later PACR headquarters staff, recalled the regiment having around ninety-two machine guns, with "about twenty-something of them placed in position for firing." The salvaged machine guns, being air-cooled, would burn out barrels after only short bursts, but the PACR had plenty of spare barrels. Bert Schwarz, interview by Doris Durbin, n.d., Bert Schwarz Collection, Veterans History Project, American Folklife Center, Library of Congress.

21. Mendelson, "Operations," 9–10, 15; Coleman, *Bataan*, 21, 27–28, 42–47; McGlothlin, *Barksdale*, 76–77; Damon Gause, *The War Journal of Major Damon "Rocky" Gause: The Firsthand Account of One of the Greatest Escapes of World War II* (New York: Hyperion, 1999), 17–18; Whitman, *Ditch*, 454; Hardee, *Bataan Survivor*, 29, 35–36, 39; Zimmerman, "Diary," 61-62, 66; and Martin and Stephenson, *Plum*, 99.

22. Mendelson, "Operations," 8.

23. Mendelson, 7–12; Coleman, *Bataan*, 21; Zimmerman, "Diary," 63–67; and Whitman, *Ditch*, 455.

24. Morton, *Philippines*, 265–95; Whitman, 155–207, 227–48; Kary C. Emerson, "The Operations of the II Philippine Corps on Bataan, 10 January–8 April 1942" (Fort Benning, GA: US Army Infantry School, 1949–1950), 13–18; Mendelson, 12–14; Coleman, 21–25; Zimmerman, 67–71; "Provisional Air Corps Regiment," Papers of Major Calvin F. Chunn, Folder 8, Box 128; Parker, Report of Operations of South Luzon Force, 34–36, Box 1157, RG407, NARA; and Martin and Stephenson, *Plum*, 107.

25. Zimmerman, 78.

26. Special Orders No. 24, 26 January 1942, Headquarters, USAFFE, Box 54, Entry 541, RG496, NARA; and General Orders No. 13, 26 January 1942, Headquarters, USAFFE, Folder 4, Box 11, Records of the Headquarters, US Army Forces in the Far East, 1941–1942, Record Group 2 (RG2), MM. The

orders assigned Harrison to the Headquarters Philippine Department to report to the commander general for duty.

27. Department of War, Adjutant General's Office, *Official Army Register*, 1 January 1943 (Washington, DC: Government Printing Office, 1943), 238; "Boche Raids Are Beaten Off Quickly; One Patrol Is Decimated," *The Pittsburgh Post*, 19 June 1918, 1, 4; "Service Orders: Army Assignments," *Washington Post*, 27 April 1923, 11; "Service Orders: Army Assignments," *Washington Post*, 19 June 1927, 18; "Army Assignments," *Washington Post*, 16 March 1930, R5; "Transfers," *Washington Post*, 23 March 1939, 28; "Organization Day: Twenty-Fifth Anniversary, Thirty-First U.S. Infantry" (program, 13 August 1941), 11; "Army Orders and Assignments, *New York Times*, 24 October 1941, 43; Oscar Shepard, "Bangor Man Fought with Famed Regimen in the Philippines," *Bangor Daily News*, 15 April 1942, 4; "Ex-Jap Prisoner Home on Globester, Phones Mother Here," *Boston Globe*, 5 October, 1945, 8; and Jonathan D. Bratten, *To the Last Man: A National Guard Regiment in the Great War, 1917–1919* (Fort Leavenworth, KS: Army University Press, 2020), 113–15.

28. Hardee, *Bataan Survivor*, xiii-xvii.

29. Hardee, 27.

30. Hardee, 27.

31. Gause, *Journal*, 8–10; Coleman, *Bataan*, 25–32; and "Provisional Air Corps Regiment," Papers of Major Calvin F. Chunn, Folder 8, Box 128, RG407, NARA.

32. Zimmerman, "Diary," 91.

33. Mendelson, "Operations," 15. The OPLR was originally located on the south bank of the San Vincente River before being advanced north of the river where it made contact with the OPLRs on the flanks of the adjacent sectors.

34. Hardee, *Bataan Survivor*, 29.

35. Hardee, 32.

36. Young, *Battle*, 7; and Hardee, 29.

37. "Philippine Escape," *The Amarillo Globe Times*, 19 November 1942, 1.

38. Gause, *Journal*, 11.

39. A map drawn by Edward Keel from 1983 lists the OPLR positioned 2,500 yards forward of the MLR, with the RRL placed 5,000 yards to the rear of the MLR. The figures cited in the text are based on an examination of a map showing the positions of the USAFFE positions as of early April 1942. McGlothlin, *Barksdale*, 75a; and Headquarters map of campaign of Bataan, Folder 1 "G3, Annex 10, Luzon Force, January to April 1942," Box 11, RG2, MM.

40. Gause, *Journal*, 9, 12–14; "Provisional Air Corps Regiment," Papers of Major Calvin F. Chunn, Folder 8, Box 128, RG407, NARA; Zimmerman, "Diary," 92, 96, 106; Hardee, *Bataan Survivor*, 28, 30–32; Mendelson, "Operations," 16–17; Whitman, *Ditch*, 455–56; and McGlothlin, *Barksdale*, 75a–76.

41. McGlothlin, 85-86; War Department, General Orders no. 25, 11 December 1947, 1; Coleman, *Bataan*, 33–35; Mendelson, 17; and Gause, 14–15.

42. Hardee, *Bataan Survivor*, 30.

43. Coleman, *Bataan*, 32–33, 37–40, 42; Gause, *Journal*, 16–17; Whitman, *Ditch*, 455–56; Mendelson, "Operations," 18–19; Hardee, 31; Calvin F. Chunn, Folder 8, Box 128, RG407, NARA; and Martin and Stephenson, *Plum*, 151–52.

44. William E. Dyess, *The Dyess Story: The Eye-Witness Account of the Death March from Bataan and the Narrative of Experiences in Japanese Prison Camps and of Eventual Escape*, ed. Charles Leavelle (New York: G. P. Putnam's Sons, 1944), 47.

45. Hiroshi Masuda, *MacArthur in Asia: The General and His Staff in the Philippines, Japan, and Korea*, trans. Reiko Yamamoto (Ithaca, NY: Cornell University Press, 2012), 22, 93–119; Morton, *Philippines*, 353–60, 387–88; George W. Smith, *MacArthur's Escape: John "Wild Man" Bulkeley and the Rescue of an American Hero* (St. Paul, MN: Zenith Press, 2005), 163–208; Franklin D. Roosevelt, "On Progress of the War," 23 February 1942, Franklin D. Roosevelt Presidential Library and Museum, http://docs.fdrlibrary.marist.edu/022342.html; Hardee, *Bataan Survivor*, 32; Gause, *Journal*, 18–19; Martin and Stephenson, *Plum*, 152; Whitman, *Ditch*, 456; and McGlothlin, *Barksdale*, 77.

46. Hardee, 33.

47. Morton, *Philippines*, 421–41; and Whitman, *Ditch*, 475–517.

48. Hardee, *Bataan Survivor*, 34.

49. Account of events of April 6–8, 1942 by William H. Maverick, attached to letter from Laura Griswold to William Bartsch, 30 June 1994, Folder "Maverick," Box 3, Record Group 127, Papers of William Bartsch, MM, hereafter cited as "Maverick Account;" Coleman, *Bataan*, 43; and McGlothlin, *Barksdale*, 87.

50. Morton, *Philippines*, 444–45; Whitman, *Ditch*, 528–31; Mendelson, "Operations," 21–22; Young, *Battle*, 212–13; Coleman, 44–46; Hardee, *Bataan Survivor*, 34–35; McGlothlin, 87–89; and "Maverick Account."

51. Hardee, *Bataan Survivor*, 35–36.

52. Hardee, 35–36.

53. Hardee, 35–36; and "Maverick Account."

54. McGlothlin, *Barksdale*, 89; and "Maverick Account."

55. Martin and Stephenson, *Plum*, 198.

56. McGlothlin, *Barksdale*, 89–90.

57. Hardee, *Bataan Survivor*, 35–38; Morton, *Philippines*, 445–47; Mendelson, "Operations," 22; Whitman, *Ditch*, 532–34, 546, 557; Young, *Battle*, 212–13, 219, 235; McGlothlin, 89–90; Coleman, *Bataan*, 47–51; Gause, *Journal*, 20; Zimmerman, "Diary," 140; "Maverick Account;" and Parker, Report of Operations of South Luzon Force, 56–58, Box 1157, RG407, NARA.

58. McGlothlin, 90–91.

59. Donald Knox, *Death March: The Survivors of Bataan* (New York: Harcourt Brace Jovanovich, 1981), 100–1.

60. Bert Schwarz, interview by Doris Durbin, n.d., Bert Schwarz Collection, Veterans History Project, American Folklife Center, Library of Congress.

61. Hardee, *Bataan Survivor*, 39–43; Coleman, *Bataan*, 51–61; McGlothlin, *Barksdale*, 91; Morton, *Philippines*, 451–59; Young, *Battle*, 220, 223–27,

239–43; Whitman, *Ditch*, 562, 568-69; Knox, *Death*, 101–8; Stanley L. Falk, *Bataan: The March of Death* (New York: W. W. Norton and Co., 1962), 18–25; Parker, Report of Operations of South Luzon Force, 58–59, Box 1157, RG407, NARA; Calvin Ellsworth Chunn, ed., *Of Rice and Men: The Story of Americans Under the Rising Sun* (Tulsa, OK: Veterans' Publishing Co., 1946), 1–13; and Jonathan M. Wainwright, *General Wainwright's Story: The Account of Four Years of Humiliating Defeat, Surrender, and Captivity*, ed. Robert Considine (Garden City, NY: Doubleday and Co., 1946), 78–85.

62. Mendelson, "Operations," 24–25; and Morton, 329. The units of the Philippine Division, the 31st Infantry (US), 45th Infantry (PS), and 57th Infantry (PS) were held in reserve for the I and II Philippine Corps.

63. The contemporary US Army considers these delaying actions "one of the most demanding of all ground combat operations." Department of the Army, Field Manual 3-90-1, *Offense and Defense*, vol. 1 (Washington, DC: 2013), 9.1–2.

64. Thomas E. Ricks, *Making the Corps* (New York: Scribner, 2007), 190.

65. The author wishes to thank James C. Burnett, Raymond Bruntmyer, Dr. Susan Dawson, Geoff Earnhart, Dr. Gregory Kupsky, and James Zobel for their assistance in researching and editing this chapter.

Chapter 10
Operation Ziethen: The Evacuation of the Demyansk Salient, February 1943

Gregory P. Liedtke

Few military operations are as hazardous as conducting a withdrawal in the face of an enemy. The movement of troops from one line of defense to the next exposes them to attacks at the very moment they are least prepared to counter them. Troops must have a high degree of confidence in themselves and their leaders to resist their own fears—of being left behind, trapped, caught, or killed. Cohesion in these circumstances, both within and among units, is vital—trusting that your neighbors will do their job exactly how and when they need to. Leaders at all levels must be stern with their men while simultaneously exuding calm confidence. Planning and cooperation must be worked out well beforehand to avoid confusion. Even the smallest glitch could result in panic and disaster. Such factors are even more crucial when evacuating a salient, whereby one is already surrounded on three sides and the only escape route might be severed by the enemy at any moment. In such circumstances, the psychological stresses on officers and men are multiplied several times over. This chapter illustrates a test case where one such operation was carried out with complete success.

By January 1943, it was time to leave. The German Army had held the Demyansk salient for almost a year. Located south of Lake Ilmen in northern Russia, the salient ballooned roughly seventy-five kilometers (forty-seven miles) into Soviet territory. Yet the most crucial feature was its long and vulnerable neck that served as the vital lifeline connecting the troops within the salient to the main German front. Named after the village of Ramushevo at the base of the salient and varying between twelve to twenty kilometers (seven to twelve miles) in width, this thin corridor had been the target of four major offensives and several smaller attacks conducted by the Soviet Red Army as it endeavored to cut the corridor and destroy German troops located within the salient. Although the extensively fortified German defenses guarding the corridor had successfully repulsed each of these assaults, evidence was mounting that the Red Army was about to launch a fifth major offensive—this time utilizing forces that were considerably larger than previous deployments. For the German defenders, the prospects of successfully repelling yet another Soviet attack appeared slim. The divisions guarding the Ramushevo corridor had been badly bloodied repelling the latest attack and were yet to fully recover. Additionally, the recent collapse of the southern portion of Germany's Eastern Front and the encirclement of its Sixth Army at Stalingrad, together with Soviet attacks elsewhere along the front, meant that no reserves were available to reinforce the Demyansk sector. Many senior German commanders feared their troops within the Demyansk salient were about to suffer the same fate that had befallen their comrades at Stalingrad. The only way of avoiding this would be to evacuate the salient, but doing so would require Hitler's acquiescence, extensive planning, skill, and a great deal of luck.

The creation of the Demyansk salient stemmed from the winter of 1941–1942; the German invasion of the Soviet Union had finally been brought to a halt and Soviet counter-offensives were beginning to ripple across the entire breadth of the Eastern Front. During January 1942, one of these counteroffensives was directed against the Sixteenth Army of Army Group North. Commanded by Colonel-General Ernst Busch, the Sixteenth Army's six divisions, equally divided into the X and II Corps, were spread thin holding a 190-kilometer (118-mile) front from Lake Ilmen southward to Lake Seliger, where it connected to the left flank of the neighboring Army Group Centre. With only a heavily depleted seventh division in reserve and an eighth still in the process of arriving, the Sixteenth Army was immediately thrown into crisis when the opposing Soviet North-Western Front began its offensive on 7 January.[1]

The focus of the Soviet attack was directed at the extreme flanks of the Sixteenth. The Soviet Eleventh Army struck the left flank of the X Corps in the north, while the Third and Fourth Shock Armies attacked the right wing of II Corps along the boundary with Army Group Centre in the south. Although the Soviets enjoyed only marginal superiority in terms of men and equipment across the entire sector, they were able to mass their forces at the critical points of attack and achieve significant local numerical superiorities. Within days, the attack had buckled the left flank of the X Corps and Soviet spearheads were within reach of Staraya Russa, a vital German logistical hub. In the south, the Third and Fourth Shock armies shattered the defenders and severed the connections between Army Groups North and Centre. Still located far forward but with Soviet troops moving rapidly around either flank, the II Corps faced the prospect of having its supply lines cut and being surrounded around the town of Demyansk. In desperation, the Army Group North commander, Field Marshal Wilhelm von Leeb, requested permission to withdraw the Sixteenth Army on 12 January, but Hitler refused and insisted the troops hold their ground. Soon thereafter, Leeb resigned and was replaced by Colonel-General Georg von Küchler.[2]

The fighting continued and on 25 February, the Soviet Thirty-Fourth Army linked up with the newly deployed First Shock Army advancing from the south to completely encircle nearly 100,000 men of the II Corps. Although an emergency airlift managed to deliver the bare minimum of supplies needed to keep the troops alive and fighting, their situation remained precarious. Fortunately, the Sixteenth Army was able to organize a relief effort; Operation Brückenslag ("bridging") began on 21 March. In heavy fighting, the relief force managed to overcome fierce Soviet resistance and harsh terrain, eventually linking up with troops fighting their way out of the pocket at the town of Ramushevo on 21 April.[3]

Although a narrow corridor had been punched through, the encircled II Corps troops remained vulnerable to any renewed Soviet effort to cut them off. Despite the precarious nature of the salient that now jutted far out into Soviet territory, Hitler refused to abandon it, insisting that it would serve as a useful launching point for a future offensive. Consequently, the Ramushevo corridor was the target of a series of Soviet offensives throughout 1942 (3–17 May, 17–24 July, and 10–21 August).[4] Despite the heavy fighting involved, the German defenses held firm and managed to inflict extremely heavy losses on the attacking Soviet troops, whose gains were usually measured in yards. While the skill and tenacity of the German troops played a significant role in the successful defense of the corridor, the Demyansk salient ranked low on the list of Soviet STAVKA priorities during this period.[5] The Soviet high command was more concerned about the relief of Leningrad, elimination of the Rzhev salient near Moscow, and in halting the German summer offensive. Consequently, Soviet troops in the Demyansk sector never received enough reinforcements and supplies to overcome the German defenses.[6]

These circumstances began to change in late 1942. Frustrated by successful local German efforts to widen the corridor and the previous string of failed Soviet offensives, the STAVKA gave Marshal Semyon Timoshenko command of the Soviet North-Western Front and ordered him to eliminate the Demyansk salient once and for all. Ultimately, Timoshenko was able to amass a total of sixteen rifle divisions, eleven rifle or ski brigades, one tank brigade, one tank regiment, five independent tank battalions, and thirty-four separate artillery regiments.[7] Opposite this host, the II Corps—now commanded by Lieutenant-General Paul Laux—controlled a total of ten infantry divisions; however, only five of these divisions guarded the corridor. To improve command and control, the latter were grouped into Group Höhne, named after its commander, Lieutenant-General Gustav Höhne. Though his preparations were incomplete due to the length of his supply lines, Timoshenko commenced his attack on 28 November. The Soviet Eleventh Army attacked from north and advanced 1.5 kilometers (one mile), while the First Shock Army achieved a smaller penetration in the south. Thereafter, fierce German resistance and counterattacks, together with continued supply problems, brought the Soviet advance to a halt. Undeterred, Timoshenko continued his attacks, turning the battle into a grinding struggle of attrition. Worried that the Ramushevo corridor defenses might collapse under the unrelenting assault, Küchler reinforced II Corps with three divisions of the Eighteenth Army stationed around Leningrad. Together with these reinforcements, Group Höhne held; Timoshenko, whose troops were now exhausted and heavily depleted, eventually suspended his offensive on 12 January.[8]

Although the fourth Soviet offensive against the Ramushevo corridor was defeated, the cost had been high. During the nearly two-month battle, II Corps sustained 17,767 combat casualties, and many of its battalions were reduced to only 100 to 200 combatants.[9] The unrelenting combat, fought during a brutal Russian winter, left the survivors both physically and mentally exhausted. Both Busch and Höhne were skeptical that their troops would endure if a fifth offensive occurred anytime soon. Making matters worse, Küchler's decision to reinforce the II Corps by stripping troops from the Eighteenth Army besieging Leningrad had left the latter army stretched thin and without significant reserves. As a result, the Red Army finally broke through the German siege lines and relieved Leningrad when it conducted Operation Spark on 12–30 January 1943. Concurrently, German fortunes elsewhere along the Eastern Front had changed for the worse and were reaching crisis proportions. The Soviet winter offensive launched in November had smashed the German lines around Stalingrad and resulted in the encirclement of the entire Sixth Army. A subsequent relief effort failed, dooming the 280,000 Sixth Army troops to death or capture. Even worse, additional Soviet offensives collapsed further sections of the German front in southern Russia, threatening to trap an entire army group that was still ensconced deep in the Caucasus region.[10] In these circumstances, the German forces deployed in the Demyansk sector could expect no further reinforcements to help with whatever future crisis they might face; the troops within the salient were now confronted by the very real possibility they would be encircled and destroyed.

The Evacuation Begins

In the midst of the bad news coming from elsewhere along the Eastern Front, German intelligence officers in the Demyansk sector detected signs that yet another Soviet offensive was brewing. These were the preparations for Operation Polar Star, an ambitious offensive designed by Soviet Marshal Georgy Zhukov to not only eliminate the II Corps at Demyansk, but to drive northwest to the Baltic coast and thereby isolate and destroy the Eighteenth Army in the Leningrad region.[11] According to Zhukov's plan, four heavily reinforced Soviet armies would overwhelm the Ramushevo corridor defenses and capture Staraya Russa, creating a massive breech in the German lines. Then the First Tank and Sixty-Eighth armies would be inserted to lead the advance on the city of Luga and then the Baltic coast. The huge force assembled for the operation, aside from a large number of artillery units, ultimately included 2 tank or mechanized corps, 39 rifle divisions, 27 ski or rifle brigades, 2 tank brigades, and 18 separate tank regiments, totalling around 327,000 personnel.[12] Originally scheduled to begin on 15 February, the attack was greatly hampered by lengthy Soviet supply lines; because Soviet railheads were located 60 to 100 kilometers (37 to 62 miles) from the front line, repositioning units and stockpiling munitions and supplies took longer than expected.[13] Although German intelligence officers could only estimate the size of forces being assembled or their broader objectives, they determined from aerial reconnaissance and prisoner interrogations that a large-scale attack was imminent.[14]

Evacuation of the Demyansk salient appears to have started on 19 January. That same day, the Red Army managed to open a corridor to Leningrad during Operation Spark. During a telephone conversation with Küchler, Chief of Staff of the High Command of the German Army (*Oberkommando des Heeres* or OKH) General Kurt Zeitzler mentioned that he intended to again raise the issue of evacuating Demyansk with Hitler. Küchler agreed, pointing out that the Soviet success around Leningrad was due to a lack of reserves and that evacuating the salient would strengthen his front considerably by freeing a number of divisions for employment elsewhere. Both also seemed to share concern that the II Corps might be cut off and destroyed by a future Soviet attack.[15]

Despite the series of recent setbacks, Zeitzler's initial effort was quickly rebuffed by Hitler. The German leader remained as obstinate as ever about voluntarily abandoning territory. However, Zeitzler persisted—repeatedly bringing up the issue for more than a week. With the Sixth Army in its final death throes and bad news continuing to come in from other

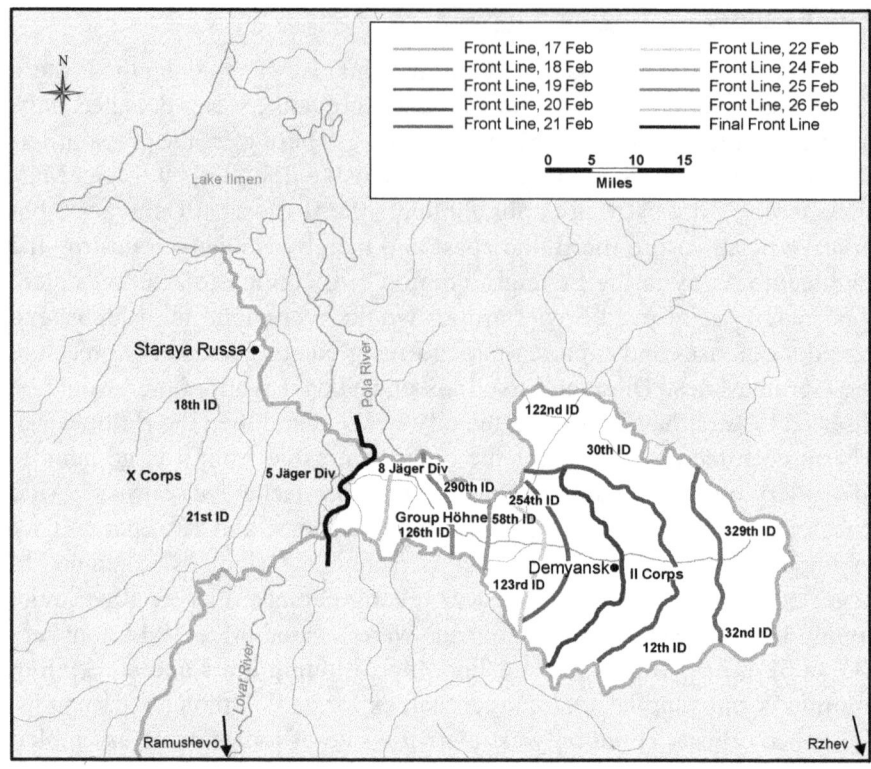

Figure 10.1. Map of the Evacuation of the Demyansk Salient, 17–26 February 1943. Created by Army University Press.

sectors of the front, Hitler finally gave in and authorized the evacuation of the salient during the night of 31 January. Worried that Hitler might change his mind, the OKH quickly notified Küchler of the decision and urged him to rapidly move his troops out of the salient even if this entailed the considerable loss of equipment and supplies.[16] Though he was relieved about finally receiving the order to evacuate the salient, Küchler was loath to abandon large amounts of precious material; he was determined to conduct a well-planned and organized operation.[17]

On 1 February, Küchler personally visited Group Höhne to speak with its commander and gain a first-hand understanding of the situation.[18] While in the sector, he likely informed both Busch and Laux about Hitler's decision to evacuate. The official orders for the operation, now codenamed Operation Ziethen, arrived at the II Corps command post that evening via special courier to prevent Soviet radio-listening stations from intercepting the message and becoming aware of the German intentions.[19]

Although Hitler's evacuation order was welcome, Sixteenth Army and II Corps commanders and staffs had quietly been moving excess equipment and material out of the salient since early January. To avoid directly contravening Hitler's standing orders, they had framed their actions as removing unserviceable or unneeded equipment to create space within the crowded salient for arriving troops and supplies. Together with a small staff, Lieutenant-Colonel Wilfried von Rosenthal, the 225th Infantry Division operations officer, was given responsibility to plan and coordinate this semi-clandestine action, which was referred to in German reports as *Entrümpelung* (clearance or clearing-out). Rosenthal also issued instructions that each division in the salient should create one new log corduroy road within their rear areas to ease traffic congestion. Exactly how much material and equipment was evacuated in the few weeks before the official order is unknown, but the *Entrümpelung* likely played an important role in Ziethen's success by easing the subsequent flow of men and equipment out of the salient.[20]

Given their previous experience, on 2 February Rosenthal and his staff were assigned responsibility for planning and coordinating the official evacuation. On the same day, Rosenthal quickly issued instructions to immediately commence an enhanced *Entrümpelung* that involved removing all units, equipment, and supplies not crucial to maintain the combat effectiveness of the frontline troops. The rear echelons of the divisions located within the salient, such as their supply, communications, headquarters, and administrative components, would be trimmed to the bare minimum required to keep the divisions functioning. All army- and corps-level support units and depots would also be removed. To keep traffic moving, military police were given strict instructions regarding who and when specific evacuation routes could be used and snow removal teams composed primarily of Russian civilians were prepositioned at various points. Orders were also issued to redistribute horses to any units for which shortages of these animals might impede movement.[21]

With the enlarged *Entrümpelung* underway, Rosenthal and his staff turned their attention to planning the final abandonment of the salient. In the meantime on 4 February, Busch ordered the X Corps to commence construction of a fortified line along the Lovat River running along the western base of the Ramushevo corridor that would become the new front line after the salient was evacuated. To help mask their evacuation preparations from the Red Army, the Germans maintained their usual levels of radio and patrol activity and conspicuously continued construction and improvement of their frontline defences. Although the *Luftwaffe* (German air force) was instructed to step up its fighter patrols over the salient to keep prowling Soviet reconnaissance planes away, only 40 German fighters were immediately available to challenge the 680 Soviet aircraft concentrated in the region; the prospects of success appeared dubious. Instead, German ground commanders hoped for an extended period of bad weather that would shield their movements and keep the Soviet Air Force grounded.[22]

On 7 February, Rosenthal met with Höhne, Laux, and other commanding officers of divisions located within the salient to discuss the evacuation. According to his plan, Operation Ziethen would occur in stages. Starting with the divisions located in the easternmost fringes of the salient, the troops would gradually pull back through a series of prepared stop lines utilizing specifically designated roads to prevent traffic jams. Each division would maintain responsibility for defending its assigned sector via strong rearguards until the retraction of the front eventually squeezed them out of the line. At that point, they would be moved back through the Ramushevo corridor. Any equipment and material that could not be evacuated in time was to be destroyed, as were all abandoned Russian villages that pursuing Soviet troops might use to shelter from the harsh weather. In the meantime, the troops defending the Ramushevo corridor would hold their positions and protect the withdrawal. The entire operation was anticipated to last two weeks.[23]

The only outstanding issue was when Operation Ziethen would finally commence. Heavy snowstorms the previous day badly impacted road conditions; many trucks struggled, breaking down or even running off the road while attempting to overcome huge snowdrifts. The result was massive traffic jams that produced columns several kilometers long. Henceforth towing vehicles would be stationed at various points along the evacuation routes to keep the columns moving, but this episode created a vexing dilemma for German planners. On the one hand, Rosenthal and his staff were certain that the huge traffic columns had been spotted by Soviet observers and that Soviet countermeasures to disrupt the evacuation were imminent. In essence, the success of the entire operation was already in jeopardy and time was running out. On the other hand, the weather's impact on the German movements already underway made it clear that a period of good or at least moderate weather was needed for the evacuation to succeed, lest a similar mishap occur during the main withdrawal and produce a disaster.[24] Although movement during good weather would expose the retreating columns to Soviet air attacks, the risk could be mitigated by reinforcing the columns with additional light anti-aircraft guns. After some debate, Rosenthal and the assembled officers agreed that commencing Ziethen should wait for a break in the weather, regardless of the risks.[25]

For Rosenthal and his staff, their fears about Soviet detection of German withdrawal preparations were confirmed the following day when Soviet troops began a series of probes and local attacks against the salient. Most were concentrated against the Ramushevo corridor and steadily increased in scale and intensity over the next several days. German aerial reconnaissance also noted a sizeable increase in Soviet supply and troop movements in the region.[26] Indeed, despite all efforts to mask the evacuation, Soviet intelligence officers apparently had deduced German intentions ever since the start of enhanced *Entrümpelung* measures; though his preparations were not yet complete, the STAVKA had already ordered Timoshenko to commence Operation Polar Star on the morning of 15 February.[27]

With Soviet pressure mounting, Küchler met with Zorn and Höhne during the afternoon of 11 February and demanded that Ziethen commence within four days. The two generals protested, insisting that their preparations were incomplete and that beginning the withdrawal early could result in substantial equipment losses. They instead argued that the earliest the operation could begin was 17 February; after further discussion, Küchler reluctantly agreed.[28]

While German preparations for the evacuation pressed on, Timoshenko rushed to get his own troops ready to attack. Constantly badgered by the STAVKA to get moving, Timoshenko's preparations were greatly hampered by long Soviet supply lines that limited how quickly he could move troops and material. Many of the new units assigned to participate in Operation Polar Star were still arriving, while those already present were recovering their strength after the previous offensive. Making matters even worse, his forward depots had yet to be fully replenished, especially in terms of the artillery shells that would be crucial to shatter the heavily fortified German defenses.[29]

Even though their preparations were far from complete, the Soviet troops commenced their attack against the Ramushevo corridor on 15 February. As anticipated, the lack of artillery shells meant the opening Soviet barrage was insufficient to destroy most of the German defenses or supress their supporting heavy weapons and artillery. Along the northern side of the corridor, most assaults staged by the Soviet Eleventh Army were repulsed, and the few that managed to gain a lodgement in the enemy positions were either sealed off or rapidly neutralized by German counterattacks. In contrast, the First Shock Army attack along the southern portion of the corridor advanced almost two kilometers (more than one mile) into 126th Infantry Division defenses before it was finally halted. While this alarmed some German commanders, the breech was quickly sealed off, and German troops regained some of the lost ground through counterattacks. During the following days, Timoshenko continued his attack, flinging fresh troops into the fighting as they arrived, but no further gains were made. The Soviets sustained heavy losses, and Group Höhne claimed to have destroyed sixty enemy tanks and knocked out another thirty-five during the first two days of the attack.[30] Although the Soviet attack continued until the Germans finished evacuating the salient on 28 February, its strength and intensity appears to have steadily wanned and never seriously threatened either the Ramushevo corridor or the German withdrawal.[31]

In the midst of the Soviet attack, the II Corps finally initiated Operation Ziethen on 17 February. This brought the *Entrümpelung* phase of the evacuation (2–16 February) to a close; a total of 8,000 tons of equipment, 5,000 horse-drawn wagons, and 1,500 motor vehicles had been successfully removed from the salient.[32] At nightfall, the troops of the 32nd, 329th and elements of the 122nd Infantry divisions quietly left their positions. By morning they had safely withdrawn to Line A, the first of the prepared stop lines. Despite their advance knowledge of the German actions, the opposing Soviet troops apparently were taken by surprise since their initial response was limited to only a handful of weak probes that the rearguards were easily able to fend off.[33]

The second day of the withdrawal was similar to the first. Now joined by the 30th Infantry Division, most of the troops began moving back to Line B while strong rearguards continued to hold Line A. Several 32nd Infantry Division battalions, the first troops to be squeezed out by the retraction of the front, were moved back by truck and assigned to Group Höhne as a reserve. Soviet ground interference with the withdrawal was once again marginal.[34] Instead, improving weather prompted an upsurge in Soviet aerial activity, especially over the Ramushevo corridor. Although the Soviet air attacks inflicted little damage on the retreating columns, they did cause concern, leading the II Corps to urgently request stronger fighter cover. The *Luftwaffe* responded and by 20 February had assembled more than 200 aircraft in the region. The result was a fierce air battle that lasted until the end of March. Subsequently, the increased *Luftwaffe* air strength, coupled with continuing bouts of bad weather, prevented the Soviet air force from effectively interdicting German road traffic throughout the withdrawal.[35]

The operation continued smoothly over the next few days, and the Germans finally abandoned the burned-out remains of Demyansk on 21 February. Although now fully cognizant of what was transpiring, the pursuing Soviet troops made no serious effort to interfere with the withdrawal; the few attacks were described as "weak" and "minor" in German reports. Thanks to the various traffic control measures instituted by the Germans and the previous expansion of the road net itself, no major traffic issues arose. By 22 February, the withdrawing troops had reached Line D. All that remained of the Demyansk salient was the Ramushevo corridor. At this point Group Höhne was disbanded, and the II Corps handed over its remaining troops to the X Corps, which assumed responsibility for the final stages of the withdrawal. On 26 February, the last German rearguards pulled back to a fortified bridgehead just east of the Lovat River.[36]

Operation Ziethen was over and by any measure was a clear success at a time when the German Army desperately needed a morale boost. In only ten days—four less than Lieutenant-Colonel Rosenthal had initially estimated—all thirteen divisions within the salient, together with their equipment and supplies, had safely evacuated. The cost was remarkably small, at least by the standards of the Eastern Front. Losses among the fifteen divisions and various support units stationed in and around the Demyansk for the period of 16–28 February amounted to only 6,402 casualties, of whom 1,585 were killed or missing.[37] Equipment losses were limited to 157 machine guns, 33 mortars, 42 anti-tank guns, and 18 artillery pieces.[38] Some 1,500 motor vehicles of all kinds were lost during the withdrawal, but almost all appear to have been ancient wrecks long rendered unserviceable that had accumulated within the salient over the course of the previous year. Around 300 tons of munitions, 700 tons of food, and 1,000 tons of other equipment and material also had to be abandoned; most were blown up by the rearguards.[39] In contrast, the Soviet armies operating in the Demyansk sector sustained 33,663 casualties, including 10,016 killed or missing, between 15–28 February.[40]

In strategic terms, the withdrawal significantly increased the stability of the northern portion of Germany's Eastern Front. Following the consolidation of the German position around Staraya Russa, the X Corps thwarted a large Soviet attack that occurred in the area in the immediate wake of the withdrawal; in return for marginal territorial gains, the Red Army sustained 103,108 casualties between 1–19 March among the 401,190 men involved.⁴¹ The shortening of the front also allowed five divisions to be deployed elsewhere along the Army Group North front or withdrawn into reserve. The availability of reserves helped this portion of the Eastern Front remain stable until early 1944.⁴²

Lessons to Remember

Despite the passage of time, the German evacuation from the Demyansk salient still offers a number of important lessons for modern military officers, especially in terms of unit cohesion. Attaining the political will to act, especially in the case of an unappealing abandonment of a position into whose retention one has devoted a considerable amount of resources and prestige, is no easy task. In the case of Demyansk, Hitler had long rejected calls by his military advisors to give it up. He only relented after German commanders convinced him that withdrawal was the only option given the deteriorating conditions.

Another important lesson is the crucial role of detailed planning and preparations for an orderly withdrawal. On many occasions during Germany's war on the Eastern Front, the decision to retreat was made too late and only after Soviet attacks had already shattered the German lines and plunged deep into their rear areas. Retreating in haste, they suffered heavy losses, especially of valuable weapons, equipment, and supplies that otherwise could have been saved with an orchestrated evacuation. In contrast, the careful planning conducted by German staff officers at Demyansk kept material losses to a minimum. Likewise, the intense advance preparations allowed troops to withdraw in a calm manner to a series of prepared positions. Panic was avoided and units withdrew with cohesion and effectiveness, regardless of enemy attempts to interfere and disrupt their movements. In short, the planning and preparations that went into the withdrawal from Demyansk allowed considerable numbers of German troops (and their equipment and supplies) to fight another day.

Another critical element was the training and experience of German officers and their men. Many of the staff officers had received rigorous training at the German Army's highly selective *Kriegsakademie* (war academy), where planned withdrawal scenarios were played out in war games. The games gave them some experience in such operations before having to conduct the real thing on the battlefield. Added to this was the doctrinal knowledge that officers gained through the German Army field manual, or *Truppenführung*; all those involved in Operation Ziethen were operating from the same guidebook.[43] With the war on the Eastern Front well into its second year, most officers were also familiar with the area's brutal weather, difficult terrain, and primitive roads, as well as the strengths and weaknesses of the Soviet enemy. Taken altogether, these elements helped make the withdrawal go smoothly.

A final issue was the morale of the rank and file, and the confidence they still had in their leaders. For most German soldiers at this point in the war, defeat still seemed far from certain, and their leaders had managed to weather each crisis that had developed. Most officers shared the same dangers and privations their men did, and in the majority of cases had prevailed over an enemy enjoying superior numbers and equipment. This boosted rank and file confidence and morale. German troops could have been crippled by the simple fear that they would fall behind and be captured by a ruthless foe. Instead, they had a high degree of confidence in both their leaders and themselves. This cohesion—in planning, leadership, doctrine, and morale—ultimately produced success. Without it, the outcome of Operation Ziethen would have been far different.

Notes

1. Very little has been written about the fighting around Demyansk, and the final evacuation of the salient tends to receive scant attention in larger studies of the Eastern Front. For example, John Erickson, *The Road to Berlin. Stalin's War with Germany,* vol. 2 (New Haven, CT: Yale University Press, 1983), 61–62, summarizes the evacuation in two paragraphs. Earl F. Ziemke, *Stalingrad to Berlin: The German Defeat in the East* (Washington, DC: US Army Center of Military History, 2002), 112–13, offers similar commentary, mostly regarding the final decision to evacuate rather than the operation itself. Though he writes about the fighting along the northern portion of the front that included events around Demyansk, even David M. Glantz, *The Battle for Leningrad, 1941–1944* (Lawrence, KS: University Press of Kansas, 2002), 297–98, offers only three paragraphs addressing the abandonment of the salient, mostly from a Soviet perspective. The two best studies are Werner Haupt, *Demjansk 1942: Ein Bollwerk im Osten* (Eggolsheim, DE: Dörfler Verlag, 2007) and Robert Forczyk, *Demyansk 1942–43: The Frozen Fortress* (Oxford, UK: Osprey Pub., 2012). Other useful sources include Andrew Koch, "Demyansk 1941–1943: A Microscopic View of the German-Soviet Conflict" (master's thesis, University of Richmond, 1994) and Jeff Rutherford, "Life and Death in the Demiansk Pocket: The 123rd Infantry Division in Combat and Occupation" *Central European History* 41 (2008), 347–80.

2. Forczyk, *Demyansk 1942–43*, 33–53; and Haupt, *Demjansk 1942*, 28–74.

3. For the best account of the relief operation, see Adolf Reinicke, *Die 5. Jäger Division.* (Eggolsheim: Dörfler Verlag, 1998), 158–205.

4. David Glantz, *Forgotten Battles of the German-Soviet War, 1941–1945*, The Summer Campaign, 12 May–18 November 1942, vol. 3 (Carlisle, PA: self-pub., 1999), 174–93.

5. The Soviet high command, more formally known as the Stavka of the Supreme Main Command (*Stavka Verkhovnogo Glavnokomandovaniya*), was located in Moscow and composed of the Soviet dictator, Joseph Stalin, and several senior military officers. As supreme commander of the Soviet military forces, Stalin had the final say in all Soviet high command decisions.

6. Throughout most of 1942, the primary focus of the STAVKA was to deal with the German offensive in the south and hold the city of Stalingrad, eliminate the German-held Rzhev salient opposite Moscow, and establish a land connection to the beleaguered Leningrad defenders. For the distribution of Soviet resources at this time, see Evan Mawdsley, *Thunder in the East: The Nazi-Soviet War, 1941–1945* (London: Hodder Arnold Pub., 2005), 150–55.

7. See Glantz, *Forgotten Battles of the German-Soviet War*, 67–82.

8. According to German estimates, Soviet losses included at least 10,000 men killed, 1,400 prisoners, and 423 tanks destroyed. Haupt, *Demjansk 1942*, 157.

9. *Deutsch-Russisches Projekt zur Digitalisierung Deutscher Dokumente in Archiven der Russischen Föderation, Dokumente zum Zweiten Weltkrieg,* Bestand 500, Findbuch 12473, Akte 81, 33.

10. These were part of a larger winter counteroffensive the STAVKA had been planning since at least early October 1942. The first and greatest were Operation Uranus around Stalingrad and Operation Mars against the Rzhev salient, with subsequent operations planned and conducted as the situation developed. For Soviet planning and accounts of smaller operations, see David M. Glantz, *After Stalingrad: The Red Army's Winter Offensive 1942–43* (Solihull, UK: Helion & Co., 2008); Glantz, *Forgotten Battles of the German-Soviet War*; and Geoffrey Roberts, *Stalin's Wars: From World War to Cold War, 1939–1953* (New Haven, CT: Yale University Press, 2006), 148–53. Regarding the Soviet offensive around Rzhev, see David M. Glantz, *Zhukov's Greatest Defeat: The Red Army's Epic Disaster in Operation Mars, 1942* (Surrey, UK: Ian Allen Pub., 2000).

11. Glantz, *After Stalingrad*, 390–427.

12. Glantz., 402, 416.

13. Forczyk, *Demyansk 1942–43*, 88.

14. Haupt, *Demjansk 1942*, 162.

15. Ziemke, *Stalingrad to Berlin,* 112.

16. Ziemke, 112–13.

17. Ziemke, 113. Also cited in Koch, "Demyansk 1941–1943," 77–78.

18. Ziemke, 81.

19. *II. Armeekorps. Kriegstagesbüch 2, Band 3. (25 August 1942–22 February 1943),* National Archives and Records Administration, hereafter cited as NARA, T314, Roll 144, Frame 000435. The operation was named after General Hans Joachim von Ziethen (1699–1786), an officer in the Prussian Army of Frederick the Great. Ziethen was famous because of his penchant for dueling and his daring military operations.

20. Haupt, *Demjansk 1942*, 159–60. Also noted in Forczyk, *Demyansk 1942–43*, 87.

21. NARA, T314, Roll 144, Frame 000449.

22. Christer Bergström, *Black Cross Red Star: Air War over the Eastern Front*, Stalingrad to Kuban, vol. 4 (Sweden: Vaktel Books, 2019), 242.

23. Koch, "Demyansk 1941–1943," 79–80.

24. NARA, T314, Roll 144, Frame 000449.

25. NARA, T314, Roll 144, Frame 000449.

26. *Deutsch-Russisches Projekt zur Digitalisierung Deutscher Dokumente in Archiven der Russischen Föderation, Dokumente zum Zweiten Weltkrieg,* Bestand 500, Findbuch 12473, Akte 81, 35.

27. Glantz, *The Battle for Leningrad, 1941–1944,* 297.

28. Koch, "Demyansk 1941–1943," 81.

29. Forczyk, *Demyansk 1942–43*, 88.

30. *Deutsch-Russisches Projekt zur Digitalisierung Deutscher Dokumente in Archiven der Russischen Föderation, Dokumente zum Zweiten Weltkrieg.* Bestand 500, Findbuch 12473, Akte 81, 35.

31. Forczyk, *Demyansk 1942–43*, 88; Haupt, *Demjansk 1942*, 165; and Koch, "Demyansk 1941–1943," 82.

32. Haupt, *Demjansk 1942*, 161.
33. Koch, "Demyansk 1941–1943," 82.
34. Koch, 82.
35. For details on the air battle over Demyansk during this period, see Bergström, *Black Cross Red Star*, 239–61.
36. NARA, T314, Roll 144, Frame 000488.
37. *Heeresgruppe Nord. Zalenmässige Gesamtverluste bis 31.3.1943*, National Archives and Records Administration, T311, Roll 105, Frames 7140020–7140021.
38. *Deutsch-Russisches Project zur Digitalisierung Deutscher Dokumente in Archiven der Russischen Föderation, Dokumente zum Zweiten Weltkrieg.* Bestand 500, Findbuch 12473, Akte 81, 72.
39. Haupt, *Demjansk 1942*, 169.
40. Glantz, *After Stalingrad*, 411.
41. Glantz, 411.
42. See Glantz, *The Battle for Leningrad, 1941–1944*, 305–23, and Steven Newton, *Retreat from Leningrad. Army Group North 1944/1945*. (Atglen, PA: Schiffer Military History, 1995), 16–25.
43. For details on pre-war development of German doctrine and training, see Matthias Strohn, *The German Army and the Defence of the Reich: Military Doctrine and the Conduct of Defensive Battle, 1918–1939* (Cambridge: Cambridge University Press, 2011).

Chapter 11

The German 7th Infantry Division and Retreat from the Rzhev Salient, February–March 1943

Jeff Rutherford

On 13 March 1943, the 7th Infantry Division reported that it had finished its retreat from the Rzhev salient, an irregularly shaped piece of German-controlled territory that pierced through Soviet lines, and completed its part in the "Buffalo Movement."[1] In about three weeks, the division—and the remainder of the Ninth, Fourth, and Third Panzer Armies deployed in the region—had evacuated the salient and established the much more defendable Buffalo line in the rear, stretching from Velizh to Kirov.[2] Army Group Center viewed the withdrawal as a complete success; shortening the front from 530 to some 200 kilometers (330 to 124 miles) allowed 21 divisional units to move into reserve.[3] IX Corps congratulated the troops for their "outstanding achievement."[4] The 7th Infantry Division commander reported that the withdrawal "increased the troops' combat value" by "escaping the stupor of positional warfare," adding that the "commanders and troops had again learned much for the conduct of a mobile war."[5] As the retreat demonstrated, the German army retained its internal cohesion despite the trials and tribulations of the first two years of war in the Soviet Union, and remained an effective fighting force able to carry out complex operations in the face of the enemy.

This was not the first retreat for the 7th Infantry Division. The unit, subordinated to Army Group Center for Operation Barbarossa, had participated in the chaotic yet ultimately successful winter 1941–42 withdrawal from the gates of Moscow.[6] While the 1943 retreat was not a singular event for the division, the manner in which the German army carried out the Buffalo Movement represented a new stage in the German army's war in the east. Building on and radicalizing the scorched earth practices that both the German and Red armies applied during 1941, the Germans systematically destroyed the area they vacated, leaving nothing of military value for the advancing Red Army. What truly differentiated this retreat from previous ones, however, was the emphasis on economic considerations. German troops removed anything of value for their war effort, ranging from foodstuffs to manpower. This focus on economics, which had animated German planning for the 1941 invasion of the Soviet Union and troop behavior throughout the campaign, now reached a new level of systematic practice. The Buffalo Movement—and the nearly simultaneous clearing of the Demyansk Pocket to the north—demonstrated that the army's conception of the war against the Soviet Union now reflected the reality of total war in the east.[7] In combination with Seventeenth Army's retreat on the Taman Peninsula, these three withdrawals established "specific evacuation and retreat scripts" that served as the basis of the army's behavior during its last two-and-a-half years of war against the Soviet Union.[8]

In the popular understanding of the conflict, the German army's war between June 1942 and July 1943 centers on the catastrophic defeats of Operation Blue and Operation Citadel. This emphasis on battlefield events is certainly well-merited, as Germany's slim chances of winning the war vanished with defeats at the Battle of Stalingrad and Kursk.[9] Even with this battlefield focus, however, the nature of German retreats has been obscured by the army's defeats. While the general outlines of withdrawals at the operational level have received attention, the actions of units at the lowest level for which adequate documentation exists—the division—still requires explanation.[10]

The German-Soviet war consisted of far more than just combat, however, and the army's occupation policies proved more important in illustrating German goals in the east. Unfortunately, this aspect of the army's experience has generally received short shrift in the literature, particularly in the years after 1941.[11] The ruthlessness and barbarity of the initial German invasion clearly illustrated the *Vernichtungskrieg* desired by Hitler and his regime. A combination of military, ideological, and economic motivations led to a war in which various German institutions—including the army—plundered the Soviet Union for food, resulting in mass starvation across the occupied territories; carried out genocidal mass shootings of Soviet Jewry; murdered Communist functionaries in cold blood; were responsible for the deaths of more than two million Soviet prisoners of war in German captivity; and unleashed savage anti-partisan sweeps that targeted tens of thousands of innocent civilians.[12] In each case, the Germans considered these policies necessary components to win the war in one blitz campaign. In this matrix, the Germans viewed and treated civilians as potential adversaries.

With the failure of Operation Barbarossa, however, the war in the east would require a more intensive mobilization of the resources under its control in order to wage yet another eastern campaign. The army needed to revise and, in some cases, transform its policies on the ground, resulting in new approaches to German occupation. In spring 1942, a "new phase of memorandums and orders that began a transition to a constructive occupation rule" heralded an attempt to actively yoke the Soviet economy and its population to the larger war effort.[13] This chapter charts the effects of this newfound approach from spring 1942 to the spring 1943 Buffalo Movement through the lens of the 7th Infantry Division. It will place the retreat into the larger context of the war and demonstrate how it represented the army's response to the increasingly tenuous situation at the front within the concept of total war. An examination of divisional level events allows for a more precise understanding of how battlefield concerns became intimately entwined with economic policies, such as the extensive plunder of economic goods and foodstuffs and the forced deportation of hundreds of thousands of civilians to be plugged into the German war economy. In other words, the army's military struggle against the Soviet Union simply cannot be disentangled from ideological and economic issues; the interaction and connections between them led to the all-encompassing war of annihilation waged by the German army in the east. The Buffalo Movement represented a new stage in the German-Soviet war, one in which the narrowly technical aspects of retreat were folded into the total war waged by the German army against Soviet state and society.

The Crisis of 1943 and the Rzhev Salient

By January 1943, the heady 1941 victories were in the distant past and a series of defeats across the front, particularly in the south, resulted in a steadily deteriorating situation for the German army in the east. *Generalleutnant* Friedrich-Georg von Rappard, commander of the 7th Infantry Division, communicated this to his officers on 22 January, declaring that the "situation in the south (Stalingrad—Don-Front), at Velikie Luki, and Leningrad forced the most extreme physical efforts."[14] His proclamation that "the effects of [this] winter are perhaps tougher than the previous one" must have been very sobering to men who had survived the winter crisis of 1941–42.[15] In many respects, however, his assessment was correct. To the north, Soviet forces destroyed the German "bottleneck" that separated Leningrad from the remainder of the Soviet Union, ending the siege, and simultaneously maintained heavy pressure on German troops in the embattled Demyansk Pocket and in the city of Velikie Luki.[16] Events to the south proved far more catastrophic. The Red Army's strangulation of Sixth Army in Stalingrad continued apace, while Army Group South—picking up the surviving remnants of German, Hungarian, and Romanian troops of Army Groups B and Don—attempted to hold the line against quantitatively superior forces.[17] With its southern flank hanging by a thread and its northern flank pinned in place, only Army Group Center held its position, despite continual Red Army efforts to destabilize it.

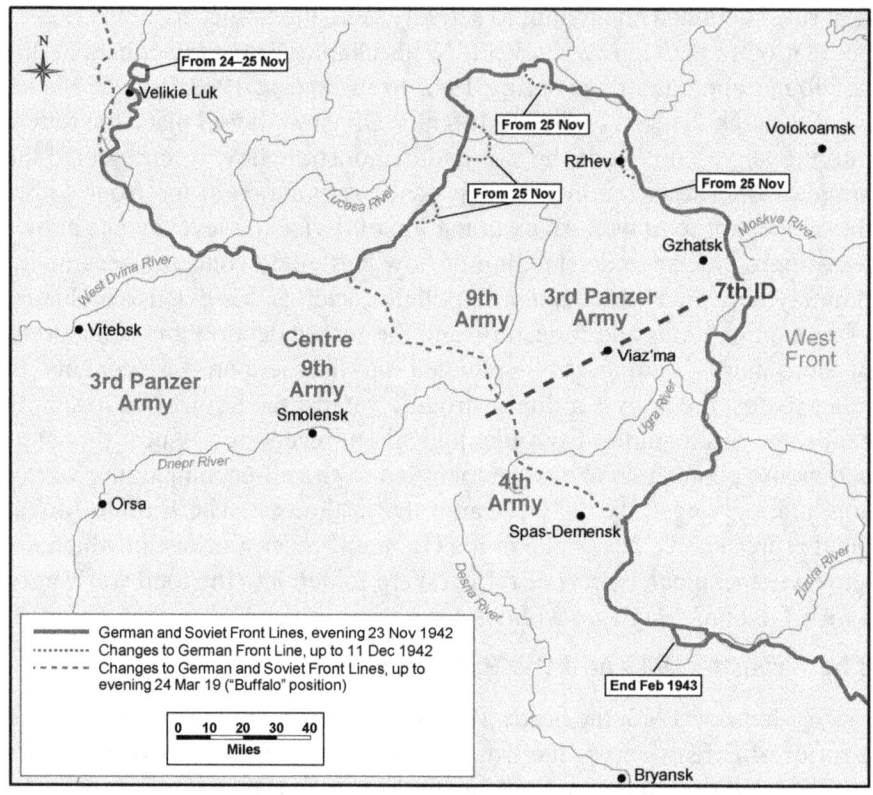

Figure 11.1. The 7th Infantry Division and the Buffalo Movement. Created by Army University Press.

At the beginning of 1943, Army Group Center's lines had been relatively settled for more than a year, though the front as it appeared on a map looked like "the work of an operations corporal gone mad."[18] The winter 1941–42 Soviet counter-attack in front of Moscow pushed German units back in pell-mell fashion, particularly on the northern wing of the army group, and the Ninth, Fourth and Third Panzer Armies occupied the Rzhev salient after the front was stabilized. The 7th Infantry Division moved into the Gzhatsk position on the right side of the salient along the Smolensk-Viaz'ma-Moscow highway in early February 1942 and remained there for the next year. Hitler adamantly maintained that the Rzhev salient needed to be held as a springboard for future operations directed at Moscow, so the German army dug in and defended the area against heavy Soviet attacks throughout the second half of 1942.

Initial Soviet attempts to crush the salient began on 31 July when the Kalinin and Western Front launched major operations.[19] These put a real strain on Ninth Army; on 16 August, its commander, *Generaloberst* Walter Model, informed *Generalfeldmarshall* Günther von Kluge, commander in chief of Army Group Center, that his formations were on their last legs and without immediate reinforcements, the responsibility would be shifted to Kluge who would have to "provide detailed instructions as to how the battle is to be continued."[20] While Ninth Army suffered grievous casualties during its defense—reaching a rate of around 1,000 dead per day during the third week of August—Third Panzer Army generally remained outside the fray; the 7th Infantry Division reported only 234 casualties for the month of August, a relatively paltry number.[21]

These casualties, however, were only the tip of a much larger iceberg. By 30 April 1942, the division had suffered nearly 7,600 casualties, including 265 officers, since the opening of the Soviet campaign. Even by May 1942, it was still short more than 345 noncommissioned officers (NCOs); many of those it received to fill the ranks failed to meet the June 1941 training standards.[22] In August 1942, Rappard reported that "the 1941–42 winter cost the blood of the infantry. The present infantry—still only sparsely infused with experienced fighters—is no longer that of 1941."[23] The predominant issues centered on losses within the low-level leadership ranks of junior officers and NCOs. This level of command provided the foundation for the German army. According to Rappard, junior officers and NCOs needed to be "fully trained soldier[s], with quick powers of observation and a quick-wittedness, considerable self-sufficiency, and an elevated understanding of the interaction between comrades and other weapons."[24] Such men could make decisions based on their own appreciation of the situation, instead of being wed to what he termed "schematic group leadership."[25] In other words, German offensives were driven forward by the initiative of low-level leaders who exploited whatever battlefield opportunities presented themselves. In addition to their battlefield role, commanders served as patriarchal figures to their men, helping them withstand the strains of modern industrial war. Rappard noted earlier in the year: "In these times of the highest combat tension and hardships, the commander's personality means everything."[26] Due to crippling shortages of experienced and effective leaders, however, the unit suffered high casualties in minor operations. As a result, Rappard deemed the division capable only of defense and "attacks with limited goals."[27]

This shift to the defensive proved vital to refashioning the division. As noted above, the German approach to warfare provided space for commanders to make their own decisions on the battlefield during the attack. On the defensive, however, this space was greatly compressed; commanders exercised firmer control over their subordinate units.[28] The 7th Infantry Division's commander made this clear in late September, demanding that "the division's position will be held until the last soldier."[29] Contrary to previous practices, the instructions emphasized that any deviations "without an order, through the independent decision by some leader or sub-leader," were out of the question.[30] The fact that this was ordered by a commander who championed the effectiveness of well-trained and self-sufficient soldiers indicates, however, that this top-down approach was prompted by a lack of men able to master the German way of war.[31] With the tone for his unit now set, the division could focus on defending its section of the front, as well as training its continually arriving replacements and re-building the camaraderie and cohesion needed to survive in the line.

While the German line held in August, the Soviets returned with real ferocity in late November. Designed to work in conjunction with Operation Uranus—the Soviet attempt to encircle German troops at Stalingrad—Operation Mars (and its second phase, Operation Jupiter), had even more grandiose hopes: the elimination of the Rzhev salient followed by the complete destruction of Army Group Center. The attack, however, resulted in a bloody debacle for the Red Army. It was called off after a month of fighting, resulting in a barely perceptible shift of the front lines—a gain that cost some 100,000 dead and 235,000 wounded Soviet soldiers.[32] Once again the 7th Infantry Division avoided the brunt of the fighting, but ferocious combat in different parts of the salient ground down other German units; the hemorrhaging of strength led Kluge to initiate preliminary investigations into evacuating the position in October 1942.[33] As the German position degenerated across the breadth of the front in early 1943, the German military leadership finally convinced Hitler to abandon the Rzhev salient in order to create urgently needed reserves. Beginning in late February 1943, Army Group Center began preparations for a March withdrawal.

The German Army's Economic Objectives in the Soviet Union

Military considerations were thus the primary motive for *why* the German army carried out the Buffalo Movement. *How* it was implemented, however, betrayed a much broader conception of the war. Operation Barbarossa's failure to defeat the Soviet Union in one decisive campaign in 1941 placed the Third Reich in an increasingly untenable position. In addition to the overwhelming bulk of its exhausted army bogged down deep in the Soviet Union, the British Empire remained an implacable enemy. Perhaps even more important, the United States added its immense industrial and financial power to the enemy coalition in December 1941. Both the army and the Reich realized that the resources of Germany and the occupied territories—including raw materials, foodstuffs, and manpower—would require more systematic and comprehensive mobilization if Germany hoped to emerge victorious. Certainly, Germany had depended on plundered Soviet food to supply its troops in 1941, and the army increasingly used Soviet prisoners of war and civilians for labor purposes as the campaign developed. Though such practices continued and intensified in 1942, German policy needed to be reformulated to address the reality of war against an enemy coalition whose economic power dwarfed that of the Reich.[34]

In spring 1942, several armies in Army Group Center issued orders designed to transform the attitudes and policies of its subsidiary formations. In the Rzhev salient itself, Fourth Army attempted to win over the population through policies ranging from distributing land and supporting the reinstitution of organized religion, to ensuring the civilian population was adequately fed and integrating native auxiliary forces into the German occupation structure.[35] Second Panzer Army reminded its troops that the struggle was directed "solely at the proponents of the Bolshevik system, the Red Army, the partisans, and the active communist functionaries and not against civilians and prisoners of war."[36] These ideas were encapsulated in a May 1942 High Command of the German Army (*Oberkommando des Heeres* or OKH) directive passed on by Third Panzer Army. Arguing that "mastery should never degenerate into contempt towards the defenseless vanquished," the directive emphasized that the troops should treat the civilian population "strictly but fairly" to ensure a "quick pacification of the country:"

> The German soldier protects the property of the laboring and peaceful population, he respects the sense of honor of Russian women and girls, he supports the reconstructive work in the rear areas. He must know that capricious acts create opposition, stir up embitterment, and therefore threaten the security of our troops.[37]

In short, the "German soldier is to prove to the civilian population that he is a member of a culturally advanced people, whose dominion will have the effect of releasing the population from the Bolshevik yoke."[38] Such thinking soon filtered down to the divisional level.

At the end of July, the division's quartermaster issued guidelines for the unit. Declaring that "this war is an economic war. It concerns the existence and future of our people," he explained:

> The securing of food independence is of decisive importance for the war. It demands the orderly exploitation of the entire economic area. The areas conquered and occupied by the Wehrmacht constitute a section of this economic area. The exploitation can take place as predatory exploitation. As the previous year's campaign has shown, it leaves behind a land sucked dry and a starving, dissatisfied population.[39]

Economic considerations thus came to rival battlefield events in the division's appreciation of the war.

While German soldiers could force Soviet civilians to work, they were not permitted to simply steal "the fruits of this work." Civilians needed sufficient food to ensure their productivity. According to the quartermaster, "In general, the Russian is eager, hard-working, and easy to control when his stomach is full and is treated correctly. It is our task to get him there."[40] The OKH further emphasized the importance of labor in an early August directive. Arguing that the "regulated and orderly deployment of civilian labor" was vital to the army's tactical performance and strategic hopes, it underscored the importance of civilians working for the army in road maintenance, construction, and in the fields.[41] In combination, the two directives demonstrated the importance which the division—and by extension the German army—ascribed to economic concerns.

With the onset of the spring sowing season, the 7th Infantry Division and other German forces became much more interventionist in local agriculture. On the same day that the division instructed its men to relocate civilians from crowded communities to smaller ones to "avoid serious foodstuff difficulties and an equitable distribution for the spring sowing," Fourth Panzer Army proclaimed that "the present supply of the troops in no way legitimizes an additional supply from the land, outside of potatoes."[42] The army was determined to preserve seeds necessary for planting and protect the area's remaining livestock to keep the civilian population alive.[43] The division placed such an emphasis on livestock that it reported the numbers of cows, calves, pigs, sheep, and goats roaming in its area of responsibility.[44] Even during the midst of the Soviet summer offensive, the division concerned itself with the rye harvest. Remembering the previous winter when fodder shortages proved quite debilitating to a unit dependent on horse-drawn artillery and supply, the quartermaster instructed the men to ensure that enough was stored for the coming cold weather. Unit leaders also wanted to ensure that civilians had enough fodder to last them until the following year.[45] In striking contrast to the previous year when German units simply watched civilians starve, the division supplied nineteen tons of flour to an area in which one person a day was dying from hunger.[46] While German actions were clearly responsible for Soviet civilians starving, the division's attempt to alleviate this suffering was a notable shift in policy from 1941.

This newfound emphasis on securing sufficient food for Soviet civilians so they could work for the Reich—almost entirely missing from the army's conduct in 1941—animated German policy in 1942. Placing Soviet agricultural production into the larger context of the German war economy, the quartermaster made clear that any unauthorized plunder of foodstuffs came at the "cost of the entire food situation that in the final result will also cost our kinsmen at home."[47] By summer 1942, the division's utilitarian approach to civilians and food indicated that it considered resources vital to victory in the war.

Food constituted one of two points of economic emphases for the army in 1942; labor was the second. Once again, Operation Barbarossa's failure led to a shift in policy. Unable to demobilize enough soldiers to fill the industrial ranks, Germany needed to turn elsewhere for labor. In March 1942, Hitler appointed Fritz Sauckel, the Gauleiter of Thuringia, as General Plenipotentiary for Labor Deployment. Charged with recruiting labor to the Reich from occupied Europe, his institution found its most fertile ground in the occupied eastern territories.[48] The 7th Infantry Division received a VII Corps directive in April concerning the gathering of labor for use at the front and in Germany itself. It argued that "the sizable shortage of workers in the *Heimat* [homeland], especially in the armaments industry and agriculture compelled the increased use of prisoners of war," as well as that of "male civilian laborers."[49] Without diminishing the numbers working for the divisions at the front, the corps required each of its units to provide 300 workers to be sent to the rear.[50] By mid-June, the division reported the rather disappointing number of 138 volunteers for work in the Reich, blaming its lack of success on manpower restrictions and poor weather.[51] This effort continued throughout the year, however, as "the creation of necessary labor power for armament production" was of "decisive importance for the war effort."[52]

More important for the division itself was the use of civilian labor for its own purposes. This was made clear in an October 1942 conference held with economic authorities. The chief of Economic Staff East, *General der Infanterie* Otto Stapf, declared that the "armaments industry needs people . . . *But the absolute priority is the requirements of the zone of operations* [emphasis in original]."⁵³ In June 1942, the 7th Infantry Division reported 440 civilians working for it in agriculture.⁵⁴ Within four months, this number had increased to 2,069 workers in the fields, 6 in factories or workshops, 12 on road maintenance, 6 in fortification construction, and 151 with the troops themselves.⁵⁵ By early February 1943, the division reported a total of 4,513 civilians working under its remit.⁵⁶ Following the end of agricultural activity in late fall, workers were increasingly shifted into preparing German defensive positions, with the division demanding the establishment of construction battalions ranging from 20 to 200 people. While the coercion implicit in German occupation remained—"the present labor situation of the division demands a ruthless combing through of the population capable of work"—the division did provide workers with food and shelter.⁵⁷ It pronounced that "the labor efforts of the civilian labor groups in winter are essentially dependent on food and shelter. The daily rations are ordered. The difficulties are known. Nevertheless, more can be achieved here than previously through some aid."⁵⁸ By the turn of the year, the 7th Infantry Division recognized the necessity of civilians working productively for its own local war effort.

These forced labor groups—augmented by other civilians seized in the region during spring 1943—carried out the bulk of the work on the Buffalo Line. Ninth Army took control of this process and instructed its subordinate units to provide labor details for the project.⁵⁹ IX Corps ordered each of its divisions to establish civilian labor groups to complete the majority of this work and provide "shelter fit for human beings and sufficient food *before* the deployment."⁶⁰ The 7th Infantry Division provided an engineer and two construction battalions charged with ensuring that the civilian laborers would be provided with rations similar to those of German troops.⁶¹ By the time the Buffalo Line was finished, some 8,500 Soviet prisoners of war and 7,500 civilians had worked on its fortifications.⁶²

The 7th Infantry Division and the Buffalo Movement

Military considerations led the army to carry out a retreat that shipped out "everything that can be of use to the troops in the Buffalo Position" and destroyed anything that could be used by the enemy.⁶³ In a fashion similar to the Demyansk Pocket evacuation described by Canadian military historian Gregory Liedtke in this volume, German forces in the Rzhev salient began a massive movement of goods and equipment. This meant that the 7th Infantry Division needed to remove a wide assortment of goods, including munitions, weapons, vehicles, and other equipment ranging from fodder and clothes to cables and tents.[64] For example, the division needed to transport some 655 tons of munitions, 150 tons of food and fodder, and 14 train cars of tents and other barracks materials to the rear.[65] Due to a lack of available transport, however, it was clear from the very beginning of the retreat that various munitions and other supplies would have to be destroyed.[66]

By recognizing the importance of economic mobilization for the war, the army transformed the retreat from a purely military movement to one that encompassed far more than traditional battlefield activities. The army's appreciation of the conflict was not the only cause of destructive scorched earth retreats. On 4 February 1943, Hitler issued *Führerbefehl* Nr. 4, which would govern all German retreats for the remainder of the war:

• Any German equipment and weapons that could not be evacuated was to be destroyed.

• All installations and shelters must either be destroyed or burned down, as the "more thorough the destruction, the more the enemy's advance will be delayed."

• All men between the ages of fifteen and sixty-five were to accompany the troops to the rear to be used as laborers for the army and the Reich; this would also prevent them from being immediately integrated into the Red Army's ranks.[67]

Retreats would thus not only be a means to improve the military situation but would also be carried out in a way to exploit Soviet economic resources for the German army.

The 7th Infantry Division's leadership first learned of the Buffalo Movement on 7 February. The division's initial thoughts corresponded with those of *Führerbefehl* Nr. 4, as the destruction of German equipment that could not be evacuated, the "seizing of all civilians (with the exception of the old and sick) and their evacuation," and establishment of staffs to work on the removal of non-mobile goods served as the basis of planning.[68] The operation's arrangements needed to be concluded by 1 March, so the division had three weeks to craft its withdrawal.[69] Unlike the hasty and ill-prepared 1941 retreats or the chaotic, dread-filled late 1942 and early 1943 flights to the rear on the southern section of the line, the 7th Infantry Division and Army Group Center had time to formulate a comprehensive withdrawal plan. This time allowed for meticulous preparations; Ninth Army, for example, created a systematic and hierarchical operation that omitted no detail, while the division carried out a war game for the retreat.[70] Through attention to detail, the division and Army Group Center planned a withdrawal that reflected the army's appreciation of the general strategic situation and laid the groundwork to regain the initiative at a later date. It also ensured that the troops were carefully prepared for each step of the retreat. This precision resulted in a confident and cohesive unit, one that effectively carried out its mission in a professional manner.[71]

On 26 February, IX Corps passed on Hitler's order to its subordinate divisions, with a special emphasis on the removal of men between fifteen and sixty-five, adding that the "ruthless seizure and removal" of civilians was vital to the operation's success.[72] A total of 10,707 civilians resided in the area under the 7th Infantry Division's control, of which 4,532 were deemed capable of work and 1,421 were between the ages of 9 and 14.[73] IX Corps planned to relocate all workers between the ages of thirteen and fifty, anyone who worked for the Germans in any capacity, and the population residing in the fifteen-kilometer area east of the Buffalo Line. The deportees were allowed to bring their livestock and food with them to ensure their nourishment during the march. Excess livestock, however, was to be immediately turned over to the economic authorities for later distribution within the army. And, as the division made clear, no animals were to be left behind for the advancing Soviets.[74] The ruthless pragmatism that characterized the evacuations was brought into sharp relief by the decision to leave the aged and sick behind and provide them with only the "most essential" foodstuffs.[75] Such policies foreshadowed later and much larger actions in which the Germans simply abandoned large numbers of elderly and sick to the advancing Red Army.[76]

The deportations ran into almost immediate difficulty. A storm deposited heavy snow that blocked the area's primary roads, and civilians living in the vicinity did not possess the "sufficient . . . physical capabilities to carry out the work."[77] This forced the division to return civilians mustered into labor columns and already fed by the division to clear the roads.[78] Because of the weather issues, those unable to work were now shipped out first and those capable of clearing roads and other such tasks remained in the region until the rear guards were ready to pull back.[79] While the Red Army reacted to the German retreat, their unimaginative attacks posed little threat and the 7th Infantry Division continued its retrograde movement.[80]

Complementing the deportation of Soviet civilians was a policy of systematic destruction: Army Group Center demanded the region be transformed into a "wasteland."[81] Model instructed his Ninth Army to create a "complete zone of destruction" in the area vacated by his troops.[82] The 7th Infantry Division used similar language, identifying that its end goal was to create "a *desert zone*."[83] IX Corps issued an order concerning the demolition activities of its subordinate divisions, identifying the objective "to exploit every opportunity to stop the enemy, to delay his movement, to disturb his supply" and emphasizing that the retreat would be "according to a precise plan of destruction."[84] Roads deemed "essential" during the mud period, as well as any structures that the Soviets could use for vehicle repair or shelter, including hospitals, were all to be destroyed.[85] The 7th Infantry Division issued its own directive concerning the destruction of the region the following day. This more specific order detailed that wells should be blown up or filled in, tents destroyed, and all ovens, stove pipes, and windows broken.[86] Next all moveable goods would be transported out of the region, including all cattle and sheep east of the Buffalo Position.[87] Then beginning on 3 March, all "towns were to be destroyed, with the exception of those needed by the troops" during their final retreat.[88] By 16 March, the "desert zone needed to be created" in front of the Buffalo Position.[89] Nothing was to be left that would help the advancing Red Army with its war effort.

Having a relatively short distance to cover, the 7th Infantry Division completed its part of the retreat ten days before the remainder of German formations fully settled into the Buffalo Line on 23 March 1943.[90] From the German viewpoint, the retreat was an overwhelming success. Ninth Army alone pulled out nearly 325,000 men at minimal cost in lives and material.[91] As previously noted, the retreat considerably shortened German lines, freeing up twenty-one German divisions; the 7th Infantry Division and eight others could now be used in the summer 1943 Operation Citadel offensive.[92] The devastation of the area slowed the Red Army's advance, leaving it with no resources to support its war effort. Russian-British journalist Alexander Werth, who toured the Rzhev salient soon after the Red Army reoccupied the area, observed that "the towns were almost totally obliterated."[93] According to the official Soviet report on the region issued about two weeks after the German withdrawal, only 300 out of 1,600 houses in Gzhatsk survived and 495 out of 5,443 in Rzhev. In the rural region of Sychevka, only 111 villages remained out of the area's original 248; the Germans burned the rest to the ground.[94] Viaz'ma felt the full impact of the German army's unbridled fury. The commander in chief of Fourth Army reported that "all installations important for the war effort have been completely destroyed" and that "owing to the location of those installations in the town . . . the destruction of the town itself could not be avoided."[95] Nothing of value was left for the advancing Red Army except "two car cemeteries of destroyed Russian vehicles originating from the Viaz'ma battles of autumn 1941."[96] Of the town's 5,500 buildings, only 51 survived the German retreat.[97]

In addition to creating a "trail of destruction," the Germans evacuated anything deemed valuable for the war effort.[98] While livestock and food stuffs were shipped out of the salient, "the deportation of the civilian population for the acquisition of labor constituted a central piece of this operation."[99] Army Group Center's forces carried out a systematic and comprehensive evacuation of the salient, with nearly 13,000 train cars bursting with plundered goods speeding west behind the Buffalo Line.[100] Just as importantly, the army deported somewhere between 170,000 to 200,000 souls to the west.[101] For the Germans, this was a dual victory; in addition to providing a reservoir of workers to draw upon, these same individuals were simultaneously denied to the Soviet war effort. After "boasting" about the trail of destruction left in its wake, Army Group Center summed up the totality of the operation's success:

> The execution of the movement was carried out like clockwork, exactly according to the army group's prescribed timetable. The preparations that had been made and the successful rearguards have given the troops a new lease on life and suffused them with a new trust in their own achievements and purposes.[102]

From the army's perspective, Operation Buffalo demonstrated the troop's resilience and continued fighting power.

The tightly proscribed nature of the retreat, which severely curtailed the autonomy of low-level leaders, played a large role in the German army's perception of its success. While the 7th Infantry Division implemented various training programs during its time on the defensive within the salient, its leadership ranks never again reached the levels of efficacy of 1941.[103] Such training, however, did suffice for the defensive tasks it faced in late 1942–early 1943, including Operation Buffalo. It also helped recreate the cohesion so important to the success of German forces during the war. A division that feared defeat in summer 1942 now confidently looked forward to 1943. As a result of both careful planning and a systematic spoiling of their former positions, the German army was now, at least temporarily, in a stronger military and economic position.

Of course, the criminal nature of Germany's war against the Soviet Union colored the army's perception of success. The Reich's war of annihilation and plunder exploded the traditional boundaries that limited violence toward civilians. Freed from such constraints, the army's conception of war swirled military operations and occupation policies into one all-encompassing whole. The Buffalo retreat clearly demonstrated that duality. Sweeping aside all moral or ethical concerns about the fate of civilians under its control, the 7th Infantry Division and other German forces in the Rzhev salient simply viewed the population and their communities in a ruthlessly utilitarian manner: everything that could support the German war effort would be forcibly removed and exploited and everything that could not would simply be destroyed. The army recognized that the war reached a new intensity in 1943, one in which the mobilization of all available resources proved vital to battlefield victory. This recognition led the 7th Infantry Division and other units in Army Group Center to carry out an extraordinarily destructive retreat, heralding a new stage in the total war waged by the German army against Soviet state and society.

Notes

1. 7. Infanterie Division, Kriegstagebuch (KTB), Ia, 13.3.43, National Archives and Record Administration (NARA), T-315, Roll 386.

2. Earl Ziemke, *Stalingrad to Berlin: The German Defeat in the East* (Washington, DC: Office of the Chief of Military History, 1966), 116.

3. Bernd Wegner, "The War against the Soviet Union," in Horst Boog et. al, *The Global War*, Germany and the Second World War, vol. 6 (Oxford: Clarendon Press, 2009), 1199.

4. Der Kommandierende General des IX. Armeekorps, Tagesbefehl, 21 March 1943, Bundesarchive-Militärarchiv (BAMA), RH 24-9/204.

5. 7. Infanterie-Division Ia, Nr. 188/43 g. Kdos., 4.4.43, Ausserterminlicher Zustandsbericht Stand 1.4.43, NARA, T-315, Roll 389.

6. For the definitive account of Army Group Center's winter crisis, see David Stahel, *Retreat from Moscow: A New History of Germany's Winter Campaign, 1941–1942* (New York: Farrar, Straus, and Giroux, 2019).

7. For an analysis of the German retreat from the Demyansk pocket, see Gregory Liedtke's contribution to the present volume and Jeff Rutherford, "Life and Death in the Demiansk Pocket: The 123rd Infantry Division in Combat and Occupation," *Central European History* 41, no. 3 (September 2008): 347-80.

8. Felix Ackermann, Janine Fubel, and Claudia Weber, "Der Zweite Weltkrieg als Evakuierungskrieg: Praktiken der Deportation, Räumung und Zerstörung im militärischen Rückzug," *Militärgeschichtliche Zeitschrift* 81, no. 1 (May 2022): 3.

9. A few highlights follow from the immense body of literature on both campaigns. On Stalingrad, see Wegner, "The War against the Soviet Union," 843–1193; Robert Citino, *Death of the Wehrmacht: The German Campaigns of 1942* (Lawrence, KS: University Press of Kansas, 2007); the Stalingrad trilogy by David Glantz and Jonathan House: *To the Gates of Stalingrad: Soviet-German Combat Operations, April–August 1942* (Lawrence, KS: University Press of Kansas, 2009); *Armageddon in Stalingrad: September–November 1942* (Lawrence, KS: University Press of Kansas, 2009); David M. Glantz and Jonathan House, *Endgame at Stalingrad: Book One: November 1942* (Lawrence, KS: University Press of Kansas, 2014); and David M. Glantz and Jonathan House, *Endgame at Stalingrad: Book Two: December 1942–February 1943* (Lawrence, KS: University Press of Kansas, 2014). On Kursk, see Karl-Heinz Frieser, "The Battle of the Kursk Salient," in *The Eastern Front 1943–1944: The War in the East and on the Neighboring Fronts*, ed. Karl-Heinz Frieser, Germany and the Second World War, vol. 8 (Oxford: Clarendon Press, 2017), 83–206; and Roman Töppel, *Kursk, 1943: Die größte Schlacht des Zweiten Weltkriegs* (Paderborn, DE: Ferdinand Schöningh, 2017).

10. Studies of this relatively neglected topic include Bernd Wegner, "The Perplexities of War: The Soviet Theater in German Policy and Strategy from the Summer of 1943," in *The Eastern Front 1943–1944*, ed. Frieser, 253–65; Armin Nolzen, "'Verbrannte Erde': Die Rückzüge der Wehrmacht in den besetzten sowjetischen Gebieten 1941–1945," in *Besatzung. Funktion und Gestalt mili-*

tärischer Fremdherrschaft von der Antike bis zum 20. Jahrhundert, eds. Günter Kronenbitter, Markus Pöhlmann und Dierk Walter (Paderborn, DE: Ferdinand Schöningh, 2006), 161–75; and Jürgen Kilian, "Wehrmacht, Partisanenkrieg und Rückzugsverbrechen an der nördlichen Ostfront im Herbst und Winter 1943," in *Vierteljahreshefte für Zeitgeschichte,* (2) 2013, 173–99. Recent contributions include Jeff Rutherford, "Germany's Total War: Combat and Occupation around the Kursk Salient, 1943," *The Journal of Military History* 85, no. 4 (October 2021): 954–79; and various articles in *Militärgeschichtliche Zeitschrift* 81, no. 1 (May 2022) devoted to German retreats across the continent.

11. Notable exceptions include Babette Quinkert and Jörg Morré, eds., *Deutsche Besatzung in der Sowjetunion 1941–1944: Vernichtungskrieg, Reaktionen, Erinnerung* (Paderborn, DE: Ferdinand Schöningh, 2014); Dieter Pohl, *Die Herrschaft der Wehrmacht: Deutsche Militärbesatzung und einheimische Bevölkerung in der Sowjetunion 1941–1944* (Munich: Oldenbourg, 2008); Jörn Hasenclever, *Wehrmacht und Besatzungspolitik in der Sowjetunion: die Befehlshaber der rückwärtigen Heeresgebiete 1941–1943* (Paderborn, DE: Ferdinand Schöningh, 2010); Manfred Oldenburg, *Ideologie und Militärisches Kalkül: die Besatzungspolitik der Wehrmacht in der Sowjetunion 1942* (Cologne, DE: Böhlau, 2004); and Jürgen Kilian, *Wehrmacht und Besatzungsherrschaft im russischen Nordwesten 1941–1944: Praxis und Alltag im Militärverwaltungsgebiet der Heeresgruppe Nord* (Paderborn, DE: Ferdinand Schöningh, 2012).

12. On the war of annihilation, see Horst Boog et al., *The Attack on the Soviet Union*, Germany and the Second World War, vol. 4 (Oxford: Clarendon Press, 2015), particularly the contributions of Jürgen Förster, Rolf-Dieter Müller; Gerd Ueberschär, and Wolfram Wette, eds., *Der deutsche Überfall auf die Sowjetunion: "Unternehmen Barbarossa" 1941* (Frankfurt am Main, DE: Fischer, 1997); Alex J. Kay, Jeff Rutherford, and David Stahel, eds., *Nazi Policy on the Eastern Front: Total War, Genocide, and Radicalization* (Rochester, NY: Rochester University Press, 2012); Christian Hartmann, *Wehrmacht im Ostkrieg: Front und militärisches Hinterland 1941–42* (Munich: Oldenbourg, 2009); Johannes Hürter, *Hitlers Heerführer: die deutschen Oberbefehlshaber im Krieg gegen die Sowjetunion 1941–42* (Munich: Oldenbourg, 2007); Christian Streit, *Keine Kameraden: Die Wehrmacht und die sowjetischen Kriegsgefangenen 1941–1945* (Bonn, DE: J. H. W. Dietz Nachf., 1997); and Ben Shepherd, *War in the Wild East: The German Army and Soviet Partisans* (Cambridge, MA: Harvard University Press, 2004).

13. Hürter, 457.

14. 7. Infanterie Division, Kommandeur-Besprechung am 22.1.43, NARA T-315, Roll 387.

15. 7. Infanterie Division.

16. Jeff Rutherford, *Combat and Genocide on the Eastern Front: The German Infantry's War, 1941–1944* (Cambridge: Cambridge University Press, 2014), 307–8; and David Glantz, *The Battle for Leningrad, 1941–1944* (Lawrence, KS: University Press of Kansas, 2002), 264–304.

17. In addition to the works cited in endnote 5, see David Glantz's two volumes on the Red Army in Operation Don: *Operation Don's Left Wing: The Trans-Caucasus Front's Pursuit of the First Panzer Army, November 1942–February 1943* (Lawrence, KS: University Press of Kansas, 2019); and *Operation Don's Main Attack: The Soviet Southern Front's Advance on Rostov, January–February 1943* (Lawrence, KS: University Press of Kansas, 2018).

18. Earl Ziemke and Magna Bauer, *Moscow to Stalingrad: Decision in the East* (Washington, DC: US Army Center of Military History, 1987), 173.

19. Wegner, "The War against the Soviet Union," 1002.

20. Cited in Ziemke and Bauer, *Moscow to Stalingrad*, 405.

21. Wegner, "The War against the Soviet Union," 1004; and 7. Infanterie Division, Meldung vom 1.9.1942, NARA T-315, Roll 379.

22. See 7. Infanterie Division Ia/Org. Nr. 059/42 g. Kdos., Betrifft: Auffrischung und Kriegsgliederung der 7. Div., Beweglichkeit der Div., 4.5.42 and 7. Infanterie-Division, Meldung 15.5.42, NARA T-315, Roll 378.

23. 7. Infanterie Division Kommandeur, Nr. 01010/42 geh., 4 August 1942, an der Generalkommando IX Armeekorps, NARA T-315, Roll 379.

24. 7. Infanterie Division Kommandeur.

25. 7. Infanterie Division Kommandeur.

26. 7. Infanterie Division Kommandeur, 9.1.42, An die Kommandeure, NARA T-315, Roll 382.

27. 7. Infanterie Division, Meldung 15.5.42, NARA T-315, Roll 378.

28. Marco Sigg, *Der Unterführer als Feldheer in Taschenformat Theorie und Praxis der Auftragstaktik im deutschen Heer 1869 bis 1945* (Paderborn, DE: Schöningh, 2014), 356.

29. 7. Infanterie Division Ia op Nr. 202, Nr. 01352/42 geh., 26.9.42, Divisionsbefehl für die weitere Vorbereitung der Abwehr gegen Großangriffe, NARA T-315, Roll 379.

30. 7. Infanterie Division Ia op Nr. 202.

31. Sigg, *Der Unterführer als Feldheer in Taschenformat*, 392.

32. David Glantz, *Zhukov's Greatest Defeat: The Red Army's Epic Disaster in Operation Mars, 1942* (Lawrence, KS: University Press of Kansas, 1999), 20; 308.

33. Nicholas Terry, "The German Army Group Centre and the Soviet Civilian Population, 1942–1944: Forced Labour, Hunger and Population Displacement on the Eastern Front" (PhD diss., King's College, London, 2005), 99–109, unless otherwise noted.

34. On the importance of economic plunder in German planning for the invasion of the Soviet Union, see Alex J. Kay, *Exploitation, Resettlement, Mass Murder: Political and Economic Planning for German Occupation Policy in the Soviet Union, 1940–1941* (New York: Berghahn, 2011); Christian Gerlach, *Kalkulierte Morde. Die deutsche Wirtschafts- und Vernichtungspolitik in Weißrußland 1941 bis 1944* (Hamburg, DE: Hamburger Edition, 2000); and Rolf-Dieter Müller, "From Economic Alliance to a War of Colonial Exploita-

tion," in Boog, *The Attack on the Soviet Union*, 118–224. On the development of the German war economy at home, see Adam Tooze, *The Wages of Destruction: The Making and Breaking of the German War Economy* (New York: Viking, 2007). On German exploitation of occupied Europe, see Jonas Scherner and Eugene White, eds., *Paying for Hitler's War: The Consequences of Nazi Hegemony for Europe* (Cambridge: Cambridge University Press, 2016).

35. Hürter, *Hitlers Heerführer*, 457–8.

36. Cited in Chris Helmecke, "Ein 'anderer' Oberbefehlshaber? Generaloberst Rudolf Schmidt und die deutsche Besatzungsherrschaft in der Sowjetunion 1941–1943," *Militärgeschichtliche Zeitschrift* 75, no. 1 (2016): 71–2.

37. Panzer Armee Oberkommando 3/Ic/A.O., Richtlinien für die Behandlung der einheimischen Bevölkerung im Osten, 31.5.42, NARA T-315, Roll 382. Reproduced in whole in Jeff Rutherford and Adrian Wettstein, eds., *The German Army on the Eastern Front: An Inner View of the Ostheer's Experiences of War* (Barnsley, UK: Pen and Sword, 2018), 128–9.

38. Panzer Armee Oberkommando 3/Ic/A.O.

39. 7. Infanterie Division Ib, Wirtschaftliche Richtlinien für die Ortskommandanten, 25.7.42, NARA T-315, Roll 383.

40. 7. Infanterie Division Ib.

41. 7. Infanterie Division, Ib, Betr,: Befriedung der besetzten Gebiete, 3.8.42, NARA T-315, Roll 383.

42. 7. Division Ic, Betr.: Behandlung der Zivilbevölkerung, 12.4.42; Der Oberbefehlshaber der 4. Panzer Armee, Abschrift, 12.4.42 both in NARA T-315, Roll 382.

43. Der Oberbefehlshaber der 4. Panzer Armee, Abschrift, 12.4.42 both in NARA T-315, Roll 382.

44. 7. Infanterie Division Ib, Betr.: Viehbestand, 8.7.42, NARA T-315, Roll 383.

45. 7. Infanterie Division Ib, Betr.: Heuerfassung, Vorbereitung der Roggenernte, 8.8.42, NARA T-315, Roll 383.

46. 7. Infanterie Division Ib, Betr.: Ernährungslage der Zivilbevölkerung an Generalkommando IX.A.K./Qu., 9.8.42, NARA T-315, Roll 383.

47. 7. Infanterie Division, Ib, Betr,: Befriedung der besetzten Gebiete, 3.8.42, NARA T-315, Roll 383.

48. Mark Spoerer, "Social Differentiation of Foreign Civilian Workers, Prisoners of War, and Detainees in the Reich," in *German Wartime Society 1939–1945: Exploitation, Interpretations, Exclusion*, Germany and the Second World War, vol. 9/2, ed. Jörg Echternkamp (Oxford: Clarendon Press, 2014), 493.

49. 7. Infanterie Division Ib/Ic, Nr. 0367/42 geh., Betr.: Arbeitskräfte, 12.4.42, NARA T-315, Roll 382.

50. 7. Infanterie Division Ib/Ic.

51. 7. Infanterie Division Ia/Ib, Betr.: Arbeitseinsatz der Zivilbevölkerung, 12.11.1942, NARA T-315, Roll 383.

52. 7. Infanterie Division Ia/Ib.

53. Cited in Terry, "The German Army Group Centre and the Soviet Civilian Population," 101.

54. 7. Infanterie Division Ib, Nr. 0657/42 geh., Betr.: Verwaltung des rückw. Korpsgebietes, 13.6.42, NARA T-315, Roll 383.

55. 7. Infanterie Division Ib, Betr.: Verwaltung des rückw. Korpsgebietes, 12.10.1942, NARA T-315, Roll 383.

56. 7. Infanterie Division Ib., Betr.: Zivile Arbeitskräfte, 3.2.1943, NARA T-315, Roll 394.

57. 7. Infanterie Division Ia, Betrifft: Zivilarbeitskommandos zum Stellungsbau, 21.11.1942, NARA T-315, Roll 381.

58. 7. Infanterie Division Ia.

59. Steven Newton, *Hitler's Commander: Field Marshal Walther Model—Hitler's Favorite General* (Cambridge, MA: Da Capo Press, 2006), 214.

60. Generalkommando IX. Armeekorps Ia, Nr.257/43 geh. Kdos., Betr.: Stellungsbau "Büffel," 31 January 1943, NARA T-315, Roll 388.

61. Generalkommando IX. Armeekorps, Qu. Nr. 01720/43 g. Kdos, Besondere Anordnungen für die Versorgung "Büffel," 2.2.43, BAMA RH 24-9/264.

62. Terry, "The German Army Group Centre and the Soviet Civilian Population," 204.

63. Generalkommando IX. Armeekorps, Qu. Nr. 01800/43 g. Kdos, Besondere Anordnungen für die Versorgung zur Studie "Büffel," 16.2.43, BAMA RH 24-9/264.

64. Generalkommando IX. Armeekorps, Qu. Nr. 01720/43 g. Kdos, Besondere Anordnungen für die Versorgung "Büffel," 2.2.43, Anlage 1, BAMA RH 24-9/264.

65. Generalkommando IX. Armeekorps, Quartiermeister-Abteilung, 19.2.43, BAMA RH 24-9/264.

66. 7. Infanterie Division, KTB Ia, 11. and 14.2.43, NARA T-315, Roll 386.

67. Norbert Müller, ed., *Deutsche Besatzungspolitik in der UdSSR* (Cologne, DE: Pahl-Rugenstein, 1980), Document 143, 334–5.

68. Punkte der Ib-Besprechung beim Korps am 7.2.43, NARA T-315, Roll 394.

69. 7. Infanterie Division, KTB Ia, 7.2.43, NARA T-315, Roll 386.

70. Newton, *Hitler's Commander*, 216; and 7. Infanterie Division, KTB Ia, 20.2.43, NARA T-315, Roll 386.

71. On the importance of control and discipline in the army's approach to retreats, see Christian Stein, "Kontrollverlust und unumkehrbare Tatsachen: Die deutschen Rückzüge an der Ostfront des Zweiten Weltkriegs," *Militärgeschichtliche Zeitschrift* 81, no. 1 (May 2022): 91–115, especially 98–101.

72. Fernschreiben von IX. A.K.—Qu. an 7. 35. 252. I.D. und Stellungsbaust. IX., 26.2.43, BAMA RH 24-9/264.

73. Generalkommando IX. Armeekorps, Qu. Nr. 01720/43 g. Kdos, Besondere Anordnungen für die Versorgung "Büffel," Anlage 3, 2.2.43, BAMA RH 24-9/264.

74. 7. Division Ia, Nr. 79/43 g. Kdos., 17.2.43, Betrifft: "Büffel," NARA T-315, Roll 388.

75. 7. Infanterie Division Ia, Nr. 367/43 geh., 11.2.43, NARA T-315, Roll 388.

76. Nicholas Terry, "'Do Not Burden One's Own Army and Its Hinterland with Unneeded Mouths!' The Fate of the Soviet Civilian Population Behind the 'Panther Line' in Eastern Belorussia, October 1943–June 1944," in *Kriegführung und Hunger 1939–1945: Zum Verhältnis von militärischen, wirtschaftlichen und politischen Interessen*, ed. Christoph Dieckmann and Babette Quinkert (Göttingen, DE: Wallstein Verlag, 2015), 185–209; and Christoph Rass, *'Menschenmaterial': Deutsche Soldaten an der Ostfront. Innenansichten einer Infanteriedivision 1939–1945* (Paderborn, DE: Ferdinand Schöningh, 2003), 386–402.

77. 7. Infanterie Division Ia, Nr. 75/43 g. Kdos., Betr.: Strassenführung "Büffel," 17.2.43, NARA T-315, Roll 388.

78. 7. Infanterie Division Ia.

79. 7. Infanterie Division Ia, Nr. 487/43 geh., An Strassenkommandant I, II, III, IV, 19.2.43, NARA T-315, Roll 388; Quartiermeister Abteilung, Nr. 053/43 g. Kdos., Erfahrungsbericht für die Versorgung des Unternehmens "Büffel," BAMA RH 24-9/264.

80. 7. Infanterie Division, KTB Ia, 5.3.43, NARA T-315, Roll 386.

81. Cited in Wegner, "The Perplexities of War," 254.

82. Rass, *Menschenmaterial*, 381.

83. No date or title; presumably 20 or 21 February, NARA T-315, Roll 388.

84. Generalkommando IX, Armeekorps, Ia Nr.496/43 geh. Kdos., Betr.: Zerstörung im Fall "Büffel," 20. February 1943, NARA T-315, Roll 388.

85. Generalkommando IX.

86. 7. Division Ib, Nr. 97/43 geh. Kdos., Besondere Anordnungen für die Versorgung für "Büffel," 21.2.1943, NARA T-315, Roll 388.

87. 7. Infanterie Division Ib/IVa, Nr. 568/43 geheim, Betr.: Fleischsammlung, 28.2.43, NARA T-315, Roll 388.

88. Generalkommando IX. Armeekorps, KTB Ia, 3.3.43, BAMA RH 24-9/96.

89. Generalkommando IX. Armeekorps, Ia Nr. 657/43 geh. Kdos., An Führer Stellungsbaustab IX. Nachrichtlich; Ko. Pi. Führer, 2. March 1943, BAMA RH 24-9/97.

90. Percy Schramm, *Kriegstagebuch des Oberkommandos der Wehrmacht 1943*, vol. I (1963; repr., Bonn, DE: Bernard & Graefe Verlag, 2002), 236.

91. Newton, *Hitler's Commander*, 213–6.

92. Robert Citino, *The Wehrmacht Retreats: Fighting a Lost War, 1943* (Lawrence, KS: University Press of Kansas, 2012), 120.

93. Alexander Werth, *Russia at War, 1941–1945* (New York: Carroll & Graf, 1964), 630–1.

94. Werth.

95. Cited in Wegner, "The Perplexities of War," 254–5.
96. Terry, "The German Army Group Centre and the Soviet Civilian Population," 204.
97. Werth, *Russia at War*, 630.
98. Terry, "The German Army Group Centre and the Soviet Civilian Population," 204.
99. Rass, *Menschenmaterial*, 381.
100. Stein, "Kontrollverlust und unumkehrbare Tatsachen," 100.
101. Terry, "The German Army Group Centre and the Soviet Civilian Population," 205.
102. See Stein, "Kontrollverlust und unumkehrbare Tatsachen," 101, for both his evaluation of the army group's perceptions and its description of the retreat.
103. See, for example, 7. Infanterie Division, Kommandeur, Betrifft: Winterausbildung, 21.10.1942, NARA T-315, Roll 396.

Chapter 12
A Fighting Retreat: The Chosin Reservoir Campaign
Charles P. Neimeyer

On 15 October 1950, General of the Army and Supreme Allied Commander in the Far East Douglas MacArthur flew to Wake Island to meet US President Harry S. Truman. Their discussion, now that United Nations (UN) forces had crossed the 38th Parallel, centered on the possibility that China would intervene in the war. MacArthur, however, brushed aside the president's concerns and informed Truman that he did not believe the risk of Chinese intervention was all that great. Moreover, even if they did intervene, he noted, "UN forces would easily prevail, in large part because of their superiority in the air."[1] Neither man was aware that Communist Chinese leader Mao Zedong had already given "the preliminary order" for Communist Chinese forces (CCF) "to move into Korea" on the 8th of October—precisely one day after non-Korean UN forces crossed the Parallel.[2]

At this same time, MacArthur and his planners were preoccupied with the northward advance of the US 8th Army on the western side of the Korean Peninsula while his X Corps, under the overall command of Maj. Gen. Edward "Ned" Almond—including the 1st US Marine Division commanded by Maj. Gen. O. P. Smith—was to make yet another major amphibious landing by 15 October at the North Korean east coast port of Wonsan. The decision to operate two widely separated and independent commands has never been fully explained. However, by 6 October, it was becoming clear that anticipating a 15 October X Corps landing at Wonsan had been wildly optimistic. Thus, D-Day kept getting "moved progressively back to a tentative date of 20 October."[3] Moreover, due to the discovery of magnetic sea mines in Wonsan harbor, the actual landing did not take place until 26 October. This eleven-day delay cost Almond's X Corps more than two weeks of good weather—a fact that no one appreciated at the time.

Army Historian Richard W. Stewart described the X Corps in Korea as "an unusual, one-of-a-kind, organization."[4] Having only been activated since the end of August, Almond soon quarreled with O. P. Smith over amphibious landing plans at Inchon and, later, Wonsan. To make matters worse, Almond had "retained his position as General Douglas MacArthur's Chief of Staff of the Far Eastern Command (FEC)."[5] Lt. Gen. Walton H. Walker, who commanded the 8th Army; resented the arrangement because Almond used his dual-hatted position to ensure his X Corps received priority over critical supplies "at the expense of the 8th Army."[6] In sum, X Corps was a hastily assembled provisional corps headquarters commanded by a fractious leader who had a penchant for "meddling . . . down to the regimental and battalion level."[7] Moreover, even during the earlier recapture of Seoul, Almond continually prodded his subordinate units (to include the Marines) to move with greater speed and aggressiveness.[8] A good example of his impetuosity was recounted by the US Army 7th Infantry Division operations officer: "We planned an orderly concentration and movement to Chosin, by first concentrating the regiments and moving them one by one . . . [but] this plan was never carried out. Before we knew it, Almond ordered our closest battalions and [even] smaller units to Chosin, individually, and as fast as they could get there."[9] It was also clear that Almond was adamant about getting his X Corps forces moving northward as soon as possible.

By early November, Almond's X Corps plunged into the heart of eastern North Korea with the 1st Marine Division representing the left flank, then drove up the main road leading from the port of Hungnam into the rugged eastern interior of North Korea. However, for the Marines, control over this single axis of advance known as the MSR (Main Supply Route) soon became a matter of life or death. As a precaution, O. P. Smith had ordered his combat engineers to begin building several rough airstrips along the way; the air power supplied by the 1st Marine Air Wing (1st MAW) later proved decisive—especially the expeditionary airfields at the key villages of Hagaru-ri and Koto-ri.

The topography of eastern North Korea presented the X Corps with a conundrum. After a relatively short, flat coastal plain that was easily dominated by US air power, the terrain broke up into inland hills, mountains, and steep inaccessible valleys. Many of the few good roads that bisected the region were carved directly into the sides of the mountains leaving little room for easy passage. This made contact between supporting and adjacent units exceptionally difficult. Almond tried to remedy this situation by hurrying the US 31st Regimental Combat Team (31st RCT), 7th Infantry Division, to take up positions east of the Chosin Reservoir. Then Smith's 5th Marines could eventually follow behind the 7th Marines west of this major terrain feature.

Before this took place, however, the 7th Marines were attacked on 2 November near the town of Sudong by a company-sized element of CCF forces. More Chinese soldiers from the 124th CCF Division, supported by tanks, soon joined the fray. The fighting continued all day and into the night of 3 November and seemed to the Marines to be serving no purpose other than to inflict casualties on their forces defending key hilltops overlooking the MSR. Nearly simultaneously, an entire Chinese Army savaged the Republic of Korea (ROK) II Corps and ferociously attacked the left wing of Walker's US I Corps and especially his exposed 21st Infantry Regiment, then just over twenty miles from the Yalu River. The ROK forces as well as the 1st Marine Division's G-2, Col. Bankson T. Holcomb Jr. (who coincidentally had grown up in China), and even Major General Almond were now convinced that the Communist Chinese had officially entered the war, but much of Walton Walker's 8th Army did not share that assessment.[10]

On the X Corps front—in a foreshadowing of even heavier fighting to come—on the morning of 3 November, Chinese troops used infiltration tactics to get between various Marine rifle companies in the hills and the MSR itself. During the fighting around Sudong, "the Marines established a tactical principle for the coming weeks: that to nullify Chinese night tactics, regardless of large-scale penetrations and infiltration, defending units only had to maintain position until daybreak."[11] At this point, the organizational firepower of the unique Marine Corps Air-Ground Task Force (MAGTF) was able to "melt down the Chinese mass to impotency."[12] However, this meltdown process did not prove as easy as it sounded. In 1/7's front alone, the Marines counted 662 enemy dead.[13] Just as swiftly as they had appeared on 2–3 November, the Chinese ceased heavy attacks on the MSR. By 6 November, the Chinese did the same in the west against much of the 8th Army; many at Walker's headquarters found this approach mystifying.

It was now the latter part of November, and the weather had grown even colder. Despite solid evidence of greater Chinese involvement in the fighting, Almond and Walker's widely separated advances to the Yalu continued northward with noticeable gaps growing between their various operating forces. On the morning of 27 November, Almond planned for his entire X Corps to resume the offensive for what he hoped would be the final drive to the Yalu. Meanwhile, Chinese generals were growing optimistic about the situation. Chinese General Peng Dehaui's Chief of Staff Xie Fang wrote: "We have over 150,000 men on the eastern front, the enemy over 90,000 giving us a 1.66 advantage over him."[14] Moreover, in the rugged terrain around the reservoir, Almond's separated X Corps elements offered the Chinese ample opportunities to use large-scale infiltration tactics. Fang further elaborated that although the CCF continued to fall back as planned in front of the X Corps, the Americans "were still far from our pre-selected killing zones."[15] That killing zone turned out to be the plateau around the Chosin (Changjin) Reservoir.

On the night of 27–28 November 1950, the CCF launched a massive assault against all UN forces in North Korea. On the eastern X Corps front, the hammer blow fell on the 31st RCT—later known as Task Force Faith after one of its last commanders, Lt. Col. Don C. Faith Jr.—and the 1st Marine Division. Strung out in positions along the eastern side of the reservoir and still minus several critical rifle companies, the 31st RCT quickly collapsed under the Chinese onslaught.[16] Surrounded by at least two Chinese divisions, the 31st RCT was authorized on 30 November to make a breakout toward the thinly held US Marine lines at Hagaru-ri. That same morning, Almond had transferred control of all 7th US Army Division forces north of Koto-ri to O. P. Smith's 1st Marine Division. At that time, however, the 7th and 5th Marine regiments were still on the road leading to the western reservoir village of Yudam-ni and had not yet consolidated with the rest of the 1st Marine Division. The 31st RCT would have to fight its way south largely on its own. The 31st Tank company and the 31st RCT rear troops reached the Marine perimeter by 1700 that day, but a huge gap remained between Task Force Faith's separated truck-bound infantry battalions and Hagaru-ri—a gap that thousands of infiltrating Chinese soldiers quickly filled.[17] Nevertheless, fifteen US Army tanks survived the clash and proved a tremendous addition to Smith's weakly defended lines at Hagaru-ri.

The overall situation for the rest of the 31st RCT rapidly grew worse, and this isolated unit—now chopped up into numerous separate enclaves—faced repeated Chinese attacks from nearly every direction. On 1 December 1950, Don Faith was mortally wounded by a Chinese fragmentation grenade. The struggling 31st RCT soldiers continued to fight their way through dozens of roadblocks and ambushes. With the death of Lieutenant Colonel Faith, however, communication between units and commanders broke down and what was left of the 31st RCT retreated across the ice of the reservoir. O. P. Smith's motor transportation officer, Lt. Col. (USMC) Olin L. Beall, drove onto the reservoir ice in his jeep and led several hundred 31st RCT soldiers to the relative safety of the Hagaru-ri lines. Beall inspected an abandoned line of US Army trucks that he estimated contained more than 300 dead soldiers. "I went through that convoy and saw dead in each vehicle, stretchers piled up with men frozen to death trying to pull themselves out from under another stretcher," he recalled. "I shall never forget it."[18] The soldiers rescued by Beall were soon placed into Smith's overextended lines at Hagaru-ri.

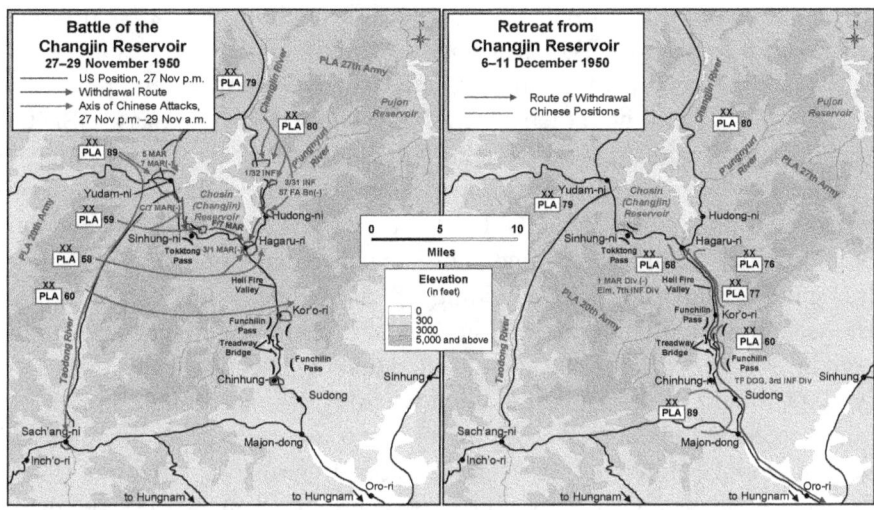

Figure 12.1. Battle of the Changjin Reservoir, 27–29 November 1950, and Withdrawal from the Reservoir, 6–11 December 1950. Courtesy of the US Army Center of Military History.

Meanwhile, the Chinese attacked the Marines to the west with astonishing ferocity. Smith ordered the 7th and 5th Marines to fight their way fourteen miles back to Hagaru-ri. Fortunately for the beleaguered Americans around the reservoir, the Chinese did not bring much supporting arms and relied predominantly on infantry assaults. Even so, by the morning of 28 November, the 1st Marine Division was in serious trouble. The turning point in the retrograde from Yudam-ni took place on 30 November. Aviation air drops resupplied the Marines with critical food, ammunition, and especially artillery and mortar shells—enough for the two regiments to complete their breakout and make it to the Hagaru-ri perimeter. Marine aviators from the 1st MAW kept the MSR relatively open during the daytime. To complete the retrograde, the 7th Marines had to secure ridgeline after ridgeline overlooking the MSR while the 5th Marines provided a rear guard.[19]

After finally consolidating at Hagaru-ri, Smith planned to fight his mostly reunited division along with 31st RCT remnants down the MSR, through Hell-Fire valley, Koto-ri, and the critical Funchilin Pass toward the safety at the port of Hungnam. However, before this could take place the F/2/7 Marines commanded by Capt. (USMC) William E. Barber had to successfully defend the critical Toktong Pass, located about halfway between Yudam-ni and Hagaru-ri. If this key chokepoint was lost, much of the 7th Marine Regiment would be cut off. Then the plan was to move as quickly as possible toward Hagaru-ri. Throughout the early morning hours of 28 November, Barber's Marines fought off repeated Chinese assaults into their company perimeter. Although overrun at several points by attackers, F/2/7 still held the pass in the morning. Pvt. 1st Class (USMC) Hector A. Cafferata Jr. recalled being jolted awake by screaming Chinese attackers overrunning his position then jumping from his sleeping bag without his parka or even boots. For the next five hours, Cafferata and another marine—temporarily blinded by grenade fragments—fought against tremendous odds, ultimately holding off the Chinese attackers. Captain Barber nominated Cafferata for the Medal of Honor. Officers who gathered information prior to the award stated that they "counted approximately 100 Chinese dead around the ditch where [Cafferata] fought that night but had decided to not put the figure into their report because they thought no one would believe it."[20] Cafferata, who suffered severe frostbite to his feet (recall he was not wearing his boots) and numerous battle wounds to his body, spent the next eighteen months recovering from his injuries.

Smith's selection of Hagaru-ri as the divisional rally point was crucial and enabled the retreat to ultimately continue toward Hungnam and the sea. Even the United Kingdom's 41 Independent Commando contributed to the effort. Smith ordered the Royal Marines to fight their way eleven miles north from Koto-ri along with a rifle company borrowed from Col. Lewis B. "Chesty" Puller's 1st Marines (G/3/1) and a previously detached 31st Infantry rifle company. Known as Task Force Drysdale for its commander, Lt. Col. Douglas B. Drysdale, the 41 Independent Commando ran into stiff resistance when the Chinese ambushed them in the "Hell-Fire Valley" along the MSR south of Hagaru-ri. The attempt to reinforce Hagaru-ri proved to be a major mistake. While both Smith and Puller had anticipated that Drysdale would be attacked during the move to Hagaru-ri, only about a third of Drysdale's original task force ultimately made it there. The remainder were killed, captured, or forced to turn back to Koto-ri. Nevertheless, Smith believed the risk was worthwhile to provide *any* infantry reinforcements for the Hagaru-ri perimeter.[21] He was that desperate.

The surviving G/3/1 marines were given the tough assignment to take and hold East Hill, a key piece of ground on the edge of the Hagaru-ri perimeter. Recently reoccupied by Chinese forces, the ground was a virtual sheet of ice that made it nearly impossible for the marines to dig in. Corp. (USMC) Robert Harbula, a G/3/1 machine gunner, noted that his crew resorted to using frozen Chinese corpses (apparently there were plenty) as a temporary breastwork for his gun section. Harbula's company commander, Capt. (USMC) Carl L. Sitter was seriously wounded by grenade fragments in the engagement but tenaciously continued to fight for nearly thirty-six continuous hours. G/3/1's stand at East Hill enabled the 1st Marine Division's combat engineers to complete and extend the critical Hagaru-ri airstrip.[22] During the period of 1–5 December, Smith's unit "air-evacuated more than 4,000 marines from Hagaru-ri, half from incapacitating frostbite."[23]

Because of the airfield, the Marine defensive perimeter needed to be large—approximately four miles. Most of the 3rd Battalion, 1st Marines (3/1), commanded by Lt. Col. Thomas L. Ridge had arrived at Hagaru-ri on 27 November—minus G/3/1, which later arrived with the remains of Task Force Drysdale. The Marines simply did not have enough available infantry to provide a credible perimeter defense. Smith admitted that "considering the mission assigned to the 1st Marine Division, an infantry component of one battalion was all that could be spared for the defense of Hagaru."[24] He noted that this single battalion "was very adequately supported by air and had sufficient artillery and tanks for its purposes."[25] Subsequently, numerous artillery batteries, engineer, and other combat service support units contributed to the overall perimeter defense of the Division HQ. In fact, Smith's combat support units were critical for holding Hagaru-ri and keeping it from being overrun for two days (28–29 November). A single USMC artillery battery attached to 3/1 recorded that it fired more

Figure 12.2. Crash landing of a Marine aircraft flown by Capt. (USMC) Paul Noel and two crew members. The crash occurred after the plane's load of ammunition shifted when the aircraft touched down on a hard-scrabble airstrip. Remarkably, all three crew members survived the crash. Courtesy of the National Archive and Records Administration.

than 1,200 rounds on the night of 29 November while two infantry companies reported expending 3,200 rounds of 60-mm mortar fire.[26] During the night of 28 November, the 7th Marines received "24.6 tons [of ammunition] in ten C-47 sorties."[27] On this same day, "the 1st MAW flew 114 sorties, 62 in support of X Corps and 52 for the Eighth Army. Up to this time attacks on enemy troops had been relatively few, but on this date CCF concentrations were attacked again and again."[28] Even though six inches of snow covered the airstrip at Yonpo the following day, the Marines had three squadrons in the air by mid-morning and flew a total of 125 sorties; "all but six were directed to the Chosin Reservoir area."[29] In sum, organic Marine aviation proved decisive throughout the entire campaign. More importantly, in the near term, the Marines were able to preserve their critical Hagaru-ri expeditionary airstrip for resupply and medical evacuation.

One of the 3/1 Marines guarding the Hagaru-ri perimeter, Pvt. 1st Class Charles Carmin, recalled the CCF attack that started about 2300:

> It was stressed that no matter what happened, no one would get out of his hole. Orders from First Lieutenant [Joseph R.] Fisher, I/3/1, said, 'If overrun, stay in your holes and shoot the bastards in the back.' . . . The first wave of Chinese ran forward throwing grenades, many of them getting entangled in the barbed wire. . . . The first wave was followed by a second wave of Chinese firing automatic weapons and rifles. In the flare light it looked like the entire valley to our front was filled with waves of Chinese.[30]

On 6 December, an entire Chinese division attempted to throw the 5th Marines, along with other combat elements, off East Hill at Hagaru-ri just

Figure 12.3. "The Eternal Band of Brothers," a combat artist rendition of the 7th Marines frozen trek toward Koto-ri. Created by Col. (USMC) Charles Waterhouse, combat artist.

as the 7th Marines were making their breakout toward Koto-ri. After twenty-two hours of combat, "the new day revealed a scene of slaughter which surpassed anything the Marines had seen since the fight for the approaches of Seoul in September."[31] The Chinese lost hundreds of men in suicidal human wave assaults. By 7 December, Smith ordered his consolidated forces to proceed down the MSR toward Koto-ri (then held by Puller's 1st Marines) and take along all their wounded, including 31st RCT members who had been lucky enough to make it to Hagaru-ri, as well as some of the dead and any operable vehicles and combat equipment. As Smith's frozen column trudged on, the weather worsened. Six squadrons of Marine Corsairs provided near-constant overhead coverage during the day. Once Smith's force made it to Koto-ri, he flew out some of the critically wounded and received some resupply in return.

The next crucial point along the MSR for the 1st Marine Division was at narrow Funchilin Pass, where the MSR literally snaked its way along the sides of steep, rocky terrain. Even more challenging, some of the surrounding high hills were occupied by the CCF. Further, a key bridge in the pass had been damaged by the enemy. If Smith's Marines could not

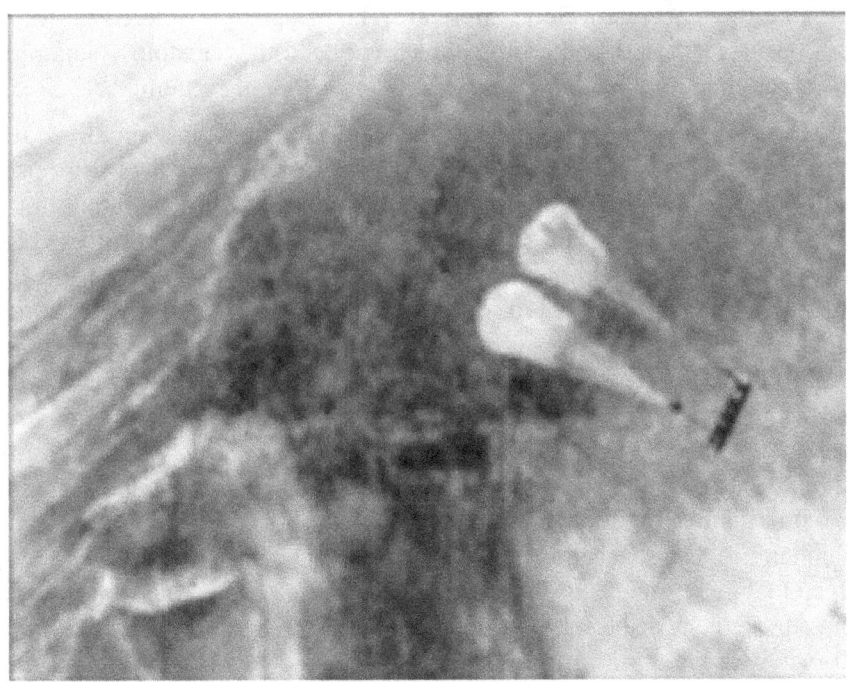

Figure 12.4. Combat Airlift Help Dates Back to Korea. Courtesy of the US Air Force.

force the Chinese from the surrounding hilltops and repair the bridge, his division would be trapped and defeated. Smith's infantry needed to take the surrounding hilltops and keep the Chinese back while his chief engineer, Lt. Col. John Partridge, arranged for the US Air Force to fly in eight 2,500-pound M-2 Treadway steel bridging sections to Koto-ri; at least four needed to arrive intact. Because such a feat had never been attempted, the Air Force conducted a test drop that resulted in a smashed bridge section. As a quick fix, two larger G-5 parachutes were attached, and this seemed to work. On 7 December, the drop proceeded as scheduled. Although one section floated into Chinese hands—alerting them to the Marine efforts at the Funchilin Pass bridge—and another smashed on impact, the remaining sections were recovered safely and trucked to the bridge site. The engineers worked around the clock and completed the bridge by 9 December.[32]

Most of the division was well across the bridge late on 10 December. However, there was still some drama as the last of Puller's 1st Marines and some heavy tanks finally crossed the span. No one had anticipated that crowds of Korean refugees would follow closely behind Puller's remaining Reconnaissance Platoon of twenty-eight Marines—his last unit to cross the span. A few armed Chinese had infiltrated the refugee group and began firing on the rear guard. Soon afterward, the bridge was ordered blown; a few Marines left on the other side of the rocky chasm were able to scramble down and then up the other side to rejoin the retreating column.[33]

The "miracle" of the Treadway Bridge at Funchilin Pass involved the joint use of US Marine, Air Force, and Army forces. To keep the MSR open, Puller ordered his 1st Battalion (1/1) to attack north from Chinhung-ni toward the north end of Funchilin Pass. To keep Chinese infiltrators from cutting off the MSR behind 1/1, Major General Almond ordered the US 3rd Army Infantry Division to form a special task force (Task Force Dog) and sent them to Chinhung-ni on 6 December to cover the withdrawal of Smith's division once it cleared Funchilin Pass. On the way north, the soldiers noted thirteen destroyed Marine trucks. Like the 31st RCT convoys east of the Chosin, the men in these vehicles had been killed in an ambush. Almond also ordered the 3rd Infantry Division to provide two battalions of its 65th Infantry Regiment to protect the MSR south of Task Force Dog and Chinhung-ni. On 8 December, 65th Infantry elements successfully repelled several Chinese attacks in the vicinity of Sudong. That same day, infiltrators attacked a Marine supply truck convoy; though the US Marine troops ultimately drove off the attackers, they sustained heavy loss of life. A timely two-man counterattack led by a US Army Artillery lieutenant colonel gave the Marine service troops time to restore the situation.[34]

Figure 12.5. Dead marines at Yudam-Ni waiting for burial. Courtesy of the US Marine Corps.

The principle of cohesion also enabled the 1st Marine Division and attached 31st Regimental Combat Team (31st RCT) elements to make it safely to US Navy shipping at Hungnam. Despite an onslaught of Chinese human wave attacks after the successful defense of Hagaru-ri, retreating US forces were never broken and even demonstrated grim and determined elan. Their relatively optimism was at least in part related to an O. P. Smith decision early in the retreat. From the start, Smith instructed that his forces should bring back marines and soldiers killed in action if at all possible, along with all their ammunition and operating rolling stock. Because of the extremely cold weather, the frozen MSR held up fairly well to the heavy vehicle and foot traffic. While most of the seriously wounded were evacuated from expeditionary airfields at Hagaru-ri and Koto-ri, the frozen bodies of deceased Marines were transported on the open beds of military trucks or even lashed to the bumpers of jeeps. While none of the Marines liked to see stacks of frozen corpses, the message sent by Smith to his troops was clear—no one would be left behind, whether dead or alive.

Following the close call at Funchilin Pass, the 1st Marine Division was nearly out of harm's way by the second week in December. However, the Marines and attached US Army forces still needed to break out into the narrow coastal plain south of the village of Chinhung-ni on the MSR. To facilitate their escape, Almond sent US 3rd Infantry "Rock of the Marne" Division elements forward to Chinhung-ni. Once the Marines and associated X Corps forces reached the lowlands, the full force of superior US airpower could be more effectively applied against the attacking Chinese. "At 1300 on 11 December the last elements of the [1st Marine] Division cleared Chinhung-ni. Majon-dong had been left behind by 1730 . . . and by 2100 all units, except for the tanks, had reached assigned assembly areas in the Hamhung-Hungnam area."[35] Just before midnight, "the armored column arrived at the LST [Landing Ship Tank] staging area . . . thus bringing to an end the breakout of the 1st Marine Division."[36] By 11–12 December, the rest of the 1st Marine Division troops were transported from the docks to the safety of US Navy amphibious vessels just offshore. Pvt. 1st Class Charles Carmin noted that the ship's galleys worked around the clock to feed the marines. At best, according

Figure 12.6. US marines march south from Hagaru-ri on 6 December 1950. Courtesy of the Department of Defense.

Figure 12.7. Korean refugees during the Hungam evacuation, circa December 1950. Courtesy of the US Navy.

to Carmin, marines would get one meal per day but could get two meals if they were willing to stand in line all day.[37]

One final act in the Chosin Reservoir saga was to evacuate remaining ROK and US Army forces, and equipment as well as approximately 98,000 Korean refugees from the port of Hungnam. The problem for the Navy and Rear Adm. James H. Doyle, the officer in charge of the evacuation, was that the Hungnam docks "could only support seven ships at a time."[38] On the bright side, the US Navy tank landing ships (LSTs) could drive directly onto the beach and backload nearly all the remaining X Corps rolling stock and even the refugees in the succeeding days. Moreover, there were no worries about the tide—"one foot [at Hungnam] as compared to Inchon's thirty foot [tidal change]."[39] The relatively fresh US 3rd Infantry Division provided a rear guard at the nearby town of Hamhung and, most importantly, military police to screen thousands of Korean refugees "attempting to leave North Korea before the communist forces arrived."[40]

Figure 12.8. USS *Begor* (APD-127) stands offshore during the evacuation and demolition of Hungnam, Korea, 24 December 1950. Courtesy of the US Navy.

By 22 December, the US 3rd Infantry Division was the sole remaining American force ashore in the region. In a series of expertly timed phased withdrawals, the 3rd Division was itself finally evacuated during the late afternoon of 24 December. US Navy destroyers moved in and provided covering fire for the last evacuees. Large-caliber naval guns from the USS *Missouri* and other US Navy vessels fired star shells that kept the lines brightly illuminated throughout the evacuation and negated the night infiltration tactics favored by the CCF. Brig. Gen. James O. Boswell later described the 3rd Division's performance at Hungnam as "essentially an exercise in improvisation . . . and a great credit to the United States Army. No school in the American military establishment had a curriculum on how to evacuate a beachhead. We had been taught how to take a beach, but not how to give one up."[41] Furthermore, the US Navy evacuated 17,500 vehicles and other equipment; plus 250,000 metric tons of supplies, including 8,635 short tons of ammunition and 29,400 drums (55 gallons) of gasoline and petroleum products in the final days at Hungnam.[42] Most importantly, they transported nearly 200,000 military personnel and 98,000 civilian refugees. Once the last American had been evacuated, the Navy demolished the Hungnam harbor facilities in a spectacular explosion.

In retrospect, the failure of the X Corps along with that of the US Eighth Army in November–December 1950 must be attributed to what military historians Eliot A. Cohen and John Gooch termed an "aggregate defeat."[43] First, General of the Army Douglas MacArthur and his chief of intelligence, Maj. Gen. Charles A. Willoughby, seriously underestimated the CCF's ability to move large numbers of troops south of the Yalu River. Moreover, they refused to change their "on to the Yalu mantra" for all UN forces even when presented with growing evidence of CCF soldiers in Korea. However, Maj. Gen. O. P. Smith deserves partial credit for the successful withdrawal of the 1st Marine Division's retreat from the Chosin Reservoir because of his increasing caution following the two-day CCF assault (2–3 November) on his 7th Marines near Sudong. On 7 November, Smith informed his corps commander, Maj. Gen. Ned Almond, that he "felt the attack had been a blocking action [which indeed it was] meant to delay his division in its march north, while the enemy brought more forces to bear."[44] Though Smith had correctly assessed the situation, Almond was not about to challenge the views of his superior, MacArthur—that is until he paid a personal visit to MacArthur in Japan on 29 November and received explicit orders to begin a general retreat to the sea. Although initially planning to continue the offensive, Almond followed MacArthur's orders and ultimately saved much of his ROK I Corps and US Army forces south and east of the Chosin Reservoir plateau.

The X Corps retreat also was greatly affected by problems with the terrain, weather, and even throngs of Korean refugees silently trudging alongside or behind the retreating American X Corps after 27 November 1950. For example, the late start at Wonsan caused all of X Corps to operate in much harsher winter conditions. Because of the extreme cold weather, an increased number of troops suffered with severe frostbite—a situation that might have been avoided if US force planners had anticipated the harsh fighting conditions in Korea and provided the troops with better pre-deployment training and in some cases adequate cold weather gear. The experience did not go unnoticed. In 1951, the US Marine Corps established its first-ever US-based mountain warfare training center at Bridgeport, California. Most USMC forces going into theater following the Chosin Reservoir campaign received some cold weather or mountain warfare training. Moreover, little or no thought had been given to what commanders should do when confronted by large throngs of refugees accompanying a major retreat. After Chosin Reservoir, the American high command established refugees as a planning factor for staffs in Korea regardless of whether American combat forces were on the offensive in or retreat.

The rough topography of eastern North Korea required most of the X Corps to generally use a single axis of advance deep into enemy territory. A single axis, however, is often a double-edged sword. If a retreat is called for, as was clearly the case at the Chosin Reservoir, an aggressive enemy will strenuously work to cut this crucial lifeline at all costs. The CCF attempted to do this first at Hagaru-ri and later at Funchilin Pass. The miracle of the Funchilin Pass bridge—created just in time by USMC combat engineers (7–10 December)—attests to the inherent strength of the budding Marine Corps Air-Ground Task Force (MAGTF) concept. Furthermore, the support of Smith's infantry by the 1st MAW was decisive throughout the retreat. Moreover, the wing flew 3,703 sorties between 26 October and 11 December, of which 599 were close air support—468 for the 1st Marine Division, 67 for the ROKs, 56 for the US 7th Infantry Division, and 8 for the US 3rd Infantry Division.[45] The 1st Marine Division's astute use of combined arms and service support enabled them to maintain a tenuous control over the MSR and ensured their future survival as a viable combat formation.

Figure 12.9. Chinese prisoners, 3–4 November 1950. Note the quilted winter uniforms and canvas tennis shoes worn by most of the Chinese soldiers. The tennis shoes were especially ineffective in the cold weather. Courtesy of the US Marine Corps.

As for the Chinese, they suffered greatly in trying to annihilate the Marines and other US Army forces operating in the eastern theater. A primary problem for forces that use infiltration as its main operating principle is that they are, by nature, poorly supported and lightly equipped. The Chinese divisions attacking the X Corps had little to no staying power, which proved advantageous to the Americans in the long run. Further, groups of horribly frostbitten and hungry Chinese soldiers sometimes surrendered during the campaign due to exposure. Other Chinese soldiers remained remarkably resilient despite being poorly clothed and suffering from extreme privation. Nevertheless, at least seven Chinese combat divisions experienced significant losses; it would be many months before they could be reconstituted and made combat-effective again.

The best after-action report on the entire Chosin campaign was provided by O. P. Smith himself in his thirteen-page personal report to the Commandant of the Marine Corps, General Clifton B. Cates. Smith recalled that on 25 November Almond informed him that his division would become the "main effort" of X Corps. Almond had ordered the 7th Infantry Division to operate east of the Reservoir and assigned the 3rd Infantry Division to provide security for the MSR "up to Hagaru-ri."[46] Smith noted that "this never transpired and to the end of the operation I had to retain one battalion of the 1st Marines at Chinhung-ni at the foot of the mountain and another battalion of the 1st Marines at Koto-ri at the top of the mountain."[47] He wrote that his 5th and 7th Marine regiments did not fully reach Hagaru-ri until 4 December; when they were finally reunited, he could begin his fighting retreat toward Puller's 1st Marines at Koto-ri. Smith's division increased its combat power as it absorbed various units (including various US Army survivors from the 31st RCT), as it moved along the MSR. The movement also required Smith to take along all his equipment and supplies, which significantly slowed his column as it traveled through Hell-Fire Valley and all the way back to Chinhung-ni and the safety provided by the more forward-deployed 3rd Infantry Division. Smith admitted that this decision probably caused an additional 500 casualties.[48] Smith believed the most critical moment in the retreat took place at the blown bridge in the Funchilin Pass. He noted that by the time his Marines had reached Hungnam, the 1st Division had suffered a total of 4,150 battle and non-battle casualties, including 400 KIA, 2,265 WIA, 90 missing, and at least 1,395 non-battle (mostly frostbite) casualties.[49] Smith offered this overall assessment of the X Corps efforts:

> I am understandably proud of the performance of this Division. The officers and men were magnificent. They came down the

mountain bearded, footsore, and physically exhausted, but their spirits were high. They were still a fighting division.[50]

In the final analysis, in an incredible feat of arms, US Marine Corps and Army forces made the icy eighty-mile fighting retreat from the Chosin Reservoir plateau to Hungnam on sheer guts and determination. Even today it remains a truly incredible story.

The X Corps and especially 1st Marine Division troops learned significant lessons during the retreat from the Chosin Reservoir. First and foremost was the problem of advancing deep into enemy territory largely using a single axis of advance that extended through difficult terrain. The later violent attacks by the Chinese to interdict this route reinforced the idea of holding and securing the MSR. Losing the MSR would mean losing your life or ending up as a prisoner of war in a Chinese prison camp. Holding the MSR was paramount. After General Smith began suspecting the Chinese were beginning to get involved in the war in increasing numbers, he detached his best regimental commander, Col. Lewis "Chesty" Puller of the 1st Marines, and charged him with holding the expeditionary airfield at Koto-Ri as well as the vitally important MSR bottleneck at the Funchilin Pass. This later proved one of the wisest decisions Smith made during the entire retreat. And Smith and his boss, Maj. Gen. Ned Almond, were reminded that a heretofore highly successful offensive can quickly be reversed by an active and alert enemy commander. The enemy always gets a vote; in this case, that vote was cast by the 250,000 soldiers of Mao's Peoples Liberation Army (PLA). In November 1950, Almond accurately assumed that the enemy in his direct front (the North Koreans) was a largely beaten force; the North Koreans, however, did not turn out to be the enemy he needed to be concerned about. Further, no one in the entire UN chain of command in Tokyo or on the ground in Korea gave much thought or serious consideration as to what their advance to the Yalu River should look like *if* the Chinese entered the war—which they ultimately did.

Next, strong leadership up and down the chain of command is an extremely desirable commodity to possess during a crisis. Continuous outstanding small unit leadership, as demonstrated by Capt. William Barber's F/2/7 at Toktong Pass, helped enable the 1st Marine Division to remain a viable fighting force despite pressure applied by more than seven Chinese divisions. For example, the Marines had strong leadership from the noncommissioned officer (NCO) ranks all the way up to the commanding general of the division—strength that was evidenced by the number of personal awards for valor received by members of the 1st Marine Division during the Chosin River campaign. However, once the unit lost its most effective leader—posthumous Medal of Honor recipient Lt. Col. Don Faith, who was killed in action during the first days of the retreat—units that lacked leadership depth tended to lose all cohesion. Leadership depth made the difference. For example, the US Army's 3rd Infantry Division (3rd ID—the "Rock of Marne") ending up saving the day for the entire X Corps and assisted the successful breakout of the 1st Marine Division from Funchilin Pass into the coastal plains below. Moreover, the critical job of defending the MSR from Chinhung-ni all the way to the port of Hungnam fell to the 3rd ID soldiers, and they performed magnificently.

Finally, throughout the epic retreat, both Smith and Almond found out that airpower matters. Smith had the foresight to create two expeditionary airfields to assist with the retreat down the MSR, the first at Koto-Ri (at the apex of critical Funchilin Pass) and the other at Hagaru-ri (near the base of the Chosin Reservoir). Both airfields allowed Smith to bring in critical supplies and evacuate his most seriously wounded, enabling the 1st Marine Division to remain viable during the worst of times throughout the long retreat to the sea. In fact, Hagaru-ri served as a rally point for all US forces east and west of the reservoir during those first dark days of the Chinese onslaught. Moreover, Almond used his land- and sea-based airpower to great effect, especially after his retreating army and Marine forces broke out into the coastal plain below Chinhung-ni. Even the attacking Chinese seemed to recognize this inherent advantage, as major attacks on US forces retreating along the MSR significantly fell off after the retreating Americans broke out of the central mountains of eastern North Korea.

The eighty-mile fighting retreat of the 1st Marine Division and other US Army X Corps elements east of the reservoir and even the performance of the British Royal Marine Commandos were among the most remarkable events of the three-year-long Korean War. After issuing a flurry of confusing orders to subordinate units, the X Corps planning staff did a credible job of organizing the general retreat to the sea. Army historian Richard W. Stewart noted that although not perfect, "in the face of possible destruction, the corps planners managed to arrange, supervise, and execute a series of complex operations beginning in early December."[51] After the initial Chinese onslaught had largely spent its force, the X Corps staff planned and supervised the evacuation of an entire corps that had been under constant attack for nearly a month by the 9th Chinese Army Group (twelve divisions). The successful evacuation of significant numbers of military, ammunition, fuel, personnel, and even refugees is a testament to the X Corps as its staff had to quickly learn how to conduct a fighting retreat under significant duress. Nevertheless, the 1st Marine Division—especially the 31st RCT—paid an extraordinarily high price for the impetuosity of MacArthur and his most faithful subordinate X Corps commander, Maj. Gen. Ned Almond.

Notes

1. William Stueck, *Rethinking the Korean War: A New Diplomatic and Strategic History* (Princeton, NJ: Princeton University Press, 2002), 89–90, 112. It should be noted that Truman and MacArthur should have seen Mao's move coming. Immediately prior to the outbreak of the Korean War, the United States had sent the US Seventh Fleet to the Taiwan Straits, declared them neutral waters, and informed Mao that an attack on Formosa [Taiwan] would not be tolerated. Mao believed that the US was intentionally meddling in the internal affairs of the PRC since he viewed the island as being illegally occupied by nationalist forces under Chiang Kai-shek.

2. Stueck, 89–90, 112.

3. Lynn Montross and Nicholas A. Canzona, *US Marine Operations in Korea, 1950–1953*, vol. III (Washington, DC: Historical Branch, G-3, HQMC, 1957), 18–19. It should be noted that one of the authors, Nicholas Canoza, was a junior officer who participated in the fighting around the Hagaru-ri perimeter. Most of the sources used were derived directly from extant USMC operational reports, November–December 1950.

4. Richard W. Stewart, *Staff Operations: The X Corps in Korea, December 1950* (Fort Leavenworth, KS: Combat Studies Institute, 1991), 1–2.

5. Stewart, 1–2.

6. Stewart, 1–2.

7. Stewart, 1–2.

8. Stewart, 1–2.

9. Stewart, 4; and Clay Blair, *The Forgotten War: America in Korea, 1950–53* (New York: Time Books, 1987), 420. Stewart did extensive research in the Clay Blair Papers located at the US Army Military History Institute, Carlisle, PA. Most of Almond's subordinates, including Deputy Chief of Staff Col. William J. McCaffrey, placed the massive intelligence failure squarely on MacArthur and his Chief of Intelligence, Maj. Gen. Charles A. Willoughby. William McCaffrey is the father of General Barry R. McCaffrey of Operation *Desert Storm* fame.

10. Allan R. Millett, *The War for Korea, 1950–1951: They Came from the North* (Lawrence, KS: University Press of Kansas, 2010), 302–4. While Almond was aware the Chinese had entered the war, he continued to demand for his subordinate commanders to continue their advance on the Yalu.

11. Montross and Canzona, *US Marine Operations in Korea,* 105–8. Although the Marine Air-Ground Task Force (MAGTF) had not yet achieved full conceptual reality in 1950, it quickly became obvious to all that USMC aviation supporting their own ground-gaining infantry forces gave the Marines an extraordinary amount of firepower as compared to the standard US Army division.

12. Montross and Canzona, 105–8.

13. Montross and Canzona, 105–8.

14. Brig. Gen. (USMC-Ret.) Edwin H. Simmons, *Frozen Chosin: The US Marines at the Changjin Reservoir*, (Washington, DC: USMC History Division, 2002), 34.

15. Simmons, 34.

16. Roy E. Appleman, *East of Chosin: Entrapment and Breakout in Korea, 1950* (College Station, TX: Texas A&M University Press, 1987), 271–99. Appleman's book remains the definitive account of what happened to the 31st RCT east of the Chosin Reservoir. Incredibly, Appleman noted that although there was discussion of a relief task force being sent out from Hagaru-ri, the problem of securing this thinly defended village and its critical airstrip prevented both the US Army and the Marines from were ever actually sending one. Task Force "Faith" was originally Task Force "MacLean," after the 31st RCT's original commander, Lieutenant Colonel Allan D. MacLean who was killed on the first day of the Chinese onslaught having mistaken Chinese soldiers for friendly forces. Command then devolved upon LTC Faith who also was killed just a few days later. Faith would later be posthumously awarded the Medal of Honor. His widow accepted the award from President Harry S. Truman.

17. Roy E. Appleman, *Escaping the Trap: The US Army X Corps in Northeast Korea, 1950* (College Station, TX: Texas A&M University, 1990), 125, 127–28.

18. Appleman, 151–53.

19. Allan R. Millett, *Semper Fidelis: The History of the Marine Corps*, New York: MacMillan Publishing Co., 1980), 493–94; Millett, *The War for Korea, 1950–1951: They Came from the North,* 492-493; Montross and Canoza, vol. III, 194–95.

20. Matt Schudel, "Hector Cafferata, Medal of Honor Recipient in Korean War, Dies at 86," *Washington Post,* 14 April 2016, https://www.washingtonpost.com/national/hector-cafferata-medal-of-honor-recipient-in-korean-war-dies-at-86/2016/04/14/9c7711a6-0259-11e6-b823-707c79ce3504_story.html. The 7th Marines retreat from Yudam-ni resulted in three Medals of Honor ultimately awarded to its members (Lt. Col. Raymond G. Davis, 1/7 Battalion commander; Capt. William E. Barber, F/2/7 commanding officer; and Pvt. 1st Class Hector A. Cafferata Jr., F/2/7). Davis's men relieved Captain Barber's Fox company at Toktong Pass and thus enabled the retreat of the 5th and 7th Marine regiments to continue to Hagaru-ri.

21. Appleman, *East of Chosin*, 164.

22. Patrick K. O'Donnell, *Give Me Tomorrow: The Korean War's Greatest Untold Story–The Epic Stand of the Marines of George Company* (Philadelphia: Da Capo Press, 2010), 143, 145–51. O'Donnell wrote his award-winning book based on first-person oral histories provided by G/3/1 survivors. Capt. (USMC) Carl L. Sitter was later awarded the Medal of Honor for his actions at East Hill.

23. Millett, *The War for Korea, 1950–1951*, 343.

24. Montross and Canoza, *US Marine Operations in Korea*, 198–202.

25. Montross and Canoza, 198–202.

26. Montross and Canoza, 215–16.

27. F. M. Berger, J. D. Lenard, W. S. Wallace, R. S. Robichaud, D. M. Mize, and W. R. Norton, *Chosin Reservoir: A Battlebook* (Fort Leavenworth, KS: Combat Studies Institute, 1983), 34.

28. Kenneth W. Condit and Ernest H. Giusti, "Marine Air Over the Chosin Reservoir," *The Marine Corps Gazette,* July 1952, http://www.koreanwar-educator.org/topics/branch_accounts/marine/p_marine_air_chosin_reservoir.htm.

29. Condit and Giusti.

30. "Memoirs of a Chosin Veteran," accessed 18 January 2021, http://www.koreanwar-educator.org/memoirs/carmin/index.htm. Carmin was later the subject of a *Time* Magazine article which noted that he had stowed away aboard one of the ships transporting 3/1 to Korea and had made himself known to Lieutenant Colonel Ridge only after his troop convoy had cleared Hawaii. Ridge assigned him to his Headquarters element. At Hagaru-ri, Headquarters Marines saw nearly as much direct combat with the Chinese as did Ridge's 3/1 rifle companies and circumstances soon placed Carmin in the front lines with I/3/1.

31. Montross and Canoza, *US Marine Operations in Korea*, 293.

32. Stanley Weintraub, *A Christmas Far from Home: An Epic Tale of Courage and Survival during the Korean War* (Boston: Da Capo Press, 2014), 201–10.

33. Weintraub, 210–14. The usually dependable Puller later came in for some mild criticism from O. P. Smith for blowing the Funchilin Pass bridge before all the rear guard had made it across the span.

34. Appleman, *Escaping the Trap*, 282, 308-309. The Army officer's name was Lt. Col. John Upshur Dennis Page. Page was an incredible combat leader and his spirited counterattack undoubtedly saved many lives of Marines further back in the convoy and gave them time to organize a counterattack. Initially awarded the Navy Cross by the Marine Corps, Page posthumously received the Medal of Honor in 1957 after more facts became known.

35. Montross and Canoza, *US Marine Operations in Korea*, 332.

36. Montross and Canoza, 332.

37. "Memoirs of a Chosin Veteran," Korean War Educator, accessed 18 January 2021, http://www.koreanwar-educator.org/memoirs/carmin/index.htm. Carmin also noted that the exhausted Marines simply laid down on just about every inch of deck space and that "the sailors did not harass us like they usually did; no complaints about bodies blocking passageways and weather decks like usual."

38. Simmons, *Frozen Chosin*, 118. It should be noted that Hungnam as an evacuation point was about the only option left for Almond's X Corps since he had ordered the destruction of Wonsan harbor facilities the same day that the Marines began crossing the Treadway bridge at Funchilin Pass (9 December).

39. Simmons, 118.

40. Glenn C. Cowart, *Miracle in Korea: The Evacuation of X Corps from the Hungnam Beachhead* (Columbia, SC: University of South Carolina Press, 1992), 77.

41. Cowart, 96.

42. Cowart, 95.

43. Eliot A. Cohen and John Gooch, *Military Misfortunes: The Anatomy of Failure in War* (New York: The Free Press, 1990), 165.

44. Gail B. Shisler, *For Corps and Country: The Life of General O. P. Smith* (Annapolis, MD: Naval Institute Press, 2009), 173.

45. Simmons, *Frozen Chosin*, 119–20.

46. Letter from Maj. Gen. (USMC) O. P. Smith to the Commandant of the Marine Corps, 17 December 1950, in *Commandership at the Chosin Reservoir: A Triumph of Optimism and Resilience* (Quantico, VA: Lejeune Leadership Institute, 2018), 132–45. See also https://www.usmcu.edu/mld-discussion-topics/commandership. Smith's letter is republished in full.

47. *Commandership at the Chosin Reservoir*, 132–45.

48. *Commandership at the Chosin Reservoir*, 132–45.

49. *Commandership at the Chosin Reservoir*, 132–45.

50. *Commandership at the Chosin Reservoir*, 132–45.

51. Stewart, *Staff Operations,* 7; and Millett, *The War for Korea*, 338–39.

Chapter 13
The Railroad Saved Our Necks: United Nations Command Retreat in Korea, Winter 1950–51
Eric Allan Sibul

In what was described as the "one of the strangest, wildest rail operations of any war," the United Nations Command (UNC) relied on rail transportation to withdraw from North Korea to the Pyongtaek-Ansong-Wonju-Samchok line in South Korea during the Chinese intervention into the Korean War, winter 1950–51.[1] Railway transportation was the responsibility of the US Army's 3rd Transportation Military Railway Service (3rd TMRS), which was the UNC's principal overland transportation organization.[2] During the retreat from the north, the UNC systemically evacuated troops, administrative personnel, casualties, and refugees as well as large amounts of supplies and equipment mainly using the railroads.[3] In conjunction with the evacuation, the 3rd TMRS had to provide supplies for the UNC forces covering the withdrawal and in contact with the enemy. This chapter examines how the 3rd TMRS successfully accomplished this evacuation—preserving UNC fighting power so it could go on the counteroffensive once the Chinese offensive culminated. Some lessons from the winter 1950–51 withdrawal were readily apparent at the time: the value of rail transportation in such operations, the importance of thorough and timely demolition of facilities, and the need for quick turnaround of railroad rolling stock. Other lessons became clear in the long-term: the value of specialized units that had largely civilian industry-acquired skills and experience and that mass movement of refugees would be part of any large-scale military withdrawal as on the Korean peninsula in winter 1950–51.

Korean Railroads

In 1950, the Korean peninsula had an extensive rail network and a less developed road system that served as local feeders to the railroads. American entrepreneurs constructed the first Korean railroad between Chemulpo (Inchon) and Seoul for the Yi Dynasty in 1899. With the Russo-Japanese War of 1904–5 and the Japanese annexation of Korea in 1910, Korea became a logistic hub for the Japanese Empire between ports on Korea's south coast near the Japanese home islands and Manchuria. Manchuria was militarily and economically important for the Japanese Empire. Manchuria served as a bulwark against Japan's principal potential adversary:

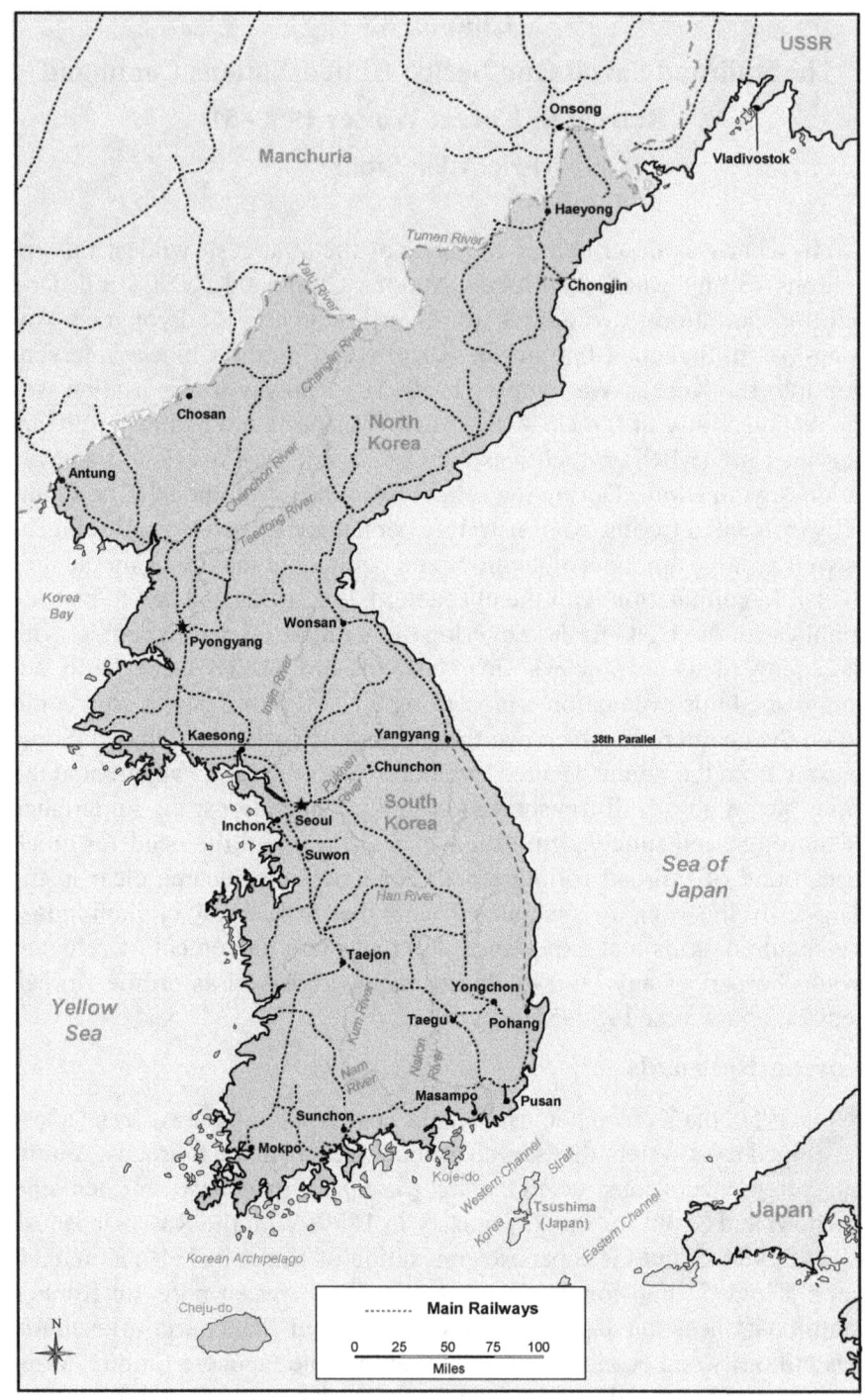

Figure 13.1. The Korean railway network. Created by Army University Press.

Tsarist and Soviet Russia.[4] Furthermore, it was home to great agricultural and mineral resources essential for the Japanese Empire. By 1945, Korea had a railway network of approximately 4,200 miles (6,720 kilometers); 10 percent of the network was double-tracked and 125 miles (200 kilometers) of standard gauge line was electrified. Double track lines were built with separate bridges and tunnels for each track to lessen the vulnerability to air attack.[5] Given distances, strategic mobility considerations, and economies of scale, the Japanese had built an extensive rail network on the Korean peninsula largely using American technology (railroad gauge, locomotives, rolling stock, couplers, signaling, etc.) and American practices. Familiarity of equipment and practices made the work of the 3rd TMRS somewhat easier during the Korean War.[6]

The 3rd TMRS

The outbreak of the Korean War on 25 June 1950 quickly overwhelmed the management abilities of both the Korean National Railroad (KNR) and the Republic of Korea Army (ROKA).[7] On 1 July 1950, the South Koreans controlled 1,404 miles (2,259 kilometers) of track, having lost 973 miles (1,566 kilometers) of track or more than two-thirds of the KNR to Communist forces since 25 June 1950. Railway equipment available consisted of 280 locomotives, 450 passenger cars, and 4,300 freight cars all in various stages of serviceability. In comparison, the North Koreans had 350 operational locomotives, 12,000 freight cars, and some 700 passenger cars.[8] With American ground troops arriving to assist the South Koreans, US Ambassador John J. Muccio negotiated to transfer operational control of KNR from the Republic of Korea (ROK) Ministry of Transportation to the Eighth US Army Korea (EUSAK).[9]

Initially, the US Army sent a railway transportation detachment of nineteen officers and ninety enlisted men from Japan to Korea. This detachment served as a movement control agency—planning and regulating military traffic on the railroad—but could not fully manage the rail system or operate trains with its limited personnel. Thus on 26 August 1950, the EUSAK formally reactivated the 3rd TMRS.[10]

As reinforcements arrived from the United States, the 3rd TMRS drew heavily on civilian expertise through the US Army's Affiliated Reserve Unit Program, where American commercial rail carriers sponsored army reserve railway operating and shop battalions.[11] Eventually the 3rd TMRS commanded two railway operating battalions, one railway shop battalion, and a military police battalion.[12] Furthermore, it supervised 32,000 KNR

Figure 13.2. Capt. Charles Mason, 3rd TMRS, gives final instructions to a Korean National Railroad conductor as a troop train readies to depart northward from Pusan, 8 September 1950. Courtesy of the US Army Transportation Corps Museum Library and Archives.

employees. However, in winter 1950–51, the 3rd TMRS was not up to full strength and relied heavily on KNR civilian employees.[13]

The KNR was a young organization as nearly all management positions and skilled trades on Korean railroads were in the hands of the Japanese before 1945. The 3rd TMRS personnel served as advisors, mentors, and trainers rather than managers, train crewmen, and maintainers. It was as much a capacity-building effort as an active transportation effort in support of combat forces. Despite cultural differences and a mix of indigenous civilians and US military personnel, the 3rd TMRS/KNR functioned successfully as a hybrid organization.[14]

During the war's early period, when UNC forces were pushed into the Pusan Perimeter, 3rd TMRS priorities were to rush reinforcements to the front lines, and evacuate casualties and refugees. The 3rd TMRS trains also moved large units around the perimeter, including moving the entire US 25th Infantry Division 150 miles (240 kilometers) in less than thirty-six hours from Waegwan to Chinju to check a North Korean advance.[15]

After the amphibious landing at Inchon and subsequent EUSAK breakout from the Pusan Perimeter, the 3rd TMRS shifted its focus to restoring recaptured railroad facilities and lines as quickly as possible to support advancing combat forces. Eight days after the Inchon landing the 33-mile (53-kilometer) Yongdongpo-Inchon railway line was restored to the outskirts of Seoul, eventually transporting 10,000 troops, 350,000 ra-

Figure 13.3. Republic of Korea marines move from Inchon toward Yongdungpo. Courtesy of the US Army Signal Corps US National Archives.

Figure 13.4. Korean National Railroad employees begin repair work at Seoul Station, the city's main railroad terminal, immediately after liberation of the city. Courtesy of the US Army Transportation Corps Museum Library and Archives.

tions, 315,000 gallons of fuel, and 1,260 tons of ammunition to support the recapture of Seoul.[16] Once recaptured, Seoul was rapidly reconnected to the rail lines within the Pusan Perimeter.

Daily operations, however, were not always smooth on the reconnected rail lines. Due to tempo, worn-out rolling stock, and the poor condition of the hastily restored tracks, derailments were a constant problem. On one single day, six trains derailed; there was only one heavy wrecking crane available on the entire railway system at the time. Fortunately, the 3rd TMRS had an experienced group of KNR personnel to clear the tracks.

These KNR employees used great ingenuity to put freight cars back onto the rails with little or no specialized equipment.[17] As the UNC advanced northward, rail lines were quickly restored.

Operations in North Korea

When UNC forces crossed the 38th Parallel on 1 October 1950 and advanced into North Korea, 3rd TMRS opened rail lines in the north with some gaps in lines covered by truck shuttles. Rail operations were restored often before the surrounding region was fully under UNC control. When trains operated in dangerous areas, 3rd TMRS placed sandbag-packed gondolas carrying troops with automatic weapons at the front and rear of the trains.[18] The US Army 1st Cavalry Division and 1st ROK Division entered Pyongyang on 19 October 1950 and secured the city in the next forty-eight hours. However, the North Korean People's Army (NKPA) had demolished bridges across the Taedong River into Pyongyang. To keep supplies moving across the river from Taedong yard on the south bank into Pyongyang, the engineers quickly constructed a pontoon bridge and began the time-intensive task of rebuilding the 2,500-foot (750-meter) Taedong railway bridge. During this period, trains were unloaded at the Taedong yard and supplies trucked across the pontoon bridge then reloaded on another train on the Pyongyang side; the 3rd TMRS was carrying four thousand tons of supplies into Taedong yard daily.[19] By late November 1950, the 3rd TMRS maintained 20 locomotives and 500 freight cars on the north side of the Taedong River.

To support 3rd TMRS efforts, detachments of KNR personnel were sent to Wonsan, Pyongyang, Harju, and Sinuiju to help manage and rehabilitate railway facilities. KNR personnel were persuasive in convincing the North Korean railway workers to work for the UNC. This was quite important because there were few 3rd TMRS personnel and the KNR was stretched thin recovering from war-related damage. Most North Korean railroaders bore no allegiance to the Communist government and were

Figure 13.5. Supply train on the Wonsan-Hamhung railway line. Courtesy of the US Army Signal Corps US National Archives.

Figure 13.6. First supply train arrives in Wonsan from Seoul, 15 November 1950. Courtesy of the US Army Signal Corps US National Archives.

willing to work with KNR employees. These railroaders proved largely loyal to the anti-Communist cause and came southward when the UNC was forced to withdraw.[20]

On 25 October 1950, the X Corps 1st Marine Division conducted an administrative landing at Wonsan. After the Inchon landing, the UNC planned another amphibious operation to capture Wonsan on the east coast. This became unnecessary when the ROKA 1st Corps captured the port city on 10 October 1950. Instead after landing at Wonsan, the 1st Marine Division pushed northward to the Manchurian border, mopping up NKPA remnants and occupying the country. The marines moved up the coast to Hamhung and then inland and farther north toward the Chosin Reservoirs. The port that Hamhung served was Hungnam. Hungnam harbor was mined and was not cleared until 19 November 1950. Thus, the 96-mile (154-kilometer) Wonsan-Hamhung railway line took on special importance.

The X Corps maintained its own rail transportation section which was supported by 3rd TMRS and KNR personnel within its area of operation. With the help of KNR personnel and local railroaders, the X Corps Rail Transportation Section began to operate daily supply trains from Wonsan to Hungnam.[21]

Figure 13.7. US Marine Corps troop train. Because of fuel and motive power shortages, US marines in Wonsan initially muscled trains together in lieu of using switching locomotives. Courtesy of the National Archives and Records Administration.

The Marine 1st Service Battalion put the Chosin branch of the narrow-gauge Shinko Railway, which formerly served the Chosin hydroelectric complex, back in service. The Korean manager of the line rounded up crews, and the first train pulled out of Hamhung on 6 November 1950 to support the advancing 7th Marine Regiment. However, blocked tunnels prevented completion of the trip. The train did not reach Sudong until three days later. By 11 November 1950, the narrow-gauge line was clear all the way to the bottom of Funchilin Pass at Chinhungni, thirty-five miles (fifty-six kilometers) from Hamhung. Previously, rolling stock was lifted to the top of the Fuchilin Pass by a cableway. The cableway's powerhouse had been destroyed during the war, however, which made it impossible to continue railway operations from that point; Chinhungni became the railhead for supplies, which were trucked the rest of the way to Hagaru. Operations were further limited by a shortage of rolling stock.[22]

Chinese Intervention

The UNC moved steadily on northern Korea's east and west coasts; EUSAK and ROKA reconnaissance units reached Chosan, a town on the Yalu River, on 26 October 1950. That same day, advancing UNC columns encountered stout resistance in various locations from Chinese troops, possibly volunteers who had reinforced NKPA remnants. By 6 Novem-

Figure 13.8. Marines load a narrow-gauge supply train on the Shinko Railway. Courtesy of the National Archives and Records Administration.

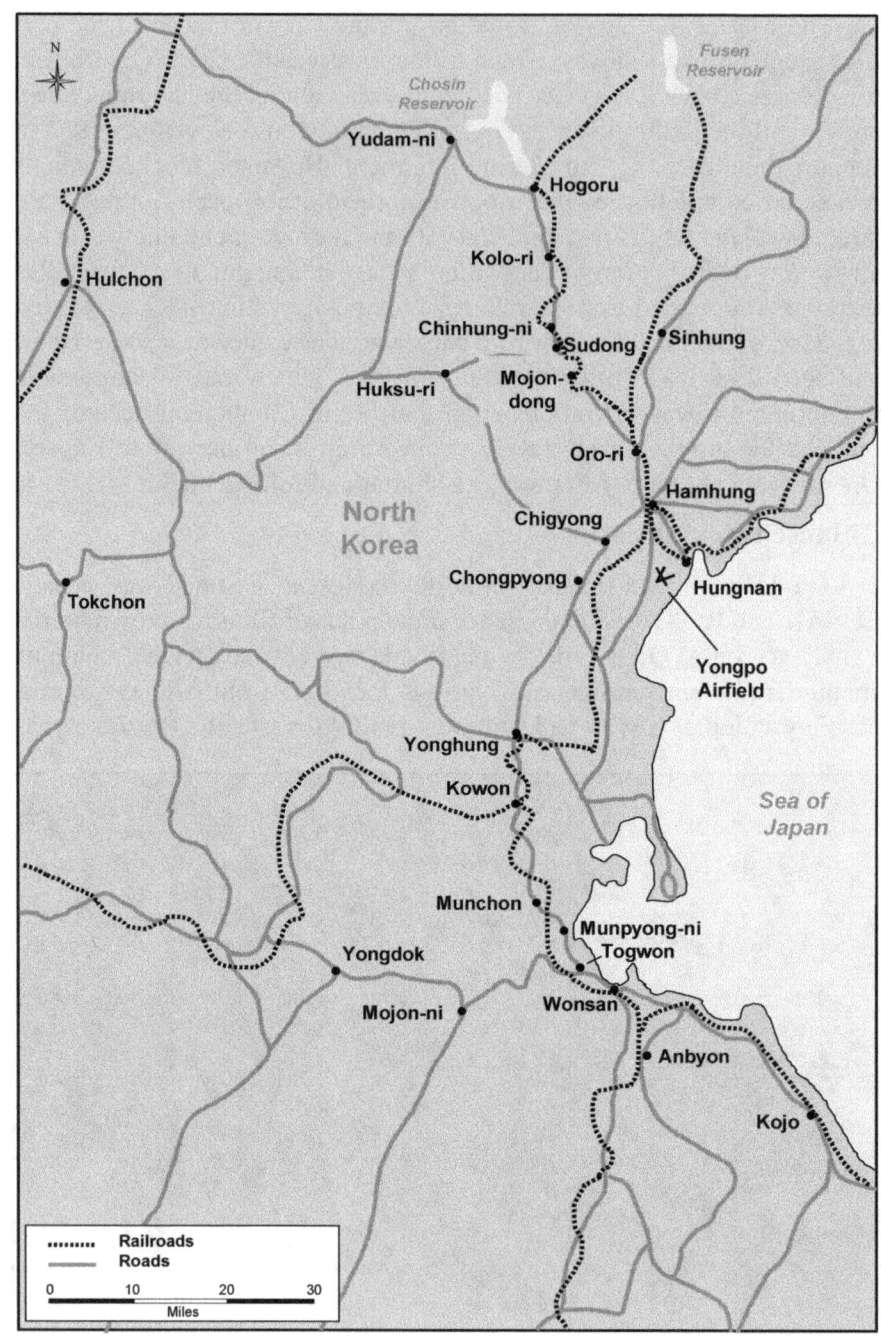

Figure 13.9. X Corps Area of Operations, October–December 1950. Created by Army University Press.

ber 1950, three divisions were believed to be in the EUSAK sector and two divisions in the X Corps area.[23] By 24 November 1950, more than 300,000 Communist Chinese Forces (CCF) troops were in Korea. Clearly the UNC was facing a new war. On 29 November 1950, General Douglas MacArthur instructed EUSAK's commander, General Walton H. Walker, to make whatever withdrawals were necessary to escape being enveloped by CCF, which was pushing hard and deep through the EUSAK eastern sector; Walker, in turn, ordered the X Corps to pull into a beachhead around Hungnam.[24]

The X Corps 1st Marine Division was hard-pressed; the Marines had gone deep into the mountains north of the Chosin Reservoir, advancing along a single narrow road. CCF units infiltrated behind portions of the 1st Marine Division, cutting the single road that led southward toward Hungnam. With the beachhead firmly in the hands of the X Corps, the Marines turned and fought both brutal arctic cold and the Chinese 3rd Field Army. They broke out and fought their way toward Hungnam, where they would be evacuated by ship. To move the Marines and their equipment to Hungnam, all available narrow-gauge freight cars were collected at Majon-dong, the new railhead southeast of Chinhung-ni.[25] Between 12 and 15 December 1950, the 1st Marine Division moved from Majondong to Hungnam and was loaded aboard 193 vessels. The X Corps began evacuating materiel at Wonsan to Hungnam as well. The X Corps Railway Transportation Section continued to keep the railway line between Wonsan and Hungnam open with the help of Korean railroaders. They assembled 400 to 500 freight cars at Wonsan and used them to move some 8,900 tons of ammunition as well as other supplies to Hungnam for loading aboard transport vessels.[26] Complicating the situation was a massive flow of refugees into Hungnam harbor. The X Corps had originally planned to evacuate only individuals serving in the ROK Armed Forces and National Police and their families as well as some North Korean civilians such as railroad workers. However, the number of refugees trying to flee the advancing Communist forces grew far beyond expectations; instead, X Corps moved them to Sohojin, a suburb southeast of Hungnam, and organized them for evacuation as soon as shipping space became available.[27] By 24 December 1950, the amphibious ships and merchant vessels carried 105,000 US and ROK troops; 17,500 vehicles; 350,000 tons of supplies; and about 100,000 refugees southward to Pusan and Ulsan.[28]

After the evacuation of Hungnam, the US Army 185th Engineer Battalion was tasked to destroy railway facilities on 15 December 1950. Based on practical experience from the Second World War, the engineers knew that lines blocked with wrecked locomotives and downed bridges would considerably slow the enemy's transportation efforts. Destroying a 21,000-foot (6,401-meter) twenty-nine-span standard gauge railway bridge and standard gauge locomotives and rolling stock in the area became a combined project. The engineers planned to destroy southern spans of the railroad bridge and push as many cars and locomotives into the void as possible. Then they would blow up the remaining spans. Korean railroaders assembled 15 locomotives and 275 freight cars. The Korean railroaders carried out the task reluctantly; in contrast, the army engineers looked forward to the destruction as a release for their pent-up emotions. The destruction began at 1545 and continued into the night. Locomotives towing freight cars, often loaded with gasoline, were pushed into the gap in the spans, and the wreckage caught fire.

The equipment and facilities of the narrow-gauge railway were destroyed in much the same way. Finally, Army engineers and US Navy Underwater Demolition Teams (UDT) destroyed the port facilities in Hungnam.[29] Four hundred tons of frozen dynamite and 500 thousand-pound bombs which could not be loaded to the evacuation fleet added to the destruction. As the last ships pulled out on 24 December 1950, the port went up in a volcanic eruption of flame, smoke, and rubble, leaving a black mushroom cloud hovering over the ruins. The X Corps left behind no serviceable equipment or usable supplies.

Figure 13.10. Hungnam destruction, 15 December 1950. Courtesy of the National Archives and Records Administration.

Figure 13.11. Final destruction of station facilities in Wonsan. Courtesy of the National Archives and Records Administration.

The X Corps evacuation from Hungnam was a spectacular logistical operation.[30] Rail transportation allowed X Corps to concentrate a large number of men and materiel in the port of Hungnam in a short period of time for evacuation by sea. According to Malcolm W. Cagle and Frank A. Manson's study of Korean War naval operations in the *Sea War in Korea*, "The value of rail transport was dramatically demonstrated at Hungnam."[31] As with the Hungnam operation, the value of rail transportation would be proven again as the EUSAK evacuated Pyongyang.

Evacuation of Pyongyang

To the west of Hungnam, the EUSAK began to systemically evacuate troops, administrative personnel, and refugees as well as supplies and equipment largely using rail transport.[32] Following the November 1950 repair of the Hanpori Bridge, railway traffic was flowing all the way to Sinuiju on the Yalu River by 1 December 1950. The gap still remained at Pyongyang, because repairs on the Taedong bridges were not yet complete. Supplies and equipment had to be unloaded at the Taedong yard and trucked across the river then reloaded on the Pyongyang side. At this time, the KNR was carrying 4,000 tons of supplies into Taedong railroad yard daily. With the beginning of the general withdrawal on 29 November 1950, the 3rd TMRS dispatched all available empty cars to Taedong yard to evacuate materiel from the north. Every available locomotive was pressed into service. Even while the various service support units were requesting empty cars to remove equipment and supplies, the 3rd TMRS

Figure 13.12. Hospital train rolling south at Pukchong, North Korea, 27 November 1950. Hospital cars initially were improvised; later purpose-built hospital cars were put in service in Korea. Courtesy of the US Army Transportation Corps Museum Library and Archives.

kept supplies flowing northward on the railway lines north and south of the Taedong River to support the combat forces in their fighting withdrawal.[33]

The withdrawal proved a difficult logistical operation as the EUSAK had a huge amount and variety of materiel brought forward to supply points and warehouses in the Pyongyang area. In allocating locomotives and rolling stock, the 3rd TMRS gave priority to trains carrying casualties and service units southward. There were heavy demands on motor transportation as well. All available trucks were needed for tactical troop movements as well as for hauling materiel from supply points to railheads. The problems of loading rolling stock, switching, and forming trains in congested railway yards were compounded by the fact that the yards had been hastily restored to service after being severely damaged by UNC aerial bombardment.[34] All freight trains going south also carried as many North Korean civilian refugees as they could. In some cases, 3rd TMRS enlisted personnel dumped and set fire to boxcar contents such as PX supplies, dining tables, and office furniture to make more room for refugees. Their superior officers largely concurred with the practice.

Figure 13.13. Refugees flock aboard an evacuation train in Sariwon, south of Pyongyang, 6 December 1950. Courtesy of the US Army Signal Corps National Archives.

Refugees rode clinging to the sides, between, and on top of freight cars. Many were crushed as loads shifted, or they fell off of or between cars.[35] As the UNC retreated, almost nothing of value was left behind for the enemy. The locomotives and rolling stock north of the Taedong River were destroyed because they could not be evacuated southward. South of the Taedong River, the 3rd TMRS made every effort to save and remove as much railway equipment as possible; engineers destroyed everything that was not moveable, including inoperative locomotives. After bridges and rail yards were stripped of all removable equipment, remaining bridges, switch points, bridges, signal towers, and other equipment were dynamited. Much of this demolition took place as railway facilities in the north were being restored to full service. Army engineers were atop the steel through-truss bridge across the Taedong River in Pyongyang, putting in the last bolts to restore it to service; they had worked three weeks, day and night, often in below-zero temperatures. At the same time, a demolition team was stringing wire to connect demolition charges to the bottom of the bridge.[36] For EUSAK Chief Engineer Officer Col. Pascal N. Strong, the order to blow up the bridge over the Taedong River was "heartbreaking."[37]

The last train out of Taedong carried remaining 3rd TMRS personnel southward—among the last UNC troops to leave the Pyongyang area.[38] At the end of December, the hope was to hold advancing CCF at the 38th Parallel. December 1950 had been a difficult month for the 3rd TMRS. The volume of railway traffic tripled from the previous month: 3rd TMRS and KNR personnel moved 3,354 passenger cars of military personnel; 7,180 cars of civilian refugees; and 39,167 freight cars loaded with military supplies and equipment.[39] The movements took a heavy toll on rolling stock—often loaded to the very margins of safety. Thirty-ton flatcars frequently were the only equipment available and were loaded with armor and heavy engineering vehicles.[40] The 3rd TMRS could not load all vehicles on flatcars for movement southward. Numerous combat units had to withdraw from the Pyongyang area as a motor-march. Though largely successful, the motor-march routes were littered with motor vehicles that broke down or were damaged in accidents then pushed off the side and set on fire. According to Capt. Ellery Anderson of the British Commonwealth Brigade:

> When Cherry-Garrard wrote *The Worst Journey in the World*, he had never driven a jeep down a Korean road at night, without lights, and in a convoy sandwiched between two American six-ton lorries driven with reckless disregard for others' safety.[41]

Although chaotic, evacuation by road and rail was largely successful. UNC forces were once again at positions near the 38th Parallel.

Unfortunately, the withdrawal cycle would soon start again. At 1700 on 31 December 1950, the CCF launched an offensive to capture Seoul. Six days after assuming command of EUSAK, General Mathew B. Ridgway issued an order to withdraw US 1st and 9th Corps to positions protecting the Seoul bridgehead and three ROKA Corps to positions along the Han River.[42] From there, UNC troops fell back to a line about forty miles south from the west coast to Pyongtaek across to Ansong and Wonju to Samchok on the east coast. General Ridgeway planned to commence offensive operations at first opportunity after forces were reorganized.[43] As soon as the evacuation order was received, the 3rd TMRS began making preparations. On 1 January 1951, the 3rd TMRS daily commitment for movement consisted of (1) forty cars of rations; (2) forty cars of petroleum, oil, and lubricants (POL); (3) forty cars of ammunition; (4) thirty-five cars of jet fuel; (5) twenty cars of replacement troops; and (6) ten hospital cars. EUSAK headquarters gave top priority for the movement of Class I (subsistence rations), Class III (POL), and Class V (ammunition) supplies. On 2 January 1951, northbound movement of empty cars was given priority in order to stage for the impending evacuation.[44]

Evacuation of the Seoul, Inchon, and Yongdungpo

The 3–4 January 1951 evacuation of Seoul was far different from the situation on 26–27 June 1950 when much of the city's population had been trapped and ROK institutions could not be effectively evacuated. In the final two weeks of 1950 when CCF were approaching the 38th Parallel, the ROK government and armed forces began evacuating North Korean refugees, government officials and their dependents, hospital patients, orphans, and prison inmates southward. In addition to evacuees, all ROK currency and money plates as well as articles from government archives, museums, and art galleries were shipped out. Much of the work was done by the KNR railway personnel working in temperatures as cold as 14°F (-10°C). A special train was designated to evacuate essential Seoul Electric Company and Seoul City Water Works employees at the last possible hour so the city would have water and electricity during the evacuation.

Many civilians were unable to board trains out of Seoul Station or the Yongsan railway yards and fled Seoul on foot, crossing the Han River on five floating footbridges maintained for that purpose. Ice on the Han was solid enough to support pedestrians but not vehicles, so many additional Korean civilians walked across the ice. Seoul went from a city of 1.5 mil-

Figure 13.14. As part of the Seoul Evacuation, evacuees prepare to board a southbound train at Seoul Station. Courtesy of the US Army Signal Corps National Archives.

Figure 13.15. Refugees climb aboard an evacuation train at Yongdungpo. Courtesy of the US Army Signal Corps National Archives.

lion to a population estimated at 200,000. Most who stayed behind were too old to travel, very young, or handicapped.[45]

By 3 January 1951, the 3rd TMRS headquarters evacuated from Seoul to its former site at Taegu.[46] On the afternoon of 4 January 1951, engineers blew up the shoofly bridge that carried the railway from Seoul to Yongdungpo.[47] Destruction of the motor vehicle and pedestrian bridges took place at the same time.[48] To move the huge volume of materiel from the Seoul area, particularly from Yongdungpo on the south bank of the Han River, the 3rd TMRS initiated fleet operations on all lines. Fleet operations entailed southward movement of loaded trains for set time periods then northward movement of returning empty trains. Trains moved in and out in fleets of three or four. Experienced noncommissioned officers were stationed at all serviceable railheads to ensure that nervous officers from other branches and services did not interfere with the systematic loading of trains, trains departed to the designated points, and empty trains arrived where needed. It was essential that the 3rd TMRS maintain strict movement control. Traffic flowed to Inchon for evacuation of materiel by sea. However, because of shipping shortages, especially specialized vessels that could handle bulky and large items such as 39-foot (11.7-meter) sections of railway rails, scores of freight cars from Inchon and Ascom City (Pupyung) had to be moved back inland for movement south, further swelling traffic at the already crowded Yongdungpo railway yard.[49]

Railway operations at Yongdungpo continued until the last possible moment. On 3 January, Lieutenant Colonels Charles O. Butler and A. T. Jordan remained with KNR personnel in the shop facility to make expedient repairs to six locomotives. CCF forces on the other side of the river began firing howitzers toward the shops; however, all rounds passed overhead without damaging the shop facilities. The shop crew finished its work at 1630, managing to return five locomotives to service. The sixth locomotive could not be repaired in time and was blown up. A number of locomotives had to be destroyed because their tenders ran dry and water facilities were no longer available. The common method of destruction was a dynamite blast through the cylinder.[50]

Col. Jesse M. McLellan, then the chief rail transportation officer on the staff of EUSAK Transportation Officer Col. Edmond C. R. Lasher, personally oversaw the final evacuation of Yongdungpo.[51] Between 0001 and 2030 hours on 4 January 1951, 23 trains of 462 cars moved southward out of Yongdungpo. EUSAK directed that no trains originating from Pusan would travel north on the central mainline except those carrying rations, POL, jet fuel, Avgas (aviation gasoline), or coal for locomotive supply. Normal operations continued on the line to Masan and on the East Coast line at Andong. By 0200 on 5 January 1951, the railway facilities at Yongdungpo were cleared and trains were moving south on both mainline tracks. Of the two last trains out, one carried all movable machinery and equipment from the KNR shops and railway yard. The other was the work train stationed at Yongdungpo plus two attached cars of demolition material and two extra cars carrying a guard detachment.[52] The final group of engineers and 3rd TMRS personnel withdrew by jeep after setting off demolition charges in the classification yard and setting the shop buildings on fire.[53]

On the night of 4 January 1951, similar operations took place at Ascom City (Pupyung) and Inchon. At Ascom City, twelve freight cars loaded with ammunition that could not be evacuated were set on fire while all stationary railway equipment and facilities were blown up. The 3rd TMRS personnel destroyed the last two switching locomotives that had worked on the docks to move material for seaborne evacuation. All other locomotives operating on the Inchon-Yongdongpo line were successfully evacuated. With their work complete, the remaining 3rd TMRS and KNR

Figure 13.16. Refugees aboard an evacuation train south of Seoul. Courtesy of the US Army Signal Corps National Archives.

personnel in Inchon and Ascom City boarded ships for evacuation southward. The US Army 50th Engineer Port Construction Company began demolishing the Inchon port facilities at 1800. All facilities except one pier and a causeway to the island of Wolmido were destroyed. The engineers blew up the tidal basin lock gates, which had compensated for the wide Yellow Sea tidal range and allowed Inchon to operate as a principal port. All demolition was completed by 0300 on 5 January 1951.[54]

The mass exodus of civilian refugees from Seoul caused a severe problem for the 3rd TMRS. Thousands of refugees overran Suwon station and railway yards, threatening to paralyze railway operations. Refugees had to be driven out of the railway yard by American MPs and Korean railroad policemen before trains could be assembled. Adding to the confusion, a huge amount of materiel needed to be loaded from supply depots in the Seoul area as well as equipment and materiel from K-13 Airfield in Suwon.

As trains were ready to leave southward, they allowed as many refugees to board as could hang on—sometimes with tragic effect. Riding on top, on the sides, and between cars proved hazardous during the withdrawal from Pyongyang. People on top of the cars were crushed in tunnels or died of exposure in sub-zero temperatures; others holding on the side of freight cars lost their grip and fell.[55] Despite the chaotic and frightful nature of the withdrawal, the 3rd TMRS maintained its supply to frontline combat units. Successive railheads were set up at points where combat units could draw POL, rations, and ammunition. When one railhead closed as the front advanced south, a new one opened farther south. This started after the withdrawal from Taedong outside of Pyongyang and continued until the final defensive line was reached on 25 January 1951 and UNC forces went on the offensive. The railhead farthest south was at Chonan. The 3rd TMRS officers felt that KNR employees working on the central mainline showed great loyalty and courage during the withdrawal.[56] Several times, the crews pulled their train out of a city at the same time as the infantry withdrew. At Sojongni just north of Pyongtaek, the infantry had taken up positions south at the end of the railway yard while a KNR crew was making up the last train and the enemy was advancing north of the yard.[57] The withdrawal on the east coast line was carried out much the same as the central mainline and on the Inchon-Yongdungpo line.[58] On 6 January 1951, the US 2nd Division defending Wonju was forced to withdraw. Railway facilities at Wonju were relatively minor but would later become an important railhead supplying the 1st Marine Division and ROKA divisions on the eastern sector of the front as UNC forces advanced again to the 38th Parallel. Railway traffic was closed, and the US 2nd Engineer Combat Battalion was assigned to destroy the railway facilities at Wonju. This included the high Killachon Bridge just south of Wonju which crossed the Wonju River. On the Killachon Bridge, which was 800 feet (240 meters) long and 120 feet (36 meters) high, the engineers placed 600 pounds of plastic explosives. TNT charges were added to sixteen ammunition-loaded boxcars near the station which could not be moved south. The engineers lit the fuses and moved five to six miles (eight to ten kilometers) south of the Killachon Bridge; at 2100, the charges went off with a horrific blast.[59]

The Communist offensive was halted in the last days of January and UNC went back on the offensive. The speed and order of the withdrawal allowed UNC to rebuild and fight another day. While often chaotic and frightful for the refugees, the evacuation saved thousands from falling to Communist occupying forces. The systematic evacuation of troops, equipment, and supplies preserved UNC combat power and allowed it to launch a counterattack once the CCF offensive culminated. According to EUSAK Transportation Officer Colonel Lasher, "There's no question that the railroad saved our necks."[60] The railway was able to continue operating under tremendously adverse conditions thanks to the technical expertise and discipline of 3rd TMRS personnel and the courage and loyalty of KNR workers. One lesson identified was not to over-demolish facilities during a retreat that would soon be retaken. EUSAK Chief Engineer Colonel Strong commented that commanders should blow up a few critical structures on a railroad but not every bridge along the line. Strong described January 1951 as a "horrible example;" the UNC destroyed twenty-three major railroad bridges over approximately forty miles (sixty-four kilometers) from Seoul south to Osan and Wonju.[61] Strong and subordinate engineer officers believed the demolition activities went far beyond the point necessary to deny the enemy the use of rail lines. Air attacks had the same effect; bridges were bombed over and over again, and engineers had to construct an entirely new bridge after the site was recaptured. A lesson identified was to ensure better liaison between Army engineers and air force targeting officers in such situations.[62] In the next phase of the war, rail transportation continued to be vital for the UNC. The 3rd TMRS and Army engineers would have to repair and rebuild damage done during the withdrawal. The reconstruction was completed on the heels of advancing UNC combat units. Some repair work and reopened tracks were in the range of CCF artillery fire. The US Army 439th Construction Engineer Battalion's reconstruction of the Killachon Bridge in April 1951 was an immensely difficult task.[63]

Figure 13.17. Supply train arrives at the 1st Marine Division Railhead at Wonju after reconstruction of the Killachon Bridge. Courtesy of the National Archives and Records Administration.

Keep Them Rolling

Another surprisingly difficult task in the aftermath of the withdrawal was sorting out everything that had been evacuated. This tedious process slowed the turnaround time for freight cars, which were always in short supply.[64] During the withdrawal, the 3rd TMRS worked to ensure that northbound cargo reached consignees and did not tie up movement. Screening points were set up along the main lines; crews removed items that were not needed or intended for units that had moved. If possible, 3rd TMRS personnel re-consigned or re-routed each car. Even with this system, however, the consignee unit often was gone when a car arrived at its destination. Another movement problem was that the urgent tactical situation had prompted disorganized loading of cars with materiel to be evacuated. Some boxcars were not marked or marked inadequately, or chalk markings on the outside of boxcars had been obliterated. While the 3rd TMRS screened cars as they moved, many were sent all the way back to the Pusan railway yards. In early January 1951, twenty to thirty trains came into the Pusan area daily. The Pusan railway yards were in danger of being swamped as 50 percent of arriving cars were unmarked. Screening teams had to open unmarked cars one by one to determine their contents. The teams often found three to four technical branches had loaded material into one car. It took months to clear the Pusan yards of the mixed car loadings. Freight cars were always in short supply, so it was imperative to unload cargo as quickly as possible and free cars for new consignment. The 3rd TMRS officers had to "drill into" commanders of consignee units that freight cars were not for storage and had to be unloaded and moved off sidings as quickly as possible. Movement priorities during the withdrawal also affected turnaround time for rolling stock. The trip to Pusan was often a slow and tedious journey for the refugees and evacuated supplies. Trains were diverted into sidings to allow northbound trains of ammunition, POL, and rations as well as southbound hospital trains to rush past. Train priorities were strictly maintained. Before the war, it took less than ten hours for trains to travel between Yongdungpo and Pusan on the KNR. During the evacuation, some trains of lesser priority made the trip in eight to ten days. Clearly for the 3rd TMRS and KNR, the need for quick turnaround time for freight cars was a lesson identified for rail transportation in support of future military operations.[65]

The Human Factor

Many hard lessons were identified for US Army combat units from winter 1950–51. During the withdrawal, cohesion of EUSAK US Army infantry units suffered greatly due to deficiencies in training, poor leadership, and lack of discipline. US Army Chief of Staff General Edward Meyer later defined unit cohesion as "the bonding together of soldiers in such a way as to sustain their will and commitment to each other, the unit, and mission accomplishment, despite combat or mission stress."[66] In a secret report to the British Chiefs of Staff after the 1950–51 withdrawal, British General Leslie Mansergh described US Army problems in Korea as "low-quality infantry" and "weak and inexperienced commanders at all levels," adding that the British contingent's "attitude to the American infantry is largely one of contempt."[67] US Army artillery units were rated far better for their professionalism and courage, and British and American observers saw US Marine units as maintaining strong cohesion and thus having effective fighting power. Historian and Korean War veteran T. R. Fehrenbach commented:

> In 1950, a Marine Corps officer was still an officer, and a sergeant behaved the way good sergeants had behaved since the time of Caesar, expecting no nonsense and allowing none. And Marine leaders had never lost sight of their primary—their only—mission, which was to fight.[68]

Like the Marines, the 3rd TMRS had better quality personnel and leadership than major Army combat units—largely due to its technical and specialized character and foundation in civilian industry, from which it drew expertise and experience. British military historian Max Hastings, while not specifically discussing 3rd TMRS, wrote regarding the US Army of winter 1950–51: "Because the American instinct for war favors a technological, managerial approach function, far too many of the ablest men are diverted to technical and managerial functions."[69] This was perhaps not so much an issue of diverting talent within the Army but more a reflection of American society. Combat arms in the peacetime Army typically did not attract the most ambitious. Army recruiting before the Korean War emphasized the opportunity to travel, be fed and secure, and be pensioned while still young.[70] In mid-twentieth century America, talented technical specialists and managers tended to choose lucrative private industry positions and not consider a career in the regular Army. However, a fair number were willing to serve in the Army Reserve where the Army could draw on their expertise when necessary.

In contrast to the many regular Army units in 1950, the affiliated Reserve railway units mobilized for service in Korea were very much understrength but had a cadre of motivated people with expertise. Reservists of

Philadelphia-based 712th TROB and 724th TROB viewed their training from 1947 to 1950 as "informative" and felt the Pennsylvania Military District and the sponsoring railroad companies took an active interest in the affiliated Reserve program. The training during monthly Reserve meetings and annual two-week summer training helped develop and maintain a cadre of experienced men. The 714th TROB and 765th TROB were active-duty units but drew heavily on expertise from the affiliated Reserve.[71]

Korean railroaders were also more steadfast and had far greater professional expertise than their fellow countrymen quickly drafted into ROK Army combat units. While rapidly organized and trained ROK Army combat units understandably had considerable cohesion problems, the KNR workforce had relatively few such problems. Being a railroader was a highly desirable profession in agrarian Korea, so KNR employees were the skilled elite of the Korean working class. Given the critical role of the railway system, the Korean government ordered railroaders to remain on the job at the outbreak of war and exempted most from mobilization into the ROK Army. North Koreans railroaders who worked with UN forces faced horrible retribution if captured by the Communists so remained loyal to ensure that they and their families would be part of the UNC withdrawal southward.[72] Col. William S. Carr, 3rd TMRS commanding officer, had a very high opinion of his KNR personnel in general and particularly their "bravery under fire and in other hazardous situations."[73] Carr and his subordinate 3rd TMRS officers considered the KNR a reliable organization with a loyal and steadfast workforce that had effectively risen to meet various crises; however, they recognized that the organization needed more development and its personnel more training. According to Colonel Lasher, EUSAK chief transportation officer, "The Korean crews weren't of the best; certainly, they don't yet measure up to our standards. But they were willing to take as great chances as our own men, which they did every day."[74] As a result of their steadfastness, the KNR railroaders won the respect of their American colleagues, providing a basis for a sound working relationship.

Although the 3rd TMRS had operational control of rail operations, in practice a parallel hierarchy of command and leadership between American and Korean personnel existed. This was useful for training and mentoring but could pose some difficulties during high-tempo operations. Despite language barriers and differing ways of doing things, the combined military-civilian rail operation functioned remarkably well. The system worked best if there was an experienced American railroader in charge and some practical diplomacy was used. It was also important to prevent officers from other branches from interfering with rail operations as much as possible. During the withdrawal, 3rd TMRS noncommissioned officers (NCOs) had to say "no" to superior officers from other commands and occasionally to inexperienced Transportation Corps officers. Toughness from experienced army railroaders was necessary to keep traffic flowing; 3rd TMRS commanders relied on the discretion of their veteran enlisted men.[75]

Equally important was mutual trust between officers and men within the command that developed mainly from their common experience in the railroad industry, which had its own specific culture rather than army command culture. For the army, the Korean War came unexpectedly; personnel and command problems that had emerged during the Second World War had not yet been resolved or had been brushed aside in the hubris of victory. The army of 1950–51 was one ruled by detailed command; it took another thirty years for the US Army to embrace mission command based on trust and initiative.[76] Despite being active-duty units, the 714th TROB and the 765th TRSB had a core cadre of officers and NCOs with considerable civilian railroad experience. Unlike with other industries which concentrated on manufacturing plants, a railroad workforce was spread out thinly over the distance of a railway line and worked with minimal supervision. Even in concentrated facilities such as locomotive and car shops, repair, maintenance, and construction tasks were generally varied; most work could not be broken down into standardized steps to permit mass production using then-in-vogue scientific management methods. While supervision might have been scant, employee discipline was expected and strictly enforced. Railroads during that era were very hierarchical organizations in which work was governed by strict operating rules.[77]

Working effectively with the KNR took a special set of skills for 3rd TMRS officers and men, a requirement for which the US Army Transportation Corps and its military railway units were not formally prepared.[78] The 3rd TMRS had a small cadre of "old Korean hands" who had served in Korea with the 737th TROB and the 770th TROB during the military government period from 1945 to 1948. They knew the reality of the rail transportation situation and could overcome language barriers and cultural differences to work effectively with KNR employees. These men proved to be of great value, particularly in winter 1950–51.[79]

Relevance for Contemporary Times

The experiences of winter 1950–51 provide a historical example for preparing operational plans with future contingencies. Logistical support for any major military operation in near future will be a combination of civilian and military personnel as well as military and civilian resources. Any future crises involving NATO's eastern flank or on the Korean peninsula allied forces will have to rely to a substantial degree on rail transportation. Rail Baltica, a 4-foot 8.5-inch (1,435-millimeter) standard gauge railway that will connect with the Baltic countries and Poland and Western Europe, will improve military mobility, according to the head of NATO's Allied Joint Force Command, Lt. Gen. Jörg Vollmer. "It is a civil and not a military project, but it will be beneficial for both purposes," he said.[80] "It will benefit both parties as the project will be favorable for both the economy and military forces."[81] The US-ROK combined forces are also working to improve military mobility via rail with recent projects such as opening a new railhead at Camp Humphreys capable of handling seventy freight cars at a time, triple the capacity of any other military railhead in the Korean theater.[82] These mobility improvements have been spurred in part by Russia and China's improved ability to move large forces across vast distances in a matter of hours.[83] As rail movement becomes an increasingly critical factor in a potential peer-to-peer conflict, recalling the events in Korea 1950–51 can help address challenges of rail operations and traffic management during a crisis.

The experienced 3rd TMRS personnel who met the crisis of winter 1950–51 had largely civilian-acquired skills from the American railroad industry. The development of the soldier-railroaders was principally through an employer-Army Reserve partnership, the Affiliated Reserve Unit Program. Another takeaway for contemporary times is the need to maintain employer-Reserve partnerships; having Reserve rail planning-advisory teams stationed in locales where there are Class 1 railroad headquarters or major rail facilities can help the Army take advantage of the expertise of railroad employees.[84]

When Russia invaded the Ukraine on 24 February 2022, Ukraine's railroads became the "vital cog" in Ukrainian defense efforts.[85] The Ukrainian railway system helped move refugees out of harm's way, military equipment and supplies to the front, and wounded soldiers to hospitals while keeping commodities and humanitarian assistance flowing as much as possible. The Ukrainians even attempted to return the Russian dead packed in refrigerator cars through third countries. Like the KNR in winter 1950–51, the Ukrainian Railways workforce has proven steadfast, according to the railway's CEO Oleksandr Kamyshin: "We are structured; we are disciplined. None of us loses control. I haven't seen a single railway man lose control. These people have iron nerves."[86] Russia also made extensive use of rail transportation, moving troops and equipment to pre-invasion staging points and invasion supplies to forward railheads. The Russians also used hospital trains to evacuate casualties and armored trains to protect captured railway lines.[87] During the initial phase of any future high-intensity conflict on NATO's eastern flank or renewed hostilities on the Korean Peninsula, Allied forces will face a situation much like the Ukrainians in winter–spring 2022 and the UNC in winter 1950–51. This well could include a withdrawal while in contact with a peer adversary until the tide of battle can be turned.

Notes

1. S. A. Levy, "Build 'Em Up—Blow 'Em Up," *Railway Progress* (February 1952): 6. President Harry S. Truman immediately ordered US Forces in Japan to come to the assistance of South Korea (Republic of Korea) after North Korea (Democratic People's Republic of Korea) attacked on 25 June 1950. After the United Nations (UN) condemned the North Korean aggression, a 7 July 1950 UN Security Council resolution recommended the establishing a unified command in Korea and requested the United States to designate a commander of these forces. On 8 July 1950, President Truman appointed General Douglas MacArthur as Commander in Chief, United Nations Command (CINCUNC).

2. J. A. Van Fleet, "Notes on Korea," n.d., James A. Van Fleet Papers, Box 105, Folder 19, George G. Marshall Research Library, Lexington, VA; and J. G. Westover, *Combat Support in Korea* (Washington, DC: Combat Force Press 1955), 65. According to Eighth US Army Korea and Transportation Corps sources, 95 percent of all overland movement in Korea was fully or partially moved by railroad.

3. Levy, "Build 'Em Up," 6. 3rd TMRS had served in Persia during WWII and supervised operation of Japanese railroads during the initial period of US occupation of Japan. It was reactivated for service in Korea.

4. S. J. Ericson, *The Sound of the Whistle: Railroads and the State in Meiji, Japan* (Cambridge, MA: Harvard University Asia Center, 1996), 268; "The Railways of Korea," *The Railway Gazette*, 21 August 1942; and Ministry of Transportation, Republic of Korea, *Transportation of Korea* (Seoul: Ministry of Transportation, 1957), 19.

5. R. B. Black, *An Evaluation of Service Support in the Korean Campaign* (Tokyo: ORO Study, 1951), 58; C. R. Gray, *Railroading in Eighteen Countries: The Story of American Railroad Men* (New York: Charles Scribner's Sons, 1955), 302–3; and A. Perlman, "Notes on South Korean Railroads," Railway Age (25 November 1950): 21.

6. Black, 58; Gray, 302–2; J. Hearst, "Rugged Peaks Termed Key in Korean Tactics," *Chicago Daily Tribune*, 29 July 1950; Perlman, 21; and "Interview with Col. Ketticus W. May Jr.," Combined Arms Center, 21 February 1946, US National Archives Record Group 334. Railroads in Korea and Manchuria were mainly 4-foot 8.5-inch (1,435-millimeter) standard gauge versus the 3-foot 6-inch (1,067-millimeter) narrow gauge used on Japanese home islands. Freight cars on the Korean and Manchurian railroads were mainly heavy American-style bogie-truck four-axle cars versus the light two-axle cars commonly used on Japanese government railways. Korean rolling stock was equipped with American-style Janney-type automatic couplers rather than European-style buffers and chain couplers. Freight equipment was equally split between boxcars, gondolas, and flatcars. These cars were thirty-three to thirty-four feet long and had a thirty-ton capacity. There was also a limited amount of specialized rolling stock such as stock (cattle) cars, petroleum tank cars, ice-cooled refrigerator cars, and heavy flat cars that could carry fifty or sixty tons. Passenger cars were

of American design; the majority were second- and third-class coaches. There were also some sleeper, diner, parlor, combination, baggage, mail, and hospital cars. Passenger cars had four or six axles with bogie-trucks. Steam locomotives were patterned after American designs and manufactured by Japanese companies. These locomotives included Mikado type and Mountain type for freight, and Pacific type for passenger service. The Mikado Type locomotives were used to pull hospital trains and also provided the most reliable steam power. All of the motive power were medium-weight locomotives; there were no heavy locomotives by American standards. Freight trains were usually fifteen cars long and passenger trains seven cars long due to steep grades. In 1950–51, however, freight trains could be up to thirty cars long, the usual upper limit being twenty-four cars using multiple locomotives. Despite being developed on an American model, the Korean railway network was not on the level of an American railroad of the period; much of the equipment was comparable to an American short-line railroad in 1920.

7. The Korean National Railroad was formally established on 10 August 1948.

8. 3rd TMRS, "Unit History and Activity Report," College Park, MD: Record Group 407, US National Archives, 1950; Rowan P. Alexander and Avery E. Kolb, "A New Concept in Military Railroad Service," *National Defense Transportation Journal* (May–June 1951): 32; and C. R. Shrader, Communist Logistics in the Korean War (Westport, CT: Greenwood Press, 1995), 116.

9. The Eighth US Army had been the occupational army for Japan, and became the US Army command for Korea.

10. US Army Forces Far East and Eighth Army, Logistics in the Korean Operations, vol. 1 (Camp Zama, JP: US Army Forces Far East, 1955), 6.

11. In 1947, with the heightening of tensions of the Cold War, the US Army established the Affiliated Reserve Unit Program based on a model developed during the Second World War. The program covered a wide array of army support functions in addition to railway operations all sponsored by appropriate organizations either in private industry or government agencies. For example, city fire departments sponsored fire-fighting engineer companies, construction contractors sponsored construction engineer battalions, and even quartermaster brewing units were sponsored by breweries. The affiliated Reserve unit members carried their civilian specialties into military service and held ranks roughly equivalent to their civilian positions. In peacetime, these reservists participated in monthly drills usually in the facilities provided by the sponsoring organization and attended two-week annual summer camps for military training at various military installations.

12. Initially the active-duty army battalions—714th Transportation Railway Operating Battalion (TROB) and the 765th Transportation Railway Shop Battalion (TRSB)—were sent from Fort Eustis, Virginia, to Korea, arriving in Pusan on 30 August 1950. The 714th TROB was rotated back to Fort Eustis in spring 1951. Two reserve battalions, the 712th TROB (Reading Railroad spon-

sored, Philadelphia) and the 724th TROB (Pennsylvania Railroad sponsored, Philadelphia) began to arrive in winter 1950–51. The 756th TRSB (Pennsylvania Railroad sponsored, Altoona, Pennsylvania) served as a replacement unit at Fort Eustis for the 765th TRSB, which remained in Korea. The TROB conducted operation and maintenance duties equivalent to a division of a Class 1 (major) American railroad operating 150 miles (240 kilometers) of railway. The commanding officer was a reserve lieutenant-colonel whose civilian job was that of division superintendent on a civilian railroad. The TRSB did the work of the general locomotive and car shops on a civilian railway. The unit did heavy repair on locomotives and car refurbishment and erection, work that could not be accomplished at repair-in-place (RIP) facilities or in outlying roundhouses. The TMRS was the higher echelon command for all rail units in a theatre or an area of operations. A TMRS had staff departments charged with the overall supervision of train movements, maintenance of locomotives and cars, and maintenance of way and structures. Each TMRS also had a stores department modelled after the purchasing and stores department of a civilian railway. The 3rd TMRS was under the EUSAK chief transportation officer, who had his own staff. Internally, the 3rd TMRS functioned much like a civilian railway with its operating procedures, and administrative and planning functions. Route and force protection and evacuation and demolition were, of course, uniquely military functions and handled accordingly by the 3rd TMRS.

13. The 3rd TMRS also worked closely with the Army Corps of Engineers. Reconstructing and repairing railway lines was a cooperative effort between the 3rd TMRS, the KNR, and the Army Corps of Engineers. Army construction engineers principally handled the repair and reconstruction of large bridges. However, no engineer units were directly in the command structure of 3rd TMRS.

14. "Headquarters 3D Transportation Military Railway Service Background," n.d., Fort Eustis, VA, United States Army Transportation Museum Research Library and Special Collections; US Army Forces Far East and Eighth Army, *Logistics in the Korean Operations*, 6; and Ministry of Transportation, *Transportation of Korea*, 40.

15. E. C. Lasher, "A Transport Miracle Saved Pusan," *National Defense Transportation* (November–December 1950): 11.

16. K. W. Condit, "Marine Supply in Korea," *Marine Corps Gazette* (January 1953): 52.

17. Westover, *Combat Support in Korea*, 66.

18. Alexander and Kolb, "A New Concept in Military Railroad Service," 34; and Edgar Ray Appleman, *United States Army in the Korean War: South to The Naktong, North to the Yalu (June–November 1950)* (Washington, DC: Office of the Chief of Military History Department of Army, 1961), 727–28.

19. Gray, *Railroading in Eighteen Countries*, 309.

20. 3rd TMRS, "Unit History and Activity Report October 1950;" *Korea: Its Land, People and Culture of All Ages* (Seoul: Hakwon-sa, 1960), 266; and Ministry of Transportation, *Transportation of Korea*, 43.

21. L. M. Canzona, *US Marine Operations in Korea*, vol. 3 (Washington, DC: Historical Branch, G-3, Headquarters, US Marine Corps, 1955–57), 126.

22. Condit, "Marine Supply in Korea," 53–54; and Canzona, 138.

23. The Chinese divisions had approximately 10,000 men each.

24. US Army Center of Military History, *American Military History* (Washington, DC: US Army Center of Military History, 1989), 557–59.

25. Canzona. *US Marine Operations in Korea*, 327.

26. Malcolm W. Cagle and Frank A. Manson. *The Sea War in Korea* (Annapolis, MD: US Naval Institute Press, 1957), 190–91; and Canzona, 327.

27. Korean Institute of Military History, *The Korean War*, vol. 2 (Lincoln, NE: University of Nebraska Press, 2000), 296.

28. Canzona. *US Marine Operations in Korea*, 343; and Korean Institute of Military History, 298.

29. B. C. Mossman, *United States Army in the Korean War: Ebb and Flow, November* (Washington, DC: US Army Center of Military History, 1988), 147; and Westover, *Combat Support in Korea*, 18–19.

30. Mossman, 175.

31. Cagle and Manson, *The Sea War in Korea*, 191.

32. Ministry of Transportation, *Transportation of Korea*, 43; and Westover, *Combat Support in Korea*, 63.

33. Levy, "Build 'Em Up," 6; and Westover, 63.

34. Korean Institute of Military History, *The Korean War*, 298; and Levy, 6).

35. C. Blair, *The Forgotten War: America in Korea, 1950–1953* (New York: Time, 1989), 503; and Ollie Atkins and Sylvia Crane Myers, "The World's Worst Railroad Headache," *Saturday Evening Post*, 14 July 1951, 126.

36. Van Fleet, "Notes on Korea;" Blair, *The Forgotten War*, 503; Levy, "Build 'Em Up," 2; and Van Fleet, *Rail Transport and the Winning of Wars*, 21.

37. Blair, 505.

38. Levy, "Build 'Em Up," 2.

39. Ministry of Transportation, *Transportation of Korea*, 43.

40. R. E. Guth, "The Korean National Railway," *National Defense Transportation Journal* (July–August 1952): 34. An M4A3(76)W HVSS Sherman Tank in service in Korea at the time weighed 30.3 tons.

41. E. Anderson, *Banner over Pusan* (London: Evan Brothers, 1960), 47.

42. General Walker, commander of the EUSAK, was killed on 22 December 1950 when the jeep in which he was riding collided with a 2½-ton truck.

43. US Army Center of Military History, *American Military History*, 560–61).

44. 714th Transportation Railway Operating Battalion, "Command Report for Month of January 1951," n.d., Record Group 407 US National Archives, College Park, MD; Korean Institute of Military History, *The Korean War*, 377–78; and Mossman, *United States Army in the Korean War*, 207–8).

45. Korean Institute of Military History, 377–78; Mossman, 202–4; S. Y. Paik, *Pusan to Panmunjom* (Washington, DC: Brassey's, 1982), 132; and Ministry of Transportation, *Transportation of Korea*, 43.

46. 714th Transportation Railway Operating Battalion, "Command Report for Month of January 1951."

47. A shoofly bridge is an expedient railroad bridge.

48. Korean Institute of Military History, *The Korean War*, 373; Mossman, *United States Army in the Korean War*, 202–4; and Ministry of Transportation, *Transportation of Korea*, 43.

49. Korean Institute of Military History, 373; Levy, "Build 'Em Up," 6–7; and Mossman, *United States Army in the Korean War*, 210. Ascom City-Army Support Command at Pupyung was a former Japanese Imperial Army compound near Incheon as support activity since 1945. Pupyung was five miles (eight kilometers) from Incheon on the Incheon–Yongdongpo Railway Line.

50. Atkins and Myers, "The World's Worst Railroad Headache," 126; and Levy, "Build 'Em Up," 7.

51. Lt. Col. Jesse M. McLellan would serve as commander of the 3rd TMRS from June 1951 to January 1954. Col. William. S. Carr had assumed command of the 3rd TMRS when it was reactivated in Korea on 26 August 1950. Before his recall to active duty on 23 July 1950, Colonel Carr was the Division Superintendent of the Boston Division of the New York, New Haven & Hartford Railroad. Colonel Carr served as the 3rd TMRS commander until June 1951. Illness forced his evacuation from Korea, and he was reassigned to the Office of the Chief of Transportation in Washington, DC. He was replaced by Lieutenant Colonel McLellan, who was an experienced "old Korea hand" as he served during the 1945–48 occupation of Korea as Chief of the Rail Transportation Department of the US military government's Transportation Bureau. He had served with the Transportation Corps during World War II in North Africa, France, and Germany and had had an extensive civilian career in the Transportation and Operations Department of the Atlantic Coast Line Railroad which ran between Richmond, Virginia, and Collier City, Florida. Col. Edmond C. R. Lasher was regular army, US Military Academy Class of 1929.

52. Maintenance of way and construction train.

53. 714th Transportation Railway Operating Battalion, "Command Report for Month of January 1951;" Levy, "Build 'Em Up," 7; Atkins and Myers, "The World's Worst Railroad Headache," 126; and Westover, *Combat Support in Korea*, 64.

54. Mossman, *United States Army in the Korean War*, 211–12; Korean Institute of Military History, *The Korean War*, 374–75; and Westover, 64.

55. Blair, *The Forgotten War*, 598); and Westover, 64.

56. Central Mainline: Seoul-Taejon-Taegu-Pusan.

57. W. T. Faricy, "Railroads—Mighty Weapon in Korea," *National Defense Transportation Journal* (March–April 1952), 30; and Westover, *Combat Support in Korea*, 65.

58. East Coast Line: Seoul-Wonju-Yongju-Pujon-Pusan.

59. M. C. Miller, "High Steel in Korea," *The Military Engineer* (September–October 1951), 332; and Westover, *Combat Support in Korea*, 65.

60. Levy, "Build 'Em Up," 8.

61. Egelhof, "Ex-Atom Chief Decries Lack of US Spirit," *Chicago Daily Tribune*, 14 September 1951, 45.

62. 3rd TMRS, "Command Report 1 March–31 March 1951," US National Archives Record Group 407, US Army 3rd Transportation Military Railway Service, *Logistics in the Korean Operations*, vol. 3 (Camp Zama, JP: US Army Forces Far East 1955), 12; and J. Egelhof, "Ex-Atom Chief Decries Lack of US Spirit," *Chicago Daily Tribune*, 14 September 1951, 45.

63. Miller, "High Steel in Korea;" and Westover, *Combat Support in Korea*, 65. The 439th Engineer Construction Battalion was an affiliated reserve unit sponsored by the Kansas Contractors Association.

64. Westover, 66. According to an estimate by Capt. Max N. Brown of the 714th TROB, the 3rd TMRS had 7,000 freight cars available during the evacuations, 500 of which were in very bad condition. Brown estimated that some 8,500 cars in good repair were needed to avoid danger of critical shortage.

65. Ministry of Transportation, *Transportation of Korea*, 43; and Westover, *Combat Support in Korea*, 65.

66. General Meyer served as Army Chief of Staff from 1979 to 1983. Quoted from F. J. Manning, "Morale and Cohesion in Military Psychiatry," in R. Zajtchuk, *Military Psychiatry Preparing in Peace for War* (Washington, DC: Office of Surgeon General Department of Army, 1994), 4.

67. M. Hastings, *The Korean War* (New York: Simon and Schuster, 1987), 174.

68. T. Fehrenbach, *This Kind of War: The Classic Korean War History* (Washington, DC: Brassey's, 1994), 128.

69. Hastings, *The Korean War*, 175.

70. "Revise Training of US Recruits, Officers Urge," *Chicago Daily* Tribune, 29 August 1950, 11.

71. A. M. Schofield, "724th TROB History," n.d., Albert M. Schofield Papers, Railroad Museum of Pennsylvania Archives; and C. U. Baum, "Back Home From Korea," *Reading Railroad Magazine* (January 1953), 4. The 714th TROB Chicago, Saint Paul Minneapolis & Omaha Railway was sponsored reserve unit and 765th TRSB was an Erie Railroad sponsored unit. Both were retained in active service in 1947. The 765th TRSB still was considered an "Erie outfit" in 1950.

72. TMRS, "Unit History and Activity Report October 1950;" Lasher, "A Transport Miracle Saved Pusan," 13; Ministry of Transportation, *Transportation of Korea*, 43; and *Korea: Its Land, People, and Culture of All Ages*, 266.

73. "Railroading Takes Direct Role in Korea," *National Defense Transportation Journal* (May–June 1951), 55.

74. Levy, "Build 'Em Up," 8.

75. Levy, 6.

76. Hastings, *The Korean War*, 175; B. Matzenbacher, "The U.S. Army and Mission Command: Philosophy Versus Practice," *Military Review* (March–April

2018): 61; and D. E. Vandergriff, *Misinterpretation and Confusion: What Is Mission Command and Can the Army Make it Work?* (Arlington, VA: Institute of Land Warfare Association of the United States Army, 2013), 6.

77. W. J. Cunningham, "Scientific Management in the Operation of Railroads," *The Quarterly Journal of Economics* (May 1911) 149–51; A. Martin, *Enterprise Denied: Origins of the Delcine of the American Railroads, 1897–1917* (New York: Columbia University Press, 1971), 211–19; and E. A. Sibul, "Forging Iron Horses and Iron Men: Rail Transport in the Korean War and the Influence of the US Army Transportation Corps on the Development of the Korean National Railroad" (PhD diss., University of York, York, UK, 2008), 171.

78. "712th TROB Command Report," 1–31 January 1951, US National Archives Record Group 407, 3rd Transportation Military Railway Service; "765th TRSB Command Report," 1–31 January 1951, US National Archives Record Group 407, 3rd Transportation Military Railway Service; and Sibul, 153.

79. US Army Military History Institute, "Conversation Between General Edmund C. R. Lasher and Lt. Col. D. R. Lasher," US Army Military History Institute, n.d., 73; and Westover, *Combat Support in Korea,* 61.

80. "Rail Baltica Will Improve Military Mobility, Says NATO Commander," *LRT English Newsletter,* 26 June 2020, https://www.lrt.lt/en/news-in-english/19/1191957/rail-baltica-will-improve-military-mobility-says-nato-commander. Railways in Estonia, Latvia. and Lithuania have a 5-foot (1,524-millimeter) gauge, a legacy of the Russia Empire. Rail Baltica is one of the priority projects of the European Union's Trans-European Transport Networks (TEN-T), scheduled to be completed in 2026.

81. "Rail Baltica Will Improve Military Mobility."

82. C. Stone, "Railhead Opening Moves Camp Humphreys Closer to Expansion," *Army News*, 29 February 2016, https://www.army.mil/article/163193/railhead_opening_moves_camp_humphreys_closer_to_expansion.

83. B. Gerdžiūnas, "Focus on Military Mobility Marks Shifting Deterrence Priorities in the Baltics," *LRT English*, 20 May 2019, https://www.lrt.lt/en/news-in-english/19/1060597/focus-on-military-mobility-marks-shifting-deterrence-priorities-in-the-baltics; and R. Beckhusen, "The Chinese Military Has a New Secret Weapon: Lightning-Fast Trains," *The Week*, 3 July 2015, https://theweek.com/articles/563699/chinese-military-new-secret-weapon-lightning-fast-trains.

84. D. T. Pollard. "The Army Reserve Expeditionary Railway Center," *Army Sustainment* (May–June 2012), https://alu.army.mil/alog/issues/MayJune12/Reserve_Expeditionary_Railway_Center.html. Class I railroads are major North American railroads with 2019 revenue of at least $505 million, according to the American Association of Railroads.

85. I. Coles, "Ukraine's Railroads Have Become Vital Cog in Kyiv's War Effort," *The Wall Street Journal*, 11 March 2022, A7; and A. Chin "On Board the Mobile Command that's Keeping Ukraine's Trains Running," *Business Insider*, 4 March 2022, https://www.businessinsider.com/on-board-the-mobile-command-

thats-keeping-ukraines-trains-running-2022-3?fbclid=IwAR3HN_u3092C6gl-foHjzzPN2dEH8-IDrDufgHAl_nKVk6gHhIzFg-MrFTmQ.

86. Chin.

87. Coles, "Ukraine's Railroads Have Become Vital Cog in Kyiv's War Effort;" E. Gershkovich, "Russia Evacuates Wounded Soldiers to Belarus as Its Casualties in Ukraine War Rise," *The Wall Street Journal,* 2 March 2022, https://www.wsj.com/articles/russia-evacuates-wounded-soldiers-to-belarus-as-its-casualties-in-ukraine-war-rise-11646239336?mod=Searchresults_pos3&page=1; A. Dangwal, "Russian 'Armored Train' Equipped With Automatic Cannons & Painted With 'Z' Mark Joins The Ukraine Invasion," *The Eurasian Times*, 9 March 2022, https://eurasiantimes.com/russian-armored-train-automatic-cannons-ukraine-invasion/; and D. A. Michaels, "Trains Help Drive Russia's Latest Gains in Ukraine," *The Wall Street Journal,* 14 June 2022, A1.

Chapter 14
Cornwallis in the 1781 Yorktown Campaign: When an Attack Becomes a Defense, a Siege, and a Surrender
Patrick H. Hannum

When it comes to lessons learned in addressing military operations, most study the victories; however, defeat often provides more insight. While each situation requiring the use of military force is unique, individuals and their institutions learn valuable lessons from the experiences of military defeat, suitable to shape thinking for future consideration. This is the case with Lt. Gen. Charles Cornwallis's 1781 Yorktown Campaign in Virginia that ended his North American experiences during the American Revolution, culminating with his surrender at Yorktown on 19 October 1781. Many of the lessons from this military failure link directly to concepts framed in contemporary joint military doctrine and

Figure 14.1. Surrender of Lord Cornwallis at Yorktown painting by John Trumbull in the US Capitol Rotunda. Courtesy of the Architect of the US Capitol.

thought. Cornwallis experienced a failed campaign in Virginia, in part, because the British lost naval superiority along the North American coast to their American-Franco adversaries for more than two months. History reflects Cornwallis learned from his experiences associated with the 1781 Yorktown Campaign and later applied those lessons from North America during his campaigns in India.[1] More importantly, a study of the 1781 Yorktown Campaign provides contemporary military officers and strategy practitioners at the operational level of warfare with valuable insight into concepts relevant in the contemporary operating environment.

In today's security environment, US civilian and military leaders face difficult choices for allocating and employing finite military resources. These circumstances are not new; past military leaders faced these same dilemmas. Nations with global security interests and military forces engaged in multiple geographic theaters often find themselves strategically overextended, requiring processes and procedures to allocate finite re-

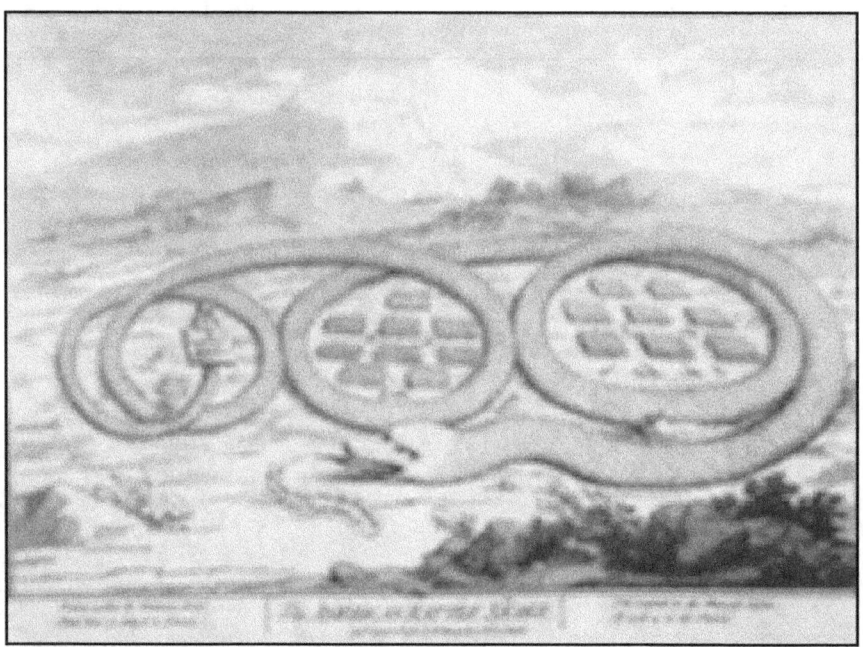

Figure 14.2. Political cartoon "The American Rattlesnake" published in London in April 1782. The snake is coiled around the two large British armies surrendered to the American Patriots at Saratoga in 1777 and Yorktown in 1781. The snake's message references a period term, "Burgoyn'd," a slang reference to the capture of General Burgoyne's Army at Saratoga, New York, in October 1777. To be "Burgoyn'd" is to be captured. "Two British Armies I have thus Burgoyn'd, And room for more I've got behind." Courtesy of the Library of Congress.

sources against priority challenges and threats.[2] Cornwallis's 1781 Yorktown Campaign highlights what can go wrong when (1) strategic and operational-level military leaders fail to synchronize their thinking and activities concerning the employment of finite military resources, (2) assumptions about the success of friendly supporting military operations prove incorrect, and (3) friendly forces lines of operation become overextended. Cornwallis's 1781 Yorktown Campaign was a well-intentioned offensive resulting in a surrender that changed the course of the American Revolution and ultimately contributed to the recognition of the United States as an independent nation.

Strategic Overview

The American-Franco road to the Yorktown victory began during a meeting between General George Washington and Lt. Gen. Jene-Baptiste-Donatien de Vimeur, comte de Rochambeau, at Wethersfield, Connecticut, on 21–22 May 1781.[3] During this meeting, Washington and Rochambeau agreed on two tentative courses of action—one involving an attack on New York and the second, an operation in the south. Both options required money, additional troops, and a maritime force.[4] Because only France possessed these capabilities, any course of action would rely heavily on the willingness and ability of the French Army and Navy to reinforce the American Patriots.[5] However, a broader overview of the American Revolution provides valuable context for why Cornwallis's 1781 Yorktown Campaign ended with British forces surrendering at Yorktown.

Great Britain's road to Yorktown began much earlier. The American Revolution transitioned from a colonial rebellion to part of a larger global shooting war in 1778 when France entered two treaties: the Treaty of Alliance, a military arrangement, and the Treaty of Amity and Commerce, a diplomatic and commercial alliance with the new United States. Prior to these treaties, both France and Spain supplied the American Patriots or Whigs with critical military resources.[6] More than ninety percent of the gunpowder provided to the American Patriots during the first two years of the revolution came from Europe, transshipped through Caribbean ports.[7] This aid is an example of operations below the level of armed conflict that enable client or proxy actors (Whigs or American Patriots in rebellion against the British government), to work in the interests of Britain's peer competitors (France and Spain) to distract and weaken Great Britain. Contemporary national and defense strategies frame this as "great power competition . . . involving revisionist powers," seeking to advance their national interests.[8] While the American Revolution was a rebellion against colonial authority, it was—

from the very beginning—a global conflict involving great powers using proxies to engage in direct conflict.[9] A colonial rebellion in North America served the interests of France, Spain, and others in competition with Great Britain for continental, global, and economic power.[10]

The sugar plantations on the Caribbean Islands were a great source of economic wealth to the European nations that colonized them, in large part because of sugar's popularity in the European market. There were more than 1,800 sugar plantations in the British Caribbean at the beginning of the American Revolution, and these plantations were very profitable.[11] To protect the economically important resource, the British Cabinet directed a shift in military resources during 1778 from the North American theater to the Caribbean to protect these colonies from French and later Spanish attacks. Although the British allocated military resources to protect their Caribbean colonies, American Patriots continued to receive war materiel through neutral Caribbean ports. The British Cabinet ultimately declared war on the Dutch, who were freely trading with the United States, and ordered the seizure of the key Dutch trading island of St. Eustatius in February 1781, to prevent the flow of war materiel and supplies into the North American theater.[12]

As a result of France's 1778 treaties with the new United States, Great Britain declared war on France—prompting Spain to openly join the conflict in support of its traditional ally. War between European powers greatly expanded the character of the conflict in North America. To address new threats to British interests around the globe, Great Britain's political leaders revised their military strategy for operations in the Western Hemisphere. During 1778, the new British Commander-in-Chief, North America, Lt. Gen. Henry Clinton, received instructions to evacuate Philadelphia and occupy New York or proceed to Rhode Island or Nova Scotia if he believed he possessed insufficient force to hold New York.[13] His instructions also required him to detach forces to protect British colonies in the Caribbean. By fall 1779, more than 7,500 British troops were serving in the Caribbean and another 7,500 in Canada, leaving 35,000 to operate in the Thirteen Colonies and East and West Florida.[14] By 1780, the number of available troops dropped to 32,000. Maintaining the fixed British bases around New York City consumed between 14,000 and 17,500 British forces leaving fewer for employment in the other Thirteen Colonies and in East and West Florida.[15] The repositioning of large numbers of land and maritime forces to the Caribbean resulted in two principle British theaters of operation in the Western Hemisphere, North America, and the Caribbe-

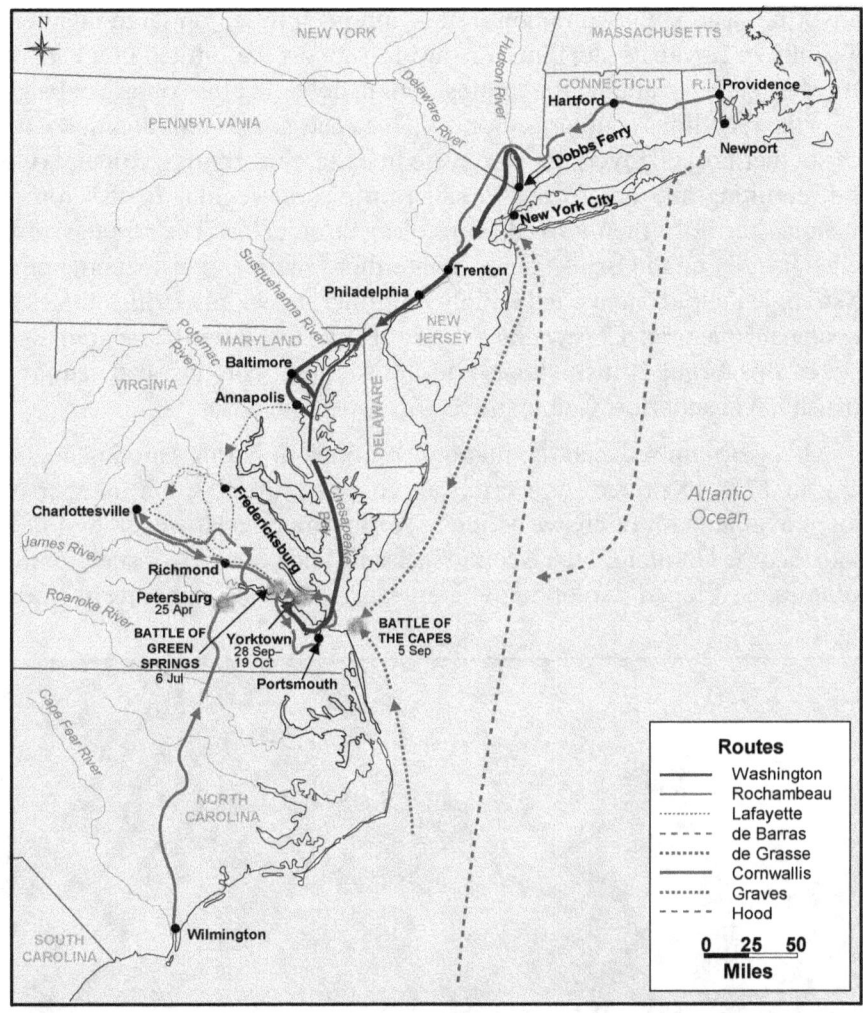

Source: National Park Service: Yorktown Battlefield Maps, Battle Map (Final Campaign 1781).

Figure 14.3. 1781 Yorktown Campaign, Operational-Level Movement and Maneuver. Created by Army University Press.

an, without an effective military command and control structure to provide unity of effort or ensure synchronization of forces and functions between these two theaters.[16]

The 1778 British strategy against the Thirteen Colonies is often referred to as the southern strategy that envisioned liberating the rebellious southern colonies beginning with Georgia and moving from South to North.[17] The key assumption in this approach relied on large numbers of southern Loyalists stepping forward to support the limited numbers of British regulars available for employment in defeating the American Patriots in the rebellious southern colonies. This necessitated coordination with the southern royal governors who were in exile, reinstituting colonial rule and recruiting and organizing Loyalist militias as regular British forces occupied territory then moved on to clear more areas. The strategy also relied heavily on the British Navy to interdict American Patriot commerce to strangle their economy and rapidly reinforce and supply British forces.[18] Lieutenant General Cornwallis's failed 1781 Yorktown Campaign was part of this larger British strategy in the southern colonies that required British naval superiority along the North American coast.

Great Britain reduced the number of troops in North America beginning in 1778 to protect its Caribbean colonies, limiting the number of troops available for offensive action in North America. However, by 1779, Lord George Germain, 1st Viscount Sackville and secretary of state for the colonies, developed a solution to his shortage of troops and units in North

Figure 14.4. Patriot Militia reenactors. Patriot Militia reinforced the Franco-American land forces at Yorktown contribution to the surrender of Cornwallis. Virginia Militia were under the command of Virginia Governor Thomas Nelson, a Yorktown resident. His home is now preserved by the National Park Service. Courtesy of the author.

America; he would rotate units between the Caribbean and North America in one grand "Western Atlantic" theater extending from Quebec to the Antilles.[19] Elements of the 50,000 deployed land forces could redeploy north during the summer and south during the winter to capitalize on the climate and extended campaigning seasons. This inter-theater movement was possible with British naval superiority supporting and complementing the transition of land forces between theaters.[20]

Unfortunately, the British lacked the joint command and control mechanisms to implement this concept. The common superiors of the land and maritime commanders resided in London, necessitating a greater degree of civilian oversight than available across the Atlantic. The campaigning seasons overlapped, and ship and fleet repositioning complicated the coordination.

Cornwallis assumed command of the British Army operating in the southern United States during the summer of 1780 and proceeded to campaign in the Carolinas. Generally successful in conventional maneuver warfare against regular formations of the Continental Army, Cornwallis struggled with an increasingly violent irregular war involving many parti-

Figure 14.5. British Dragoon reenactors. British Dragoons clashed with their French counterparts in the Battle of the Hook, on Gloucester Point, as part of the siege of Yorktown. Courtesy of the author.

san actors and local militia that complicated the conduct of conventional military operations.[21] He faced an elusive enemy. After engaging but failing to defeat the highly mobile Continental Army commanded by Maj. Gen. Nathanael Greene, Cornwallis decided to move to Virginia, arriving at Petersburg during May 1781.

Contemporary military doctrine emphasizes the need to understand the operating environment and, as part of this understanding, gain an appreciation for the nature of the population.[22] The vast geographic expanse of the Thirteen Colonies and the lack of large population centers, particularly in Virginia and the south, necessitated large, dispersed formations to control the countryside.[23] The British did not possess the numbers of ground troops needed to seize, pacify, and secure the countryside. Great Britain's government leaders failed to fully appreciate the nature of the environment and problems associated with controlling the population in North America. The lack of infrastructure and navigable inland waterways, poor roads, distances, poor logistics, and limited sustainment sources all impacted British forces' ability to conduct sustained military operations away from the coast and the British Navy.

Even more important was a fundamental misunderstanding of the nature of the population.[24] Although eighty-five percent of the white population of America's Thirteen Colonies were of British ancestry, these regional groups represented a very diverse set of cultural norms and behaviors. While most spoke English, they considered themselves British citizens, not subjects. The political autonomy afforded the Colonies through the end of the Great War for Empire (1754–63) produced a degree of self-governance and independence across all cultural regions and groups.[25] In general, the various regional British cultures responded similarly to attempts to restrict self-governance and "joined together in the movement that led to the American Revolution."[26] In 1777, William Pitt, the Elder, the architect of Great Britain's victory in the French and Indian War in North America, summed up the complexities of military operations to restore British rule over the Thirteen Colonies: "My lords, you cannot conquer America."[27] The human and physical terrain in the colonies was extremely diverse, helping to create a complex operating environment.[28]

Military Leaders Fail to Synchronize their Approach

Successful military campaigns require synchronization of all military activities as well as integration of military activities with the other elements of national power. Senior military leaders must work closely with civilian government leaders to produce globally integrated and coordinated military action.[29] Examining the effectiveness of the British forces in synchronizing their military activities with strategic guidance provides insight into why Lieutenant General Cornwallis failed in his efforts during the 1781 Yorktown Campaign and the American-Franco force succeeded. Contemporary and emerging US doctrine emphasizes the importance of integrating campaign design elements with a thorough understanding of the political-military environment, continuous analysis and adaptation, and integrated force employment.[30]

Although there were political disagreements within the Parliament of Great Britain over the war in America, British King George III was consistent in his policy to use military force to crush the American rebellion. He selected a like-minded individual to implement this colonial policy; Lord Germain, a former general officer with a court martial and relief from command in his background, assumed responsibility for implementing the grand strategy developed by the Cabinet and approved by the king.[31] Germain's duties included appointing land component commanders, allocating forces between various theaters, and prioritizing sustainment. The complexities of his challenges increased exponentially in 1778 when France recognized US independence, expanding the rebellion in North America into a global conflict involving a traditional enemy and competitor. By 1781, Great Britain and its few allies faced the rebellious Americans, French, Spanish, and Dutch in a global conflict highly dependent on maritime power to support land forces.

"Mission command," a tenet of contemporary joint command and control doctrine, is also a fundamental component for policymakers providing guidance to military commanders around the globe who are geographically separated by time and distance.[32] Shortly after assuming his position, Lord Germain stated: "The distance from the seat of Government necessarily leaves much to the discretion and resources of the General."[33] Unfortunately, he faced numerous challenges beyond those associated with time and distance from the North American theater of operations that impacted his effectiveness and efficiency in translating strategic policy guidance into decisive military actions.

While Lord Germain was the architect of the grand colonial military strategy and controlled land forces allocation, he did not control the maritime resources needed to effectively synchronize all military activities; he relied on close collaboration with John Montagu, 4th Earl of Sandwich, First Lord of the Admiralty, to gain necessary maritime resources. Germain and Sandwich differed on how to effectively employ the British

Navy. Germain advocated deploying the fleet globally and engaging the enemy in forward regions, while Sandwich preferred a maritime strategy focused on meeting the French Navy in European waters and first protecting the British Isles.[34] Additionally, the British Cabinet did not provide timely guidance necessary to resolve differences between the key commanders at critical decision points.[35] At the operational-level, the senior land component commander in North America and the senior maritime component commander also had to collaborate. There was no overall joint commander in the North American theater.[36] The personality and professional disconnects resulting from this command structure hampered effective operations and helped create some disconnects between grand strategy and policy and operational-level implementation.[37]

While the British Cabinet directed the war in America, Germain and Sandwich did not always have enough talent or resources to meet the conditions existing in the operating environment, or effectively influence the command relationships between their key commanders. For example, Lieutenant General Clinton collaborated but did not exercise command authority over the North American maritime commanders. This created some significant challenges, particularly during the Yorktown Campaign. By the summer of 1781, the relationship between Clinton and Vice Admiral of the White Marriott Arbuthnot, who commanded the Royal Navy's North American Station, deteriorated to the point that communication failures between land and maritime forces prevented collaborative and coordinated operations.[38] Rear Adm. Thomas Graves replaced Arbuthnot in early July 1781, relieving some of the animosity. However, American historian William B. Willcox noted that poor relations between key military leaders prevented effective employment of land and maritime assets: "The tragedy of Great Britain in America was not that her military leaders were fools, but that they lacked the qualities required for effective teamwork. Although they had individual virtues, they could not pool them to solve their common problems."[39] Contemporary doctrine emphasizes the importance of understanding commander's intent and building trust between commanders. These elements were clearly lacking in the British command structure during the Yorktown Campaign.

While there were synchronization issues between the land and maritime component commanders in North America, there were also significant issues inside the land component. This difference became known as the Clinton-Cornwallis Controversy.[40] Lieutenant General Cornwallis abandoned the Carolinas in April 1781 after a series of engagements and a winter campaign that left him with less than 2,000 troops, contributing to his

Figure 14.6. 1781 plan of the Town of York with land and water features in shaded relief. The British interior defensive position (center) is bounded on the north by the York River. The map also displays the siege lines of the American and French forces. Portions of the siege lines were reconstructed during the 1930's by the Civilian Conservation Corps. The original description reads: "Plan of York Town and Gloucester in Virginia, shewing the works constructed for the defence of those posts by the Rt. Honble: Lieut. General Earl Cornwallis, with the attacks of the combined army of French and rebels under the command of the Generals Count de Rochambaud and Washington which capitulated October 1781." Courtesy of the Library of Congress.

decision to campaign in Virginia.[41] Unable to defeat Maj. Gen. Nathanael Greene's Southern Army, Cornwallis failed to pacify or secure the Carolinas as instructed by Lieutenant General Clinton. Cornwallis, tiring of the indecisive civil war in the Carolinas, moved north to Virginia. Clinton, displaying his inability to act decisively, provided a series of conflicting orders and ultimately ordered Cornwallis to establish a base of operations in Virginia to support a deep-water anchorage for ships of the line.[42] Because Clinton and Cornwallis failed to share a common operational approach, their 8,000 soldiers and sailors ultimately were left in a vulnerable position at Yorktown, where the more agile American-Franco forces fixed them in a defensive position and cut off any chance of escape by land or sea.

Clinton was Cornwallis's senior. However, because they were geographically separated between New York and the Carolinas during 1780–81, Clinton authorized direct communication between Cornwallis and Lord Germain in London to speed the information flow.[43] Clinton and Cornwallis differed in how to pursue victory in the south and failed to share a common view of the operational environment. Cornwallis corresponded directly with Lord Germain, who favored his aggressive approach and his move to Virginia; this process marginalized Clinton's authority. Clinton was the methodical planner who had difficulty executing operations that involved risk.[44] Cornwallis was the bold commander who believed in the power of the offense and favored defeating American Patriot forces with speed and aggressive offensive maneuver. Relations soured between the two men during 1780, creating an acrimonious climate that resulted in a lack of unity of effort in the southern theater culminating at Yorktown.

Assumptions about Supporting Operations Prove Incorrect

The 1781 Yorktown Campaign was a joint and multinational operation involving US and French land and maritime forces opposing those of Great Britain. Great Britain ruled the sea at the end of the Great War for Empire (1754–63).[45] However, post-war fiscal austerity reduced the readiness of the British fleet, and global commitments made it difficult for naval forces to employ adequate numbers of ships of the line (warships with sixty-four or more guns) in North American waters after declaration of war on France in 1778.[46] The Caribbean, with its numerous island colonies and rich sugar plantations, consumed the bulk of the warships allocated to the Western Hemisphere as the war progressed. For several months between early September and early November 1781, the French Navy shifted its focus from the Caribbean to the North American coast.[47] As a result, Great Britain lost naval superiority along the North American coast for this two-month period. This invalidated the assumption of successful friendly supporting maritime operations required to resupply and support or reposition land forces operating in Virginia under Cornwallis's command.[48]

Control of the Chesapeake Bay during the Yorktown Campaign was a decisive point.[49] The planning assumption both Clinton and Cornwallis accepted was the British Navy would control this decisive point and provide local naval superiority along the North American coast, enabling freedom of movement for land forces. The 5 September 1781 Battle of the Chesapeake Capes (also known as the Battle of the Capes) was a naval engagement near the entrance to the Chesapeake Bay between the French fleet of Adm. François Joseph Paul, comte de Grasse, and the British fleet commanded by Rear Admiral Graves. The French fleet's ability to prevent the British fleet from entering the Chesapeake Bay and drawing them away from the bay allowed freedom of movement for American-Franco land forces ashore and synchronized arrival of supplies by sea required to conduct and sustain a siege. This decisive maritime action allowed the French fleet to occupy the Chesapeake Bay, which set the conditions for the Siege of Yorktown and Cornwallis's surrender. After the engagement and several subsequent days of maneuver at sea and a council of war by the admirals, the British fleet withdrew to New York to recover from battle damage.[50] Repairs to the British fleet took a month to complete because of the extensive damage from two intense hours of combat. Adm. Jacques-Melchior Saint-Laurent, comte de Barras, transporting critical siege supplies protected by eight ships of the line, entered the bay unchallenged as Admirals de Grasse and Graves maneuvered their fleets south off the Outer Banks of North Carolina.[51] Admiral de Grasse deliberately headed south to draw Graves away from the entrance to the Chesapeake and allow Admiral de Barras to enter unmolested. The naval engagement, tactically a draw, had profound strategic and operational-level impact on operations ashore. As the British fleet approached the entrance to the Chesapeake Bay, they faced twenty-four French ships of the line to their nineteen warships. The British fleet mistakenly assumed they faced combined French fleets of de Grasse from the Caribbean and de Barras from Newport, Rhode Island. That was an incorrect assumption because de Grasse brought his entire Caribbean fleet north after careful consultation with Spanish diplomats; de Barras was several days away in the North Atlantic.[52]

Without the support and mobility provided by the British Navy, Lieutenant General Cornwallis had no ability to escape. His small supporting maritime component was not capable of lifting his combat forces or challenging the French warships of the line anchored at the mouth of the Chesapeake Bay.[53] Ashore, Cornwallis continued to strengthen his defensive positions in anticipation of the British fleet's return. On several occasions prior to his surrender, Lieutenant General Clinton assured him a relief force was on the way.[54] However, repairs to British warships in New York took longer than expected, delaying the relief attempt until after Cornwallis's surrender. Cornwallis now faced thirty-six French ships of the line holding the Chesapeake Bay and blocking British maritime reinforcements; hoping to prevent unnecessary death and destruction ashore, he surrendered when the American-Franco siege turned the eastern flank of his defensive line and subjected his position to incessant fire from American-Franco cannons.[55]

Adm. George Brydges Rodney, commanding the British Caribbean Fleet, controlled the most capable British maritime force in the Western Hemisphere. However, at a critical point in the summer of 1781, he returned to Great Britain to settle accounts associated with the seizure of commercial property on the island of St. Eustatius. During his absence, he turned command of the fleet over to Rear Adm. Samuel Hood.[56] Hood appropriately deployed his fleet north under the assumption that the French

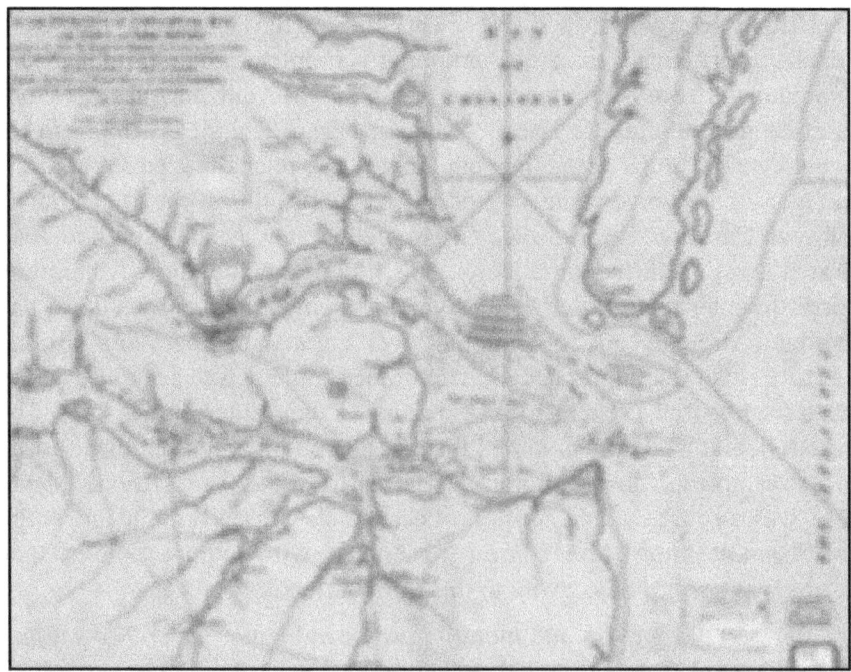

Figure 14.7. Plan of the entrance to the Chesapeake Bay. Courtesy of the Library of Congress.

Caribbean Fleet commanded by Admiral de Grasse was moving north to support Franco-Americans land forces. However, after combining with the British North American fleet in New York and transiting south to engage the French, the ensuing tactical engagement left the French fleet in control of the Chesapeake Bay, resulting in control of a decisive point.

Friendly Lines of Operation Become Overextended[57]

Operational reach, a component of the direct or indirect approach, and lines of operation are contemporary elements of operational design that link to the concepts of French military theorist Antoine-Henri Jomini.[58] Although Great Britain had nearly 50,000 land forces operating in the Western Hemisphere in 1781, these forces were geographically separated and depended on the British Navy for transport. To control the tempo of operations in more than twenty-five different colonies from Canada to the Antilles, they separated their land forces geographically and relied heavily on the British Navy for the mobility needed to resupply and consolidate their available land forces. Because General Washington had few maritime forces available, he relied heavily on the capabilities and resources of the French Navy.

Large elements of the British Army and supporting German Auxiliary and loyal Provincial forces were in pockets around the hemisphere and in the Thirteen Colonies.[59] Because of the dispersion of forces—an attempt to influence and control numerous locations—forces were unable to mutually support each other. This limited flexibility to move forces and maneuver effectively.[60] In order to concentrate forces, the British needed to maintain their maritime dominance. The British Navy provided the freedom of movement and ability to reinforce and sustain these geographically separated units as envisioned in the grand strategy developed in 1778. Loss of maritime superiority, for even a brief period, could spell disaster for any of these widely separated forces. The British garrison of West Florida found themselves in this situation; the British commander, Maj. Gen. John Campbell, surrendered his force to the Spanish forces in May 1781 after a siege of Pensacola.[61] Lieutenant General Cornwallis would suffer a similar outcome in October 1781, only with a much larger British force.

The loss of British naval superiority resulting from the 5 September 1781 Battle of the Capes placed Cornwallis's British forces operating in Virginia in a vulnerable position. While Cornwallis experienced relative freedom of movement in Virginia between May and August 1781, the British Navy lost complete maritime control of the Chesapeake Bay during a two-month period from September to November 1781. This loss, set the conditions for American-Franco forces to move adequate land forces for a siege and force Cornwallis to surrender twenty-five percent of the British land forces available for employment against the American-Franco allies.

The decision to employ the entire French Caribbean fleet of Admiral de Grasse in support of an American-Franco offensive in the United States resulted from intervention by the Spanish diplomat, Don Francisco Saavedra de Sangronis.[62] Saavedra based his actions and recommendations to de Grasse on guidance from the Spanish Minister of the Indies, Don Jose de Galvez.[63] Moving the French fleet north during the peak of the hurricane season was also a practical force protection measure. This series of decisions by Great Britain, France, and Spain, culminated in the loss of British maritime superiority along the North American coast. The decision by de Grasse to move his entire fleet north left the British fleet outnumbered and outgunned during the Battle of the Capes. The British were unable to operate inside the decision cycle of the more agile American-Franco forces who made more timely decisions about where and in what strength to move and maneuver their available forces.[64] Saavedra summarized the conditions

Figure 14.8. French Infantry reenactors fire a volley. French Infantry and American Militia conducted successful combined operations against the British on Gloucester Point to prevent foraging for supplies, contributing to Cornwallis's surrender. Courtesy of the author.

facing the British in his 18 July 1781 diary entry, which referenced de Grasse sending his entire fleet north from Haiti to engage the British fleet: "And never in order to save resources ought one risk the success of an expedition that was perhaps going to decide the outcome of the fortune of the entire war."[65] While Saavedra respected the power of the British forces, he was not afraid to articulate the reason the Spanish were willing, on this occasion, to fully support their French allies and weaken the British in the Western Hemisphere, even if it involved empowering the United States.

The British had no single joint force commander to synchronize operations in the Western Hemisphere in multiple warfighting domains. The American-Franco alliance suffered from the same problem and had the added burden of a coalition structure with no formal overall joint commander. What made the difference between the two opponents was that the American-Franco forces were able to efficiently synchronize and maneuver their land and maritime forces and act with a unity of effort while the British forces struggled to develop a cohesive approach.

Figure 14.9. 76th Highland reenactors. Members of the 76th Highland Regiment who surrendered at Yorktown became prisoners of war under the Articles of Surrender. Members of this unit were interred at Camp Security in York County, Pennsylvania, guarded by Pennsylvania Militia. Several members of the local militia who guarded these prisoners were ancestors of the author. Courtesy of the author.

With no overall British joint commander in the Western Hemisphere, effective joint operations designed to employ movement and maneuver to defeat American-Franco forces depended on collaboration—and cooperation—between land and maritime commanders.[66] Contemporary joint military doctrine seeks to achieve "unity of effort" or "coordination and cooperation toward common objectives, even if the participants are not part of the same command or organization."[67] The key senior British commanders during the summer of 1781 included Lieutenant Generals Clinton and Cornwallis and Admirals Graves, Rodney, and Hood. Lacking unity of command, successful operations relied on unity of effort between geographically separated land and maritime forces to execute timely and coordinated decisions.[68] Over the years, historians concluded senior British leaders in the Western Hemisphere "were often as much absorbed in quarreling with one another as in fighting the enemy."[69] Unfortunately, for the British, the American-Franco forces operated more efficiently with a degree of unity of effort the British forces could not match; additionally, the British failed to effectively reinforce their vulnerable forces.

Conclusion

Today's national security leaders face challenges concerning the allocation of finite military resources—challenges that require clear policy and strategic guidance to ensure the employment of military force against priority challenges and threats.[70] These are not new problems for nations with global security interests. Lieutenant General Cornwallis's attack into Virginia was not synchronized with the intent of his immediate commander, Lieutenant General Clinton.[71] Clinton and Lord Germain were also of different minds on the conduct of the 1781 Yorktown Campaign. Once in Virginia, Cornwallis did not decisively engage military forces there or sufficiently damage the infrastructure supporting American Continental forces operating in the Carolinas, who worked in relative harmony with many partisans forces also operating there. The failure of strategic and operational-level military leaders to synchronize their thinking and activities concerning the employment of finite military resources contributed significantly to the failure of the British 1781 Yorktown Campaign.

The British efforts in Virginia were highly dependent on the support and mobility of the British Navy. The loss of control of the Chesapeake Bay resulting from the 5 September 1781 Battle of the Capes placed Cornwallis's land forces in a position from which there was little chance of escape. British land and maritime forces—operating from Canada to the Antilles—produced overextended lines of operation. The assumption that the British Navy would dominate the North American coast proved incorrect during this critical two-month period; British lines of operation became overextended. The timely and strategic approach taken by the Spanish forces in the Western Hemisphere contributed significantly to the success of the allies and Cornwallis's surrender. The British found themselves reacting to allied actions rather than setting the conditions for military success. Cornwallis's Virginia Campaign was a well-intentioned attack that turned into a siege and surrender that changed the course of the American Revolution and ultimately contributed to the recognition of the United States as an independent nation.

Notes

1. Franklin and Mary Wickwire, *Cornwallis: The Imperial Years* (Chapel Hill, NC: The University of North Carolina Press, 1980), 12–18. Perhaps the most important lesson Lieutenant General Cornwallis learned in North America was the value of one individual exercising both civil and military authority when managing a colony.

2. Chairman of the Joint Chiefs of Staff, *Joint Concept for Integrated Campaigning* (Washington, DC: 2018), v. The *Joint Concept for Integrated Campaigning* is an effort by the Chairman of the Joint Chiefs of Staff to "develop a methodology, with associated capabilities, that enables the Joint Force to collaborate and synchronize with interorganizational partners and conduct globally integrated operations to achieve acceptable and sustainable outcomes." From Chairman of the Joint Chiefs of Staff, Chairman of the Joint Chiefs of Staff Guide 3130, *Adaptative Planning and Execution Overview and Policy Framework* (Washington, DC: 2019), A-6: "Global Force Management (GFM) procedures allow proactive, resource- and risk-informed planning assumptions and estimates and execution decision-making regarding military forces."

3. Lt. Gen. Jene-Baptiste-Donatien de Vimeur, comte de Rochambeau, commanded the French Expeditionary Forces in America during the American Revolution. *The American Campaigns of Rochambeau's Army 1780, 1781, 1782, 1783*, vol. 1, trans and ed. Howard C. Rice and Anne S. K. Brown (Princeton, NJ: Princeton University Press, 1972), 323.

4. George Washington, *The Diaries of George Washington, 1748–1799*, ed. John C. Fitzpatrick (Boston: Houghton Mifflin Company, 1925, II, 208 and 217–18. General Washington kept no diary during most of the revolution unlike other periods in his life. This makes his 1 May to 5 November 1781 diary unique and particularly valuable for the study of the Yorktown Campaign. This diary is also important to researchers because these dates align almost perfectly with the Yorktown Campaign and provide insights into the mind of the commander that complement other primary source records. Washington opened his 1781 diary on 1 May and acknowledged that for a successful campaign he would need money, ships, and troops from France. Fortunately for Washington, the French provided all three. In his 21–22 May meeting with Lieutenant General Rochambeau, the two men set into motion a campaign design that would culminate with the defeat of a major British force at Yorktown in October. For more specifics on Washington's campaign design, see Patrick H. Hannum, "George Washington's 1781 Campaign Design Revealed," *Journal of the American Revolution,* 30 January 2018, https://allthingsliberty.com/2018/01/george-washingtons-1781-campaign-design-revealed/.

5. For a discussion of Lieutenant General Rochambeau's effort to create a functional American-Franco command and control structure, see Louis Gottschalk, *Lafayette and the Close of the American Revolution* (Chicago: University of Chicago Press, 1965), 96–97. For an analysis of the command and control structure during the Yorktown Campaign using contemporary doctrine,

see Patrick H. Hannum, "Command and Control During the Yorktown Campaign," *Journal of the American Revolution*, 18 May 2016, https://allthingsliberty.com/2016/05/command-and-control-during-the-yorktown-campaign/.

6. Because the American Revolution was a civil war, one must be clear in identifying participants and their military or political association. The term American Patriots or Whigs refers to the rebellious Americans who took up arms against the British government during the American Revolution. Loyalists or Tories supported the British government.

7. Andrew Jackson O'Shaughnessy, *An Empire Divided: The American Revolution in the British Caribbean* (Philadelphia: University of Pennsylvania Press, 2000), 213.

8. Donald J. Trump, *National Security Strategy of the United States of America* (Washington, DC: The White House, 2017), 25 and 27; and Jim Mattis, *Summary of the National Defense Strategy of the United States, Sharpening the Military's Competitive Edge* (Washington, DC: 2018), 2 and 5.

9. Larrie D. Fierro, *Brothers at Arms: American Independence and the Men of France and Spain Who Saved It* (New York: Alfred A. Knopf, 2016), 21–31, 36–74, and 75–116.

10. Andrew F. Krepinevich and Barry T. Watts, *Regaining Strategic Competence: Strategy for the Long Haul* (Washington, DC: Center for Strategy and Budgetary Assessments, 2009), 36, www.CSBAonline.org. The authors reference the work of Richard Rumelt, who postulates a weakness of strategy is failing to envision the competitive nature of strategic challenges.

11. O'Shaughnessy, *An Empire Divided,* 58.

12. O'Shaughnessy, 213–14 and 216–20.

13. Prior to the American Revolution, the position of British commander-in-chief of North America included the command of all land forces on the North American continent. During the revolution, the continent was split between a commander-in-chief America, responsible for West Florida to Nova Scotia—Lieutenant General Clinton's position—and a commander-in-chief Quebec, responsible for Canada minus Nova Scotia.

14. O'Shaughnessy, *An Empire Divided,* 169–70.

15. Ian Saberton, "Britain's Last Throw of the Dice Begins—The Charlestown Campaign of 1780," *Journal of the American Revolution*, 12 October 2020, https://allthingsliberty.com/2020/10/britains-last-throw-of-the-dice-begins-the-charlestown-campaign-of-1780/. Also see Chairman of the Joint Chiefs of Staff, Joint Publication (JP) 5-0, *Joint Planning* (Washington, DC: 2017), IV-39–40, for a discussion of Forces and Functions as elements of operational design.

16. William B. Willcox, *Portrait of a General: Sir Henry Clinton in the War of Independence* (New York: Alfred A. Knopf, 1962), 273.

17. There were sixteen British North American Colonies and ten Caribbean colonies. Only thirteen of the twenty-six colonies in the Western Hemisphere were in rebellion against the British government. In addition to the thirteen colonies in rebellion, North American British colonies included Canada and east and

west Florida. For more detail on the British Caribbean Colonies, see O'Shaughnessy, *An Empire Divided*. Paul H. Smith, *Loyalists and Red Coats: A Study in British Revolutionary Policy* (New York: W. W. Norton and Company), 82–99.

18. Smith, 82–99.

19. Piers Mackesy, *The War for America, 1775–1783* (Lincoln, NE: University of Nebraska Press, 1964), 258.

20. Mackesy, 257–59.

21. Walter Edgar, *Partisans & Redcoats* (New York: Harper Collins Publishers, 2001), 83–143. Between July 1780 and January 1781, there were at least twenty-four different engagements in South Carolina involving militia—creating an irregular environment where heavy British infantry formations designed for conventional operations had to adapt to unconventional backcountry warfare better suited to light infantry formations. To face the lighter more mobile Continental Infantry and militia operating under Major General Greene and his militia commanders, Lieutenant General Cornwallis burned his supplies and wagons, conducted an opposed nighttime river crossing on 1 February 1781, and began an unsuccessful pursuit of Greene across the state of North Carolina.

22. Chairman of the Joint Chiefs of Staff, JP 5-0, V-6–V-14.

23. For more details on the destruction of the largest city in Virginia in 1775–76, see Patrick H. Hannum, "Norfolk, Virginia Sacked by North Carolina and Virginia Troops," *Journal of the American Revolution*, 6 November 2017, https://allthingsliberty.com/2017/11/norfolk-virginia-sacked-north-carolina-virginia-troops/.

24. Krepinevich and Watts, *Regaining Strategic Competence*, 40–41. The authors reference the work of Richard Rumelt and his strategic premise that effective strategy must reflect an understanding of the adversary.

25. The Great War for Empire (1754–63) was a global conflict—also known as the Seven Years' War in Europe and the French and Indian War in North America. See Fred Anderson, *Crucible of War* (New York: Vintage Books, 2000) for a comprehensive contemporary study.

26. David Hackett Fisher, *Albion's Seed: Four British Folkways in North America* (New York: Oxford University Press, 1991), 826.

27. William Jennings Bryan and Francis Whiting Halsey, eds., "On Affairs in America, William Pitt, Earl of Chatham (1708–78), 1777," in *World's Famous Orations*—Great Britain (New York: Funk and Wagnalls, 1906), https://www.bartleby.com/268/3/24.html. A study of the 1758 Campaign in North America, designed under Pitt's guidance, reveals the complexities and tremendous resources associated with successful military operations in North America; Pitt understood this all too well. For a contemporary analysis of the Seven Years' War in North America, see Anderson, *Crucible of War*.

28. For a contemporary view of the importance of the human aspects of military operations, see Chairman of the Joint Chiefs of Staff, *Joint Concept for Human Aspects of Military Operations (JC-HAMO)* (Washington, DC: Chairman of the Joint Chiefs of Staff, 2016), 13–14. "Influencing the will and decisions of relevant actors" is one of the imperatives in warfare. This requires the

development of "a foundational understanding of the elements shaping human behavior," as well as understanding the broader operational environment.

29. Chairman of the Joint Chiefs of Staff, JP 5-0, I-2.

30. US Joint Chiefs of Staff, *Joint Concept for Integrated Campaigning* (Washington, DC: Joint Chiefs of Staff, 2018), v–vii. This document introduces the competition as a form of warfare and includes the concept of competition below the level of armed conflict.

31. Mackesy, *The War for America*, 13.

32. From Chairman of the Joint Chiefs of Staff, Joint Publication (JP) 1, *Doctrine for the Armed Forces of the United States* (Washington, DC: 2017), V-15: "Mission command is the conduct of military operations through decentralized execution based upon mission-type orders. It empowers individuals to exercise judgment in how they carry out their assigned tasks and it exploits the human element in joint operations, emphasizing trust, force of will, initiative, judgment, and creativity. Successful mission command demands that subordinate leaders at all echelons exercise disciplined initiative and act aggressively and independently to accomplish the mission. They focus their orders on the purpose of the operation rather than on the details of how to perform assigned tasks. They delegate decisions to subordinates wherever possible, which minimizes detailed control and empowers subordinates' initiative to make decisions based on understanding what the commander wants rather than on constant communications. Essential to mission command is the thorough understanding of the commander's intent at every level of command and a command climate of mutual trust and understanding."

33. Mackasey, *The War for America*, 56.

34. David Syrett, *The Royal Navy in European Waters During the American Revolutionary War* (Columbia, SC: University of South Carolina Press, 1988), 18–22; and Harold W. Larrabee, *Decision at the Chesapeake* (New York: Clarkson N. Potter, 1964), 41–43.

35. Willcox, *Portrait of a General*, xiii.

36. Willcox, 91. The lack of an overall joint commander to coordinate land and maritime operations surfaced early in the war and was a constant obstacle to British success.

37. The manifestation of these disconnects surfaced in two major military defeats for the British in North America: Saratoga in 1777 and Yorktown in 1781.

38. Willcox, *Portrait of a General*, xiii. During this period of the American Revolution, the British Navy maintained two geographic commands in the Western Hemisphere: the North American Station and the West Indian Station.

39. William B. Willcox, "The British Road to Yorktown: A Study in Divided Command," *American Historical Review* (October 1946): LII, 1, 3.

40. Mark M. Boatner III, ed., *Encyclopedia of the American Revolution* (Mechanicsville, PA: Stackpole Books, 1994), s.v. "Clinton-Cornwallis Controversy;" and Henry Clinton, Benjamin and Franklin Stevens, eds., *The Clinton-Cornwallis Controversy*, 2 vols. (London: B. F. Stevens, 1888).

41. Ian Saberton, "The Decision that Lost Britain the War: An Enigma Now Resolved," *Journal of the American Revolution*, 28 January 2019, https://allthingsliberty.com/2019/01/the-decision-that-lost-britain-the-war-an-enigma-now-resolved/.

42. Ian Saberton, "The Aborted Virginia Campaign and Its Aftermath, May to August 1781," *Journal of the American Revolution*, 23 November 2020, https://allthingsliberty.com/2020/11/the-aborted-virginia-campaign-and-its-aftermath-may-to-august-1781/.

43. Henry Clinton, *The American Rebellion*, ed. William B. Willcox (New Haven, CT: Yale University Press, 1954), 222.

44. Willcox, *Portrait of a General*, x and xiii.

45. Anderson, *Crucible of War*, 777, n1.

46. Smith, *Loyalists and Red Coats*, 94–95.

47. Charles Lee Lewis, *Admiral de Grasse and American Independence* (Annapolis, MD: Naval Institute Press, 1945), 117–55.

48. From Willcox, *The British Road to Yorktown*, 35: "Out of the sea came the force which" defeated Cornwallis.

49. From Chairman of the Joint Chiefs of Staff, JP 5-0, IV-26–28: "A decisive point is a geographic place, specific key event, critical factor, or a function that, when acted upon, allows a commander to gain a marked advantage over an enemy or contributes materially to achieving success."

50. Thomas Graves, *The Graves Papers and Other Documents Relating to the Naval Operations of the Yorktown Campaign, July to October 1781*, ed. French Ensor Chadwick (New York: Printed for the Naval History Society of New York by the De Vinne Press, 1916) 65–66 and 83–84.

51. De Barras and de Grasse held two separate commands. De Barras commanded the smaller of the two French fleets based out of Newport, Rhode Island, and de Grasse commanded the larger of the two fleets with primary responsibility for protecting France's interests and engaging the British fleet in the Caribbean; at the time of the Yorktown Campaign, de Grasse used Haiti as his base of operations.

52. Don Francisco Saavedra de Sangronis, *The Journal of Don Francisco Saavedra de Sangronis 1780–1786*, ed. Francisco Morales Padron and trans. Aileen Moore Topping (Gainesville, FL: University of Florida Press, 1989), 192–212.

53. The thirty-six ships of the line represented the combined French fleets of de Barras and de Grasse.

54. Clinton, *The American Rebellion*, 570, 573, 576–77, and 579–81.

55. British redoubts 9 and 10 protected the eastern flank of the British defensive position at Yorktown. A combined American-Franco assault overran the positions on the evening of 14 October 1781, forcing Lieutenant General Cornwallis to request a secession of hostilities on the 17th to work out surrender terms. His formal surrender took place on 19 October 1781. For one of the more detailed and scholarly analyses of the Yorktown battlefield and associated

events, see Jerome A. Greene, *The Guns of Independence* (New York: Savas Beatie, 2005).

56. O'Shaughnessy, *An Empire Divided*, 231–32.

57. Chairman of the Joint Chiefs of Staff, JP 5-0, IV-28–V-30. Lines of operation generally possess a physical orientation while lines of effort tend to be functional.

58. Chairman of the Joint Chiefs of Staff, IV 28–IV-34; and Antoine-Henri Jomini, *Treatise on Grand Military Operations: Or A Critical and Military History of the Wars of Frederick the Great as Contrasted with the Modern System*, trans. Col. S. B. Holabird (New York: D. van Nostrand, 1865), 2, 9–13, http://www.memory.loc.gov/service/gdc/scd0001/2010/20100414001tr/20100414001tr.pdf.

59. Many incorrectly refer to the German troops as mercenaries. The term "Auxiliary" best describes them. Today they would be more like contract troops from a nation-state offered to a coalition. Loyal provincial force consisted of American Loyalists formed for service to augment the regular British Army. Because the American Revolution was a civil war, Americans fought on both sides. It is incorrect to refer to the Patriot forces as Americans because there were Americans on both sides.

60. Willcox, *Portrait of a General*, 91. Movement and maneuver is one of the seven joint functions outlined in contemporary joint military doctrine, defined as supporting "the disposition of joint forces to conduct operations by securing positional advantages before or during combat operations and by exploiting tactical success to achieve operational and strategic objectives." See Chairman of the Joint Chiefs of Staff, Joint Publication (JP) 3-0, *Operations* (Washington, DC: Joint Chiefs of Staff, 2017), III-37–39.

61. Kathleen DuVal, *Independence Lost: Lives on the Edge of the American Revolution* (New York: Random House, 2016), 215.

62. Saavedra, *The Journal of Don Francisco Saavedra de Sangronis*, xxii–xxiv. Saavedra was a fourth-grade diplomatic official in the Ministry of the Indies; today we might consider him a special envoy. Don Jose de Galvez was one of several members of the Galvez family who held important political and military positions in the Spanish government during this period. The Ministry of the Indies had responsibility for diplomacy in the Western Hemisphere. Galvez selected Saavedra as his representative and instructed him to coordinate Spanish military activities in the hemisphere with the French force operating there—a task that Saavedra accomplished effectively.

63. Saavedra, 192 and 201–2.

64. For a contemporary and detailed discussion of the maneuver of Patriot forces under command of General Lafayette and British forces of Lieutenant General Cornwallis in Virginia during the summer of 1781, see John R. Maass, *The Road to Yorktown* (Charleston, SC: The History Press, 2015).

65. Saavedra, *The Journal of Don Francisco Saavedra de Sangronis*, 202.

66. Willcox, *Portrait of a General*, 91.

67. *Department of Defense Dictionary of Military and Associated Terms,* June 2020, 225, https://www.jcs.mil/Portals/36/Documents/Doctrine/pubs/dictionary.pdf?ver=2020-06-18-073638-727.

68. *Department of Defense Dictionary of Military and Associated Terms.* Unity of command is defined as "the operation of all forces under a single responsible commander."

69. Willcox, *Portrait of a General,* xii.

70. Chairman of the Joint Chiefs of Staff, *Joint Concept for Integrated,* v; and Chairman of the Joint Chiefs of Staff, Chairman of the Joint Chiefs of Staff Guide 3130, A-6.

71. On the importance of a contemporary view of "commander's intent" from a strategic leader, see Jim Mattis and Bing West, *Call Sign Chaos* (New York: Random House, 2019), 44.

Chapter 15

Disaster on the Scheldt, 1809: A British Defeat in Holland

Jason D. Lancaster

Britain's 1809 expedition to the Scheldt Estuary was an avoidable disaster. After successful expeditions on the European periphery, Britain overestimated its ability to project power onto the European Continent. The consequences of the campaign did not equal the financial and human cost of the campaign or the results achieved by Great Britain. The failed campaign cost 10 million British pounds (almost 1 billion US dollars in today's currency) and 15,000 British casualties.[1] During deployments to the Iberian Peninsula, British soldiers who had fought in the campaign were less resistant to campaign ardors than other troops. Political disputes between rival cabinet ministers over the failed campaign resulted in a duel between the Secretary of State for War and the Foreign Minister. Britain partially achieved one campaign objective, reducing Dutch shipbuilding capabilities in Flushing until 1812. Dutch consequences were also significant. Severe bombardment by the British force essentially destroyed the Dutch city of Flushing. French military leader Napoleon Bonaparte considered the Dutch response to the attack insufficient. He was disappointed in his brother Louis Bonaparte's performance as King of Holland and thought he had become too Dutch. In November 1810, Napoleon incorporated the Kingdom of Holland into France.

The French Revolution and Napoleonic Wars had engulfed Europe and its colonial empires since 1793. By 1809, France's borders extended from the Niemen River on the Russian border to Portugal. On the Iberian Peninsula, a small British army was in Portugal, and another British army had retreated from Salamanca to La Coruna, Spain, and been evacuated by sea. Meanwhile, French forces fought Spanish and Portuguese guerrillas across the Iberian Peninsula. In central Europe, Austria prepared to fight the French again, and would defeat the French at Aspern-Essling in May then lose to France at Wagram in July. Following Wagram, the Austrians signed an armistice and negotiated a peace treaty with the French.

France occupied the Netherlands, and Napoleon hoped to exploit Dutch shipyards in his continued quest to wrest sea control from Great Britain. Antwerp was the third largest port and dockyard complex in the French Empire—capable of both building a fleet and protecting it. Antwerp was a vital cog in the French naval machine, situated more than forty miles up the Scheldt River from the North Sea. The city was protected by a series of islands at the mouth of the river and numerous batteries and fortifications along the river. The Scheldt River Estuary was a maze of islands, shoals, and narrow channels. The main islands included Walcheren with the major port city of Flushing, North and South Beveland, and Schouen. Walcheren was on the North Sea. The mouth of the Scheldt River contained navigational hazards including shallow waters, currents, and ever-shifting sandbanks that required expert local knowledge to ascend the river to Antwerp.

Sea control was the British government's highest priority. British security depended on sea control. British trade subsidized allies like Austria, Portugal, and Spain in their wars against Napoleon. In 1801 and 1807, Britain attacked neutral Denmark to prevent its fleet from falling into French hands. The Scheldt River Estuary was in a French satellite state ruled by Napoleon's brother Louis. Britain considered a French fleet in the Scheldt—only eighty-seven nautical miles from Dover—a threat. The British government resolved to launch an expedition to seize ships, destroy shipyards, and explore the possibility of capturing Antwerp.

The planning, size, timing, and leadership of the expedition meant there was little likelihood of success. The British expedition was both too large and too small to succeed. More than 40,000 troops embarked in 616 ships was too large for a rapid assault up the difficult-to-navigate Scheldt River to seize Antwerp. In addition to the navigational complication presented by the fleet's size, it took Britain six months to assemble that force. Though too large for a rapid assault, the force was too small for a methodical invasion of the continent. At the battle of Wagram, 172,000 French, Saxon, and Italian troops battled 136,000 Austrian soldiers; each side sustained roughly the same number of casualties as the size of the British Expeditionary Force.

Lord Castlereagh, British Secretary of State for War, planned the Walcheren Expedition, and the British cabinet approved it, retaining the authority to end the campaign and evacuate captured territory. The proximity of Walcheren to London played a role in limiting the on-scene commander's authority. Unlike the British evacuation at La Coruna, Spain, the decision to evacuate and end the campaign was a political decision held at cabinet.[2] The commander of the expedition, Lord Chatham, had authority to expand the campaign or hold Walcheren but did not have the authority to end the campaign and evacuate. Castlereagh's plans contained branch plans for the army to maintain positions at Antwerp or Walcheren or ex-

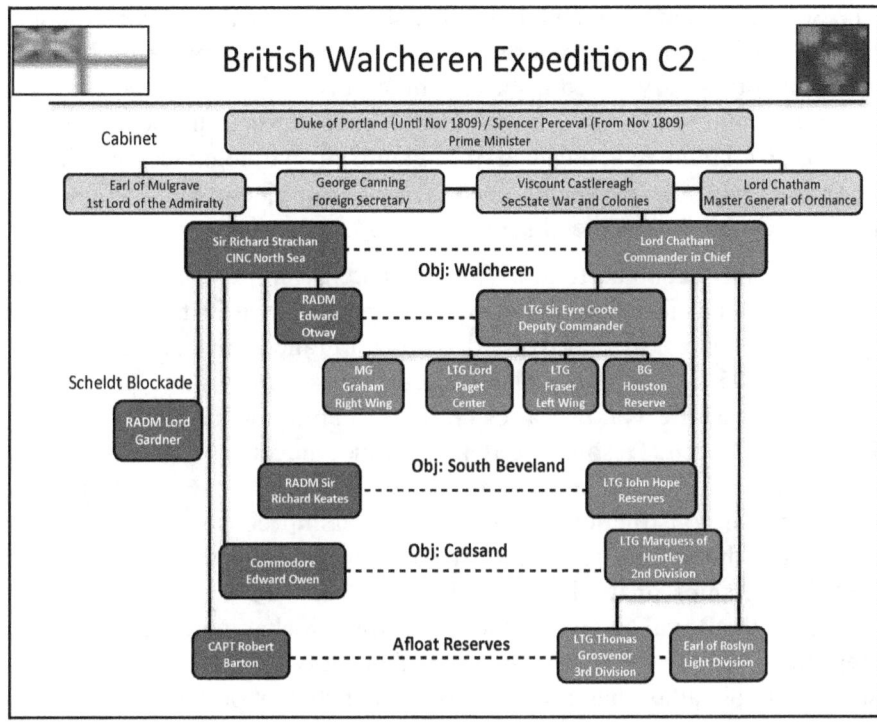

Figure 15.1. British Walcheren Expedition Command and Control. Created by the author.

pand the campaign into Germany. Lord Chatham could land at Walcheren and attack Antwerp or march into Germany, but he could not abandon Walcheren without permission. Maintaining a position at Walcheren was a military decision that Lord Chatham could make; however, the decision to evacuate Walcheren was a political decision. The delay of the decision to retreat resulted in rampant disease within the British army.

The campaign for Antwerp ended 27 August 1809, and the last British troops left Walcheren on 23 December 1809. The delay demonstrated not only the danger of delaying the decision to retreat in the face of defeat, but the danger to military forces during government administration changes. Two months after the last soldiers evacuated Walcheren, 37 percent of the force had become casualties: 4,000 soldiers had died of disease and 11,000 were still mustered as sick.[3]

Why Walcheren?

From 1793 to 1809, Great Britain conducted four campaigns in the Netherlands to protect the Netherlands or eliminate the French naval threat.

The Scheldt Estuary contained multiple shipyards capable of constructing large warships. Antwerp was the second-largest naval arsenal in France. The Scheldt Estuary posed a serious threat, because ships could threaten London within twenty-four hours. Napoleon described the Scheldt as "a cocked pistol pointed at the head of England."[4] Its strategic location meant that throughout the eighteenth century, Britain frequently campaigned in the Low Countries to defend itself.

Sea control enabled trade. Without trade, Britain could not subsidize its allies, fund its forces, or maintain its economy. Great Britain established general sea control by decisively defeating a Franco-Spanish fleet at Trafalgar in 1805. The British captured twenty-one of thirty-three ships in the Franco-Spanish fleet and, as a result, fears of an immediate cross-channel invasion subsided. Despite the defeat, France never stopped attempting to gain temporary local sea control in the English Channel. Additionally, French naval construction never ceased. Warship construction occurred throughout the empire from Antwerp to Venice. Bonaparte believed that 150 French ships of the line would force Britain to make peace.[5] After Trafalgar, the Royal Navy stretched itself thin blockading ports from Antwerp to Venice. The Royal Navy blockaded every port where France constructed ships rather than risk that completed ships would escape. France augmented its domestic fleet with foreign fleets like the Dutch, and ships constructed in occupied ports.

Britain would go to great lengths to prevent the expansion of the French Navy, preserve British control of the seas, and achieve victory. In 1801 and 1807, Britain attacked Denmark to prevent France from seizing the Danish fleet. In 1808, Britain helped the Portuguese royal family and their fleet escape to Brazil to avoid capture by the French. Historian Richard Glover calculated that seizing the Danish fleet and supporting the evacuation of the Portuguese Royal Family prevented fifty Danish, Portuguese, Swedish, and Russian ships of the line from falling into Napoleon's hands.[6]

Perceived Franco-Dutch weakness, the potential to seize French ships and eliminate the French invasion threat, and the campaign's projected cheapness were major points in support of the Scheldt Campaign. In 1809, Britain had troops available for a campaign with limitations. The exchequer could not fund another distant expedition. The four campaign options were northern Germany, the Scheldt, Portugal, or Italy.[7] Austrian diplomat Prince Starhemberg lobbied for a British landing in northern Germany to distract Napoleon from a campaign against Austria in the Danube River Valley. British reinforcements to Portugal or Sicily could have improved offensive capabilities in the Mediterranean, except the exchequer did not believe they were affordable options. Britain's decision to attack the Scheldt was partially strategic and partially budget-driven, but reinforcing the Duke of Wellington's small army in Portugal would have improved his position on the peninsula. One of the invasion consequences was that the Duke of Wellington's position was more precarious than it would have been with an additional 30,000 troops. Even after winning the 1809 battle of Talavera, he had to return to Portugal for lack of support in Spain.

Seizing the ships with land forces and destroying the shipyards required a balance of force and speed. A smaller force could move faster but might not be able to achieve all the objectives and was vulnerable a larger French force. The larger the force, the longer it took to organize and move but the greater the likelihood of success. British success in the 1807 amphibious operation to capture the Danish fleet at Copenhagen encouraged the cabinet to consider an amphibious descent on the Scheldt. The difference between Copenhagen and the Scheldt was that Copenhagen was far from metropolitan France; Copenhagen was located on an island removed from the rest of the country. The Scheldt Estuary combined multiple islands with proximity to France.

Secretary of State for War and the Colonies Robert Stewart, Viscount Castlereagh, planned the Scheldt Expedition for the British government. Previously, he had proposed attacks on the Scheldt in 1805, 1807, and again in 1809. Castlereagh envisioned a *coup de main*, a sudden attack with two objectives: support Austria with a diversion on Napoleon's flank and eliminate Antwerp's naval threat.

Austria joined the Fifth Coalition on 24 April 1809, although its troops attacked French ally Bavaria on 9 April. Austria had coordinated with the British for a diversion in north Germany or the Netherlands. Because Napoleon was concerned about the state of Dutch defenses, a diversion prior to Austria's campaign could have forced him to leave more troops in Holland. Unfortunately, the time required to form the British expedition meant that British force landed at Walcheren three weeks after defeat at Wagram ended the campaign in Austria.[8]

Eliminating the naval threat in the Scheldt River Estuary entailed three sub-objectives: capturing warships, destroying dockyard facilities at Flushing and Antwerp, and rendering the Scheldt unnavigable. Achieving one or two of the objectives would temporarily relieve the threat to Great Britain but would not completely remove it. Accomplishing all three would eliminate the threat for at least a decade.

Analyzing Intelligence to Prepare for Operations

Today's US Joint Publication (JP) 2.0, *Joint Intelligence*, defines the Joint Intelligence Preparation of the Operational Environment (JIPOE) as "the continuous process through which J-2 manages the analysis and development of products that help the commander and staff understand the complex and interconnected Operating Environment.[9] The J-2 analyzes input from intelligence planners and other staff directorates, including medical and engineering, to create a coherent picture of the area the force will operate in, including the physical environment, the medical environment, the political-social environment, enemy order of battle, and courses of action.[10] The resulting nuanced understanding of where the force will operate helps operation planners predict required force levels and logistics support to those forces.[11]

Modern staffs have multiple people to gather and fuse this data together, but Lord Castlereagh conducted his analysis independently. He received updated intelligence on the area from multiple sources: details about blockading ships via the Admiralty, diplomatic reports, and private reports from smugglers who provided intelligence to both sides for money or licenses to smuggle. Despite years of planning, the expedition sailed without a clear picture of the situation in most portions of the JIPOE. The expedition lacked a clear understanding of the physical environment on land and sea as well as medical risks to the force, and a false view of the political-social environment ashore. Significantly, the enemy order of battle and courses of action were woefully inaccurate.

Both on land and at sea, the expedition lacked a clear picture of the theater's terrain. Despite a continuous blockade of the Dutch coast and four amphibious operations over twenty years of war, the Royal Navy still lacked accurate charts of the Scheldt Estuary. Maneuvering a fleet of 600 sailing ships is complex; without adequate charts of a dangerous littoral and pilots, the task was exponentially more difficult.

Scheldt is the Dutch word for shallow, a name that accurately reflects the hydrography of the river and estuary. The North Sea and Scheldt River are full of shifting sandbanks. Adm. Sir Richard Strachan told the First Lord of the Admiralty, Henry Phipps, Earl of Mulgrave, that he had no knowledge of the navigation of the Scheldt. The First Lord told Sir Richard to rely on Capt. Sir Home Popham, a subordinate familiar with the area and amphibious operations.[12] Amphibious operations require specific beach conditions for putting troops ashore. Several times planned landing locations proved unfeasible due to conditions on the beaches. These failed landings and delays slowed the campaign, allowing French forces to increase their size and build fortifications.

Additionally, disease caused 15,000 casualties to the 40,000-strong British force. Lord Castlereagh did not consult the Army Sick Board, which was responsible for medical planning. Britain had already conducted three campaigns in the Netherlands since 1793, and plenty of professionals understood risks inherent with the climate. The medical men would have told Castlereagh that August and September were the sickly season on Walcheren. They also would have sent more medical personnel and medical supplies.

The expedition sailed with 95 percent of its surgeons but only 50 percent of its hospital corpsmen. The timing of the campaign during the sickly season and the understaffing of medical personnel exacerbated the disease impact. During the Lord Commissioner's 23 January 1810 speech, Adm. John Jervis, Lord St. Vincent, hero of the battle of St Vincent and former First Naval Lord, commented that the sickly season on Walcheren was well-known. The climate during that time is so unhealthy that Swiss mercenaries in the Dutch army contractually refuse to serve there.[13]

Further, Lord Castlereagh's planning in the political, economic, and social realms was incorrect. Dutch involvement in the war was an economic disaster. The Netherlands lost its overseas colonies and eventually its role as a neutral shipper to belligerent nations. Britain conquered many Dutch colonies: Ceylon (1796), St Maarten (1801), St. Eustatius (1801), Surinam (1799 and 1804), and South Africa (1795 and 1806). The loss of colonies impacted employment rates and production in the Netherlands, resulting in recession and unemployment. Nevertheless, the Dutch resisted the British attack on their homeland.

The Netherlands had always relied on trade. The British blockade and the French Continental System drastically reduced Dutch overseas commercial opportunities. The announcement of Napoleon's Continental System banning trade with Britain was devastating for Dutch commerce. Merchant ship arrivals in Amsterdam fell from 1,349 in 1806 to 310 in 1809.[14] The loss of colonial trade and commercial opportunities caused economic disruption. Because trade with Britain was crucial, smuggling was the only way to sustain Holland's economy.[15] To help clamp down on smuggling, Napoleon crowned his brother Louis King of Holland in 1806. Napoleon expected his brother to strictly enforce the continental blockade.

Although the Dutch were not enthusiastic about Louis, they preferred independence and Louis to French annexation. Louis worked to protect the Dutch economy from the deprivations of war.

Based on intelligence reports, the British assumed the Dutch would be reluctant to fight them because of economic challenges resulting from the blockade. Despite the hardships, the Dutch did not want British interference. The British expected to be hailed as liberators but, instead, met stubborn resistance during the siege of Flushing. Although the Dutch wanted their trade restored and economic prosperity, they valued their independence more. Instead of being welcomed as they anticipated, the British faced fierce resistance and delaying actions, which slowed their advance and bought time for French reinforcements to arrive.

Although, initial British estimates of local Franco-Dutch strength were accurate, Castlereagh miscalculated how quickly France would reinforce the Scheldt River Estuary. Britain gathered intelligence in the Netherlands from several sources, including reports from smugglers, fishermen, secret agents, correspondents, and newspapers. Different British agencies received different reports from different sources. Britain had several highly stove-piped intelligence organizations that sometimes shared information. Castlereagh did not share his private smuggler intelligence with the senior officers he consulted while planning the expedition.

In March 1809, Castlereagh's intelligence reported the number of troops in the Scheldt Estuary was less than 9,000. Throughout the planning phase, Castlereagh received reports of Franco-Dutch troop departures. These numbers were accurate. Napoleon denuded coastal defenses to concentrate his army along the Danube for war against Austria.[16] Castlereagh's intelligence on Antwerp's naval strength was second-hand from Dutch fishermen and smugglers. They reported twelve ships of the line in the Scheldt and more under construction; this was four more than the number of British ships blockading the Scheldt. The threat of the French fleet escaping was a constant.

With French forces concentrated on the Danube and the Iberian Peninsula, Castlereagh expected that a rapid assault up the river would prevent the French and Dutch from reinforcing the area before Britain accomplished its objectives. British generals feared that delaying the assault could enable the French to rush reinforcements to the region.

Modern planning doctrine is a formulaic and repeatable process. This repeatability helps planners ensure they do not forget key pieces of information. Since Lord Castlereagh conducted most of the planning himself without modern planning doctrine, he overlooked key intelligence planning elements. These oversights compromised the expedition from the start. Lack of reliable intelligence on beaches resulted in delayed and canceled amphibious landings, which resulted in plan alterations. Lack of proper medical planning doomed thousands of soldiers to death and disease. The effects of the compromised intelligence plan reverberated through the rest of the campaign.

Planning the Expedition

The seeds of defeat were sown during the expedition's planning phase. Castlereagh conducted most of the planning alone. A quality JIPOE creates the conditions for successful planning. Since Castlereagh's intelligence was flawed, those flaws carried through the planning phase—errors that were compounded through the planning and execution phases of the operation.

The French campaign in the Danube Valley had denuded Holland of troops. The small number of French and Dutch troops in the Scheldt Estuary made the ships a tempting target; however, the size of the British expedition made a rapid assault almost impossible. Castlereagh's initial plan was complex and required multiple simultaneous landings, but the British force did not have sufficient landing craft to execute multiple simultaneous landings. Scholars debate whether the campaign ever could have succeeded. Late nineteenth-century/early twentieth-century scholar John Fortescue, author of the thirteen-volume *History of the British Army*, wrote: "The British force was sent upon an errand in which success was at best precarious and practically impossible".[17] Professor Gordon Bond, author of *The Grand Expedition*, said that the campaign could have succeeded with better weather and aggressive leadership—boldly advancing to Antwerp before France could organize its defense.[18] Fortescue's argument that there was little likelihood of success resonates. The complexity of coordinated simultaneous landings beyond the line of sight without radio communications or sufficient landing craft significantly reduced the likelihood of operational success. This complex operation would have challenged the amphibious warfare experts of the Second World War like Adm. Richmond Kelly Turner.

Nine days after Castlereagh received reports that French troops in Zeeland had departed, Sir Henry Dundas, Commander in Chief of the Army, attended a cabinet meeting where Castlereagh asked for 15,000 troops for an immediate assault on the Scheldt. Sir Henry stated that such a force did not exist. Most regular forces in Great Britain had recently returned from Spain and were not ready for a new campaign.[19] Sir John Moore's army of 33,000 had sustained 21-percent casualties during the retreat from Salamanca to Coruna and required reconstitution after its disastrous winter retreat.[20]

In May, Castlereagh consulted a host of high-ranking British officers, including the Chief of the Army and two generals who would participate in the expedition. These men generally agreed that the best approach would be to simultaneously capture the islands of Walcheren, South Beveland, and Cadsand to protect passage up the Scheldt, then disembark at Sandvliet, which was twenty miles from Antwerp. Though the officers agreed this was the best approach, they considered the expedition "a desperate enterprise" and doubted its success.[21] Few eighteenth-century amphibious operations used more than one landing beach. In contrast, Castlereagh's plan was to land on four separate beaches simultaneously—a highly complex undertaking since the beaches had different times for high tides and were not visible from each other. In discussions with the Earl Mulgrave, Sir Strachan predicted the troops would seize Flushing on Walcheren Island but achieve nothing else.[22] The complexity of the landings and the

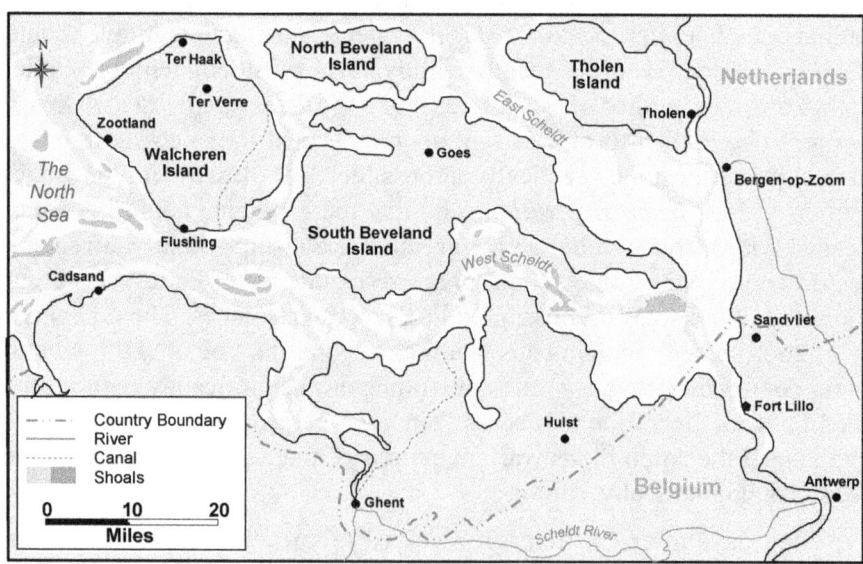

Figure 15.2. Map of the Scheldt Estuary. Created by Army University Press.

slow pace of large bodies of sailing ships in unknown waters would preclude the "coup de main" plan.

During the first week of June, Castlereagh learned about the Austrian victory at Aspern-Essling. News of this victory encouraged Castlereagh to move forward with the expedition to support Austria on the continent. He persuaded the cabinet to attack Antwerp and eliminate the Scheldt naval threat. Cabinet approval had "a propendering influence with His Majesty's Government in the consideration of the question."[23] After receiving royal approval in June, Castlereagh made his final preparations then began the campaign six weeks later.

On 18 June 1809, Castlereagh wrote to Sir Dundas requesting 35,000 infantrymen and 1,800 cavalry to be prepared for immediate embarkation and transport to the Scheldt.[24] The scope of planning was immense: 352 transport ships had to be procured. During the parliamentary inquiry following the expedition, Sir Rupert George testified that the difficulty of acquiring vessels was probably due to an overall "scarcity of vessels."[25] In early June 1809, Sir Home Popham, one of the lead Royal Navy planners, was also concerned about the shortage of vessels for the expedition.[26] It took months to charter the ships required for the expedition. The demand for transports was so high that it drastically increased the lease rate. The final cavalry transports didn't arrive from Portugal until 15 July. During the Lord Commissioner's speech, Lord St. Vincent stated that the expected war between Austria and France was predictable in 1808, and the expedition should have been planned to complement that war.[27]

Knowing his desired size of force and the time it would take to procure troops and transports, Lord Castlereagh should have begun organizing troops and transports far earlier, even though there were no troops available until June. Because of the difficulty raising sufficient troops and transports, the objective to provide a continental diversion in support of the Austrian campaign on the Danube was moot. The expedition did not sail from England until after an armistice between France and Austria had already been signed.

Once delays in finding troops and transports were solved and troops moved to embark, the next problem was that of weather. Sir Home Popham frequently wrote to Castlereagh concerning bad weather's impact on the campaign. Continued delays increased risks of bad weather and increased the risk that the expedition's destination would be exposed, increasing the possibility of French reinforcements.

The Master General of the Ordnance, General John Pitt, Earl of Chatham, was appointed to command the army. As Commander in Chief, North Sea, Sir Strachan commanded the naval force. Chatham's initial organization divided the army into four separate units—one for each landing. This organization supported Castlereagh's original plan: a rapid multi-prong assault capturing Cadsand and South Beveland while isolating Flushing; this would enable the fleet to ascend the West Scheldt River—landing at Sandvliet—then attack Antwerp, capture the ships, destroy the dockyards, and finally decide whether to remain or return to England.

The Amphibious Assault

On 28 and 29 July, the British fleet set sail for the Dutch coast. Lord Chatham had a rough sketch of where his forces would land; however, there was no plan beyond the initial landings and objectives. A French general stated: "If the British would have advanced rapidly . . . they would have found the forces and defenses of the Scheldt unprepared."[28] Instead, the British force slowed down to deal with problems encountered during the campaign.

This shifting of responsibility and understanding of landing force requirements reinforce the importance of good relations between landing force and naval force commanders. Modern amphibious doctrine places the admiral in charge of the fleet in charge of the landings; only after the landing force commander has established himself ashore does the role reverse. At Walcheren, Sir Richard also maintained responsibility for the landings until the force established itself ashore. Landing a force is a balance of distance to the objective and suitable beaches. Success in the desperate British enterprise required rapid execution of four landings spread over 700 square miles with no ability to communicate with each force. As the campaign unfolded, weather, poor communications, lack of intelligence on French strength, and insufficient landing craft disrupted the plan. Simultaneous landings became sequenced landings.[29]

Essentially, landing craft shortages ruined the plan. At Walcheren, the Navy could not conduct two dispersed landings of sufficient size. The navy could land 3,000 men at Zoutland and 1,100 at Ter Haak, but the second wave would land 90 minutes after the first wave at Ter Haak. Uncertainty about French strength caused reluctance to land so few men at once. Sir Richard suggested a single landing site would enable the landing of 4,000 men. Because of bad weather and beach surf at Zoutland, Ter Haak would be the single landing beach—the farthest point from Flushing on Walcheren. British troops would have to capture Fort Ter Haak and the fortified city of Ter Veere before advancing across the island to lay siege to Flushing. This branch plan would have required the force laying siege to Flushing to capture two other fortified areas during the twelve-mile march to Flushing instead of immediately beginning the siege.

Sir Richard suggested Sir John Hope's army remain in Roompots Bay until Sir Eyre Coote's forces captured Ter Veere. At this point, the simultaneous landings became sequenced landings, as the force gradually advanced toward Antwerp. Lord Chatham was not present but concurred with the alterations.[30] Although Ter Haak fell rapidly, Ter Veere's defenders delayed the British for two days. Sir Coote's organic nine-pounder field artillery proved insufficient to breach the walls of Ter Veere. The Royal Navy landed heavier twenty-four-pounders from a ship and deployed gunboats earmarked to support Lt. Gen. John Hope's descent on South Beveland to bombard Ter Haak. Artillery fire from the gunboats was effective until wind and tide forced them off station. Sir Strachan attributed Ter Veere's capitulation to the captain of *Caesar* and his direction of the naval battery's heavy guns landed to bombard the city.[31] British forces captured Middleburg without a fight then began the siege of Flushing several days behind schedule.

No landing occurred on Cadsand. Because of bad weather, lack of landing craft, and sizeable French forces, Lord Huntley had to cancel the landings. From 30 July until 4 August, his force remained afloat off Cadsand as Huntley desperately tried to correspond with Lord Chatham. On 4 August, the force proceeded to Roompots Bay. With French and Dutch batteries controlling the West Scheldt, the British fleet would not risk transports running the batteries under sail. As a result, Flushing could not be isolated. French reinforcements flowed into the city, prolonging the siege and delaying the descent on Antwerp.[32]

Sir Richard Keats seized 150 local Dutch sailboats to transport General Hope's force to South Beveland. Weather delayed the navy's ability to transfer the army to the small boats, costing two days. The small boat fleet proceeded up the East Scheldt on 1 August. Unfamiliar with the channel, the Navy rushed to take soundings in advance of the force. Despite their best efforts, many ships ran aground during the ascent, luckily with no major damage.

General Hope's forces opened the route to Antwerp after they landed without incident on South Beveland. The city of Goes surrendered without a fight and the French evacuated Fort Batz on 2 August. South Beveland was in British hands. Napoleon condemned the French commander of Fort Batz for withdrawing without a fight. From South Beveland, British officers could observe the French fleet withdrawing upriver beyond Fort Lillo's protection.[33]

Lord Chatham and Sir Richard met on the 1st and 6th of August to discuss the campaign. Fortescue argued that Sir Richard's navigational concerns prevented the ascent of the Scheldt.[34] Strachan's biographer noted that Sir Richard proposed leaving the siege of Flushing to 10,000 men, ascending the river with the remainder, and landing either directly across from Antwerp at Tete de Flanders or Slough, about thirty-five miles from Antwerp. In the end, Lord Chatham responded, "We had better wait."[35] The spirit of the garrison at Ter Veere caught the British by surprise, as did the resistance at Flushing. The 6 August conference confirmed the resequencing of the campaigns; Flushing would fall before the assault on Antwerp.

The consequences of Castlereagh's poor JIPOE demonstrated Prussian military theorist Carl von Clausewitz's friction and fog of war. A combination of bad weather and unknown enemy troop numbers prompted the cancellation of one landing. Because of a landing craft shortage, planners merged two landings into one. Unexpectedly strong Dutch resistance at Ter Haak and Flushing spooked the British into caution. These difficulties caused Lord Chatham to sequence landings and focus on capturing one individual objective at a time. Instead of a rapid ascent and coup de main in Antwerp, the British adopted a methodical sequenced advance. These delays gave the French time to receive reinforcements, reorganize, and respond.

French Reinforcements and British Culmination

Louis requested Napoleon send a French marshal to supervise the defense. Louis arrived in Antwerp on 3 August and took command of 7,000 troops throughout the region. Louis expected the commander of Fort Batz would buy time for him to organize a defense; instead, the commander abandoned Fort Batz.[36] In Paris, Minister of Police Joseph Fouche called out 60,000 National Guard soldiers. Fortescue asserted that Fouche raised forces to fight the British but also prepared to seize power in the event of a British victory.[37]

The siege of Flushing was brutal. The British bombardment of Flushing used 100 guns and rockets. This bombardment left nearly every house roofless; fires started by rockets destroyed houses.[38] Despite the destruction, the garrison held out, defying the British. On 10 August, the Flushing garrison cut the dikes of Walcheren, flooding the surrounding countryside. The garrison of Flushing hoped that the flood would break the British siege, but it continued. Although Flushing capitulated on 15 August, the flooding combined with the destruction of the town, led to sickness in the British ranks.

Napoleon sent Marshal Jean Baptiste Bernadotte to Antwerp; he arrived on 15 August. Marshall Bernadotte found 35,000 National Guard and other soldiers in Antwerp, with more arriving daily—most of them untrained. Bernadotte dedicated himself to training, organizing, and improving the region's defenses.[39]

With Flushing finally in British hands, Lord Chatham decided to advance on Antwerp via South Beveland. Lieutenant General Fraser remained at Flushing while the remainder of Sir Coote's force crossed to South Beveland. Hampered by lack of transports, the infantry crossing took three days; weather delayed the artillery and supplies even longer.[40] On 23 and 24 August, the Royal Navy probed the Antwerp defenses, bombarding outlying batteries, but the defenses were stronger than expected.

Heavily damaged Flushing—surrounded by flooded fields—was a poor location for billeting a garrison. Crowded, damp, and damaged buildings increased the spread of disease. The first cases of what became known as Walcheren Fever were reported on 19 August on South Beveland and 22 August on Walcheren. Doctors today believe Walcheren Fever was actually several diseases: malaria, typhus, and typhoid. Sickness drastically reduced the size of the army.[41]

A subsequent landing near Sandvliet required fortifications to protect depots and a force to watch Bergen-op-Zoom; these additional requirements combined with casualties limited Lord Chatham's striking force, juxtaposed against ever-increasing French army strength. Lord Chatham no longer believed he had a force large enough to advance on Antwerp.

The consequences of Lord Chatham's shift of strategy from a simultaneous assault to a sequenced assault slowed the British advance. As days turned into weeks, the French were able to concentrate forces in the area. This rapid buildup of defense forces prevented the British from capitalizing on their surprise landings and initial strength. By mid-August, the British lacked the manpower to advance on Antwerp in the face of French reinforcements.

British Retreat

The decision to retreat was made on two separate levels. At the operational level, Lord Chatham and Admiral Strachan controlled the pace of advance from Walcheren Island to Antwerp. At the strategic level, the Cabinet and Castlereagh determined whether to evacuate Walcheren Island. The fall of the Portland government and the expected Franco-Austrian peace treaty delayed the decision to evacuate.

The war's outlook in Central Europe was grim. France had achieved notable success in Germany that threatened the safety of the British force in the Netherlands. On 6 July 1809, Napoleon smashed the Austrian army at Wagram. Subsequently, Austria and France signed a ceasefire and began peace negotiations. Even though it was negotiating an exit from the war, Austria asked Britain to hold onto Walcheren for exchange in their peace negotiations. In Westphalia, Frederick William, Duke of Brunswick, had failed in his rebellion against French rule.[42] He retreated to Bremen and was evacuated by the Royal Navy.[43] The fires of resistance in Germany that had encouraged the landings in the Netherlands had been extinguished.

Lord Chatham and Admiral Strachan convened a council of war on 27 August. The Quartermaster General, General Sir Robert Brownrigg, detailed the situation. The campaign assumptions had proved faulty. The initial plan called for a sudden assault that left 10,000 British troops to isolate Flushing; the remaining 30,000 would advance on Antwerp after landing in multiple locations then seize the Scheldt River mouth. Instead, the army sequenced the advance and only proceeded after the capture of each objective. The British force besieged Flushing but did not advance to South Beveland until after Flushing surrendered.

Following the occupation of South Beveland, the generals considered an assault on Antwerp. The British force, however, could not concentrate enough men to take Antwerp. After accounting for garrisons on Walcheren and South Beveland, the garrisoning of Sandvliet after capture, and the increasing number of sick, only 10,000 British soldiers remained to attack Antwerp. According to their initial estimates, the British would face a small and demoralized Franco-Dutch force of 9,000 spread across the region amidst crumbling defenses. Instead, 35,000 French troops garrisoned stout fortifications in Antwerp, Bergen-op-Zoom, and Breda. Without the men to take Antwerp, the British expedition stalled. The Army command did not believe they could advance, domestic and international politics prevented the withdrawal from Walcheren, and sickness reduced their ranks.

With the exception of naval commander Sir Richard, the consensus was to retreat. Sir Richard proposed attacking Fort Lillo.[44] He hoped some chance development would enable the British to capture the French fleet or at least achieve something, but the Franco-Dutch defenses were too strong. Lord Chatham did not concur; if the army was not strong enough to take Antwerp, it was not strong enough to take Fort Lillo.[45] Lord Chatham's rebuff prompted a complete breakdown in relations between Sir Richard and Lord Chatham.[46] Cooperation between the landing force commander and the amphibious task force commander is vital to a successful operation; during the most stressful part of the expedition—when strong leadership was needed most—that bond was severed.

After deciding to cancel the assault on Antwerp, the army had two choices: complete withdrawal to England or retreat to Flushing. Lord Chatham's orders allowed flexibility in whether to advance, but evacuation from Flushing required governmental approval.[47] After the decision was made not to advance, the next decision was the speed of withdrawal to Walcheren. Sir Richard wanted to delay withdrawal from South Beveland long enough to wreck the channel and prevent navigation to Antwerp. Wrecking navigation of the Scheldt to Antwerp would trap twelve ships of the line at Antwerp and reduce the French naval threat, partially accomplishing at least one of the expedition's campaign objectives.

In the end, the rapid withdrawal to Walcheren coupled with the government's delayed decision to evacuate cost many soldier lives without achieving campaign objectives. Lord Chatham wanted to evacuate as soon as possible and minimize losses to Walcheren Fever, which was spreading through the army. By 28 August, more than 3,000 soldiers mustered as sick, but suspected numbers were far higher.[48] There were several causes of tension in withdrawal. Sir Richard wanted to accomplish as many naval objectives as possible by wrecking the channel near Fort Batz. Army commanders were concerned about South Beveland's defensibility. Across all objectives, there was a desire to minimize British losses to Walcheren Fever, but an inability to limit the losses while still on Walcheren.

The army expeditiously withdrew from South Beveland. The French noticed the decreasing fleet anchored near Fort Batz—sixty ships on 30 August and almost none on 4 September.[49] Despite entreaties from Sir Richard, no effort was made to obstruct the channel. With the exception of the artillery left to defend the debarkation point, the evacuation of South Beveland ended 2 September. Britain only retained control of Walcheren Island.

France could retake Walcheren at will. One 81st Infantry Regiment officer wrote: "15,000 troops might hold Walcheren, but the mainland controlled South Beveland, and South Beveland controlled Walcheren; the island garrison was completely dependent on Britain for supplies."[50] Lord Chatham returned to England on 14 September, leaving Sir Eyre Coote in command. Because of the proximity to London, the army lacked the same agency for withdrawal as Sir John Moore's army in Spain. The army at Walcheren had to await permission from civilian leadership in London to return to England.

Austria asked Britain to retain Walcheren as leverage for its peace treaty with France. The British government hoped Walcheren could be exchanged to prevent the loss of Austrian territory. While Britain awaited the results of the Austro-French peace treaty, the British government experienced "perfect anarchy."[51] The Prime Minister, the Duke of Portland, had suffered from ill health throughout the year. In late August, he suffered a stroke and resigned in early September. The formation of the new government distracted Parliament from its warfighting responsibilities. While the new government formed, the Foreign Secretary, George Canning, executed his plot to remove his rival Castlereagh from office.

Political rivalries are common. Canning had plotted for months to remove Castlereagh from office and replace him with someone else; he also blamed Castlereagh for the disaster in Walcheren. Castlereagh learned about the plans and also that Canning schemed to form a new government with himself as Prime Minister instead of Spencer Perceval. Canning and Castlereagh fought a duel. Castlereagh wounded Canning in the thigh with a pistol ball. London society was shocked and both men resigned from government. These political machinations further delayed the decision to withdraw from Walcheren. The decision to withdraw to Walcheren finally occurred on 26 August; the subsequent decision to withdraw from Walcheren was made in November. It took more than two months for the British government to decide to withdraw, because the British government was paralyzed by these distractions.

Although delay proved deadly for the British force at Walcheren, it was politically expedient. Domestic concerns with forming a new government took priority. Spencer Perceval formed a new government on 4 October. Lord Liverpool assumed the post of Secretary of State for War and the Colonies. Richard Wellesley, the Duke of Wellington's brother, assumed the post of Foreign Secretary. The newly formed government needed time to establish itself and did not care to begin with a failed expedition. In addition, the Austrians wanted Britain to occupy Walcheren for the peace conference. Austria hoped Walcheren could be traded for a territorial concession in their peace treaty. The decision was delayed by a month of government paralysis and then a month of procrastination. The Austrian request proved a convenient excuse to delay making a decision.

Throughout October, London ignored the army's recommendation to withdraw. Instead, Lord Liverpool offered reinforcements and replacements. The Treaty of Schönbrunn, signed on 14 October, removed any requirement to hold Walcheren for Austrian peace negotiations. Austria lost its maritime provinces in Illyria and parts of Tyrol. Napoleon married a Habsburg princess, and Austria joined Napoleon's continental system. Unfortunately, word of the treaty only reached Britain in early November.

The British army on Walcheren was overwhelmed by the sick and dying. By 7 September, more than a quarter of the British force was sick—11,000 men—overwhelming the British medical corps. The expedition had sailed with twenty-three of twenty-four surgeons and thirty of sixty corpsmen, many of whom caught the disease while tending the wounded.[52] The cramped, damp living conditions and poorer diet for enlisted soldiers made them more susceptible to the disease combination than officers.

Between 21 August and 16 December, 12,863 sick soldiers were evacuated from Walcheren.[53] Sir Eyre required 20,000 troops to defend the island while even more in the garrison continued to fall ill.[54] From August to December 1809, 38 to 60 percent of the garrison was sick with Walcheren Fever.[55] Sir Eyre was concerned that British newspapers would reveal the army's weakness and encourage a French attack. He pleaded with Castlereagh for more doctors, medical supplies, and reinforcements, additionally arguing that the army could be lost if it was not evacuated.[56]

When General Sir George Don replaced Sir Eyre Coote on 27 October, his dispatches sent to the government were dire:

> The Island is almost in a defenseless state and the Army is so much reduced as not to be able to cope with the enemy in the field; and only capable of holding the town of Flushing until the enemy can open mortars and ricochet batteries against it.[57]

Don further stated that without strong naval support, he would be forced to flood significant portions of Walcheren to protect his force. The government in London did not mind flooding Walcheren, but flooding would have destroyed the island's crops; Don was loathe to anger the local population.

On 3 November, Lord Liverpool responded to General Don, indicating that the island of Walcheren should be evacuated. The following week, Lord Liverpool clarified his instruction to evacuate. Lord Liverpool sent 100 artificers to Flushing to wreck the Walcheren dockyards and fortifications. The objective was to prevent military use of Flushing for two years.[58] The artificers achieved their objective; it took the French two years to restore the port of Flushing.[59] The last British troops evacuated Walcheren on 23 December 1809.[60]

The Scheldt Expedition disaster led to a parliamentary inquiry. As is common in democratic nations, the inquiry rapidly became political. The inquiry initially sought to understand why the expedition occurred and why it failed. The opposition party, the Whigs, attempted to use the inquiry to topple the government. A whole-house committee of inquiry convened twenty times between February and March 1810. A new government had formed in October, however, and many independents in Parliament were not ready to topple the new government, particularly since the responsible ministers no longer held roles in the new government. *The Edinburgh Review* wrote: "The government majority acquitted itself, but condemned parliament."[61]

The inquiry culminated with three resolutions that absolved the government and military of blame for the disaster. Two resolutions failed—1) a censure of the government's plan and execution of the expedition and 2) a censure for retaining Walcheren; the committee of inquiry passed a third resolution, which placed no blame on government ministers for the expedition.[62] Once it became clear that the government would survive, the inquiry faded away.[63] Politically, there were no serious consequences for the government. George Canning eventually became Prime Minister in 1827, and Castlereagh served as Foreign Minister from 1812 to 1822. Along with Prince Metternich of Austria, Castlereagh was responsible for the post-Napoleonic Wars world order.

Conclusion

The Scheldt Expedition was a disaster entirely of Britain's making. The force was defeated by itself rather than the French. The British met only one of their three objectives: destroying the dockyards and arsenals of Flushing. Two years of repairs were required to make them operational. The French fleet remained in the navigable Scheldt River, and the shipyards of Antwerp continued to build ships. The campaign provided no value as a decoy for the Austrian campaign on the Danube, and Napoleon had no interest in exchanging Walcheren for any Austrian territory.

Remaining until December had been a political decision. The campaign ended at the 27 August War Council, but troops remained at Walcheren until 26 December 1809. Tentatively, the political decision to retreat was made on 3 November and confirmed the next week. Flushing's proximity to London meant the government did not delegate as much authority to the expedition commander as an overseas expedition. The authority to abandon the campaign was maintained in London, making it a political decision instead of a military one.

British commanders on the scene were not allowed to abandon the campaign. They were forced to wait for distracted London politicians to decide to end the campaign, a decision delayed for multiple political reasons. Holding Walcheren to support Austrian peace negotiations was a convenient excuse for a new government focused on organizing itself and unwilling for a military defeat to be its first act. The ministry offered additional reinforcements, additional medical personnel, and anything else the army required to prolong the Walcheren occupation and delay the decision.

The consequences of the defeat were not felt by the leaders. They were suffered by enlisted soldiers forced to remain in ruined buildings throughout the sickly season with insufficient medical care, waiting to be overtaken by sickness. Meanwhile, government leaders who planned the expedition went on to long and distinguished government careers. Insufficient intelligence led to insufficient planning of requirements. Insufficient landing craft and lack of familiarity with enemy orders of battle led to the campaign's shift from multiple simultaneous landings to a sequenced advance from Walcheren to Antwerp. The delayed decision to abandon the campaign combined with the lack of medical personnel and supplies resulted in 15,000 British casualties.

There are parallels between the end of the war in Afghanistan and the Walcheren campaign. Despite offensive action having concluded, the force remained in country because politicians were not willing to make the difficult decision to leave. At Walcheren, that decision took two months. In Afghanistan, both Democrat and Republican presidents passed the decision to their successors over the course of twenty years. In the end, the inquiry into the withdrawal was a heavily politicized as a way to attack the sitting administration. The French did not defeat Britain at the Scheldt; British leaders defeated themselves.

Notes

1. Eric W. Nye, *Pounds Sterling to Dollars: Historical Conversion of Currency*, accessed 19 October 2022, https://www.uwyo.edu/numimage/currency.htm.

2. Charles Oman, *A History of the Peninsular War Volume I 1807–1809: From the Treaty of Fontainbleau to the Battle of Corunna* (Oxford: Clarendon Press, 1802), 526.

3. T. H. McGuffie, "The Walcheren Expedition and the Walcheren Fever," *The English Historical Review* (1947): 191–202, 191.

4. Gordon C. Bond, *The Grand Expedition: The British Invasion of Holland in 1809* (Athens, GA: The University of Georgia Press, 1979), 9.

5. Bond, 234.

6. Richard Glover, "The French Fleet, 1807–1814: Britain's Problem and Madison's Opportunity," *Journal of Modern History* (1967): 233–52, 233–35.

7. T. C. Hansard, *The Parliamentary Debates from the Year 1803 to the Present Time Vol XV Comprising the Period from the Twenty-Third Day of January to The Firrst Day of March 1810* (London: Hansard, 1812), 27.

8. J. W. Fortescue, *A History of the British Army*, vol. 7 (Uckfield, UK: The Naval and Military Press, 2004, 36.

9. Joint Chiefs of Staff, Joint Publication (JP) 2-0, *Joint Intelligence* (Washington, DC: 2013), I-16–17.

10. JP 2-0, I-16–17.

11. JP 2-0, I-16–17.

12. Thomas A. Wise, "Life and Career of Admiral Sir Richard J. Strachan, Baronet, G. C. B.," *Transactions of the Royal Historical Society* 2 (1873): 32–53, 45

13. Hansard, *The Parliamentary Debates*, 19–20.

14. Owen Connelly, *Napoleon's Satellite Kingdoms* (Toronto: The Free Press, 1965), 144.

15. Connelly, 137.

16. Hansard, *The Parliamentary Debates*, 16–17.

17. Fortescue, *A History of the British Army*, 95.

18. Martin R. Howard, *Walcheren 1809: The Scandalous Destruction of a British Army* (Croydon, UK: Pen and Sword, 2012), 216.

19. John Bew, *Castlereagh: Enlightenment, War, and Tyranny* (Toronto: Quercus, 2019), 250.

20. Oman *A History of the Peninsular War*, 646–47.

21. Bew, *Castlereagh*, 250.

22. Wise, "Life and Career of Admiral Sir Richard J. Strachan," 45

23. Bond, *The Grand Expedition*, 16.

24. Bond, 11–13.

25. Christopher T. Golding, "Amphibians At Heart: The Battle of Copenhagen (1807), The Walcheren Expedition (1809), and the War Against Napoleon," *Journal of the Society for Army Historical Research* (2012): 167–88, 180.

26. Golding, 167–88, 180.

27. Hansard, *The Parliamentary Debates*, 17

28. Howard, *Walcheren 1809*, 177.

29. Andrew Limm, *Walcheren to Waterloo: The British Army in the Low Countries during the French Revolutionary and Napoleonic Wars, 1793–1815* (Barnsley, UK: Pen and Sword, 2018), 109.

30. Limm, 43.

31. Howard, *Walcheren 1809*, 79.

32. Limm, *Walcheren to Waterloo*, 110–13.

33. Limm, 95–99.

34. Limm, 93.

35. Wise, "Life and Career of Admiral Sir Richard J. Strachan," 46–47.

36. Connelly, *Napoleon's Satellite Kingdoms*, 168.

37. Fortescue, *A History of the British Army*, 96.

38. Anonymous, *The Walcheren Expedition: The Experiences of a British Officer of the 81st Regt. during the Campaign in the Low Countries of 1809* (Cheshire, UK: Leonaur, 2008), 51.

39. Howard, *Walcheren 1809*, 141–42.

40. Howard, 143.

41. John Lynch, "The Lessons of Walcheren Fever," *Military Medicine* (2009): 316–19, 315.

42. John Kuehn, *Napoleonic Warfare: The Operational Art of Great Campaigns*, 140.

43. Connelly, *Napoleon's Satellite Kingdoms*, 205.

44. Howard, *Walcheren 1809*, 156, 157.

45. "Cobbett's Weekly Political Register," 23 September 1809, 415.

46. Bond, *The Grand Expedition*, 121.

47. Bond, 24.

48. Howard, *Walcheren 1809*, 177.

49. Howard, 177.

50. Anonymous, *The Walcheren Expedition*, 278.

51. Anonymous, 190.

52. Bond, *The Grand Expedition*, 127.

53. Bond, 317.

54. Howard, *Walcheren 1809*, 185.

55. Lynch, "The Lessons of Walcheren Fever," 316.

56. Howard, *Walcheren 1809*, 186.

57. Howard, 192.

58. Howard, 193–94.

59. Bond, *The Grand Expedition*, 164.

60. Howard, *Walcheren 1809*, 194–96.

61. Howard, 211.

62. Bond, *The Grand Expedition*, 157–58.

63. David Fisher, The Scheldt Divisions 1810," History of Parliament Online, accessed 23 December 2020, https://www.historyofparliamentonline.org/periods/hanoverians/scheldt-divisions-1810.

Chapter 16
"We Did Retreat but Were Not Beat": The Irish-American Experience at Bull Run as Told through Civil War Songs

Catherine V. Bateson

"Most of my troops are demoralized by the defeat at Bull Run; some regiments even mutinous," General George B. McClellan observed to his wife in August 1861.[1] Almost a month after the Civil War's first major engagement, the mood was downcast. Not only had the Union lost the conflict's opening battle to Confederate forces of the seceded southern slave states, but their retreat from the fields around Manassas, Virginia, had been nothing short of "terrible havoc."[2] Although President Abraham Lincoln turned the loss into a galvanizing recruiting tool, the Federal government force's failure and disorganized 21 July 1861 retreat was remembered as a significant beating. The immediate consequence of this was made clear by wartime contemporaries who reflected that whatever happened elsewhere in the soon-to-be-all-enveloping conflict, "that never-to-be-forgotten spot, Bull Run . . . witnessed the success of armies hostile" to the unity of the American nation. Though the United States eventually won the Civil War in 1865, the Federal failure haunted the war's earliest memories. The fields of Manassas would forever remain "a spot . . . baptized in [the] blood" of its sons.[3]

Out of what many contemporaries described as a disastrous loss, one group of Federal Army soldiers viewed their experiences at the First Battle of Bull Run as a noteworthy victory that altered perceptions about them and their future wartime service. Amidst the growing confusion of a scrambled retreat, this body of men remained firm in the middle of the battlefield. The 69th New York State Militia maintained their cohesion while other regimental formations broke around them. Formed from New York City's Irish-born and second/third-generation Irish-American diaspora population, the 69th New York was one of the initial units to enlist. They were subsequently one of the last to retreat from the war's opening encounter. Their actions in what was principally an early military blow to the northern states had a consequential impact on their brethren's actions for the remainder of the conflict. Widespread and beneficial perceptions about their actions spread through society and wartime culture in the 1860s.

Indeed, these soldiers and their commanding officers laid the foundation for an oft-repeated scene during the next four years: Irish-Americans demonstrated their ultimate commitment to maintain United States unity by forming rearguard actions during various retreats across the Civil War's large and small engagements. What began at Bull Run in July 1861—celebrated in Irish-American and non-Irish-American reports of the battle—subsequently inspired and encouraged other soldiers from the Irish-American diaspora to sustain final lines of defense. Their actions prompted a wealth of acclaim for their battlefield behavior beyond the front-line. This, in turn, helped create a cultural reputation and admiration for competent and brave Irish-American performance in Federal service that lasted throughout the whole of the conflict. Unlike the German-Americans who fought at Chancellorsville in May 1863 (discussed in Chapter 17 on the XI Corps in this collection), the Irish-American experience in the conflict's first major battle earned positive praise and celebration. Their legacy has affected how both scholars and military observers might think about immigrant wartime histories and service; they were not, and should not, be viewed with pre-existing explanatory prejudice when assessing actions.

This chapter discusses how specific contemporary Irish-American songs written in the aftermath of the First Battle of Bull Run interpreted the 69th New York State Militia's actions as a success amidst what was, in reality, defeat for Federal forces. These lyrical outputs countered contemporary northern state society's despair regarding the Confederate Army triumph. Instead of blaming military organization, the Irish diaspora used song to exalt their fighting contributions. They perceived their battle actions as a win, despite the overall loss. Certainly, as with any historical source and cultural writing, ballads should not be seen as fully factual, accurate accounts of what occurred on the battlefield. They are interpretations of memory, maneuvers, and particular messages of fighting bravery that supported a pro-Irish-American agenda; these accounts, at times, differ from the historical record. That does not, however, take away the critical merit of close lyrical reading.

Songs about the sons of the Irish-American diaspora transformed their role in the Federal Army retreat—and the crucial fact that they did not surrender—into their own wartime gain and promotion. These cultural recollections of what happened on the fields around Manassas, including the retreat itself, were emphasized and molded into messages designed to bolster morale, recruitment, and overall collaboration within defeat. In doing so, they presented an effective message of victory that motivated Irish-American military service. What happened at the First Battle of Bull Run was celebrated by the Irish in the United States as a winning aspect of an otherwise "disastrous battle" and ignoble withdrawal.[4] This chapter will demonstrate how critical this lyrical messaging was, and the impact it had on the events of 21 July 1861.

The 69th New York State Militia's First Battle of Bull Run

The focal point of Irish-American Civil War enlistment was encapsulated in the 69th New York State Militia, which developed out of several Irish immigrant community companies in the late 1840s and 1850s.[5] By 1861, the well-established 69th New York was ready to serve in the coming civil conflict under Col. Michael Corcoran, their charismatic commander from County Sligo, Ireland. At the war's outbreak, Corcoran offered his militia when President Lincoln called for troops. He mustered the regiment to parade down Broadway "amid deafening cheers," leaving their home city in a spirit of triumphant energy as "flags and banners streamed from the windows" and women "flung bouquets on the marching column."[6] More than a thousand Irish-born and descended 69th New York soldiers and officers, and additional units of Irish Zouave companies organized by Capt. Thomas Francis Meagher, journeyed by boat, rail, and road to Washington, DC. Alongside those already in the militia, many northeastern state residents were spurred to join by recruitment posters that emphasized Irish fighting spirit. One such advertisement called for Massachusetts Irishmen to "carry the American Eagle over the Potomac, down like an avalanche through the land of Dixie."[7]

This burning proud sense of wanting to exhibit devotion to the United States through military action was also depicted in an early wartime song, "Glorious 69th," a ballad with a title that recalled the praise and adulation given to the unit in the war's first months. Written in May 1861, its lyrics described the militia's journey from their home city:

> On the 22nd of April, the Boys they sailed away;
> They made a glorious turn-out, a going down Broadway. . . .
> For they were bound for Washington, straightway unto the wars!

Commanded in the ballad by "our President," "Glorious 69th" stressed how the diaspora's soldiers would "put down Secession" and "fight hand-to-hand, until we plant the Stars and Stripes way down in Dixie's Land."[8] This song was the first of more than 200 written specifically about the Irish-American wartime experience between 1861 and 1865. More than any other artistic form of cultural output, ballads played an incredibly important role in Irish-American articulations about the ethnic migrant community's place in the country.[9]

During the Civil War itself, the experiences of the approximately 180,000 Irish-born and greater number of descended generation Irish-Americans who fought for the Union—and to a considerably lesser extent the experiences of 20,000 Irish-born Confederate soldiers—were written into popular and well-published ballad outputs.[10] In addition to maintaining the diaspora's heritage of song singing, lyrics addressed conflict, experiences, realities, sentiments, and encounters. The majority of Irish-American Civil War songs focused on specific moments of Civil War history, namely 1861 and 1862 battle engagements. Songs about the 69th New York State Militia at the First Bull Run in July 1861 were complemented from late 1861 onward by ballads about the Federal Army's Irish Brigade throughout the rest of the conflict.

Lyrical battle reports and song stories followed traditional balladry news reporting styles, providing accounts that could be disseminated and sung around home-front society to supplement official war and newspaper reports.[11] Songs provided distinct interpretations of battles, skirmishes, and overall war conduct, presenting differing cultural source examples that compared, and (sometimes) ran counter to, official accounts of Irish-American Civil War and mid-nineteenth century history.[12] As observed in the aftermath of the First Bull Run, ballads carried instantaneous emotive messages about particular fighting encounters, and played a significant role in forming views of Irish-American commitment and specific versions of their battle memories.

After spending a few months in encampment around Arlington Heights, Virginia, the 69th New York State Militia moved out around 16 July 1861 and headed to Manassas, via a few skirmishes around the town of Centreville. Approximately thirty miles from Washington, and just over ninety miles to the new seceded capital at Richmond, Manassas Junction was an important railroad town and constituted a militarily essential area for the Confederacy to gain and for Federal forces to hold. The July 1861 battlefield, and the overlapping area of the August 1862 Second Battle of Bull Run, was a combination of rolling hills, fields, "dark, gloomy woods, deep ravens, wood-covered runs [streams], and elevated plateaus."[13] From the Confederacy's stronger position on the higher ground, these "afforded excellent covering" for infantry and artillery.[14] The Confederacy mostly took its battle name from the town/railroad junction closest to the fighting; hence Bull Run also was called the First Battle of Manassas. By comparison, the Federal government named the battle after the nearby narrow Bull Run creek, which numerous soldiers crossed as they entered the fray and again as they retreated.

When the US Army's overall commander, General Irvin McDowell, assembled his forces and marched on Manassas in the morning of 21 July, hopes of success were high and their strength appeared to match and surpass Confederate opposition. Nevertheless, most military assessments of Bull Run conclude that McDowell's failure to coordinate consistent attacks and press on following individual regimental successes "prevented him from driving the foe from the field."[15] He was further hindered by the timely arrival of Joseph E. Johnston's reinforcements from the Shenandoah Valley, which bolstered Confederate ranks. Young soldiers and untested commanders were additionally met with a cacophony of warfare and "unbelievable noise, with the cannon roaring and biting and killing for hour upon hour, with the men screaming, with smoke absorbing every line of vision, with relentless musket fire."[16] The Federals attacked Confederate forces in waves, attempting to both strike head-on and flank opposing batteries; but by mid-afternoon, and as the temperature rose on a stiflingly hot summer day, the Federals lost cohesion. The fighting became far more disjointed and was prosecuted in an incredibly muddled manner.[17] Soldiers witnessed "immense confusion, with mistakes and failures and brilliance and bravery all swirled together."[18] Confederate Eugene Blackford described the scene as "truly awful, an immense cloud of smoke and dust . . . the field, literally covered with bodies for five miles," with many "piled in heaps."[19]

Figure 16.1. "The Battle at Bull's Run—The Gallant 69th N.Y.S.M. Assaulting A Rebel Battery" illustration from *Frank Leslie's Illustrated Newspaper*, 3 August 1861. Courtesy of the Library of Congress.

Colonel Corcoran's 69th New York State Militia was mustered under the overall command of then-Col. William Tecumseh Sherman's Third Brigade. When battle was engaged, the immigrant unit was eager to join the fray: "from daylight up to the moment of our entering the conflict," they waited to throw "themselves fiercely against the rebel ranks;" then once "stripped of knapsacks and overcoats," they went on "a gallant charge, gallantly led and gallantly sustained."[20] Undeterred by "murderous batteries" of Confederate gunfire and cannons, and "with terrific shouts and yells," the 69th New York charged straight into the opposing line.[21] The militia demonstrated its courage, maintaining assaults against reinforced counter-attacks during the "hard-contested fight on the 21st."[22]

In his postbellum writings, Irish-American Civil War soldier and correspondent Capt. David Power Conyngham described how "after each repulse, the regiment formed and charged right upon the batteries" of Confederate cannon.[23] Its soldiers "bravely but vainly struggled to capture the batteries and drive the enemy from the shelter of the wood" at the top edge of a ridgeline where Confederate forces held a commanding position.[24] Corcoran encouraged his men "in every assault," being "everywhere conspicuous, cheering on and rallying the troops."[25] One newspaper correspondent from *The World* called the 69th New York "determined fellows" in their actions, and noted that even Confederate opponents "spoke of [their] fighting . . . in the highest terms."[26] Not all of the attacks were futile either. Then-United States Col. Ambrose Burnside officially reported: "It was Sherman's brigade, with the Sixty-Ninth New York Militia in advance . . . by a most deadly fire assisted in breaking the enemy's lines" along some areas of the Confederate position.[27]

Irish-American ballads produced after the battle also immortalized the memory of this fierce fighting display. Written in late 1861, "The Gallant Sons of Erin" was "dedicated to the 69th Regt. N.Y.S.M." and extolled their "brave behavior."[28] While their actions excelled "what pen can write or tongue can tell," lyrics still managed to applaud:

These sporting boys from Paddies' land . . .
Who at the battle of last July, when other troops did quickly fly,
Who stood and did the foes defy . . .
At famed Manassas and Bull-run, where glorious laurels they have won,
Not a man being absent from his gun . . .
Each Captain boldly did maintain and dauntless soldier's station:
And stood the plain for many an hour, though shot and shell like

rain did shower,
To prove their valor, tact, and power as gallant sons of Erin.[29]

"To the Glorious 69th!" provided a similar depiction of the militia unit's courage under Confederate fire:

In the Battle of Bull Run, their chivalry was seen,
And, with a brave Commander, faced rebels that were mean;
They stood in the hot battle, where balls like hailstones flew,
Until the rebel ambush-host with balls did pierce them through.[30]

"Over ten long hours we fought most manfully," the "Battle of Bull Run" explained, referring to the long day of engagements. Written by lyricist F. Collins, who produced several wartime ballads about the Irish, "Battle of Bull Run" was yet another song that described "the glorious Sixty Ninth" as "the terror of Bull Run."[31] The unit maintained its fighting honor on "the field of fame . . . against an enemy, conceal'd in woods and ambuscades and their masked batteries," Collins recounted.[32]

The 69th New York's battlefield experiences at the First Bull Run became a common and reinforced lyrical story in the northern states. More than a year after the engagement, Collins penned "The 69th Brigade, sung from the personal perspective of fictional Irish-born "patriot and soldier" William, who served with the militia at the start of the war.[33] "At the battle of Bull-Run," William "conquer'd with each blow with his bayonet and his gun" and "laid those Rebels low" in the process; this made him "a credit to his country"—both to America and his old homeland of Ireland.[34] In late 1862, similar pride could be heard in William P. Ferris's "Return of Gen. Corcoran, of the Glorious 69th." The ballad's lyrics recalled the "battle of Bull-Run" more than fifteen months before, where the militia unit "first . . . met the foe":

They charged the rebels with cold steel, and laid their columns low;
And while the Northern ranks were broke, mid showers of shot and shell
The Gallant Sixty Ninth still stood, nor flinched, but nobly fell.[35]

The Battle at Henry House Hill and Federal Army Retreat

The 69th New York State Militia's foremost moment at the First Battle of Bull Run came as they joined Federal waves of attack against the Confederate defensive ridgeline position around Henry House Hill, named after the Henry family farmhouse situated near the crest of the mound.[36]

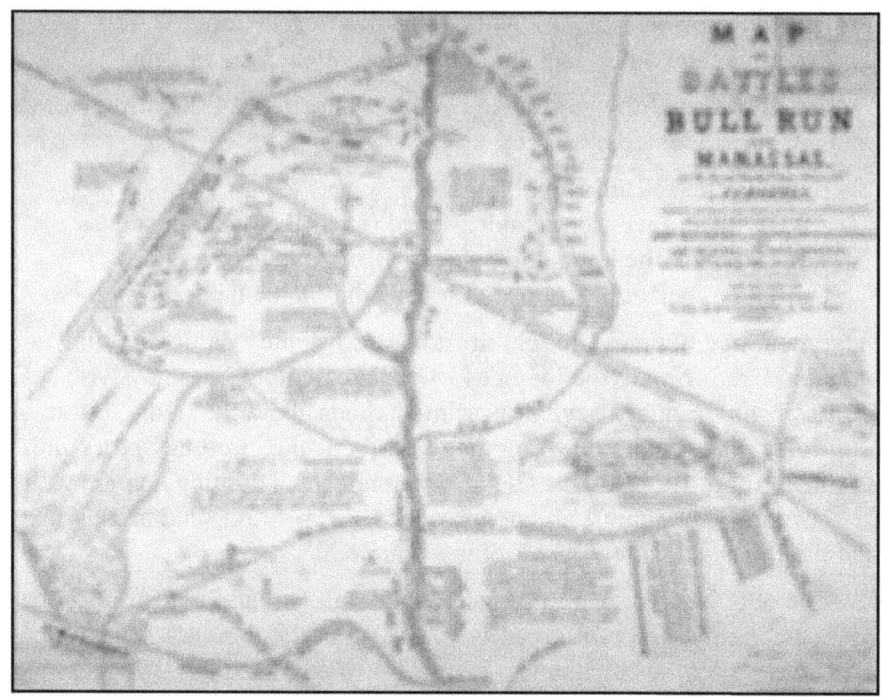

Figure 16.2. Map of the Battles of Bull Run near Manassas, March 1862. Courtesy of the Library of Congress.

Conditions here were ferociously difficult. Ahead of the 69th New York went the Scottish-American 79th New York Regiment; one of their soldiers, Private William Todd, later described how his unit was met "with the constant fire of shells . . . [that] somewhat staggered us."[37] As a fourteenth wave of attack on Henry House Hill was launched, the only "last unscathed regiment" that commanding Col. (later General) Sherman could call on was the one containing Corcoran's men. With the same enthusiasm exhibited earlier in the day, they charged up the hill and began to break through the Confederate line.[38] Adding to their struggle, they attacked over the bodies of the fallen, injured and the "demoralized wreckage of the previous assaults."[39]

Given the battle's chaotic and confused atmosphere, the fact that the 69th New York survived relatively unscathed and conducted their fighting in such a fierce manner was itself praiseworthy. To be sure, songs emphasized this fact but also recounted how the militia faced hard Confederate defenses at various points in the battle. Corcoran noted one precise moment where "we pushed them rapidly, and would have entirely cleared the field of them had a battery not opened upon us with great fury and disseminated our ranks."⁴⁰ "Battle of Bull Run" echoed this, arguing that if the Confederate opposition had not "turned our scale of battle . . . we'd gain the victory."⁴¹ Thomas Francis Meagher detailed the ferocity in even more blunt terms:

> It was impossible for men to override that tempest. Three times did the 69th launch itself against it. Three times, having plunged head-foremost into its deadliest showers, was it hurled back . . . we beat their men—their batteries beat us. That is the story of the day.⁴²

Due to the confusion of the battle and those who recalled it subsequently— along with competing and conflicting accounts, the tracking of specific unit movements across the battlefield to and from Henry House Hill is, at times, unclear in the historical record. This is especially true of accounts by the main Irish-American military figures who detailed the encounter in their remembrances.⁴³ Nonetheless, accounts indicate consistently that the 69th New York State Militia was defeated by superior odds on the Confederate side, emphasizing observations about the "tenacity of the New York Irish on the battlefield" as they struggled against an increasingly dominant opposing force.⁴⁴ "Against four-to-one a fearful odds of men we could not see," as "Battle of Bull Run" stressed, it was impossible for the 69th New York to keep attacking.⁴⁵ "We Will Have the Union Still" explained this simply: "though from Bull Run we retreated, did they not fight ten-to-one?"⁴⁶

The odds being referenced here related to eventual increases in Confederate manpower as the battle wore on and Federal soldiers were repulsed. Indeed, for much of the engagement during the day, both armies were fairly evenly matched: United States and Confederate forces engaged approximately 18,000 soldiers respectively.⁴⁷ As the fighting reached its zenith, however, the numerical advantage of Confederate reinforcements began to be seen. Yet, unlike the Chancellorsville example assessed elsewhere in this collection, Irish-American and non-Irish-American accounts of events at Henry House Hill do not include any notion of cowardice against superior enemy odds.⁴⁸

Corcoran equally used the superior odds defense in disclosures about why he twice called for his unit to retreat from Henry House Hill. He rationalized that "under the circumstances, I knew it would only insure a useless waste of life to hold our position, and I was therefore obliged to order a retreat."⁴⁹ His men "went back slowly and apparently with dissatisfaction" at being asked to withdraw, reinforcing the impression that Irish-born and descended soldiers were eager to keep fighting.⁵⁰ Through-

Figure 16.3. Ruins of Mrs. Henry's House, Battlefield of Bull Run, March 1862. Courtesy of The Met Museum Collection. Perhaps the most famous image of the ruined Henry House, this George N. Barnard photo shows the devastation on the fields around Manassas, Virginia, seven months after the First Bull Run. This photograph initially was attributed to Irish-born Matthew Brady.

out the "fearful contest . . . right gallantly did the men of the Sixty-Ninth maintain their proud distinction."[51] Nevertheless, Corcoran's order was a prudent move with the presence of a Confederate cavalry charge "galloping down upon us with the most fearful fire imaginable. . . . Valor must often give way to prudence, and so the retreat was continued."[52] By half-past-four on the afternoon of 21 July, a Confederate reinforcement "overran the Union forces" across much of the field.[53] Regiments retreated, and eventually the proud Irish-American militia "was ordered by Colonel Sherman to fall back to shelter" thus reinforcing Corcoran's personal calls for his men to leave the field.[54]

In much the same way as the battle had first started for the United States Army, what "began in an orderly way . . . broke down into chaos."[55] In part, this was due to continued lack of clear organization across the battlefield, compounded additionally by the fact the entire affair was being observed by intrigued civilians. As Conyngham recalled, when "the news spread that the army was retreating," Federal military suppliers, teamsters, and "a good many" people watching the battle "rushed frantically forward . . . soon joined by the panic-stricken army."[56] This led to "mingling and confusion of soldiers without arms, members of Congress and editors . . . ladies in buggies . . .special correspondents" all combined together on the routes away from Manassas.[57] "Battle of Bull Run" chastised the teamsters specifically in its lyrics, suggesting that it was "amongst . . . [them] a panic had began."[58] This then created a rush away from the battlefield, and the retreat quickly became a rout of military men and startled civilians.

Cornelia McDonald, whose husband served with the Confederate 7th Virginia Cavalry at Bull Run, recalled "many laughable accounts of how the luxurious non-combatants made good their escape" by casting aside picnic hampers, champagne, clothing, and carriages as they were engulfed by the flight.[59] Moreover, Confederate amusement at the Federal retreat was depicted in a mocking southern version of the traditional folk song "Yankee Doodle," noting that: "Yankee Doodle ran away—Dixie, he ran after."[60] During the "retiring at Manassas when hordes of Yankees ran away" from their battle "licking," they escaped slowly in the congestion back to Washington "like streams of thick molasses."[61]

For the 69th New York, the final retreat was not a joking matter. If anything, the retreat itself was one of the most consequential moments of the unit's immediate history; this action cemented their fighting glory, ensuring that the Irish in Federal forces ranks ended their service with their heads held victoriously high. Corcoran personally "conducted [the retreat] in an orderly manner," so his unit remained mostly intact through the process.[62] This retreating cohesion was a crucial aspect in subsequent Irish-American versions of events, especially as it countered Sherman's account that while "the Sixty-ninth held ground for some time," they too "finally fell back in disorder."[63] Overall, Sherman concluded there had been "no positive order to retreat" for his entire brigade.[64]

The Irish-American view, by comparison, was that *they* at least were *not* disordered. Contrary to Sherman's opinion, Thomas Francis Meagher, for instance, complained that "the whole assault collapsed in a general rout" for the United States Army; if anything, he said, it was a tumult in which he and his fellow Irishmen just happened to be "swept back" by the weight of other retreating soldiers and units.[65] The 69th New York fell back not in the disorder that Sherman had suggested, but by sheer force of the whole army instead. The message emphasis was clear: the Irish New Yorkers, at least, did not retreat in disorder by themselves.[66]

Irish-American veterans who survived the battle were eager to stress that the 69th New York troops were dragged unintentionally into the army's messy retreat due to forces beyond their control. Retreating on the losing side was, therefore, not their fault. Conyngham emphasized this highlighted how "the Sixty-ninth left the field in good order, with colors flying."[67] "Battle of Bull Run" summarized the same message succinctly in its proud refrain: "then we did retreat but were not beat at the battle of Bull Run."[68]

Civil War historian James McPherson has observed that Sherman's brigade "probably fought better than any other Union brigade" at the First Bull Run, in no small part due to the role of ethnic regiments such as the Scottish-American 79th New York and the Irish-American 69th New York State Militia.[69] Thanks to Corcoran's coordinated organizational ability, his men formed the still-fighting "protective rearguard" retreat for the whole army; they were one of the last units to leave the field.[70] They maintained this defensive position for other disorderly regimental units all the way back to the Federal encampments at Arlington Heights outside Washington.[71] In so doing, they earned more praise for the unit and the diaspora's sense that *they* were at least victorious in the midst of wider defeat—a point that songs stressed above all.

Even with pro-Irish/pro-69th New York bias influencing remembrance of their actions as being nobler than the reality of events, undeniably, some of the militia unit's soldiers stayed on the field while others left. Corcoran certainly organized his men to repulse advancing Confederate cavalry charges and protect their retreating army's rearguard. Corcoran himself commented about using "a small house as a means of defense" while opposing cavalry surrounded his "little band" of remaining men.[72] "Return of Gen. Corcoran" recounted: "Against the odds of two-to-one he fought, but could not yield," even as Corcoran was injured in the process.[73] Similarly, "The Gallant Sons of Erin" recalled: "Brave Corcoran, wounded on the plain, called to his men to charge again."[74] Not for nothing was the Irish officer's wartime memoir subtitled "The Hero Of Bull Run." Corcoran was a fundamental part of the Irish fighting display that day, and in the subsequent ensuing memory of his unit's actions.

In an 1862 anniversary/recruiting speech commemorating the 69th New York Irish's actions at the First Bull Run, Meagher recalled the "staunch loyalty, the patient courage and stern nerve of Michael Corcoran."[75] Wartime songs about Corcoran frequently echoed the same sentiments. However, Corcoran did not immediately hear Meagher's praise and devotional lyrics about him. During his stand, Corcoran, along with thirty privates and four fellow officers, was captured by Confederate forces and interned in the southern states. He remained a Confederate captive for thirteen months until being released in August 1862. Although losing the colonel was a huge personal blow to the 69th New York, the unit's maintenance of order and Corcoran's wise leadership ensured a strong remnant of the militia unit survived.

For northern Irish-Americans, the other notable officer loss at the First Bull Run was the death of Lt. Col. James Haggerty from County Donegal, Ireland. Haggerty's memory was recalled for the remainder of the conflict by prominent Irish-American officers and in ballads. Described "as fine a specimen of a Celt as Ireland could produce," Haggerty fell "shot through the heart" during the 69th New York's first waves of attack.[76] News of his death, along with the Federal loss and Irish battle involvement, was part of initial battle reports that spread beyond the warring United States to Ireland in the weeks following the engagement. One example, printed in Cork, Ireland, in late July/early August 1861, was "Our Brave Irish Champions—A New Song on the Great Battle Fought in America!" The lyrical tribute gave a very immediate, visceral account of what happened around Manassas:

> The great battle in America, to you I will explain,
> On the 21st of July, there was 20,000 slain.
> By the dawn on Sunday morning, that battle did take place.
> 'Till Six o'Clock that Evening, the firing did not cease . . .
> And many a valiant Irishman lay bleeding on the plain . . .
> The dreadful slaughter on that day, was awful to behold
> The moans of dying and wounded, would make your blood run cold . . .
> A scene of horrid slaughter was the battle field that day,
> The 69th brave Irishmen were all near cut away.[77]

The last line that nearly all the 69th New York's soldiers had been killed at the First Bull Run was an exaggeration but shows how quickly transnational songs could be produced during the Civil War. A little misinformation did not hinder the desire to report events via traditional ballad forms. As long as wider messages about brave fighting service, composure in the face of the enemy and unprecedented fighting, and maintaining order in the midst of chaotic retreat could be extolled, some lyrical inaccuracy could be forgiven. What was certainly true is that by the time the 69th New York returned to their base at Fort Corcoran around three in the morning on 22 July, they were "weary and worn, famished . . . and after a battle which lasted for eight hours and more, and march of five and thirty miles, laid themselves down to sleep" for much-needed rest.[78]

First Battle of Bull Run, 21 July 1861	Federal Army	Confederate Army
Total Dead	470	387
Total Wounded	1,071	1,582
Total Missing	1,793 (includes about 1,200 prisoners of war)	13
Henry House Casualties	285 killed 647 wounded	193 killed 326 wounded
69th New York State Militia Casualties (United States only)	38 killed 59 wounded 95 missing	N/A

Figure 16.4. The Cost of the First Battle of Bull Run for the United States Federal Army, Confederate Army, and 69th New York State Militia. Created by Army University Press.

Victorious Memory in Defeat

For northern society as a whole, immediate reactions to the First Battle of Bull Run were "shame and despair" at the loss, the disorganized nature of the United States attack, and the chaos of the retreat.[79] For the 69th New York, such feelings were irrelevant. Their service was instantaneously commended, reinforcing the message that *their* battlefield experience had more victorious aspects than the rest of the army. Captain Conyngham's account indicated that General McDowell, "a spectator of the charge" and their fighting retreat, "rode up to the Sixty-ninth and personally thanked them" for their actions.[80] In the following days, President Lincoln and the soon-to-be-promoted Sherman visited military encampments around Arlington Heights, including the 69th New York at Fort Corcoran. When he addressed each Federal unit, Lincoln referred to "our late disaster at Bull Run" but also reassured the army that there would be "brighter days to come."[81] When the president reached the Irish soldiers, he made "the same feeling address" as he had done to other units, but included "more personal allusions" for the 69th New York "because of their special gallantry in the battle under Corcoran."[82]

The 69th New York's "special gallantry" was celebrated with massive ovation when the soldiers returned to New York City. On their journey home, they were met with universal expressions of joy across the northern states: "Their reception in Washington, Philadelphia, and even Baltimore, which at that time favored secession, was enthusiastic."[83] Civil and military organizations in New York recreated the parade environment from a few months earlier, this time with the 69th New York marching up Broadway homeward instead of down toward to the war. They were, according to Conyngham, "heroes of the occasion . . . cheered and fêted, and graced a New York holiday."[84] The 69th New York even received a sixty-nine-gun salute in their honor—hardly the reaction a losing side would expect to receive.[85] These celebratory aspects of the unit's return intersect with McPherson's observations about how the story of what happened at the First Battle of Bull Run "became an important part of the psychology of the war in the eastern theatre" for both "collective southern and northern memories."[86]

While the Confederacy claimed the actual victory, groups in the northern states such as the Irish diaspora used their battlefield service to again stress their loyalty to their adopted homeland. They took great pride in the fact they behaved with a high level of credibility. "Battle of Bull Run" described this clearly: not only had they "gone to face the enemy and put rebellion down," but they had personally returned "victoriously and [wore] a laurel crown" of success.[87] "Our gallant soldiers they are gone to the battle field of fame" and came back to receive a befitting homecoming that strengthened their reputation.[88] All thoughts of the Federal Army's retreat and loss were removed.[89]

In his study of New York Irish songs, Dan Milner commented that "a vast number of Irish-American songs first published during the Civil War focused on the military" aspects as their central subject matter.[90] Stories and "accounts of Irish heroics at Bull Run flooded" newspapers and printing presses, furthering the acclaim "won . . . on the battlefield in the summer" of 1861.[91] In *The Last Days of the 69th in Virginia*, Thomas Francis Meagher recalled the 69th New York's journey to Manassas just weeks after the unit returned to their home city. Additionally, he made frequent public addresses throughout the second half of 1861 that "gave vivid account of the operations" at Bull Run.[92] He eulogized the 69th New York's "noble behavior in the battle" in these speeches.[93] Similarly, other Irish-American servicemen devoted the first few pages and chapters of their wartime memoirs to tales of the militia unit's continued steadfastness from the start of the conflict. Such contemporary recounting while the war raged on ensured yet another consequence of the retreat for the diaspora. These persistent positive references in print publications galvanized continual recruitment.

Throughout the fall and winter of 1861, the 69th New York State Militia was reshaped and evolved into the 69th New York Regiment, the founding unit of the US Army's famed Irish Brigade. Comprised eventually of three New York regiments and one each from Massachusetts and Pennsylvania, the Irish Brigade was first commanded by Meagher himself. The soldiers' actions were extolled in their own ballad accounts, with "highly optimistic" cultural outputs "praising bravery and encouraging recruitment" for the remainder of the conflict.[94] Furthermore, they ensured that the First Bull Run and the 69th New York's service there would not be forgotten.[95] To fire "up the spirits of the people" during 1862, Meagher continued to make regular use of the "powerful influence" of tales about the fighting at Henry House Hill, Michael Corcoran, and the 69th New York State Militia.[96] These stories made a substantial impression, inspiring the diaspora's sons and "inducing them to join the army."[97]

The Irish Brigade became the subject of numerous wartime songs and lyrical expressions and, in turn, ensured that the unbeaten, victorious spirit of the 69th New York State Militia lived on beyond 21 July 1861. In the middle of the conflict, "The Irish Brigade in America"—a ballad first produced in the British Isles about the Irish-American diaspora's wartime experiences—praised the "gallant sons of Erin's isle . . . who are fighting in the American states to put down slavery."[98] It stressed that while they were fighting "in the loyal cause of freedom on the American shore," they were also following in the footsteps of their earlier wartime brethren.[99] According to the song's lyrical commemoration, it was at "the battle of Bull's Run they fought right manfully."[100]

The shorter-titled "The Irish Brigade" went even further in January 1862 with its recollection of the 69th New York's Bull Run service. Sung to the American anthemic tune of "Red, White, and Blue" to reinforce the message of loyalty to the United States Union cause, "The Irish Brigade" echoed past lyrics about how the 69th New York remained unbeaten through retreat and loss at the start of the conflict. Above all others, this ballad typified all the sentiments about what Bull Run meant to the diaspora, to American remembrance of their service, and to the creation of a cultural memory that ensured Irish-American battlefield actions in the Civil War would be honored with great pride and respect:

> Surrounded by carnage and slaughter,
> At Bull Run . . . They poured out their life-blood like water,
> Upholding the Red, White, and Blue.
> Although by large forces o'erpowered,
> No soldier or chief was afraid:
> *Chorus*
> There ne'er was a traitor or coward,
> In the ranks of the Irish Brigade.[101]

Conclusion

If Irish-American Civil War song examples reveal anything about how messages of the United States Army's First Battle of Bull Run retreat were perceived in the aftermath of 21 July, it is that *their* version of the battle's events carry vastly different reactions that run counter to official military reports, memoirs, news accounts and historical scholarship. In *Pickett's Charge in History and Memory*, American military historian Carol Reardon assessed veterans' selective recollection of events at Pickett's Charge during 3 July 1863, the third day of the Battle of Gettysburg. She discussed how subsequent histories related to successes vs. failures, wins vs. defeats, advances vs. retreats, and that such binary distinctions can impact memories of military events. In the process, they forget other realities and perceptions held by those mostly closely involved at the time.[102]

Wider, collective retreats include individual moments of personal and collective—in the case of the 69th New York State Militia at the First Bull Run—success. Such praiseworthy service and actions were considered as victories for the specific units and soldiers involved. For the 69th, brave conduct such as staying on the field around Henry House, Corcoran's defense to the point of imprisonment, and James Haggerty's death was lauded in ballads. At least for the Irish-American diaspora in their northern state enclaves, *their retreat* (within the broader Federal forces retreat) was *not* a failure. Subsequently, this view shaped a different understanding and immediate narratives across the home-front and built perceptions of heroic service. Recounting such sentiments at recruitment rallies, in the diaspora's newspapers, and in songs strengthened Irish-American morale behind the Union cause.

The consequence of Irish-American ballads about Bull Run was that retreat was not viewed as a complete and outright disaster. Irish-Americans across New York, Massachusetts, Pennsylvania, Connecticut, and Illinois used it to rouse the diaspora after the Federal withdrawal around Manassas, turning what happened into a powerful inspiration to enlist in the war effort. The survivors were depicted as gallant heroes; their actions—as told through songs that commemorated their service—generated home-front support and honored those involved. The power of this combat legacy carried through for the remainder of the conflict, building on the reality that the retreat came with positive consequences for this migrant community.

The Civil War experience is an important lesson not just for how battles are discussed, but how the words "retreat" and "failure" are not always synonymous. This is as true in the twenty-first century as it was more than 160 years ago. Though the sense of noble loss and defeat pervades military historical memory, ballads about the 69th New York's actions at the First Bull Run and other wartime examples expose something deeper than mere rhetorical opinion. Honorable service in the retreat was itself used to project both the argument and the reality that the Irish in America were willing to assert their loyalty and citizenship to their new home nation of the United States via their steadfast behavior on the battlefield. Very literally, as "Battle of Bull Run" stressed, they "were not beat;" they took ownership of their more successful actions within the wider loss to emphasize that point repeatedly in the months and years after the fighting moved on from the fields around Manassas.[103] Furthermore, the ballads reinforced that if the soldiers of the 69th New York could hold rearguards successfully, they could also bring the national union back together again through their continued brave wartime actions.

The 69th New York State Militia's behavior in the retreat proved that Irish-American Federal soldiers—beyond an already (and continued) willingness to volunteer for military service—were prepared to join the fray again, avenge fallen comrades, and push for future victories in their new homeland. Retreat, then, was a temporary step back. It boosted, not weakened, morale. The Civil War songs discussed in this chapter, therefore, highlight how withdrawal should not always be seen as simply "not winning." Retreat can have positive impacts as well. The legacy of more optimistic views, and moments of individual and military unit successes, carried long in the memory of those closest to the events. Defeat was certainly *not* the 69th New York State Militia's lyrical assessment of the United States Federal Army retreat at the First Battle of Bull Run in July 1861.

Notes

1. "George B. McClellan letter to his wife, 16 August 1861," quoted in Bob Blaisdell, ed., *Civil War Letters: From Home, Camp & Battlefield* (New York: Dover Publications, 2021), 26.

2. Thomas Francis Meagher, *The Last Days of the 69th in Virginia—A Narrative in Three Parts* (New York: Lynch & Cole, 1861), 13.

3. Michael Corcoran, *The Captivity of General Corcoran: The Only Authentic and Reliable Narratives of the Trials and Suffering Endured During His Twelve Months' Imprisonment in Richmond and Other Southern Cities, by Brig-General Michael Corcoran—The Hero of Bull Run* (Philadelphia: Barclay & Co, 1864), 22.

4. Michael Cavanagh, *Memoirs of Gen. Thomas Francis Meagher, Comprising the Leading Events of His Career: Chronologically Arranged, With Selections from his Speeches, Lectures, and Miscellaneous Writings, Including Personal Reminiscences* (Worcester, MA: The Messenger Press, 1892), 406.

5. David Power Conyngham, *The Irish Brigade and Its Campaigns: With Some Account of the Corcoran Legion, and Sketches of the Principal Officers* (New York: William McSorley & Co., 1867), 19.

6. Conyngham, 21.

7. Third Irish Regiment recruitment poster (Boston, 1861), National Park Service Manassas Museum, Virginia.

8. Unknown lyricist, "Glorious 69th" (New York: H. De Marsan, 1861).

9. The immediacy of lyrics extolling loyal service also harked back to older martial music traditions; lyrical poetry has long been a cultural product of conflict with origins in classical and ancient warfare history. By the mid-1800s, traditional folk ballads—especially from Celtic cultures such as Ireland and its transnational diaspora—were the chief outlet for warring pride and battlefield bravery sentiments. See Catherine V. Bateson, "Music and War," *Oxford Bibliographies in Military History* online edition, ed. Dennis Showalter (New York: Oxford University Press, 2019).

10. For greater detail and study of the Irish-American Civil War experience, see Damian Shiels, *The Irish in the American Civil War* (Dublin: The History Press, 2013); and Dr. Shiels's work via *Irish in the American Civil War: Exploring Irish Involvement in the American Civil War,* http://irishamericancivilwar.com. For specific United States Union Irish-American history, see Susannah J. Ural, *The Harp and the Eagle: Irish-American Volunteers and the Union Army, 1861–1865* (New York: New York University Press, 2006). For specific Confederate Irish-American history, see David T. Gleeson, *The Green and the Gray: The Irish in the Confederate States of America* (Chapel Hill, NC: The University of North Carolina Press, 2013). Confederate lyrical output in the Civil War tended to focus more on Confederate/secessionist nationalism and wartime sentiments rather than singing about battle encounters (a marked difference from northern Union ballad counterparts), hence no comparative Confederate ballads are discussed in this chapter.

11. For further exploration of the history and culture of general Civil War songs and music, see Christian McWhirter, *Battle Hymns: The Power and Popularity of Music in the Civil War* (Chapel Hill, NC: University of North Carolina Press, 2012); and Steven H. Cornelius, *Music of the Civil War Era* (Westport, CT: Greenwood Press, 2004).

12. For more on the specific sentiments and culture of Irish-American Civil War songs and music production, see Catherine V. Bateson, *Irish American Civil War Songs: Identity, Loyalty, and Nationhood* (Baton Rouge, LA: Louisiana State University Press, 2022).

13. This chapter uses current American Civil War historiographical convention of favoring the Federal Union names to reflect their ultimate conflict victory; hence it will be referred to as the First Battle of Bull Run—and variations of this—throughout. Manassas will be used when discussing the wider area and the railway junction town.

14. Conyngham, *Irish Brigade and Its Campaigns*, 32–33.

15. Brooks D. Simpson, *America's Civil War* (Wheeling, IL: Harlan Davidson, 1996), 38. This chapter focuses on the individual example of the 69th New York State Militia and Irish-American ballads about the battle. For wider study and military history of the events at the First Battle of Bull Run, see Edward G. Longacre, *The Early Morning of War: Bull Run, 1861* (Norman, OK: University of Oklahoma Press, 2014); John Hennessy, *First Battle of Manassas: An End to Innocence, July 18–21, 1861* (Mechanicsburg, PA: Stackpole Books, 2015); and Ted Ballad, *Battle of Bull Run* (Washington, DC: US Army Center of Military History, 2007).

16. Edward L. Ayers, "The Meaning of Bull Run," in *Disunion: 106 Articles from The New York Times Opinionator—Modern Historians Revisit and Reconsider the Civil War from Lincoln's Election to the Emancipation Proclamation*, eds. Ted Widmer, Clay Risen, and George Kalogeraki (New York: Black Dog & Leventhal Publishers, 2013), 163. William Tecumseh Sherman's first account of the battle was written three days later at Fort Corcoran and recalled the sounds of fighting. He noted that "the firing was very severe, and the roar of cannon, muskets, and rifles incessant," William Tecumseh Sherman, First Bull Run Report, 25 July 1861. The average age of the untested Federal and Confederate soldiers fighting on 21 July 1861 was just twenty-one years old.

17. James M. McPherson, *Battle Cry of Freedom: The Civil War Era* (Oxford: Oxford University Press & Penguin Books, 1990), 344. McPherson described 21 July 1861 as "a brutally hot, sultry day" even before the heat of battle took hold.

18. Ayres, "Meaning of Bull Run," 164.

19. "Eugene Blackford letter to his father, 22 July 1861," quoted in *Major Problems in the Civil War and Reconstruction: Documents and Essays*, eds. Michael Perman and Amy Murrell Taylor (Independence, KY: Wadsworth Cengage Learning, 2011), 182–83. Blackford's letter commented with relief that his regiment "arrived too late to take any considerable part in the action.

". . . Had we been an hour earlier, many would not have lived to tell the tale." However in his correspondence, the unsatisfied soldier complained more about the "hard bread and intensely salty meat to eat" than the fact that he missed the height of the battle.

20. Conyngham, *Irish Brigade and Its Campaigns*, 36–37.

21. Corcoran, *Captivity of General Corcoran*, 23.

22. "Michael Corcoran letter to Capt. James B. Kirker, 24 July 1861," quoted in Cavanagh, *Memoirs of Gen. Thomas Francis Meagher*, 402.

23. Conyngham, *Irish Brigade and Its Campaigns*, 37, 41.

24. Conyngham, 37, 41.

25. Conyngham, 37, 41.

26. Special Correspondent, *The World* (July 1861), quoted in Conyngham, *Irish Brigade and Its Campaigns*, 42–43. Confederate Irish-born and descended soldiers were credited similarly for their display of "Irish fighting ability" during the battle, David T. Gleeson, *The Green and the Gray: The Irish in the Confederate States of America* (Chapel Hill, NC: University of North Carolina Press, 2013), 76.

27. Col. Ambrose Burnside (July 1861), quoted in Cal McCarthy, *Green, Blue, and Grey: The Irish in the American Civil War* (Cork, IE: The Collins Press, 2009), 23.

28. Unknown lyricist, "The Gallant Sons of Erin" (New York: H. De Marsan, 1861).

29. Unknown lyricist.

30. Unknown lyricist, "To the Glorious 69th!" (New York: H. De Marsan, 1861).

31. F. Collins, "Battle of Bull Run" (New York, James Wrigley, 1861).

32. Collins.

33. F. Collins, "The 69th Brigade" (New York: James Wrigley, c.1862–1863).

34. Collins.

35. William P. Ferris, "Return of Gen. Corcoran, of the Glorious 69th" (Boston: Horace Partridge, 1862). This ballad was set to the tune of "To the Glorious 69th!"

36. The farmhouse belonged to eighty-five-year-old widow Judith Carter Henry. Suffering continual fire, the property was completely destroyed by the end of the engagement. For Henry, who decided to stay inside the house as the battle raged, it "proved to be no shelter at all;" she was killed by a shell, Ayres, "Meaning of Bull Run," 163. The heavily annotated observational map of the First Bull Run from a Confederate perspective in Figure 16.2 details the position and movements of both Federal and Confederate positions across the morning and afternoon of 21 July 1861. The "N.Y. 69th" appear by a road bend in the upper central left portion of the map near the detail of the "BATTLE FIELD in the morning." On the other side of the Turnpike farther to the middle left, the "BATTLE FIELD IN THE AFTERNOON" portion of the map shows the posi-

tion of Sherman and Jackson's mutual brigades, along with a house described as "Old woman killed in this house." This is the Henry House and the site of the 69th New York State Militia's afternoon attacks. Elsewhere, the map depicts the misspelled "MCLANE'S HOUSE" owned by Wilmer McLean (who famously moved to Appomattox Court House after the battle where his home witnessed the surrender of Lee in April 1865), the headquarters of both sides, some notable deaths and injuries to key battle figures, and the retreats along the Turnpike and main roads away from the battlefield. Bamberger's annotations by the Stone Bridge state: "When the retreating [Federal] column reached this point and saw our [Confederate] cavalry on the turnpike the panic seized the entire column.... Everything was abandoned to facilitate their retreat."

37. Private William Todd, 79th New York, quoted in JoAnna M. McDonald, *'We Shall Meet Again': The First Battle of Manassas (Bull Run), July 18–21 1861* (New York: Oxford University Press), 140. Adding to the 79th New York's shock, their commander—Col. James Cameron (brother to Lincoln's first Secretary of War Simon Cameron)—was fatally shot in the chest. A plaque near the Henry's farmhouse marks the spot where "Colonel Cameron of the 79th New York Regiment was killed here on July 21, 1861," National Park Service Manassas Museum, Virginia.

38. McDonald, *We Shall Meet Again*, 144–45.

39. Joseph G. Bilby, *The Irish Brigade in the Civil War: The 69th New York and Other Irish Regiments of the Army of the Potomac* (Cambridge, MA: Da Capo Press, 1997), 13.

40. Corcoran, *Captivity of General Corcoran*, 24.

41. Collins, "Battle of Bull Run."

42. Meagher, *Last Days of the 69th in Virginia*, 13.

43. For more on the confusion of accurate reporting, fighting remembrances, and Civil War military memory in the height of battle, see Carole Reardon, *Pickett's Charge in History and Memory* (Chapel Hill, NC: University of North Carolina Press, 2003).

44. Ryan W. Keating, *Shades of Green: Irish Regiments, American Soldiers, and Local Communities in the Civil War Era* (New York: Fordham University Press, 2017), 51.

45. Collins, "Battle of Bull Run."

46. Robert Smith, *We Will Have the Union Still* (New York: James Wrigley, 1861).

47. Figures relating to how many men actually fought at the First Battle of Bull Run vary. McDonald estimated conservatively that both Federal and Confederate forces engaged less than half of their available soldiers during the battle; "while the combined Confederate forces totaled almost 30,000, the actual troops directly involved in the fighting numbered approximately 14,050." By comparison in the United States Army, "only about 13,000 to 15,000 men actually participated in the fighting" out of a possible 32,000 to 35,000 available to McDowell. The discrepancy in availability versus fighting was due to ineffective

use of men by commanders, too many held back in reserve, many being "too exhausted from marching" to Manassas, and soldiers dropping out of service due to their initial ninety-day enlistment terms ending prior to the battle (something that also impacted the 69th New York State Militia), McDonald, *We Will Meet Again*, 15, 17.

48. As this was the war's first major battle (compared to Chancellorsville almost two years later—and two years into the conflict itself), criticism of *Irish* soldiers and commanders was not very vocal in any sections (be that military, political, or home front) after Bull Run. This added to the relative "success" of their performance.

49. Corcoran, *Captivity of General Corcoran*, 23–24.

50. Corcoran, 23–24.

51. Corcoran, 23–24.

52. Corcoran, 23–24.

53. Conyngham, *Irish Brigade and Its Campaigns*, 37.

54. Conyngham, 37.

55. Ayres, "Meaning of Bull Run," 164.

56. Conyngham, *Irish Brigade and Its Campaigns*, 38–39.

57. Conyngham, 38–39.

58. Collins, "Battle of Bull Run."

59. Cornelia McDonald, quoted in B.A. Botkin, ed, *A Civil War Treasury of Tales, Legends and Folklore* (New York: Promontory Press, 1981), 28–29.

60. Unknown lyricist, "Yankee Doodle," in *Songs of the South* (Richmond, VA: J. W. Randolph, 1864), 59. The song also noted that news of the battle reached international audiences thanks to the presence of *The Times* journalist William Howard Russell. The global humiliation of the Federal loss was described as being "a funny yarn" in which "Russell . . . stood looking on, and split his sides with laughter."

61. Unknown lyricist.

62. Corcoran, *Captivity of General Corcoran*, 23.

63. Sherman, First Bull Run Report.

64. Sherman.

65. Denis Gwynn, *Thomas Francis Meagher: O'Donnell Lecture Delivered at University College Cork, July 17th 1961* (Dublin: National University of Ireland, 1961), 49.

66. Gwynn, 49.

67. Conyngham, *Irish Brigade and Its Campaigns*, 40.

68. Collins, "Battle of Bull Run."

69. McPherson, *Battle Cry of Freedom*, 344

70. Keating, *Shades of Green*, 4; and McCarthy, *Green, Blue, and Grey*, 27.

71. Keating, 4; and McCarthy, 27.

72. Corcoran to Kirker, *Memoirs of Gen. Thomas Francis Meagher*, 402.

73. Ferris, "Return of Gen. Corcoran."

74. Unknown lyricist, "The Gallant Sons of Erin."

75. "Ceade Mille Failthe—General Meagher Recruiting the Irish Brigade—Enthusiastic Gathering of the Seventh New York Regiment Armory– Speech by General Meagher—A Rousing Meeting!," *The New York Herald*, 25 July 1862.

76. Conyngham, *Irish Brigade and Its Campaigns*, 37. Meagher and Corcoran were impacted deeply by their friend's death: Meagher often used Haggerty's memory to inspire his Irish soldiers at future battles. Corcoran likewise recalled how the loss "fills me with the deepest sorrow [that] my beloved acting Lieutenant-Colonel was the first who fell," Corcoran to Kirker, *Memoirs of Gen. Thomas Francis Meagher*, 402. Haggerty is listed in some military reports as a captain prior to Bull Run.

77. Thomas Walsh, *Our Brave Irish Champions—A New Song on the Great Battle Fought in America! On Sunday, 21st of July, 1861* (Cork, IE: Haly, 1861).

78. Meagher, *Last Days of the 69th in Virginia*, 13.

79. McPherson, *Battle Cry of Freedom*, 347.

80. Conyngham, *Irish Brigade and Its Campaigns*, 37.

81. William Tecumseh Sherman, *Memoirs of General W. T. Sherman* (1885), quoted in Botkin, *Civil War Treasury*, 13.

82. Sherman, 13. Lincoln was said to be so impressed by Sherman's conduct during these post-Bull Run visits to the Federal Army encampments that it encouraged the colonel's promotion to brigadier general, awarded despite the fact that Sherman himself doubted his own leadership capabilities following the battle defeat. His conduct for the rest of the conflict, particularly with his (in)famous march through Georgia and the Carolinas, proved this wrong; regardless of the July 1861 events, Sherman became one of the leading generals in the Civil War and in US military history.

83. Conyngham, *Irish Brigade and Its Campaigns*, 47.

84. Conyngham, 47.

85. Thomas J. Craughwell, *The Greatest Brigade: How the Irish Brigade Cleared the Way to Victory in the American Civil War* (Beverly, MA: Fair Winds Press, 2011), 63.

86. McPherson, *Battle Cry of Freedom*, 349.

87. Collins, "Battle of Bull Run."

88. Collins.

89. It can be argued that this message was emphasized to resist any latent mid-nineteenth century American anti-immigrant nativism (as explored in *Armies in Retreat* Chapter 17 on German-Americans in the XI Corps at Chancellorsville). However, several Irish-American scholars have observed how nativist views toward the Irish were waning in the 1860s. They argue that by the late 1850s, "anti-Catholicism had receded as a public passion" in the United States as the stance took "a subordinate position to the sectional tensions between North and South," Lawrence J. McCaffrey, *The Irish Diaspora in America* (Bloomington, IN: Indiana University Press, 1976), 95.

90. Dan Milner, *The Unstoppable Irish: Songs and Integration of the New York Irish, 1783–1883* (Notre Dame, IN: University of Notre Dame Press, 2019), 134.

91. Keating, *Shades of Green*, 61, 71.

92. Conyngham, *Irish Brigade and Its Campaigns*, 49.

93. Conyngham, 49.

94. Milner, *Unstoppable Irish*, 134.

95. Milner, 134.

96. Conyngham, *Irish Brigade and Its Campaigns*, 49.

97. Conyngham, 49.

98. Unknown lyricist, "The Irish Brigade in America" (Glasgow: James Lindsay, 1863). The song was also published as "The Soldier's Letter from America."

99. Unknown lyricist.

100. Unknown lyricist.

101. Unknown lyricist.

102. Reardon, *Pickett's Charge in History and Memory*.

103. Collins, "Battle of Bull Run."

Chapter 17

The Flight into History: The XI Corps at Chancellorsville

Anthony J. Cade II

In May 1863, General Joseph Hooker encircled the town of Chancellorsville, Virginia, to destroy southern forces positioned around the city. Hooker had multiple units under his command, but the one that became the most famous for its actions was the XI Corps led by General Oliver Otis Howard. The unit, which had a high proportion of German immigrants or soldiers whose parents immigrated a decade prior, broke ranks on the evening of 2 May 1863 when enemy forces executed a pincer maneuver on its unsecured flank. The XI Corps' actions that day followed all German immigrants for decades, with one soldier writing nearly thirty years after that "The burning shame of that stigma has followed us nearly twenty-eight years, and will follow us on to the grave, and still on to the end of time."[1] Private Gottfried Rentschler wrote about the consequences of their actions soon after the battle:

> The treatment or rather mistreatment of the Germans in the army has recently demanded the attention of the German press more than usual. If a full company is needed for an easy service, a German company is never taken. If an entire company is required for rough service, . . . a German company will be ordered whenever possible. . . . As a rule, the German has to wade through the mud, while the American walks on the dry road. The German is a "Dutch soldier" and as a "Dutchman" he is, if not despised, is disrespected, and not regarded or treated as an equal.[2]

Misunderstandings about what caused the rout of the XI Corps not only affected the treatment of all German immigrants for the remainder of the war; it also has tainted the legacy of their actions in the face of insurmountable obstacles. Twenty-first century military leaders can learn from the mistakes of Chancellorsville to understand why an inclusive and equitable command environment is necessary to avoid a similar retreat from a battlefield or stigma within the ranks.

"Divisiveness Leads to Defeat"

American history is permeated with an unending list of people discriminated against both politically and within the military. During the nineteenth century, Germans were one of those many groups. More than 243,000 German immigrants and German Americans fought for the Federal Army during the war—the largest of all the ethnic groups in the Army; they were considered at the time to be inferior to American soldiers, despite the fact many had military experience from a failed revolution in Germany and were politically motivated to support the Federal cause.[3] This belief in German inferiority had its roots in the politicized nativist beliefs of the mid-nineteenth century, which disparaged immigrants from most nations. German anti-slavery sentiment was the largest issue that made Germans a target for most of the early nineteenth century.[4] During the war, these nativist beliefs were prevalent within the Army of the Potomac, and they influenced command decisions by US Army generals at the Battle of Chancellorsville.[5]

The consequences of the events at Chancellorsville were multifold for the military as a whole and XI Corps soldiers in particular. The 2 May 1863 events were an embarrassment for the Federal military, and the entire Army was seen as weak because of it. Enemy forces used the campaign as proof of southern superiority in combat rather than recognizing that an enemy mistake and good timing allowed them to win. Buoyed by the Chancellorsville victory, southern forces were confident they had the capability to invade farther north—misplaced confidence which led to the bloodiest battle ever fought on American soil at Gettysburg. If they had been defeated in May, Confederate forces would not have had the manpower or the will to attempt such an act. Thus, Chancellorsville was a tactical defeat for the Federal Army that resulted in the deaths of many while prolonging the Civil War itself. Additionally, soon after campaign officers were questioned for their command ability, German soldiers were treated as cowards and, like Private Rentschler, felt they did not belong in the Army anymore. German culture itself was attacked, and racist epithets followed many both in and outside of the military for the remainder of the war. Their morale was at its lowest ebb for many months after Chancellorsville; some left the military to avoid the prejudicial onslaught. The cultural, morale, and tactical repercussions of the Battle of Chancellorsville affected many in 1863—circumstances that could have been avoided if different choices had been made prior to and during the campaign.

This chapter contains two explicit arguments: one for historians and the other for military leaders. The first is that the German members of the XI Corps should not be remembered as the "Flying Dutchmen." This negative and discriminatory moniker has followed them since the Civil War, despite contemporary historian efforts to revise the historiography.[6] Rather, the men were not utilized properly during the battle, and the generals in command that day did not follow battle manual instructions for placement and responding to reports. Historian James S. Pula writes in *Under the Crescent Moon with the XI Corps in the Civil War*: "Their comrades-in-arms in the Army of the Potomac never fully accepted them as part of 'their' army, much less as equals."[7] His work demonstrates that unequal treatment was prevalent from the unit's inception and affected not only their treatment but equipment and use. Pula argues there were multiple reasons the XI Corps retreated on 2 May 1863, none of which were the fault of the men involved in the battle.[8] In *Chancellorsville and the Germans*, military historian Christian Keller presents a similar argument focused on Chancellorsville specifically. This chapter builds on the work of Keller and Pula to demonstrate how the negative events at Chancellorsville can be traced to nativist sentiments in the Federal Army that were prevalent during the war. Adding another layer to the discussion, authors Walter D. Kamphoefner, and Wolfgang Helbich suggest that the German soldiers may have invited the harsh treatment: "The unpopular Germans insisted on believing they were the better soldiers and could thus win the respect of the Americans, and many Americans were eagerly waiting for a chance to prove that these incompetent foreigners were inferior to real Yankees."[9] The Army's retreat at Chancellorsville became the chance that many were looking for, and nineteenth-century nativist reactions have followed the German soldiers through the historiography.[10] This chapter builds on these multiple writings to show that the men in the XI Corps were not at fault when they choose to retreat from Chancellorsville; rather their superior officers made command decisions that led to the retreat.

The second argument is that biases can cloud effective judgment in military leaders, and perceived bias by those leaders can negatively affect the fighting spirit of those who serve under them. A person in command who allows personal feelings about a subordinate's race, gender, ethnicity, political affiliation, sexual orientation, or any other discriminatory factor to affect the way they treat their troops or place them in relation to battle invites defeat while causing a schism between themselves and those who report to them. When soldiers believe their command cannot be trusted, a unit's combat effectiveness suffers as well—because of a phenomenon often referred to as Social Identity Theory. The theory posits that "an individual's attachment to members of their own group serves to validate their own social identity and helps determine the ways in which they will interact with and interpret the actions of others."[11] Social Identity Theory is seen in the XI Corps' German immigrants, who accepted the identity of "German" when there was no Germany; nativist views of this communal identity influenced how these men were treated prior to and during the Battle of Chancellorsville. Additionally, these soldiers believed their commanding officers did not support their social identity, and this belief affected the men's morale for months after the battle. The primary function of this chapter is to provide a historical example of potential consequences when military leaders do not respect all those under their command; any direct or perceived disrespect of a shared community identity can affect the use of specific soldiers and create a toxic command environment.[12]

The events at Chancellorsville became infamous because nearly everyone who was there—as well as historians commenting after the event—agree the Federals should have won that battle. Robert E. Lee and his men were heavily outnumbered, in poor position for an all-out assault, and had limited supplies.[13] However, the XI Corps was placed in a poor position on the battlefield and "Dutch Corps" reports about enemy forces possibly being near their position were ignored for hours until it was too late. The general in charge of the field did not abide by military convention, and his missteps caused a defeat. Twenty-first century military leaders should observe this historical lesson about what can occur if an officer in command allows personal feelings about the ancestry of the soldiers under them affect their judgment. Furthermore, the men lost respect for their commanders because they felt ill-treated by their leaders both during and after the battle. This perception, intentional or not, affected enlisted and officer alike, lowering their morale; many would still be upset about it years after the war. Modern military leaders need to be reminded to avoid a situation where an army retreats from a battlefield because of prejudicial reasons. In 2020 comments to the House Armed Services Committee, the Chairman of the Joint Chiefs of Staff, General Mark A. Milley, condemned racism and prejudice within the military, acknowledging that "Divisiveness leads to defeat."[14] If the Union generals at Chancellorsville had understood this, they might have won the battle that day.

The XI Army Corps

From the constitution of the XI Corps in the Federal Army, it was an outlier.[15] Originally constituted September 1861, the XI Corps was led by multiple German officers—arguably, the most famous among them was General Franz Sigel, a German war hero and revolutionary. The unit was understrength for a corps and manned by multiple regiments of ethnic Germans. Sigel was a man with many ambitions, and he used his personality to galvanize thousands of Germans to join the Northern cause to help further their placement in the country and also his own political career.[16] Sigel's status as a hero to his fellow Germans cannot be overstated. He was among the most prominent Germans in the country, and President Abraham Lincoln made him a general specifically because he was aware Sigel would garner the enthusiasm of German immigrants. Although the XI Corps is known as a German unit, less than 60 percent of the Corps was German or had German ancestry. Despite this fact, they were known as The German Corps; the unit was used as a litmus test for all Germans serving in the Federal Army. Most German immigrants in the Corps were combat veterans or at least had military training prior to coming to the United States; during the war they served in a number of both large and small battles ranging from the Battle of Cross Keys to the Second Bull Run campaign.[17] The combination of their training, experience, and leadership convinced the men they were prepared for anything going into 1863. The German almanac *Lahrer Hinkender Bote* summarized the sentiment of their Corps: "The Germans have won such respect from their enemies that when the cry is heard, 'the Germans are coming, Sigel is coming!' entire regiments turn and flee without firing a shot."[18] Evidently, even the enemy knew to be aware of the distinctive corps.

Prior to Chancellorsville, Sigel's ambitions and personality alienated him from Lincoln and Secretary of War Edwin Stanton. Sigel thought

Figure 17.1. Maj. Gen. Franz Sigel. Courtesy of the Library of Congress.

his command was too small for a major general and requested to expand his unit to the full size of the other corps. After multiple rejections, he requested to be reassigned as he felt insulted by the treatment of his unit and himself. Furthermore, his strong anti-slavery stance caused a rift with the General in Chief, Henry Halleck, which all contributed to his removal from command. His replacement, General Oliver Otis Howard—not of German ancestry—did not sit well with the men of the XI Corps, who believed they should have another German in charge. The loss of Sigel as their leader lowered the men's morale and prompted negative comments from XI Corps soldiers at all levels and the media as well. Capt. Theodore Howell wrote: "I would rather fight under Sigel than any other Gen'l [sic] in the army as he tries to save his men and don't go in blind."[19] Pvt. William Charles, a German-American serving in the XI Corps, commented: "I have heard yesterday that Gen. Sigel resigned. For one I am very sorry for I believe him to be a very good General and one that wishes to put down this rebellion."[20] In a letter to his parents, Sergeant Albert Krause shared what many Germans in the north believed, that Sigel was the best Federal general.[21] Maj. Gen. Samuel Ryan Curtis, who commanded one of the divisions, wrote to Maj. Gen. Peter Osterhaus, another division commander, asking if they should both resign in support of Sigel.[22] German newspaper *Der Demokrat* was outraged that Sigel was not allowed to return to the XI Corps, which he had trained, and told its readers Sigel only resigned to help his men.[23] *Der Demokrat* called for Sigel to return or be replaced by another German. They feared the nativist sentiment of the time would lead to a new commander who did not respect the Germans in his command. By April, *Der Demokrat* recognized that Sigel would not return, leaving Schurz as their next choice; the paper expressed its expectation that his tutelage under Sigel and his involvement in Lincoln's election would make him a good replacement.[24]

General Carl Schurz initially took command of the XI Corps in Sigel's absence, and he and his fellow officers thought Lincoln would give him permanent command of the unit. Lt. Col. Alwin von Matzdorff wrote to a fellow German officer: "In this case [Sigel's resignation], Genr'l Schurz will probably take command of the corps."[25] Schurz wrote to Lincoln requesting permanent command of the XI Corps.[26] However, he was not the only contender. General Adolph von Steinwehr hoped he could get the position and wrote to Lincoln as well.[27] Northern papers such as the Chicago *Daily Tribune* commented that Schurz was the only choice to command Sigel's old corps because of his recent promotion to major general.[28] However, Stanton and General Halleck petitioned Lincoln that another German

Figure 17.2. General Oliver Otis Howard. Courtesy of the Library of Congress.

would only cause trouble. Alarmed by Sigel's use of the position as a political means to advance his own career, Stanton and Halleck believed that another German, such as Schurz, would share a similar agenda. Instead, they coordinated with General Hooker to appoint General Howard as the new commander of the Corps, an American who had never worked with German soldiers before.

Howard's appointment prior to the Battle of Chancellorsville generated optimistic reactions in the North and, thanks to early victories under Sigel, the Corps had earned a good reputation with northern newspapers. Howard assumed command of the XI Corps on 2 April 1863. The governor of Pennsylvania met with Howard two days after his appointment, and the crowd in attendance cheered for Howard and his German soldiers. The crowd applauded when the governor referred to Howard's Corps as "One of God's Christian Regiments."[29] However, not everyone felt optimistic regarding Howard's placement. General Schurz wrote to President Lincoln days after the appointment and requested that all Germans be removed from under Howard and put under either General Ambrose Burnside or William Rosecrans because he feared Howard's personal prejudice against Germans.[30] Lincoln rejected his request, believing Howard could lead the Corps.[31] Subsequent events at Chancellorsville demonstrated that Lincoln's confidence was misplaced.

The Battle of Chancellorsville

Rain fell day and night on 27 April 1863, muddying the ground and giving the sky a grim overcast. The XI Corps marched south toward Kelly's Ford on the Rappahannock River at the head of the Army of the Potomac. General Joseph Hooker, then-commander of the Army of the Potomac, assigned the Corps as the lead for the march. However, Howard had never directed such a large unit, and his newly formed staff could not compensate for their leader's inexperience. For example, Howard moved the Corps' equipment and cattle with the main body instead of leaving it with the rear, an error that caused the unit to move more slowly than expected. When the men reached the Germanna Ford on the Rapidan River after two days of rain and marching, the river was too high to cross, and the Army had to halt and sleep in mud and water.[32]

The XI Corps reached Chancellorsville on 1 May after two additional days of marching in the rain and mud; finally, the rain stopped. Hooker marched two of his corps forward to help secure the field then took a defensive posture instead of attacking the bulk of Lee's forces, even though he outnumbered the Confederate troops. General Howard had his men set

Figure 17.3. "The Battle of Chancellorsville" sketch showing the junction of US Ford Road and the road to Rapidan River. Courtesy of the Library of Congress.

up defensive positions west, along the Orange Turnpike. This position secured the Federal Army's right flank; they would not be in direct contact with the main enemy force in Chancellorsville once the battle commenced. All the Corps regiments camped facing south of Orange Turnpike, which was the presumed direction of attack should enemy forces move toward their position. The German regiments entrenched themselves for nearly two miles facing south of the Turnpike—and rested because Hooker assured Howard that the battle would be in the center.

By 0930 the next morning, Hooker's Aide-de-Camp, General James Van Alen sent a message to Howard warning that the enemy might attack his flank through the woods and destroy his right instead of attacking his front. At 1000, two Corps scouts reported that Confederate troops appeared to be moving west across the unit's front to flank them. The XI Corps flank was of major concern because General Hooker understood that if the Corps broke ranks, their retreat would take them through his center. He feared the entire Army could be disrupted by confusion and demoralization if such an event occurred. General Van Alen cautioned Howard to examine his front and adjust his flank because of multiple reports of enemy troops in the area:

> The right of your line does not appear to be strong enough. No artificial defenses worth naming have been thrown up, and there appears to be a scarcity of troops at this point, and not, in the general's opinion, as favorably posted as might be."[33]

Whether because of inexperience, Howard's suspicion of the Germans recently put under his command, or because he did not understand the significance of the message, Howard only adjusted his artillery while making no change to the Corps front.[34] His inaction would have a lasting effect on the reputation of the XI Corps.

Corps officers pressed Howard to reposition the unit. General Carl Schurz was the loudest among them, but Howard rejected the suggestions based on prior orders and his desire to rest. By 1100, Howard received additional reports from his right of movement and sounds from the forest, but he continued to ignore these indications of trouble. When Schurz requested Howard to at least adjust his own lines in case of an enemy attack, Howard rejected the recommendations. Howard had his reasons; Major General Sickles had reported to his fellow commanders that the enemy was in retreat and he was pursuing them.[35] Howard was not alone in thinking the culminating point of attack was 180 degrees from where his men reported noises. Thus, Howard assumed any disturbances in the forest

Figure 17.4. Hooker at Chancellorsville, 3 May 1863. Courtesy of the Library of Congress.

were animals, an extremely small force, or stragglers attempting to escape capture. Dozens of animals leaped from the forest for hours, and their scurrying seemed to confirm Howard's belief that the tumult was caused primarily by wildlife. Schurz adjusted his brigades anyway; by noon, his were the only units in the entire Corps facing west. Between 1500 and 1600 in the afternoon, units near the western front continued to send reports of enemy infantry amassing near their position; however, Howard had left his headquarters to move with a nearby brigade. Those left behind in both his and Hooker's headquarters dismissed the reports as skittish Germans overestimating an enemy in retreat; Hooker had incorrectly told his officers the battle was won. On the evening of 2 May, most of the Corps was ordered to eat so they would be ready to pursue the retreating enemy once called upon; the men slaughtered deer running through their camp, looking forward to eating real meat while they relaxed around a fire.[36]

At approximately 1800, 70 enemy regiments—26,000 soldiers—attacked the Corps' exposed right flank, which was facing the wrong direction and cooking dinner. Although Howard's 8,500 men were stretched out over two miles and heavily outnumbered, the exposed German divisions attempted to form lines and stand their ground. Capt. Theodore Howell swore that the enemy marched in so close that "they struck some of the men with the butts of their rifles;" the Germans did not retreat until their lines were completely overwhelmed.[37]

Other lines saw mixed results, as expressed by Col. Leopold Von Gilsa, the officer in charge of securing the flank:

> The whole line was at once engaged furiously, and my brigade stood coolly and bravely, fired three times, and stood still after they had outflanked me already on the right . . . . The enemy attacked now from the front and rear, and then of course, my brave boys were obliged to fall back.[38]

Von Gilsa commented that other units had already retreated from the field of battle: "Retreating, I expected surely to rally my brigade behind our second line, formed by [Schurz's] Divisions, but I did not find the second line; it was abandoned before we reached it."[39] With the flank failing and units abandoning their positions, confusion set in on the battlefield, further demoralizing the outnumbered men.

As the westernmost regiments broke position, those in the east were facing south—still awaiting orders to turn west or retreat. Fleeing soldiers

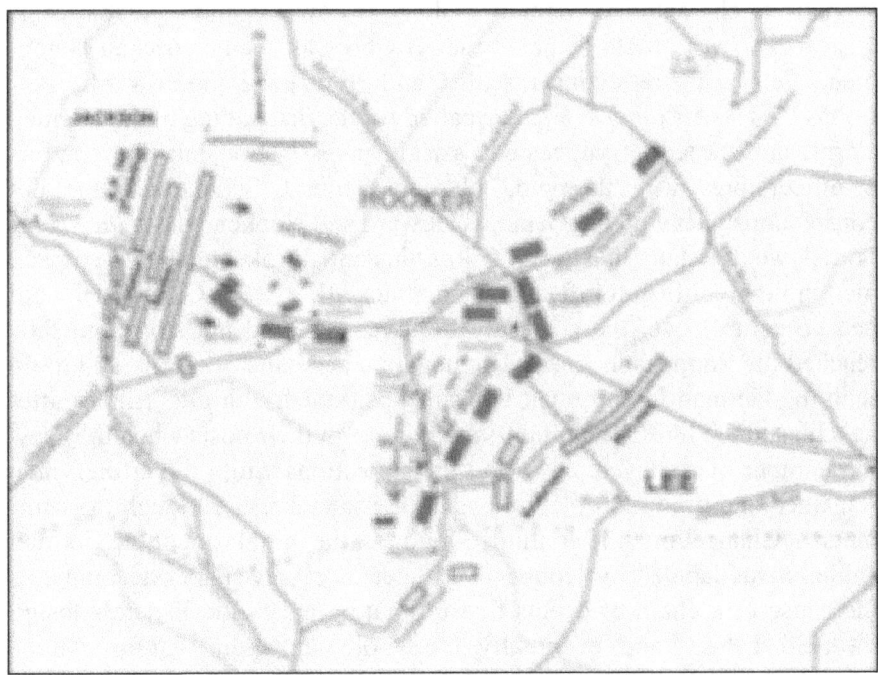

Figure 17.5. Map of Jackson's Flank Attack, 1700–1800 on 2 May. Courtesy of The National Park Service Civil War Series.

broke the ranks of regiments attempting to hold their positions; more than that, the fleeing soldiers shattered the army's combat spirit. Despite this, multiple regiments attempted to hold their position. The 119th Regiment withstood the onslaught for nearly twenty minutes before enemy forces breached their position, and the Ohio battery held for almost as long before it lost too many men to maintain combat effectiveness. Sgt. Fredrick Kappelman wrote to his parents after the battle: "Our regiment would have stood its ground better, but the attack came unforeseen, and we were caught down."[40] Although many officers were shot from their horses, a few led the men in organized retreats that prevented a complete rout. The enemy outnumbered the Germans three-to-one and, because of their size and position, enveloped the Corps until the flank broke and exposed the center. By 2100 that evening, the Corps could only account for 3,200 men; the rest were either in retreat, captured, or dead.[41] Pushed back along with Hooker's center, they retreated from the battlefield, unaware of how their actions would affect Germans throughout the country.

The Consequences for German Soldiers

Nativist Americans exploited the collapse of the XI Corps at Chancellorsville to characterize German soldiers as cowards and mercenaries. A *New York Times* article depicted the XI Corps as "panic-stricken Dutchmen," "cowardly retreating rascals," and "retreating and cowardly poltroons."[42] The *Alexandria Gazette* called for the disbanding of the German Corps, and the editor suggested "a rigid investigation into the conduct of officers present on the field," blaming Generals Schurz and Sigel but conspicuously leaving out Generals Howard and Hooker.[43] The *Gazette* reported two days later that the XI Corps "instantly broke into panic-stricken men in utter confusion [after Jackson attacked].... For General Howard had no control over the cowardly fugitives who did not stop until they reached the Rappahannock."[44] The negative accounts primarily had to do with the German infantrymen Howard positioned with the artillery after he adjusted the lines. The infantrymen ran from their posts when they saw the number of troops approaching their positions while the artillerymen remained and fired multiple volleys at their attackers. Although the campaign at Chancellorsville continued for days, the initial rout of the German soldiers was labeled by Hooker, and later most newspaper accounts, as the cause of a chain of events that ultimately led to the Federals losing the field that day and, eventually, the whole campaign.[45] Unfortunately, some historians cite these nativist reactions to Chancellorsville as a full account of the campaign. Similarly, one sign at the Chancellorsville battle site labeled "The Flying Dutchmen" marks the point of retreat for the XI Corps—helping to keep the derogatory moniker alive.[46] However, some modern historians have worked to correct this view, helping to demonstrate that the men of the XI Corps were not solely responsible for the Army of the Potomac retreat.

The *Ohio Democrat* described the democratic disposition in regards to Sigel and the XI Corps after Chancellorsville:

> President [Lincoln] should not let the whims of a confirmed and established failure control important military appointments . . . . Sigel has demonstrated his ability as a soldier, his countrymen in the army and out of it are attached to him, and the services of such officers just now, appear to be much needed. The falling back of the Germans under Carl S[c]hurz we attribute to no want of pluck upon their part; but to a want of confidence in their leader. . . . Those who are disposed to censure this case should remember German soldiers throughout the war, while at the first Bull Run and other places some of our best troops gave way. . . . In the next engagement in which these Germans soldiers are placed with Sigel in command, we confidently expect to hear of them wiping out the advantage which the fiery Stonewall Jackson obtained.[47]

The article was a warning to Southern soldiers not to become complacent when dealing with the German Corps.

Private correspondence of soldiers after the battle reveals conflicting viewpoints regarding Chancellorsville. Most believed the Germans broke without any attempt to halt Jackson's assault. One captain reported to General Hooker: "Sigel's Dutchmen broke and ran, all of them, at the first shot, as I always knew they would. . . . It is horrible awful. Everyman in Sigel's Corps ought to be hauled off the face of the earth."[48] Another captain decided his report should be publicized and wrote: "I never saw men as did these Dutchmen. Our boys stood, all American regiments did, but the panic among the Dutch was fearful. It shows where their mettle is . . . . Americans will make a stand even if outflanked and surprised."[49] Even some German soldiers believed it was a complete rout with little to no resistance. Carl Uterhard, a Federal surgeon who fought and was captured at Chancellorsville, wrote to his family after his release that the battle was a slaughter, the Corps was massacred, officers were shot off of their horses, soldiers fled the field by shooting behind them and running, the wounded lay on the battlefield screaming—dying from dehydration, hunger, and madness from the sun's rays because the enemy refused to help them and they would not allow him to help his men for eight days; and after fourteen days of this in enemy hands, he was ready to resign and go back to Germany.[50] Adam Muenzenberger agreed with Uterhard's assessment of the battle:

> When we reached our camp again [after retreating from Chancellorsville], and pitched our tents, we saw only misery.... One-third of the tents in the camp were empty. And why? Because those who had occupied them were no more. Where are they? Dead! In the hospitals. Captured by the rebels. That is the worst thing that could happen to a regiment that was once so excellent.[51]

August Horstman, a captain at the time of Chancellorsville, wrote to his family that the battle was bloody and merciless but the men held their lines against the onslaught despite being outnumbered.[52] Corp. Wilhelm Albrecht, an artillery noncommissioned officer who was among the forward-deployed soldiers utilized by Hooker, was proud of his unit's ability to hold their own against the superior enemy cannons that day.[53] Schurz, and many of his men, laid most of the blame on poor leadership and prejudice against Germans.

Figure 17.6. Men of Company C, 41st New York Infantry from Manassas, Virginia. Courtesy of the Library of Congress.

The soldiers publicly expressed their strong belief that Howard's orders were the cause of retreat, and a German commander—specifically Schurz or Sigel—would have positioned his troops better. An unnamed soldier wrote a letter to the *New York Tribune* that was later published in *The Spirit of Democracy*:

> It cannot be denied that a needless disaster was permitted to happen at Chancellorsville. Upon whom rest the fault? Our own correspondents in all the journals have attributed it in turn to the disaffection, the panic, the cowardice of the eleventh corps.... That one brigade (German) behaved badly is admitted; that they ran panic-stricken though the lines of other brigades, disorganizing them is true, but that the fault was the commanders'—or a commander's—and that the result must have been the same with any troops, of any condition of discipline or nationality, in from three to five minutes, is most certain.... If Sigel had been in command of his old corps, none believe such a surprise could have happened.[54]

This feeling that Howard and his fellow commanders were to blame was shared by many Germans in the Corps, and they felt this way directly because of their heritage. This fostered the belief that a German commander would have protected his men rather than leaving their flank exposed to enemy attack. One of Howard's men wrote: "[General Howard] wanted to have us slaughtered, because most of us are Germans."[55] The Pittsburgh *Freiheitsfreund* published a letter that claimed: "A comprehensive bitterness against Howard is evident that borders on insubordination—as expected, morale is quite depressed, especially among the officers who without exception feel offended and outraged in the aftermath of the strenuous denunciations from the American Press."[56] In tune with the sentiment of his men, Schurz conducted his own plan to ensure German soldiers were not blamed for Chancellorsville.

Carl Schurz personally responded to attacks on his leadership and his men. Leslie Combs, a former Army captain, Whig Speaker of the House, and, at the time, a Republican politician in Kentucky, published a scathing letter: "Our children [Americans] have fought in every battlefield, and never one fled as Carl Schurz and his gang of freedom-shirkers did at Chancellorsville."[57] Schurz called Combs a liar, insinuated he could kill him in a duel, and then invited Combs to share his tent and the field of battle with him so Schurz could observe Combs's ability to stand his ground in the next battle.[58] Schurz consistently stressed that he acted properly on the battlefield, and took responsibility for the actions of his men who

Figure 17.7. General Carl Schurz. Courtesy of the National Archives and Records Administration.

stood and fought as well as those who retreated before ordered to do so. Schurz later requested and obtained a public inquiry to challenge Hooker's and Howard's reports on the actions of the XI Corps at Chancellorsville. During the inquiry, Schurz proved that he and his men were following the orders of their superiors.[59]

Within weeks of the failed campaign, Schurz commenced a letter-writing campaign seeking justice for his men and the removal of Howard. Schurz wrote to Hooker regarding the battle, asking for the ejection of Howard and expressing the effect the battle had on the men:

> The Battle of Chancellorsville is not a thing that happened yesterday in order to be forgotten tomorrow. . . . It will fill a prominent page in the history of this Republic, on which every incident and the conduct of every commander and every command ought to be presented in their true light. You may believe me, General, when I say that the spirit of the corps is broken, and something must be done to revive it or the Corps will lose its efficacy. Too much humiliation destroys the morale of the men. . . . Every private in

this command knows and appreciated them as well, that it would be looked upon as the grossest injustice if they were ignored in their official publications.[60]

Schurz asked Hooker to publish his report blaming Howard, and requested an official inquiry where he could prove that his men were not at fault.[61] After Hooker and Stanton refused to publish his report, Schurz wrote letters to politicians and newspapers explaining that German soldiers were not at fault for the Federals' rout.[62] Schurz also wrote to President Lincoln asking him to reinstate Sigel because he was the only man the men had faith in and the only man Germans in America would follow onto any battlefield. Schurz also reported inadequacies in Howard's command and his inability to galvanize the Germans of the XI Corps the way Sigel did.[63] However, Lincoln rejected Schurz's request and instead relied on the advice of Stanton, who was already fed up with Germans in command because of his experience with Sigel.

Schurz's assertion that the XI Corps soldiers questioned the command ability of high-ranking officers is also reflected in personal correspondence by the rank and file. Federal surgeon Carl Uterhard wrote to his family that there was no longer a "penny's worth of trust or respect for the generals," for every soldier came to believe the colonels and generals were only interested in making as much money as possible.[64] Corporal Albrecht sent a similar message to his family: "If our generals were even half as much soldiers and military leaders as the enemy, the Union cause would be in a much better position today."[65] As modern commanders are well aware, once soldiers lose confidence in their leadership, a unit loses its combat effectiveness. One soldier wrote, "It was clear a regiment like this cannot win a battle, as we will find out soon."[66] As predicted, flawed generalship and placement once again caused the XI Corps to retreat on the first day of the Battle of Gettysburg, demonstrating that poor leadership and prejudice can reduce a once powerful unit to depths of despair and defeat.

Reverberations through History

Historians are often cautioned against the practice of presentism, or using hindsight to judge the past, but even in the nineteenth century, it was known that improper position on the battlefield and ignoring good intelligence could spell defeat. Antoine Jomini, the most prominent military strategist read by Federal officers during the war, warned against aligning an army next to a heavily wooded forest as the result could be disastrous should the enemy exploit the poor position.[67] Jomini and other nineteenth-century military strategists offered similar maxims regarding the use of good intelligence reports and proper placement of troops in a major campaign; however, these directives were all ignored at Chancellorsville. Hooker placed the XI Corps far out on his western flank and failed to press Howard to properly defend against a possible enemy assault. Furthermore, he did not listen to officers within his command who warned they thought the enemy was approaching their positions—disregarding their counsel, perhaps because of biases against Germans that he brought with him to his command.[68] One of the officers who commanded Von Gilsa's lines concluded that the cause of their defeat "was the persistent neglect of the plainest precepts of military foresight; the utter disregard of even elementary principles of flank defense; the deaf ear to the remonstrances and entreaties of Brigade and Division Chiefs; the inexplicable contempt of reports," and their commanders ignoring "the sternest warnings of imminent assault."[69] Thus, it is not presentism to say Hooker and Howard should have followed certain military doctrine in terms of placement and the use of personnel because they were both trained on those subjects prior to the campaign.

The feelings and perceptions of those being commanded are a factor in how soldiers react to their commanding officers. General Schurz may have said it best: "Too much humiliation destroys the morale of the men."[70] Humiliation comes in many forms, as seen by the treatment of the XI Corps and Germans in the Army after the Battle of Chancellorsville; some of the humiliation that Schurz wrote about after the battle can be summarized into the contemporary definition of discrimination. Unfortunately, racism and discrimination are still prevalent in the twenty-first century military, and some psychological studies have even concluded that such humiliation can cause psychological trauma in soldiers.[71] Reflecting a combination of defeat in battle and discrimination within the ranks, officers such as Capt. Frederick Winkler of the 26th Wisconsin, wrote: "The army, at least our corps, is demoralized; officers talk of resigning, and a spirit of depression and lack of confidence manifests itself everywhere."[72] Numerous studies have identified systemic racism within the military rank structure and promotion system, and some degree of discrimination within the military persists today.[73] Similar to the nativism that existed during the nineteenth-century, there are multiple debates in Congress, public discourse, and by extension, within the military regarding women in combat, immigrants, transgender individuals, and those of differing religions which emboldens those in command to question those who report to them.[74] For service members who are the subjects of these debates, this only adds to their humiliation, and as Schurz pointed out, destroys their morale.[75]

The Battle of Chancellorsville was detrimental to the morale of thousands of German service members in the Federal Army; as the largest ethnic group serving in the military at that time, this prejudice affected the tactical use of many units going forward. Furthermore, if the battle itself had been handled differently, Lee and his forces would not have been able to go farther north toward Gettysburg, Pennsylvania; thousands more lives could have been spared during the summer of 1863. Additionally, Germans felt culturally attacked by the prevalent deleterious sentiment within the military which curtailed their faith in their fellow soldiers and vice versa. When soldiers do not trust one another on the battlefield—or the officers leading them—the entire army is poised for defeat. The tactical corollaries for the campaign were multifold and avoidable. All must feel welcome and trusted within the ranks, and most importantly, within the nation they choose to serve.

The XI Corps at Chancellorsville demonstrates potential consequences when personal prejudice enters the command structure of a field army. The nation's nativist sentiment in the nineteenth century was pervasive enough to influence the placement of an entire corps and caused the officers to question the veracity of German reports. The fault at Chancellorsville does not lie with the "Flying Dutchmen" but with their corps commander and army commander. Historians need to take this into account when they write histories of the Civil War, and modern leaders must learn not to make a similar mistake. Steps must be taken—both politically and within the US Armed Forces—to prevent discrimination against any group.

Notes

1. James H. Peabody, quoted in John F. Krumwiede, "The 'Burning Shame' of Chancellorsville," *America's Civil War* 14, no. 4, (May 2001), 32.

2. Private Gottfried Rentschler, Letter 8, in, Joseph R. Reinhart, ed., *Two Germans in the Civil War: The Diary of John Daeuble and the Letters of Gottfried Rentschler, 6th Kentucky Volunteer Infantry* (Knoxville, TN: The University of Tennessee Press, 2004), 67.

3. This chapter discusses the initial motivations of German immigrants and German Americans who choose to fight for the Federal Army during the Civil War in a previous paper. For those interested in exploring this topic further see, Anthony J. Cade II, "Why They Fought: The Initial Motivations of German American Soldiers who Fought for the Union in the American Civil War," *European Review of History: Revue européenne d'histoire* 27 (2020): 1–2, 65–87. For clarity and ease of reading, both German immigrants and German Americans are referred to as simply Germans in this chapter.

4. For further information on German anti-slavery and its roots in American nativism, see Allison Clark Efford, *German Immigrants, Race, and Citizenship in the Civil War Era* (New York: Cambridge University Press, 2013); and Zachary Stuart Garrison, *German Americans on the Middle Border: From Antislavery to Reconciliation, 1830–1877* (Carbondale, IL: Southern Illinois University Press, 2019).

5. Chancellorsville was a multi-day campaign; however, the defeat of the XI Corps on 2 May 1863 is the moment most consider the campaign was lost.

6. At the Battle of Chancellorsville site, the battle marker for Stop 8 on the tour is titled "The Flying Dutchmen." The marker does not adequately explain why the XI Corps was given this sobriquet after the battle. Many Civil War history buffs who do not know the full history of the battle still refer to the men of the Corps by this derogatory pseudonym. The appellation needs to be retired by both the battle site and the historiography as it does not reflect the events of that day.

7. James S. Pula, *Under the Crescent Moon with the XI Corps in the Civil War*, From the Defenses of Washington to Chancellorsville, 1862–1863, vol. 1 (El Dorado Hills, CA: Savas Beatie, 2017), vii.

8. Pula, 210–11. Pula lists up to six reasons for the retreat: 1) General Oliver Otis Howard chose the wrong position and failed to entrench his lines, 2) General Joseph Hooker believed the enemy was in retreat, 3) Howard failed to rearrange his command to form an adequate reserve force, 4) Howard allowed supply trains and cattle herds to come too close to the front lines, 5) Deven's failed to heed the warnings of his own officers, and 6) the I Corps failed to support the XI Corps exposed flank. This chapter builds on this work by adding a seventh contributing factor: nativism within the ranks affected their placement, which led to the first and primary cause of the defeat.

9. Walter D. Kamphoefner and Wolfgang Helbich, eds., *Germans in the Civil War: The Letters They Wrote Home* (Chapel Hill, NC: The University of North Carolina Press, 2006), 25.

10. For examples of historians who suggest that the XI Corps' ethnicity was a contributing factor to the retreat, see John Bigelow, *The Campaign of Chancellorsville: A Strategic and Tactical Study* (New Haven, CT: Yale University Press, 1910); Edward J. Stackpole, *Chancellorsville: Lee's Greatest Battle* (Harrisburg, PA.: Stackpole Books, 1958); Ernest B. Ferguson, *Chancellorsville: The Souls of the Brave* (New York: Aldred A. Knopf, 1993); and Stephen W. Sears, *Chancellorsville* (Boston: Houghton Mifflin, 1996). There are examples of contemporary studies that are working to correct this view. Two worth the read are Christian B. Keller, *Chancellorsville and the Germans: Nativism, Ethnicity and Civil War Memory* (New York: Fordham University Press, 2007); and James S. Pula, *Under the Crescent Moon with the XI Corps in the Civil War,* From the Defenses of Washington to Chancellorsville, 1862–1863: vol. 1 (El Dorado Hills, CA: Savas Beatie, 2017).

11. Girvin L. Liggins et al., "Diversity and Inclusion Efforts in Federal Agencies: A Context for Exploring Perceptions of Military Veterans," *Journal of Veteran Studies* 3, no. 1 (2018), 145.

12. This chapter is not meant to be a full battle history of Chancellorsville; thus, there are many elements of the battle which will not be discussed for brevity's sake.

13. Despite what previous studies indicated, Lee was never made a general officer when he served the United States of America; perpetuating the myth that Lee was a General or the Confederacy a true nation only validates the Lost Cause narrative of the Civil War. Confederate ranks used in this chapter are merely to explain Confederate hierarchy and chain of command, and are not meant to further this myth. For additional information on how incorrect vocabulary legitimizes the idea the Confederacy was a nation, see David W. Blight, *Race and Reunion: The Civil War in American Memory* (Cambridge, MA: Harvard University Press, 2001). There is also a good summation of this argument in Christopher Wilson, "We Legitimize the 'So-Called' Confederacy with our Vocabulary, and that's a Problem," *Smithsonian Magazine* (12 September 2017), https://www.smithsonianmag.com/smithsonian-institution/we-legitimize-so-called-confederacy-vocabulary-thats-problem-180964830/.

14. Jim Garamone, "No Place for Racism, Discrimination in U.S. Military, Milley Says," *DOD News*, 9 July 2020.

15. The XI Corps was built on an amalgamation of Maj. Gen. John Fremont's Army of the Mountain Department and Brig. Gen. Louis Blenker's brigade. Both were primarily German units, and it was an easy decision to combine the two as they both had large numbers of German-speaking soldiers. When President Lincoln ordered the formation of a corps led by Fremont under John Pope's Army of Virginia, Fremont resigned as he saw an order to serve under someone he outranked as a dismissal of his prowess and rank. Maj. Gen. Franz Sigel assumed command of the newly formed I Corps, which was redesignated the XI Corps by September 1862. Soon after, the unit was attached to the Army of the Potomac and served under Hooker for the Battle of Chancellorsville.

16. David K. Work, *Lincoln's Political Generals* (Urbana, IL: University of Illinois Press, 2009), 212.

17. Pula, *Under the Crescent Moon*, 16.

18. *Lahrer Hinkender Bote* (1863), 253, quoted in Kamphoefner and Helbich eds., *Germans in the Civil War*, 24.

19. Christian B. Keller, *Chancellorsville and the Germans: Nativism, Ethnicity and Civil War Memory* (New York: Fordham University Press, 2007), 47.

20. Keller, 47.

21. Albert Krause to his parents, 27 July 1861, in *Germans in the Civil War*, ed. Kamphoefner and Helbich, 197.

22. Mary Bobbitt Townsend, *Yankee Warhorse: A Biography of Major General Peter Osterhaus* (Columbia, MO: University of Missouri Press, 2010), 49.

23. "General Sigel," *Der Demokrat*, 12 March 1863.

24. "General Sigel," *Der Demokrat*, 9 April 1863.

25. Alwin von Matzdorff to David Strother, US Army War Department, *The War of the Rebellion: A Compilation of the Official Records of the Union and Confederate Armies,* 127 vols. (Washington, DC: Government Printing Office, 1880–1901), hereafter cited as *OR*.

26. Carl Schurz to Abraham Lincoln, 24 February 1863, in Abraham Lincoln Papers at the Library of Congress, Library of Congress, hereafter cited as Lincoln Papers.

27. Adolf von Steinwehr to Abraham Lincoln, 30 January 1863, in Lincoln Papers.

28. "The Army in Virginia," *Daily Tribune*, 17 March 1863.

29. John S. Hart, "Soldiers' Reading," *The Sunday-School Times*, Philadelphia, 4 April 1863, in Howard Collection.

30. Carl Schurz to Abraham Lincoln, 6 April 1863, in Lincoln Papers.

31. Abraham Lincoln to Carl Schurz, 11 April 1863, in Lincoln Papers.

32. Oliver Otis Howard, *Autobiography of Oliver Otis Howard*, Classic Reprint Series, vol. 1 (1907; repr., Freeport, NY: Books for Libraries Press, 1971), 354–78.

33. Maj. Gen. J. H. Van Alen to Major Generals Howard and Slocum, 2 May 1863 in *OR*, vol. 25, Part 2, 360–61.

34. Van Alen to Howard and Slocum.

35. D. E. Sickles to Major General Howard, 2 May 1863 in *OR*, vol. 25, Part 2, 370.

36. Sickles to Howard; and Pula, *Under the Crescent Moon*, 134–35.

37. Keller, *Chancellorsville and the Germans*, 94.

38. Col. Leopold von Gilsa report, quoted in Ernest B. Ferguson, *Chancellorsville 1863: The Souls of the Brave* (New York: Alfred A. Knopf, 1992), 175–76.

39. Gilsa report.

40. Keller, *Chancellorsville and the Germans*, 63.

41. O. O. Howard, *Autobiography of Oliver Otis Howard*, 354–78; and Pula, *Under the Crescent Moon*, 186–87. The Chancellorsville Campaign

continued until 6 May 1863. In *Under the Crescent Moon with the XI Corps at Chancellorsville*, author James Pula gives a detailed analysis of the campaign from the first day until the last.

42. *New York Times*, 5 May 1863.

43. *Alexandria Gazette*, 9 May 1863. Interestingly, the article does not ensure its readers know Sigel was no longer in command of the Corps. A passive reader not abreast of the current military situation would assume Sigel was entirely at fault and that he and all his Germans were cowards.

44. *Alexandria Gazette*, 11 May 1863.

45. Ferguson, *Chancellorsville 1863*, 177–78.

46. While the "Flying Dutchmen" marker does include a disclaimer, the plaque helps reinforce a discriminatory nickname for the XI Corps.

47. *The Ohio Democrat*, 15 May 1863.

48. Quoted in *Germans in the Civil War*, eds. Kamphoefner and Helbich, 24

49. Quoted in *Germans in the Civil War*, 24.

50. Carl Uterhard to his Mother and his Wife Maria, 17 May 1863, in *Germans in the Civil War*, ed. Kamphoefner and Helbich, 158.

51. Adam Muenzenberger to his wife, quoted in James S. Pula, *The Sigel Regiment: A History of the Twenty-Sixth Wisconsin Volunteer Infantry, 1862–1865* (El Dorado Hills, CA: Savas, 2014), 135.

52. August Horstman to his Parents, 18 September 1863, in *Germans in the Civil War*, ed. Kamphoefner and Helbich, 124–25.

53. Wilhelm Albrecht to his family, 22 August 1864, in Kamphoefner and Helbich, 109.

54. Albrecht to his family, 109.

55. A. Wilson Greene, "From Chancellorsville to Cemetery Hill" *The First Day at Gettysburg: Essays on Confederate and Union Leadership*, ed. Gary W. Gallagher (Kent, OH: Kent State University Press, 1992), 59.

56. *Freiheitsfreund und Courier*, 17 June 1863, quoted in Keller, *Chancellorsville and the Germans*, 96.

57. Carl Schurz, "Carl Schurz in Self Defense," *The New York Daily Tribune*, 19 November 1863.

58. Schurz.

59. Keller, *Chancellorsville and the Germans*, 129–30.

60. Carl Schurz to General Hooker, 17 May 1863, *OR*.

61. Schurz to Hooker.

62. Keller, *Chancellorsville and the Germans*, 97.

63. Carl Schurz to Abraham Lincoln, 28 May 1863, in Lincoln Papers.

64. Carl Uterhard to his Mother, 27 May 1863, in *Germans in the Civil War*, ed. Kamphoefner and Helbich, 161–62.

65. Wilhelm Albrecht to his family, 30 May 1863, in *Germans in the Civil War*, 108.

66. Carl Uterhard to his friends, 3 June 1863, in *Germans in the Civil War*, ed. Kamphoefner and Helbich, 162.

67. Antoine Henri baron de Jomini, *The Art of War*, trans. Capt. G. H. Mendell and Lt. W. P. Craighill (Philadelphia: J. B. Lippincott & Co., 1862), 182.

68. Schurz, *The Reminiscences of Carl Schurz*, 420.

69. Owen Rice, *Afield with the XI Army Corps at Chancellorsville* (Cincinnati: H. C. Sherick & Co., 1885), 7.

70. Carl Schurz to General Hooker, 17 May 1863. *OR*.

71. M. Carlson et al., "Addressing the Impact of Racism on Veterans of Color: A Race-Based Stress and Trauma Intervention," *Psychology of Violence* 8, no. 6 (2018): 749–50.

72. Capt. Frederick Winkler, quoted in Pula, *Under the Crescent Moon with the XI Corps*, 215.

73. Lt. Col. Anthony D. Reyes, *Strategic Options for Managing Diversity in the U.S. Army* (Washington, DC: Joint Center for Political and Economic Studies, 2006), 14–16. Lieutenant Colonel Reyes addressed this issue in his 2006 study, and the Army took some steps toward achieving this goal later in the decade. See Department of the Army, Army Regulation (AR) 690-12, *Equal Employment Opportunity and Diversity* (Washington, DC: 2019) for the Army's current opportunity and diversity initiatives. However, there are multiple editorials which show these steps are not enough. See Kori Schake, "The Military and the Constitution Under Trump," *Survival* 62 no. 4, (2020): 33; Helene Cooper, "African-Americans are Highly Visible in the Military, but Almost Invisible at the Top," *New York Times*, 9 June 2020. Numerous studies have proven that diversity within an organization broadens and uplifts all; see Robert L. Lattimer, "The Case for Diversity in Global Business, and the Impact of Diversity on Team Performance," *Competitiveness Review* 8, no. 2 (1998) for more information on the topic.

74. Because of space constraints, this chapter cannot explore each of these debates. For examples that demonstrate current debates, see "Congress Nominates Far Fewer Women than Men to Military Service Academies," *Yale Law School*, 23 July 2019; Richard Sisk, "Military's De Facto Transgender Ban Is Hurting Readiness, Advocacy Group Report Finds," *Military.com*, 25 November 2020; Prabhjot Singh, "Religious Discrimination by the Military Must End," *Huffington Post*, 13 November 2015; Melissa del Bosque, "The Military's Failure to Reckon with White Supremacy in its Ranks," *The Intercept*, 7 March 2021; and Andrea Mazzarino, "The US Military Also has a Racism Problem," *The Nation*, 23 June 2020.

75. In 2020, the US Army released the *Army People Strategy: Diversity, Equity, and Inclusion Annex*, designed to address this issue within the next five years. Hopefully chapters such as this one will spur officers that such changes are needed.

Chapter 18
Evacuating Gallipoli: Military Advice and the Politics of Decision-Making, 1915–16
Aimée Fox

Writing in October 1915, the former First Lord of the Admiralty Winston Churchill, one of the prime architects of the Dardanelles campaign, decried the possibility of evacuation from the Gallipoli peninsula:

> No more terrible decision . . . has been wrung from a British government since the loss of the American colonies. All the specific disasters of our history . . . rolled into one, do not exceed the moral and material loss involved in it.[1]

Yet despite Churchill's fears, the British forces completed evacuation with only a handful of casualties. Mediterranean Expeditionary Force (MEF) formations were redeployed to other operational theaters, allaying some of the anxieties associated with the decision to withdraw. The Dardanelles Commission, established in 1916 by the British government to investigate the failure of the Gallipoli campaign, endorsed the decision to abandon the peninsula. The commissioners reserved their criticism for the time taken to decide on evacuation, and what that seemingly belated decision revealed about the civil-military relations that produced it.[2] The decision to evacuate raises several questions: how much time should be taken to decide on retreat? Whose interests and what factors need to be considered? Which interests and factors should be prioritized? With these questions in mind, this chapter will examine the decision-making process behind the evacuation from Gallipoli and explore the military advice provided to the British government, highlighting the consequences of the campaign and offering insights on the challenges associated with military advice in modern militaries.

Scholarship on the evacuation has tended to focus on several broad themes: first, that the evacuation was a success in spite of Britain's political decision-makers. The politicians were "dithering" and "vacillating" in contrast to clear-sighted military efforts on the peninsula.[3] Secondly, that the decision to evacuate revealed the inherent limitations of Cabinet government as a wartime decision-making apparatus—flaws especially evident under the leadership of then-British Prime Minister Herbert Asquith.[4] Finally, that the evacuation was a pyrrhic victory in an otherwise disastrous campaign. In each case, the military is cast in a positive light with its "thoroughly well-planned and successfully executed" evacuation.[5]

By re-examining the sources and nature of military advice offered to political decision-makers during the autumn of 1915, this chapter argues that the civil-military dialogue was more effective than has often been portrayed. Military advice from commanders on the Gallipoli peninsula was scrutinized and probed by both the War Committee and Cabinet, rather than accepted unthinkingly. It was, after all, just one element in the broader strategic picture. The example of the Gallipoli evacuation reaffirms the need for military commanders to provide advice that is politically aware or at least situates itself within a broader context—be that economic, cultural, or political. Isolating military advice from this context can undermine effective policy- and strategy-making as it divorces war from its inherently political nature.[6]

The Decision to Evacuate: A Narrative

The Gallipoli peninsula is a narrow and mountainous strip of land which runs in a south-westerly direction from Thrace into the Aegean Sea. It defines the Dardanelles straits to its south and commands the entrance to the Black Sea, making it a key geostrategic position. From 19 February 1915 to 9 January 1916, the Gallipoli peninsula and the Dardanelles straits were the site of an Anglo-French campaign—known interchangeably as the Gallipoli or Dardanelles campaign—in which British and French imperial forces sought to wrest control of the peninsula from the Ottoman Empire to secure access to the Sea of Marmara and the Black Sea. Historians have debated the reasons for launching the Gallipoli campaign in considerable depth.[7] There was no monocausal reason for the campaign, but rather its genesis was the result of a confluence of factors: first, the continuing stalemate on the Western Front led members of the British government, notably Winston Churchill (First Lord of the Admiralty, 1911–15), to argue that opportunities for breaking the impasse lay elsewhere; secondly, following the 1908 Young Turk revolution, along with Anglo-French colonial attitudes toward the Ottoman Empire, the Ottomans were viewed as a weak link within the Central Powers—an alliance which included Germany and Austria-Hungary (and later the Kingdom of Bulgaria); and finally, Russia—a member of the Triple Entente alongside France and Britain—had requested help from its allies to ease the pressure it was facing from Ottoman forces in the Caucasus.[8]

Against this backdrop, a naval campaign was launched in February 1915 to force the Dardanelles straits, which involved bombarding Otto-

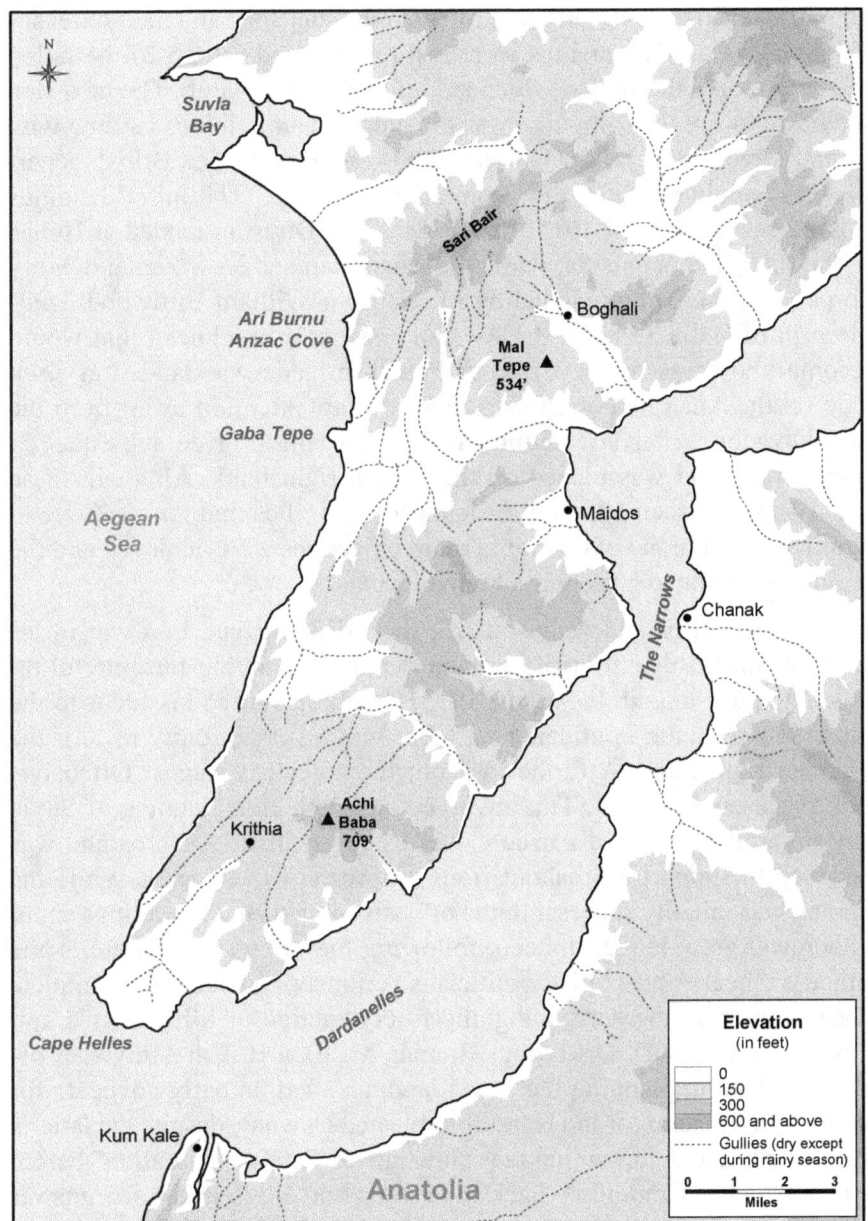

Figure 18.1. Gallipoli peninsula. Created by Army University Press.

man coastal forts and clearing minefields, then proceeding to Constantinople—the Ottoman capital. Campaign supporters hoped these actions would topple the government and thereby remove the Ottoman Empire from the war; however, Ottoman forces were tenacious and their defenses effective. Six allied warships were lost or damaged as part of the failed attempt to force the straits, which culminated on 18 March. The next step in the Anglo-French campaign was to launch an amphibious landing with ground forces. General Sir Ian Hamilton—an experienced British general—was appointed the MEF's commander-in-chief. The initial landings took place on 25 April 1915: the British 29th Division landed at Helles on the tip of the peninsula, while the Australian and New Zealand Army Corps (ANZAC), commanded by Lt. Gen. Sir William Birdwood, landed north of Gaba Tepe on the Aegean coast at a beachhead that would become known as Anzac Cove. A French brigade was landed at Kum Kale on the Anatolian coast as a feint to draw attention away from the 29th Division. After succeeding in this task, the brigade subsequently re-embarked and was placed on the British right flank. Although these initial landings secured small beachheads at Helles and Anzac Cove at significant cost, none of the initial main objectives were achieved and the peninsula remained largely in Ottoman hands.[9]

Between April and August 1915, the MEF engaged in a war of attrition against a determined Ottoman defense, stymying meaningful attempts to push inland. In August 1915, Hamilton shifted his focus to the Anzac Cove sector, confident that there was an opportunity to turn the Ottoman right flank. A further assault, the so-called August Offensive, took place on 6 August. This involved an amphibious landing at Suvla Bay (five miles north of Anzac Cove) by the British IX Corps and was designed to support a breakout from the Anzac Cove sector. While the landing was initially successful, the offensive failed, and mutterings about withdrawal grew louder. Indeed, following the offensive's failure, some military officers and British politicians seriously considered a complete evacuation or, at the least, a significant contraction of MEF lines. Capt. Guy Dawnay (GSO2, Operations Branch, MEF), a British Army staff officer involved in planning the Suvla landings, was an early advocate for evacuation. General Sir Ian Hamilton selected Dawnay, despite the latter's reservations about continuing the campaign, to "lay [the] situation" before the Dardanelles Committee back in London and advised him to "answer all questions truthfully but in no way pessimistically."[10] This committee was the body in charge of the British strategic direction of the war. Arriving in London on 10 September, Dawnay spent three weeks meeting with and apprising various ministers and senior generals, as well as the King.

Shortly after Dawnay returned to Gallipoli, Hamilton and his chief of staff were recalled to London and replaced. The new commander-in-chief,

Figure 18.2. Troops from the Australian 13th Battalion with a Turkish dog in the Aghyl Dere valley, a position captured during the 1915 August Offensive. Courtesy of the Australian War Memorial.

Lt. Gen. Sir Charles Monro, and his chief of staff, Maj. Gen. Sir Arthur Lynden-Bell, had thus far spent the war on the Western Front—widely regarded in military circles as the main theater. Lord Herbert Kitchener (Secretary of State for War, 1914–16) asked Monro to "report fully and frankly on [the] military situation" following his 27 October arrival at Mudros harbor on the island of Lemnos.[11] By 31 October, Monro cabled his report to Kitchener recommending the complete evacuation of the Gallipoli peninsula. While senior military opinion on the peninsula broadly favored evacuation, the same could not be said of British officials in Egypt, who were inclined to veto evacuation, fearing a "Mahommedan uprising."[12] To offset their concerns, Monro and his staff proposed a "scheme for an invasion of Asia Minor from Alexandretta"—a plan that had been on the table throughout 1915.[13] This plan initially proposed

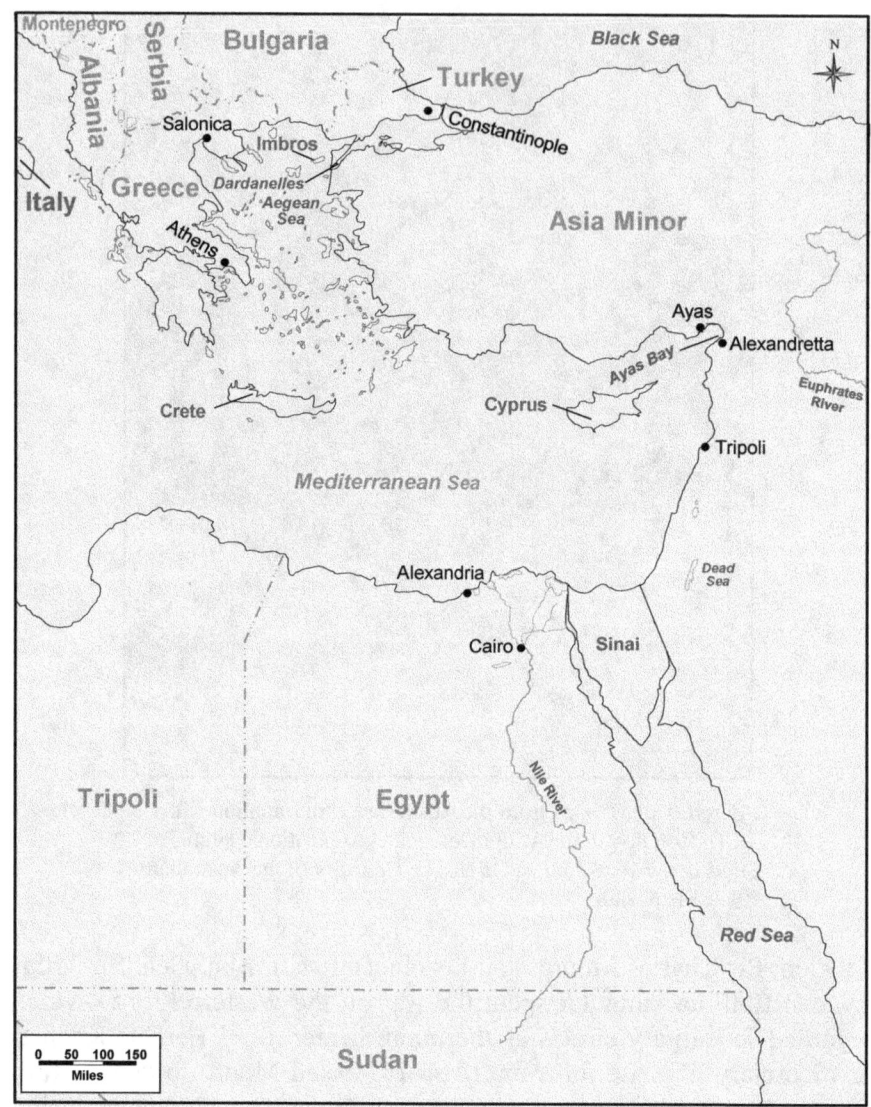

Figure 18.3. Eastern Mediterranean map showing location of Alexandretta and Ayas Bay. Created by Army University Press.

landing two divisions drawn from Gallipoli with two drawn from Egypt at Ayas Bay, located in the Gulf of Alexandretta in the eastern Mediterranean.[14] The Ayas Bay project, as it was called, would cut Ottoman railway communications to Egypt and Mesopotamia, as well as strike vital passes through the Taurus and Amanus mountains.[15] There was disagreement within MEF headquarters over the feasibility of the project. Dawnay, however, rationalized that it was "militarily possible, *given certain conditions*" and that, without some "set off," evacuation would remain unpalatable to political decision-makers.[16]

Back in London, Kitchener and the War Committee were unimpressed with Monro's report. Though evacuation was viewed with some equanimity, Monro's suggestion that evacuation might result in 30 to 40 percent casualties was deemed unacceptable. Kitchener was, therefore, sent to Egypt to "provide more palatable advice."[17] When he arrived on Gallipoli on 9 November, Kitchener originally thought that evacuation might not be necessary. A tour of the peninsula, however, proved sobering. Reporting to the Prime Minister on 15 November, Kitchener noted that his position had shifted, adding that "careful and secret preparations for the evacuation of the Peninsula are being made."[18] Despite Kitchener's support for both evacuation and the Ayas Bay project, Asquith and the War Committee (the Dardanelles Committee was renamed in October 1915) dismissed the project as a viable alternative—a decision strengthened by French objections and the strain it would place on the Royal Navy. On 22 November, Kitchener formally recommended evacuating Suvla and Anzac but advised to hold onto Helles, which was deemed important to the navy. Kitchener's advice was reinforced by the General Staff, which reached similar conclusions but recommended evacuating Helles.[19]

On 23 November, the War Committee met to consider the advice. Overwhelmingly in favor of evacuation, the War Committee suggested all three landing sites, including Helles, be abandoned. Several politicians commented that the Cabinet should simply be "'informed' of the Committee's decision and not 'consulted.'"[20] Asquith, however, was unmoved: "This was a large question of policy, and it had been arranged that such should be left to the Cabinet. *Military considerations were dominating*."[21] In theory, Cabinet committees such as the Dardanelles Committee or War Committee should have expedited decision-making, but they lacked executive authority; policies had to be discussed and ratified by the full Cabinet—more than twenty members.[22] Unlike the War Committee, several Cabinet members were anti-evacuation. Some requested to delay any decision to consider other avenues of advice and ensure that memoranda—for and against evacuation—be fully considered.[23] Unsurprisingly, events beyond Whitehall and the Gallipoli peninsula also weighed heavily on the minds of decision-makers. With Bulgaria declaring for the Central Powers, Germany could now directly assist the Ottomans; meanwhile in

Mesopotamia, British imperial forces had been repulsed by the Ottomans at Ctesiphon on the eastern bank of the River Tigris and were in retreat to Kut-al-Amara, an eastern Iraq town that would be the site of a siege between British and Ottoman forces.

The gloomy international situation was mirrored by a turn in weather at Gallipoli. From the end of November onward, storms and blizzards whipped across the peninsula. Trenches flooded and thousands of men were evacuated with severe frostbite. Some decision-makers believed the force should remain on the defensive until spring due to the potential for catastrophic loss of life if evacuation was attempted in increasingly inclement weather.[24] Others, however, advocated for offensive operations. Kitchener, for example, proposed sending four divisions from the Salonika front (which ran through parts of modern-day Greece, North Macedonia, and Albania) to improve the position at Suvla, with the Royal Navy taking the offensive in cooperation. Monro, however, believed such an operation did not offer a "reasonable chance of success."[25] Because of back-channelling by naval officers such as Rear Adm. Rosslyn Wemyss (Senior Naval Officer, Mudros) and Commodore Roger Keyes (Chief of Staff, Eastern Mediterranean Squadron), the possibility of a naval offensive remained on the table even after the Cabinet decided to evacuate. This decision eventually occurred on 7 December prior to discussions at the inter-allied Chantilly conference—a forum for Britain, France, Russia, Serbia, and Italy to form a coordinated strategy for the next year of the war.

Figure 18.4. Photo showing the aftermath of heavy storms that swept the Gallipoli peninsula in November 1915. The bad weather severely damaged many piers and drove many vessels ashore. Courtesy of the Australian War Memorial.

Between 18 and 20 December, ten days after the Cabinet decision, Suvla and Anzac were evacuated with a handful of casualties. Helles, however, remained in British hands. The incoming Chief of the Imperial General Staff (CIGS), Lt. Gen. Sir William Robertson, argued that the peninsula should be "entirely evacuated, and with the least possible delay."[26] Despite further petitions by naval officers, the evacuation of Helles was ordered on 28 December and carried out between 8 and 9 January 1916. "We could have done no more there," concluded Dawnay. "It was, and always will be, very pathetic to all of us who served through the campaign from the beginning . . . the sorrow and the suffering for no tangible result."[27] The campaign might have been over, but its legacy cast a long shadow over British strategy and military personnel alike.

The Timeliness of Military Advice and Decision-Making

A key criticism of the evacuation was the time taken to reach a decision. This highlights an inherent tension in the provision and interpretation of military advice; policymakers seldom act rapidly enough to give armed forces adequate time to plan how to implement their decisions.[28] British academic Lawrence Freedman argued that policymakers need to understand that prevarication—though it improves the quality of decision-making through inclusivity—can undermine timeliness.[29] The Gallipoli case study provides two examples of timeliness: first, the time Lt. Gen. Sir Charles Monro took to deliver his advice, and second, how long it took for the War Committee and Cabinet to decide on evacuation.

When he was appointed, Monro was asked to report whether "in his opinion, on purely military grounds, it was better to evacuate Gallipoli or make another attempt to carry it."[30] Kitchener cautioned Monro about "the effect that Gallipoli had on the Moslem and Oriental world" and stressed that a withdrawal "might operate unpleasantly for us."[31] Withdrawal was clearly an unpalatable option for some military and political figures. Time was of the essence to Kitchener and the government. Two days after his arrival, Monro received a telegram from Kitchener asking when his report would be ready. "K[itchener] always in such a hurry," remarked one officer. "How can a reasonable man expect Monro to have formed an opinion yet."[32] The same officer noted that Monro was worried at "being hustled into giving his very important decision."[33] Contemporary commentators have questioned whether Monro spent enough time on the peninsula and had enough information. Some noted that he barely set foot on the peninsula, while others suggested he spent only a few hours looking around.[34]

Either way, his telegram on 31 October—four days after his arrival—concluded that the forces should be withdrawn:

> On purely military grounds, I recommend the evacuation of the Peninsula . . . I have endeavoured in the expression of my opinion to give full weight to the effect which will be created in the East by our evacuation, and I consider that the force . . . would be more favourably placed in Egypt.[35]

Monro offered his advice quickly and decisively. It was now up to policymakers to decide how to proceed.

Members of the Cabinet and the Admiralty pounced on the relative rapidity—indeed, the very timeliness—of Monro's report. In a memorandum to the Cabinet, George Curzon, Marquess Curzon (a former viceroy of India) noted that Monro's knowledge of the situation was "confined to a hurried visit on one morning to the three British beaches" where he made "the most cursory examination of the trenches."[36] This, combined with the rapid nature of Monro's report, seemingly undermined the rigor of his advice. According to Commodore Roger Keyes, Monro and his chief of staff had only visited the peninsula once. Keyes, who continued to believe in the possibility of offensive action, was astonished: "[Monro and Lynden-Bell] had quite made up their minds before they left England etc. It really is amazing."[37] In many respects, Monro was put in an invidious position: Kitchener and the Cabinet pushed him to report as soon as possible then criticized him for not taking enough time to form his opinion.

Where the War Committee and Cabinet are concerned, the criticism was the opposite: they took too long to reach a decision. After receiving Monro's report on 31 October, the government took thirty-seven days to decide on evacuation. The Dardanelles Commission's final report was damning in this respect, concluding that once Kitchener affirmed Monro's advice, "the decision to evacuate should have been taken at once".[38] Some senior generals despaired over the "difficulty of getting the Gov[ernmen]t to make up their minds," with one remarking: "We have four enemies to contend with—the Bosches, the Turks, the Bulgars, and [His Majesty's] Government—and the last is the most deadly."[39] For Lt. Gen. Sir William Robertson, who advocated withdrawal, the delay was the result of inefficient and unwieldy bureaucratic structures: "Prompt decision and prompt action are required, and for these a small responsible body is essential."[40] It was clear to Robertson that Cabinet government was not working.

While there were dissenters on and off the peninsula, the overwhelming military advice was to evacuate. However, as American political science professor Peter Feaver argues, military expertise is "still only one (albeit very important) factor that belongs in the strategic calculus."[41] Concerns over loss of imperial prestige weighed heavily on the minds of Cabinet members, as did the potential impact that a full or partial evacuation might have on relations with French and Russian allies. The precarious situation in Serbia, Salonika, and Mesopotamia further complicated matters. For Curzon, the evacuation could not be decided by "'cold calculations of military strategy' alone, but by the largest considerations of political expediency and moral effect."[42] It is understandable that because so many different political and strategic factors were at play, more time was required to decide whether evacuation was necessary or, indeed, desirable.

Not surprisingly, the implications of this lengthy period of challenge and discussion were keenly felt by military personnel on the peninsula. There was increasing criticism of the coalition government and its seeming lack of policy in the eastern Mediterranean. Capt. Guy Dawnay despaired at the "utter confusion and disorganisation of the Government... IF ONLY there were policy and some general direction from home!"[43] With the narrowing window for evacuation, a timely decision was more pressing than ever. Monro urged the Cabinet that the "late season makes time a matter of great urgency."[44] One staff officer noted that "precious, precious time is being wasted," criticizing the government's failure to understand that further disembarkation of forces "cannot be made with any chance of success."[45] As the evacuation reveals, time is an important but often neglected aspect of decision-making. Military advice can be offered too quickly, and thus undermine its credibility by conveying a sense of a fait accompli. Though rapid decisions are important, decision-makers should not shy away from taking time to think and decide, nor should they view challenging advice as time wasted. Indeed, the passage of time can help reveal new information that may improve or change assessments.[46] Military officials need to be mindful of the time involved and realities of strategic decision-making associated with withdrawal; military operations are usually only part of the decision. Similarly, though, civilian decision-makers must consider the time-sensitive nature of withdrawal, particularly when taking more time equates to possible loss of life.

Weighing Experience and Expertise

When offering and receiving military advice, both military leaders and political decision-makers need to distinguish between experience and expertise. Military leaders must make a distinction between offering personal opinion versus a formal military assessment. Passing off the former as the

Figure 18.5. Australian soldiers stand in snow outside a dugout after inclement weather and storms battered the peninsula, narrowing the window for evacuation, November 1915. Courtesy of the Australian War Memorial.

latter can undermine their credibility—even if the point where professional and personal judgment merge is inevitably somewhat arbitrary.[47] Military advice can have a "self-interested" aspect—promoting a particular agenda or course of action.[48] Interrogation and questioning help reveal assumptions and motivations that underpin military advice.[49] However, experience and expertise cuts across both civil and military spheres. Political decision-makers may have little knowledge or experience of the military, potentially impacting how they assess military advice. It can, therefore, become easier for the military, "for better or for worse, to influence policy."[50] In the Gallipoli evacuation, tensions were at play in which experience (or lack thereof) was used to both legitimize and delegitimize expertise.

Military professionals who claimed to possess expertise which "politicians had no right to question" caused significant tensions within civil-military relations during World War I.[51] For contemporary commentators, the political and the military inhabited separate spheres. William Robertson, then commandant of the Staff College from 1910 to 1913, stressed that "discussion of questions of policy and political matters generally leads to no practical result, nor benefit of any kind to the soldier, nor is it his business."[52] Most political decision-makers had no experience of war and little understanding of the inner workings of armed forces, which seemingly gave military advisors a "profound moral advantage" over their political masters.[53] In 1907, for example, then-Secretary of State for War Richard Haldane remarked that "the soldier is the only ultimate judge of military necessities. If he presses the matter, the civilian must accept what he says."[54] For Lt. Gen. Sir Gerald Ellison, a senior staff officer at Gallipoli, military strategists must have power to "plan without due interference; power to advise freely, fearlessly, and as an equal; power to act swiftly, secretly, and decisively."[55] Both Haldane's and Ellison's statements are problematic, undermining civilian primacy and advocating for the military to act in isolation, free from sustained challenge. These opinions also overlook the fundamental nature of war—that the use of force is a political act.[56]

Throughout the course of the war, there was, however, a shift from the posture Haldane espoused in 1907. While some Conservative and Unionist Party politicians were more sympathetic and willing to accept military advice, such as Andrew Bonar Law (Colonial Secretary, 1915–16) who pleaded with his Cabinet colleagues to approve evacuation, it was not always so clear cut.[57] Some Conservative and Unionist peers like Curzon and Henry Petty-Fitzmaurice, Marquess of Lansdowne, as well as Liberal peer Robert Crewe-Milnes, Marquess of Crewe, were skeptical of Monro's advice to evacuate. Military expediency was only one part of the strategic calculus and, as Curzon remarked, advice was not unanimous regarding evacuation. Such sentiments were echoed by the Prime Minister himself. In a statement to Parliament on 2 November 1915, Asquith, who had received Monro's advice to evacuate, argued that "you cannot determine your policy or your course of action entirely and exclusively by military and naval considerations."[58] It was the duty of the government, he continued, to "rely upon the advice of its military and naval advisers" but that it was sometimes necessary "to run risks and encounter dangers which purely naval or military policy would warn them against."[59] He reassured Parliament that the situation on the peninsula was receiving "our most careful and anxious consideration, not as an isolated thing, but as part and parcel of a larger strategic question."[60] Yet, for soldiers like Ellison and General Sir George Barrow (Monro's biographer), Monro's advice should have been accepted and acted on immediately. Barrow wrote:

> One would have thought that his report would have settled the business. One would have pictured the War Council [sic.] as saying, "Thank God, we now know definitely what we ought to do.

> Here is the opinion of our expert, our selected man . . . There is only one thing to do . . . to follow this opinion, and the sooner we commence to act the better for all concerned."⁶¹

Once again, the political decision-makers were depicted as unthinking ciphers; there was no need for them to think because the military had done that for them. All they needed to do was act.

Monro's expertise as an advisor seemingly benefited from his detachment from the Gallipoli campaign. Indeed, his experience in another theater was viewed positively by some, enhancing his expertise. In his evidence to the Dardanelles Commission, Monro remarked that Kitchener had sent him because "he wanted an independent opinion."⁶² An outsider who was less invested in the marginal gains made on the peninsula would provide a different perspective. Monro had a solid reputation, starting the war as a divisional commander in August 1914 and rising to command the British Third Army in July 1915. On the surface, his advice was based purely on what he heard and saw on the peninsula, and considered the MEF's lack of power and surprise, its morale and health, and the strengthening Ottoman position. When pushed by Kitchener on 1 November to ensure that his corps commanders were of the same opinion, Monro was unequivocal in his response:

> I hold very strongly that our course of military action must be governed by our military resources and that it should be our endeavour to avoid frittering away of men and be in full strength at vital points. My judgment, having these views, is that we should act on the defensive in Egypt and collect there all available troops (without impairing the operations in France *which I regard as the main theatre*).⁶³

Monro's opinion of the Western Front as the "main theatre" was not a particularly controversial one in most military circles. Yet, because of these views—coupled with his previous service there—some politicians and even some military personnel were less convinced by his expertise. In a memorandum to the Cabinet, Curzon remarked that Monro "arrived from France, as do all officers who have served in that theatre of war, with no very friendly feelings to the Dardanelles campaign."⁶⁴ Additionally, some naval personnel admonished Monro for his precipitous decision to evacuate. They—along with Monro's predecessor, Ian Hamilton—believed his focus on the Western Front impeded his judgment.⁶⁵ Here we can see the challenges of disentangling experience from expertise. Decision-makers were theoretically right to challenge his advice. However, just because

Monro endorsed the primacy of the Western Front, it did not necessarily mean his advice was inexpert.

While advice may prove both expert and well-grounded, political decision-makers need to understand the extent to which advice rests on "considerations within military expert competence and how much does not."[66] Not surprisingly, Monro's advice was subject to further interrogation; alternative views and advice were sought. This raises interesting questions about the nature and source of military advice. Curzon, for example, questioned whether a "Cabinet decision upon evacuation without any attempt to ascertain officially the views of either Sir Ian Hamilton or [Hamilton's chief of staff] [would] strike the public as a somewhat peculiar proceeding."[67] Additionally, it appeared sensible to broaden the scope of advice beyond Monro and the General Staff since the latter seemed to be increasingly aligned with the primacy of the Western Front. Dissent is necessary in the search for good advice, particularly as "no individual, no matter how senior, can possess sufficient knowledge and experience to offer a 'one-size-fits-all' view for the military."[68] Military professionals and policymakers can benefit from learning about each other's experiences and expertise, realized through robust, unencumbered dialogue.

Maintaining Effective Civil-Military Dialogue

The ways in which military personnel and policymakers engage in dialogue with one another has proven a fruitful area of discussion within political science, particularly in the United States. Whether conceived of as Eliot Cohen's "unequal dialogue" or Richard Betts's "equal dialogue with unequal authority," dialogue is an essential component of healthy civil-military relations.[69] As part of that dialogue, military advice should be "iterative, responsive, and interactive."[70] It needs to evolve with policy direction and options, rather than delivering an ultimatum that unhelpfully constrains decision-makers. While strategy-making is the product of dialogue between politicians and soldiers, there is a chicken-and-egg challenge: civilians often demand options without offering clear strategic guidance, while military leaders expect clear direction before generating options.[71] Though the decision to evacuate the Gallipoli peninsula speaks to the fraught nature of civil-military relations, there was a dialogue of sorts between politicians and soldiers even though such interactions were tense and inconsistent.

Personalities and bureaucratic structures proved challenging to effective civil-military dialogue. In early autumn 1915, with the increasingly acute situation in the Dardanelles and Balkans, Kitchener ordered General Sir Ian Hamilton "not to telegraph his plans to London lest ministers might learn from them."[72] Kitchener's action was an example of a broader climate of distrust and suspicion within the corridors of power—a climate made more challenging because no military advisors served on key Cabinet committees. Indeed, the nature of Cabinet government at that time was "too little representation for the views of the armed services themselves."[73] The Dardanelles Committee, established in May 1915, was limited to ministers for much of its tenure and was often "starved of information by the War Office" despite the Committee's "explicit interest" in military matters.[74] A brewing political crisis in late September 1915 forced Prime Minister Asquith to reconstruct the Dardanelles Committee with a different and smaller membership, renaming it the War Committee. Both the CIGS and the First Sea Lord—the professional heads of the British Army and Royal Navy respectively—were always present to give information, providing decision-makers with continuous military advice.

Unsurprisingly, a culture of withholding information and mutual suspicion had negative effects on civil-military relations. As previously illustrated, contemporary and post-war commentators were shocked that Monro's advice was not immediately acted on. Yet, military advice should never be made "too easy for politicians;" nor should soldiers only expect civilians to "modify their thoughts and positions after receiving military advice."[75] Monro's advice was certainly not too easy to act on. In many ways, it limited decision-makers' choices, providing them with only one option: to evacuate and place the force in Egypt. Throughout the final months of 1915 and beyond, Monro unequivocally supported evacuation, which likened his advice to an ultimatum. In his evidence to the Dardanelles Commission, he was asked if he ever "swerved" in his opinion; "No, no more than I do now," he replied.[76] Though staunch in his assessment, Monro engaged in a stilted back-and-forth dialogue with Kitchener regarding other options, usually dismissing them without suggesting alternatives. The lone exception was the Ayas Bay project. Critics referred to the project as a cynical attempt by Monro and his staff to play for time as they planned for evacuation.[77] Monro testified to the Dardanelles Commission that he had put plans in place as he "did not want to be jumped."[78] Ayas Bay was a military possibility—the plans having been considered in early 1915. A scheme was worked out detailing the military commitments, but, importantly, with no comment on whether the navy could support it. Despite some military and political support for the scheme, decision-makers in London rejected the plan because it would strain Britain's resources and the French objected because a British landing near Syria would encroach on their sphere of influence.[79]

During the tense back-and-forth discussion over evacuation, a dialogue existed, but it was often fraught, inconsistent, and determined by key personalities. Personal suspicion and lack of mutual respect persisted throughout the conflict despite the creation of committees and fora to facilitate civil-military dialogue.[80] Monro's unwavering views on evacuation, Kitchener's imperious and centralizing nature, and Asquith's reticence to challenge military advice created a critical situation exacerbated by limited communications and powerless government committees. Communication between Monro and decision-makers in London was via telegram. While relatively rapid, telegrams are a blunt instrument, without the nuance of a telephone call or face-to-face meeting. As has been noted, government committees like the War Committee lacked the executive authority to decide military matters, adding another layer of bureaucracy to proceedings. In this respect, the failure at Gallipoli was one of several factors that contributed to calls to realign the British government's decision-making machinery for developing strategy. In late 1916, following the collapse of Asquith's coalition government in December, incoming Prime Minister David Lloyd George established a War Cabinet with five members, including himself as Prime Minister, charged to oversee the war. The service chiefs also attended War Cabinet meetings. Though fiery and far from harmonious, discussions were constructive in producing a strategy that led to eventual victory.[81]

Military advice should not be an ultimatum, nor should it necessarily be defined as recommendations.[82] Advisors should present decision-makers with information, assessments, and a series of options, rather than just one course of action. Adapting or modifying advice in response to new policy guidance or external factors does not show inconsistency or weakness; rather, it is an important part of the iterative and responsive nature of military advice.

Conclusion: Consequences and Implications

The Gallipoli evacuation begs fundamental questions about the political and military dynamics of retreat, highlighting some of the decision-making tensions between civilian and military spheres. The campaign had several consequences: a formal inquiry was established to investigate the campaign's inception and conduct. Prior to the establishment of the Dardanelles Commission, there were calls in Parliament to ensure the inquiry was "going to bring the matter home to the people who have done wrong" and that "the people who are incapable are severely dealt with."[83] The Commission produced two reports—the first in 1917 and the final report in 1919. While an initial aspiration was to hold individuals to account, ultimately this did not happen. British historian Jenny Macleod argued, it was not deemed appropriate in wartime to impugn the reputations of those still holding political or military office; accordingly, the two reports were "purposefully bland."[84] What criticism the reports did contain was largely directed at the time taken to decide on the evacuation, and toward the then-deceased Lord Kitchener's tendency to ignore the General Staff, which led to "confusion and want of efficiency."[85] Beyond these points, there was very little censure or purposeful holding to account of military or political figures involved in the campaign. Sir Thomas Mackenzie, a former Prime Minister of New Zealand who had sat on the Commission, placed on record his dissent over the findings of the final report, remarking on the reticence of some of the witnesses: "Probably their reticence arose from a sense of loyalty to the Service . . . and a disinclination to say anything against their comrades."[86] Despite noble intentions, the Dardanelles Commission reports had very little consequence for those involved, highlighting the inherent challenges of ensuring accountability for military and political decision-makers during—and, sometimes, even after—war.

The campaign had more meaningful consequences for the broader contours of civil-military relations during the war. As noted above, the campaign contributed to a general sense that the British government lacked appropriate bureaucratic structures and machinery for wartime decision-making. Throughout 1915, rumbles of dissatisfaction and discontent with the conduct of the war had grown—often accompanied by calls for more rapid decision-making, enabled through a smaller, select group responsible for strategy.[87] British historian Hew Strachan observed: the "true evil in war is the inability to hammer out" how military and civilian priorities are to be reconciled, a charge that can certainly be leveled at the British government in this period.[88] The failures at Gallipoli provided further evidence that Britain's higher direction of war was at fault, presaging a series of changes to the way the war effort was managed. Most directly, because of dissatisfaction at the performance of the War Office and General Staff under Kitchener, he was increasingly marginalized; ultimately the CIGS's powers were strengthened in late 1915, making that officer the sole source of professional military advice to the government and thereby re-linking professional staff work with the overall direction of the war.[89]

A further step was taken later in 1916 with the formation of the War Cabinet, which represented a more effective means to reconcile civil and military priorities and partially mitigated some of the challenges to civil-military relations evident during the decision to evacuate Gallipoli. None of these structural adjustments were sufficient to resolve civil-military tensions inherent in war, however. One British general called before the War Cabinet in 1917 remarked that it was "an extraordinary show and it would make one laugh if it were not quite so serious. To think that at this crisis in the country's history its war policy should be run by a pack of ignorant civilians is too tragic for words."[90] As these remarks suggest, despite the advent of new structures, civil-military relations were constantly subject to the whims and clashes of different personalities—much as they had been in the winter of 1915. Lt. Gen. Sir William Robertson who, as CIGS, had called for the establishment of a small responsible body for rapid decision-making, had an infamously poor relationship with David Lloyd George; Lloyd George reflected in his memoirs that he believed a cabal led by Robertson had sought to oust his government.[91] The clashes between Lloyd George and Robertson underpinned—for good or ill—many of Britain's strategic decisions throughout 1916 and 1917, including the Somme campaign (launched in July 1916), the Third Battle of Ypres (also known as the Passchendaele campaign, launched in the summer of 1917), and the decision to send British troops to the Italian front in November 1917. Ultimately, then, the Gallipoli campaign can be seen as one of many factors that impacted the balance and conduct of civil-military relations within the British government, and which resulted in military advisors playing a more significant role in the conduct of the war. This proved valuable in certain respects, yet erected new barriers to effective dialogue in others.

The campaign also raises several relevant points for current and future conflicts. First, different sources of advice are needed. Monro's voice was one among many. It was entirely right and appropriate for the War Committee and Cabinet to go beyond Monro and Kitchener. Expanding the provision of military advice opens decision-making to new perspectives and opinions. All participants benefit from hearing multiple perspectives. The challenge here is two-fold: deciding whose advice and voice matters, and balancing that advice against the need to be timely. When retreat is considered, time must be balanced against combined factors such as the sunk cost of materiel, high actual and potential casualties, and future civil-military recriminations. Yet such a formulation raises questions as to how much time should be taken, whose interests need to be considered, and which interests and factors should be prioritized.

Secondly, the impact of personalities and experience cannot be ignored as factors in the decision-making process. General Sir George Barrow remarked: "The decision to be made frequently resolves itself into a battle between two strong personalities;" this supports military historian David French's argument that, to understand World War I civil-military relations, the people rather than the formal machinery of government need to be examined.[92] Such concerns are no less important today and in the future. Policy and strategy are not made in bureaucratic isolation. They are collaborative, human endeavors—often fiery and combative. As such, taking the time to understand each other's perspectives and limitations—with humility and respect—is vital for effective dialogue.

Finally, military advice needs to be politically informed and policy aware. Monro's advice was "purely military" and did not consider broader political matters, which was a consistent problem with British civil-military relations at the time. The military are partners in strategy-making. The provision of "policy aware" military advice should consider political factors to aid in good strategy.[93] It is vital, however, that such advice is never made too easy for politicians to accept—for that marks out a path to bad decisions and bad strategy, creating a legacy that can weaken civil-military relations in the future.

Notes

1. The National Archives of the UK, hereafter TNA, CAB 37/136/12, Winston Churchill to Cabinet, 15 October 1915, 1–2.

2. TNA, CAB 19/1, Dardanelles Commission: Final Report, Part II, 1917, 88.

3. R. Prior, *Gallipoli: The End of the Myth* (London: Yale University Press, 2009), 226–27; and T. Travers, *Gallipoli 1915* (2001; repr., Stroud, UK: History Press, 2009), 277.

4. D. French, *British Strategy and War Aims 1914–1916* (London: Allen & Unwin, 1986), 159–60; and J. Turner, "Cabinets, Committees and Secretariats: The Higher Direction of War," in K. Burk, ed., *War and the State: The Transformation of British Government, 1914–1919* (London: Allen & Unwin, 1982), 61.

5. J. Macleod, *Gallipoli* (Oxford: Oxford University Press, 2015), 65.

6. J. Golby and M. Karlin, "Why 'Best Military Advice' Is Bad for the Military—and Worse for Civilians," *Orbis* 62, no. 1 (2008): 143.

7. For the latest in this debate, see N. A. Lambert, *The War Lords and the Gallipoli Disaster: How Globalized Trade Led to Britain's Worst Defeat of the First World War* (Oxford: Oxford University Press, 2021).

8. Prior, *Gallipoli*, 13–14.

9. R. Crawley, *Climax at Gallipoli: The Failure of the August Offensive* (Norman, OK: University of Oklahoma Press, 2014), 6.

10. Imperial War Museum, hereafter IWM, Diary of Captain Orlo Williams, 69/78/1, 2 September 1915.

11. TNA, CAB 19/1, Final Report, 53.

12. IWM, Papers of Major-General G. Dawnay, 69/21/1, Dawnay to wife, 30 June 1916

13. D. Whittingham, *Charles E. Callwell and the British Way in Warfare* (Cambridge: Cambridge University Press, 2020), 170.

14. P. G. Halpern, *A Naval History of World War I* (Annapolis, MD: Naval Institute Press, 1994), 122–23.

15. Whittingham, *Callwell*, 186; and French, *War Aims*, 149.

16. IWM, 69/78/1, Williams diary, 12 November 1915. Emphasis in the original.

17. Prior, *Gallipoli*, 218.

18. TNA, CAB 19/31, Kitchener to Asquith, 15 November 1915, 131.

19. Whittingham, *Callwell*, 188.

20. TNA, CAB 42/5/20, War Committee minutes, 23 November 1915, 5.

21. TNA, CAB 42/5/20, 5. Emphasis added.

22. D. French, "A One-Man Show? Civil-Military Relations during the First World War," in Paul Smith, ed., *Government and the Armed Forces in Britain 1856–1990* (London: Hambledon Press, 1996), 79–80.

23. TNA, CAB 37/138/7, Asquith to King George V, 24 November 1915.

24. TNA, CAB 42/5/25, "The Future Military Policy at the Dardanelles," 29 November 1915.

25. TNA, CAB 19/31, Dardanelles Commission: Evidence, Monro to Kitchener, 3 December 1915, 134.

26. TNA, CAB 19/30, Dardanelles Commission: Evidence, "Memorandum by CIGS," 23 December 1915, 197–98.

27. IWM, 69/21/2/13–14, Dawnay to his wife, 6 January 1916.

28. W. E. Rapp, "Civil-Military Relations: The Role of Military Leaders in Strategy Making," *Parameters* 45, no. 3 (2015): 19.

29. L. Freedman, "On Military Advice," *RUSI Journal* 162, no. 3 (2017): 17.

30. TNA, CAB 19/1, Final report, 53.

31. TNA, CAB 19/33, Dardanelles Commission: Minutes, Monro evidence, Q123–24.

32. IWM, 69/78/1, Williams diary, 30 November 1915.

33. IWM, 69/78/1.

34. For example, see Winston S. Churchill, *1915, The World Crisis*, vol. 2 (London: Thornton Butterworth, 1923), 488–89.

35. TNA, CAB 19/1, Final report, 54.

36. TNA, CAB 37/138/12, Curzon memorandum, 25 November 1915, 2–3.

37. G. Halpern, ed., *1914–1918, The Keyes Papers*, vol. 1 (London: George Allen and Unwin, 1979), 301 (Keyes to his wife, 31 December 1915).

38. Cmd 371, *Final Report*, 88.

39. Quoted in Whittingham, *Callwell*, 189.

40. TNA, CAB 19/30, W. R. Robertson, "Memorandum on the Conduct of the War," 5 November 1915.

41. D. Feaver, "The Right to Be Right: Civil-Military Relations and the Iraq Surge Decision," *International Security* 35, no. 4 (2011): 97.

42. TNA, CAB 37/138/12, Curzon memorandum, 25 November 1915, 1.

43. IWM, 69/21/1, Dawnay to his wife, 1–2 November 1915.

44. TNA, CAB 19/31, Dardanelles Commission: Evidence, Monro to Kitchener, 1 December 1915, 133.

45. IWM, 69/78/1, Williams diary, 4 December 1915.

46. A. Carr, "It's about Time: Strategy and Temporal Phenomena," *Journal of Strategic Studies* (2018): 10, https://doi.org/10.1080/01402390.2018.1529569.

47. Golby and Karlin, "Best Military Advice," 151.

48. Freedman, "Military Advice," 12.

49. Feaver, "Right to Be Right," 116.

50. J. Kiszely, "The Political-Military Dynamic in the Conduct of Strategy," *Journal of Strategic Studies* 42, no. 2 (2019): 248.

51. French, "One-Man Show," 90.

52. Quoted in H. Strachan, *The Politics of the British Army* (Oxford: Clarendon Press, 1997), 132–33.

53. French, "One-Man Show," 77.

54. Quoted in M. Johnson, *Militarism and the British Left, 1902–1914* (Basingstoke, UK: Palgrave, 2013), 58.

55. G. Ellison, *The Perils of Amateur Strategy* (London: Longmans, 1926), 127.

56. C. von Clausewitz, *On War*, trans. and ed. M. Howard and Peter Paret (Princeton, NJ: Princeton University Press, 1976), 605.

57. TNA, CAB 37/139/12, Bonar Law memorandum, 4 December 1915. The Conservative and Unionist Party was the main center-right party in British politics. It joined a multi-party wartime coalition government in May 1915 until December 1916 when the coalition collapsed.

58. "Dardanelles," House of Commons debate, 2 November 1915, *Hansard*, vol. 75, 509–15.

59. "Dardanelles," 509–15.

60. "Dardanelles," 509–15.

61. G. Barrow, *The Life of General Sir Charles Carmichael Monro* (London: Hutchinson, 1931), 71.

62. TNA, CAB 19/33, Dardanelles Commission: Minutes, Monro evidence, Q143, 4.

63. TNA, CAB 19/31, Dardanelles Commission: Evidence, Monro to Kitchener, 2 November 1915, 127. Emphasis added.

64. TNA, CAB 37/138/12, Curzon memorandum, 25 November 1915, 2.

65. Halpern, *1914–1918*, I, 266 (Keyes to his wife, 2 December 1915) and 268 (Wemyss to Jackson, n.d.); and TNA, CAB 19/33, Dardanelles Commission: Minutes, Hamilton evidence, Q2538–39, 1321–22.

66. Feaver, "Right to Be Right," 116.

67. TNA, CAB 37/138/22, Curzon memorandum, 27 November 1915, 5.

68. Golby and Karlin, "Best Military Advice," 147.

69. E. Cohen, *Supreme Command: Soldiers, Statesmen and Leadership in Wartime* (New York: Free Press, 2002); and R. K. Betts, *American Force: Dangers, Delusions, and Dilemmas in National Security* (New York: Columbia University Press, 2012).

70. Rapp, "The Role of Military Leaders," 21–24.

71. J. Davidson, "Civil-Military Friction and Presidential Decision Making: Explaining the Broken Dialogue," *Presidential Studies Quarterly* 43, no. 1 (2013): 134–35.

72. Quoted in French, "One-Man Show," 92.

73. H. Strachan, "Making Strategy: Civil-Military Relations after Iraq," *Survival* 48, no. 3 (2006): 68.

74. Turner, "Cabinets, Committees, and Secretariats," 59–60.

75. Freedman, "Military Advice," 18; and Rapp, "The Role of Military Leaders," 22.

76. TNA, CAB 19/33, Dardanelles Commission: Minutes, Monro evidence, Q128, 7.

77. For example, see G. Halpern, *The Naval War in the Mediterranean: 1914–1918* (Abingdon, UK: Routledge, 1987), 186.

78. TNA, CAB 19/33, Dardanelles Commission: Minutes, Monro evidence, Q131, 7.

79. G. H. Cassar, *Asquith as War Leader* (London: Hambledon Press, 1994), 135.

80. French, "One-Man Show," 107.

81. Strachan, "Making Strategy," 68.

82. Golby and Karlin, "Best Military Advice," 150.

83. "Special Commissions (Dardanelles and Mesopotamia) Bill," House of Commons debate, 26 July 1916, *Hansard*, vol. 84, 1714–15.

84. J. Macleod, "General Sir Ian Hamilton and the Dardanelles Commission," *War in History* 8, no. 4 (2001), 437.

85. Cmd 8490, *First Report of the Dardanelles Commission*, 1917, 43; and Cmd 371, *Final Report*, 88.

86. Cmd 371, 95.

87. Turner, "Cabinets, Committees and Secretariats," 62.

88. Strachan, "Making Strategy," 68.

89. French, "One-Man Show," 88, 94–95; and D. R. Woodward, *Field Marshal Sir William Robertson: Chief of the Imperial General Staff in the Great War* (Westport, CT: Praeger, 1998), 29–30.

90. Private Collection of the Dawnay Family, Maj. Gen. Sir A. Lynden-Bell to Dawnay, 13 October 1917.

91. Quoted in French, "One-Man Show," 98.

92. Barrow, *Monro*, 93; and French, 106–7.

93. Kiszely, "Political-Military Dynamic," 252.

Chapter 19

The Retreat of Cyber Forces after Offensive Operations

J. D. Work

Despite millennia of human experience, the nature and causation of defeat in conflict remains a subject of study and debate. Although each victory may have countless claimants seeking credit, the orphans of defeat compel deeper study into the unique factors and pivotal decisions that saw forces routed and the field conceded. Not surprisingly, contemporary planners grapple with these questions in the much-newer warfare domain of cyberspace. With mere decades of operational history, many foundational questions of cyber operations have not been touched by theory—let alone resolved by case analysis or other theory testing. Among these unresolved questions is how cyber mission forces behave when facing prospective loss, a topic that has been largely overlooked. Yet just as in kinetic fights, the range of decision options becomes critically important as operators disengage. The way a retreat is conducted may transform retrograde and retrenchment into a rout, or provide critical time to rally forces for new campaigns.

Professionals who study war are familiar with the valor of the last stand on the bridge as a delaying action such as at Pons Sublicius in Rome, or the bitter grind of maneuver groups kettled in unanticipated salient at Kursk.[1] Historians have studied fighting retreats across unthinkable distances that became the stuff of legends, such as the March of the Ten Thousand.[2] Yet they have not looked at the hard decisions of an operator commanding implants moving laterally throughout industrial control systems within an adversary's electrical grid at the height of a militarized crisis, when detection alarms begin to sound—as in recent engagements observed between Chinese cyber intrusions and Indian network defenders concurrent to clashes at Ladakh.[3] When do leaders directing such actions give the order to pull back, even if the face of potential loss of all access to a target? Under what conditions might they stand fast, even as their careful pre-positioning may rapidly become untenable, with detected malware no longer able to deliver potential military effects disrupting power distribution due to defensive responses? How does good decision-making mitigate consequences of loss, or bad leadership turn setbacks into catastrophe?

It is difficult to understand what defeat looks like in virtual conflict, especially for warfighting communities rooted in "breaking things and killing people." The centrality of destroying personnel and materiel in combat operations has long been framed as "the only true aim in war."[4] Many commentators have therefore assumed that the difficulty of envisioning such destruction in the cyber domain means that things are not broken, and that people do not die as a result. In turn, commentators offer differing explanations as to why this would be so, despite manifest and sustained military effort toward definitive ends. This has spawned a robust debate within academic literature over the character of cyber conflict.[5]

Of course, much of this debate is premised on the fallacy that virtual effects do not have real-world consequences. But offensive cyber capabilities can and have been employed to degrade and destroy systems and networks, and the higher-order effects of losing confidentiality, integrity, and availability of these assets may lead to lethal outcomes. Notable and widely publicized recent examples include alteration to safety systems that control highly energetic physical processes in industrial control systems architectures, as well as the compromise of artillery fire control applications as part of integrated counter-battery fires efforts, destruction of port and railway infrastructure, and loss of military satellite communications in conflict.[6] Even as this long-running international relations theory debate is settled in ongoing contemporary engagements, cyber forces are increasingly manned, equipped, and deployed to conduct missions that states believe are worth the level of investment. States have set out to build and buy warfighting capabilities—and use them. As these forces seek opposing objectives, there will be winners and losers as in any fight.

But how will the losers behave in defeat? Military history offers countless examples of armies forced to quit the field, and their various fates. Many of the cases documented across other chapters in this volume highlight catastrophe through compounding failures under enemy pressure, but also how strong leadership, imaginative innovation, uncompromising discipline, and tactical brilliance ensured a single battle gone badly did not decide the war. These histories offer critical lessons regarding kinetic engagements to inform doctrine, planning, and future leader decisions. Yet there is almost no equivalent literature encompassing behavior in defeat in the cyber domain—although not for lack of contact between opposing forces.

Retreat in cyber engagements is very different than in other domains. Yet the reasons why an officer commanding cyber forces orders a retreat shares many characteristics—in the face of prospective defeat, where combat power is no longer sustainable, or where an action may preserve a larger force or enable continued pursuit of larger objectives beyond the present engagement. How an officer recognizes and thinks about these conditions is as important for study as movements on land, at sea, in air, or in space—both for analyzing future adversary problems and with hard choices faced by friendly forces.

This chapter looks at the breaking point for adversary offensive cyber capabilities, considering the thresholds at which an intrusion or cyber-attack campaign is no longer combat-effective. It is not a given that such conditions may be recognized by either operators or their leadership (let alone opposing forces) given the ambiguity, deception, fog, and friction that is characteristic in cyber engagements. Cyber operations are constrained by access options, and by limited arsenals of offensive capabilities. Adversary operators act differently as these resources are depleted, and planners and leadership face difficult decisions when these resources are exhausted. When an adversary disengages from further offensive operations, difficult decisions must be made on whether to tear down hard-gained access and existing infrastructure supporting these accesses, or simply abandon the compromised systems in place. This chapter will consider scenarios where adversaries do so in an orderly and even covert/clandestine manner to preserve footholds for future re-engagement, as well as cases in which adversaries destructively terminate intrusion access as a deliberate measure to inflict harm on the victor, deny insight into as-yet-undetected capabilities and their employment, or seek other objectives. Also considered is the near-term future when autonomous forces may continue to fight even as operators and planners disengage—and where the multi-actor environment may see such forces leveraged in new ways even as the initiating conflict fades. Lastly, this examination will consider the fate of former operator cadres and developers who control yet-unused access and arsenals in the face of retreat and loss, as they face uncertain futures, unknown liabilities, and unclear employment.

Breaking the Intrusion Set

Understanding defeat in cyber engagements is just one facet of how modern warfare has blurred distinctions of victory across many domains.[7] The intangibles of the cyber domain merely magnify these trends. But as in any military engagement, there is a threshold at which an offensive cyber operations force becomes combat ineffective. This threshold sometimes depends on secrecy, in that "victory in information warfare depends on knowing something that your adversaries do not and using this advantage to confound, coerce, or kill them; lose the secrecy, and you lose your advantage."[8] The knowns and unknowns here encompass system and network vulnerabilities, the means by which these vulnerabilities may be exploited, detection of weaponized tooling use in exploitation, and disruptive or destructive effects introduced by such exploitation. In addition to deliberate obfuscation, such secrets also stem from complex interactions across different environments that may cause a target to be unaware of the dependencies that underpin its critical functions. Eliminating such secrecy may be considered the first objective for operations against cyber forces "in the field." Sustaining secrecy is a key requirement, if not the *sine qua non* driver, of successful offensive cyber operations.[9] Losing secrecy may halt ongoing campaigns, or even prevent future operations from ever launching. The latter condition may represent a more common failure mode from earlier defeats than may generally be recognized, due to the lack of studies focused on decisions not to conduct operations.[10]

The general assumption is that the advantage of secrecy can be lost due to disclosures driven by defensive cyber operations. An extensive research ecosystem driven by global investment exists to find and highlight previously unknown security vulnerabilities; substantial personal and market incentives publicize these findings.[11] Even governments must consider coordinated disclosure of their unique insight regarding potentially exploitable vulnerabilities—particularly since private sector equities may be harmed by withholding such disclosures.[12] Likewise, significant government and private sector intelligence efforts are to identify exploitation of these vulnerabilities in the wild, and to recognize and track the offensive tooling ("cyber weapons") used in intrusion and attack incidents that leverage these vulnerabilities.[13]

The loss of secrecy around a threat capability is thus seen as essential to stop exploitation and delivery of cyber effects against protected targets that are aware of, and appropriately postured, to defeat known vulnerabilities and identified tactics, techniques, and procedures. At scale, these may render an adversary offensive capability portfolio relatively nonviable due to widespread detection and prevention of access using known implants or previously observed C2 infrastructure. While a capability may remain viable with some modification where defender visibility lags, or against lesser defended targets for some period thereafter, this declining offensive utility is generally counted as loss under presumption of defender responsiveness. This loss is predicated on a given point where operations against defended targets fail. That is, there is a curve where the work factor required to exploit defended targets overtakes adversary operator abilities to achieve effects against enough nodes, or against critical nodes pursuing specific operational or overall campaign objectives.[14] The point can be reached where offensive options of otherwise successful capabilities are rendered *de minimis* because they cannot deliver effects against functions supported by target systems and networks. Key lower thresholds include the inability to sustain exfiltration in compromise of confidentiality (for espionage), conduct disruption of availability, or manipulate integrity—or to do so but only in a manner that does not impact supported organizational processes or decision-making.

However, defensive cyber operations alone do not defeat adversary intrusion sets. Extended engagements encompassing defensive cyber operations-response actions (DCO-RA), and other offensive cyber operations conducted for counter-cyber operations (CCO) objectives, may be conducted forward of friendly systems and networks to provide improved warning of adversary action, better characterization of ongoing operations, or other objectives to deny and degrade infrastructure and tooling in live intrusions.[15] These actions often are essential where the compounded coordination and re-posturing effort to react to systematic vulnerability within large systems and network deployments requires more extensive time and effort than the adversary will permit. This reality lies at the heart of the shift in the US government strategic approach to defend forward through the doctrine of persistent engagement.[16]

Further, offensive cyber operations (OCO) may be conducted for counterforce objectives, targeting adversary military and intelligence services (as well as their contractors and proxies) responsible for ongoing threats. This may extend to adversary leadership command, control, and communications (C3) arrangements providing direction to hostile operators, as well as to finance, logistics, and other supporting functions enabling cyber threat activity.[17]

Recognizing and Reaching Adversary Breaking Points

In kinetic engagements, adversary losses are generally obvious in the shattered forms of combatants and machines left on the battlefield. The key questions about when an adversary force breaks are centered on its ability to sustain operations in the face of losses through reserves or reinforcement, or when the situation becomes untenable because of logistics, leadership, or morale. But these factors are difficult to translate into the cyber domain, and harder still to recognize in the abstracts of code. What is the breaking point of a given cyber force? What are the signs an adversary has reached that point?

Observers may consider the correlation of forces in an engagement. However, the term "cyberweapon" remains stubbornly ambiguous due to the inherent overlap with common administrative and other functional tooling in common use within industry.[18] So, too, is the manner in which such capabilities are aggregated in force. Narrow consideration of uniquely weaponized portfolios may be a first approximation. This formulation would measure combat power by the availability of specific offensive cyber components (often focusing on 0-day vulnerabilities and novel payloads) within an adversary's ready mission force, reserve magazines, and overall arsenals. Loss of such capabilities due to disclosure and associated defeat through detection eventually leads to depleted inventories that prevent an adversary from continuing effective engagements. Quantified capability must be therefore considered only in relative terms against the state of the art of a defenders' technical investment in intrusion countermeasures. These concepts also reach beyond operational uncertainties, underpinning much of the literature around the strategic level of cyber conflict, shaping debates over offensive advantage (or offense persistence) relative to the systemic features of defended network ecosystems, or specific defenders.[19]

Such attrition models are complicated by the continuing utility of many exploits long after disclosure. Such 1-day (or n-day) vulnerability windows, where specific exploits remain viable because of lagging efforts to patch insecure systems, are a near-constant reality of deployed networks. So too are so-called forever-day exploits, in which a system cannot be patched but instead must be entirely replaced so that the vulnerabilities are not "immortal."[20] Likewise, payloads may be modified to extend useful lifespan even when malware family has been identified through obfuscation. While a point is reached where defensive responses drive the obsolescence of given capabilities, it is not a simple matter to "count warheads," whether observed on launch or estimated in adversary "bunkers." Neither offensive forces nor defenders may rely on immediate material considerations for determining disengagement.

Alternatively, given the limited utility of attrition models, planners may consider position and maneuver as determinants of loss. The concept, definition, and identification of "key terrain" in cyberspace.[21] Yet undeniably there are pivotal nodes, essential processes, and critical services in any network that must be controlled to achieve specific effects and objectives. The struggle to deny these options to an adversary defines tactical actions "on the wire." Yet the adversary controls this key terrain through offensive capabilities exercised at a given point in time across a discrete attack surface. This results in conditional access—effectively a binary question of whether the adversary can exercise its will by controlling the target application, service, or hardware. Stepping back from the intricacies of mapping these access conditions for situational awareness and representation, the underlying contest involves the relative viability of an offensive capability—not merely across the arsenal in some abstract correlation, but at the sticking place. Cyber "combat power" is thus brought to bear through these accesses, or the adversary does not achieve its objectives and must decide on a further course of action. If options are sufficiently foreclosed through capabilities and accesses that have been rendered nonviable, the engagement is decided (at least in this iteration).

This is not to say positional factors become irrelevant. Even if denied key terrain, an adversary's control of secondary or tertiary network nodes can provide advantage in shifting approaches to direct offensive capabilities against less-well-defended elements, or introduce novel capabilities for which defenders are unprepared. Looking at broader campaigns, these are rarely two-player contests. An adversary will often target a variety of states and private organizations concurrently using the same capabilities set. Even facing defeat in one target or operational phase, a given access option may be leveraged to succeed against other targets. Understanding these decisions and their iterations, particularly as an adversary faces mounting losses, becomes critical to describing, explaining, and estimating cyber conflict events as they unfold.

Adversary Recognition of Losses

Offensive cyber operators are acutely aware that potential access to target systems and networks, and actions on these objectives, may fail. Simple mistakes and operational friction may compound. Likewise, they face constant pressure from defensive countermeasures intended to deny and degrade the effectiveness of tactics, techniques, and procedures. Planners and operators select postures and objectives based on these considerations—balancing tradeoffs of access and effect against probability of detection.[22] Many offensive successes at the technical, tactical levels are fragile—an awareness that underpins a sense of the domain as transitory.[23] This awareness is coupled with the fact that offensive operators frequently do not know why an action failed to result in a desired outcome. Environment, configuration, and state variables must all be correct, and offensive tooling must be appropriately tailored to successfully execute specific instructions—a demanding task even in single instances.[24] This complexity is magnified across broadly sustained operations involving larger numbers of targets, especially heterogenous objectives across organizations with distinct hardening postures. Offensive operators, therefore, highly value intelligence on the reasons for a failure, and the degree to which this failure was driven by specific internal defensive measures taken by the target.[25]

These uncertainties also create scenarios where adversaries may not know their forces have been defeated, or realize this with some degree of lag. As a result, when failing against core objectives they may continue to expend efforts (and inflict damage) on relatively peripheral targets. For example, Iranian-attributed intrusion sets launched destructive cyber-attacks against Saudi Arabia in 2017 in which wiper malware deployment was relatively ineffective against primary objectives that had substantially improved hardening and recovery postures after suffering severe impacts in earlier incidents dating back to 2012.[26] Further efforts to stage destructive effects during this campaign against other critical infrastructure networks, including financial sector systems, also reportedly failed because operators did not have experience with specialized target environments.[27] Despite their inability to inflict economic damage on industrial targets, the adversary operators were particularly aggressive in their further destructive actions against interlinked administrative and government networks.[28]

The adversary revisited these targets repeatedly in future years but, despite experiencing declining effectiveness over sustained campaigns, failed to recognize diminishing returns. This likely impacted the choices operators made as they fell back, reassessed, and re-postured for renewed efforts with different infrastructure, tooling selection, and engagement plans. These challenges were magnified by disconnects between what Iranian Revolutionary Guard Corps officers and their contractors knew, and what was communicated and understood by the regime's leadership.[29] Disconnects between leadership awareness and the actions of those with hands on keyboard may be observed in other campaigns involving declining effectiveness. If operators are still able to report some success metrics, they can forestall recognition of loss—at least until it becomes apparent they cannot deliver against higher value targets, or detection and defeat of a campaign becomes public through defender attribution (whether deliberately acknowledged in the open, or through private backchannels).

Failure to recognize defeat in these cases—including distorted narratives that Iranian offensive cyber operators provided to management—delay adaptation and innovation in future operations. Thus, the adversary learned more slowly than would otherwise have been the case, and repeated many of the same mistakes in new intrusions—especially where effects were intended. These cascading failures were likely not limited to the original contractors or even sponsoring service, but almost certainly continued into future operations planning by other Iranian services, including within the Ministry of Intelligence and Security (MOIS) and its contractors and proxies.

Retrograde on the Grid

Writings that describe various cyber operation maneuvers, including flanking, envelopment, infiltration, penetration, and turning movements, are assigned as core reading to teach new cyber operators how to think about the domain.[30] Conspicuously, retrograde maneuver has not been covered. Yet the behavior of adversary forces at these moments is critical to understanding how a retreat will develop.

Adversaries facing mounting losses to deployed cyber capabilities must make hard choices. Even those who are not driven solely by attrition logic must deal with inescapable realities related to narrowed exploitation and access options. In one sense, these are nothing like the hard choices facing decimated units pressed by the burden of dead and wounded. Rather, a better analogy may be a unit at the edge of its logistics envelope—not the hard calculus of a last stand but instead the unforgiving flight operation limits imposed by limited fuel or ordnance. In aviation brevity code, these conditions are known as BINGO (minimum fuel state for return to base) and WINCHESTER (expenditure of all available munitions). Although significant, an adversary can continue activities to some degree after reaching these mission states. But pressing on will generally have a poor outcome—resulting in loss of the ability to make choices about implant behavior (much as an aircraft ceases controlled flight when it runs out of fuel), or the inability to deliver further effects due to nonviability of exploit and/or payload tooling (when weapon stations are empty or cannot effectively engage relevant targets).

This admittedly simple analogy elides much of the complexity of cyber exploitation and attack. The full scope of required calculations encompasses far more than combustion and detonation. One must consider an array of technical factors in detail. These include both current and future probability of exploitation of identical or similar targets, the availability and efficacy of other exploit options, the likelihood that other new exploitable vulnerabilities may be present, the difficulty involved in identifying such vulnerabilities and weaponizing new exploit options, the probability of defender hardening due to prior pressure, the lifespan of exploits in inventory or those likely to be discovered, and the relative longevity of these timelines against other target engineering configuration changes. Similar considerations must be weighed regarding offensive payloads, encompassing not only the current use of the tooling but the entire prior operational history of implant families and any related codebase.[31] Operators will have different priorities regarding factors which achieve immediate effects or preserve future options, although some general principles may dictate recurring patterns of decisions.[32]

Manual interactive commands abusing functionality present on target systems and networks, including techniques for "living off the land," may allow some degree of continued effects delivery even where prepared tooling may no longer be viable. Likewise, living off the land may become critical where rate of other expenditures and volume of targets to be serviced within compressed timelines place untenable demands on operational elements.[33] For example, in the Russia-Ukraine conflict in late February 2022, Windows Sysinternals tools were used for destructive effects against Ukrainian government targets by an attributed Russian nexus intrusion set, even as other unique destructive implants were deployed against other targets at a high rate of expenditure.[34] However, the timing of this incident likely matters. Here, initial commitment of other more tailored destructive capabilities inventories was likely preplanned in the opening phase of the war under the first concept of operations (modeled on earlier seizure of capital cities through rapid intervention as seen in Storm-333 and similar prior "special military operations"). By the time of the incident, this CONOPS was clearly no longer viable.[35] This likely forced operators to service some targets through manually interactive commands, even as the main thrust faltered and planners were forced into a protracted and more conventional fight beyond the operation's initial reported timeline (as the planners apparently anticipated decisive success within days, and an overall campaign of no more than two weeks).[36]

But analogy does illustrate that operator behavior changes under these conditions. Just as pilots cannot ignore loss of engines, adversary cyber forces make different decisions when they lose capabilities. Planners, knowing that these changes will likely be forced upon them at a given point in a campaign, generally develop contingency options. Even absent such pre-planned responses, operators will have a limited range of courses of action available in extremis. Similarly, the combatants making these calls will generally be afforded a degree of abstracted distance, in contrast to the press of immediate personal survival concerns in other fights. Such more dispassionate decision-making is often overlooked for responses when facing defeat. Yet emotional dynamics such as surprise, stress, and ego may well play out in new ways.[37]

Hard Choices in Retreat

Adversaries who recognize their positions are untenable will generally face constrained options on the wire. The first decision will be whether to go quietly or "bring the noise." That is, operators may attempt to maximize nondetection to preserve yet-undetected capability, and concurrently extend defender uncertainty regarding prior success (particularly important for intelligence collection operations), or maximize disruptive/destructive effects on target systems (including when such effects were not the initial intrusion objective).

When attempting quiet withdrawal, operators remove existing implants and sanitize logs, disk, and memory space to eliminate any artifacts that might be identified during defender digital forensics incident response (DFIR). Mature capabilities developers often design such functionality directly into tooling, reducing the likelihood of mistake or unintended consequences. Indeed, a fast, clean, and consistent teardown was the core driver of the earliest automation in scripted offensive capabilities deployment.[38] Automation does, however, impose a risk tradeoff for designers. With "killswitch" features, deployed implants are vulnerable to DCO-RA and other CCO actions that trigger removal of detected implants whose command and control authentication protocols are known. Adversary planners are now acutely aware of this potential risk after high-profile killswitches triggered by defenders halted the uncontrolled spread of the Wannacry malware in 2017, and were part of the Retadup botnet takedown in 2019.[39] Whether such removal is manual or automated, in any operational act friction does occur, and collateral damage may result from target systems that are incompletely sanitized, or enter other failure states. In the cases of a quiet withdrawal, this can compromise stealth.

More critically, such friction can impair an adversary's potential options to preserve a foothold that will allow return when conditions change. Footholds for resumption of intrusion activities using alternative tooling likely gain importance to adversary planners as capability losses mount due to evictions across multiple related targets within a relatively narrow time period. Variable emphasis may also be placed on higher value objectives, where threat actors may view sustainment of future options as more important than potential risk of a foothold being detected and left in place by defenders as an early-warning tripwire. A detected foothold could result in cascading detection of retooled capabilities deployed to re-establish access at a later date.

Similar considerations apply beyond specific targeted systems and networks, as adversaries must assess every infrastructure element that supported a given operation, weighing the probability that a defender may detect enabling intrusions, proxy nodes, staging servers, exfiltration drops, and other distributed functions. Some operators may keep more of this infrastructure in retreat due to effort expended in setup, or based on varying degrees of confidence in segmentation and other operational security practices during employment. The ease of acquiring replacement infrastructure and effort required to secure such infrastructure against potential CCO pressures (including red-on-red threats) also likely plays a role in these decisions. Operators may choose to sanitize supporting infrastructure less frequently if perceived risk to core operations is low. In fact, adversaries often abandon supporting infrastructure in place, as it is not worth the effort to tear down once compromised. Of course, such legacy infrastructure also offers potential latent utility for future campaigns—especially after "aging out" of common transient periods for indicators of compromise (IOC) and log retention.[40]

Operators who do not go quietly in retreat may instead pursue destructive termination of intrusion access. Such scorched-earth tactics typically delay incident response and recovery and may help obfuscate the scope of compromise, employed tooling, or mechanisms of effects. Introducing delays may preserve other operational infrastructure, extend the nondetection period for implants, or remove critical forensics artifacts that would disclose otherwise-unknown exploitation mechanisms. Destructive retreat also imposes additional punishment on the victim through technical pain points as well as financial and political dimensions. One notable example of destructive withdrawal was attributed to the Democratic People's Republic of Korea (DPRK); where a HIDDEN COBRA/LAZARUS intrusion set delivered malware to wipe systems and destroy networks, including prominent financial institution victims, following conclusion of active operations.[41]

Destructive options may also contribute to other delaying actions, where an adversary campaign may continue to sustain intrusion efforts against other victims, or even acquire new victims, using burned capabilities that they are aware defenders will focus on. Such tactics may prolong the viability of offensive capabilities against lower sophistication defenders, as well as attrit a more sophisticated defender's response capacity regardless of actual espionage or attack utility. This is especially apparent where limited coordination exists between multiple targeted organizations and their supporting intelligence and countermeasures functions. Just as in a child's soccer game, the continuing chase after known threat activity may occupy disproportionate attention.

One example may be observed in 2016 to early 2017 campaigns conducted by the Russian Foreign Intelligence Service (SVR) intrusion set known as APT29/COZY BEAR/IRON HEMLOCK. Although operators almost certainly became increasingly aware their actions were being detected, they continued intrusion activity largely unchanged. Operators reacted only when widespread compromise of their intrusion infrastructure (including pivoting against the operators themselves) by Dutch General Intelligence and Security Service counter-cyber operations was publicly disclosed.[42] Because of such disclosures, the operators abandoned common infrastructure and tooling to allow retrenchment and retooling in 2018 to mid-2019. During this time, however, some operations against less-well-defended targets continued using legacy capabilities that had received less scrutiny from Western intelligence services, including private sector players.[43] This retreat proved substantially successful; it forced the service to focus on better-designed implants offering lower probability of detection, and also on more complex operations intended to exploit positional advantage against multiple targets going into 2019 and 2020. As a result, subsequent APT29 operations against medical sector research and development targets were poorly detected, and largely unattributed by industry until government intelligence services furnished warning.[44] Other substantial industry and government compromises through subversion of software update mechanisms also came to light only much later with the detection of the HOLIDAY BEAR campaign. Even after detection, these changes in adversary tradecraft resulted in continuing attribution uncertainty in the private sector.[45] The attribution debate was conclusively resolved for some participants only after government disclosure.[46] The case illustrates the utility of continued delaying operations using burned capabilities closely tracked by defenders, buying time to introduce and leverage alternative new options even in the face of a catastrophic setback.

Operators Disengage While the Fight Goes on

Cyber forces in retreat that abandon active implant and associated C2 infrastructure in place may create the equivalent of cyber "unexploded ordnance" (UXO). Such still-live intrusion access may continue to threaten defenders even as adversary operators abandon direct interaction with the architecture. Hostile implants can continue to execute pre-planned effects logic, including disruptive and destructive options with time or other conditional triggers (once known as "logic bombs").[47] DPRK-origin wiper malware deployed across Republic of Korea networks in the infamous "Independence Day" cyber attacks of 2009 was designed to be triggered on a specific anniversary date, but a year later, systems whose internal clock settings were not properly synchronized suffered re-attack from previously dormant infection.[48] The US government likely considered such history in 2019 when it degraded the DPRK-attributed Joanap botnet that by that point had been largely abandoned.[49]

Unlike conventional kinetic UXO, however, hostile implants may continue to be directed if they still interact with C2 infrastructure; or other actors may successfully pass commands in the right protocol to be executed by the malware. Attempts to discover and control live implants are not uncommon in complex campaigns.[50] Adversary capabilities abandoned in retreat can be likely attractive targets worth the potential effort for n^{th} parties involved in hijacking of abandoned C2 servers, or defeating command authentication at the implant level. These latent force elements may be leveraged for espionage or attack in complex conflicts involving multiple coalition, allied, and other partners—and their rivals in and beyond immediate hostilities. Such actions may prolong militarized disputes, degrade post-conflict stability and reconstruction, and risk renewed conflict for extended periods after the initial operators have retreated. Planners must consider and manage the consequences of a retreat, although this is less likely when decisions are made by individual operators under pressure.

These problems may exist absent deliberate intervention, as future campaigns increasingly incorporate autonomous offensive capabilities. In these cases, ongoing cyber fires may be delivered from surviving infrastructure and deployed implants acting according to previously established targeting and effects criteria. Although debate continues on how to ensure operational limits absent human-in-the-loop or human-on-the-loop, technologies have far outpaced norms. Deployed capabilities might be triggered based on dynamic decision logic regarding target conditions, crisis events, or other factors outside the immediate conflict (even factors such as stock prices or other market movements). The prospect that friendly forces must contend with autonomous adversary capabilities long after the operators have quit the field is sobering—and especially so when considering the potential adoption of "Dead Hand" style retaliatory architectures intended to deliver widespread destructive effects upon loss of positive C2.[51]

These conditions may also be exploited to minimize political or other retreat costs for still-extant cyber forces directed by parties already involved in ongoing engagements. In one case, industry researchers observed that an SVR-attributed intrusion set displaced prior access attributed to Russian Armed Forces General Staff Main Intelligence Directorate (GRU) operators then itself entirely removed all implants—abandoning the victim network.[52] While multiple explanations may be advanced for this unusual scenario, it is possible here that one Russian intelligence service handled the problems of retreat for another. This action may have been executed without deconfliction or even GRU awareness, as the military intelligence service has been generally acknowledged as less focused on nondetection.[53]

Conclusion and Outlook

The nature of war remains unchanged in the cyber domain; defeat ultimately rests on breaking the enemy's will to continue the fight. The problem of understanding that breaking point, and an adversary's reactions, is compounded in the transient virtual environment. Yet morale and intention are also intangible, and advantage is often fleeting. This has not stopped generations of military theorists from considering the problem.[54]

The retreat of cyber forces also creates issues beyond the virtual world, and beyond specific conflicts between opposing elements. These consequences must be considered. Even after an adversary has been defeated, the disposition of the talent that sustained offensive campaigns must be considered. Operators, planners, developers, and intelligence officers involved in targeting, capabilities generation, access, and effects delivery may be at loose ends in a post-conflict environment—but with continuing access to deployed infrastructure and surviving footholds within high-value networks. Many retain knowledge of still-current vulnerabilities and insecure target architectures that could be exploited in the future, or may even have pre-operational reconnaissance and targeting intelligence that could help identify new options for other interested parties.

Even if active operations terminate in a manner that previous positions and plans are entirely untenable, an adversary force may still have some capabilities inventory. As a result, former cadres may possess unsecured arsenals with unused exploits and undetected implants that would command value on the commercial market. Even if such offensive capabilities were partially disclosed because of prior use, certain unique features and design logics may still be in demand. And beyond the profit motive, public release may inflict continuing damage on now-victorious former enemies, as cyber criminals and other players attempt to take advantage of the situation. As was seen in the case of the infamous Shadowbrokers leak of tooling allegedly stolen from the US government, the compounding damage from such opportunistic actors could far exceed the initial impact.[55]

In the rarified circles of offensive malware development, such tooling may be leveraged not merely for its immediate value, but as a unique branding for those who claim credit for, or association, with detected operations. This points to perhaps the hardest challenge that must be addressed in retreat: the post-conflict futures of abandoned operators, now free to ply their trade for other sponsors. It is increasingly the proliferation of this talent—rather than any specific exploit or implant—that has driven maturity across multiple states' emerging offensive cyber programs. A substantial defeat that realigns economic incentives, personal interests, or market positions may accelerate these dynamics, with difficult implications for conflicts yet to come.

For too long, adversary cyber threats have been viewed as a recurring problem that cannot be considered or addressed in military terms. While this may or may not hold true for operations below the threshold of armed conflict, there have been operations conducted during regional hostilities, and there will almost certainly be other future campaigns that reach or exceed whatever definition of "war-like" actions one chooses to consider. These future operations may be conducted in conjunction with kinetic engagements, or perhaps entirely within and through the virtual environment. Inevitably, such operations will end. As demonstrated throughout military history, not all such endings are conclusive—producing stalemates, frozen conflicts, and unresolved ceasefires that never result in armistice. However, in many contests of arms there are indeed winners and losers. Understanding the events that bring an adversary to the point of defeat, and can shape the conditions under which a force disengages, will be vital to post-conflict stability. Rather, these forces in retreat will likely remain critical factors for resilience and security throughout globally interconnected technology ecosystems, long after hostile cyber fires have gone dark.

Notes

1. Polybius, *Histories*, trans. William Roger Paton (Cambridge, MA: Harvard University Press, 1922); and Valeriy Zamulin, "The Battle of Kursk: New Findings," *Journal of Slavic Military Studies* 25 (2012):409–17.

2. Xenophon, *Anabasis*, trans. Carleton L. Brownson and John Dillery (Cambridge, MA: Harvard University Press, 1998).

3. Recorded Future, "China-Linked Group RedEcho Targets the Indian Power Sector Amid Heightened Border Tensions," February 2021.

4. B. H. Liddell Hart, *The Decisive Wars in History: A Study in Strategy* (London: G. Bell & Sons. 1929).

5. John Arquilla and David Ronfeldt, "Cyberwar is Coming!." *Comparative Strategy* 12, no. 2 (1993): 141–65; Winn Schwartau, *Information Warfare* (New York: Thunder's Mouth Press, 1994); Martin Libiciki. "Information War, Information Peace," *Journal of International Affairs* 51, no. 2 (1998): 411–28; Gregory J. Rattray, *Strategic Warfare in Cyberspace* (Cambridge, MA: MIT Press, 2001); Thomas Rid, *Cyber War Will Not Take Place* (Oxford: Oxford University Press, 2013); Erik Gartzke, "The Myth of Cyberwar: Bringing War in Cyberspace Back Down to Earth," *International Security* 38, no. 2 (2013): 41–73; Brandon Valeriano and Ryan C. Maness, *Cyber War Versus Cyber Realities: Cyber Conflict in the International System* (Oxford: Oxford University Press, 2015); and James J. Wirtz, "The Cyber Pearl Harbor," *Intelligence and National Security* 32, no. 6 (2017): 758–67.

6. Dragos, "TRISIS Malware: Analysis of Safety System Targeted Malware," 13 December 2017; FireEye, "Attackers Deploy New ICS Attack Framework 'TRITON' and Cause Operational Disruption to Critical Infrastructure," 14 December 2017; CrowdStrike, "Danger Close: Fancy Bear Tracking of Ukrainian Field Artillery Units," 22 December 2016; Laboratory of Cryptography and System Security (CrySyS Lab), Budapest University of Technology and Economics, "Technical details on the Fancy Bear Android malware," 3 January 2017; Bryan Pietesch, "Hacking group claims control of Belarusian railroads in move to 'disrupt' Russian troops heading near Ukraine," *Washington Post*, 25 January 2022; SentinelOne, "MeteorExpress—Mysterious Wiper Paralyzes Iranian Trains with Epic Troll," 29 July 2021; Handelsblatt, "Black Cat-Erpressersoftware: Staatsanwaltschaft ermittelt nach Angriff auf Tankstellen-Zulieferer," 2 February 2022; Spiegel, "Satellitennetzwerk Viasat offenbar gezielt in Osteuropa gehackt," 5 March 2022; and Mandiant, "First Glance: Threat Actor 'Predatory Sparrow' Claims to Attack Iranian Steel Industry and Cause Physically Destructive Impacts," 30 June 2022.

7. Raymond G. O'Connor, "Victory in Modern War," *Journal of Peace Research*, 6 no. 4 (1969): 367–84; Michael Howard, "When are wars decisive?," *Survival* 41, no. 1 (1999): 126–35; Colin S. Gray, "Defining and Achieving Decisive Victory," Strategic Studies Institute, US Army War College, April 2002; Jan Angstrom and Isabelle Duyvesteyn, *Understanding Victory and Defeat in Contemporary War* (Oxfordshire, UK: Routledge, 2007); Robert Mandel,

"Reassessing Victory in Warfare," *Armed Forces and Society* 33, no. 4 (2007): 461–95; and Gabriella Blum, "The Fog of Victory," *European Journal of International Law* 24, no. 1 (2013): 391–421.

8. Bruce D. Berkowitz, "War Logs On: Girding America for Computer Combat," *Foreign Affairs* (May–June 2000).

9. Michael Warner, "The Character of Cyber Conflict," *Texas National Security Review* (September 2020).

10. Max Smeets, "A US History of Not Conducting Cyber Attacks," *Bulletin of the Atomic Scientists* 78, no. 4 (2022): 208–13.

11. Rainer Bohme, "Vulnerability Markets: What is the economic value of a zero-day exploit?," 22C3, Berlin, 27–30 December 2005; Rainer Böhme, "A Comparison of Market Approaches to Software Vulnerability Disclosure," Emerging Trends in Information and Communication Security (ETRICS), Freiburg, Germany, 6–9 June 2006; Jaziar Radianti and Jose. J. Gonzalez, "A Preliminary Model of the Vulnerability Black Market," 25th International System Dynamics Conference, Boston, 29 July–2 August 2007; David McKinney, "Vulnerability Bazaar," *IEEE Security & Privacy* 5, no. 6 (November–December 2007); Stefan Frei et al., "Modeling the Security Ecosystem—The Dynamics of (In)Security," Workshop on the Economics of Information Security (WEIS), University College London, 2009; and Jaziar Radianti, Jose. J. Gonzalez, and Eliot Rich, "Vulnerability Black Markets: Empirical Evidence and Scenario Simulation," 42nd Hawaii International Conference on System Sciences, Big Island, HI, 5–8 January 2009.

12. Jason Healey, "The US Government and Zero Day Vulnerabilities," *Journal of International Affairs* (November 2016); Tristan Caulfield, Christos Ioannidis, and David Pym, "The U.S. Vulnerabilities Equities Process: An Economic Perspective,". 8th International Conference on Decision and Game Theory for Security (GameSec), Vienna, 23–25 October 2017; and Matthias Schulze, "The State of Cyber Arms Control: An International Vulnerabilities Equities Process as the Way to go Forward?," *S&F Sicherheit und Frieden* 38, no. 1 (2020): 17–21.

13. J. D. Work, "Evaluating Commercial Cyber Intelligence Activity," *International Journal of Intelligence and CounterIntelligence* 33, no. 2 (2020): 278–308; and Sasha Romanosky and Benjamin Boudreaux, "Private-Sector Attribution of Cyber Incidents: Benefits and Risks to the U.S. Government," *International Journal of Intelligence and CounterIntelligence* (2020).

14. Concepts of work factor analysis are owed to Jon Mallery.

15. Department of Defense, Joint Publication (JP) 3-12, *Cyberspace Operations* (Washington, DC: 2018); Jason Healey, Neil Jenkins, and J. D. Work, "Defenders Disrupting Adversaries: Framework, Dataset, and Case Studies of Disruptive Counter-Cyber Operations," 12th International Conference on Cyber Conflict (CyCon), Tallinn, 2020; and J. D. Work, "Burned and Blinded: Escalation Risks of Intelligence Loss from Countercyber Operations in Crisis," *International Journal of Intelligence and Counterintelligence* (2022).

16. Michael P. Fischerkeller and Richard J Harknett, "Persistent Engagement, Agreed Competition, Cyberspace Interaction Dynamics, and Escalation," Institute for Defense Analyses, May 2018; Nina Kollars and Jacquelyn Schneider, "Defending Forward: The 2018 Cyber Strategy Is Here," *War on the Rocks*, 20 September 2018; and Paul M. Nakasone and Michael Sulmeyer, "How to Compete in Cyberspace: Cyber Command's New Approach," *Foreign Affairs* (August 2020).

17. Austin Long, "A cyber SIOP? Operational considerations for strategic offensive cyber planning," *Journal of Cybersecurity* 3, no. 1 (2017): 19–28; and Max Smeets, "The Strategic Promise of Offensive Cyber Operations," *Strategic Studies Quarterly* 12, no. 3 (2018): 90–113.

18. Dorothy Denning, "Reflections on Cyberweapons Controls," *Computer Security Journal* 16, no. 4 (2000): 43–53; Dale Peterson, "Offensive Cyber Weapons: Construction, Development, and Employment," *Journal of Strategic Studies* (2013); Dusan Repel and Steven Hersee, "The Ingredients of Cyber Weapons," 10th International Conference on Cyber Warfare and Security, Kruger National Park, South Africa, 24–25 March 2015; Robert E. Schmidle Jr., Michael Sulmeyer, and Ben Buchanan, "Nonlethal Weapons and Cyber Capabilities," in *Understanding Cyber Conflict: Fourteen Analogies*, ed. George Perkovich and Ariel E. Levite (Washington, DC: Georgetown University Press, 2017); and Lucas Kello, *The Virtual Weapon* (New Haven, CT: Yale University Press, 2017).

19. Patrick J. Malone, "Offense-defense balance in cyberspace: a proposed model," Naval Postgraduate School, December 2012; Richard Harknett and Emily Goldman, "The Search for Cyber Fundamentals," *Journal of Information Warfare* 15, no. 2 (2016): 81–86; Rebecca Slayton, "What Is the Cyber Offense-Defense Balance? Conceptions, Causes, and Assessment," International Security 41, no. 3 (Winter 2016/17): 72–109; and Jason Healey, "Understanding the Offense's Systemwide Advantage in Cyberspace," *Lawfare*, 22 December 2021.

20. Lillian Ablon and Andy Bogart, "Zero Days, Thousands of Nights: The Life and Times of Zero-Day Vulnerabilities and Their Exploits," RAND, 2017.

21. Scott D. Applegate, "The principle of maneuver in cyber operations," 4th International Conference on Cyber Conflict (CyCon), Tallinn, 2012; John R. Mills, "The Key Terrain of Cyber," *Georgetown Journal of International Affairs* (2012); David Raymond et al., "Key terrain in cyberspace: Seeking the high ground," 6th International Conference on Cyber Conflict (CyCon), Tallinn, 2014; David Gioe, "Can the Warfare Concept of Maneuver be Usefully Applied in Cyber Operations?," *Cyber Defense Review* (2016); Jeffrey Guion and Mark Reith, "Cyber terrain mission mapping: Tools and methodologies," International Conference on Cyber Conflict (CyCon U.S.), Washington, DC, 2017; Brian Thompson and Richard E. Harang, "Identifying Key Cyber-Physical Terrain," 3rd ACM on International Workshop on Security And Privacy Analytics (ISWPA), Scottsdale, AZ, March 2017; Scott D. Applegate, Christopher L. Carpenter, and David C. West, "Searching for Digital Hilltops," *Joint Forces Quar-*

terly 84 (2017): 18–23; Brian R. Raike. "Maneuver Warfare in Cyberspace," *Marine Corps Gazette* (October 2018); Kenton G. Fasana, "Another manifestation of cyber conflict: attaining military objectives through cyber avenues of approach," *Defence Studies* 18, no.:2 (2018): 167–87; Giorgio Bertoli and Stephen Raio, "The Elusive Nature of 'Key Cyber Terrain,'" *Journal of Cyber Security and Information Systems* 6, no. 2 (2018); and Maxim Kovalsky, Robert J. Ross, and Greg Lindsay, "Contesting Key Terrain: Urban Conflict in Smart Cities of the Future," *Cyber Defense Review* 5, no. 3 (2020): 133–50.

22. Robert Axelrod and Rumen Iliev, "Timing of cyber conflict," *PNAS* 111, no. 4 (2014): 1298–1303; and Max Smeets and J. D. Work, "Operational Decision-Making for Cyber Operations: In Search of a Model," *Cyber Defense Review* 5, no. 1 (2020): 95–112.

23. Max Smeets. "A Matter of Time: On the Transitory Nature of Cyberweapons," *Journal of Strategic Studies* 41, no. 1–2 (2018): 6–32.

24. Matthew Monte, *Network Attacks & Exploitation: A Framework* (Hoboken, NJ: Wiley & Sons, 2015), 73–77.

25. Remarks under Chatham House Rule, GlassHouse Center, 17 December 2020.

26. Robert Falcone, "Shamoon 2: Return of the Disttrack Wiper," Palo Alto Networks, 30 November 2016; Robert Falcone, "Second Wave of Shamoon 2 Attacks Identified," Palo Alto Networks, 9 January 2017; FireEye, "Wiper Malware, SHAPESHIFT, Targets Saudi Arabia," 23 March 2017; and CrowdStrike, "Charming Kitten Campaign Linked to Recent Waves of Shamoon Attacks," 4 April 2017.

27. Interview with an Iranian defector previously involved in offensive cyber operations, December 2016.

28. Remarks under Chatham House Rule, OODA Network, 18 December 2020.

29. J. D. Work, "Offensive cyber confidence, competition and escalation in recent Gulf crisis events," Workshop on Crisis Stability and Cyber Conflict, Columbia University, 25 February 2020.

30. Gregory Conti and David Raymond, *On Cyber: Towards an Operational Art for Cyber Conflict* (New York: Kopidion Press, 2017).

31. J. D. Work, "Calculating the Fast Equations: Arsenal Management Considerations in Sustained Offensive Cyber Operations," Cyber Security Project, Belfer Center for Science and International Affairs, Harvard University, April 2019.

32. Robert Koch and Mario Golling, "Silent Battles: Towards Unmasking Hidden Cyber Attack," 11th International Conference on Cyber Conflict (CyCon), Tallinn, 2019.

33. Christopher Campbell and Matthew Graeber, "Living Off the Land: A Minimalist's Guide to Windows Post-Exploitation," DerbyCon, Louisville, KY, 2013.

34. FireEye, "Dormant EMPIRE Infection Reactivated to Trigger Wiping," 21 March 2022.

35. For more information on STORM-333 planning, see Yu. V. Romashova and M. G. Stepanov, "Soviet Intelligence Activities in Afghanistan in the 1970s," The Phenomenon of War in the Historical Process: Interdisciplinary Discourse, Abakan, 13–23 October 2020; and Mark Galeotti, "Storm-333: KGB and Spetsnaz seize Kabul, Soviet-Afghan War 1979," Bloomsbury Publishing, 2021.

36. Ministry of Defense Ukraine, "The situation regarding the Russian invasion," 2 March 2022.

37. Rose McDermott, "Some emotional considerations in cyber conflict," *Journal of Cyber Policy* 4, no. 3 (2019): 309–25.

38. Remarks under Chatham House Rule, Glasshouse Center, 4 January 2021.

39. Lily Hay Newman, "How an Accidental 'Kill Switch' Slowed Friday's Massive Ransomware Attack," *Wired* (13 May 2017); and Jan Vojtesek, "Putting an end to Retadup: A malicious worm that infected hundreds of thousands," AVAST, 28 August 2019.

40. MISP Project, "Decaying of Indicators—MISP improved model to expire indicators based on custom models," 12 September 2019.

41. BAE Systems, "Taiwan Heist: Lazarus Tools and Ransomware," 16 October 2017; Christopher DiGiamo, Nalani Fraser, and Jacqueline O'Leary, "Unmasking APT X," FireEye Cyber Defense Summit, 1–4 October 2018.

42. Matthew Dunwoody, "No Easy Breach," DERBYCON, Louisville, KY, 21–25 September 2016; NRK, "Norge utsatt for et omfattende hackerangrep," 3 February 2017; and Huib Modderkolk, "Dutch agencies provide crucial intel about Russia's interference in US-elections," *Volkskrant,* 25 January 2018.

43. ESET, "Operation Ghost: The Dukes aren't back—they never left," 17 October 2019; and FireEye, "Not So Cozy: An Uncomfortable Examination of a Suspected APT29 Phishing Campaign," 19 November 2018.

44. National Cyber Security Centre, Communications Security Establishment, and National Security Agency, "Advisory: APT29 targets COVID-19 vaccine development," 16 July 2020; and Cyber Infrastructure Security Agency, "Malicious Activity Targeting COVID-19 Research, Vaccine Development," 16 July 2020.

45. FireEye, "Highly Evasive Attacker Leverages SolarWinds Supply Chain to Compromise Multiple Global Victims with SUNBURST Backdoor," 13 December 2020; Ellen Nakashima and Craig Timberg, "Russian government hackers are behind a broad espionage campaign that has compromised U.S. agencies, including Treasury and Commerce," *Washington Post*, 14 December 2020; and Microsoft, "Analyzing Solorigate, the compromised DLL file that started a sophisticated cyberattack," 18 December 2020.

46. White House, "Imposing Costs for Harmful Foreign Activities by the Russian Government," 15 April 2021.

47. Donn Parker, "Integrated Test Facility," *Computer Fraud & Security Bulletin* 1, no. 7 (1–3 May 1979); Donn B. Parker, "Vulnerabilities of EFTs to intentionally caused losses," Communications of the ACM, December 1979; Jan Hruska, "Data viruses, Trojan horses and logic bombs—How to combat them?,"

Computer Fraud & Security Bulletin 10, no. 6 (1988); Eugene H. Spafford, "The Internet Worm Program: An Analysis," *ACM SIGCOMM Computer Communication Review* (January 1989); Stanley A. Kurzban, "Viruses and worms—What Can They Do?," *ACM SIGSAC Review* (February 1989); and Peter J. Denning, "The Science of Computing: Stopping Computer Crimes," *American Scientist* 78, no. 1 (1990): 10–12.

48. AFP, "S. Korea attacked by reactivated computer virus," 8 July 2010.

49. Department of Justice, "Justice Department Announces Court-Authorized Efforts to Map and Disrupt Botnet Used by North Korean Hackers," 30 January 2019.

50. Juan Andrés Guerrero-Saade, "Walking in your Enemy's Shadow: When Fourth-Party Collection Becomes Attribution Hell," Virus Bulletin, Madrid, 4–6 October 2017.

51. J. D. Work, "Autonomy & Conflict Management in Offensive & Defensive Cyber Engagement," IWCon, Nashville, TN, April 2016.

52. Yonathan Klijnsma, "GRU implant pushing in an SVR attributed implant," Twitter, 19 August 2020, https://twitter.com/ydklijnsma/status/1296120044879937543.

53. Patrick Tucker, "Russia Wanted to be Caught, Says Company Waging War on the DNC Hackers," DefenseOne, 28 July 2016; and F-Secure, "Deconstructing the Dukes: A Researcher's Retrospective of APT29," 5 June 2020.

54. David A. Grossman, "Defeating the Enemy's Will: The Psychological Foundations of Maneuver Warfare," in *Maneuver Warfare: An Anthology*, ed. R. D. Hooker (Novato, CA: Presidio Press, 1994); Wayne Michael Hall, *The Power of Will in International Conflict: How to Think Critically in Complex Environments* (Westport, CT: Praeger, 2018); and Ben Connable et al., "Will to Fight: Analyzing, Modeling, and Simulating the Will to Fight of Military Units," RAND, 2018.

55. Rebekah Brown, "The Shadow Brokers Leaked Exploits Explained," Rapid7, 18 April 2017; and Ben Buchanan, *The Hacker and the State* (Cambridge, MA: Harvard University Press, 2020).

Chapter 20
Conclusion
Walker D. Mills

While editing the chapters for this volume and preparing to send it to editors at Army University Press, it became impossible to ignore the ongoing withdrawal of US troops from Afghanistan and the connection to these chapters. Creating an edited volume on retreats and withdrawals takes on a different, more personal character when the US military is in the middle of its own, highly public, withdrawal. Between the two editors, we know countless marines, soldiers, airmen, sailors, and civilians who deployed and fought in Afghanistan—a number that expands exponentially among the other authors, making the US withdrawal an almost-personal event. Then as work was in progress on the revised manuscript, Russian forces invaded Ukraine while the world watched, reinforcing the need for historical case studies on large-scale combat operations. As esteemed military historian Jeremy Black explained in *Land Warfare Since 1860*, "Told from the present, looking back, history, including military history, inevitably shifts to reflect changing perspectives."[1] This shift in perspectives and dominant narratives has become obvious over the course of writing and editing this volume. Without a doubt these perspectives and narratives can, and likely will, shift again in the years ahead.

The Afghanistan operation—initially called a "retrograde" by US Central Command—became a hasty rush to withdraw all US military personnel, diplomatic and Coalition personnel, and Afghan allies and partners and their families as Kabul fell in late August 2021. For a few brief weeks, the eyes of the world focused on Afghanistan as foreign militaries scrambled to evacuate and overcome the difficulties of space and time. It was a tragic validation of one of the initial sparks for this volume: that the US military needed to study historical cases of withdrawals and retreats because it would one day need to draw on that knowledge. Furthermore, retreats and withdrawals are not simple or easy. Speaking about the difficulties of withdrawing from Afghanistan, one retired US general commented: "It's a lot easier to invade a country than to leave it in an orderly manner."[2] The excellent chapters in this volume recount a range of outcomes, but all of the operations were trying and difficult for those involved.

The question of how the United States will remember Afghanistan is ongoing, and likely will not be settled in our lifetimes. But the battle for the narrative has already begun. The US government promoted the view that US troops "accomplished the mission for which [they] were sent to Afghanistan, and that was to disrupt and defeat Al-Qaeda and the threat that Al-Qaeda represented to the homeland."[3] But the withdrawal was somber and without public ceremony. Early on, the White House acknowledged: "We're not going to have a 'Mission Accomplished' moment . . . It's a twenty-year war that has not been won militarily. . . . We are not having a moment of celebration," a reference to President George W. Bush's infamous speech aboard the USS *Abraham Lincoln*.[4] But controlling the narrative is difficult; as one journalist remarked: "The military wants to show itself in a victorious way. When you're leaving a field of battle, it never looks victorious."[5] America's complicated legacy in Afghanistan is unlikely to avoid the bifurcated debates regarding history and memory that have occurred with each facet of American history. Americans—veterans and civilians alike—will ask whether the retreat, including the tragic deaths of thirteen US marines defending the Kabul airport in its final days and countless Afghans, was worth the price.[6]

Certainly, the way US forces withdrew from the country has shaped how the departure will be remembered. Should the spotlight be on the soldiers and marines defending the airport; the commanders in Kabul, Tampa, and Washington, DC; or the Afghans left behind? For months the withdrawal was orderly and largely out of sight as the military worked to avoid a repeat of the Vietnam embassy helicopters-on-the-roof evacuation. Journalists had complained that the military imposed a "near blackout" for the press covering Afghanistan.[7] Apparently even the Afghan military was taken by surprise when the US military finally left Bagram air base in the middle of the night. Afghan forces reportedly did not know US forces had left until they turned off the lights in a move that satirical publication *The Onion* had predicted a decade to the day before.[8] The publication's story included a fictional quote from Secretary of Defense James Mattis: "Sometimes it's hard to remember why we even got involved in the first place."[9] But in the end, the withdrawal couldn't avoid the international media spotlight; videos from the Kabul airport went viral, and news outlets provided near hourly coverage of the evacuation. Ultimately, 123,000 people were evacuated in the airlift out of Kabul airport before the last US forces withdrew just before midnight on 31 August 2021.[10]

The withdrawal from Afghanistan echoes other infamous withdrawals and pullouts. It is compared to the Army of the Republic of Vietnam collapse and subsequent US evacuation of Saigon during "Black April" nearly fifty years ago, and the Soviet withdrawal from Afghanistan nearly twenty years after that. Regarding the 1989 Soviet withdrawal, the Russian General Staff wrote in its study of the war:

> On 15 February 1989, the last unit left the territory Afghanistan. Thus, these forces returned to their people, having been sent to another country on the whims of a few Kremlin politicians. Their history is written in the blood of thousands of people on the soil of Afghanistan.[11]

What will an official history of the US withdrawal from Afghanistan say? How will it portray the final days at Hamid Karzai International Airport? Fuzzy videos of Afghans falling from a US transport plane are the Afghan pullout's equivalent of images of the US withdrawal from Vietnam—with thousands of Vietnamese clamoring for a ride out of Saigon on a US helicopter.[12] One enduring lesson of withdrawals and retreats is that they are almost always messy and chaotic.

In their introduction to *Past as Prologue: The Importance of Military History to the Profession*, military historians Williamson Murray and Richard Hart Sinnreich wrote: "It is the very repetitive quality of many of military history's worst disasters that can make reading it so depressing."[13] That's why *Armies in Retreat* is an important project. As noted in the book's introduction, military disasters and defeats—including withdrawals and retreats—are chronically understudied. This is true even though most casualties happen during retreats or withdrawals; they can be just as decisive as other engagements, often more so. Historians and practitioners typically study victories—the encirclements, and the breakthroughs, the Normandies and the Gettysburgs from the perspective of the victors. While the eighteen case studies in *Armies in Retreat* will not reverse that trend, hopefully this new information will help liven discussion about retreats. Central to US military thought, the concept of maneuver warfare overly focuses on decisive combat as the primary way of winning wars. This overfocus is what military historian Cathal Nolan calls "the allure of battle," or a cult of the decisive battle, and it's a distraction from other important parts of warfare.[14] For every smashing victory there is often a crushing defeat that includes a withdrawal or retreat. Historians typically study Napoleon's campaigns in Europe but not his retreat from Moscow. They learn about the German blitzkrieg but not the army's amphibious evacuation of Sicily or Rommel's retreat to Tobruk. As military historian John Keegan wisely suggested: "All battles are in some degree . . . disasters."[15] Studying historical examples can help avoid the pitfall of overly focusing on the present, which looks radically different now than when it was the future, or how it will look when it fades into the past.

In his *War on the Rocks* essay, author Edward Geist, a researcher at the RAND Corporation, argued: "If the United States is to have a reasonable hope of winning a war, it needs to think very seriously about what it would be like to lose."[16] Hopefully this volume provides an opportunity to ruminate on often-overlooked operations that can be nearly taboo to discuss—retreat and withdrawal—and learn from the mistakes and successes of others. As one Marine leader recently wrote in a commentary on Afghanistan: "I had been taught how to lead Marines to victory. No one had ever taught me how to lead Marines through defeat."[17] These cases are intended at the very least to "light what is often a dark path ahead."[18] Beyond the Afghanistan withdrawal, tactical defeats and retreats of Russian and Ukrainian forces in the Ukraine are another indication that military professionals need to think more about the other side of the coin.

These eighteen case studies address successful withdrawals like Lt. Gen. Johann Dietrich von Hülsen's 1760 campaign in which the Prussians artfully traded space for time and occupied a larger force. The range of cases cover a wide swath of time and space, though with an admittedly Western and twentieth-century focus. Also included are failures like the XI Corps' inability to hold the line at Chancellorsville and others from a purely military perspective such as analysis of the British 1809 campaign in Holland and the Continental Army's Northern Campaigns during the American Revolution. Additionally, *Armies in Retreat* addresses political developments and civil-military relations regarding the withdrawal from Gallipoli, as well as retreats celebrated in folk songs and what it means to retreat in the cyber domain.

The book editors made difficult choices about which chapters to include, and in doing so only kept the very best. These eighteen cases represent not only the operational view, but also discussions of the strategic impact and the impact on cultural memory and how the events were memorialized. Inevitably, *Armies in Retreat* cannot cover these cases in sufficient depth, or provide a sufficient number of cases to create anything close to a comprehensive study.

Far more research and writing are required on the subject of retreats, especially in bringing cases from outside of the Western experience and drawn from non-English sources that were beyond this book's reach. Many more examples of retreats and withdrawals, as John T. Kuehn and David W. Holden suggested, have been "poorly chronicled, lost to history, or have yet to be more fully discovered and articulated."[19] Additionally, this book focuses on terrestrial case studies; this choice leaves a broad range of retreats and withdrawals to cover—especially in the maritime domain. For example, an additional volume could be filled with amphibious retreats, from George Washington's evacuation of Long Island to Operation KE and the Japanese evacuation of Guadalcanal.

There is no single right answer to the question, "What causes a military or a unit to collapse during a retreat or withdrawal?" The *Armies in Retreat* editors echo this sentiment shared by American military theorists Eliot A. Cohen and John Gooch in *Military Misfortunes: The Anatomy of Failure in War*: "The only feature many defeats have in common is their outcome."[20] But across all these themes, one constant stands out: leadership. In retreat, as in war and conflict generally, good leadership is essential. In their introduction to *The 100 Worst Military Disasters in History,* military historians John T. Kuehn and David W. Holden acknowledged the importance of effective leadership: "It is rare that a professional or well-trained army, navy, or air force prevails when its senior leadership is incompetent or just plain bad."[21] During the confused chaos of a retreat or collapse, armies and units are held together by their leaders—whether generals, admirals, captains or sergeants. These leaders—more than any other single factor—determine whether cohesion is maintained or lost. And of course, there is always the immeasurable importance of chance. Prussian military theorist Carl von Clausewitz wrote: "War is the realm of chance. No other human activity gives it greater scope: no other has such incessant and varied dealings with this intruder."[22] There is no certainty in warfare.

The cases in this book do not represent the final word on retreats and withdrawals but rather a starting point for discussing operations that are often overlooked, but that need to be studied and understood nonetheless. Further, the editors cannot offer a full and complete answer to questions about why and how armies retreat and what turns a retreat into a rout. The intention is for this collection of case studies to start a broader discussion and help bring more balance into historical case studies and military touchstones discussed by military historians and practitioners alike.

Notes

1. Jeremy Black, *Land Warfare Since 1860: A Global History of Boots on the Ground* (London: Rowman and Littlefield, 2019), 1.

2. James Kitfield, "The Last Commander," *Politico Magazine* (16 July 2021), https://www.politico.com/news/magazine/2021/07/16/scott-miller-general-afghanistan-profile-499490.

3. John F. Kirby, "Pentagon Press Secretary John F. Kirby Holds a Press Briefing," transcript (9 August 2021), https://www.defense.gov/Newsroom/Transcripts/Transcript/Article/2725063/pentagon-press-secretary-john-f-kirby-holds-a-press-briefing/.

4. Steve Beynon, "No 'Mission Accomplished' Moment: Biden Plans to End Afghan War with No Fanfare," *Military.com* (8 July 2021), https://www.military.com/daily-news/2021/07/08/no-mission-accomplished-moment-biden-plans-end-afghan-war-no-fanfare.html.

5. Megan K. Stack, "A Near Press Blackout in Afghanistan," *The New Yorker* (4 August 2021), https://www.newyorker.com/news/daily-comment/a-near-press-blackout-in-afghanistan.

6. Eliot A. Cohen, "How Does One Process Defeat?" *The Atlantic* (29 July 2021), https://www.theatlantic.com/ideas/archive/2021/07/how-do-you-reconcile-yourself-defeat/619596/.

7. Stack, "A Near Press Blackout in Afghanistan."

8. "U.S. Quietly Slips Out of Afghanistan in the Dead of Night," *The Onion* (18 July 2011), https://www.theonion.com/u-s-quietly-slips-out-of-afghanistan-in-dead-of-night-1819572778.

9. "U.S. Quietly Slips Out of Afghanistan in the Dead of Night," *The Onion*.

10. Guy Davies, "Historic Afghan Evacuation Wraps Up, with Fate of Those Left Behind Uncertain," *ABC News* (2 September 2021, https://abcnews.go.com/International/historic-afghanistan-evacuation-wraps-fate-left-uncertain/story?.

11. The Russian General Staff, *The Soviet-Afghan War: How a Superpower Fought and Lost*, ed. Lester Grau and Michael A. Gress (Lawrence, KS: University of Kansas Press, 2002), 29.

12. Kirk Wallace Johnson, "How Joe Biden Could Save Tens of Thousands of Afghan Allies," *The New Yorker* (9 August 2021), https://www.newyorker.com/news/daily-comment/how-joe-biden-could-save-tens-of-thousands-of-afghan-allies.

13. Williamson Murray and Richard Hart Sinnreich, *The Past as Prologue: The Importance of History to the Military Profession* (Cambridge: Cambridge University Press, 2006) 3.

14. Cathal J. Nolan, *The Allure of Battle: A History of How Wars Have Been Won and Lost* (Oxford, UK: Oxford University Press, 2017).

15. John Keegan, *The Face of Battle* (New York: Viking Press, 1976), 199, quoted in Eliot A. Cohen and John Gooch, *Military Misfortunes: The Anatomy of Failure in War* (New York: Free Press, 1990), 1.

16. Edward Geist, "Defeat Is Possible," *War on the Rocks* (17 June 2021), https://warontherocks.com/2021/06/defeat-is-possible/.

17. Brian Kerg, "Leading Through Defeat," *USNI Proceedings* (April 2022), https://www.usni.org/magazines/proceedings/2022/april/leading-through-defeat.

18. "General Mattis on Professional Reading and the Study of Military History," *The Cove* (31 August 2017), https://cove.army.gov.au/article/general-mattis-professional-reading-and-study-military-history.

19. John T. Kuehn and David W. Holden, *The 100 Worst Military Disasters in History* (Santa Barbara, CA: ABC-CLIO, 2020), ix.

20. Eliot A. Cohen and John Gooch, *Military Misfortunes: The Anatomy of Failure in War* (New York: Free Press, 1990), 2.

21. Kuehn and Holden, *The 100 Worst Military Disasters in History*, x.

22. Carl von Clausewitz, *On War*, trans. Peter Paret and Michael Howard (Princeton, NJ: Princeton University Press, 1986), 101.

About the Authors

Catherine V. Bateson

Dr. Catherine V. Bateson is an associate lecturer of American history at the University of Kent. She researches and teaches the American Civil War, 1700s to early 1900s US social and cultural topics, slavery, civil rights and indigenous history, and American studies. She published *Irish-American Civil War Songs: Identity, Loyalty, and Nationhood* (Baton Rouge, LA: LSU Press, 2022) and has written articles about the Irish-American wartime experience and the importance of music in military history. She is associate editor of the Irish in the American Civil War project and co-founder of the Stuff of War Society.

Frank A. Blazich Jr.

Dr. Frank A. Blazich Jr. is a curator of modern military history at the Smithsonian Institution's National Museum of American History. He earned his doctorate from The Ohio State University. He is author of *"An Honorable Place in American Air Power": Civil Air Patrol Coastal Patrol Operations, 1942–1943* (Maxwell Air Force Base, AL: Air University Press, 2020) and editor of *Bataan Survivor: A POW's Account of Japanese Captivity in World War II* (Columbia, MO: University of Missouri Press, 2017).

Jonathan D. Bratten

Jonathan D. Bratten is a National Guard officer and works full-time as an Army historian. His book *To the Last Man: A National Guard Regiment in the Great War, 1917–1919* (Fort Leavenworth, KS: Combat Studies Institute, 2020) received the Army Historical Foundation's 2021 award for best unit history. He has also published in the *Washington Post* and the *New York Times*. Bratten served as the Army Center of Military History's first scholar-in-residence at the US Military Academy at West Point from 2021 to 2022.

Alexander S. Burns

Dr. Alexander S. Burns is a visiting assistant professor in American history at Franciscan University of Steubenville, Ohio. In 2022, he was the editor of *The Changing Face of Old Regime War: Essays in Honour of Christopher Duffy* (Warwick, UK: Helion & Company, 2022). During his doctoral work at West Virginia University, Burns developed a long-standing partnership with the Reserve Officer Training Corps Mountaineer Battalion, and was a featured speaker at the Senior Enlisted Leader International Summit 2022 in Washington, DC. His research focuses on the intersection of violence, militaries, and the state in the Atlantic World during the eighteenth century. He has published articles on the British, Hessian, and Prussian militaries, and his next monograph will explore the international culture of military professionalism that allowed the United States to triumph during the American War of Independence.

Anthony J. Cade II

Anthony J. "A. J." Cade II is a retired US Marine and military historian with the federal government. He completed his PhD at the George Washington University, and his research focused on the subaltern of the American Civil War, specifically immigrants and African Americans. Cade is the author of a number of articles on subaltern military history, and his dissertation addressed the Louisiana Native Guards, the first successfully constituted regiments of African American soldiers in the Union Army during the American Civil War.

Aimée Fox

Dr. Aimée Fox is an associate professor in the Defence Studies Department at King's College London. She is the author of the award-winning *Learning to Fight: Military Innovation and Change in the British Army, 1914–1918* (Cambridge: Cambridge University Press, 2018), and recently edited the military correspondence of Maj. Gen. Guy Dawnay (Woodbridge, UK: Boydell & Brewer, forthcoming). She is a nonresident fellow at the Brute Krulak Center for Innovation and Creativity at the Marine Corps University.

Nikolas E. Gardner

Nikolas E. Gardner is professor of strategy at the UAE National Defence College in Abu Dhabi. He is the author of *Trial by Fire: Command and the British Expeditionary Force in 1914* (Westport, CT: Praeger, 2003) and *The Siege of Kut-al-Amara: At War in Mesopotamia, 1915–16* (Bloomington, IN: Indiana University Press, 2014), co-editor of *Turning Point 1917: The British Empire at War* (Vancouver: University of British Columbia Press, 2017), and is writing a book on Clausewitzian friction in twenty-first century wars.

Patrick H. Hannum

Dr. Patrick H. Hannum, lieutenant colonel (US Marine Corps-Retired), completed a twenty-nine-year Marine Corps career as an amphibious assault vehicle officer with service in all four Marine divisions, including service as commanding officer, Combat Assault Battalion, 3rd Marine

Division, Okinawa, Japan. After leaving active duty, Hannum continued service in the Department of Defense as a professor at National Defense University, where he specialized in Phase II Joint Professional Military Education at the Joint Forces Staff College in Norfolk, Virginia. He recently retired as a civilian professor, culminating a forty-five-year Department of Defense career. Hannum continues to research, write, speak, present, and advocate for the study of American military history, concentrating on the revolutionary period, and focuses on linking enduring lesson of warfare to the contemporary operating environment.

Timothy G. Heck

An artillery officer by training, Timothy G. Heck is a graduate of several military command and staff schools. As a reservist, he is a joint historian with the Marine Corps History Detachment and Joint History Office. He is co-editor of *On Contested Shores: The Evolving Role of Amphibious Operations in the History of Warfare* (Quantico, VA: Marine Corps University Press, 2020) and wrote chapters in *Deep Maneuver: Historical Case Studies of Maneuver in Large-Scale Combat Operations* (Fort Leavenworth, KS: Army University Press, 2018) and *Enduring Success: Consolidation of Gains in Large-Scale Combat Operations* (Fort Leavenworth, KS: Army University Press, 2022).

Jason D. Lancaster

Lt. Cdr. Jason D. Lancaster is a US Navy surface warfare officer. He is command, control, communications, computers, combat systems and interoperability (C5I) officer aboard the USS *America*. Afloat, he previously was operations officer at Destroyer Squadron 26, weapons officer aboard the USS *Stout*, training officer aboard the USS *Tortuga*, and plank owner main propulsion division officer aboard the USS *New York*. Ashore, he served in the N5 at the Office of the Chief of Naval Operations and Commander, Naval Forces Korea. He also was an instructor at the Surface Warfare Officers' School in Newport, Rhode Island. An alumnus of Mary Washington College, he has a master's in history from the University of Tulsa.

Gregory P. Liedtke

Gregory P. Liedtke is a military historian and researcher specializing in German military history and the Russian Front during World War Two. He has an MA and a PhD in war studies from the Royal Military College of Canada, and is the author of *Enduring the Whirlwind: The German Army and the Russo-German War 1941–1943* (West Midlands, UK: Helion & Company, 2016).

Walker D. Mills

A Marine Corps infantry officer, Capt. Walker D. Mills is a nonresident fellow at Marine Corps University's Brute Krulak Center for Innovation and Future War and a nonresident fellow with the Irregular Warfare Initiative, a collaboration between West Point's Modern War Institute and the Princeton Empirical Studies of Conflict Project. He has a BA in history from Brown University and an MA in international relations and modern war from King's College in London. He has written more than sixty articles on military affairs and three previous book chapters.

Charles P. Neimeyer

Following graduation from the University of Maryland, Charles P. Neimeyer began his professional career as a military officer with the US Marine Corps in 1976. During his twenty-year active-duty military career, he served in all three Marine Corps divisions to include service as a strategic plans officer at Headquarters, Marine Corps; on the White House military staff for Presidents George H. W. Bush and William J. Clinton; and as an instructor at the US Naval Academy and Naval War College. Neimeyer retired from active service in 1996 then returned to the Naval War College in 1997 as a professor of national security affairs. In 2006, he became the director and chief of Marine Corps history, Quantico, Virginia. He remained in that capacity until retiring from civilian federal service in 2018. He teaches strategy and policy for the Naval War College in the Fleet Support Program, Washington, DC, and at Georgetown and Catholic Universities. He wrote *America Goes to War: A Social History of the Continental Army, 1775–1783* (New York: New York University Press, 1996), *The Revolutionary War* (Westport, CT: Greenwood Press, 2007), and *War in the Chesapeake: The British Campaigns to Control the Bay, 1813–1814* (Annapolis, MD: Naval Institute Press, 2015).

Jeff Rutherford

Jeff Rutherford teaches history at Xavier University. He specializes in the military and ideological aspects of the German-Soviet war. He is author of *Combat and Genocide on the Eastern Front: The German Infantry's War* (Cambridge: Cambridge University Press, 2014), co-author of *The German Army on the Eastern Front: An Inner View of the Ostheer's Experiences of War* (Barnsley, UK: Pen & Sword Books, 2018), co-editor of *Nazi Policy on the Eastern Front, 1941: Total War, Genocide, and Radicalization* (Rochester, NY: University of Rochester Press, 2014), and is writing a history of the German army during the Second World War for Cambridge University Press.

Eric A. Sibul

Eric A. Sibul has a BA in international relations from Penn State University, an MA in history from San Jose State University, and a PhD in history from the University of York in the United Kingdom. He served as an assistant professor of military theory and history at the Baltic Defence College in Tartu, Estonia, from 2006 to 2015 and as principal lecturer on sea power theory, naval history, and strategy at the Baltic Naval Command and Staff Course in Riga, Latvia. Prior to his academic appointment in Estonia, Dr. Sibul was a military English instructor at the Republic of Korea Army Intelligence School in Songnam, Republic of Korea. As a US Navy Reserve member, he served in the Office of Naval Intelligence unit and Amphibious Construction Battalion Two. He is an instructor of history, business, and economics at the City Colleges of Chicago.

Jonathan H. Warner

Jonathan H. Warner is a classicist and ancient historian who studies Greek and Roman military history and literature, Roman imperial administration, and late-antique Christianity. In 2020, he received his PhD from Cornell University, where he wrote his dissertation on martial descriptions of church and state service in the fourth and fifth centuries. He lives in New Jersey with his family and teaches Latin and classical literature at Millburn High School.

Tyler D. Wentzell

Tyler D. Wentzell is a Canadian infantry officer and a doctoral candidate at the University of Toronto. He is the author of *Not for King or Country: Edward Cecil-Smith, the Communist Party of Canada, and the Spanish Civil War* (Toronto: University of Toronto Press, 2020). He teaches at the Canadian Forces College.

Marcin Wilczek

Dr. Marcin Wilczek has degrees in history from the University of Warsaw and the Polish Academy of Sciences. As an independent researcher, he is especially interested in military-industrial relations, twentieth-century armed conflicts, economic issues, and digital humanities. He is also a graduate of a reserve officers training course at the Wrocław Military University and a Polish Army reserve infantry officer.

J. D. Work

J. D. Work is a professor at the National Defense University, College of Information and Cyberspace. His research focuses on cyber intelligence and decision advantage, operational art in offensive and counter-cyber campaigns, and strategy in conflict and competition. He has more than twenty-five years' experience working in cyber intelligence and operations roles for the private sector and US government. Work has additional affiliations with the Saltzman Institute of War and Peace Studies in the School of International and Public Affairs at Columbia University, the Atlantic Council's Cyber Statecraft Initiative, and the Krulak Center for Innovation and Future Warfare at Marine Corps University.

Andrew O. G. Young

Andrew O. G. Young is a former Royal Navy officer who specializes in professional military education. He has worked at the Royal United Services Institute on Whitehall and lectured at Britannia Royal Naval College Dartmouth, Commando Training Centre Royal Marines, Joint Services Command and Staff College, and RAF College Cranwell. He is the fellowships officer for the Royal Navy Strategic Studies Centre.

www.ingramcontent.com/pod-product-compliance
Lightning Source LLC
Chambersburg PA
CBHW080049190426
43201CB00035B/2143